core
JavaServer™ Faces

Third Edition

core
JavaServer™ Faces

Third Edition

DAVID GEARY
CAY HORSTMANN

PRENTICE
HALL

Upper Saddle River, NJ • Boston • Indianapolis • San Francisco
New York • Toronto • Montreal • London • Munich • Paris • Madrid
Capetown • Sydney • Tokyo • Singapore • Mexico City

The publisher offers excellent discounts on this book when ordered in quantity for bulk purchases or special sales, which may include electronic versions and/or custom covers and content particular to your business, training goals, marketing focus, and branding interests. For more information, please contact:

U.S. Corporate and Government Sales
(800) 382-3419
corpsales@pearsontechgroup.com

For sales outside the United States, please contact:

International Sales
international@pearsoned.com

Visit us on the Web: informit.com/ph

Library of Congress Cataloging-in-Publication Data

Geary, David M.
  Core JavaServer faces / David Geary, Cay Horstmann.—3rd ed.
     p.   cm.
  Includes index.
  ISBN 978-0-13-701289-3 (pbk. : alk. paper)
  1. JavaServer pages. 2. Web site development. 3. Web sites—Design.
I. Horstmann, Cay S., 1959- II. Title.
  TK5105.8885.J38G433 2010
  006.7'8—dc22

                                        2010011569

ISBN-13: 978-0-13-701289-3
ISBN-10:   0-13-701289-6

Text printed in the United States on recycled paper at Edwards Brothers in Ann Arbor, Michigan.
First printing, May 2010

Contents

Preface

When we heard about JavaServer Faces (JSF) at the 2002 JavaOne conference, we were very excited. Both of us had extensive experience with client-side Java programming—David in *Graphic Java™*, and Cay in *Core Java™*, both published by Sun Microsystems Press—and we found web programming with servlets and JavaServer Pages (JSP) to be rather unintuitive and tedious. JSF promised to put a friendly face in front of a web application, allowing programmers to think about text fields and menus instead of dealing with page flips and request parameters. Each of us proposed a book project to our publisher, who promptly suggested that we should jointly write the Sun Microsystems Press book on JSF.

In 2004, the JSF Expert Group (of which David is a member) released the JSF 1.0 specification and reference implementation. A bug fix 1.1 release emerged shortly afterward, and an incremental 1.2 release added a number of cleanups and convenience features in 2006.

The original JSF specification was far from ideal. It was excessively general, providing for use cases that turned out to be uninteresting in practice. Not enough attention was given to API design, forcing programmers to write complex and tedious code. Support for GET requests was clumsy. Error handling was plainly unsatisfactory, and developers cursed the "stack trace from hell".

JSF had one saving grace, however. It was highly extensible, and therefore it was very attractive to framework developers. Those framework developers built cutting edge open-source software that plugged into JSF, such as Facelets, Ajax4jsf, Seam, JSF Templates, Pretty Faces, RichFaces, ICEFaces, and so on.

JSF 2.0, released in 2009, is built on the experience of those open-source frameworks. Nearly all of the original authors of the aforementioned frameworks participated on the JSF 2 Expert Group, so JSF 2.0, unlike JSF 1.0, was forged from the crucible of real-world open-source projects that had time to mature.

JSF 2.0 is *much* simpler to use and better integrated into the Java EE technology stack than JSF 1.0. Almost every inch of JSF 1.0 has been transformed in JSF 2.0 in some way for the better. In addition, the specification now supports new web technologies such as Ajax and REST.

JSF is now the preeminent server-side Java web framework, and it has fulfilled most of its promises. You really can design web user interfaces by putting components on a form and linking them to Java objects, without having to mix code and markup. A strong point of JSF is its extensible component model, and a large number of third-party components have become available. The flexible design of the framework has allowed it to grow well and accommodate new technologies.

Because JSF is a specification and not a product, you are not at the mercy of a single vendor. JSF implementations, components, and tools are available from multiple sources. We are very excited about JSF 2.0, and we hope you will share in this excitement when you learn how this technology makes you a more effective web application developer.

About This Book

This book is suitable for web developers whose main focus is on implementing user interfaces and business logic. This is in stark contrast to the official JSF specification, a dense and pompously worded document whose principal audience is framework implementors, as well as long-suffering book authors. JSF is built on top of servlets, but from the point of view of the JSF developer, this technology merely forms the low-level plumbing. While it can't hurt to be familiar with servlets, JSP, or Struts, we do not assume any such knowledge.

The first half of the book, extending through Chapter 7, focuses on the JSF *tags*. These tags are similar to HTML form tags. They are the basic building blocks for JSF user interfaces. Anyone with basic HTML skills (for web page design) and standard Java programming (for the application logic) can use the JSF tags to build web applications.

The first part of the book covers these topics:

- Setting up your programming environment (Chapter 1)
- Connecting JSF tags to application logic (Chapter 2)
- Navigating between pages (Chapter 3)
- Using the standard JSF tags (Chapter 4)
- Using Facelets tags for templating (Chapter 5) **NEW**
- Data tables (Chapter 6)
- Converting and validating input (Chapter 7)

Starting with Chapter 8, we begin JSF programming in earnest. You will learn how to perform advanced tasks, and how to extend the JSF framework. Here are the main topics of the second part:

- Event handling (Chapter 8)
- Building composite components—reusable components with sophisticated behavior that are composed from simpler components (Chapter 9) **NEW**
- Ajax (Chapter 10) **NEW**
- Implementing custom components (Chapter 11)
- Connecting to databases and other external services (Chapter 12)

We end the book with a chapter that aims to answer common questions of the form "How do I . . . ?" (Chapter 13). We encourage you to have a peek at that chapter as soon as you become comfortable with the basics of JSF. There are helpful notes on debugging and logging, and we also give you implementation details and working code for features that are missing from JSF, such as file uploads, pop-up menus, and a pager component for long tables.

All chapters have been revised extensively in this edition to stress the new and improved features of JSF 2.0. Chapters 5, 9, and 10 are new to this edition.

Required Software

All software that you need for this book is freely available. You can use an application server that supports Java EE 6 (such as GlassFish version 3) or a servlet runner (such as Tomcat 6) together with a JSF implementation. The software runs on Linux, Mac OS X, Solaris, and Windows. Both Eclipse and NetBeans have extensive support for JSF development with GlassFish or Tomcat.

Web Support

The web site for this book is http://corejsf.com. It contains:

- The source code for all examples in this book
- Useful reference material that we felt is more effective in browseable form than in print
- A list of known errors in the book and the code
- A form for submitting corrections and suggestions

Acknowledgments

First and foremost, we'd like to thank Greg Doench, our editor at Prentice Hall, who has shepherded us through this project, never losing his nerve in spite of numerous delays and complications. Many thanks to Vanessa Moore for turning our messy manuscript into an attractive book and for her patience and amazing attention to detail.

We very much appreciate our reviewers for this and previous editions who have done a splendid job, finding errors and suggesting improvements in various drafts of the manuscript. They are:

- Gail Anderson, Anderson Software Group, Inc.
- Larry Brown, LMBrown.com, Inc.
- Damodar Chetty, Software Engineering Solutions, Inc.
- Frank Cohen, PushToTest
- Brian Goetz, Sun Microsystems, Inc.
- Rob Gordon, Crooked Furrow Farm
- Marty Hall, author of *Core Servlets and JavaServer Pages™, Second Edition*, (Prentice Hall, 2008)
- Steven Haines, CEO/Founder, GeekCap, Inc.
- Charlie Hunt, Sun Microsystems, Inc.
- Jeff Langr, Langr Software Solutions
- Jason Lee, Senior Java Developer, Sun Microsystems, Inc.

- Bill Lewis, Tufts University
- Kito Mann, author of *JavaServer Faces in Action* (Manning, 2005) and founder of JSFCentral.com
- Jeff Markham, Markham Software Company
- Angus McIntyre, IBM Corporation
- John Muchow, author of *Core J2ME™* (Prentice Hall, 2001)
- Dan Shellman, BearingPoint
- Sergei Smirnov, principal architect of Exadel JSF Studio
- Roman Smolgovsky, Flytecomm
- Stephen Stelting, Sun Microsystems, Inc.
- Christopher Taylor, Nanshu Densetsu
- Kim Topley, Keyboard Edge Limited
- Michael Yuan, coauthor of *JBoss® Seam: Simplicity and Power Beyond Java™ EE* (Prentice Hall, 2007)

Finally, thanks to our families and friends who have supported us through this project and who share our relief that it is finally completed.

core
JAVASERVER™ FACES

THIRD EDITION

GETTING STARTED

Topics in This Chapter

Chapter 1

Why JavaServer Faces?

Nowadays, you can choose among many frameworks for developing the user interface of a web application. JavaServer Faces (JSF) is a *component-based* framework. For example, if you want to display a table with rows and columns, you do not generate HTML tags for rows and cells in a loop, but you add a table component to a page. (If you are familiar with client-side Java development, you can think of JSF as "Swing for server-side applications.") By using components, you can think about your user interface at a higher level than raw HTML. You can reuse your own components and use third-party component sets. And you have the option of using a visual development environment in which you can drag and drop components onto a form.

JSF has these parts:

- A set of prefabricated UI (user interface) components
- An event-driven programming model
- A component model that enables third-party developers to supply additional components

Some JSF components are simple, such as input fields and buttons. Others are quite sophisticated—for example, data tables and trees.

JSF contains all the necessary code for event handling and component organization. Application programmers can be blissfully ignorant of these details and spend their effort on the application logic.

JSF is not the only component-based web framework, but it is the view layer in the Java EE standard. JSF is included in every Java EE application server, and it can be easily added to a standalone web container such as Tomcat.

Unlike most web frameworks, JSF is a standard with multiple implementations. This gives you a choice of vendors. Another advantage is that a standards committee has given considerable thought to the design of the framework, and that JSF is continuously improved and updated.

This book focuses on JSF 2.0, a major improvement over previous versions. JSF 2.0 is much simpler to use than JSF 1.x, and it provides new and powerful features, such as easy Ajax integration and composite component authoring.

A Simple Example

Let us have a look at a simple example of a JSF application. Our example starts with a login screen, shown in Figure 1–1.

Figure 1–1   A login screen

The file that describes the login screen is essentially an HTML file with a few additional tags (see Listing 1–1). Its visual appearance can be easily improved by a graphic artist who need not have any programming skills.

Listing 1-1   `login/web/index.xhtml`

```
1. <?xml version="1.0" encoding="UTF-8"?>
2. <!DOCTYPE html PUBLIC "-//W3C//DTD XHTML 1.0 Transitional//EN"
3. "http://www.w3.org/TR/xhtml1/DTD/xhtml1-transitional.dtd">
4. <html xmlns="http://www.w3.org/1999/xhtml"
5.       xmlns:h="http://java.sun.com/jsf/html">
6.    <h:head>
7.       <title>Welcome</title>
8.    </h:head>
9.    <h:body>
10.      <h:form>
11.         <h3>Please enter your name and password.</h3>
12.         <table>
13.            <tr>
14.               <td>Name:</td>
15.               <td><h:inputText value="#{user.name}"/></td>
16.            </tr>
17.            <tr>
18.               <td>Password:</td>
19.               <td><h:inputSecret value="#{user.password}"/></td>
20.            </tr>
21.         </table>
22.         <p><h:commandButton value="Login" action="welcome"/></p>
23.      </h:form>
24.   </h:body>
25. </html>
```

We discuss the contents of this file in detail in the section "JSF Pages" on page 17. For now, note the following points:

- A number of the tags are standard HTML tags: p, table, and so on.

- Some tags have *prefixes*, such as h:head and h:inputText. These are JSF tags. The xmlns attribute declares the JSF namespace.

- The h:inputText, h:inputSecret, and h:commandButton tags correspond to the text field, password field, and submit button in Figure 1–1.

- The input fields are linked to object properties. For example, the attribute value="#{user.name}" tells the JSF implementation to link the text field with the name property of a user object. We discuss this linkage in more detail in the section "Beans" on page 16.

When the user enters the name and password, and clicks the "Login" button, the welcome.xhtml file is displayed, as specified in the action attribute of the h:commandButton tag. (See Figure 1–2 and Listing 1–2.)

> **JSF 2.0** NOTE: Before JSF 2.0, you had to add a "navigation rule" in a file WEB-INF/ faces-config.xml file in order to specify the page that should be displayed when a button is clicked. In JSF 2.0, you can specify the page name directly in the action attribute of the button. (You can still use navigation rules; we discuss them in Chapter 3.)

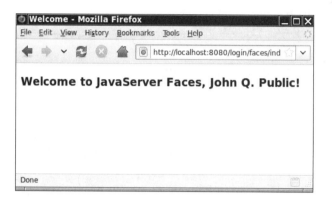

Figure 1–2   A welcome page

The second JSF page of our application is even simpler than the first (see Listing 1–2). We use the #{user.name} expression to display the name property of the user object that was set in the first page. The password is ignored for now.

Listing 1–2   login/web/welcome.xhtml

```
 1. <?xml version="1.0" encoding="UTF-8"?>
 2. <!DOCTYPE html PUBLIC "-//W3C//DTD XHTML 1.0 Transitional//EN"
 3. "http://www.w3.org/TR/xhtml1/DTD/xhtml1-transitional.dtd">
 4. <html xmlns="http://www.w3.org/1999/xhtml"
 5.       xmlns:h="http://java.sun.com/jsf/html">
 6.    <h:head>
 7.       <title>Welcome</title>
 8.    </h:head>
 9.    <h:body>
10.       <h3>Welcome to JavaServer Faces, #{user.name}!</h3>
11.    </h:body>
12. </html>
```

The purpose of this application is, of course, not to impress anyone, but to illustrate the various pieces that are necessary to produce a JSF application.

Ingredients

Our sample application consists of the following ingredients:

- Pages that define the login and welcome screens. We call them index.xhtml and welcome.xhtml.

- A bean that manages the user data (in our case, username and password). A *bean* is a Java class that exposes properties, by following a simple naming convention for the getter and setter methods. The code is in the file UserBean.java (see Listing 1–3). Note the @Named or @ManagedBean annotation that specifies the name by which an object of this class is referenced in the JSF pages. (For compatibility reasons, there are two alternative annotations for naming a bean. @Named is the best choice with a Java EE 6 compliant application server. @ManagedBean is intended for use with legacy application servers and standalone servlet runners.)

- Configuration files web.xml and beans.xml that are needed to keep the application server happy.

 NOTE: Before JSF 2.0, you had to declare beans in a file WEB-INF/faces-config.xml. This is no longer necessary, and this application does not need a faces-config.xml file.

More advanced JSF applications have the same structure, but they can contain additional Java classes, such as event handlers, validators, and custom components. Additional configuration parameters can be placed in a file WEB-INF/faces-config.xml that we will describe in the next chapter. For a simple application, this file is not required.

Listing 1–3   login/src/java/com/corejsf/UserBean.java

```
1. package com.corejsf;
2.
3. import java.io.Serializable;
4. import javax.inject.Named;
5.    // or import javax.faces.bean.ManagedBean;
6. import javax.enterprise.context.SessionScoped;
7.    // or import javax.faces.bean.SessionScoped;
8.
9. @Named("user") // or @ManagedBean(name="user")
10. @SessionScoped
11. public class UserBean implements Serializable {
12.    private String name;
```

```
13.    private String password;
14.
15.    public String getName() { return name; }
16.    public void setName(String newValue) { name = newValue; }
17.
18.    public String getPassword() { return password; }
19.    public void setPassword(String newValue) { password = newValue; }
20. }
```

Directory Structure

A JSF application is deployed as a *WAR file*: a zipped file with extension .war and a directory structure that follows a standardized layout:

XHTML files

resources/

   └── *CSS files, JavaScript, images*

WEB-INF/

   ├── *servlet and JSF configuration files*

   ├── classes/

   │   ├── *class files*

   │   └── META-INF/

   │   └── *application server configuration files*

   └── lib/

       └──*library files*

For example, the WAR file of our sample application has the directory structure shown in Figure 1–3. Note that the UserBean class is in the package com.corejsf.

> NOTE: When you use Tomcat or another servlet runner, the lib directory contains the JAR files of the JSF implementation. This is not necessary with GlassFish and other Java EE application servers since they already have JSF built in.

Figure 1–3 Directory structure of the sample WAR file

It is customary to package the application *source* in a different directory structure. In this book, we follow the Java Blueprints conventions (http://java.sun.com/blueprints/code/projectconventions.html). This packaging makes it easy to import our projects into IDEs, such as Eclipse or NetBeans. The source code is contained in a src/java directory, and the JSF pages and configuration files are contained in a web directory (see Figure 1–4).

Figure 1–4 Directory structure of the sample application source

Building a JSF Application

We now walk you through the steps required for building JSF applications with your bare hands. Of course, you will usually want to use an IDE or a build script. However, it is a good idea to know what your IDE does under the hood so that you can troubleshoot problems effectively.

You need the following software packages to get started:

- JDK (Java SE Development Kit) 5.0 or higher (http://java.sun.com/j2se)
- JSF 2.0 (either included with your application server or separately available at http://javaserverfaces.dev.java.net)
- The sample code for this book, available at http://corejsf.com

We assume that you have already installed the JDK and that you are familiar with the JDK tools. For more information on the JDK, see Cay Horstmann and Gary Cornell, *Core Java™*, 8th ed., Santa Clara, CA: Sun Microsystems Press/ Prentice Hall, 2008.

Since JSF 2.0 is part of the Java EE 6 specification, the easiest way to try out JSF is to use an application server that is compatible with Java EE 6, such as Glass-Fish version 3 (http://glassfish.dev.java.net).

If you do not want to install a complete application server, you can use a servlet runner, such as Tomcat (http://tomcat.apache.org), together with the JSF reference implementation (available at http://javaserverfaces.dev.java.net).

If you use another application server or servlet runner, you will need to adjust the instructions that follow.

Here are the build instructions for the sample JSF application.

1. Launch a command shell.
2. Change to the *corejsf-examples* directory—that is, the directory that contains the sample code for this book.
3. If you use GlassFish or another Java EE 6 compliant application server, change to the javaee subdirectory. If you use Tomcat, change to the tomcat subdirectory.
4. Change to the source directory and make the directory for holding the class files:

    ```
    cd ch01/login/src/java
    mkdir ../../web/WEB-INF/classes
    ```

    On Windows, use backslashes as file separators.
5. If you use GlassFish, run

    ```
    javac -d ../../web/WEB-INF/classes -classpath .:glassfish/modules/\*
        com/corejsf/UserBean.java
    ```

On Windows, use a semicolon in the classpath, and don't escape the * wildcard:

```
javac -d ..\..\web\WEB-INF\classes -classpath .;glassfish\modules\*
    com\corejsf\UserBean.java
```

If you use Tomcat, use the following command to compile your code:

```
javac -d ../../web/WEB-INF/classes -classpath .:jsf-ref-impl/lib/jsf-api.jar
    com/corejsf/UserBean.java
```

6. If you use Tomcat, you need to include the JSF libraries:

```
mkdir ../../web/WEB-INF/lib
cp jsf-ref-impl/lib/*.jar ../../web/WEB-INF/lib
```

Skip this step if you use a Java EE 6 compliant application server.

7. Run the following commands (and note the period at the end of the jar command, indicating the current directory):

```
cd ../..
jar cvf login.war .
```

Deploying a JSF Application

Install your server and start it. For example, to start GlassFish on Unix/Linux, you use the command:

```
glassfish/bin/asadmin start-domain
```

(See Figure 1–5.) To start Tomcat on Unix/Linux, use:

```
tomcat/bin/startup.sh
```

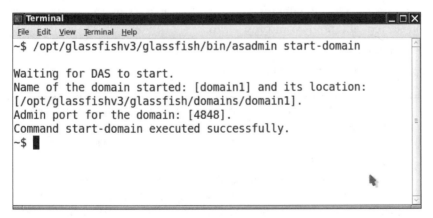

Figure 1–5   Starting GlassFish

To test that your server runs properly, point your browser to a default URL. With GlassFish and Tomcat, that is `http://localhost:8080`. You should see a welcome page (see Figure 1–6).

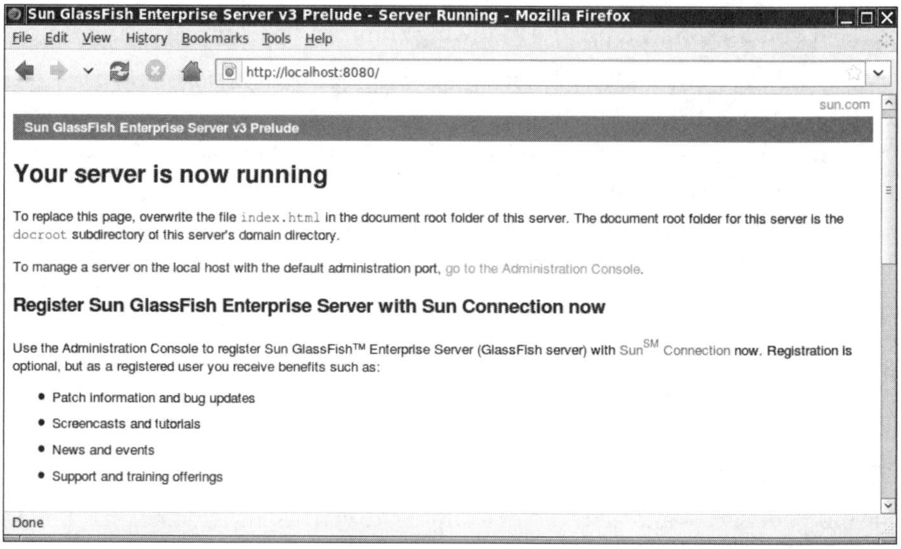

Figure 1–6   GlassFish welcome page

Most servers let you deploy applications by copying WAR files to a deployment directory. In GlassFish, that directory is *glassfish*/domains/domain1/autodeploy. With Tomcat, you deploy WAR files in the *tomcat*/webapps directory.

Copy the `login.war` file to the deployment directory, make sure that your server has been started, and point your browser to:

```
http://localhost:8080/login
```

The application should start up at this point.

> NOTE: If something goes wrong with deploying the example program, you should consult the log file for clues. GlassFish logs all messages in the file *glassfish*/domains/domain1/logs/server.log. Tomcat keeps logs in the *tomcat*/logs/catalina.out file.
>
> As you start developing your own applications, it is useful to know that the logs contain all output that was sent to `System.out` and `System.err`. In the default configuration, that includes all logging messages with level `INFO` or higher.
>
> In other words, you can simply include calls to `System.out.println` or `Logger.get-Global().info` for debugging purposes, and the output will appear in the logs.

Development Environments for JSF

You can produce the pages and configuration files for a simple JSF application with a text editor. However, as your applications become more complex, you will want to use more sophisticated tools.

IDEs, such as Eclipse or NetBeans, are deservedly popular with programmers. Support for autocompletion, refactoring, debugging, and so on, can dramatically increase programmer productivity, particularly for large projects.

As this book is written, both Eclipse and Netbeans have good JSF support. Netbeans gives you one-stop shopping: it is already fully integrated with GlassFish and Tomcat. With Eclipse, install GlassFish or Tomcat separately and use a server plugin. (The GlassFish plugin is at https://glassfishplugins.dev.java.net.) Eclipse has fairly basic JSF support. Several commercial Eclipse derivatives (such as MyEclipse, JBoss Developer Studio, and Rational Application Developer) as well as Oracle JDeveloper have advanced JSF features. They all have trial versions that you can download.

When you load one of the sample projects from the book's companion code into your IDE, choose the option for importing a web project from existing sources. Select the source directory, such as *corejsf-examples*/javaee/ch01/login. Netbeans automatically picks up the correct source and web directories, but with Eclipse, you need to change the defaults src and WebContent to src/java and web (see Figure 1–7).

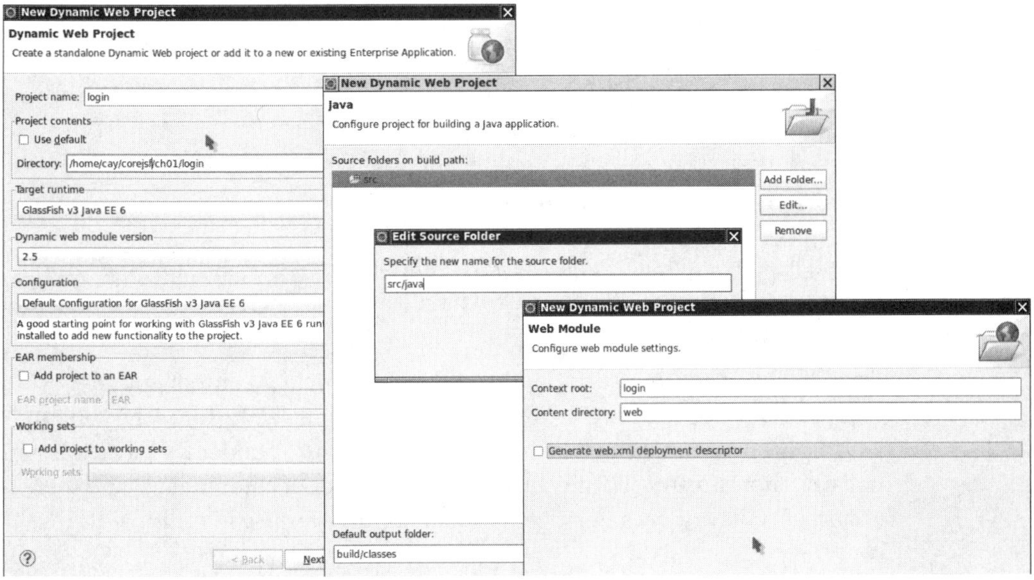

Figure 1–7   Importing a project into Eclipse

With an IDE, it is very easy to run and debug applications. Figure 1–8 shows the Eclipse debugger, stopped at a breakpoint in the UserBean class. Both Eclipse and Netbeans support *hot fixes*, the ability to make changes to JSF pages and Java code that are instantly reflected in the running program. (Fair warning: Hot fixes can't always be applied, and you will occasionally need to redeploy your application or even restart the application server.)

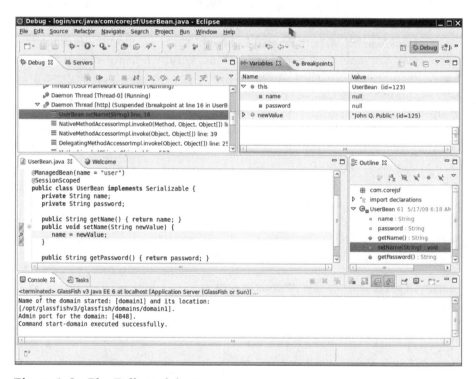

Figure 1–8   The Eclipse debugger

Some IDEs have a *visual builder tool* that allows a designer to drag and drop components from a palette onto a JSF page. Figure 1–9 shows the visual builder in JDeveloper.

Visual JSF builders are usually optimized for a particular component set. For example, JDeveloper uses the ADF Faces components. Unfortunately, you cannot simply add your favorite component set to a visual builder tool. The JSF standard does not currently specify design time behavior of components, and there is no standard way of packaging component libraries for use in multiple IDEs.

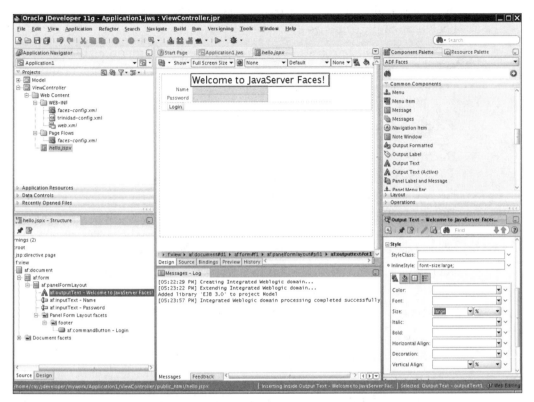

Figure 1–9   Visual JSF development

An Analysis of the Sample Application

You have now seen a simple JSF application, and you now know how to build and run it. Now let us have a closer look at the structure of the application.

Web applications have two parts: the *presentation layer* and the *business logic*. The presentation layer is concerned with the look of the application. In the context of a browser-based application, the look is determined by the HTML tags that specify layout, fonts, images, and so on. The business logic is implemented in the Java code that determines the behavior of the application.

Some web technologies intermingle HTML and code. That approach is seductive since it is easy to produce simple applications in a single file. But for serious applications, mixing markup and code poses considerable problems.

Professional web designers know about graphic design, but they typically rely on tools that translate their vision into HTML. They would certainly not want to deal with embedded code. On the other hand, programmers are notoriously unqualified when it comes to graphic design. (The example programs in this book bear ample evidence.)

Thus, for designing professional web applications, it is important to *separate* the presentation from the business logic. This allows both web designers and programmers to focus on their core competencies.

In the context of JSF, the application code is contained in beans, and the design is contained in web pages. We look at beans first.

Beans

A Java *bean* is a class that exposes properties and events to a framework, such as JSF. A *property* is a named value of a given type that can be read and/or written. The simplest way to define a property is to use a standard naming convention for the reader and writer methods, namely, the familiar get/set convention. The first letter of the property name is changed to uppercase in the method names.

For example, the UserBean class has two properties, name and password, both of type String:

```
public class UserBean implements Serializable {
   . . .
   public String getName() { . . . }
   public void setName(String newValue) {. . . }

   public String getPassword() { . . . }
   public void setPassword(String newValue) { . . . }
}
```

The get/set methods can carry out arbitrary actions. In many cases, they simply get or set an instance field. But they might also carry out some computations or even access a database.

> NOTE: According to the bean specification, it is legal to omit a getter or setter method. For example, if getPassword is omitted, then password is a write-only property. That might be desirable for security reasons. However, JSF does not support write-only properties. You always use read/write properties for input components, though you can use read-only properties for output components.

A *managed bean* is a Java bean that can be accessed from a JSF page. A managed bean must have a *name* and a *scope*. The bean in our example has name user and *session* scope. This means that the bean object is available for one user across multiple pages. Different users who use the web application are given different instances of the bean object. You will encounter additional bean scopes in Chapter 2.

The beans are "managed" in the following sense: When the bean name occurs in a JSF page, the JSF implementation locates the object with that name, or constructs it if it does not yet exist in the appropriate scope. For example, if a second user connects to our sample application, another UserBean object is constructed.

The easiest way of specifying the name and scope of a managed bean is to use attributes:

```
@Named("user") // or @ManagedBean(name="user")
@SessionScoped
public class UserBean implements Serializable
```

In JSF applications, you use managed beans for all data that needs to be accessible from a page. The beans are the conduits between the user interface and the backend of the application.

JSF Pages

You need a JSF page for each browser screen. For historical reasons, there are several different mechanisms for authoring JSF pages. JSF 1.x was based on JavaServer Pages (JSP), which caused some unpleasant technical problems. However, JSF allows programmers to replace the "view handler" that processes JSF pages. The Facelets project did just that, providing better error messages, a mechanism for factoring out common page parts, and an easier mechanism for writing your own components. Facelets has become a part of JSF 2.0, and we use it in this book.

When you author a Facelets page, you add JSF tags to an XHTML page. An XHTML page is simply an HTML page that is also proper XML. We use the extension .xhtml for Facelets pages.

Have another look at the first page of our sample application in Listing 1–1. At the top of the page, you will find a namespace declaration:

```
<html xmlns="http://www.w3.org/1999/xhtml" xmlns:h="http://java.sun.com/jsf/html">
```

The second line declares the h: prefix for the JSF HTML tags.

The JSF implementation also defines a set of core tags that are independent of HTML. If you need such a tag in your page, you must add a namespace declaration:

```
xmlns:f="http://java.sun.com/jsf/core"
```

If you use tag libraries from other vendors, you supply additional namespace declarations.

NOTE: You can choose any tag prefixes that you like, such as `html:inputText` instead of `h:inputText`. In this book, we always use `h` for the HTML tags and `f` for the core tags.

A JSF page is similar to an HTML form. Note the following differences:

• Your page must be properly formatted XHTML. Unlike a browser, the JSF implementation is not forgiving of syntax errors.

• You use `h:head`, `h:body`, and `h:form` instead of `head`, `body`, and `form`.

• Instead of using the familiar `input` HTML tags, use `h:inputText`, `h:inputSecret`, and `h:commandButton`.

NOTE: Instead of using a JSF tag such as:

`<h:inputText value="#{user.name}"/>`

you can use a regular HTML tag with a `jsfc` attribute:

`<input type="text" jsfc="h:inputText" value="#{user.name}"/>`

That feature is intended to facilitate page authoring in a web design tool. However, it only works for those JSF components that directly correspond to HTML components. In this book, we always use the JSF tags.

NOTE: If you are familiar with earlier versions of JSF, you may have seen JSF pages defined with the JSP syntax:

```
<html>
    <%@ taglib uri="http://java.sun.com/jsf/core" prefix="f" %>
    <f:view>
        <head>...</head>
        <body>...</body>
    </f:view>
</html>
```

You can still use JSP in JSF 2.0, but we do not recommend it. One disadvantage is that you can get very cryptic error messages if a page has a syntax error. More importantly, some JSF 2.0 features (such as templating) only work with Facelets.

We discuss all standard JSF tags and their attributes in Chapters 4 and 5. In the first three chapters, we can get by with input fields and command buttons.

The input field values are bound to properties of the bean with name user:

```
<h:inputText value="#{user.name}"/>
```

The #{...} delimiters enclose expressions in the JSF "expression language," which we discuss in detail in Chapter 2.

When the page is displayed, the JSF implementation locates the user bean and calls the getName method to obtain the current property value. When the page is submitted, the JSF implementation invokes the setName method to set the value that was entered into the form.

The h:commandButton tag has an action attribute whose value indicates which page should be displayed next:

```
<h:commandButton value="Login" action="welcome"/>
```

Servlet Configuration

When you deploy a JSF application inside an application server, you need to supply a configuration file named web.xml. Fortunately, you can use the same web.xml file for most JSF applications. Listing 1–4 shows the file.

Listing 1–4   login/web/WEB-INF/web.xml

```
1. <?xml version="1.0" encoding="UTF-8"?>
2. <web-app xmlns:xsi="http://www.w3.org/2001/XMLSchema-instance"
3.    xmlns="http://java.sun.com/xml/ns/javaee"
4.    xmlns:web="http://java.sun.com/xml/ns/javaee/web-app_2_5.xsd"
5.    xsi:schemaLocation="http://java.sun.com/xml/ns/javaee
6.       http://java.sun.com/xml/ns/javaee/web-app_2_5.xsd"
7.    version="2.5">
8.    <servlet>
9.       <servlet-name>Faces Servlet</servlet-name>
10.       <servlet-class>javax.faces.webapp.FacesServlet</servlet-class>
11.    </servlet>
12.    <servlet-mapping>
13.       <servlet-name>Faces Servlet</servlet-name>
14.       <url-pattern>/faces/*</url-pattern>
15.    </servlet-mapping>
16.    <welcome-file-list>
17.       <welcome-file>faces/index.xhtml</welcome-file>
18.    </welcome-file-list>
19.    <context-param>
20.       <param-name>javax.faces.PROJECT_STAGE</param-name>
21.       <param-value>Development</param-value>
22.    </context-param>
23. </web-app>
```

All JSF pages are passed to the Faces servlet that is a part of the JSF implementation code. To ensure that the correct servlet is activated when a JSF page is requested, the JSF URLs have a special format. In our configuration, they have a prefix /faces. The `servlet-mapping` element ensures that all URLs with that prefix are processed by the Faces servlet.

For example, you cannot simply point your browser to `http://localhost:8080/login/index.xhtml`. The URL has to be `http://localhost:8080/login/`**`faces`**`/index.xhtml`. The mapping rule activates the Faces servlet, which is the entry point to the JSF implementation. The JSF implementation strips off the /faces prefix, loads the `index.xhtml` page, processes the tags, and displays the result.

 CAUTION: If you view a JSF page without the /faces prefix, the browser will display the HTML tags in the page, but it will simply skip the JSF tags.

 NOTE: You can also define an *extension mapping* instead of the /faces prefix mapping. Use the following directive in your `web.xml` file:

```
<servlet-mapping>
    <servlet-name>Faces Servlet</servlet-name>
    <url-pattern>*.faces</url-pattern>
</servlet-mapping>
```

Then use the URL `http://localhost:8080/login/index.faces`. That URL activates the Faces servlet. The JSF implementation strips off the `faces` prefix and loads the file `/login/index.xhtml`.

NOTE: Strictly speaking, JSF pages are not XHTML files—they only aim to produce such files. If you want to use a `.jsf` extension for JSF page files, then add the following entry to the `web.xml` file:

```
<context-param>
    <param-name>javax.faces.DEFAULT_SUFFIX</param-name>
    <param-value>.jsf</param-value>
</context-param>
```

Note that this configuration affects only the web developers, not the users of your web application. The URLs still have a `.faces` extension or `/faces` prefix.

The `web.xml` file specifies a *welcome page*, the page that is loaded when the user enters the URL of the web application. For example, if a user enters the

URL http://localhost:8080/login, the application server automatically loads the page /faces/index.xhtml.

Finally, we specify a parameter that adds support for debugging a JSF application:

```
<context-param>
   <param-name>javax.faces.PROJECT_STAGE</param-name>
   <param-value>Development</param-value>
</context-param>
```

The choices for the project stage are Development, UnitTest, SystemTest, and Production. In the development stage, you get more informative error messages.

NOTE: The PROJECT_STAGE parameter was introduced in JSF 2.0.

NOTE: Some application servers (including GlassFish) automatically provide a servlet mapping for the /faces/*, *.faces, and *.jsf patterns, provided that any of the following conditions applies:

- Any of the classes in the web application uses a JSF annotation
- Any initialization parameters start with javax.faces
- The WEB-INF/faces-config.xml file is present

It's not necessary to supply a web.xml file if you don't need to set other parameters. However, since we recommend to set the project stage to Development, we will supply web.xml files in our examples. If you know that your application server automatically detects JSF applications, then you can omit the declaration of the Faces servlet and the servlet mapping from your web.xml file.

A First Glimpse of Ajax JSF 2.0

Asynchronous JavaScript with XMLHttpRequest (Ajax) is a technology for updating a web page in the browser client without submitting a form and rendering the response. The web page contains JavaScript code that communicates with the server and makes incremental changes to the structure of the page. The result is a smoother user experience without the dreaded "page flip".

We will discuss Ajax in detail in Chapter 10. Fortunately, JSF 2.0 lets you use Ajax without having to understand the considerable complexities of the Ajax communication channel. Here, we give you a quick flavor to whet your appetite.

We will restructure our login application so that the Login button makes an
Ajax request instead of submitting the form. As soon as the user has logged in,
a greeting will appear (see Figure 1–10).

Figure 1–10   With Ajax, the welcome message appears without a page flip

Each component that is accessed by the client code needs an ID, which we
declare with the id attribute, like this:

```
<h:outputText id="out" value="#{user.greeting}"/>
```

We also give IDs to the name and password input fields.

By default, the form ID is prepended to the IDs of its components. We turn this
process off in order to have simpler ID names, by setting the prependId attribute
of the form to false (see Listing 1–5).

We add a read-only greeting property to the UserBean class:

```
public String getGreeting() {
    if (name.length() == 0) return "";
```

```
      else return "Welcome to JSF2 + Ajax, " + name + "!";
}
```

This greeting will be displayed in the text field.

Now we are ready to implement the Ajax behavior for the Login button:

```
<h:commandButton value="Login">
    <f:ajax execute="name password" render="out" />
</h:commandButton>
```

When the Login button is clicked, the form is not submitted. Instead, an Ajax request is sent to the server.

The execute and render attributes specify lists of component IDs. The execute components are processed exactly as if the form had been submitted. In particular, their values are sent to the server and the corresponding bean properties are updated. The render components are processed as if the page had been displayed. In our case, the getGreeting method of the user bean is called, and its result is sent to the client and displayed.

Note that the user bean is located on the server. The greeting is *not* computed on the client. Instead, the client code sends component values to the server, receives updated HTML for the components to be rendered, and splices those updates into the page.

When you run this application, you can see that there is no "page flip" when you press the login button. Only the greeting is updated; the remainder of the page stays unchanged.

As you just saw, using Ajax with JSF is pretty straightforward. You write the program logic in Java and use the same mechanism for interacting with the Java code as you would in a regular JSF page.

Listing 1–5 login-ajax/web/index.xhtml

```
 1. <?xml version="1.0" encoding="UTF-8"?>
 2. <!DOCTYPE html PUBLIC "-//W3C//DTD XHTML 1.0 Transitional//EN"
 3. "http://www.w3.org/TR/xhtml1/DTD/xhtml1-transitional.dtd">
 4. <html xmlns="http://www.w3.org/1999/xhtml"
 5.       xmlns:h="http://java.sun.com/jsf/html"
 6.       xmlns:f="http://java.sun.com/jsf/core">
 7.   <h:head>
 8.     <title>Welcome</title>
 9.   </h:head>
10.   <h:body>
11.     <h:form prependId="false">
12.       <h3>Please enter your name and password.</h3>
```

```
13.        <table>
14.          <tr>
15.            <td>Name:</td>
16.            <td><h:inputText value="#{user.name}" id="name"/></td>
17.          </tr>
18.          <tr>
19.            <td>Password:</td>
20.            <td><h:inputSecret value="#{user.password}" id="password"/></td>
21.          </tr>
22.        </table>
23.        <p><h:commandButton value="Login">
24.          <f:ajax execute="name password" render="out"/>
25.        </h:commandButton></p>
26.        <h3><h:outputText id="out" value="#{user.greeting}"/></h3>
27.      </h:form>
28.    </h:body>
29. </html>
```

JSF Framework Services

Now that you have seen your first JSF application, it is easier to explain the services that the JSF framework offers to developers. Figure 1–11 gives a high-level overview of the JSF architecture. As you can see, the JSF framework is responsible for interacting with client devices, and it provides tools for tying together the visual presentation, application logic, and business logic of a web application. However, the scope of JSF is restricted to the presentation tier. Database persistence, web services, and other backend connections are outside the scope of JSF.

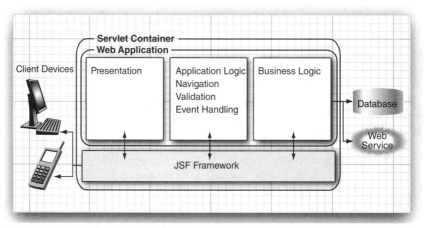

Figure 1–11   High-level overview of the JSF framework

Here are the most important services that the JSF framework provides:

- **Model-view-controller architecture**—All software applications let users manipulate certain data, such as shopping carts, travel itineraries, or whatever data is required in a particular problem domain. This data is called the *model*. Just as artists create paintings of a model in a studio, a web application displays *views* of the data model. In a web application, HTML (or a similar rendering technology) is used to paint these views.

  JSF connects the view and the model. As you have seen, a view component can be wired to a bean property of a model object, such as:

  ```
  <h:inputText value="#{user.name}"/>
  ```

  The JSF implementation operates as the *controller* that reacts to the user by processing action and value change events, routing them to code that updates the model or the view. For example, you may want to invoke a method to check whether a user is allowed to log on. Use the following JSF tag:

  ```
  <h:commandButton value="Login" action="#{user.check}"/>
  ```

  When the user clicks the button and the form is submitted to the server, the JSF implementation invokes the check method of the user bean. That method can take arbitrary actions to update the model, and it returns the ID of the next page to be displayed. We discuss this mechanism further in Chapter 3.

  Thus, JSF implements a model-view-controller architecture.

- **Data conversion**—Users enter data into web forms as text. Business objects want data as numbers, dates, or other data types. As explained in Chapter 7, JSF makes it easy to specify and customize conversion rules.

- **Validation and error handling**—JSF makes it easy to attach validation rules for fields such as "this field is required" or "this field must be a number". Of course, when users enter invalid data, you need to display appropriate error messages. JSF takes away much of the tedium of this programming task. We cover validation in Chapter 7.

- **Internationalization**—JSF manages internationalization issues, such as character encodings and the selection of resource bundles. We cover resource bundles in Chapter 2.

- **Custom components**—Component developers can develop sophisticated components that page designers simply drop into their pages. For example, suppose a component developer produces a calendar component with all the usual bells and whistles. You just use it in your page, with a command, such as:

```
<acme:calendar value="#{flight.departure}" startOfWeek="Mon"/>
```

Chapter 11 covers custom components in detail.

- **Ajax support**—JSF provides a standard Ajax communication channel that transparently invokes server-side actions and updates client-side components. See Chapter 10 for more information.

- **Alternative renderers**—By default, JSF generates markup for HTML pages. But it is possible to extend the JSF framework to produce markup for another page description language such as WML or XUL. When JSF was first developed, this flexibility seemed quite intriguing. However, we have never seen a compelling use of this generality and do not cover it in this book.

Behind the Scenes

Now that you have read about the "what" and the "why" of JSF, you may be curious about just how the JSF implementation does its job.

Let us look behind the scenes of our sample application. We start at the point when the browser first connects to `http://localhost:8080/login/faces/index.xhtml`. The JSF implementation initializes the JSF code and reads the `index.xhtml` page. That page contains tags, such as `h:form` and `h:inputText`. Each tag has an associated *tag handler* class. When the page is read, the tag handlers are executed. The JSF tag handlers collaborate with each other to build a *component tree* (see Figure 1–12).

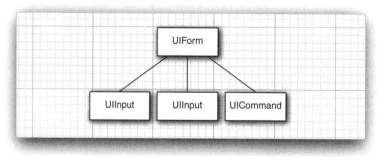

Figure 1–12   Component tree of the sample application

The component tree is a data structure that contains Java objects for all user interface elements on the JSF page. For example, the two UIInput objects correspond to the h:inputText and h:inputSecret fields in the JSF file.

Rendering Pages

Next, the HTML page is *rendered*. All text that is not a JSF tag is passed through. The h:form, h:inputText, h:inputSecret, and h:commandButton tags are converted to HTML.

As we just discussed, each of these tags gives rise to an associated component. Each component has a *renderer* that produces HTML output, reflecting the component state. For example, the renderer for the component that corresponds to the h:inputText tag produces the following output:

```
<input type="text" name="unique ID" value="current value"/>
```

This process is called *encoding*. The renderer of the UIInput object asks the JSF implementation to look up the unique ID and the current value of the expression user.name. By default, ID strings are assigned by the JSF implementation. The IDs can look rather random, such as _id_id12:_id_id21.

The encoded page is sent to the browser, and the browser displays it in the usual way (see Figure 1–13).

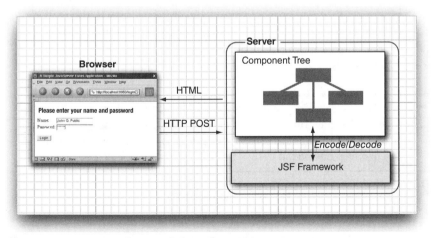

Figure 1–13 Encoding and decoding JSF pages

TIP: Select "View -> Page source" from the browser menu to see the HTML output of the rendering process. Figure 1–14 shows a typical output. This is useful for debugging JSF problems.

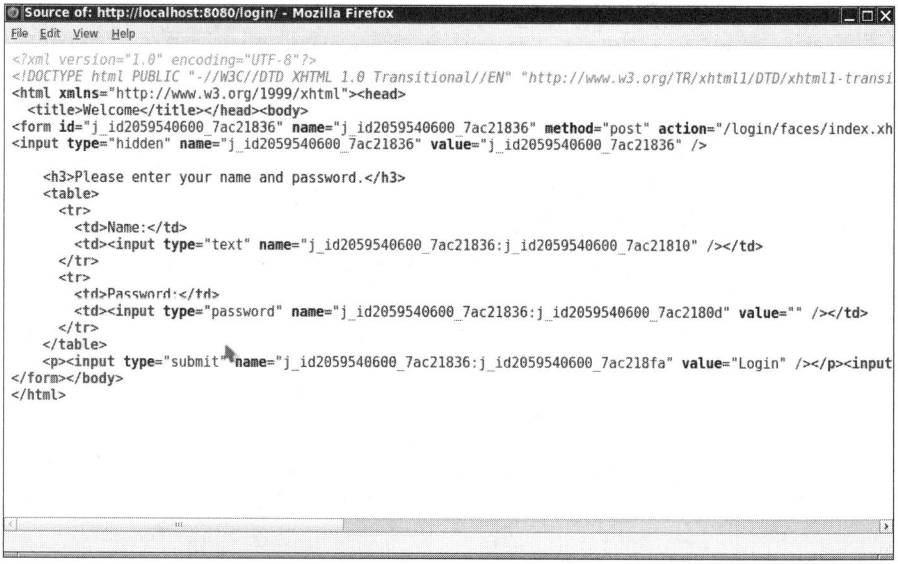

Figure 1–14   Viewing the source of the login page

Decoding Requests

After the page is displayed in the browser, the user fills in the form fields and clicks the login button. The browser sends the *form data* back to the web server, formatted as a *POST request*. This is a special format, defined as part of the HTTP protocol. The POST request contains the URL of the form (/login/faces/index.xhtml), as well as the form data.

> NOTE: The URL for the POST request is the same as that of the request that renders the form. Navigation to a new page occurs after the form has been submitted. (For this reason, the URL displayed in the browser is usually one step behind the URL of the JSF page that is being displayed.)

The form data is a string of ID/value pairs, such as:

id1=me&*id2*=secret&*id3*=Login

As part of the normal request processing, the form data is placed in a hash table that all components can access.

Next, the JSF implementation gives each component a chance to inspect that hash table, a process called *decoding*. Each component decides on its own how to interpret the form data.

The login form has three component objects: two UIInput objects that correspond to the text fields on the form and one UICommand object that corresponds to the submit button.

- The UIInput components update the bean properties referenced in the value attributes: they invoke the setter methods with the values that the user supplied.

- The UICommand component checks whether the button was clicked. If so, it fires an *action event* to launch the login action referenced in the action attribute. That event tells the navigation handler to look up the successor page, welcome.xhtml.

Now the cycle repeats.

You have just seen the two most important processing steps of the JSF implementation: encoding and decoding. However, the processing sequence (also called the *life cycle*) is a bit more intricate. If everything goes well, you do not need to worry about the intricacies of the life cycle. However, when an error occurs, you will definitely want to understand what the JSF implementation does. In the next section, we look at the life cycle in greater detail.

The Life Cycle

The JSF specification defines six distinct *phases*:

1. Restore View
2. Apply Request Values
3. Process Validations
4. Update Model Values
5. Invoke Application
6. Render Response

Here we discuss the most common flow through the life cycle (see Figure 1–15). You will see a number of variations throughout the book.

The *Restore View* phase retrieves the component tree for the requested page if it was displayed previously or constructs a new component tree if it is displayed for the first time.

If there are no request values, the JSF implementation skips ahead to the *Render Response* phase. This happens when a page is displayed for the first time.

Otherwise, the next phase is the *Apply Request Values* phase. In this phase, the JSF implementation iterates over the component objects in the component tree. Each component object checks which request values belong to it and stores them.

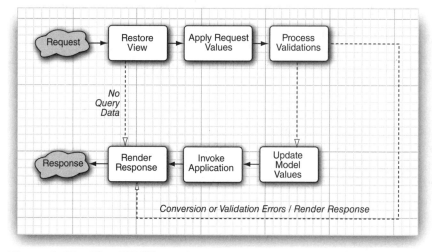

Figure 1–15   The JSF life cycle

The values stored in the component are called "local values". When you design a JSF page, you can attach validators that perform correctness checks on the local values. These validators are executed in the *Process Validations* phase. If validation passes, the JSF life cycle proceeds normally. However, when conversion or validation errors occur, the JSF implementation invokes the Render Response phase directly, redisplaying the current page so that the user has another chance to provide correct inputs.

> NOTE: To many programmers, this is the most surprising aspect of the JSF life cycle. If a converter or validator fails, the current page is redisplayed. You should add tags to display the validation errors so that your users know why they see the old page again. See Chapter 7 for details.

After the converters and validators have done their work, it is assumed that it is safe to update the model data. During the *Update Model Values* phase, the local values are used to update the beans that are wired to the components.

In the *Invoke Application* phase, the action method of the button or link component that caused the form submission is executed. That method can carry out arbitrary application processing. It returns an outcome string that is passed to the navigation handler. The navigation handler looks up the next page.

Finally, the *Render Response* phase encodes the response and sends it to the browser. When a user submits a form, clicks a link, or otherwise generates a new request, the cycle starts anew.

> **NOTE:** In the Ajax example, the Ajax request added the input components to the execute list and the output component to the render list. For components on the execute list, all phases except for "Render Response" are carried out. In particular, during the "Update Model Values" phase, the model bean is updated. Conversely, for components on the render list, the "Render Response" phase of the lifecycle is executed, and the result is sent back to the Ajax request.

Conclusion

You have now seen the basic mechanisms that make the JSF magic possible. In the following chapters, we examine the various parts of the life cycle in more detail.

MANAGED BEANS

Chapter 2

A central theme of web application design is the separation of presentation and business logic. JSF uses *beans* to achieve this separation. JSF pages refer to bean properties, and the program logic is contained in the bean implementation code. Because beans are so fundamental to JSF programming, we discuss them in detail in this chapter.

The first half of the chapter discusses the essential features of beans that every JSF developer needs to know. We then present an example program that puts these essentials to work. The remaining sections cover more technical aspects about bean configuration and value expressions. You can safely skip these sections when you first read this book and return to them when the need arises.

Definition of a Bean

According to the JavaBeans specification (available at http://java.sun.com/ products/javabeans/), a Java bean is "a reusable software component that can be manipulated in a builder tool". That is a pretty broad definition and indeed, as you will see in this chapter, beans are used for a variety of purposes.

At first glance, a bean seems to be similar to an object. However, beans serve a different purpose. Objects are created and manipulated inside a Java program when the program calls constructors and invokes methods. Yet, beans can be created and manipulated *without programming*.

> NOTE: You may wonder where the term "bean" comes from. Well, Java is a synonym for coffee (at least in the United States), and coffee is made from beans that encapsulate its flavor. You may find the analogy cute or annoying, but the term has stuck.

The "classic" application for JavaBeans is a user interface builder. A palette window in the builder tool contains component beans such as text fields, sliders, checkboxes, and so on. Instead of writing Java code, you use a user interface designer to drag and drop component beans from the palette into a form. Then you can customize the beans by selecting property values from a *property sheet* dialog (see Figure 2–1).

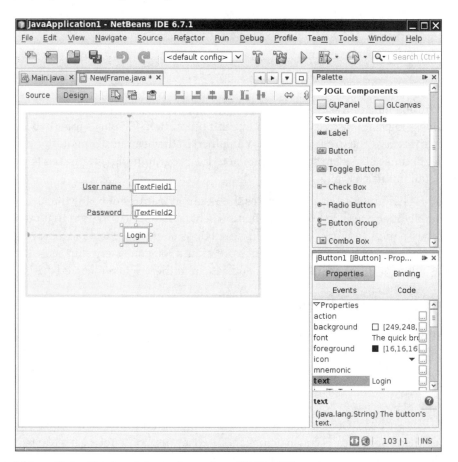

Figure 2–1   Customizing a bean in a GUI builder

In the context of JSF, beans store the state of web pages. Bean creation and manipulation is under the control of the JSF implementation. The JSF implementation does the following:

- Creates and discards beans as needed (hence the term "managed beans")
- Reads bean properties when displaying a web page
- Sets bean properties when a form is posted

Consider the login application in Chapter 1, shown in "A Simple Example" on page 4. An input field reads and updates the password property of the user bean:

```
<h:inputSecret value="#{user.password}"/>
```

The JSF implementation needs to locate a bean class for the bean named user. In our example, a UserBean class was declared as follows:

```
@ManagedBean(name="user")
@SessionScoped
public class UserBean implements Serializable {
   ...
}
```

You can omit the name attribute in the @ManagedBean annotation. In that case, the bean name is derived from the class name by turning the first letter into lowercase. For example, if you omit (name = "user") in the example above, the bean name becomes userBean.

CAUTION: The @ManagedBean annotation is in the javax.faces.bean package. Java EE 6 defines another @ManagedBean annotation in the javax.annotation package that does not work with JSF.

When an expression with name user is first encountered, the JSF implementation constructs an object of the class UserBean. The object stays alive for the duration of the *session*—that is, for all requests that originate from the same client, lasting until the session is either terminated explicitly or it times out. Throughout the session, the bean name user references the previously constructed object.

At any given point in time, different sessions that belong to different clients may be active on the server. Each of them has its own UserBean object.

NOTE: The UserBean class implements the Serializable interface. This is not a requirement for a JSF managed bean, but it is nevertheless a good idea for session-scoped beans. Application servers can provide better management for serializable beans, such as clustering.

As you can see, the JSF developer does not need to write any Java code to construct and manipulate the user bean. The JSF implementation constructs the beans and accesses them, as described by the expressions in the JSF pages.

Bean Properties

Bean classes need to follow specific programming conventions to expose features that tools can use. We discuss these conventions in this section.

The most important features of a bean are the properties that it exposes. A *property* is any attribute of a bean that has:

- A name
- A type
- Methods for getting and/or setting the property value

For example, the UserBean class of the preceding chapter has a property with name password and type String. The methods getPassword and setPassword access the property value.

Some programming languages, in particular Visual Basic and C#, have direct support for properties. However, in Java, a bean is simply a class that follows certain coding conventions.

The JavaBeans specification puts a single demand on a bean class: It must have a public constructor without parameters. However, to define properties, a bean must either use a *naming pattern* for property getters and setters, or it must define a companion *bean info* class. (Bean info classes are not commonly used, and we will not discuss them here. See Cay Horstmann and Gary Cornell, *Core Java™*, *Eighth Edition*, Santa Clara, CA: Sun Microsystems Press/Prentice Hall, 2008, Vol. 2, Chapter 8, for more information.)

Defining properties with naming patterns is straightforward. Consider the following pair of methods:

```
public T getFoo()
public void setFoo(T newValue)
```

The pair corresponds to a read-write property with type *T* and name foo. If you have only the first method, then the property is read-only. If you have only the second method, then the property is write-only.

The method names and signatures must match the pattern precisely. The method name must start with get or set. A get method must have no parameters. A set method must have one parameter and no return value. A bean class can have other methods, but the methods do not yield bean properties.

Note that the name of the property is the "decapitalized" form of the part of the method name that follows the get or set prefix. For example, getFoo gives rise to a property named foo, with the first letter turned into lowercase. However, if the first *two* letters after the prefix are uppercase, then the first letter stays unchanged. For example, the method name getURL defines a property URL and not uRL.

For properties of type boolean, you have a choice of prefixes for the method that reads the property. Both

```
public boolean isConnected()
```

and

```
public boolean getConnected()
```

are valid names for the reader of the connected property.

> NOTE: The JavaBeans specification also defines indexed properties, speci-
> fied by method sets such as the following:
>
> ```
> public T[] getFoo()
> public T getFoo(int index)
> public void setFoo(T[] newArray)
> public void setFoo(int index, T newValue)
> ```
>
> However, JSF provides no support for accessing the indexed values.

The JavaBeans specification is silent on the *behavior* of the getter and setter methods. In many situations, these methods simply manipulate an instance field. But they may equally well carry out more sophisticated operations, such as database lookups, data conversion, validation, and so on.

A bean class may have other methods beyond property getters and setters. Of course, those methods do not give rise to bean properties.

Value Expressions

As you already saw in Chapter 1, you can use an expression, such as #{user.name}, to access a property of a bean. In JSF, such an expression is called a *value expression*. For example, the welcome.xhtml page contains the fragment:

```
Welcome to JavaServer Faces, #{user.name}!
```

When the JSF implementation renders that page, it invokes the getName method of the user object.

A value expression can be used both for reading and writing a value. Consider this input component:

```
<h:inputText value="#{user.name}"/>
```

When the JSF implementation renders the component, it calls the property getter is invoked when the component is rendered. When the user submits the page, the JSF implementation invokes the property setter.

We will discuss value expressions in detail in the section "The Expression Language Syntax" on page 63.

 NOTE: JSF value expressions are related to the expression language used in JSP. Those expressions are delimited by ${...} instead of #{...}. As of JSF 1.2 and JSP 2.1, the syntax of both expression languages has been unified. (See "The Expression Language Syntax" on page 63 for a complete description of the syntax.)

The ${...} delimiter denotes *immediate* evaluation of expressions. When the page is processed, the expression's value is computed and inserted. In contrast, the #{...} delimiter denotes *deferred* evaluation. With deferred evaluation, the JSF implementation retains the expression and evaluates it whenever a value is needed.

As a rule of thumb, you always use deferred expressions for JSF component properties, and you use immediate expressions in plain JSP or JSTL (JavaServer Pages Standard Tag Library) constructs. (These constructs are rarely needed in JSF pages.)

Backing Beans

Sometimes it is convenient to design a bean that contains some or all component objects of a web form. Such a bean is called a *backing bean* for the web form.

For example, we can define a backing bean for the quiz form by adding properties for the form component:

```
@ManagedBean(name="quizForm")
@SessionScoped
public class QuizFormBean {
   private UIInput answerComponent;
   private UIOutput scoreComponent;

   public UIInput getAnswerComponent() { return answerComponent; }
   public void setAnswerComponent(UIInput newValue) { answerComponent = newValue; }

   public UIOutput getScoreComponent() { return scoreComponent; }
   public void setScoreComponent(UIOutput newValue) { scoreComponent = newValue; }
   ...
}
```

Input components belong to the UIInput class and output components belong to the UIOutput class. We discuss these classes in greater detail in Chapter 11.

Some visual JSF development environments use backing beans. These environments automatically generate property getters and setters for all components that are dragged onto a form.

When you use a backing bean, you need to wire up the components on the form to those on the bean. You use the binding attribute for this purpose:

```
<h:inputText binding="#{quizForm.answerComponent}" .../>
```

When the component tree for the form is built, the getAnswerComponent method of the backing bean is called, but it returns null. As a result, an output component is constructed and installed into the backing bean with a call to setAnswerComponent.

CDI Beans CDI

JSF pioneered the concept of "managed beans" in web applications. However, JSF managed beans are fairly limited. JSR 299 ("Contexts and Dependency Injection", often abbreviated as CDI) defines a more flexible model for beans that are managed by the application server. These beans are bound to a *context* (such as the current request, a browser session, or even a user-defined life cycle context). CDI specifies mechanisms for injecting beans, intercepting and decorating method calls, and firing and observing events. Because CDI is a much more powerful mechanism than JSF managed beans, it makes sense to use CDI beans if you deploy your application in a Java EE application server. A Java EE 6 compliant application server, such as GlassFish, automatically supports CDI.

NOTE: You can also add the CDI reference implementation to Tomcat. See http://seamframework.org/Weld for the details.

You use a CDI bean in the same way as a JSF managed bean. However, you declare it with the @Named annotation, like this:

```
@Named("user")
@SessionScoped
public class UserBean implements Serializable {
    ...
}
```

You can then use value expressions #{user} or #{user.name} in the same way as with JSF managed beans.

Here, the @SessionScoped annotation is from the javax.enterprise.context package, not the javax.faces.bean package.

Note that session-scoped CDI beans must implement the Serializable interface.

> NOTE: You must include a file WEB-INF/beans.xml to activate CDI beans processing. This file can be empty, or it can optionally contain instructions for configuring the beans. See the CDI specification at http://jcp.org/en/jsr/summary?id=299 for details about the beans.xml file.

It is a historical accident that there are two separate mechanisms, CDI beans and JSF managed beans, for beans that can be used in JSF pages. We suggest that you use CDI beans unless your application must work on a plain servlet runner such as Tomcat. The source code for the book comes in two versions, one with CDI beans (for Java EE 6 application servers) and one with JSF managed beans (for servlet runners without CDI support).

Message Bundles

When you implement a web application, it is a good idea to collect all message strings in a central location. This process makes it easier to keep messages consistent and, crucially, makes it easier to localize your application for other locales. In this section, we show you how JSF makes it simple to organize messages. In the section "A Sample Application" on page 45, we put managed beans and message bundles to work.

You collect your message strings in a file in the time-honored *properties* format:

```
guessNext=Guess the next number in the sequence!
answer=Your answer:
```

> NOTE: Look into the API documentation of the load method of the java.util.Properties class for a precise description of the file format.

Save the file together with your classes—for example, in src/java/com/corejsf/messages.properties. You can choose any directory path and file name, but you must use the extension .properties.

You can declare the message bundle in two ways. The simplest way is to supply a file named faces-config.xml in the WEB-INF directory of your application, with the following contents:

```
<?xml version="1.0"?>
<faces-config xmlns="http://java.sun.com/xml/ns/javaee"
    xmlns:xsi="http://www.w3.org/2001/XMLSchema-instance"
    xsi:schemaLocation="http://java.sun.com/xml/ns/javaee
        http://java.sun.com/xml/ns/javaee/web-facesconfig_2_0.xsd"
    version="2.0">
    <application>
        <resource-bundle>
            <base-name>com.corejsf.messages</base-name>
            <var>msgs</var>
        </resource-bundle>
    </application>
</faces-config>
```

 NOTE: The faces-config.xml file can be used for configuring numerous aspects of your JSF application. It is important that you use the correct version of the schema declaration. Here we show the declaration for JSF 2.0. If you use an older schema version, the JSF implementation may view this as an indication to fall back into a compatibility mode for an older JSF version.

Instead of using a global resource bundle declaration, you can add the f:loadBundle element to each JSF page that needs access to the bundle, like this:

```
<f:loadBundle basename="com.corejsf.messages" var="msgs"/>
```

In either case, the messages in the bundle are accessible through a map variable with the name msgs. (The base name com.corejsf.messages looks like a class name, and indeed the properties file is loaded by the class loader.)

You can now use value expressions such as #{msgs.guessNext} to access the message strings.

That is all there is to it! When you are ready to localize your application for another locale, you simply supply localized bundle files.

NOTE: The resource-bundle element is more efficient than the f:loadBundle action, since the bundle can be created once for the entire application.

When you localize a bundle file, you need to add a locale suffix to the file name: an underscore followed by the lowercase, two-letter ISO-639 language code. For example, German strings would be in `com/corejsf/messages_de.properties`.

NOTE: You can find a listing of all two- and three-letter ISO-639 language codes at `http://www.loc.gov/standards/iso639-2/`.

As part of the internationalization support in Java, the bundle that matches the current locale is automatically loaded. The default bundle without a locale prefix is used as a fallback when the appropriate localized bundle is not available. See Cay Horstmann and Gary Cornell, *Core Java™*, 8th ed., Santa Clara, CA: Sun Microsystems Press/Prentice Hall, 2008, Vol. 2, Chapter 5, for a detailed description of Java internationalization.

NOTE: When you prepare translations, keep one oddity in mind: Message bundle files are not encoded in UTF-8. Instead, Unicode characters beyond 127 are encoded as \uxxxx escape sequences. The Java SDK utility `native2ascii` can create these files.

You can have multiple bundles for a particular locale. For example, you may want to have separate bundles for commonly used error messages.

Messages with Variable Parts

Often, messages have variable parts that need to be filled. For example, suppose we want to display the sentence "You have n points.", where n is a value that is retrieved from a bean. Make a resource string with a placeholder:

```
currentScore=Your current score is {0}.
```

Placeholders are numbered {0}, {1}, {2}, and so on. In your JSF page, use the `h:outputFormat` tag and supply the values for the placeholders as `f:param` child elements, like this:

```
<h:outputFormat value="#{msgs.currentScore}">
  <f:param value="#{quizBean.score}"/>
</h:outputFormat>
```

The `h:outputFormat` tag uses the `MessageFormat` class from the standard library to format the message string. That class has several features for locale-aware formatting.

You can format numbers as currency amounts by adding a suffix `number,currency` to the placeholder, like this:

```
currentTotal=Your current total is {0,number,currency}.
```

In the United States, a value of 1023.95 would be formatted as $1,023.95. The same value would be displayed as €1.023,95 in Germany, using the local currency symbol and decimal separator convention.

The `choice` format lets you format a number in different ways, such as "zero points", "one point", "2 points", "3 points", and so on. Here is the format string that achieves this effect:

```
currentScore=Your current score is {0,choice,0#zero points|1#one point|2#{0} points}.
```

There are three cases: 0, 1, and ≥ 2. Each case defines a separate message string.

Note that the `0` placeholder appears twice, once to select a choice, and again in the third choice, to produce a result such as "3 points".

Listings 2–5 and 2–6 on page 51 illustrate the choice format in our sample application. The English locale does not require a choice for the message, "Your score is . . . ". However, in German, this is expressed as "Sie haben . . . Punkte" (You have . . . points). Now the choice format is required to deal with the singular form "einen Punkt" (one point).

For more information on the `MessageFormat` class, see the API documentation or Cay Horstmann and Gary Cornell, *Core Java™*, *Eighth Edition*, Santa Clara, CA: Sun Microsystems Press/Prentice Hall, 2008, Vol. 2, Chapter 5.

Setting the Application Locale

Once you have prepared your message bundles, you need to decide how to set the locale of your application. You have three choices:

1. You can let the browser choose the locale. Set the default and supported locales in `WEB-INF/faces-config.xml`:

```
<faces-config>
  <application>
    <locale-config>
      <default-locale>en</default-locale>
      <supported-locale>de</supported-locale>
    </locale-config>
  </application>
</faces-config>
```

When a browser connects to your application, it usually includes an `Accept-Language` value in the HTTP header (see `http://www.w3.org/International/questions/qa-accept-lang-locales.html`). The JSF implementation reads the header and finds the best match among the supported locales. You can test this feature by setting the preferred language in your browser (see Figure 2–2).

2. You can set the locale programatically. Call the `setLocale` method of the `UIViewRoot` object:

```
UIViewRoot viewRoot = FacesContext.getCurrentInstance().getViewRoot();
viewRoot.setLocale(new Locale("de"));
```

See "Using Command Links" on page 141 of Chapter 4 for an example.

3. You can set the locale for an individual page by using the `f:view` element with a `locale` attribute—for example:

```
<f:view locale="de">
```

The locale can be dynamically set:

```
<f:view locale="#{user.locale}"/>
```

Now the locale is set to the string that the `getLocale` method returns. This is useful in applications that let the user pick a preferred locale.

Place your entire page—both the `h:head` and the `h:body` tags—inside `f:view`.

JSF 2.0 NOTE: Before JSF 2.0, all JSF pages had to be enclosed in `f:view` tags. Nowadays, this is no longer necessary. However, the `f:view` tag is still occasionally useful; for example, for setting the locale.

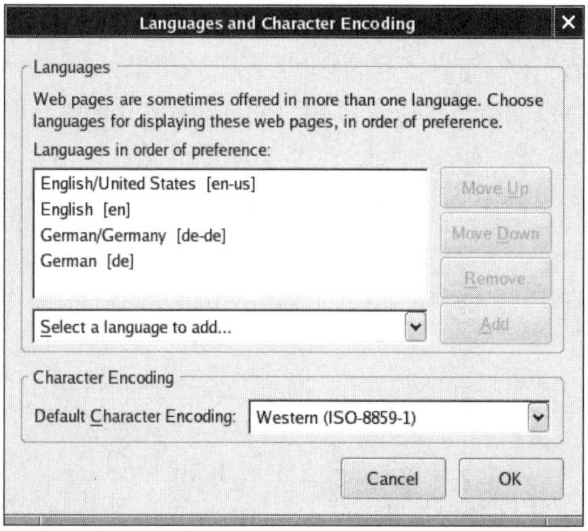

Figure 2–2 Selecting the preferred language

A Sample Application

After all these rather abstract rules and regulations, it is time for a concrete example. The application presents a series of quiz questions. Each question displays a sequence of numbers and asks the participant to guess the next number of the sequence.

For example, Figure 2–3 asks for the next number in the sequence:

```
3 1 4 1 5
```

You often find puzzles of this kind in tests that purport to measure intelligence. To solve the puzzle, you need to find the pattern. In this case, we have the first digits of π.

Type in the next number in the sequence (9), and the score goes up by one.

 NOTE: There is a Java-compatible mnemonic for the digits of π: "Can I have a small container of coffee? Thank you." Count the letters in each word, and you get 3 1 4 1 5 9 2 6 5 3.

NumberQuiz - Mozilla Firefox

File Edit View History Bookmarks Tools Help

http://localhost:8080/ch02-numberquiz/

Have fun with NumberQuiz!

Your current score is 0.

Guess the next number in the sequence!

[3, 1, 4, 1, 5]

Your answer:

Next

Done

Figure 2–3   The number quiz

In this example, we place the quiz questions in the QuizBean class. Of course, in a real application, you would be more likely to store this information in a database. But the purpose of the example is to demonstrate how to use beans that have complex structure.

We start out with a ProblemBean class. A ProblemBean has two properties: solution, of type int, and sequence, of type ArrayList (see Listing 2–1).

Listing 2–1 numberquiz/src/java/com/corejsf/ProblemBean.java

```
1. package com.corejsf;
2.
3. import java.io.Serializable;
4. import java.util.ArrayList;
5.
6. public class ProblemBean implements Serializable {
7.    private ArrayList<Integer> sequence;
8.    private int solution;
9.
10.    public ProblemBean() {}
11.
12.    public ProblemBean(int[] values, int solution) {
13.       sequence = new ArrayList<Integer>();
14.       for (int i = 0; i < values.length; i++)
15.          sequence.add(values[i]);
16.       this.solution = solution;
17.    }
18.
19.    public ArrayList<Integer> getSequence() { return sequence; }
20.    public void setSequence(ArrayList<Integer> newValue) { sequence = newValue; }
21.
22.    public int getSolution() { return solution; }
23.    public void setSolution(int newValue) { solution = newValue; }
24. }
```

Next, we define a bean for the quiz with the following properties:

*   problems: a write-only property to set the quiz problems
*   score: a read-only property to get the current score
*   current: a read-only property to get the current quiz problem
*   answer: a property to get and set the answer that the user provides

The problems property is unused in this sample program—we initialize the problem set in the QuizBean constructor. However, under "Configuring Managed Beans with XML" on page 58, you will see how to set up the problem set inside faces-config.xml, without having to write any code.

The current property is used to display the current problem. However, the value of the current property is a ProblemBean object, and we cannot directly display that object in a text field. We make a second property access to get the number sequence as #{quizBean.current.sequence}.

The value of the sequence property is an ArrayList. When it is displayed, it is converted to a string by a call to the toString method. The result is a string of the form:

```
[3, 1, 4, 1, 5]
```

Finally, we do a bit of dirty work with the answer property. We tie the answer property to the input field:

```
<h:inputText value="#{quizBean.answer}"/>
```

When the input field is displayed, the getter is called, and we define the getAnswer method to return an empty string.

When the form is submitted, the setter is called with the value that the user typed into the input field. We define setAnswer to check the answer, update the score for a correct answer, and advance to the next problem:

```
public void setAnswer(String newValue) {
    try {
        int answer = Integer.parseInt(newValue.trim());
        if (getCurrent().getSolution() == answer) score++;
        currentIndex = (currentIndex + 1) % problems.size();
    }
    catch (NumberFormatException ex) {
    }
}
```

Strictly speaking, it is a bad idea to put code into a property setter that is unrelated to the task of setting the property. Updating the score and advancing to the next problem should really be contained in a handler for the button action. However, we have not yet discussed how to react to button actions, so we use the flexibility of the setter method to our advantage.

Another weakness of our sample application is that we have not yet covered how to stop at the end of the quiz. Instead, we just wrap around to the beginning, letting the user rack up a higher score. You will learn in the next chapter how to do a better job. Remember—the point of this application is to show you how to configure and use beans.

Finally, note that we use message bundles for internationalization. Try switching your browser language to German, and the program will appear as in Figure 2–4.

This finishes our sample application. Figure 2–5 shows the directory structure. The remaining code is in Listings 2–2 through 2–6.

Figure 2–4   The number quiz with the German locale

📁 **numberquiz.war**
   📄 index.xhtml
▼ 📁 WEB-INF
      📄 beans.xml
      📄 faces-config.xml
      📄 web.xml
   ▼ 📁 classes
      ▼ 📁 com
         ▼ 📁 corejsf
               📄 ProblemBean.class
               📄 QuizBean.class
               📄 messages.properties
               📄 messages_de.properties

Figure 2–5   The directory structure of the number quiz example

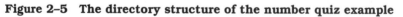
| Listing 2–2 | numberquiz/web/index.xhtml |

```
1. <?xml version="1.0" encoding="UTF-8"?>
2. <!DOCTYPE html PUBLIC "-//W3C//DTD XHTML 1.0 Transitional//EN"
3. "http://www.w3.org/TR/xhtml1/DTD/xhtml1-transitional.dtd">
4. <html xmlns="http://www.w3.org/1999/xhtml"
5.      xmlns:f="http://java.sun.com/jsf/core"
6.      xmlns:h="http://java.sun.com/jsf/html">
7.   <h:head>
8.      <title>#{msgs.title}</title>
9.   </h:head>
```

```
10.    <h:body>
11.       <h:form>
12.          <h3>#{msgs.heading}</h3>
13.          <p>
14.             <h:outputFormat value="#{msgs.currentScore}">
15.                <f:param value="#{quizBean.score}"/>
16.             </h:outputFormat>
17.          </p>
18.          <p>#{msgs.guessNext}</p>
19.          <p>#{quizBean.current.sequence}</p>
20.          <p>
21.             #{msgs.answer}
22.             <h:inputText value="#{quizBean.answer}"/>
23.          </p>
24.          <p><h:commandButton value="#{msgs.next}"/></p>
25.       </h:form>
26.    </h:body>
27. </html>
```

Listing 2–3   numberquiz/src/java/com/corejsf/QuizBean.java

```
 1. package com.corejsf;
 2.
 3. import java.io.Serializable;
 4. import java.util.ArrayList;
 5.
 6. import javax.inject.Named;
 7.    // or import javax.faces.bean.ManagedBean;
 8. import javax.enterprise.context.SessionScoped;
 9.    // or import javax.faces.bean.SessionScoped;
10.
11. @Named // or @ManagedBean
12. @SessionScoped
13. public class QuizBean implements Serializable {
14.    private ArrayList<ProblemBean> problems = new ArrayList<ProblemBean>();
15.    private int currentIndex;
16.    private int score;
17.
18.    public QuizBean() {
19.       problems.add(
20.          new ProblemBean(new int[] { 3, 1, 4, 1, 5 }, 9)); // pi
21.       problems.add(
22.          new ProblemBean(new int[] { 1, 1, 2, 3, 5 }, 8)); // fibonacci
23.       problems.add(
24.          new ProblemBean(new int[] { 1, 4, 9, 16, 25 }, 36)); // squares
25.       problems.add(
```

```
26.          new ProblemBean(new int[] { 2, 3, 5, 7, 11 }, 13)); // primes
27.       problems.add(
28.          new ProblemBean(new int[] { 1, 2, 4, 8, 16 }, 32)); // powers of 2
29.    }
30.
31.    public void setProblems(ArrayList<ProblemBean> newValue) {
32.       problems = newValue;
33.       currentIndex = 0;
34.       score = 0;
35.    }
36.
37.    public int getScore() { return score; }
38.
39.    public ProblemBean getCurrent() { return problems.get(currentIndex); }
40.
41.    public String getAnswer() { return ""; }
42.    public void setAnswer(String newValue) {
43.       try {
44.          int answer = Integer.parseInt(newValue.trim());
45.          if (getCurrent().getSolution() == answer) score++;
46.          currentIndex = (currentIndex + 1) % problems.size();
47.       }
48.       catch (NumberFormatException ex) {
49.       }
50.    }
51. }
```

Listing 2–4   numberquiz/web/WEB-INF/faces-config.xml

```
1. <?xml version="1.0"?>
2. <faces-config xmlns="http://java.sun.com/xml/ns/javaee"
3.    xmlns:xsi="http://www.w3.org/2001/XMLSchema-instance"
4.    xsi:schemaLocation="http://java.sun.com/xml/ns/javaee
5.       http://java.sun.com/xml/ns/javaee/web-facesconfig_2_0.xsd"
6.    version="2.0">
7.    <application>
8.       <locale-config>
9.          <default-locale>en</default-locale>
10.          <supported-locale>de</supported-locale>
11.       </locale-config>
12.       <resource-bundle>
13.          <base-name>com.corejsf.messages</base-name>
14.          <var>msgs</var>
15.       </resource-bundle>
16.    </application>
17. </faces-config>
```

Listing 2–5 `numberquiz/src/java/com/corejsf/messages.properties`

```
1. title=NumberQuiz
2. heading=Have fun with NumberQuiz!
3. currentScore=Your current score is {0}.
4. guessNext=Guess the next number in the sequence!
5. answer=Your answer:
6. next=Next
```

Listing 2–6   `numberquiz/src/java/com/corejsf/messsages_de.properties`

```
1. title=Zahlenquiz
2. heading=Viel Spa\u00df mit dem Zahlenquiz!
3. currentScore=Sie haben {0,choice,0#0 Punkte|1#einen Punkt|2#{0} Punkte}.
4. guessNext=Raten Sie die n\u00e4chste Zahl in der Folge!
5. answer=Ihre Antwort:
6. next=Weiter
```

Bean Scopes

For the convenience of the web application programmer, a JSF container provides separate scopes, each of which manages a table of name/value bindings.

These scopes typically hold beans and other objects that need to be available in different components of a web application.

When you define a bean, you need to specify its scope. Three scopes are common to JSF and CDI beans:

• Session scope
• Request scope
• Application scope

JSF 2.0 adds a view scope and custom scopes. These are not supported in CDI, which instead has a far more useful conversation scope.

In JSF 2.0, you can use annotations, such as the following, for defining bean scopes:

```
@SessionScoped
@RequestScoped
@ApplicationScoped
```

Note that these annotations are in the package javax.faces.bean for JSF managed beans and in the package javax.enterprise.context for CDI beans.

We discuss these scopes in the following sections.

Session Scope

Recall that the HTTP protocol is *stateless*. The browser sends a request to the server, the server returns a response, and then neither the browser nor the server has any obligation to keep any memory of the transaction. This simple arrangement works well for retrieving basic information, but it is unsatisfactory for server-side applications. For example, in a shopping application, you want the server to remember the contents of the shopping cart.

For that reason, servlet containers augment the HTTP protocol to keep track of a *session*—that is, repeated connections by the same client. There are various methods for session tracking. The simplest method uses *cookies*: name/value pairs that a server sends to a client, hoping to have them returned in subsequent requests (see Figure 2–6).

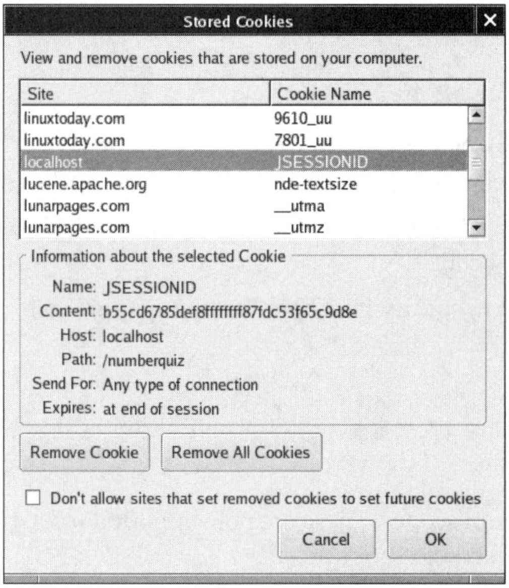

Figure 2–6   The cookie sent by a JSF application

As long as the client does not deactivate cookies, the server receives a session identifier with each subsequent request.

Application servers use fallback strategies, such as *URL rewriting*, for dealing with those clients that do not return cookies. URL rewriting adds a session identifier to a URL, which looks somewhat like this:

```
http://corejsf.com/login/faces/index.xhtml;jsessionid=b55cd6...d8e
```

> NOTE: To see this behavior, tell your browser to reject cookies from the
> `localhost`, then restart the web application and submit a page. The next
> page will have a `jsessionid` attribute.

Session tracking with cookies is completely transparent to the web developer,
and the standard JSF tags automatically perform URL rewriting if a client does
not use cookies.

The *session scope* persists from the time that a session is established until session
termination. A session terminates if the web application invokes the `invalidate`
method on the `HttpSession` object, or if it times out.

For example, a `UserBean` can contain information about users that is accessible
throughout the entire session. A `ShoppingCartBean` can be filled up gradually
during the requests that make up a session.

Keep in mind that an excessively large session state can be a performance
bottleneck. See the following sections for alternatives.

Request Scope

The *request scope* is short-lived. It starts when an HTTP request is submitted
and ends after the response is sent back to the client. If you place a managed
bean into request scope, a new instance is created with each request. It is worth
considering request scope if you are concerned about the cost of session scope
storage.

Request scope works fine when all bean data is also stored in a page. For example, in the login application of Chapter 1, we could have placed the `UserBean` into
request scope. When the login page is submitted, a new `UserBean` is created. The
bean is available for rendering the welcome page, and the user name will be
displayed correctly. However, in a more realistic application, the user name
would probably be needed for multiple pages, and request scope would not be
sufficient.

Data for error and status messages can often be placed in request scope. They
are computed when the client submits the form data and displayed when the
response is rendered. Similarly, the `f:loadBundle` tag places the bundle variable
in request scope. The variable is needed only during the *Render Response* phase
in the same request.

If you have complex data, such as the contents of a table, then request scope may not be appropriate since you would need to regenerate the data with every request.

CAUTION: Only request scope beans are single-threaded and, therefore, inherently threadsafe. Perhaps surprisingly, session beans are *not* single-threaded. For example, a user can simultaneously submit responses from multiple browser windows. Each response is processed by a separate request thread. If you need thread safety in your session scoped beans, you must provide locking mechanisms.

Application Scope

The *application scope* persists for the entire duration of the web application. That scope is shared among all requests and all sessions.

You place managed beans into the application scope if a single bean should be shared among all instances of a web application. The bean is constructed when it is first requested by any user of the application, and it stays alive until the web application is removed from the application server.

However, if an application-scoped bean is marked as *eager*, then it must be constructed before the first page of the application is displayed. Use the annotation:

```
@ManagedBean(eager=true)
```

The eager attribute is a feature of JSF 2.0.

Conversation Scope CDI

A conversation scope ranges over a set of related pages. This provides data persistence until a particular goal has been reached, without having to store the data for the entire session. A conversation is tied to a particular browser page or tab. A single session can have multiple conversations in different pages. This is an important requirement in practice. Users often branch out to a new tab so that they can explore two parts of your application in parallel.

To see the importance of supporting multiple conversations, start up the number quiz application in two browser windows and play two rounds of the quiz in parallel. This plainly does not work. When you hit the "Next" button in either window, you can see that the session has a single QuizBean instance, with one score and one current index.

Conversation scope is easy to use. Follow these rules:

*   Use a CDI bean—this is a feature of CDI, not JSF.
*   Use the @ConversationScoped annotation.
*   Add an instance variable:

    private @Inject Conversation conversation;

    The instance variable will be automatically initialized with a Conversation object when the bean is constructed.

*   Call conversation.begin() to elevate the scope of the bean from request scope to conversation scope.
*   Call conversation.end() to remove the bean from conversation scope.

For example, here is how you can use conversation scope in the number quiz:

```
@Named
@ConversationScoped
public class QuizBean implements Serializable {
    @Inject Conversation conversation;
    ...
    public void setAnswer(String newValue) {
        try {
            if (currentIndex == 0) conversation.begin();
            int answer = Integer.parseInt(newValue.trim());
            if (getCurrent().getSolution() == answer) score++;
            currentIndex = (currentIndex + 1) % problems.size();
            if (currentIndex == 0) conversation.end();
        }
        catch (NumberFormatException ex) {
        }
    }
}
```

Try running the quiz in two browser windows again. Now each quiz keeps its own score and current index. When you reach the end of the quiz, the conversation ends.

View Scope JSF 2.0

View scope was added in JSF 2.0. A bean in view scope persists while the same JSF page is redisplayed. (The JSF specification uses the term *view* for a JSF page.) As soon as the user navigates to a different page, the bean goes out of scope.

If you have a page that keeps getting redisplayed, then you can put the beans that hold the data for this page into view scope, thereby reducing the size of the session scope. This is particularly useful for Ajax applications.

Custom Scopes

Ultimately, a scope is simply a map that binds names to objects. What distinguishes one scope from another is the lifetime of that map. The lifetimes of the four standard JSF scopes (session, application, view, and request) are managed by the JSF implementation. As of JSF 2.0, you can supply custom scopes—maps whose lifetimes you manage. A bean is placed into such a map with the annotation:

```
@CustomScoped("#{expr}")
```

where #{expr} yields the scope map. Your application is responsible for removing objects from the map.

NOTE: We are unenthusiastic about custom scopes. In most applications, the CDI conversation scope is a better choice.

Configuring Beans

In the following sections, we cover in detail how you can configure beans with Java annotations and XML descriptors.

Injecting CDI Beans CDI

It often happens that you need to wire beans together. Suppose you have a User-Bean that contains information about the current user, and an EditBean needs to know about that user. You "inject" the UserBean instance into the EditBean. In its simplest form, you can use the following annotation:

```
@Named
@SessionScoped
public class EditBean {
    @Inject private UserBean currentUser;
    ...
}
```

Instead of annotating a field, you can annotate a property setter or a constructor.

When the EditBean is constructed, an appropriate UserBean instance is located—in this situation, the UserBean in the current session. The currentUser instance variable is then set to that UserBean.

While this simple setup is fine for basic applications, the CDI specification gives you great flexibility in controlling the injection process. Using annotations and deployment descriptors, you can inject different beans for particular deployments or for testing. We refer you to the excellent documentation of the reference implementation at http://docs.jboss.org/weld/reference/1.0.0/en-US/html for details.

Injecting Managed Beans JSF 2.0

JSF managed beans don't have a rich set of controls for dependency injection, but there is a basic mechanism—the @ManagedProperty annotation.

Suppose you have a UserBean with name user that contains information about the current user. Here is how you can inject it into a field of another bean:

```
@ManagedBean
@SessionScoped
public class EditBean implements Serializable {
    @ManagedProperty(value="#{user}")
    private UserBean currentUser;

    public void setCurrentUser(UserBean newValue) { currentUser = newValue; }
    . . .
}
```

Note that you annotate the currentUser field, but you *must* supply a setCurrentUser method. When an EditBean instance is constructed, the value expression #{user} is evaluated, and the result is passed to the setCurrentUser method.

> CAUTION: Programmers who are familiar with Java EE annotations may be bewildered by the fact that the @ManagedProperty annotation is applied to a field when in fact the property setter is invoked. If you have a property that doesn't correspond to a field, you will need to create a bogus field so you can place the annotation.

When you set a managed bean as the property of another, you must make sure that their scopes are compatible. The scope of the property must be no less than that of the containing bean. Table 2–1 lists the permissible combinations.

Table 2–1   Compatible Bean Scopes

When defining a bean of this scope . . .	. . . you can set its properties to beans of these scopes.
none	none
application	none, application
session	none, application, session
view	none, application, session, view
request	none, application, session, view, request

Bean Life Cycle Annotations

Using the @PostConstruct and @PreDestroy annotations, you can specify bean methods that are automatically called just after a bean has been constructed and just before a bean goes out of scope:

```
public class MyBean {
    @PostConstruct
    public void initialize() {
        // initialization code
    }
    @PreDestroy
    public void shutdown() {
        // shutdown code
    }

    // other bean methods
}
```

The @PostConstruct annotation is useful for beans that need to pull in data for display on a page. Another common use is for beans that establish connections to external resources, such as databases.

 NOTE: The @PreDestroy and @PostDestruct annotations work both with JSF managed beans and CDI beans.

Configuring Managed Beans with XML

Before JSF 2.0, all beans had to be configured with XML. Nowadays, you have the choice between annotations and XML configuration. The XML configuration is rather verbose, but it can be useful if you want to configure beans at deployment time. Feel free to skip this material if you are not interested in configuring beans with XML.

You can place XML configuration information into the following files:

*   WEB-INF/faces-config.xml

*   Files named faces-config.xml or having a name ending with .faces-config.xml inside the META-INF directory of a JAR file. (You use this mechanism if you deliver reusable components in a JAR file.)

- Files listed in the javax.faces.CONFIG_FILES initialization parameter inside WEB-INF/web.xml. For example:

```
<web-app>
   <context-param>
      <param-name>javax.faces.CONFIG_FILES</param-name>
      <param-value>WEB-INF/navigation.xml,WEB-INF/managedbeans.xml</param-value>
   </context-param>
   ...
</web-app>
```

This mechanism is attractive for builder tools because it separates navigation, beans, and so on.

Defining Beans

You use the managed-bean element to define a managed bean in an XML configuration file. For example:

```
<faces-config>
   <managed-bean>
      <managed-bean-name>user</managed-bean-name>
      <managed-bean-class>com.corejsf.UserBean</managed-bean-class>
      <managed-bean-scope>session</managed-bean-scope>
   </managed-bean>
</faces-config>
```

The scope can be request, view, session, application, none, or a value expression that yields a custom scope map. (See "Custom Scopes" on page 56.)

The none scope denotes a bean that is not kept in a scope map. Whenever an object of the none scope is requested in a value expression, a new object is created. This can be useful for specifying beans that are set as properties of other beans.

An application-scoped bean can be marked as "eager" (see page 54) with the attribute:

```
<managed-bean eager="true">
```

Setting Property Values

You can configure property values with XML, similar to the use of the @ManagedProperty annotation. Here we customize a UserBean instance:

```
<managed-bean>
   <managed-bean-name>user</managed-bean-name>
   <managed-bean-class>com.corejsf.UserBean</managed-bean-class>
   <managed-bean-scope>session</managed-bean-scope>
   <managed-property>
```

```
    <property-name>name</property-name>
    <value>troosevelt</value>
  </managed-property>
  <managed-property>
    <property-name>password</property-name>
    <value>jabberwock</value>
  </managed-property>
</managed-bean>
```

When the user bean is first looked up, it is constructed with the UserBean() constructor. Then the setName and setPassword methods are executed.

To initialize a property with null, use a null-value element. For example:

```
<managed-property>
  <property-name>password</property-name>
  <null-value/>
</managed-property>
```

The value elements can be value expressions, such as:

```
<managed-bean>
  <managed-bean-name>editBean</managed-bean-name>
  <managed-bean-class>com.corejsf.EditBean</managed-bean-class>
  <managed-bean-scope>session</managed-bean-scope>
  <managed-property>
    <property-name>user</property-name>
    <value>#{user}</value
  </managed-property>
</managed-bean>
```

In this example, the setUser method is invoked with the value of the expression #{user}.

Initializing Lists and Maps

A special syntax initializes values that are of type List or Map. Here is an example of a list:

```
<list-entries>
  <value-class>java.lang.Integer</value.class>
  <value>3</value>
  <value>1</value>
  <value>4</value>
  <value>1</value>
  <value>5</value>
</list-entries>
```

Here we use the java.lang.Integer wrapper type since a List cannot hold values of primitive type.

The list can contain a mixture of value and null-value elements. The value-class is optional. If it is omitted, a list of java.lang.String objects is produced.

A map is more complex. You specify optional key-class and value-class elements (again, with a default of java.lang.String). Then you provide a sequence of map-entry elements, each of which has a key element, followed by a value or null-value element.

Here is an example:

```
<map-entries>
    <key-class>java.lang.Integer</key-class>
    <map-entry>
       <key>1</key>
       <value>George Washington</value>
    </map-entry>
    <map-entry>
       <key>3</key>
       <value>Thomas Jefferson</value>
    </map-entry>
    <map-entry>
       <key>16</key>
       <value>Abraham Lincoln</value>
    </map-entry>
    <map-entry>
       <key>26</key>
       <value>Theodore Roosevelt</value>
    </map-entry>
</map-entries>
```

You can use list-entries and map-entries elements to initialize either a managed-bean or a managed-property, provided that the bean or property type is a List or Map.

Figure 2–7 shows a syntax diagram for the managed-bean element and all of its child elements. Follow the arrows to see which constructs are legal inside a managed-bean element. For example, the second graph tells you that a managed-property element starts with zero or more description elements, followed by zero or more display-name elements, zero or more icons, then a mandatory property-name, an optional property-class, and exactly one of the elements value, null-value, map-entries, or list-entries.

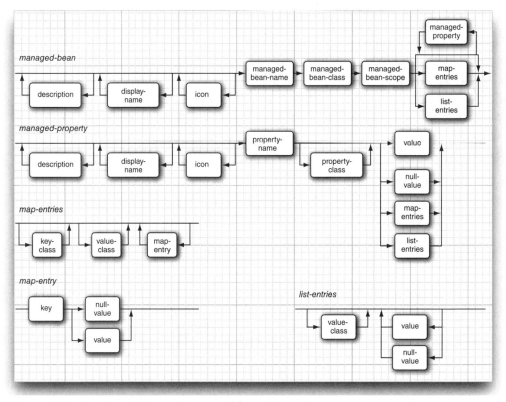

Figure 2–7   Syntax diagram for managed-bean elements

String Conversions

You specify property values and elements of lists or maps with a value element that contains a string. The enclosed string needs to be converted to the type of the property or element. For primitive types, this conversion is straightforward. For example, you can specify a string, such as 10 or true, and have it converted to a number or boolean value.

Starting with JSF 1.2, values of enumerated types are supported as well. The conversion is performed by calling Enum.valueOf(*propertyClass*, *valueText*).

For other property types, the JSF implementation attempts to locate a matching PropertyEditor. If a property editor exists, its setAsText method is invoked to convert strings to property values. Defining a property editor is somewhat involved, and we refer the interested reader to Cay Horstmann and Gary Cornell, *Core Java™*, 8th ed., Santa Clara, CA: Sun Microsystems Press/Prentice Hall, 2008, Vol. 2, Chapter 8.

Table 2–2 summarizes these conversion rules. They are identical to the rules for the jsp:setProperty action of the JSP specification.

> CAUTION: The string conversion rules are fairly restrictive. For example, if you have a property of type URL, you cannot simply specify the URL as a string, even though there is a constructor URL(String). You would need to supply a property editor for the URL type or reimplement the property type as String.

Table 2–2   String Conversions

Target Type	Conversion
int, byte, short, long, float, double, or the corresponding wrapper type	The valueOf method of the wrapper type, or 0 if the string is empty.
boolean or Boolean	The result of Boolean.valueOf, or false if the string is empty.
char or Character	The first character of the string, or (char) 0 if the string is empty.
String or Object	A copy of the string; new String("") if the string is empty.
bean property	A type that calls the setAsText method of the property editor if it exists. If the property editor does not exist or it throws an exception, the property is set to null if the string is empty. Otherwise, an error occurs.

The Expression Language Syntax

In the following sections, we discuss the syntax for value and method expressions in gruesome detail. These sections are intended for reference. Feel free to skip them at first reading.

Lvalue and Rvalue Modes

We start with an expression of the form a.b. For now, we will assume that we already know the object to which a refers. If a is an array, a list, or a map, then special rules apply (see "Using Brackets" on page 64). If a is any other object, then b must be the name of a property of a. The exact meaning of a.b depends on whether the expression is used in *rvalue mode* or *lvalue mode*.

This terminology is used in the theory of programming languages to denote that an expression on the *right-hand side* of an assignment is treated differently from an expression on the *left-hand side*.

Consider the assignment:

```
left = right;
```

A compiler generates different code for the left and right expressions. The right expression is evaluated in rvalue mode and yields a value. The left expression is evaluated in lvalue mode and stores a value in a location.

The same phenomenon happens when you use a value expression in a user interface component:

```
<h:inputText value="#{user.name}"/>
```

When the text field is rendered, the expression user.name is evaluated in rvalue mode, and the getName method is called. During decoding, the same expression is evaluated in lvalue mode and the setName method is called.

In general, the expression a.b in rvalue mode is evaluated by calling the property getter, whereas a.b in lvalue mode calls the property setter.

Using Brackets

Just as in JavaScript, you can use brackets instead of the dot notation. That is, the following three expressions all have the same meaning:

```
a.b
a["b"]
a['b']
```

For example, user.password, user["password"], and user['password'] are equivalent expressions.

Why would anyone write user["password"] when user.password is much easier to type? There are a number of reasons:

- When you access an array or map, the [] notation is more intuitive.
- You can use the [] notation with strings that contain periods or dashes—for example, msgs["error.password"].
- The [] notation allows you to dynamically compute a property: a[b.propname].

 TIP: Use single quotes in value expressions if you delimit attributes with double quotes: value="#{user['password']}". Alternatively, you can switch single and double quotes: value='#{user["password"]}'.

Map and List Expressions

The value expression language goes beyond bean property access. For example, let m be an object of any class that implements the Map interface. Then m["key"] (or the equivalent m.key) is a binding to the associated value. In rvalue mode, the value

```
m.get("key")
```

is fetched. In lvalue mode, the statement

```
m.put("key", right);
```

is executed. Here, right is the *right-hand side* value that is assigned to m.key.

You can also access a value of any object of a class that implements the List interface (such as an ArrayList). You specify an integer index for the list position. For example, a[i] (or, if you prefer, a.i) binds the ith element of the list a. Here i can be an integer, or a string that can be converted to an integer. The same rule applies for array types. As always, index values start at zero.

Table 2–3 summarizes these evaluation rules.

Table 2–3   Evaluating the Value Expression a.b

Type of a	Type of b	lvalue Mode	rvalue Mode
null	any	error	null
any	null	error	null
Map	any	a.put(b, right)	a.get(b)
List	convertible to int	a.set(b, right)	a.get(b)
array	convertible to int	a[b] = right	a[b]
bean	any	call setter of property with name b.toString()	call getter of property with name b.toString()

CAUTION: Unfortunately, value expressions do not work for indexed properties. If p is an indexed property of a bean b, and i is an integer, then b.p[i] does not access the ith value of the property. It is simply a syntax error. This deficiency is inherited from the JSP expression language.

Calling Methods and Functions JSF 2.0

Starting with JSF 2.0, you can invoke methods in value expressions. Simply supply the method name and parameters. For example, if the stockQuote bean has a method double price(String), then you can use the following expression:

```
#{stockQuote.price("ORCL")}
```

Overloaded methods are not supported. The bean must have a unique method with the given name.

You can also invoke useful functions from the JSTL functions library. They are shown in Table 2–4. If you use these functions, remember to add

```
xmlns:fn="http://java.sun.com/jsp/jstl/functions"
```

to the html element in your page.

Table 2–4   JSTL Functions

Functions	Description
fn:contains(str, substr)	Returns true if the string str contains substr.
fn:containsIgnoreCase(str, substr)	Returns true if the string str contains substr, ignoring letter case.
fn:startsWith(str, substr)	Returns true if the string str starts with substr.
fn:endsWith(str, substr)	Returns true if the string str ends with substr.
fn:length(str)	Returns the length of the string str.
fn:indexOf(str, substr)	Returns the index of the first occurrence of substr in str, -1 if not found.
fn:join(strArray, separator)	Joins the strings in the given string array, placing the separator string between them.
fn:split(str, separator)	Splits the string into an array of strings, removing all occurrences of the separator.
fn:substring(str, start, pastEnd)	Returns the substring of str at positions start . . . pastEnd - 1.
fn:substringAfter(str, separator)	Returns the substring of str after the first occurrence of separator.
fn:substringBefore(str, separator)	Returns the substring of str before the first occurrence of separator.

Table 2–4   JSTL Functions (cont.)

Functions	Description
`fn:replace(str, from, to)`	Returns the result of replacing all occurrences of `from` in `str` with `to`.
`fn:toLowerCase(str)`	Returns the lowercase of `str`.
`fn:toUpperCase(str)`	Returns the uppercase of `str`.
`fn:trim(str)`	Returns `str` with leading and trailing whitespace removed.
`fn:escapeXml(str)`	Returns `str` with characters < > & escaped as XML entities.

Resolving the Initial Term

Now you know how an expression of the form a.b is resolved. The rules can be applied repetitively to expressions such as a.b.c.d (or, of course, a['b'].c["d"]). We still need to discuss the meaning of the initial term a.

In the examples you have seen so far, the initial term referred to a bean or to a message bundle map. Those are indeed the most common situations. But it is also possible to specify other names.

There are a number of predefined objects, called *implicit objects* in the JSF specification. Table 2–5 shows the complete list. For example:

```
header['User-Agent']
```

is the value of the User-Agent parameter of the HTTP request that identifies the user's browser.

If the initial term is not one of the predefined objects, the JSF implementation looks for it in the request, view, session, and application scopes, in that order. In particular, all instantiated managed beans are located in these scope maps.

If the search is still not successful, the JSF implementation attempts to construct a managed bean or a resource bundle with the given name.

It is also possible for an application to define custom "resolvers" that recognize additional names. We briefly discuss this in the section "How do I extend the JSF expression language?" on page 596 of Chapter 13.

Table 2–5   Predefined Objects in the Expression Language

Variable Name	Meaning
header	A Map of HTTP header parameters, containing only the first value for each name.
headerValues	A Map of HTTP header parameters, yielding a String[] array of all values for a given name.
param	A Map of HTTP request parameters, containing only the first value for each name.
paramValues	A Map of HTTP request parameters, yielding a String[] array of all values for a given name.
cookie	A Map of the cookie names and values of the current request.
initParam	A Map of the initialization parameters of this web application. Initialization parameters are discussed in Chapter 12.
requestScope	A Map of all request scope attributes.
viewScope **JSF 2.0**	A Map of all view scope attributes.
sessionScope	A Map of all session scope attributes.
applicationScope	A Map of all application scope attributes.
flash **JSF 2.0**	A Map for forwarding objects to the next view. See Chapter 3.
resource **JSF 2.0**	A Map of application resources. Resources are described in Chapter 4.
facesContext	The FacesContext instance of this request. This class is discussed in Chapter 7.
view	The UIViewRoot instance of this request. This class is discussed in Chapter 8.
component **JSF 2.0**	The current component (see Chapter 9).
cc **JSF 2.0**	The current composite component (see Chapter 9).

Consider, for example, the following expression:

```
#{user.password}
```

The term user is not one of the predefined objects. When it is encountered for the *first* time, it is not an attribute name in request, view, session, or application scope.

Therefore, the JSF implementation locates the managed bean with name user and calls the constructor with no parameters of the corresponding class. Next, it adds an association to the sessionScope map. Finally, it returns the constructed object as the result of the lookup.

When the term user needs to be resolved again in the same session, it is located in the session scope.

Composite Expressions

You can use a limited set of operators inside value expressions:

- Arithmetic operators + - * / %. The last two operators have alphabetic variants div and mod.
- Relational operators < <= > >= == != and their alphabetic variants lt le gt ge eq ne. The first four variants are required for XML safety.
- Logical operators && || ! and their alphabetic variants and or not. The first variant is required for XML safety.
- The empty operator. The expression empty a is true if a is null, an array or String of length 0, or a Collection or Map of size 0.
- The ternary ?: selection operator.

Operator precedence follows the same rules as in Java. The empty operator has the same precedence as the unary - and ! operators.

Generally, you do not want to do a lot of expression computation in web pages—that would violate the separation of presentation and business logic. However, occasionally, the presentation layer can benefit from operators. For example, suppose you want to hide a component when the hide property of a bean is true. To hide a component, you set its rendered attribute to false. Inverting the bean value requires the ! (or not) operator:

```
<h:inputText rendered="#{!bean.hide}" ... />
```

Finally, you can concatenate plain strings and value expressions by placing them next to each other. Consider, for example:

```
<h:commandButton value="#{msgs.clickHere}, #{user.name}!"/>
```

The statement concatenates four strings: the string returned from #{messages. greeting}, the string consisting of a comma and a space, the string returned from #{user.name}, and the string consisting of an exclamation mark.

You have now seen all the rules that are applied to resolve value expressions. Of course, in practice, most expressions are of the form #{bean.property}. Just come back to this section when you need to tackle a more complex expression.

Method Expressions

A *method expression* denotes an object and a method that can be applied to it.

For example, here is a typical use of a method expression:

```
<h:commandButton action="#{user.checkPassword}"/>
```

We assume that user is a value of type UserBean and checkPassword is a method of that class. The method expression is a convenient way of describing a method invocation that needs to be carried out at some future time.

When the expression is evaluated, the method is applied to the object.

In our example, the command button component will call user.checkPassword() and pass the returned string to the navigation handler.

Syntax rules for method expressions are similar to those of value expressions. All but the last component are used to determine an object. The last component must be the name of a method that can be applied to that object. Table 2–6 shows the attributes that require method expressions.

Table 2–6   Method Expression Attributes

Tag	Attribute	Method Expression Type	See Chapter
Buttons and links	action	String action()	3
	actionListener	void listener(ActionEvent)	8
Input components	valueChangeListener	void listener(ValueChangeEvent)	9
	validator	void validator(FacesContext, UIComponent, Object)	7
f:event **JSF 2.0**	listener	void listener(ComponentSystemEvent)	8
f:ajax **JSF 2.0**	listener	void listener(AjaxBehaviorEvent)	10

> NOTE: The EL syntax for method expression types (shown in Table 2–6) contains not just the method parameter and return types, but also a method name, such as void **listener**(ActionEvent). These names are intended to document the purpose of the method.

Method Expression Parameters JSF 2.0

Starting with JSF 2.0, you can provide parameter values in method expressions. This feature is useful for providing parameters to the actions of buttons and links. For example,

```
<h:commandButton value="Previous" action="#{formBean.move(-1)}"/>
<h:commandButton value="Next" action="#{formBean.move(1)}"/>
```

The action method must then be declared with a parameter:

```
public class FormBean {
    ...
    public String move(int amount) { ... }
}
```

When the method reference is evaluated, the parameters are evaluated and passed to the method.

> CAUTION: Method parameters will *not* work on Tomcat 6 with just the JSF JAR files. The expression language (EL) is not a part of JSF but instead defined in JSR 245 (JavaServer Pages). Method parameters are a feature of EL 2.2, which is not supported by Tomcat 6. In order to use the EL 2.2 features, obtain the JARs from http://uel.dev.java.net, add them to the WEB-INF/lib directory of your web application, and add the following to your web.xml file:
>
> ```
> <context-param>
>     <param-name>com.sun.faces.expressionFactory</param-name>
>     <param-value>com.sun.el.ExpressionFactoryImpl</param-value>
> </context-param>
> ```

Conclusion

This completes our discussion of managed beans. We would like to reassure you that most of the technical issues raised here are not important to be productive with JSF development. Start out with using message bundles and session-scoped named beans, and come back to this chapter when you have more advanced needs.

Next, you will learn how your JSF applications navigate between pages.

NAVIGATION

Chapter 3

In this short chapter, we discuss how you configure the navigation of your web application. In particular, you will learn how your application can move from one page to the next, depending on user actions and the outcomes of decisions in the business logic.

Static Navigation

Consider what happens when the user of a web application fills out a web page. The user might fill in text fields, click radio buttons, or select list entries.

All these edits happen inside the user's browser. When the user clicks a button that posts the form data, the changes are transmitted to the server.

At that time, the web application analyzes the user input and must decide which JSF page to use for rendering the response. The *navigation handler* is responsible for selecting the next JSF page.

In a simple web application, navigation is static. That is, clicking a particular button always selects a fixed JSF page for rendering the response. In "A Simple Example" on page 4 of Chapter 1, you saw the simplest mechanism for wiring up static navigation between JSF pages.

You give each button an `action` attribute—for example:

```
<h:commandButton label="Login" action="welcome"/>
```

 NOTE: As you will see in Chapter 4, navigation actions can also be attached to hyperlinks.

The value of the action attribute is called the *outcome*. As you will see in the section "Mapping Outcomes to View IDs" on page 75, an outcome can be optionally mapped to a *view ID*. (In the JSF specification, a JSF page is called a *view*.)

If you don't provide such a mapping for a particular outcome, the outcome is transformed into a view ID, using the following steps:

1. If the outcome doesn't have a file extension, then append the extension of the current view.

2. If the outcome doesn't start with a /, then prepend the path of the current view.

For example, the welcome outcome in the view /index.xhtml yields the target view ID /welcome.xhtml.

NOTE: The mapping from outcomes to view IDs is optional since JSF 2.0. Prior to JSF 2.0, you had to specify explicit navigation rules for every outcome.

Dynamic Navigation

In most web applications, navigation is not static. The page flow does not just depend on which button you click but also on the inputs that you provide. For example, submitting a login page may have two outcomes: success or failure. The outcome depends on a computation—namely, whether the username and password are legitimate.

To implement dynamic navigation, the submit button must have a *method expression*, such as:

```
<h:commandButton label="Login" action="#{loginController.verifyUser}"/>
```

In our example, loginController references a bean of some class, and that class must have a method named verifyUser.

A method expression in an action attribute has no parameters. It can have any return type. The return value is converted to a string by calling toString.

NOTE: In JSF 1.1, an action method was required to have return type `String`. As of JSF 1.2, you can use any return type. In particular, using enumerations is a useful alternative since the compiler can catch typos in the action names.

Here is an example of an action method:

```
String verifyUser() {
    if (...)
        return "success";
    else
        return "failure";
}
```

The method returns an outcome string such as `"success"` or `"failure"`, which is used to determine the next view.

 NOTE: An action method may return `null` to indicate that the same view should be redisplayed. In this case, the view scope (which was discussed in Chapter 2) is preserved. Any non-`null` outcome purges the view scope, even if the resulting view is the same as the current one.

In summary, here are the steps that are carried out whenever the user clicks a command button whose `action` attribute is a method expression:

1. The specified bean is retrieved.
2. The referenced method is called and returns an outcome string.
3. The outcome string is transformed into a view ID.
4. The page corresponding to the view ID is displayed.

Thus, to implement branching behavior, you supply a reference to a method in an appropriate bean class. You have wide latitude about where to place that method. The best approach is to find a class that has all the data that you need for decision making.

Mapping Outcomes to View IDs

One key design goal of JSF is to separate presentation from business logic. When navigation decisions are made dynamically, the code that computes the outcome should not have to know the exact names of the web pages. JSF provides a mechanism for mapping *logical outcomes*, such as `success` and `failure`, to actual web pages.

This is achieved by adding `navigation-rule` entries into `faces-config.xml`. Here is a typical example:

```
<navigation-rule>
   <from-view-id>/index.xhtml</from-view-id>
   <navigation-case>
      <from-outcome>success</from-outcome>
      <to-view-id>/welcome.xhtml</to-view-id>
   </navigation-case>
</navigation-rule>
```

This rule states that the `success` outcome navigates to `/welcome.xhtml` if it occurred inside `/index.xhtml`.

NOTE: The view ID strings start with a `/`. If you use extension mapping (such as a suffix `.faces`), the extension must match the file extension (such as `.xhtml`), not the URL extension.

If you pick the outcome strings carefully, you can group multiple navigation rules together. For example, you may have buttons with action `logout` sprinkled throughout your application's pages. You can have all these buttons navigate to the `loggedOut.xhtml` page with the single rule:

```
<navigation-rule>
   <navigation-case>
      <from-outcome>logout</from-outcome>
      <to-view-id>/loggedOut.xhtml</to-view-id>
   </navigation-case>
</navigation-rule>
```

This rule applies to all pages because no `from-view-id` element was specified.

You can merge navigation rules with the same `from-view-id`. Here is an example:

```
<navigation-rule>
   <from-view-id>/index.xhtml</from-view-id>
   <navigation-case>
      <from-outcome>success</from-outcome>
      <to-view-id>/welcome.xhtml</to-view-id>
   </navigation-case>
   <navigation-case>
      <from-outcome>failure</from-outcome>
      <to-view-id>/newuser.xhtml</to-view-id>
   </navigation-case>
</navigation-rule>
```

NOTE: For simple applications, you probably don't need to use navigation rules. As your applications get more complex, it makes sense to use logical outcomes in your managed beans, together with navigation rules for mapping outcomes to target views.

The JavaQuiz Application

In this section, we put navigation to use in a program that presents the user with a sequence of quiz questions (see Figure 3–1).

Figure 3–1   A quiz question

When the user clicks the "Check Answer" button, the application checks whether the user provided the correct answer. If the answer is not correct, the user has one additional chance to answer the same problem (see Figure 3–2).

Figure 3–2   One wrong answer: Try again

After two wrong answers, the next problem is presented (see Figure 3–3).

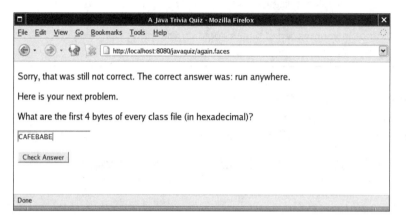

Figure 3–3   Two wrong answers: Move on

And, of course, after a correct answer, the next problem is presented as well. Finally, after the last problem, a summary page displays the score and invites the user to start over (see Figure 3–4).

Our application has two classes. The Problem class, shown in Listing 3–1, describes a single problem, with a question, an answer, and a method to check whether a given response is correct.

The QuizBean class describes a quiz that consists of a number of problems. A QuizBean instance also keeps track of the current problem and the total score of a user. You will find the complete code in Listing 3–2.

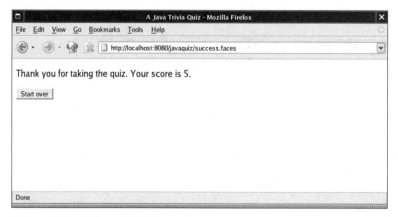

Figure 3–4   Done with the quiz

Listing 3–1 javaquiz/src/java/com/corejsf/Problem.java

```
1. package com.corejsf;
2.
3. import java.io.Serializable;
4.
5. public class Problem implements Serializable {
6.    private String question;
7.    private String answer;
8.
9.    public Problem(String question, String answer) {
10.       this.question = question;
11.       this.answer = answer;
12.    }
13.
14.    public String getQuestion() { return question; }
15.
16.    public String getAnswer() { return answer; }
17.
18.    // override for more sophisticated checking
19.    public boolean isCorrect(String response) {
20.       return response.trim().equalsIgnoreCase(answer);
21.    }
22. }
```

In this example, the QuizBean is the appropriate class for holding the navigation methods. That bean has all the knowledge about the user's actions, and it can determine which page should be displayed next.

The answerAction method of the QuizBean class carries out the navigation logic. The method returns one of the strings "success" or "done" if the user answered the question correctly, "again" after the first wrong answer, and "failure" or "done" after the second wrong try.

```
public String answerAction() {
   tries++;
   if (problems.get(currentProblem).isCorrect(response)) {
      score++;
      nextProblem();
      if (currentProblem == problems.size()) return "done";
      else return "success";
   }
   else if (tries == 1) return "again";
   else {
      nextProblem();
      if (currentProblem == problems.size()) return "done";
```

```
        else return "failure";
    }
}
```

We attach the `answerAction` method expression to the buttons on each of the pages. For example, the `index.xhtml` page contains the following element:

```
<h:commandButton value="#{msgs.checkAnswer}" action="#{quizBean.answerAction}"/>
```

Figure 3–5 shows the directory structure of the application. Listing 3–3 shows the main quiz page `index.xhtml`. The `success.xhtml` and `failure.xhtml` pages are omitted. They differ from `index.xhtml` only in the message at the top of the page.

The `done.xhtml` page in Listing 3–4 shows the final score and invites the user to play again. Pay attention to the command button on that page. It looks as if we could use static navigation, since clicking the "Start over" button always returns to the `index.xhtml` page. However, we use a method expression:

```
<h:commandButton value="#{msgs.startOver}" action="#{quizBean.startOverAction}"/>
```

The `startOverAction` method carries out useful work that needs to take place to reset the game. It reshuffles the response items and resets the score:

```
public String startOverAction() {
    Collections.shuffle(problems);
    currentProblem = 0;
    score = 0;
    tries = 0;
    response = "";
    return "startOver";
}
```

In general, action methods have two roles:

- To carry out the model updates that are a consequence of the user action
- To tell the navigation handler where to go next

NOTE: As you will see in Chapter 8, you can also attach action listeners to buttons. When the user clicks the button, the code in the `processAction` method of the action listener is executed. However, action listeners do not interact with the navigation handler.

Listing 3–5 shows the application configuration file with the navigation rules. To understand the rules better, have a look at the page transitions in Figure 3–6.

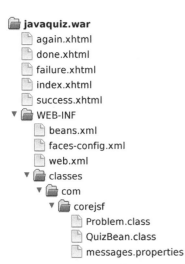

Figure 3–5 Directory structure of the Java Quiz application

Three of our outcomes ("success", "again", and "done") have no navigation rules. They always lead to /success.xhtml, /again.xhtml, and /done.xhtml. We map the "startOver" outcome to /index.xhtml. The failure outcome is a bit tricker. It initially leads to /again.xhtml, where the user can have a second try. However, if failure occurs in that page, then the next page is /failure.xhtml:

```
<navigation-rule>
    <from-view-id>/again.xhtml</from-view-id>
    <navigation-case>
        <from-outcome>failure</from-outcome>
        <to-view-id>/failure.xhtml</to-view-id>
    </navigation-case>
</navigation-rule>
<navigation-rule>
    <navigation-case>
        <from-outcome>failure</from-outcome>
        <to-view-id>/again.xhtml</to-view-id>
    </navigation-case>
</navigation-rule>
```

Note that the order of the rule matters. The second rule matches when the current page is not /again.xhtml.

Finally, Listing 3–6 shows the message strings.

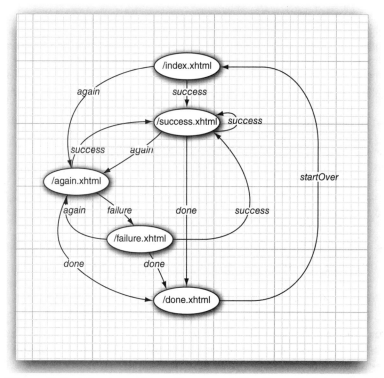

Figure 3–6   The transition diagram of the Java Quiz application

Listing 3–2   javaquiz/src/java/com/corejsf/QuizBean.java

```
1. package com.corejsf;
2.
3. import java.io.Serializable;
4.
5. import java.util.ArrayList;
6. import java.util.Arrays;
7. import java.util.Collections;
8.
9. import javax.inject.Named;
10.    // or import javax.faces.bean.ManagedBean;
11. import javax.enterprise.context.SessionScoped;
12.    // or import javax.faces.bean.SessionScoped;
13.
14. @Named // or @ManagedBean
15. @SessionScoped
16. public class QuizBean implements Serializable {
17.    private int currentProblem;
```

```
18.   private int tries;
19.   private int score;
20.   private String response = "";
21.   private String correctAnswer;
22.
23.   // Here, we hardwire the problems. In a real application,
24.   // they would come from a database
25.   private ArrayList<Problem> problems = new ArrayList<Problem>(Arrays.asList(
26.      new Problem(
27.         "What trademarked slogan describes Java development? Write once, ...",
28.         "run anywhere"),
29.      new Problem(
30.         "What are the first 4 bytes of every class file (in hexadecimal)?",
31.         "CAFEBABE"),
32.      new Problem(
33.         "What does this statement print? System.out.println(1+\"2\");",
34.         "12"),
35.      new Problem(
36.         "Which Java keyword is used to define a subclass?",
37.         "extends"),
38.      new Problem(
39.         "What was the original name of the Java programming language?",
40.         "Oak"),
41.      new Problem(
42.         "Which java.util class describes a point in time?",
43.         "Date")));
44.
45.   public String getQuestion() { return problems.get(currentProblem).getQuestion(); }
46.
47.   public String getAnswer() { return correctAnswer; }
48.
49.   public int getScore() { return score; }
50.
51.   public String getResponse() { return response; }
52.   public void setResponse(String newValue) { response = newValue; }
53.
54.   public String answerAction() {
55.      tries++;
56.      if (problems.get(currentProblem).isCorrect(response)) {
57.         score++;
58.         nextProblem();
59.         if (currentProblem == problems.size()) return "done";
60.         else return "success";
61.      }
62.      else if (tries == 1) return "again";
63.      else {
64.         nextProblem();
```

```
65.          if (currentProblem == problems.size()) return "done";
66.          else return "failure";
67.       }
68.    }
69.
70.    public String startOverAction() {
71.       Collections.shuffle(problems);
72.       currentProblem = 0;
73.       score = 0;
74.       tries = 0;
75.       response = "";
76.       return "startOver";
77.    }
78.
79.    private void nextProblem() {
80.       correctAnswer = problems.get(currentProblem).getAnswer();
81.       currentProblem++;
82.       tries = 0;
83.       response = "";
84.    }
85. }
```

Listing 3–3   javaquiz/web/index.xhtml

```
1. <?xml version="1.0" encoding="UTF-8"?>
2. <!DOCTYPE html PUBLIC "-//W3C//DTD XHTML 1.0 Transitional//EN"
3. "http://www.w3.org/TR/xhtml1/DTD/xhtml1-transitional.dtd">
4. <html xmlns="http://www.w3.org/1999/xhtml"
5.       xmlns:h="http://java.sun.com/jsf/html">
6.    <h:head>
7.       <title>#{msgs.title}</title>
8.    </h:head>
9.    <h:body>
10.      <h:form>
11.         <p>#{quizBean.question}"/></p>
12.         <p><h:inputText value="#{quizBean.response}"/></p>
13.         <p>
14.            <h:commandButton value="#{msgs.checkAnswer}"
15.                             action="#{quizBean.answerAction}"/>
16.         </p>
17.      </h:form>
18.   </h:body>
19. </html>
```

Listing 3–4   javaquiz/web/done.xhtml

```
1. <?xml version="1.0" encoding="UTF-8"?>
2. <!DOCTYPE html PUBLIC "-//W3C//DTD XHTML 1.0 Transitional//EN"
3.    "http://www.w3.org/TR/xhtml1/DTD/xhtml1-transitional.dtd">
4. <html xmlns="http://www.w3.org/1999/xhtml"
5.      xmlns:f="http://java.sun.com/jsf/core"
6.      xmlns:h="http://java.sun.com/jsf/html">
7.    <h:head>
8.       <title>#{msgs.title}</title>
9.    </h:head>
10.   <h:body>
11.      <h:form>
12.         <p>
13.            #{msgs.thankYou}
14.            <h:outputFormat value="#{msgs.score}">
15.               <f:param value="#{quizBean.score}"/>
16.            </h:outputFormat>
17.         </p>
18.         <p>
19.            <h:commandButton value="#{msgs.startOver}"
20.                             action="#{quizBean.startOverAction}"/>
21.         </p>
22.      </h:form>
23.   </h:body>
24. </html>
```

Listing 3–5   javaquiz/web/WEB-INF/faces-config.xml

```
1. <?xml version="1.0"?>
2. <faces-config xmlns="http://java.sun.com/xml/ns/javaee"
3.    xmlns:xsi="http://www.w3.org/2001/XMLSchema-instance"
4.    xsi:schemaLocation="http://java.sun.com/xml/ns/javaee
5.       http://java.sun.com/xml/ns/javaee/web-facesconfig_2_0.xsd"
6.    version="2.0">
7.    <navigation-rule>
8.       <navigation-case>
9.          <from-outcome>startOver</from-outcome>
10.         <to-view-id>/index.xhtml</to-view-id>
11.      </navigation-case>
12.   </navigation-rule>
13.   <navigation-rule>
14.      <from-view-id>/again.xhtml</from-view-id>
15.      <navigation-case>
16.         <from-outcome>failure</from-outcome>
17.         <to-view-id>/failure.xhtml</to-view-id>
```

```
18.      </navigation-case>
19.    </navigation-rule>
20.    <navigation-rule>
21.      <navigation-case>
22.        <from-outcome>failure</from-outcome>
23.        <to-view-id>/again.xhtml</to-view-id>
24.      </navigation-case>
25.    </navigation-rule>
26.
27.    <application>
28.      <resource-bundle>
29.        <base-name>com.corejsf.messages</base-name>
30.        <var>msgs</var>
31.      </resource-bundle>
32.    </application>
33. </faces-config>
```

Listing 3–6   javaquiz/src/java/com/corejsf/messages.properties

```
1. title=A Java Trivia Quiz
2. checkAnswer=Check Answer
3. startOver=Start over
4. correct=Congratulations, that is correct.
5. notCorrect=Sorry, that was not correct. Please try again!
6. stillNotCorrect=Sorry, that was still not correct.
7. correctAnswer=The correct answer was: {0}.
8. score=Your score is {0}.
9. nextProblem=Here is your next problem.
10. thankYou=Thank you for taking the quiz.
```

Redirection

You can ask the JSF implementation to *redirect* to a new view. Then the JSF implementation sends an HTTP redirect to the client. The redirect response tells the client which URL to use for the next page. The client then makes a GET request to that URL.

Redirecting is slow because another round trip to the browser is involved. However, the redirection gives the browser a chance to update its address field.

Figure 3–7 shows how the address field changes when you use redirection.

Without redirection, the original URL (localhost:8080/javaquiz/faces/index.xhtml) is unchanged when the user moves from the /index.xhtml page to the /success.xhtml face. With redirection, the browser displays the new URL (`localhost:8080/javaquiz/faces/success.xhtml`).

Figure 3–7   Redirection updating the URL in the browser

If you don't use navigation rules, add the string

```
?faces-redirect=true
```

to the outcome string, for example:

```
<h:commandButton label="Login" action="welcome?faces-redirect=true"/>
```

In a navigation rule, you add a `redirect` element after `to-view-id`, as follows:

```
<navigation-case>
   <from-outcome>success</from-outcome>
   <to-view-id>/success.xhtml</to-view-id>
   <redirect/>
</navigation-case>
```

Redirection and the Flash JSF 2.0

To minimize session scope bloat, it makes sense to use request scope as much as possible. Without the redirect element, you can use request scoped beans for data that are shown in the next view.

However, consider what happens with a redirect.

1.   The client sends a request to the server.
2.   The request scope map is populated with request scoped beans.

3. The server sends an HTTP 302 (Moved temporarily) status to the client, together with the redirect location. This ends the current request, and the request scoped beans are removed.

4. The client makes a GET request to the new location.

5. The server renders the next view. However, the previous request scoped beans are no longer available.

To overcome this problem, JSF 2.0 provides a *flash* object that can be populated in one request and used in the next. (The flash concept is borrowed from the Ruby on Rails web framework.) A common use of the flash is for messages. For example, a button handler can put a message into the flash:

```
ExternalContext.getFlash().put("message", "Your password is about to expire");
```

The `ExternalContext.getFlash()` method returns an object of the class `Flash` which implements `Map<String, Object>`.

In a JSF page, you reference the flash object with the `flash` variable. For example, you can display the message as:

```
#{flash.message}
```

After the message has been rendered and the redirected view has been delivered to the client, the message string is automatically removed from the flash.

You can even keep a value in the flash for more than one request. The expression

```
#{flash.keep.message}
```

yields the value of the `message` key in the flash and adds it back for another request cycle.

 NOTE: If you find yourself shoveling large amounts of data between the flash and a bean, consider using a conversation scope instead.

RESTful Navigation and Bookmarkable URLs JSF 2.0

By default, a JSF application makes a sequence of POST requests to the server. Each POST contains form data. This makes sense for an application that collects lots of user input. But much of the web doesn't work like that. Consider for example a user browsing a shopping catalog, clicking from one link to the next. No user input is involved other than selecting the links that are being clicked. These links should be *bookmarkable*, so that a user can return to the same page when revisiting the URL. And the pages should be *cacheable*. Caching is an important part of building efficient web applications. Of course, POST requests do not work with bookmarking or caching.

An architectural style called REST (Representational State Transfer) advocates that web applications should use HTTP as it was originally envisioned. Lookups should use GET requests. PUT, POST, and DELETE requests should be used for creation, mutation, and deletion.

REST proponents tend to favor URLs, such as

```
http://myserver.com/catalog/item/1729
```

but the REST architecture does not require these "pretty URLs". A GET request with a parameter

```
http://myserver.com/catalog?item=1729
```

is every bit as RESTful.

Keep in mind that GET requests should never be used for updating information. For example, a GET request for adding an item to a cart

```
http://myserver.com/addToCart?cart=314159&item=1729
```

would not be appropriate. GET requests should be *idempotent*. That is, issuing a request twice should be no different from issuing it once. That's what makes the requests cacheable. An "add to cart" request is not idempotent—issuing it twice adds two copies of the item to the cart. A POST request is clearly appropriate in this context. Thus, even a RESTful web application needs its share of POST requests.

Currently, JSF does not have a standard mechanism for producing or consuming "pretty URLs", but since JSF 2.0, there is support for GET requests. We describe that support in the following sections.

View Parameters

Consider a GET request for displaying information about a particular item:

```
http://myserver.com/catalog?item=1729
```

An item ID is supplied as a query parameter. When the request is received, the parameter value must be transferred to an appropriate bean. You can use *view parameters* for this purpose.

At the top of your page, add tags such as the following:

```
<f:metadata>
  <f:viewParam name="item" value="#{catalog.currentItem}"/>
</f:metadata>
```

When the request is processed, the value of the item query parameter is passed to the setCurrentItem method of the catalog bean.

A JSF page can have any number of view parameters. View parameters can be converted and validated, just like any other request parameters. (See chapter 7 for details on conversion and validation.)

It is often necessary to fetch additional data after the view parameters have been set. For example, after setting the item view parameter, you may want to retrieve item properties from a database so that you can render the page that describes the item. In Chapter 8, you will see how to carry out this kind of work in a handler for the preRenderView event.

GET Request Links

In the preceding section, you saw how JSF processes a GET request. In a RESTful application, you want to enable your users to navigate with GET requests. Therefore, you need to add buttons and links to your pages that issue GET requests. You use the h:button and h:link tags for this purpose. (In contrast, h:commandButton and h:commandLink generate POST requests.)

You will want to control the target view ID and the query parameters for these requests. The target view ID is specified by the outcome attribute. This can be a fixed string:

```
<h:button value="Done" outcome="done"/>
```

Alternatively, you can supply a *value expression*:

```
<h:button value="Skip" outcome="#{quizBean.skipOutcome}"/>
```

The getSkipOutcome method is invoked. It must yield an outcome string. The outcome string is then fed into the navigation handler in the usual way, yielding a target view ID.

There is an essential difference between the outcome attribute of an h:button and the action attribute of an h:commandButton. The outcome attribute is evaluated before the page is rendered, so that the link can be embedded into the page. However, the action attribute is only evaluated if the user actually clicked on the command button. For that reason, the JSF specification uses the term *preemptive navigation* for computing the target view IDs for GET requests.

CAUTION: The EL expression in the `outcome` attribute is a value expression and *not* a method expression. Conceptually, a command button action may mutate the state of the application in some way. However, computing the outcome of a GET request link should not do any mutation—after all, the link is just computed for potential use at a later time.

Specifying Request Parameters

Often, you will want to include parameters with a GET request link. These parameters can come from three sources:

- The outcome string
- View parameters
- Nested `f:param` tags

If the same parameter is specified more than once, the latter one in this list takes precedence.

Let us look at these choices in detail.

You can specify parameters in an outcome string, such as:

```
<h:link outcome="index?q=1" value="Skip">
```

The navigation handler strips off the parameters from the outcome, computes the target view ID, and appends the parameters. In this example, the target view ID is `/index.xhtml?q=1`.

If you supply multiple parameters, be sure to escape the & separator:

```
<h:link outcome="index?q=1&amp;score=0" value="Skip">
```

Of course, you can use value expressions in the outcome string, like this:

```
<h:link outcome="index?q=#{quizBean.currentProblem + 1}" value="Skip">
```

There is a convenient shortcut for including all view parameters in the query string. Simply add an attribute:

```
<h:link outcome="index" includeViewParams="true" value="Skip">
```

In this way, you can carry all view parameters from one page to another, which is a common requirement in a RESTful application.

You can use the `f:param` tag to override view parameters. For example:

```
<h:link outcome="index" includeViewParams="true" value="Skip">
    <f:param name="q" value="#{quizBean.currentProblem + 1}"/>
</h:link>
```

A redirect link, also being a GET request, can similarly benefit from inclusion of view parameters. However, instead of setting an attribute in the tag, you add a parameter to the outcome:

```
<h:commandLink action="index?faces-redirect=true&amp;includeViewParams=true"
   value="Skip"/>
```

Unfortunately, nested f:param tags are *not* included in the request.

If you specify navigation rules in the XML configuration, use the include-view-params attribute and nested view-param tags, like this:

```
<redirect include-view-params=true>
   <view-param>
      <name>q</name>
      <value>#{quizBean.currentProblem + 1}</value>  ·
   </view-param>
</redirect>
```

Do not be alarmed by the minor inconsistencies in the syntax. They are meant to heighten your level of attention and thereby make you a better programmer.

Adding Bookmarkable Links to the Quiz Application

Consider the quiz application that we used earlier in this chapter to demonstrate navigation. Can we make it more RESTful?

A GET request would not be appropriate for submitting an answer because it is not idempotent. Submitting an answer modifies the score. However, we can add RESTful links for navigating among the questions.

In order to keep the application simple, we provide a single bookmarkable link for skipping to the next question. We use a view parameter:

```
<f:metadata>
   <f:viewParam name="q" value="#{quizBean.currentProblem}"/>
</f:metadata>
```

The link is given by:

```
<h:link outcome="#{quizBean.skipOutcome}" value="Skip">
   <f:param name="q" value="#{quizBean.currentProblem + 1}"/>
</h:link>
```

The getSkipOutcome method of the QuizBean returns index or done, depending on whether there are additional questions available:

```
public String getSkipOutcome() {
   if (currentProblem < problems.size() - 1) return "index";
```

```
    else return "done";
}
```

The resulting link looks like this (see Figure 3–8):

```
http://localhost:8080/javaquiz-rest/faces/index.xhtml?q=1
```

You can bookmark the link and return to any question in the quiz.

Figure 3–8   A RESTful link

Listing 3–7 shows the index.xhtml page with the view parameter and the h:link tag. Listing 3–8 shows the modified QuizBean. We added a setCurrentProblem method and modified the mechanism for computing the score. Since it is now possible to visit the same question multiple times, we need to make sure that a user doesn't receive points for answering the same question more than once.

Listing 3–7   javaquiz-rest/web/index.xhtml

```
1. <?xml version="1.0" encoding="UTF-8"?>
2. <!DOCTYPE html PUBLIC "-//W3C//DTD XHTML 1.0 Transitional//EN"
3. "http://www.w3.org/TR/xhtml1/DTD/xhtml1-transitional.dtd">
4. <html xmlns="http://www.w3.org/1999/xhtml"
5.     xmlns:f="http://java.sun.com/jsf/core"
6.     xmlns:h="http://java.sun.com/jsf/html">
7.   <f:metadata>
8.     <f:viewParam name="q" value="#{quizBean.currentProblem}"/>
9.   </f:metadata>
10.   <h:head>
11.     <title>#{msgs.title}</title>
12.   </h:head>
13.   <h:body>
```

```
14.    <h:form>
15.        <p>#{quizBean.question}</p>
16.        <p><h:inputText value="#{quizBean.response}"/></p>
17.        <p><h:commandButton value="#{msgs.checkAnswer}"
18.        action="#{quizBean.answerAction}"/></p>
19.        <p><h:link outcome="#{quizBean.skipOutcome}" value="Skip">
20.           <f:param name="q" value="#{quizBean.currentProblem + 1}"/>
21.        </h:link>
22.        </p>
23.    </h:form>
24.  </h:body>
25.</html>
```

Listing 3–8   javaquiz-rest/src/java/com/corejsf/QuizBean.java

```java
1. package com.corejsf;
2.
3. import java.io.Serializable;
4.
5. import java.util.ArrayList;
6. import java.util.Arrays;
7. import java.util.Collections;
8. import javax.inject.Named;
9.    // or import javax.faces.bean.ManagedBean;
10. import javax.enterprise.context.SessionScoped;
11.    // or import javax.faces.bean.SessionScoped;
12.
13. @Named // or @ManagedBean
14. @SessionScoped
15. public class QuizBean implements Serializable {
16.    private int currentProblem;
17.    private int tries;
18.    private String response = "";
19.    private String correctAnswer;
20.
21.    // Here, we hardwire the problems. In a real application,
22.    // they would come from a database
23.    private ArrayList<Problem> problems = new ArrayList<Problem>(Arrays.asList(
24.       new Problem(
25.          "What trademarked slogan describes Java development? Write once, ...",
26.          "run anywhere"),
27.       new Problem(
28.          "What are the first 4 bytes of every class file (in hexadecimal)?",
29.          "CAFEBABE"),
30.       new Problem(
31.          "What does this statement print? System.out.println(1+\"2\");",
32.          "12"),
```

```
33.        new Problem(
34.            "Which Java keyword is used to define a subclass?",
35.            "extends"),
36.        new Problem(
37.            "What was the original name of the Java programming language?",
38.            "Oak"),
39.        new Problem(
40.            "Which java.util class describes a point in time?",
41.            "Date")));
42.
43.    private int[] scores = new int[problems.size()];
44.
45.    public String getQuestion() {
46.        return problems.get(currentProblem).getQuestion();
47.    }
48.
49.    public String getAnswer() { return correctAnswer; }
50.
51.    public int getScore() {
52.        int score = 0;
53.        for (int s : scores) score += s;
54.        return score;
55.    }
56.
57.    public String getResponse() { return response; }
58.    public void setResponse(String newValue) { response = newValue; }
59.
60.    public int getCurrentProblem() { return currentProblem; }
61.    public void setCurrentProblem(int newValue) { currentProblem = newValue; }
62.
63.    public String getSkipOutcome() {
64.        if (currentProblem < problems.size() - 1) return "index";
65.        else return "done";
66.    }
67.
68.    public String answerAction() {
69.        tries++;
70.        if (problems.get(currentProblem).isCorrect(response)) {
71.            scores[currentProblem] = 1;
72.            nextProblem();
73.            if (currentProblem == problems.size()) return "done";
74.            else return "success";
75.        }
76.        else {
77.            scores[currentProblem] = 0;
78.            if (tries == 1) return "again";
```

```
79.         else {
80.            nextProblem();
81.            if (currentProblem == problems.size()) return "done";
82.            else return "failure";
83.         }
84.      }
85.   }
86.
87.   public String startOverAction() {
88.      Collections.shuffle(problems);
89.      currentProblem = 0;
90.      for (int i = 0; i < scores.length; i++)
91.         scores[i] = 0;
92.      tries = 0;
93.      response = "";
94.      return "startOver";
95.   }
96.
97.   private void nextProblem() {
98.      correctAnswer = problems.get(currentProblem).getAnswer();
99.      currentProblem++;
100.     tries = 0;
101.     response = "";
102.  }
103.}
```

Advanced Navigation Rules

The techniques of the preceding sections should be sufficient for most practical navigation needs. In this section, we describe the remaining rules for the navigation elements that can appear in the faces-config.xml file. Figure 3–9 shows a syntax diagram of the valid elements.

> NOTE: As you saw in "Configuring Beans" on page 56 of Chapter 2, it is also possible to place the navigation information into configuration files other than the standard faces-config.xml file.

As you can see from the syntax diagram in Figure 3–9, each navigation-rule and navigation-case element can have an arbitrary description, a display-name, and icon elements. These elements are intended for use in builder tools, and we do not discuss them further.

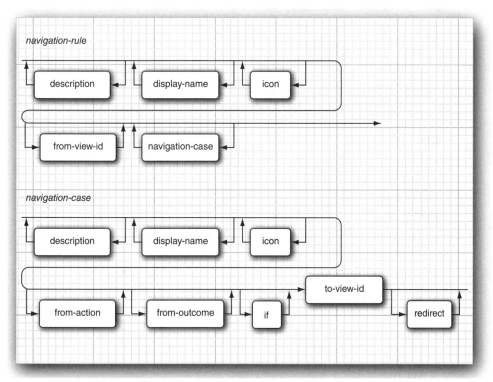

Figure 3–9 Syntax diagram for navigation elements

Wildcards

You can use *wildcards* in the from-view-id element of a navigation rule, for example:

```
<navigation-rule>
  <from-view-id>/secure/*</from-view-id>
  <navigation-case>
    . . .
  </navigation-case>
</navigation-rule>
```

This rule applies to all pages that start with the prefix /secure/. Only a single * is allowed, and it must be at the end of the ID string.

If there are multiple matching wildcard rules, the longest match is taken.

> NOTE: Instead of leaving out a `from-view-id` element, you can also use one of the following to specify a rule that applies to all pages:
>
> `<from-view-id>/*</from-view-id>`
>
> or
>
> `<from-view-id>*</from-view-id>`

Using `from-action`

The structure of the `navigation-case` element is more complex than we previously discussed. In addition to the `from-outcome` element, there is also a `from-action` element. That flexibility can be useful if you have two separate actions with the same outcome string.

For example, suppose that in our quiz application, the `startOverAction` returns the string `"again"` instead of `"startOver"`. The same string can be returned by the `answerAction`. To differentiate between the two navigation cases, you can use a `from-action` element. The contents of the element must be identical to the method expression string of the `action` attribute:

```
<navigation-case>
    <from-action>#{quizBean.answerAction}</from-action>
    <from-outcome>again</from-outcome>
    <to-view-id>/again.xhtml</to-view-id>
</navigation-case>
<navigation-case>
    <from-action>#{quizBean.startOverAction}</from-action>
    <from-outcome>again</from-outcome>
    <to-view-id>/index.xhtml</to-view-id>
</navigation-case>
```

> NOTE: The navigation handler does *not* invoke the method inside the #{...} delimiters. The method has been invoked before the navigation handler kicks in. The navigation handler merely uses the `from-action` string as a key to find a matching navigation case.

Conditional Navigation Cases JSF 2.0

As of JSF 2.0, you can supply an if element that activates a navigation case only when a condition is fulfilled. Supply a value expression for the condition. Here is an example:

```
<navigation-case>
    <from-outcome>previous</from-outcome>
    <if>#{quizBean.currentQuestion != 0}</if>
    <to-view-id>/main.xhtml</to-view-id>
</navigation-case>
```

Dynamic Target View IDs JSF 2.0

The to-view-id element can be a value expression, in which case it is evaluated. The result is used as the view ID. For example:

```
<navigation-rule>
    <from-view-id>/main.xhtml</from-view-id>
    <navigation-case>
        <to-view-id>#{quizBean.nextViewID}</to-view-id>
    </navigation-case>
</navigation-rule>
```

In this example, the getNextViewID method of the quiz bean is invoked to get the target view ID.

Conclusion

You have now seen all features that JSF offers for controlling navigation. Keep in mind that the simplest case is very straightforward: the actions of command buttons and links can simply return an outcome that specifies the next page. However, if you want more control, the JSF framework gives you the necessary tools.

In the next chapter, you will learn all about the standard JSF components.

STANDARD JSF TAGS

Topics in This Chapter

Chapter 4

Development of compelling JSF applications requires a good grasp of the JSF tag libraries. JSF 1.2 had two tag libraries: core and HTML. As of JSF 2.0, there are six libraries with over 100 tags—see Table 4–1. In this chapter, we cover the core library and most of the HTML library. One HTML library component—the data table—is so complex that it is covered separately in Chapter 6.

Table 4–1   JSF Tag Libraries

Library	Namespace Identifier	Commonly Used Prefix	Number of Tags	See Chapter
Core	http://java.sun.com/jsf/core	f:	27	See Table 4–2
HTML	http://java.sun.com/jsf/html	h:	31	4 and 6
Facelets JSF 2.0	http://java.sun.com/jsf/facelets	ui:	11	5
Composite Components JSF 2.0	http://java.sun.com/jsf/composite	composite:	12	9
JSTL Core JSF 2.0	http://java.sun.com/jsp/jstl/core	c:	7	13
JSTL Functions JSF 2.0	http://java.sun.com/jsp/jstl/functions	fn:	16	2

An Overview of the JSF Core Tags

The core library contains the tags that are independent of HTML rendering.
The core tags are listed in Table 4–2.

Table 4–2   JSF Core Tags

Tag	Description	See Chapter
attribute	Sets an attribute (key/value) in its parent component.	4
param	Adds a parameter child component to its parent component.	4
facet	Adds a facet to a component.	4
actionListener	Adds an action listener to a component.	8
setPropertyActionListener **JSF 1.2**	Adds an action listener that sets a property.	8
valueChangeListener	Adds a value change listener to a component.	8
phaseListener **JSF 1.2**	Adds a phase listener to the parent view.	8
event **JSF 2.0**	Adds a component system event listener.	8
converter	Adds an arbitrary converter to a component.	7
convertDateTime	Adds a datetime converter to a component.	7
convertNumber	Adds a number converter to a component.	7
validator	Adds a validator to a component.	7
validateDoubleRange	Validates a double range for a component's value.	7
validateLength	Validates the length of a component's value.	7
validateLongRange	Validates a long range for a component's value.	7
validateRequired **JSF 2.0**	Checks that a value is present.	7
validateRegex **JSF 2.0**	Validates a value against a regular expression.	7

Table 4–2　JSF Core Tags (cont.)

Tag	Description	See Chapter
validateBean **JSF 2.0**	Uses the Bean Validation API (JSR 303) for validation.	7
loadBundle	Loads a resource bundle, stores properties as a Map.	2
selectitems	Specifies items for a select one or select many component.	4
selectitem	Specifies an item for a select one or select many component.	4
verbatim	Turns text containing markup into a component.	4
viewParam **JSF 2.0**	Defines a "view parameter" that can be initialized with a request parameter.	3
metadata **JSF 2.0**	Holds view parameters. May hold other metadata in the future.	3
ajax **JSF 2.0**	Enables Ajax behavior for components.	11
view	Use for specifying the page locale or a phase listener.	2 and 7
subview	Not needed with facelets.	

Most of the core tags represent objects you add to components, such as the following:

- Attributes
- Parameters
- Facets
- Listeners
- Converters
- Validators
- Selection items

All of the core tags are discussed at length in different places in this book, as shown in Table 4–1.

Attributes, Parameters, and Facets

The f:attribute, f:param, and f:facet tags are general-purpose tags to add information to a component. Any component can store arbitrary name/value pairs in its *attribute map*. You can set an attribute in a page and later retrieve it programatically. For example, in "Supplying Attributes to Converters" on page 289 of Chapter 7, we set the separator character for credit card digit groups like this:

```
<h:outputText value="#{payment.card}">
   <f:attribute name="separator" value="-" />
</h:outputText>
```

The converter that formats the output retrieves the attribute from the component.

The f:param tag also lets you define a name/value pair, but the value is placed *in a separate child component*, a much bulkier storage mechanism. However, the child components form a list, not a map. You use f:param if you need to supply a number of values with the same name (or no name at all). You saw an example in "Messages with Variable Parts" on page 42 of Chapter 2, where the h:outputFormat component contains a list of f:param children.

 NOTE: the h:commandlink component turns its f:param children into HTTP request name/value pairs. The event listener that is activated when the user clicks the link can then retrieve the name/value pairs from the request map. We demonstrate this technique in Chapter 8.

Finally, f:facet adds a named component to a component's *facet map*. A facet is not a child component; each component has *both* a list of child components and a map of named facet components. The facet components are usually rendered in a special place. The root of a Facelets page has two facets named "head" and "body". You will see in "Headers, Footers, and Captions" on page 212 of Chapter 6 how to use facets named "header" and "footer" in data tables.

Table 4–3 shows the attributes for the f:attribute, f:param, and f:facet tags.

Table 4–3   Attributes for f:attribute, f:param, **and** f:facet

Attribute	Description
name	The attribute, parameter component, or facet name
value	The attribute or parameter component value (does not apply to f:facet)
binding, id	See Table 4–5 on page 107 (f:param only)

> NOTE: All tag attributes in this chapter, except for var and id, accept value or method expressions. The var attribute must be a string. The id attribute can be a string or an immediate ${...} expression.

An Overview of the JSF HTML Tags

Table 4–4 lists all HTML tags. We can group these tags in the following categories:

- Inputs (input...)
- Outputs (output..., graphicImage)
- Commands (commandButton and commandLink)
- GET Requests (button, link, outputLink)
- Selections (checkbox, listbox, menu, radio)
- HTML pages (head, body, form, outputStylesheet, outputScript)
- Layouts (panelGrid, panelGroup)
- Data table (dataTable and column); see Chapter 6
- Errors and messages (message, messages)

The JSF HTML tags share common attributes, HTML pass-through attributes, and attributes that support dynamic HTML.

Table 4–4   JSF HTML Tags

Tag	Description
head **JSF 2.0**	Renders the head of the page
body **JSF 2.0**	Renders the body of the page
form	Renders a HTML form
outputStylesheet **JSF 2.0**	Adds a stylesheet to the page
outputScript **JSF 2.0**	Adds a script to the page
inputText	Single-line text input control
inputTextarea	Multiline text input control
inputSecret	Password input control
inputHidden	Hidden field

Table 4–4   JSF HTML Tags (cont.)

Tag	Description
outputLabel	Label for another component for accessibility
outputLink	Link to another web site
outputFormat	Like outputText, but formats compound messages
outputText	Single-line text output
commandButton	Button: submit, reset, or pushbutton
commandLink	Link that acts like a pushbutton
button **JSF 2.0**	Button for issuing a GET request
link **JSF 2.0**	Link for issuing a GET request
message	Displays the most recent message for a component
messages	Displays all messages
graphicImage	Displays an image
selectOneListbox	Single-select listbox
selectOneMenu	Single-select menu
selectOneRadio	Set of radio buttons
selectBooleanCheckbox	Checkbox
selectManyCheckbox	Set of checkboxes
selectManyListbox	Multiselect listbox
selectManyMenu	Multiselect menu
panelGrid	Tabular layout
panelGroup	Two or more components that are laid out as one
dataTable	A feature-rich table control (see Chapter 6)
column	Column in a dataTable (see Chapter 6)

> NOTE: The HTML tags may seem overly verbose—for example,
> selectManyListbox could be more efficiently expressed as multiList. But those
> verbose names correspond to a component/renderer combination, so
> selectManyListbox represents a selectMany component paired with a listbox
> renderer. Knowing the type of component a tag represents is crucial if you
> want to access components programmatically.

Common Attributes

Three types of tag attributes are shared among multiple HTML component
tags:

- Basic
- HTML 4.0
- DHTML events

Next, we look at each type.

Basic Attributes

As you can see from Table 4–5, basic attributes are shared by the majority of JSF
HTML tags.

Table 4–5   Basic HTML Tag Attributes[a]

Attribute	Component Types	Description
id	A (*31*)	Identifier for a component
binding	A (*31*)	Links this component with a backing bean property
rendered	A (*31*)	A Boolean; false suppresses rendering
value	I, O, C (*21*)	A component's value, typically a value expression
valueChangeListener	I (*11*)	A method expression to a method that responds to value changes
converter	I, O (*15*)	Converter class name
validator	I (*11*)	Class name of a validator that is created and attached to a component

Table 4–5   Basic HTML Tag Attributes[a] (cont.)

Attribute	Component Types	Description
required	I (*11*)	A Boolean; if true, requires a value to be entered in the associated field
converterMessage, validatorMessage, requiredMessage **JSF 1.2**	I (*11*)	A custom message to be displayed when a conversion or validation error occurs, or when required input is missing

a. A = all, I = input, O = output, C = commands, (*n*) = number of tags with attribute

All components can have id, binding, and rendered attributes, which we discuss in the following sections.

The value and converter attributes let you specify a component value and a means to convert it from a string to an object, or vice versa.

The validator, required, and valueChangeListener attributes are available for input components so that you can validate values and react to changes to those values. See Chapter 7 for more information about validators and converters.

IDs and Bindings

The versatile id attribute lets you do the following:

- Access JSF components from other JSF tags
- Obtain component references in Java code
- Access HTML elements with scripts

In this section, we discuss the first two tasks listed above. See "Form Elements and JavaScript" on page 120 for more about the last task.

The id attribute lets page authors reference a component from another tag. For example, an error message for a component can be displayed like this:

```
<h:inputText id="name" .../>
<h:message for="name"/>
```

You can also use component identifiers to get a component reference in your Java code. For example, you could access the name component in a listener like this:

```
UIComponent component = event.getComponent().findComponent("name");
```

The preceding call to findComponent has a caveat: The component that generated the event and the name component must be in the same form. There is another way to access a component in your Java code. Define the component as an instance field of a class. Provide property getters and setters for the component. Then use the binding attribute, which you specify in a JSF page, like this:

```
<h:inputText binding="#{form.nameField}" .../>
```

The binding attribute is specified with a value expression. That expression refers to a read-write bean property, such as this one:

```
private UIComponent nameField = new UIInput();
public UIComponent getNameField() { return nameField; }
public void setNameField(UIComponent newValue) { nameField = newValue; }
```

See "Backing Beans" on page 38 of Chapter 2 for more information about the binding attribute. The JSF implementation sets the property to the component, so you can programatically manipulate components.

Values, Converters, and Validators

Inputs, outputs, commands, and data tables all have values. Associated tags in the HTML library, such as h:inputText and h:dataTable, come with a value attribute. You can specify values with a string, like this:

```
<h:commandButton value="Logout" .../>
```

Most of the time you will use a value expression—for example:

```
<h:inputText value="#{customer.name}"/>
```

The converter attribute, shared by inputs and outputs, lets you attach a converter to a component. Input tags also have a validator attribute that you can use to attach a validator to a component. Converters and validators are discussed at length in Chapter 7.

Conditional Rendering

You use the rendered attribute to include or exclude a component, depending on a condition. For example, you may want to render a "Logout" button only if the user is currently logged in:

```
<h:commandButton ... rendered="#{user.loggedIn}"/>
```

To conditionally include a group of components, include them in an h:panelGrid with a rendered attribute. See "Panels" on page 115 for more information.

> TIP: Remember, you can use operators in value expressions. For example, you might have a view that acts as a tabbed pane by optionally rendering a panel depending on the selected tab. In that case, you could use `h:panelGrid` like this:
>
> `<h:panelGrid rendered="#{bean.selectedTab == 'Movies'}"/>`
>
> The preceding code renders the movies panel when the user selects the `Movies` tab.

> NOTE: Sometimes, you will see the JSTL `c:if` construct used for conditional rendering. However, that is less efficient than the `rendered` attribute.

HTML 4.0 Attributes

JSF HTML tags have appropriate HTML 4.0 pass-through attributes. Those attribute values are passed through to the generated HTML element. For example, `<h:inputText value="#{form.name.last}" size="25".../>` generates this HTML: `<input type="text" size="25".../>`. Notice that the `size` attribute is passed through to HTML.

The HTML 4.0 attributes are listed in Table 4–6.

Table 4–6 HTML 4.0 Pass-Through Attributes[a]

Attribute	Description
accesskey (*16*)	A key, typically combined with a system-defined metakey, that gives focus to an element.
accept (*1*)	Comma-separated list of content types for a form.
acceptcharset (*1*)	Comma- or space-separated list of character encodings for a form. The HTML `accept-charset` attribute is specified with the JSF attribute named `acceptcharset`.
alt (*5*)	Alternative text for nontextual elements such as images or applets.
border (*4*)	Pixel value for an element's `border` width.
charset (*3*)	Character encoding for a linked resource.
coords (*3*)	Coordinates for an element whose shape is a rectangle, circle, or polygon.
dir (*26*)	Direction for text. Valid values are `"ltr"` (left to right) and `"rtl"` (right to left).

Table 4–6 HTML 4.0 Pass-Through Attributes[a] (cont.)

Attribute	Description
disabled (14)	Disabled state of an input element or button.
hreflang (3)	Base language of a resource specified with the href attribute; hreflang may only be used with href.
lang (26)	Base language of an element's attributes and text.
maxlength (2)	Maximum number of characters for text fields.
readonly (11)	Read-only state of an input field; text can be selected in a read-only field but not edited.
rel (3)	Relationship between the current document and a link specified with the href attribute.
rev (3)	Reverse link from the anchor specified with href to the current document. The value of the attribute is a space-separated list of link types.
rows (1)	Number of visible rows in a text area. h:dataTable has a rows attribute, but it is not an HTML pass-through attribute.
shape (3)	Shape of a region. Valid values: default, rect, circle, poly (default signifies the entire region).
size (4)	Size of an input field.
style (26)	Inline style information.
styleClass (26)	Style class; rendered as HTML class attribute.
tabindex (16)	Numerical value specifying a tab index.
target (5)	The name of a frame in which a document is opened.
title (25)	A title, used for accessibility, that describes an element. Visual browsers typically create tooltips for the title's value.
type (4)	Type of a link—for example, "stylesheet".
width (3)	Width of an element.

a. (*n*) = number of tags with attribute

The attributes listed in Table 4–6 are defined in the HTML specification, which you can access online at http://www.w3.org/TR/REC-html40. That web site is an excellent resource for deep digging into HTML.

Styles

You can use CSS styles, either inline (style) or classes (styleClass), to influence how components are rendered:

```
<h:outputText value="#{customer.name}" styleClass="emphasis"/>
<h:outputText value="#{customer.id}" style="border: thin solid blue"/>
```

CSS style attributes can be value expressions—that gives you programmatic control over styles.

Resources JSF 2.0

You can include a stylesheet in the usual way, with an HTML link tag. But that is tedious if your pages are at varying directory nesting levels—you would always need to update the stylesheet directory when you move a page. More importantly, if you assemble pages from different pieces—as described in Chapter 5—you don't even know where your pieces end up.

Since JSF 2.0, there is a better way. You can place stylesheets, JavaScript files, images, and other files into a resources directory in the root of your web application. Subdirectories of this directory are called *libraries*. You can create any libraries that you like. In this book, we often use libraries css, images, and javascript.

To include a stylesheet, use the tag:

```
<h:outputStylesheet library="css" name="styles.css"/>
```

The tag adds a link of the form

```
<link href="/context-root/faces/javax.faces.resource/styles.css?ln=css"
    rel="stylesheet" type="text/css"/>
```

to the header of the page.

To include a script resource, use the outputScript tag instead:

```
<h:outputScript name="jsf.js" library="javascript" target="head" />
```

If the target attribute is head or body, the script is appended to the "head" or "body" facet of the root component, which means that it appears at the end of the head or body in the generated HTML. If there is no target element, the script is inserted in the current location.

To include an image from a library, you use the graphicImage tag:

```
<h:graphicImage name="logo.png" library="images"/>
```

There is a *versioning* mechanism for resource libraries and individual resources. You can add subdirectories to the library directory and place newer versions of files into them. The subdirectory names are simply the version numbers. For example, suppose you have the following directories:

```
resources/css/1_0_2
resources/css/1_1
```

Then the latest version (resources/css/1_1) will be used. Note that you can add new versions of a library in a running application.

Similarly, you can add new versions of an individual resource, but the naming scheme is a bit odd. You replace the resource with a directory of the same name, then use the version name as the file name. You can add an extension if you like. For example:

```
resources/css/styles.css/1_0_2.css
resources/css/styles.css/1_1.css
```

The version numbers must consist of decimal numbers, separated by underscores. They are compared in the usual way, first comparing the major version numbers and using the minor numbers to break ties.

There is also a mechanism for supplying localized versions of resources. Unfortunately, that mechanism is unintuitive and not very useful. Localized resources have a prefix, such as resources/de_DE/images, but the prefix is *not* treated in the same way as a bundle suffix. There is no fallback mechanism. That is, if an image is not found in resources/de_DE/images, then resources/de/images and resources/images are *not* consulted.

Moreover, the locale prefix is *not* simply the current locale. Instead, it is obtained by a curious lookup, which you enable by following these steps:

1. Add the line

   <message-bundle>*name of a resource bundle used in your application*</message-bundle>

   inside the application element of faces-config.xml

2. Inside each localized version of that resource bundle, place a name/value pair

   javax.faces.resource.localePrefix=*prefix*

3. Place the matching resources into resources/*prefix*/*library*/...

For example, if you use the message bundle com.corejsf.messages, and the file com.corejsf.messages_de contains the entry

   javax.faces.resource.localePrefix=german

then you place the German resources into resources/german. (The prefix need not use the standard language and country codes, and in fact it is a good idea not to use them so that you don't raise false hopes.)

> CAUTION: Unfortunately, this localization scheme is unappealing in practice. Once you define a locale prefix, that prefix is used for *all* resources. Suppose you wanted to have different images for the German and English versions of your site. Then you would also have to duplicate *every other* resource. Hopefully, this will be fixed in a future version of JSF.

DHTML Events

Client-side scripting is useful for all sorts of tasks, such as syntax validation or rollover images, and it is easy to use with JSF. HTML attributes that support scripting, such as onclick and onchange are called *dynamic HTML (DHTML) event attributes*. JSF supports DHTML event attributes for nearly all of the JSF HTML tags. Those attributes are listed in Table 4–7.

Table 4–7   DHTML Event Attributes[a]

Attribute	Description
onblur (*16*)	Element loses focus
onchange (*11*)	Element's value changes
onclick (*17*)	Mouse button is clicked over the element
ondblclick (*21*)	Mouse button is double-clicked over the element
onfocus (*16*)	Element receives focus
onkeydown (*21*)	Key is pressed
onkeypress (*21*)	Key is pressed and subsequently released
onkeyup (*21*)	Key is released
onload (*1*)	Page is loaded
onmousedown (*21*)	Mouse button is pressed over the element
onmousemove (*21*)	Mouse moves over the element
onmouseout (*21*)	Mouse leaves the element's area
onmouseover (*21*)	Mouse moves onto an element
onmouseup (*21*)	Mouse button is released
onreset (*1*)	Form is reset

Table 4–7   DHTML Event Attributes[a] (cont.)

Attribute	Description
onselect (11)	Text is selected in an input field
onsubmit (1)	Form is submitted
onunload (1)	Page is unloaded

a. (n) = number of tags with attribute

The DHTML event attributes listed in Table 4–7 let you associate client-side scripts with events. Typically, JavaScript is used as a scripting language, but you can use any scripting language you like. See the HTML specification for more details.

> TIP: You will probably add client-side scripts to your JSF pages soon after you start using JSF. One common use is to submit a request when an input's value is changed so that value change listeners are immediately notified of the change, like this: <h:selectOneMenu onchange="submit()"...>

Panels

Up to this point, we have used HTML tables to lay out components. Creating table markup by hand is tedious, so now we'll look at alleviating some of that tedium with h:panelGrid, which generates the HTML markup for laying out components in rows and columns.

> NOTE: The h:panelGrid tag uses HTML tables for layout, which some web designers find objectionable. You can certainly use CSS layout instead of h:panelGrid. A future version of h:panelGrid may have an option for using CSS layout as well.

You can specify the number of columns with the columns attribute, like this:

```
<h:panelGrid columns="3">
   ...
</h:panelGrid>
```

The columns attribute is not mandatory—if you do not specify it, the number of columns defaults to 1. The h:panelGrid tag places components in columns from left to right and top to bottom. For example, if you have a panel grid with three columns and nine components, you will wind up with three rows, each containing three columns. If you specify three columns and 10 components, you will have four rows, and in the last row only the first column will contain the tenth component.

Table 4–8 lists h:panelGrid attributes.

Table 4–8   Attributes for h:panelGrid

Attributes	Description
bgcolor	Background color for the table
border	Width of the table's border
cellpadding	Padding around table cells
cellspacing	Spacing between table cells
columnClasses	Comma-separated list of CSS classes for columns
columns	Number of columns in the table
footerClass	CSS class for the table footer
frame	Specification for sides of the frame surrounding the table that are to be drawn; valid values: none, above, below, hsides, vsides, lhs, rhs, box, border
headerClass	CSS class for the table header
rowClasses	Comma-separated list of CSS classes for rows
rules	Specification for lines drawn between cells; valid values: groups, rows, columns, all
summary	Summary of the table's purpose and structure used for nonvisual feedback, such as speech
captionClass **JSF 1.2**, captionStyle **JSF 1.2**	CSS class or style for the caption; a panel caption is optionally supplied by a facet named "caption"
binding, id, rendered, value	Basic attributes[a]
dir, lang, style, styleClass, title, width	HTML 4.0[b]

Table 4–8   Attributes for h:panelGrid **(cont.)**

Attributes	Description
onclick, ondblclick, onkeydown, onkeypress, onkeyup, onmousedown, onmousemove, onmouseout, onmouseover, onmouseup	DHTML events[c]

a. See Table 4–5 on page 107 for information about basic attributes.
b. See Table 4–6 on page 110 for information about HTML 4.0 attributes.
c. See Table 4–7 on page 114 for information about DHTML event attributes.

You can specify CSS classes for different parts of the table: header, footer, rows, and columns. The columnClasses and rowClasses specify lists of CSS classes that are applied to columns and rows, respectively. If those lists contain fewer class names than rows or columns, the CSS classes are reused. That makes it possible to specify classes, like this:

```
rowClasses="evenRows, oddRows"
```

and

```
columnClasses="evenColumns, oddColumns"
```

The cellpadding, cellspacing, frame, rules, and summary attributes are HTML pass-through attributes that apply only to tables. See the HTML 4.0 specification for more information.

h:panelGrid is often used with h:panelGroup, which groups two or more components so they are treated as one. For example, you might group an input field and its error message, like this:

```
<h:panelGrid columns="2">
    ...
    <h:panelGroup>
        <h:inputText id="name" value="#{user.name}">
        <h:message for="name"/>
    </h:panelGroup>
    ...
</h:panelGrid>
```

Grouping the text field and error message puts them in the same table cell. (We discuss the h:message tag in the section "Messages" on page 171.)

h:panelGroup is a simple tag with only a handful of attributes. Those attributes are listed in Table 4–9.

Table 4–9   Attributes for `h:panelGroup`

Attributes	Description
layout **JSF 1.2**	If the value is "block", use an HTML div to lay out the children; otherwise, use a span
binding, id, rendered	Basic attributes[a]
style, styleClass	HTML 4.0[b]

a. See Table 4–5 on page 107 for information about basic attributes.
b. See Table 4–6 on page 110 for information about HTML 4.0 attributes.

The Head, Body, and Form Tags

Table 4–10 shows the attributes of the `h:head` and `h:body` tags. All of them are basic or HTML/DHTML attributes.

Table 4–10   Attributes for `h:head` and `h:body`

Attributes	Description
id, binding, rendered	Basic attributes[a]
dir, lang h:body only: style, styleClass, target, title	HTML 4.0[b] attributes
h:body only: onclick, ondblclick, onkeydown, onkeypress, onkeyup, onload, onmousedown, onmousemove, onmouseout, onmouseover, onmouseup, onunload	DHTML events[c]

a. See Table 4–5 on page 107 for information about basic attributes.
b. See Table 4–6 on page 110 for information about HTML 4.0 attributes.
c. See Table 4–7 on page 114 for information about DHTML event attributes.

Web applications run on form submissions, and JSF applications are no exception. Table 4–11 lists all `h:form` attributes.

Table 4–11   Attributes for `h:form`

Attributes	Description
`prependId` **JSF 1.2**	true (default) if the ID of this form is prepended to the IDs of its components; `false` to suppress prepending the form ID (useful if the ID is used in JavaScript code)
`binding, id, rendered`	Basic attributes[a]
`accept, acceptcharset, dir, enctype, lang, style, styleClass, target, title`	HTML 4.0[b] attributes
`onclick, ondblclick, onfocus, onkeydown, onkeypress, onkeyup, onmousedown, onmousemove, onmouseout, onmouseover, onmouseup, onreset, onsubmit`	DHTML events[c]

a. See Table 4–5 on page 107 for information about basic attributes.
b. See Table 4–6 on page 110 for information about HTML 4.0 attributes.
c. See Table 4–7 on page 114 for information about DHTML event attributes.

Although the HTML `form` tag has `method` and `action` attributes, `h:form` does not. Because you can save state in the client—an option that is implemented as a hidden field—posting forms with the GET method is disallowed. The contents of that hidden field can be quite large and may overrun the buffer for request parameters, so all JSF form submissions are implemented with the POST method.

There is no need for an `anchor` attribute since JSF form submissions always post to the current page. (Navigation to a new page happens after the form data have been posted.)

The `h:form` tag generates an HTML `form` element. For example, if, in a JSF page named `/index.xhtml`, you use an `h:form` tag with no attributes, the `Form` renderer generates HTML like this:

```
<form id="_id0" method="post" action="/faces/index.xhtml"
    enctype="application/x-www-form-urlencoded">
```

If you do not specify the `id` attribute explicitly, a value is generated by the JSF implementation, as is the case for all generated HTML elements. You can explicitly specify the `id` attribute for forms so that it can be referenced in stylesheets or scripts.

Form Elements and JavaScript

Java*Server* Faces is all about *server*-side components, but it is also designed to work with scripting languages, such as JavaScript. For example, the application shown in Figure 4–1 uses JavaScript to confirm that a password field matches a password confirm field. If the fields do not match, a JavaScript dialog is displayed. If they do match, the form is submitted.

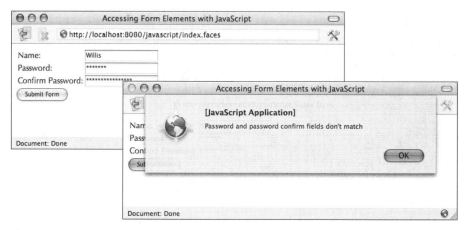

Figure 4–1   Using JavaScript to access form elements

We use the id attribute to assign names to the relevant HTML elements so that we can access them with JavaScript:

```
<h:form>
    ...
    <h:inputSecret id="password" .../>
    <h:inputSecret id="passwordConfirm" .../>
    ...
    <h:commandButton type="button" onclick="checkPassword(this.form)"/>
    ...
</h:form>
```

When the user clicks the button, a JavaScript function checkPassword is invoked. Here is the implementation of the function:

```
function checkPassword(form) {
    var password = form[form.id + ":password"].value;
    var passwordConfirm = form[form.id + ":passwordConfirm"].value;

    if (password == passwordConfirm)
        form.submit();
```

```
else
    alert("Password and password confirm fields don't match");
}
```

To understand the syntax used to access form elements, look at the HTML produced by the preceding code:

```
<form id="_id0" method="post"
    action="/javascript/faces/index.xhtml"
    enctype="application/x-www-form-urlencoded">
    ...
    <input id="_id0:password"
        type="text" name="registerForm:password"/>
    ...
    <input type="button" name="_id0:_id5"
        value="Submit Form" onclick="checkPassword(this.form)"/>
    ...
</form>
```

All form controls generated by JSF have names that conform to

formName:componentName

where *formName* represents the name of the control's form and *componentName* represents the control's name. If you do not specify id attributes, the JSF implementation creates identifiers for you. In our case, we didn't specify an id for the form. Therefore, to access the password field in the preceding example, the script uses the expression:

```
form[form.id + ":password"]
```

NOTE: The ID values generated by the JSF implementation seem to get more complex with every version of JSF. In the past, they were fairly straightforward (such as _id0), but more recent versions use IDs such as j_id2059540600_7ac21823. For greater clarity, we use the simpler IDs in our examples.

The directory structure for the application shown in Figure 4–1 is shown in Figure 4–2. The JSF page is listed in Listing 4–1. The JavaScript code, stylesheets, and resource bundle are listed in Listings 4–2 through 4–4.

Figure 4–2   The JavaScript example directory structure

Listing 4–1   javascript/web/index.xhtml

```
1. <?xml version="1.0" encoding="UTF-8"?>
2. <!DOCTYPE html PUBLIC "-//W3C//DTD XHTML 1.0 Transitional//EN"
3. "http://www.w3.org/TR/xhtml1/DTD/xhtml1-transitional.dtd">
4. <html xmlns="http://www.w3.org/1999/xhtml"
5.     xmlns:h="http://java.sun.com/jsf/html">
6.   <h:head>
7.     <title>#{msgs.windowTitle}</title>
8.     <h:outputStylesheet library="css" name="styles.css"/>
9.     <h:outputScript library="javascript" name="checkPassword.js"/>
10.   </h:head>
11.   <h:body>
12.     <h:form>
13.       <h:panelGrid columns="2" columnClasses="evenColumns, oddColumns">
14.         #{msgs.namePrompt}
15.         <h:inputText/>
16.         #{msgs.passwordPrompt}
17.         <h:inputSecret id="password"/>
18.         #{msgs.confirmPasswordPrompt}
19.         <h:inputSecret id="passwordConfirm"/>
20.       </h:panelGrid>
21.       <h:commandButton type="button" value="Submit Form"
22.                       onclick="checkPassword(this.form)"/>
23.     </h:form>
24.   </h:body>
25. </html>
```

Listing 4–2   javascript/web/resources/javascript/checkPassword.js

```
1. function checkPassword(form) {
2.    var password = form[form.id + ":password"].value;
3.    var passwordConfirm = form[form.id + ":passwordConfirm"].value;
4.
5.    if (password == passwordConfirm)
6.       form.submit();
7.    else
8.       alert("Password and password confirm fields don't match");
9. }
```

Listing 4–3   javascript/web/resources/css/styles.css

```
1. .evenColumns {
2.    font-style: italic;
3. }
4.
5. .oddColumns {
6.    padding-left: 1em;
7. }
```

Listing 4–4   javascript/src/java/com/corejsf/messages.properties

```
1. windowTitle=Accessing Form Elements with JavaScript
2. namePrompt=Name:
3. passwordPrompt=Password:
4. confirmPasswordPrompt=Confirm Password:
```

Text Fields and Text Areas

Text inputs are the mainstay of most web applications. JSF supports three varieties represented by the following tags:

- h:inputText
- h:inputSecret
- h:inputTextarea

Since the three tags use similar attributes, Table 4–12 lists attributes for all three.

Table 4–12   Attributes for h:inputText, h:inputSecret, h:inputTextarea, **and** h:inputHidden

Attributes	Description
cols	For h:inputTextarea only—number of columns.
immediate	Process validation early in the life cycle.
redisplay	For h:inputSecret only—when true, the input field's value is redisplayed when the web page is reloaded.
required	Require input in the component when the form is submitted.
rows	For h:inputTextarea only—number of rows.
valueChangeListener	A specified listener that is notified of value changes.
label **JSF 1.2**	A description of the component for use in error messages. Does not apply to h:inputHidden.
binding, converter, converterMessage **JSF 1.2**, id, rendered, required, requiredMessage **JSF 1.2**, value, validator, validatorMessage **JSF 1.2**	Basic attributes.[a]
accesskey, alt, dir, disabled, lang, maxlength, readonly, size, style, styleClass, tabindex, title	HTML 4.0 pass-through attributes[b]— alt, maxlength, and size do not apply to h:inputTextarea. None apply to h:inputHidden.
autocomplete	If the value is "off", render the nonstandard HTML attribute autocomplete="off" (h:inputText and h:inputSecret only).
onblur, onchange, onclick, ondblclick, onfocus, onkeydown, onkeypress, onkeyup, onmousedown, onmousemove, onmouseout, onmouseover, onmouseup, onselect	DHTML events. None apply to h:inputHidden.[c]

a. See Table 4–5 on page 107 for information about basic attributes.
b. See Table 4–6 on page 110 for information about HTML 4.0 attributes.
c. See Table 4–7 on page 114 for information about DHTML event attributes.

All three tags have immediate, required, value, and valueChangeListener attributes. The immediate attribute is used primarily for value changes that affect the user interface and is rarely used by these three tags. Instead, it is more commonly used by other input components such as menus and listboxes. See "Immediate Components" on page 320 of Chapter 8 for more information about the immediate attribute.

Three attributes in Table 4–12 are each applicable to only one tag: cols, rows, and redisplay. The rows and cols attributes are used with h:inputTextarea to specify the number of rows and columns, respectively, for the text area. The redisplay attribute, used with h:inputSecret, is a boolean that determines whether a secret field retains its value—and therefore redisplays it—when the field's form is resubmitted.

Table 4–13 shows sample uses of the h:inputText and h:inputSecret tags.

Table 4–13 h:inputText **and** h:inputSecret **Examples**

Example	Result
<h:inputText value="#{form.testString}" readonly="true"/>	12345678901234567890
<h:inputSecret value="#{form.passwd}" redisplay="true"/>	********** (shown after an unsuccessful form submit)
<h:inputSecret value="#{form.passwd}" redisplay="false"/>	 (shown after an unsuccessful form submit)
<h:inputText value="inputText" style="color: Yellow; background: Teal;"/>	inputText
<h:inputText value="1234567" size="5"/>	123456
<h:inputText value="1234567890" maxlength="6" size="10"/>	123456

The first example in Table 4–13 produces the following HTML:

```
<input type="text" name="_id0:_id4" value="12345678901234567890"
    readonly="readonly"/>
```

The input field is read-only, so our form bean defines only a getter method:

```
private String testString = "12345678901234567890";
public String getTestString() {
    return testString;
}
```

The h:inputSecret examples illustrate the use of the redisplay attribute. If that attribute is true, the text field stores its value between requests and, therefore, the value is redisplayed when the page reloads. If redisplay is false, the value is discarded and is not redisplayed.

The size attribute specifies the number of visible characters in a text field. But because most fonts are variable width, the size attribute is not precise, as you can see from the fifth example in Table 4–13, which specifies a size of 5 but displays six characters. The maxlength attribute specifies the maximum number of characters a text field will display. That attribute is precise. Both size and maxlength are HTML pass-through attributes.

Table 4–14 shows examples of the h:inputTextarea tag.

The h:inputTextarea has cols and rows attributes to specify the number of columns and rows, respectively, in the text area. The cols attribute is analogous to the size attribute for h:inputText and is also imprecise.

Table 4–14   h:inputTextarea Examples

Example	Result
`<h:inputTextarea rows="5"/>`	
`<h:inputTextarea cols="5"/>`	
`<h:inputTextarea value="123456789012345" rows="3" cols="10"/>`	456789012345
`<h:inputTextarea value="#{form.dataInRows}" rows="2" cols="15"/>`	line one line two line three

If you specify one long string for h:inputTextarea's value, the string will be placed in its entirety in one line, as you can see from the third example in Table 4–14. If you want to put data on separate lines, you can insert newline characters (\n) to force a line break. For example, the last example in Table 4–14 accesses the dataInRows property of a backing bean. That property is implemented like this:

```
private String dataInRows = "line one\nline two\nline three";
public void setDataInRows(String newValue) {
    dataInRows = newValue;
}
public String getDataInRows() {
    return dataInRows;
}
```

Hidden Fields

JSF provides support for hidden fields with h:inputHidden. Hidden fields are often used with JavaScript actions to send data back to the server. The h:inputHidden tag has the same attributes as the other input tags, except that it does not support the standard HTML and DHTML tags.

Using Text Fields and Text Areas

Next, we take a look at a complete example that uses text fields and text areas. The application shown in Figure 4–3 uses h:inputText, h:inputSecret, and h:inputTextarea to collect personal information from a user. The values of those components are wired to bean properties, which are accessed in the thankYou.xhtml page that redisplays the information the user entered.

Three things are noteworthy about the following application. First, the JSF pages reference a user bean (com.corejsf.UserBean). Second, the h:inputTextarea tag transfers the text entered in a text area to the model (in this case, the user bean) as one string with embedded newlines (\n). We display that string by using the HTML <pre> element to preserve that formatting. Third, for illustration, we use the style attribute to format output. A more industrial-strength application would presumably use stylesheets exclusively to make global style changes easier to manage.

Figure 4–3   Using text fields and text areas

Figure 4–4 shows the directory structure for the application shown in Figure 4–3. Listings 4–5 through 4–8 show the pertinent JSF pages, managed beans, faces configuration file, and resource bundle.

Figure 4–4   Directory structure of the text fields and text areas example

---

Listing 4–5   personalData/web/index.xhtml

```
1. <?xml version="1.0" encoding="UTF-8"?>
2. <!DOCTYPE html PUBLIC "-//W3C//DTD XHTML 1.0 Transitional//EN"
3. "http://www.w3.org/TR/xhtml1/DTD/xhtml1-transitional.dtd">
4. <html xmlns="http://www.w3.org/1999/xhtml"
5.     xmlns:h="http://java.sun.com/jsf/html">
6.   <h:head>
7.     <title>#{msgs.indexWindowTitle}</title>
8.   </h:head>
9.   <h:body>
10.     <h:outputText value="#{msgs.indexPageTitle}"
11.                 style="font-style: italic; font-size: 1.5em"/>
12.     <h:form>
13.       <h:panelGrid columns="2">
14.         #{msgs.namePrompt}
15.         <h:inputText value="#{user.name}"/>
16.         #{msgs.passwordPrompt}
17.         <h:inputSecret value="#{user.password}"/>
18.         #{msgs.tellUsPrompt}
19.         <h:inputTextarea value="#{user.aboutYourself}" rows="5" cols="35"/>
20.       </h:panelGrid>
21.       <h:commandButton value="#{msgs.submitPrompt}" action="thankYou"/>
22.     </h:form>
23.   </h:body>
24. </html>
```

Listing 4–6   personalData/web/thankYou.xhtml

```
1. <?xml version="1.0" encoding="UTF-8"?>
2. <!DOCTYPE html PUBLIC "-//W3C//DTD XHTML 1.0 Transitional//EN"
3. "http://www.w3.org/TR/xhtml1/DTD/xhtml1-transitional.dtd">
4. <html xmlns="http://www.w3.org/1999/xhtml"
5.     xmlns:h="http://java.sun.com/jsf/html">
6.   <h:head>
7.     <title>#{msgs.thankYouWindowTitle}</title>
8.   </h:head>
9.   <h:body>
10.     <h:outputText value="#{msgs.namePrompt}" style="font-style: italic"/>
11.     #{user.name}
12.     <br/>
13.     <h:outputText value="#{msgs.aboutYourselfPrompt}" style="font-style: italic"/>
14.     <br/>
15.     <pre>#{user.aboutYourself}</pre>
16.   </h:body>
17. </html>
```

Listing 4–7   personalData/src/java/com/corejsf/UserBean.java

```java
 1. package com.corejsf;
 2.
 3. import java.io.Serializable;
 4.
 5. import javax.inject.Named;
 6.    // or import javax.faces.bean.ManagedBean;
 7. import javax.enterprise.context.SessionScoped;
 8.    // or import javax.faces.bean.SessionScoped;
 9.
10. @Named("user") // or @ManagedBean(name="user")
11. @SessionScoped
12. public class UserBean implements Serializable {
13.    private String name;
14.    private String password;
15.    private String aboutYourself;
16.
17.    public String getName() { return name; }
18.    public void setName(String newValue) { name = newValue; }
19.
20.    public String getPassword() { return password; }
21.    public void setPassword(String newValue) { password = newValue; }
22.
23.    public String getAboutYourself() { return aboutYourself; }
24.    public void setAboutYourself(String newValue) { aboutYourself = newValue; }
25. }
```

Listing 4–8   personalData/src/java/com/corejsf/messages.properties

```
1. indexWindowTitle=Using Textfields and Textareas
2. thankYouWindowTitle=Thank you for submitting your information
3. thankYouPageTitle=Thank you!
4. indexPageTitle=Please enter the following personal information
5. namePrompt=Name:
6. passwordPrompt=Password:
7. tellUsPrompt=Please tell us about yourself:
8. aboutYourselfPrompt=Some information about you:
9. submitPrompt=Submit your information
```

Displaying Text and Images

JSF applications use the following tags to display text and images:

- h:outputText
- h:outputFormat
- h:graphicImage

The h:outputText tag is one of JSF's simplest tags. With only a handful of attributes, it does not typically generate an HTML element. Instead, it generates mere text—with one exception: If you specify the style or styleClass attributes, h:outputText will generate an HTML span element.

In JSF 2.0, you don't usually need the h:outputText tag since you can simply insert value expressions, such as #{msgs.namePrompt} into your page. You would use h:outputText in the following circumstances:

- To produce styled output
- In a panel grid to make sure that the text is considered one cell of the grid
- To generate HTML markup

The h:outputText and h:outputFormat tags have one attribute that is unique among all JSF tags: escape. By default, the escape attribute is true, which causes the characters < > & to be converted to < > and & respectively. Changing those characters helps prevent cross-site scripting attacks. (See http://www.cert.org/advisories/CA-2000-02.html for more information about cross-site scripting attacks.) Set this attribute to false if you want to programmatically generate HTML markup.

NOTE: The value attribute of h:outputText can never contain < characters. The only way to produce HTML markup with h:outputText is with a value expression.

NOTE: When you include a value expression such as #{msgs.namePrompt} in your page, the resulting value is always escaped. You must use h:outputText if you want to generate HTML markup.

Table 4–15 lists all h:outputText attributes.

Table 4–15 Attributes for h:outputText **and** h:outputFormat

Attributes	Description
escape	If set to true (default), escapes <, >, and & characters
binding, converter, id, rendered, value	Basic attributes[a]
style, styleClass, title, dir **JSF 1.2**, lang **JSF 1.2**	HTML 4.0[b]

a. See Table 4–5 on page 107 for information about basic attributes.
b. See Table 4–6 on page 110 for information about HTML 4.0 attributes.

The h:outputFormat tag formats a compound message with parameters specified in the body of the tag—for example:

```
<h:outputFormat value="{0} is {1} years old">
  <f:param value="Bill"/>
  <f:param value="38"/>
</h:outputFormat>
```

In the preceding code fragment, the compound message is {0} is {1} years old and the parameters, specified with f:param tags, are Bill and 38. The output of the preceding code fragment is: Bill is 38 years old. The h:outputFormat tag uses a java.text.MessageFormat instance to format its output.

The h:graphicImage tag generates an HTML img element. You can specify the image location with the url or value attribute, as a context-relative path—meaning relative to the web application's context root. As of JSF 2.0, you can place images into the resources directory and specify a library and name:

```
<h:graphicImage library="images" name="de_flag.gif"/>
```

Here, the image is located in resources/images/de_flag.gif. Alternatively, you can use this:

```
<h:graphicImage url="/resources/images/de_flag.gif"/>
```

You can also use the resources map:

```
<h:graphicImage value="#{resources['images:de_flag.gif']}"/>
```

Table 4–16 shows all the attributes for h:graphicImage.

Table 4–16 Attributes for h:graphicImage

Attributes	Description
binding, id, rendered, value	Basic attributes[a]
alt, dir, height, ismap, lang, longdesc, style, styleClass, title, url, usemap, width	HTML 4.0[b]
onclick, ondblclick, onkeydown, onkeypress, onkeyup, onmousedown, onmousemove, onmouseout, onmouseover, onmouseup	DHTML events[c]
library, name **JSF 2.0**	The resource library and name for this image

a. See Table 4–5 on page 107 for information about basic attributes.
b. See Table 4–6 on page 110 for information about HTML 4.0 attributes.
c. See Table 4–7 on page 114 for information about DHTML event attributes.

Table 4–17 shows some examples of using h:outputText and h:graphicImage.

Table 4–17 ** h:outputText **and ** h:graphicImage **Examples

Example	Result
<h:outputText value="#{form.testString}"/>	12345678901234567890
<h:outputText value="Number #{form.number}"/>	Number 1000
<h:outputText value="#{form.htmlCode}" escape="false"/> where the getHtmlCode method returns the string "<input type='text' value='hello'/>"	hello
<h:outputText value="#{form.htmlCode}"/> where the getHtmlCode method returns the string "<input type='text' value='hello'/>"	<input type="text" value="hello">
<h:graphicImage value="/tjefferson.jpg"/>	
<h:graphicImage library="images" name="tjefferson.jpg" style="border: thin solid black"/>	

The third and fourth examples in Table 4–17 illustrate use of the escape attribute. If the value for h:outputText is <input type='text' value='hello'/>, and the escape attribute is false—as is the case for the third example in Table 4–17—the h:outputText tag generates an HTML input element. Unintentional generation of HTML elements is exactly the sort of mischief that enables miscreants to carry out cross-site scripting attacks. With the escape attribute set to true—as in the fourth example in Table 4–17—that output is transformed to harmless text, thereby thwarting a potential attack.

The final two examples in Table 4–17 show you how to use h:graphicImage.

Buttons and Links

Buttons and links are ubiquitous among web applications, and JSF provides the following tags to support them:

- h:commandButton
- h:commandLink
- h:button
- h:link
- h:outputLink

The h:commandButton and h:commandLink are the primary components for navigating within a JSF application. When a button or link is activated, a POST request sends the form data back to the server.

JSF 2.0 introduced the h:button and h:link components. These components also render buttons and links, but clicking on them issues a bookmarkable GET request instead. We discussed this mechanism in Chapter 3.

The h:outputLink tag generates an HTML anchor element that points to a resource such as an image or a web page. Clicking the generated link takes you to the designated resource without further involving the JSF framework. These links are most suitable for navigating to a different web site.

Table 4–18 lists the attributes shared by h:commandButton, h:commandLink, h:button, and h:link.

Table 4–18 **Attributes for** h:commandButton, h:commandLink, h:button, **and** h:link

Attribute	Description
action (h:commandButton and h:commandLink only)	*If specified as a string:* Directly specifies an outcome used by the navigation handler to determine the JSF page to load next as a result of activating the button or link.
	If specified as a method expression: The method has this signature: String methodName(); the string represents the outcome.
	If omitted: Activating the button or link redisplays the current page.
outcome (h:button and h:link only)	The outcome, used by the navigation handler to determine the target view when the component is rendered.
fragment (h:button and h:link only)	A fragment that is to be appended to the target URL. The # separator is applied automatically and should not be included in the fragment.
actionListener	A method expression that refers to a method with this signature: void methodName(ActionEvent).
image (h:commandButton and h:button only)	The path to an image displayed in a button. If you specify this attribute, the HTML input's type will be image. If the path starts with a /, the application's context root is prepended.
immediate	A Boolean. If false (the default), actions and action listeners are invoked at the end of the request life cycle; if true, actions and action listeners are invoked at the beginning of the life cycle. See Chapter 8 for more information about the immediate attribute.
type	For h:commandButton—The type of the generated input element: button, submit, or reset. The default, unless you specify the image attribute, is submit.
	For h:commandLink and h:link—The content type of the linked resource; for example, text/html, image/gif, or audio/basic.

Table 4–18   Attributes for h:commandButton, h:commandLink, h:button, and h:link (cont.)

Attribute	Description
value	The label displayed by the button or link. You can specify a string or a value expression.
binding, id, rendered	Basic attributes.[a]
accesskey, charset (h:commandLink and h:link only), coords (h:commandLink and h:link only), dir `JSF 1.1`, disabled (h:commandButton only in JSF 1.1), hreflang (h:commandLink and h:link only), lang, rel (h:commandLink and h:link only), rev (h:commandLink and h:link only), shape (h:commandLink and h:link only), style, styleClass, tabindex, target (h:commandLink and h:link only), title	HTML 4.0.[b]
onblur, onclick, ondblclick, onfocus, onkeydown, onkeypress, onkeyup, onmousedown, onmousemove, onmouseout, onmouseover, onmouseup	DHTML events.[c]

a. See Table 4–5 on page 107 for information about basic attributes.
b. See Table 4–6 on page 110 for information about HTML 4.0 attributes.
c. See Table 4–7 on page 114 for information about DHTML event attributes.

Using Buttons

The h:commandButton and h:button tags generate an HTML input element whose type is button, image, submit, or reset, depending on the attributes you specify. Table 4–19 illustrates some uses of these tags.

The third example in Table 4–19 generates a push button—an HTML input element whose type is button—that does not result in a form submit. The only way to attach behavior to a push button is to specify a script for one of the DHTML event attributes, as we did for onclick in the example.

Table 4–19 h:commandButton **and** h:button **Examples**

Example	Result
`<h:commandButton value="submit" type="submit"` `action="#{form.submitAction}"/>`	submit
`<h:commandButton value="reset" type="reset"/>`	reset

`<h:commandButton value="click this button..."`
    `onclick="alert('button clicked')"`
    `type="button"/>`
	click this button to execute JavaScript

`<h:commandButton value="disabled"` `disabled="#{not form.buttonEnabled}"/>`	disabled
`<h:button value="#{form.buttonText}"` `outcome="#{form.pressMeOutcome}"/>`	press me

CAUTION: In JSF 1.1, there was an inconsistency in the handling of image paths between h:graphicImage and h:commandButton. The context root is automatically added by h:graphicImage, but not by h:commandButton. For example, for an application named myApp, here is how you specified the same image for each tag:

```
<h:commandButton image="/myApp/imageFile.jpg"/> <!-- JSF 1.1 -->
<h:graphicImage value="/imageFile.jpg"/>
```

This was annoying because it required the page to know the context root. The h:commandButton behavior changed in JSF 1.2. Now the context root is automatically added if the path starts with a /.

To preserve a level of annoyance, this feature interacts poorly with a resource map. You cannot use

```
<h:commandButton image="#{resources['images:imageFile.jpg']}"/>
```

because the string returned by the resource map starts with /*context-root*. The result would be <input type="image" src="/*context-root/context-root/*..."/>

The h:commandLink and h:link tags generates an HTML anchor element that acts like a form submit button. Table 4–20 shows some examples.

Table 4–20   `h:commandLink` **and** `h:link` **Examples**

Example	Result
`<h:commandLink>register</h:commandLink>`	register

`<h:commandLink style="font-style: italic">`
`   #{msgs.linkText}>`
`</h:commandLink>`
	click here to register

`<h:commandLink>`
`   #{msgs.linkText}`
`   <h:graphicImage value="/registration.jpg"/>`
`</h:commandLink>`
	
	click here to register

`<h:commandLink value="welcome"`
`   actionListener="#{form.useLinkValue}"`
`   action="#{form.followLink}"/>`
	welcome

`<h:link value="welcome"`
`   outcome="#{form.welcomeOutcome}">`
`   <f:param name="id" value="#{form.userId}"/>`
`</h:link>`
	welcome

The `h:commandLink` and `h:link` tags generate JavaScript to make links act like buttons. For example, here is the HTML generated by the first example in Table 4–20:

```
<a href="#" onclick="document.forms['_id0']['_id0:_id2'].value='_id0:_id2';
   document.forms['_id0'].submit()">register</a>
```

When the user clicks the link, the anchor element's value is set to the `h:commandLink`'s client ID, and the enclosing form is submitted. That submission sets the JSF life cycle in motion and, because the `href` attribute is "#", the current page will be reloaded unless an action associated with the link returns a non-`null` outcome.

You can place as many children as you want in the body of an `h:commandLink` tag—each corresponding HTML element is part of the link. So, for example, if you click on either the text or image in the third example in Table 4–20, the link's form will be submitted.

The next-to-last example in Table 4–20 attaches an action listener, in addition to an action, to a link. Action listeners are discussed in "Action Events" on page 312 of Chapter 8.

The last example in Table 4–20 embeds an f:param tag in the body of the
h:link tag. When you click the link, a request parameter with the name and
value specified with the f:param tag is created by the link. In Chapter 2, we discussed how the request parameters can be processed. You can also use request
parameters with an h:commandLink or h:commandButton. See "Passing Data from the
UI to the Server" on page 324 of Chapter 8 for an example.

Like h:commandLink and h:link, h:outputLink generates an HTML anchor element. But
unlike h:commandLink, h:outputLink does not generate JavaScript to make the link act
like a submit button. The value of the h:outputLink value attribute is used for the
anchor's href attribute, and the contents of the h:outputLink body are used to
populate the body of the anchor element. Table 4–21 lists all attributes for
h:outputLink., and Table 4–22 shows some h:outputLink examples.

Table 4–21   Attributes for h:outputLink

Attributes	Description
binding, converter, id, lang, rendered, value	Basic attributes[a]
accesskey, charset, coords, dir, disabled **JSF 1.2**, hreflang, lang, rel, rev, shape, style, styleClass, tabindex, target, title, type	HTML 4.0[b]
onblur, onclick, ondblclick, onfocus, onkeydown, onkeypress, onkeyup, onmousedown, onmousemove, onmouseout, onmouseover, onmouseup	DHTML events[c]

a. See Table 4–5 on page 107 for information about basic attributes.
b. See Table 4–6 on page 110 for information about HTML 4.0 attributes.
c. See Table 4–7 on page 114 for information about DHTML event attributes.

Table 4–22   h:outputLink Examples

Example	Result
``<h:outputLink value="http://java.net">
<h:graphicImage value="java-dot-net.jpg"/>
<h:outputText value="java.net"/>
</h:outputLink>```	java.net
``<h:outputLink value="#{form.welcomeURL}">
#{form.welcomeLinkText}
</h:outputLink>```	go to welcome page

Table 4–22   `h:outputLink` **Examples (cont.)**

Example	Result
```<h:outputLink value="#introduction">` ` <h:outputText value="Introduction"` ` style="font-style: italic"/>` `</h:outputLink>```	*Introduction*
```<h:outputLink value="#conclusion"` ` title-"Go to the conclusion">` ` Conclusion` `</h:outputLink>```	Conclusion Go to the conclusion
```<h:outputLink value="#toc"` ` title="Go to the table of contents">` ` <h2>Table of Contents</h2>` `</h:outputLink>```	**Table of Contents**

The first example in Table 4–22 is a link to http://java.net. The second example uses properties stored in a bean for the link's URL and text. Those properties are implemented like this:

```
private String welcomeURL = "/outputLinks/faces/welcome.jsp";
public String getWelcomeURL() {
   return welcomeURL;
}
private String welcomeLinkText = "go to welcome page";
public String getWelcomeLinkText() {
   return welcomeLinkText;
}
```

The last three examples in Table 4–22 are links to named anchors in the same JSF page. Those anchors look like this:

```
<a name="introduction">Introduction</a>
...
<a name="conclusion">Conclusion</a>
...
<a name="toc">Table of Contents</a>
...
```

> CAUTION: If you use JSF 1.1, you need to use the `f:verbatim` tag when you want to place text inside a tag. For example, the last example in Table 4–22 had to be:
>
> `<h:outputLink...><f:verbatim>Table of Contents</f:verbatim></h:outputLink>`
>
> In JSF 1.1, the text would appear outside the link. The remedy is to place the text inside another component, such as `h:outputText` or `f:verbatim`. This problem has been fixed in JSF 1.2.

Using Command Links

Now that we have discussed the details of JSF tags for buttons and links, we take a look at a complete example. Figure 4–5 shows the application discussed in "Using Text Fields and Text Areas" on page 127, with two links that let you select either English or German locales. When a link is activated, an action changes the view's locale and the JSF implementation reloads the current page.

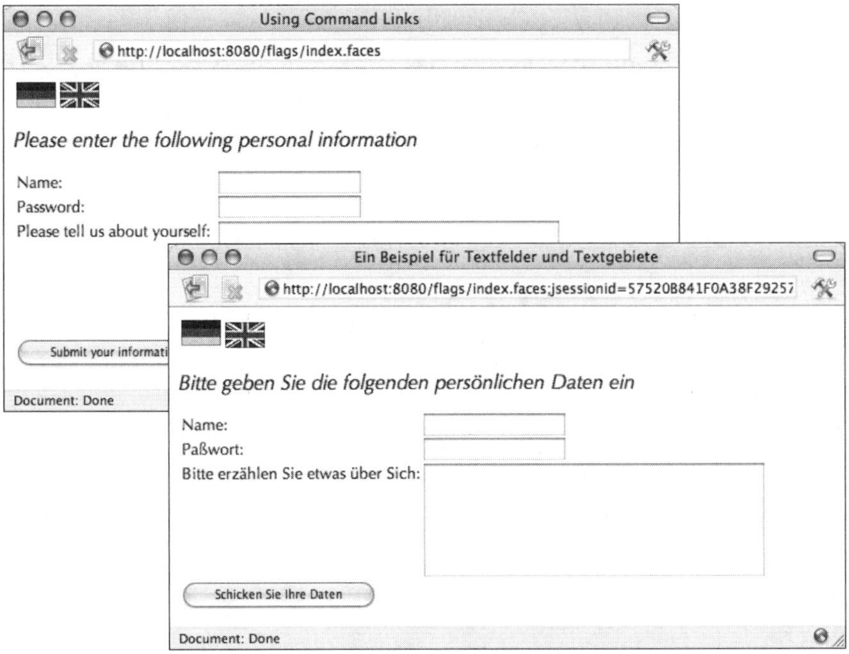

Figure 4–5   Using command links to change locales

The links are implemented like this:

```
<h:commandLink action="#{localeChanger.englishAction}">
   <h:graphicImage library="images" name="en_flag.gif" style="border: 0px" />
</h:commandLink>
```

Both links specify an image and an action method. The method to change to the English locale looks like this:

```
public class LocaleChanger {
   ...
   public String englishAction() {
      FacesContext context = FacesContext.getCurrentInstance();
      context.getViewRoot().setLocale(Locale.ENGLISH);
      return null;
   }
}
```

Because we have not specified any navigation for this action, the JSF implementation will reload the current page after the form is submitted. When the page is reloaded, it is localized for English or German, and the page redisplays accordingly.

Figure 4–6 shows the directory structure for the application, and Listings 4–9 through 4–11 show the associated JSF pages and Java classes.

Figure 4–6   Directory structure of the flags example

Listing 4–9   `flags/web/index.xhtml`

```
1. <?xml version="1.0" encoding="UTF-8"?>
2. <!DOCTYPE html PUBLIC "-//W3C//DTD XHTML 1.0 Transitional//EN"
3. "http://www.w3.org/TR/xhtml1/DTD/xhtml1-transitional.dtd">
4. <html xmlns="http://www.w3.org/1999/xhtml"
5.     xmlns:h="http://java.sun.com/jsf/html">
6.   <h:head>
7.     <title>#{msgs.indexWindowTitle}</title>
8.   </h:head>
9.   <h:body>
10.     <h:form>
11.       <h:commandLink action="#{localeChanger.germanAction}">
12.         <h:graphicImage library="images" name="de_flag.gif"
13.                     style="border: 0px; margin-right: 1em;"/>
14.       </h:commandLink>
15.       <h:commandLink action="#{localeChanger.englishAction}">
16.         <h:graphicImage library="images"
17.                     name="en_flag.gif" style="border: 0px"/>
18.       </h:commandLink>
19.       <p><h:outputText value="#{msgs.indexPageTitle}"
20.       style="font-style: italic; font-size: 1.3em"/></p>
21.       <h:panelGrid columns="2">
22.         #{msgs.namePrompt}
23.         <h:inputText value="#{user.name}"/>
24.         #{msgs.passwordPrompt}
25.         <h:inputSecret value="#{user.password}"/>
26.         #{msgs.tellUsPrompt}
27.         <h:inputTextarea value="#{user.aboutYourself}" rows="5" cols="35"/>
28.       </h:panelGrid>
29.       <h:commandButton value="#{msgs.submitPrompt}" action="thankYou"/>
30.     </h:form>
31.   </h:body>
32. </html>
```

Listing 4–10   `flags/src/java/com/corejsf/UserBean.java`

```
1. package com.corejsf;
2.
3. import java.io.Serializable;
4.
5. import javax.inject.Named;
6.   // or import javax.faces.bean.ManagedBean;
7. import javax.enterprise.context.SessionScoped;
8.   // or import javax.faces.bean.SessionScoped;
9.
```

```
10. @Named("user") // or @ManagedBean(name="user")
11. @SessionScoped
12. public class UserBean implements Serializable {
13.    private String name;
14.    private String password;
15.    private String aboutYourself;
16.
17.    public String getName() { return name; }
18.    public void setName(String newValue) { name = newValue; }
19.
20.    public String getPassword() { return password; }
21.    public void setPassword(String newValue) { password = newValue; }
22.
23.    public String getAboutYourself() { return aboutYourself; }
24.    public void setAboutYourself(String newValue) { aboutYourself = newValue; }
25. }
```

Listing 4–11   flags/src/java/com/corejsf/LocaleChanger.java

```
1. package com.corejsf;
2.
3. import java.io.Serializable;
4. import java.util.Locale;
5.
6. import javax.inject.Named;
7.    // or import javax.faces.bean.ManagedBean;
8. import javax.enterprise.context.SessionScoped;
9.    // or import javax.faces.bean.SessionScoped;
10. import javax.faces.context.FacesContext;
11.
12. @Named // or @ManagedBean
13. @SessionScoped
14. public class LocaleChanger implements Serializable {
15.    public String germanAction() {
16.       FacesContext context = FacesContext.getCurrentInstance();
17.       context.getViewRoot().setLocale(Locale.GERMAN);
18.       return null;
19.    }
20.
21.    public String englishAction() {
22.       FacesContext context = FacesContext.getCurrentInstance();
23.       context.getViewRoot().setLocale(Locale.ENGLISH);
24.       return null;
25.    }
26. }
```

Selection Tags

JSF has seven tags for making selections:

- h:selectBooleanCheckbox
- h:selectManyCheckbox
- h:selectOneRadio
- h:selectOneListbox
- h:selectManyListbox
- h:selectOneMenu
- h:selectManyMenu

Table 4–23 shows examples of each tag.

Table 4–23   Selection Tag Examples

Tag	Generated HTML	Examples
h:selectBooleanCheckbox	`<input type="checkbox">`	Receive email: ☑

h:selectManyCheckbox	`<table>`
	`    ...`
	`    <label>`
	`        <input type="checkbox"/>`
	`    </label>`
	`    ...`
	`</table>`
		☐ Red ☑ Blue ☐ Yellow

h:selectOneRadio	`<table>`
	`    ...`
	`    <label>`
	`        <input type="radio"/>`
	`    </label>`
	`    ...`
	`</table>`
		○ High School
		● Bachelor's
		○ Master's
		○ Doctorate

h:selectOneListbox	`<select>`
	`    <option value="Cheese">`
	`        Cheese`
	`    </option>`
	`    ...`
	`</select>`
		Cheese
		Pickle
		Mustard
		Lettuce

h:selectManyListbox	`<select multiple>`
	`    <option value="Cheese">`
	`        Cheese`
	`    </option>`
	`    ...`
	`</select>`
		Cheese
		Pickle
		Mustard
		Lettuce
		Onions

Table 4–23   Selection Tag Examples (cont.)

Tag	Generated HTML	Examples

h:selectOneMenu	```<select size="1">```
	   ```<option value="Cheese">```
	     Cheese
	   ```</option>```
	   ...
	```</select>```
		Pickle ▾
		Cheese
		Pickle
		Mustard
		Lettuce
		Onions

h:selectManyMenu	```<select multiple size="1">```
	   ```<option value="Sunday">```
	     Sunday
	   ```</option>```
	   ...
	```</select>```
		Sunday
		Monday
		Tuesday
		Wednesday

The h:selectBooleanCheckbox is the simplest selection tag—it renders a checkbox you can wire to a boolean bean property. You can also render a set of checkboxes with h:selectManyCheckbox.

Tags whose names begin with selectOne let you select one item from a collection. The selectOne tags render sets of radio buttons, single-select menus, or listboxes. The selectMany tags render sets of checkboxes, multiselect menus, or listboxes.

All selection tags share an almost identical set of attributes, listed in Table 4–24.

Table 4–24   Attributes for h:selectBooleanCheckbox, h:selectManyCheckbox, h:selectOneRadio, h:selectOneListbox, h:selectManyListbox, h:selectOneMenu, **and** h:selectManyMenu

Attributes	Description
enabledClass, disabledClass **JSF 2.0**	CSS class for enabled or disabled elements—for h:selectOneRadio and h:selectManyCheckbox only.
selectedClass, unselectedClass **JSF 2.0**	CSS class for selected or unselected elements—for h:selectManyCheckbox only.
layout	Specification for how elements are laid out: lineDirection (horizontal) or pageDirection (vertical)—for h:selectOneRadio and h:selectManyCheckbox only.

Table 4–24 Attributes for h:selectBooleanCheckbox, h:selectManyCheckbox, h:selectOneRadio, h:selectOneListbox, h:selectManyListbox, h:selectOneMenu, **and** h:selectManyMenu **(cont.)**

Attributes	Description
label **JSF 1.2**	A description of the component for use in error messages.
collectionType **JSF 2.0**	(selectMany tags only) A string or a value expression that evaluates to a fully qualified collection class name, such as java.util.TreeSet. See "The value Attribute and Multiple Selections" on page 162.
hideNoSelectionOption **JSF 2.0**	Hide any item that is marked as the "no selection option". See "The f:selectItem Tag" on page 153.
binding, converter, converterMessage **JSF 1.2**, requiredMessage **JSF 1.2**, id, immediate, required, rendered, validator, validatorMessage **JSF 1.2**, value, valueChangeListener	Basic attributes.[a]
accesskey, border, dir, disabled, lang, readonly, style, styleClass, size, tabindex, title	HTML 4.0[b]—border is applicable to h:selectOneRadio and h:selectManyCheckbox only. size is applicable to h:selectOne-Listbox and h:selectManyListbox only.
onblur, onchange, onclick, ondblclick, onfocus, onkeydown, onkeypress, onkeyup, onmousedown, onmousemove, onmouseout, onmouseover, onmouseup, onselect	DHTML events.[c]

a. See Table 4–5 on page 107 for information about basic attributes.
b. See Table 4–6 on page 110 for information about HTML 4.0 attributes.
c. See Table 4–7 on page 114 for information about DHTML event attributes.

Checkboxes and Radio Buttons

Two JSF tags represent checkboxes:

- h:selectBooleanCheckbox
- h:selectManyCheckbox

The h:selectBooleanCheckbox tag represents a single checkbox that you can wire to a boolean bean property. Here is an example:

Contact me   ☑

In your JSF page, you do this:

```
<h:selectBooleanCheckbox value="#{form.contactMe}"/>
```

In your backing bean, provide a read-write property:

```
private boolean contactMe;
public void setContactMe(boolean newValue) { contactMe = newValue; }
public boolean getContactMe() { return contactMe; }
```

The generated HTML looks something like this:

```
<input type="checkbox" name="_id2:_id7"/>
```

You can create a group of checkboxes with h:selectManyCheckbox. As the tag name implies, you can select one or more of the checkboxes in the group. You specify that group within the body of h:selectManyCheckbox, either with one or more f:selectItem tags or one f:selectItems tag. See "Items" on page 153 for more information about those core tags. For example, here is a group of checkboxes for selecting colors:

☐ Red ☑ Blue ☐ Yellow ☐ Green ☑ Orange

The h:selectManyCheckbox tag looks like this:

```
<h:selectManyCheckbox value="#{form.colors}">
    <f:selectItem itemValue="Red" itemLabel="Red"/>
    <f:selectItem itemValue="Blue" itemLabel="Blue"/>
    <f:selectItem itemValue="Yellow" itemLabel="Yellow"/>
    <f:selectItem itemValue="Green" itemLabel="Green"/>
    <f:selectItem itemValue="Orange" itemLabel="Orange"/>
</h:selectManyCheckbox>
```

The checkboxes are specified with f:selectItem (page 153) or f:selectItems (page 155).

The h:selectManyCheckbox tag generates an HTML table element; here is the generated HTML for our color example:

```
<table>
  <tr>
    <td>
      <label for="_id2:_id14">
        <input name="_id2:_id14" value="Red" type="checkbox"> Red</input>
      </label>
    </td>
  </tr>
  ...
</table>
```

Each color is an input element, wrapped in a label for accessibility. That label is placed in a td element.

Radio buttons are implemented with h:selectOneRadio. Here is an example:

○ High School ○ Bachelor's ⊙ Master's ○ Doctorate

The value attribute of the h:selectOneRadio tag specifies the currently selected item. Once again, we use multiple f:selectItem tags to populate the radio buttons:

```
<h:selectOneRadio value="#{form.education}">
  <f:selectItem itemValue="High School" itemLabel="High School"/>
  <f:selectItem itemValue="Bachelor's" itemLabel="Bachelor's"/>
  <f:selectItem itemValue="Master's" itemLabel="Master's"/>
  <f:selectItem itemValue="Doctorate" itemLabel=Doctorate"/>
</h:selectOneRadio>
```

Like h:selectManyCheckbox, h:selectOneRadio generates an HTML table. Here is the table generated by the preceding tag:

```
<table>
  <tr>
    <td>
      <label for="_id2:_id14">
        <input name="_id2:_id14" value="High School" type="radio">
          High School
        </input>
      </label>
    </td>
  </tr>
  ...
</table>
```

Besides generating HTML tables, h:selectOneRadio and h:selectManyCheckbox have something else in common—a handful of attributes unique to those two tags:

- border
- enabledClass
- disabledClass
- layout

The border attribute specifies the width of the border. For example, here are radio buttons and checkboxes with borders of 1 and 2, respectively:

The enabledClass and disabledClass attributes specify CSS classes used when the checkboxes or radio buttons are enabled or disabled, respectively. For example, the following picture shows an enabled class with an italic font style, blue color, and yellow background:

The layout attribute can be either lineDirection (horizontal) or pageDirection (vertical). For example, the following checkboxes on the left have a pageDirection layout and the checkboxes on the right are lineDirection:

NOTE: You might wonder why layout attribute values are not horizontal and vertical, instead of lineDirection and pageDirection, respectively. Although lineDirection and pageDirection are indeed horizontal and vertical for Latin-based languages, that is not always the case for other languages. For example, a Chinese browser that displays text top to bottom could regard lineDirection as vertical and pageDirection as horizontal.

Menus and Listboxes

Menus and listboxes are represented by the following tags:

- `h:selectOneListbox`
- `h:selectManyListbox`
- `h:selectOneMenu`
- `h:selectManyMenu`

The attributes for the preceding tags are listed in Table 4–24 on page 146, so that discussion is not repeated here.

Menu and listbox tags generate HTML select elements. The menu tags add a size="1" attribute to the select element. That size designation is all that separates menus and listboxes.

Here is a single-select listbox:

The corresponding listbox tag looks like this:

```
<h:selectOneListbox value="#{form.year}" size="5">
   <f:selectItem itemValue="1900" itemLabel="1900"/>
   <f:selectItem itemValue="1901" itemLabel="1901"/>
   ...
</h:selectOneListbox>
```

Notice that we've used the size attribute to specify the number of visible items. The generated HTML looks like this:

```
<select name="_id2:_id11" size="5">
   <option value="1900">1900</option>
   <option value="1901">1901</option>
   ...
</select>
```

Use h:selectManyListbox for multiselect listboxes like this one:

The listbox tag looks like this:

```
<h:selectManyListbox value="#{form.languages}">
    <f:selectItem itemValue="English" itemLabel="English"/>
    <f:selectItem itemValue="French" itemLabel="French"/>
    <f:selectItem itemValue="Italian" itemLabel="Italian"/>
    <f:selectItem itemValue="Spanish" itemLabel="Spanish"/>
    <f:selectItem itemValue="Russian" itemLabel="Russian"/>
</h:selectManyListbox>
```

This time we do not specify the size attribute, so the listbox grows to accommodate all its items. The generated HTML looks like this:

```
<select name="_id2:_id11" multiple>
    <option value="English">English</option>
    <option value="French">French</option>
    ...
</select>
```

Use h:selectOneMenu and h:selectManyMenu for menus. A single-select menu looks like this:

```
Wednesday
```

h:selectOneMenu created the preceding menu:

```
<h:selectOneMenu value="#{form.day}">
    <f:selectItem itemValue="1" itemLabel="Sunday"/>
    <f:selectItem itemValue="2" itemLabel="Monday"/>
    <f:selectItem itemValue="3" itemLabel="Tuesday"/>
    <f:selectItem itemValue="4" itemLabel="Wednesday"/>
    <f:selectItem itemValue="5" itemLabel="Thursday"/>
    <f:selectItem itemValue="6" itemLabel="Friday"/>
    <f:selectItem itemValue="7" itemLabel="Saturday"/>
</h:selectOneMenu>
```

Here is the generated HTML:

```
<select name="_id2:_id17" size="1">
    <option value="1">Sunday</option>
    ...
</select>
```

The h:selectManyMenu tag is used for multiselect menus. That tag generates HTML, which looks like this:

```
<select name="_id2:_id17" multiple size="1">
    <option value="1">Sunday</option>
    ...
</select>
```

That HTML does not yield consistent results among browsers. For example, here is h:selectManyMenu on Internet Explorer (left) and Netscape (right):

Sunday
Monday
Tuesday
Wednesday

Sunday

NOTE: In HTML, the distinction between menus and listboxes is artificial. Menus and listboxes are both HTML select elements. The only distinction: Menus always have a size="1" attribute.

Browsers consistently render single-select menus as drop-down lists, as expected. But they do not consistently render multiple select menus, specified with size="1" and multiple attributes. Instead of rendering a drop-down list with multiple selection, as you might expect, some browsers render absurdities such as tiny scrollbars that are nearly impossible to manipulate (Internet Explorer) or no scrollbar at all, leaving you to navigate with arrow keys (Firefox).

Items

Starting with "Checkboxes and Radio Buttons" on page 148, we have used multiple f:selectItem tags to populate select components. Now that we are familiar with the visual appearance of selection tags, we take a closer look at f:selectItem and the related f:selectItems tags.

The f:selectItem Tag

You use f:selectItem to specify single selection items, like this:

```
<h:selectOneMenu value="#{form.condiments}">
    <f:selectItem itemValue="Cheese" itemLabel="Cheese"/>
    <f:selectItem itemValue="Pickle" itemLabel="Pickle"/>
    <f:selectItem itemValue="Mustard" itemLabel="Mustard"/>
    <f:selectItem itemValue="Lettuce" itemLabel="Lettuce"/>
    <f:selectItem itemValue="Onions" itemLabel="Onions"/>
</h:selectOneMenu>
```

The values—Cheese, Pickle, etc.—are transmitted as request parameter values when a selection is made from the menu and the menu's form is subsequently submitted. The itemLabel values are used as labels for the menu items. Sometimes you want to specify different values for request parameter values and item labels:

```
<h:selectOneMenu value="#{form.condiments}">
    <f:selectItem itemValue="1" itemLabel="Cheese"/>
    <f:selectItem itemValue="2" itemLabel="Pickle"/>
    <f:selectItem itemValue="3" itemLabel="Mustard"/>
    <f:selectItem itemValue="4" itemLabel="Lettuce"/>
    <f:selectItem itemValue="5" itemLabel="Onions"/>
</h:selectOneMenu>
```

In the preceding code, the item values are strings. "Binding the value Attribute" on page 161 shows you how to use different data types for item values.

In addition to labels and values, you can also supply item descriptions and specify an item's disabled state:

```
<f:selectItem itemLabel="Cheese" itemValue="#{form.cheeseValue}"
        itemDescription="used to be milk"
        itemDisabled="true"/>
```

Item descriptions are for tools only—they do not affect the generated HTML. The itemDisabled attribute, however, is passed to HTML. The f:selectItem tag has the attributes shown in Table 4–25.

As of JSF 2.0, there is a noSelectionOption attribute for marking an item that is included for navigational purposes, such as "Select a condiment". This attribute is used in conjunction with validation. If an entry is required and the user selects the "no selection option", a validation error occurs.

Table 4–25 Attributes for f:selectItem

Attribute	Description
binding, id	Basic attributes[a]
itemDescription	Description used by tools only
itemDisabled	Boolean value that sets the item's disabled HTML attribute
itemLabel	Text shown by the item
itemValue	Item's value, passed to the server as a request parameter
value	Value expression that points to a SelectItem instance
escape **JSF 1.2**	true if special characters in the value should be converted to character entities (default), false if the value should be emitted without change
noSelectionOption **JSF 2.0**	true if this item is the "no selection" option that, when selected, indicates that the user intends to made no selection

a. See Table 4–5 on page 107 for information about basic attributes.

You can use f:selectItem's value attribute to access SelectItem instances created in a bean:

```
<f:selectItem value="#{form.cheeseItem}"/>
```

The value expression for the value attribute points to a method that returns a javax.faces.model.SelectItem instance:

```
public SelectItem getCheeseItem() { return new SelectItem("Cheese"); }
```

 javax.faces.model.SelectItem

- SelectItem(Object value)
  Creates a SelectItem with a value. The item label is obtained by applying toString() to the value.

- SelectItem(Object value, String label)
  Creates a SelectItem with a value and a label.

- SelectItem(Object value, String label, String description)
  Creates a SelectItem with a value, label, and description.

- SelectItem(Object value, String label, String description, boolean disabled)
  Creates a SelectItem with a value, label, description, and disabled state.

- SelectItem(Object value, String label, String description, boolean disabled, boolean noSelectionOption) **JSF 2.0**
  Creates a SelectItem with a value, label, description, disabled state, and "no selection option" flag.

The f:selectItems Tag

As we saw in "The f:selectItem Tag" on page 153, f:selectItem is versatile, but it is tedious for specifying more than a few items. The first code fragment shown in that section can be reduced to the following with f:selectItems:

```
<h:selectOneRadio value="#{form.condiments}">
   <f:selectItems value="#{form.condimentItems}"/>
</h:selectOneRadio>
```

The value expression #{form.condimentItems} could point to an array of SelectItem instances:

```
private static SelectItem[] condimentItems = {
   new SelectItem(1, "Cheese"),
   new SelectItem(2, "Pickle"),
   new SelectItem(3, "Mustard"),
   new SelectItem(4, "Lettuce"),
```

```
    new SelectItem(5, "Onions")
};

public SelectItem[] getCondimentItems() {
    return condimentItems;
}
```

The f:selectItems value attribute must be a value expression that points to one of the following:

- A single SelectItem instance
- A collection
- An array
- A map whose entries represent labels and values

The first option is not very useful. We discuss the other options in the following sections.

NOTE: Can't remember what you can specify for the f:selectItems value attribute? It's a SCAM: Single select item, Collection, Array, or Map.

NOTE: A single f:selectItems tag is usually better than multiple f:selectItem tags. If the number of items changes, you have to modify only Java code if you use f:selectItems, whereas f:selectItem may require you to modify both Java code and JSF pages.

Table 4–26 summarizes the attributes of the f:selectItems tag.

Table 4–26   Attributes for f:selectItems

Attribute	Description
binding, id	Basic attributes[a]
value	Value expression that points to a SelectItem instance, an array or collection, or a map
var 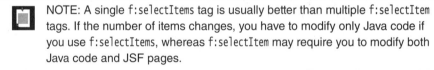 **JSF 2.0**	The name of a variable, used in the value expressions below when traversing an array or collection of objects other than SelectItem
itemLabel **JSF 2.0**	Value expression yielding the text shown by the item referenced by the var variable

Table 4–26   Attributes for f:selectItems **(cont.)**

Attribute	Description
itemValue **JSF 2.0**	Value expression yielding the value of the item referenced by the var variable
itemDescription **JSF 2.0**	Value expression yielding the description of the item referenced by the var variable; the description is intended for use by tools
itemDisabled **JSF 2.0**	Value expression yielding the disabled HTML attribute of the item referenced by the var variable
itemLabelEscaped **JSF 2.0**	Value expression yielding true if special characters in the item's value should be converted to character entities (default), false if the value should be emitted without change
noSelectionOption **JSF 2.0**	Value expression that yields the "no selection option" item or string that equals the value of the "no selection option" item

a. See Table 4–5 on page 107 for information about basic attributes.

Using Collections and Arrays with f:selectItems

Before JSF 2.0, collections and arrays had to contain SelectItem instances. That was unfortunate because it coupled your business logic to the JSF API. As of JSF 2.0, the value of f:selectItems can be a collection or array containing objects of *any* type.

If they are instances of SelectItem, no further processing is done. Otherwise, the labels are obtained by calling toString on each object.

Alternatively, you cau use the var attribute to define a variable that iterates over the array or collection. Then you supply value expressions for the label and value in the attributes itemLabel and itemValue.

For example, suppose you want users to select objects of the following class:

```
public class Weekday {
    public String getDayName() { ... } // name in current locale, such as "Monday"
    public int getDayNumber() { ... } // number such as Calendar.MONDAY (2)
    ...
}
```

Use the following tag:

```
<f:selectItems value="#{form.daysOfTheWeek}"
    var="w"
```

```
itemLabel="#{w.dayName}"
itemValue="#{w.dayNumber}" />
```

Here, `#{form.daysOfTheWeek}` yields an array or collection of Weekday objects. The variable w is set to each of the elements. Then a SelectItem object is constructed with the results of the itemLabel and itemValue expressions.

JSF 2.0 NOTE: The var attribute in the f:selectItems tag is conceptually similar to the use of the var attribute in the h:dataTable which we will discuss in Chapter 6.

Using Maps with f:selectItems

If the value attribute of the f:selectItems tag yields a map, the JSF implementation creates a SelectItem instance for every entry in the map. The entry's key is used as the item's label, and the entry's value is used as the item's value. For example, here are condiments specified with a map:

```
private static Map<String, Object> condimentItems;
static {
    condimentItems = new LinkedHashMap<String, Object>();
    condimentItems.put("Cheese",  1);  // label, value
    condimentItems.put("Pickle",  2);
    condimentItems.put("Mustard", 3);
    condimentItems.put("Lettuce", 4);
    condimentItems.put("Onions",  5);
}

public Map<String, Object> getCondimentItems() {
    return condimentItems;
}
```

Note that you cannot specify item descriptions or disabled status when you use a map.

Pay attention to these two issues when using a map:

1. You will generally want to use a LinkedHashMap, not a TreeMap or HashMap. In a LinkedHashMap, you can control the order of the items because items are visited in the order in which they were inserted. If you use a TreeMap, the labels that are presented to the user (which are the keys of the map) are sorted alphabetically. That may or may not be what you want. For example, days of the week would be neatly arranged as Friday Monday Saturday Sunday Thursday Tuesday Wednesday. If you use a HashMap, the items are ordered randomly.

2.　Map keys are turned into item labels and map values into item values. When a user selects an item, your backing bean receives a value in your map, not a key. For example, in the example above, if the backing bean receives a value of 5, you would need to iterate through the entries if you wanted to find the matching "Onions". Since the value is probably more meaningful to your application than the label, this is usually not a problem, just something to be aware of.

Item Groups

You can group menu or listbox items together, like this:

```
Burgers
Qwarter pounder
Single
Veggie
Beverages
Coke
Pepsi
Water
Coffee
Tea
Condiments
cheese
pickle
mustard
lettuce
onions
```

Here are the JSF tags that define the listbox:

```
<h:selectManyListbox>
  <f:selectItems value="#{form.menuItems}"/>
</h:selectManyListbox>
```

The menuItems property is a SelectItem array:

```
public SelectItem[] getMenuItems() { return menuItems; }
```

The menuItems array is instantiated like this:

```
private static SelectItem[] menuItems = { burgers, beverages, condiments };
```

The burgers, beverages, and condiments variables are SelectItemGroup instances that are instantiated like this:

```
private SelectItemGroup burgers =
    new SelectItemGroup("Burgers",      // value
        "burgers on the menu",          // description
        false,                          // disabled
        burgerItems);                   // select items
```

```
private SelectItemGroup beverages =
   new SelectItemGroup("Beverages", // value
      "beverages on the menu",      // description
      false,                        // disabled
      beverageItems);               // select items

private SelectItemGroup condiments =
   new SelectItemGroup("Condiments", // value
      "condiments on the menu",      // description
      false,                         // disabled
      condimentItems);               // select items
```

Notice that we are using SelectItemGroups to populate an array of SelectItems. We can do that because SelectItemGroup extends SelectItem. The groups are created and initialized like this:

```
private SelectItem[] burgerItems = {
   new SelectItem("Qwarter pounder"),
   new SelectItem("Single"),
   new SelectItem("Veggie"),
};
private SelectItem[] beverageItems = {
   new SelectItem("Coke"),
   new SelectItem("Pepsi"),
   new SelectItem("Water"),
   new SelectItem("Coffee"),
   new SelectItem("Tea"),
};
private SelectItem[] condimentItems = {
   new SelectItem("cheese"),
   new SelectItem("pickle"),
   new SelectItem("mustard"),
   new SelectItem("lettuce"),
   new SelectItem("onions"),
};
```

SelectItemGroup instances encode HTML optgroup elements. For example, the preceding code generates the following HTML:

```
<select name="_id0:_id1" multiple size="16">
   <optgroup label="Burgers">
      <option value="1" selected>Qwarter pounder</option>
      <option value="2">Single</option>
      <option value="3">Veggie</option>
   </optgroup>
```

```
<optgroup label="Beverages">
   <option value="4" selected>Coke</option>
   <option value="5">Pepsi</option>
   <option value="6">Water</option>
   <option value="7">Coffee</option>
   <option value="8">Tea</option>
</optgroup>

<optgroup label="Condiments">
   <option value="9">cheese</option>
   <option value="10">pickle</option>
   <option value="11">mustard</option>
   <option value="12">lettuce</option>
   <option value="13">onions</option>
</optgroup>
</select>
```

> NOTE: The HTML 4.01 specification does not allow nested optgroup elements,
> which would be useful for things like cascading menus. The specification
> does mention that future HTML versions may support that behavior.

 javax.faces.model.SelectItemGroup

- `SelectItemGroup(String label)`
  Creates a group with a label but no selection items.

- `SelectItemGroup(String label, String description, boolean disabled, SelectItem[] items)`
  Creates a group with a label, a description (which is ignored by the JSF Reference Implementation), a boolean that disables all the items when true, and an array of select items used to populate the group.

- `setSelectItems(SelectItem[] items)`
  Sets a group's array of SelectItems.

Binding the value Attribute

Whether you are using a set of checkboxes, a menu, or a listbox, you will want to keep track of the item or items selected by the user. For that purpose, you use the value attribute of the selectOne and selectMany tags. Consider this example:

```
<h:selectOneMenu value="#{form.bestDay}">
   <f:selectItems value="#{form.weekdays}"/>
</h:selectOneRadio>
```

The `value` attribute of `h:selectOneMenu` refers to the value that the user selects. The `value` attribute of `f:selectItems` specifies all possible values.

Suppose the radio buttons were specified with an array of `SelectItem` objects, containing the following:

```
new SelectItem(1, "Sunday"),   // value, label
new SelectItem(2, "Monday"),
...
```

The user sees the labels (Sunday, Monday, ...), but the application uses the values (1, 2, ...).

There is an important but subtle issue about the Java type of the values. In the web page, *the values are always strings*:

```
<option value="1">Sunday</option>
<option value="2">Monday</option>
```

When the page is submitted, the server receives the selected string and must convert it to an appropriate type. The JSF implementation knows how to convert to numbers and enumerated types, but for other types you need to define a converter. (We discuss converters in Chapter 7.)

In our example, the `#{form.bestDay}` value expression should refer to a property of type `int` or `Integer`. Listing 4–13 has an example where the value is an enumerated type.

CAUTION: Because the value of a `SelectItem` is an `Object`, it can be tempting to set it to the value that you actually need in your application. However, keep in mind that the value is turned into a string when it is sent to the client. For example, consider a `SelectItem(Color.RED, "Red")`. The client receives the client is the string `"java.awt.Color[r=255,g=0,b=0]"`. That string is returned when the user selects the option with label `"Red"`. You would have to parse it to turn it back into a color. It is easier to send the RGB value of the color instead.

The `value` Attribute and Multiple Selections

You can keep track of multiple selections with a `selectMany` tag. These tags have a `value` attribute that specifies zero or more selected items, using an array or collection.

Consider an `h:selectManyListbox` that lets a user choose multiple condiments:

```
<h:selectManyListbox value="#{form.condiments}">
   <f:selectItems value="#{form.condimentItems}"/>
</h:selectManyListbox>
```

Here are the condimentItems and condiments properties:

```
private static SelectItem[] condimentItems = {
   new SelectItem(1, "Cheese"),
   new SelectItem(2, "Pickle"),
   new SelectItem(3, "Mustard"),
   new SelectItem(4, "Lettuce"),
   new SelectItem(5, "Onions"),
};
public SelectItem[] getCondimentItems() {
   return condimentItems;
}

private int[] condiments;
public void setCondiments(int[] newValue) {
   condiments = newValue;
}
public int[] getCondiments() {
   return condiments;
}
```

Instead of an int[] array for the condiments property, you could have used an Integer[] array.

The value of a selectMany tag can be a collection instead of an array, but there are two technical issues that you need to keep in mind. Most importantly, the elements cannot be converted because the collection's element type is not known at runtime. (This is an unfortunate aspect of Java generics. At runtime, an ArrayList<Integer> or ArrayList<String> is only a raw ArrayList, and there is no way of determining the element type. In contrast, Integer[] and String[] are distinct types at runtime.) That means, you should use collections only for strings.

The other complexity is more subtle. When the JSF application receives the user choices, it must construct a new instance of the collection, populate it, and pass the collection to the property setter. But suppose the property type is Set<String>. What kind of Set should be constructed?

Before JSF 2.0, this was not clearly specified. JSF 2.0 lays down the following rules:

1. If the tag has a collectionType attribute, its value must be a string or a value expression that evaluates to a fully qualified classname, such as java.util.TreeSet. Instantiate that class.

2. Otherwise, get the existing value and try cloning and clearing it.

3. If that fails (perhaps because the existing value was null or not cloneable), look at the type of the value expression. If that type is SortedSet, Set, or Queue, construct a TreeSet, HashSet, or LinkedList.

4. Otherwise, construct an ArrayList.

For example, suppose you define a languages property:

```
private Set<String> languages; // initialized with null
public Set<String> getLanguages() {
   return languages;
}
public void setLanguages(Set<String> newValue) {
   languages = newValue;
}
```

When the form is submitted for the first time, the property setter is called with a HashSet that contains the user choices (step 3). In subsequent invocations, that set is cloned (step 2). However, suppose you initialize the set:

```
private Set<String> languages = new TreeSet();
```

Then a clone of that TreeSet is always returned.

All Together: Checkboxes, Radio Buttons, Menus, and Listboxes

We close out our section on selection tags with an example that exercises nearly all those tags. That example, shown in Figure 4–7, implements a form requesting personal information. We use an h:selectBooleanCheckbox to determine whether the user wants to be contacted, and h:selectOneMenu lets the user select the best day of the week for us to do so.

The year listbox is implemented with h:selectOneMenu, and it demonstrates the use of a "no selection" item. The language checkboxes are implemented with h:selectManyCheckbox; the education level is implemented with h:selectOneRadio.

Note that the languages are collected in a Set<String>. Also note the styles in the color selector. The disabled Orange option is colored gray, and the selected colors are marked in bold. We use the attribute onchange="submit()" in order to update the styles immediately upon selection.

When the user submits the form, JSF navigation takes us to a JSF page that shows the data the user entered.

The directory structure for the application shown in Figure 4–7 is shown in Figure 4–8. The JSF pages, RegisterForm bean, faces configuration file, and resource bundle are shown in Listings 4–12 through 4–16.

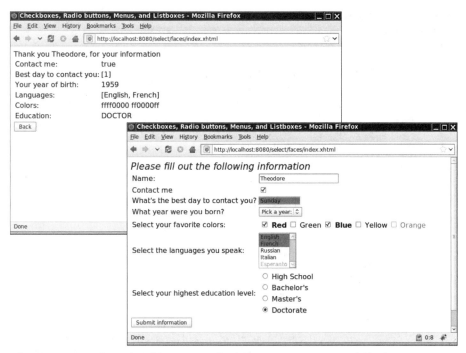

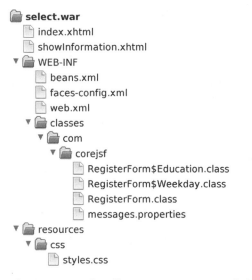

Figure 4–7   Using checkboxes, radio buttons, menus, and listboxes

📁 **select.war**
  📄 index.xhtml
  📄 showInformation.xhtml
▼ 📁 WEB-INF
    📄 beans.xml
    📄 faces-config.xml
    📄 web.xml
  ▼ 📁 classes
    ▼ 📁 com
      ▼ 📁 corejsf
          📄 RegisterForm$Education.class
          📄 RegisterForm$Weekday.class
          📄 RegisterForm.class
          📄 messages.properties
▼ 📁 resources
  ▼ 📁 css
      📄 styles.css

Figure 4–8   The directory structure of the selection example

Listing 4–12 select/web/index.xhtml

```
 1. <?xml version="1.0" encoding="UTF-8"?>
 2. <!DOCTYPE html PUBLIC "-//W3C//DTD XHTML 1.0 Transitional//EN"
 3. "http://www.w3.org/TR/xhtml1/DTD/xhtml1-transitional.dtd">
 4. <html xmlns="http://www.w3.org/1999/xhtml"
 5.       xmlns:f="http://java.sun.com/jsf/core" xmlns:h="http://java.sun.com/jsf/html">
 6.    <h:head>
 7.       <h:outputStylesheet library="css" name="styles.css"/>
 8.       <title>#{msgs.indexWindowTitle}</title>
 9.    </h:head>
10.
11.    <h:body>
12.       <h:outputText value="#{msgs.indexPageTitle}" styleClass="emphasis"/>
13.       <h:form>
14.          <h:panelGrid columns="2">
15.             #{msgs.namePrompt}
16.             <h:inputText value="#{form.name}"/>
17.             #{msgs.contactMePrompt}
18.             <h:selectBooleanCheckbox value="#{form.contactMe}"/>
19.             #{msgs.bestDayPrompt}
20.             <h:selectManyMenu value="#{form.bestDaysToContact}">
21.                <f:selectItems value="#{form.daysOfTheWeek}" var="w"
22.                               itemLabel="#{w.dayName}" itemValue="#{w.dayNumber}"/>
23.             </h:selectManyMenu>
24.             #{msgs.yearOfBirthPrompt}
25.             <h:selectOneMenu value="#{form.yearOfBirth}" required="true">
26.                <f:selectItems value="#{form.yearItems}"/>
27.             </h:selectOneMenu>
28.             #{msgs.colorPrompt}
29.             <h:selectManyCheckbox value="#{form.colors}"
30.                                   selectedClass="selected" disabledClass="disabled"
31.                                   onchange="submit()">
32.                <f:selectItems value="#{form.colorItems}"/>
33.             </h:selectManyCheckbox>
34.             #{msgs.languagePrompt}
35.             <h:selectManyListbox size="5" value="#{form.languages}">
36.                <f:selectItems value="#{form.languageItems}"/>
37.             </h:selectManyListbox>
38.             #{msgs.educationPrompt}
39.             <h:selectOneRadio value="#{form.education}"
40.                               selectedClass="selected" layout="pageDirection">
41.                <f:selectItems value="#{form.educationItems}"/>
42.             </h:selectOneRadio>
43.          </h:panelGrid>
44.          <h:commandButton value="#{msgs.buttonPrompt}" action="showInformation"/>
```

```
45.        </h:form>
46.        <h:messages/>
47.    </h:body>
48. </html>
```

Listing 4–13   select/web/showInformation.xhtml

```
1. <?xml version="1.0" encoding="UTF-8"?>
2. <!DOCTYPE html PUBLIC "-//W3C//DTD XHTML 1.0 Transitional//EN"
3. "http://www.w3.org/TR/xhtml1/DTD/xhtml1-transitional.dtd">
4. <html xmlns="http://www.w3.org/1999/xhtml"
5.      xmlns:f="http://java.sun.com/jsf/core" xmlns:h="http://java.sun.com/jsf/html">
6.    <h:head>
7.        <title>#{msgs.indexWindowTitle}</title>
8.    </h:head>
9.    <h:body>
10.       <h:form>
11.           <h:outputStylesheet library="css" name="styles.css" target="head"/>
12.           <h:outputFormat value="#{msgs.thankYouLabel}">
13.               <f:param value="#{form.name}"/>
14.           </h:outputFormat>
15.           <h:panelGrid columns="2">
16.               #{msgs.contactMeLabel}
17.               <h:outputText value="#{form.contactMe}"/>
18.               #{msgs.bestDayLabel}
19.               <h:outputText value="#{form.bestDaysConcatenated}"/>
20.               #{msgs.yearOfBirthLabel}
21.               <h:outputText value="#{form.yearOfBirth}"/>
22.               #{msgs.languageLabel}
23.               <h:outputText value="#{form.languages}"/>
24.               #{msgs.colorLabel}
25.               <h:outputText value="#{form.colorsConcatenated}"/>
26.               #{msgs.educationLabel}
27.               <h:outputText value="#{form.education}"/>
28.           </h:panelGrid>
29.           <h:commandButton value="#{msgs.backPrompt}" action="index"/>
30.       </h:form>
31.    </h:body>
32. </html>
```

Listing 4–14 select/src/java/com/corejsf/RegisterForm.java

```
 1. package com.corejsf;
 2.
 3. import java.awt.Color;
 4. import java.io.Serializable;
 5. import java.text.DateFormatSymbols;
 6. import java.util.ArrayList;
 7. import java.util.Arrays;
 8. import java.util.Calendar;
 9. import java.util.Collection;
10. import java.util.LinkedHashMap;
11. import java.util.Map;
12. import java.util.Set;
13. import java.util.TreeSet;
14.
15. import javax.inject.Named;
16.    // or import javax.faces.bean.ManagedBean;
17. import javax.enterprise.context.SessionScoped;
18.    // or import javax.faces.bean.SessionScoped;
19. import javax.faces.model.SelectItem;
20.
21. @Named("form") // or @ManagedBean(name="form")
22. @SessionScoped
23. public class RegisterForm implements Serializable {
24.    public enum Education { HIGH_SCHOOL, BACHELOR, MASTER, DOCTOR };
25.
26.    public static class Weekday {
27.       private int dayOfWeek;
28.       public Weekday(int dayOfWeek) {
29.          this.dayOfWeek = dayOfWeek;
30.       }
31.
32.       public String getDayName() {
33.          DateFormatSymbols symbols = new DateFormatSymbols();
34.          String[] weekdays = symbols.getWeekdays();
35.          return weekdays[dayOfWeek];
36.       }
37.
38.       public int getDayNumber() {
39.          return dayOfWeek;
40.       }
41.    }
42.
43.    private String name;
44.    private boolean contactMe;
```

```
45.   private int[] bestDaysToContact;
46.   private Integer yearOfBirth;
47.   private int[] colors;
48.   private Set<String> languages = new TreeSet<String>();
49.   private Education education = Education.BACHELOR;
50.
51.   public String getName() { return name; }
52.   public void setName(String newValue) { name = newValue; }
53.
54.   public boolean getContactMe() { return contactMe; }
55.   public void setContactMe(boolean newValue) { contactMe = newValue; }
56.
57.   public int[] getBestDaysToContact() { return bestDaysToContact; }
58.   public void setBestDaysToContact(int[] newValue) { bestDaysToContact = newValue; }
59.
60.   public Integer getYearOfBirth() { return yearOfBirth; }
61.   public void setYearOfBirth(Integer newValue) { yearOfBirth = newValue; }
62.
63.   public int[] getColors() { return colors; }
64.   public void setColors(int[] newValue) { colors = newValue; }
65.
66.   public Set<String> getLanguages() { return languages; }
67.   public void setLanguages(Set<String> newValue) { languages = newValue; }
68.
69.   public Education getEducation() { return education; }
70.   public void setEducation(Education newValue) { education = newValue; }
71.
72.   public Collection<SelectItem> getYearItems() { return birthYears; }
73.
74.   public Weekday[] getDaysOfTheWeek() { return daysOfTheWeek; }
75.
76.   public SelectItem[] getLanguageItems() { return languageItems; }
77.
78.   public SelectItem[] getColorItems() { return colorItems; }
79.
80.   public Map<String, Education> getEducationItems() { return educationItems; }
81.
82.   public String getBestDaysConcatenated() {
83.      return Arrays.toString(bestDaysToContact);
84.   }
85.
86.   public String getColorsConcatenated() {
87.      StringBuilder result = new StringBuilder();
88.      for (int color : colors) result.append(String.format("%06x ", color));
89.      return result.toString();
90.   }
91.
```

```
 92.    private SelectItem[] colorItems = {
 93.       new SelectItem(Color.RED.getRGB(), "Red"), // value, label
 94.       new SelectItem(Color.GREEN.getRGB(), "Green"),
 95.       new SelectItem(Color.BLUE.getRGB(), "Blue"),
 96.       new SelectItem(Color.YELLOW.getRGB(), "Yellow"),
 97.       new SelectItem(Color.ORANGE.getRGB(), "Orange", "", true) // disabled
 98.    };
 99.
100.    private static Map<String, Education> educationItems;
101.    static {
102.       educationItems = new LinkedHashMap<String, Education>();
103.       educationItems.put("High School", Education.HIGH_SCHOOL); // label, value
104.       educationItems.put("Bachelor's", Education.BACHELOR);
105.       educationItems.put("Master's", Education.MASTER);
106.       educationItems.put("Doctorate", Education.DOCTOR);
107.    };
108.
109.    private static SelectItem[] languageItems = {
110.       new SelectItem("English"),
111.       new SelectItem("French"),
112.       new SelectItem("Russian"),
113.       new SelectItem("Italian"),
114.       new SelectItem("Esperanto", "Esperanto", "", true) // disabled
115.    };
116.
117.    private static Collection<SelectItem> birthYears;
118.    static {
119.       birthYears = new ArrayList<SelectItem>();
120.       // The first item is a "no selection" item
121.       birthYears.add(new SelectItem(null, "Pick a year:", "", false, false, true));
122.       for (int i = 1900; i < 2020; ++i) birthYears.add(new SelectItem(i));
123.    }
124.
125.    private static Weekday[] daysOfTheWeek;
126.    static {
127.       daysOfTheWeek = new Weekday[7];
128.       for (int i = Calendar.SUNDAY; i <= Calendar.SATURDAY; i++) {
129.          daysOfTheWeek[i - Calendar.SUNDAY] = new Weekday(i);
130.       }
131.    }
132.}
```

Listing 4–15   select/src/java/com/corejsf/messages.properties

```
 1. indexWindowTitle=Checkboxes, Radio buttons, Menus, and Listboxes
 2. indexPageTitle=Please fill out the following information
 3.
 4. namePrompt=Name:
 5. contactMePrompt=Contact me
 6. bestDayPrompt=What's the best day to contact you?
 7. yearOfBirthPrompt=What year were you born?
 8. buttonPrompt=Submit information
 9. backPrompt=Back
10. languagePrompt=Select the languages you speak:
11. educationPrompt=Select your highest education level:
12. emailAppPrompt=Select your email application:
13. colorPrompt=Select your favorite colors:
14.
15. thankYouLabel=Thank you {0}, for your information
16. contactMeLabel=Contact me:
17. bestDayLabel=Best day to contact you:
18. yearOfBirthLabel=Your year of birth:
19. colorLabel=Colors:
20. languageLabel=Languages:
21. educationLabel=Education:
```

Listing 4–16   select/web/resources/css/styles.css

```
 1. .emphasis {
 2.    font-style: italic;
 3.    font-size: 1.3em;
 4. }
 5. .disabled {
 6.    color: gray;
 7. }
 8. .selected {
 9.    font-weight: bold;
10. }
```

Messages

During the JSF life cycle, any object can create a message and add it to a queue of messages maintained by the faces context. At the end of the life cycle—in the Render Response phase—you can display those messages in a view. Typically, messages are associated with a particular component and indicate either conversion or validation errors.

Although error messages are usually the most prevalent message type in a JSF application, messages come in four varieties:

- Information
- Warning
- Error
- Fatal

All messages can contain a summary and a detail. For example, a summary might be Invalid Entry and a detail might be The number entered was greater than the maximum.

JSF applications use two tags to display messages in JSF pages: h:messages and h:message.

The h:messages tag displays all messages that were stored in the faces context during the course of the JSF life cycle. You can restrict those messages to global messages—meaning messages not associated with a component—by setting h:message's globalOnly attribute to true. By default, that attribute is false.

The h:message tag displays a single message for a particular component. That component is designated with h:message's mandatory for attribute. If more than one message has been generated for a component, h:message shows only the last one.

JSF 2.0 NOTE: When you use JSF 2.0 and your project stage is set to Development, then an h:messages child is automatically added to your page (provided you didn't add one yourself).

The h:message and h:messages tags share many attributes. Table 4–27 lists all attributes for both tags.

Table 4–27 ■ Attributes for h:message and h:messages

Attributes	Description
errorClass	CSS class applied to error messages.
errorStyle	CSS style applied to error messages.
fatalClass	CSS class applied to fatal messages.
fatalStyle	CSS style applied to fatal messages.

Table 4–27   Attributes for h:message and h:messages (cont.)

Attributes	Description
for	The id of the component for which to display the message (h:message only).
globalOnly	Instruction to display only global messages—applicable only to h:messages. Default is false.
infoClass	CSS class applied to information messages.
infoStyle	CSS style applied to information messages.
layout	Specification for message layout: "table" or "list"—applicable only to h:messages.
showDetail	A Boolean that determines whether message details are shown. Defaults are false for h:messages, true for h:message.
showSummary	A Boolean that determines whether message summaries are shown. Defaults are true for h:messages, false for h:message.
tooltip	A Boolean that determines whether message details are rendered in a tooltip; the tooltip is only rendered if showDetail and showSummary are true.
warnClass	CSS class for warning messages.
warnStyle	CSS style for warning messages.
binding, id, rendered	Basic attributes.[a]
style, styleClass, title, dir **JSF 1.2**, lang **JSF 1.2**	HTML 4.0.[b]

a. See Table 4–5 on page 107 for information about basic attributes.
b. See Table 4–6 on page 110 for information about HTML 4.0 attributes.

The majority of the attributes in Table 4–27 represent CSS classes or styles that h:message and h:messages apply to particular types of messages.

You can also specify whether you want to display a message's summary or detail, or both, with the showSummary and showDetail attributes, respectively.

The h:messages layout attribute can be used to specify how messages are laid out, either as a list or a table. If you specify true for the tooltip attribute and you have also set showDetail and showSummary to true, the message's detail will be wrapped in a tooltip that is shown when the mouse hovers over the error message.

Now that we have a grasp of message fundamentals, we take a look at an application that uses the h:message and h:messages tags. The application shown in Figure 4–9 contains a simple form with two text fields. Both text fields have required attributes.

Moreover, the "Age" text field is wired to an integer property, so its value is converted automatically by the JSF framework. Figure 4–9 shows the error messages generated by the JSF framework when we neglect to specify a value for the "Name" field and provide the wrong type of value for the Age field.

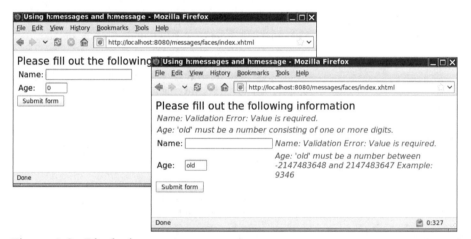

Figure 4–9   Displaying messages

At the top of the JSF page, we use h:messages to display all messages. We use h:message to display messages for each input field:

```
<h:form>
    <h:messages layout="table" errorClass="errors"/>
    ...
    <h:inputText id="name"
        value="#{user.name}" required="true" label="#{msgs.namePrompt}"/>
    <h:message for="name" errorClass="errors"/>

    ...
    <h:inputText id="age"
        value="#{form.age}" required="true" label="#{msgs.agePrompt}"/>
    <h:message for="age" errorClass="errors"/>

    ...
</h:form>
```

Note that the input fields have `label` attributes that describe the fields. These labels are used in the error messages—for example, the `Age:` label (generated by `#{msgs.agePrompt}`) in this message:

`Age:` 'old' must be a number between -2147483648 and 2147483647 Example: 9346

Both message tags in our example specify a CSS class named `errors`, which is defined in `styles.css`. That class definition looks like this:

```
.errors {
    font-style: italic;
    color: red;
}
```

We have also specified `layout="table"` for the `h:messages` tag. If we had omitted that attribute (or alternatively specified `layout="list"`), the output would look like that shown in Figure 4–10.

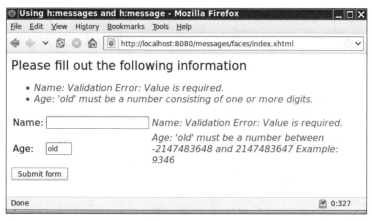

Figure 4–10   Messages displayed as a list

The `list` layout encodes the error messages in an unnumbered list (whose appearance you can control through styles).

 CAUTION: In JSF 1.1, the "`list`" style placed the messages one after the other, without any separators, which was not very useful.

Figure 4–11 shows the directory structure for the application shown in Figure 4–9. Listings 4–17 through 4–19 list the JSF page, resource bundle, and stylesheet for the application. For this example, we added `getAge` and `setAge` methods to the `UserBean` class.

NOTE: By default, h:messages shows message summaries but not details. h:message, on the other hand, shows details but not summaries. If you use h:messages and h:message together, as we did in the preceding example, summaries will appear at the top of the page, with details next to the appropriate input field.

📁 **messages.war**
  📄 index.xhtml
▼ 📁 WEB-INF
    📄 beans.xml
    📄 faces-config.xml
    📄 web.xml
  ▼ 📁 classes
    ▼ 📁 com
      ▼ 📁 corejsf
          📄 UserBean.class
          📄 messages.properties
▼ 📁 resources
  ▼ 📁 css
      📄 styles.css

Figure 4–11   Directory structure for the messages example

Listing 4-17   messages/web/index.xhtml

```
1. <?xml version="1.0" encoding="UTF-8"?>
2. <!DOCTYPE html PUBLIC "-//W3C//DTD XHTML 1.0 Transitional//EN"
3. "http://www.w3.org/TR/xhtml1/DTD/xhtml1-transitional.dtd">
4. <html xmlns="http://www.w3.org/1999/xhtml"
5.       xmlns:f="http://java.sun.com/jsf/core" xmlns:h="http://java.sun.com/jsf/html">
6.   <h:head>
7.     <title>#{msgs.windowTitle}</title>
8.     <h:outputStylesheet library="css" name="styles.css"/>
9.   </h:head>
10.  <h:body>
11.    <h:form>
12.      <h:outputText value="#{msgs.greeting}" styleClass="emphasis"/>
13.      <br/>
14.      <h:messages errorClass="errors" layout="table"/>
15.      <h:panelGrid columns="3">
16.        #{msgs.namePrompt}:
17.        <h:inputText id="name" value="#{user.name}" required="true"
18.                     label="#{msgs.namePrompt}"/>
```

```
19.          <h:message for="name" errorClass="errors"/>
20.          #{msgs.agePrompt}:
21.          <h:inputText id="age" value="#{user.age}" required="true"
22.                      size="3" label="#{msgs.agePrompt}"/>
23.          <h:message for="age" errorClass="errors"/>
24.       </h:panelGrid>
25.       <h:commandButton value="#{msgs.submitPrompt}"/>
26.    </h:form>
27.   </h:body>
28. </html>
```

Listing 4–18	messages/src/java/com/corejsf/messages.properties

```
1. windowTitle=Using h:messages and h:message
2. greeting=Please fill out the following information
3. namePrompt=Name
4. agePrompt=Age
5. submitPrompt=Submit form
```

Listing 4–19	messages/web/resources/css/styles.css

```
1. .errors {
2.    font-style: italic;
3.    color: red;
4. }
5. .emphasis {
6.    font-size: 1.3em;
7. }
```

Conclusion

You have now seen all HTML tags in the standard library with the exception of the tags used for tables, which are covered in Chapter 6. In the next chapter, you will learn how to use the Facelets tags.

FACELETS

JSF 2.0

Topics in This Chapter

Chapter 5

User interfaces are typically a web application's most volatile aspect during development, and they are often comprised of brittle code that is difficult to change, making user interfaces expensive to develop. This chapter shows you how to implement flexible UIs with Facelets.

Facelets Tags

Facelets was originally developed as an alternative to the JSP-based view handler in JSF 1.x. In JSF 2.0, Facelets replaces JSP as JSF's default view technology. In addition to being a better view handler, Facelets supports a number of tags for templating and other purposes. These tags are the topic of this chapter.

Facelets tags can be grouped in these categories:

- Including content from other XHTML pages (`ui:include`)
- Building pages from templates (`ui:composition`, `ui:decorate`, `ui:insert`, `ui:define`, `ui:param`)
- Creating custom components without writing Java code (`ui:component`, `ui:fragment`)
- Miscellaneous utilities (`ui:debug`, `ui:remove`, `ui:repeat`)

To use Facelets tags, add the following namespace declaration to your JSF page:

```
xmlns:ui="http://java.sun.com/jsf/facelets"
```

Table 5–1 gives a brief summary of the Facelets tags. We will discuss these tags in detail in this chapter, except for ui:repeat, which is covered in Chapter 6.

Table 5–1 Facelets Tags

Tag	Description
ui:include	Includes content from another XML file.
ui:composition	When used without a template attribute, a composition is a sequence of elements that can be inserted somewhere else. The composition can have variable parts (specified with ui:insert children).
	When used with a template attribute, the template is loaded. The children of this tag determine the variable parts of the template. The template contents replaces this tag.
ui:decorate	When used without a template attribute, ui:decorate specifies a page into which parts can be inserted. The variable parts are specified with ui:insert children.
	When used with a template attribute, the template is loaded. The children of this tag determine the variable parts of the template.
ui:define	Defines content that is inserted into a template with a matching ui:insert.
ui:insert	Inserts content into a template. That content is defined inside the tag that loads the template.
ui:param	Specifies a parameter that is passed to an included file or a template.
ui:component	This tag is identical to ui:composition, except that it creates a component that is added to the component tree.
ui:fragment	This tag is identical to ui:decorate, except that it creates a component that is added to the component tree.
ui:debug	The ui:debug tag lets users display a debug window, with a keyboard shortcut, that shows the component hierarchy for the current page and the application's scoped variables.
ui:remove	JSF removes everything inside of ui:remove tags.
ui:repeat	Iterates over a list, array, result set, or individual object. See Chapter 6.

Templating with Facelets

Most web applications follow a similar pattern, in which all pages have a common layout and styling. For example, it is typical for pages to have the same header, footer, and sidebars.

Facelets lets you encapsulate that commonality in a *template*, so that you can update the look of your site by making changes to the template, not the individual pages.

> NOTE: Facelets templates encapsulate functionality that is shared by multiple pages, so you don't have to specify that functionality individually for each page. Encapsulation is the cornerstone of both object-oriented programming, and the well-known DRY (Don't Repeat Yourself) principle.

As a simple example, we will dissect an application that displays information about the planets in our solar system (see Figure 5–1 and Figure 5–2).

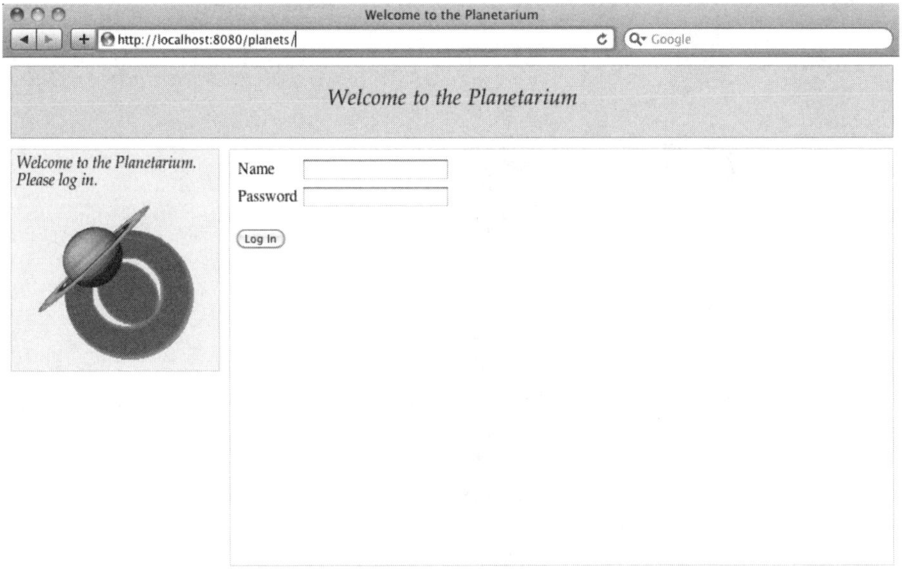

Figure 5–1 Logging into the planetarium

The planets application has a total of 10 pages: a login page, a welcome page, and a page for each of the planets. All of those pages share a common layout, with a header at the top, a sidebar on the left, and a content area to the right of the sidebar. The pages also share some content (all planet pages have an identical header and sidebar) and a CSS stylesheet.

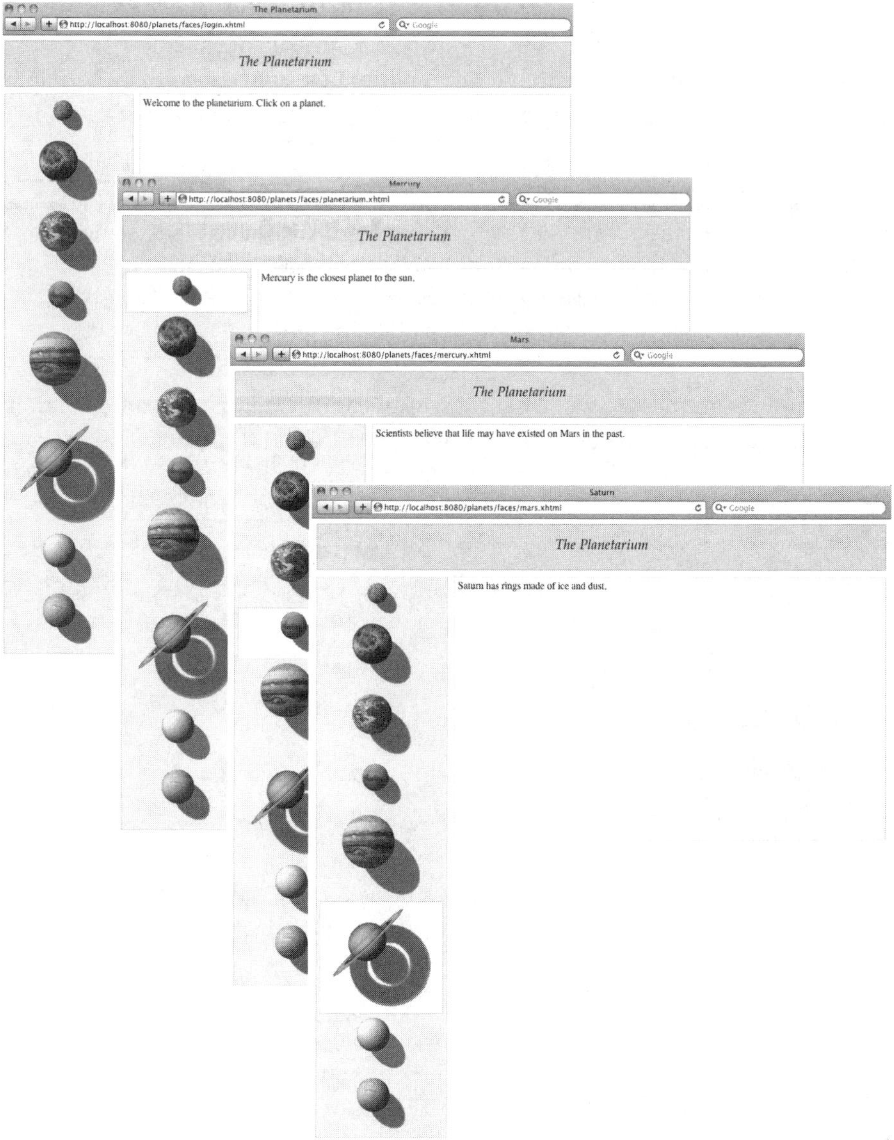

Figure 5–2   All planetarium views share a common template

Building Pages from Common Templates

Listing 5–1 shows the template for the planets application.

Listing 5–1	planets/web/templates/masterLayout.xhtml

```
1. <!DOCTYPE html PUBLIC "-//W3C//DTD XHTML 1.0 Transitional//EN"
2. "http://www.w3.org/TR/xhtml1/DTD/xhtml1-transitional.dtd">
3.
4. <html xmlns="http://www.w3.org/1999/xhtml"
5.      xmlns:ui="http://java.sun.com/jsf/facelets"
6.      xmlns:h="http://java.sun.com/jsf/html">
7.
8.   <h:head>
9.      <title><ui:insert name="windowTitle"/></title>
10.     <h:outputStylesheet library="css" name="styles.css"/>
11.   </h:head>
12.
13.   <h:body>
14.     <div id="heading">
15.       <ui:insert name="heading">
16.         <ui:include src="/sections/planetarium/header.xhtml"/>
17.       </ui:insert>
18.     </div>
19.
20.
21.     <div id="sidebarLeft">
22.       <ui:insert name="sidebarLeft">
23.         <ui:include src="/sections/planetarium/sidebarLeft.xhtml"/>
24.       </ui:insert>
25.     </div>
26.
27.     <div id="content">
28.       <ui:insert name="content"/>
29.     </div>
30.     <ui:debug/>
31.   </h:body>
32. </html>
```

The template uses the `ui:insert` tag four times, to insert:

• The window title
• The heading
• The left sidebar
• The main content

The template also inserts a stylesheet into the head of the page. The stylesheet defines the layout for the heading, the sidebar, and the main content.

You can specify default content inside the body of a ui:insert tag. For example:

```
<ui:insert name="header">
    Default header goes here
</ui:insert>
```

The default is used if no replacement for header is specified when the template is used.

It is common to use a ui:include tag to include default content from another file:

```
<ui:insert name="header">
    <ui:include src="/sections/planetarium/header.xhtml">
</ui:insert>
```

We use a default for the header and the left sidebar.

To make use of a template, you use a ui:composition tag with a template attribute, as shown in Listing 5–2.

Listing 5–2   planets/web/saturn.xhtml

```
 1. <!DOCTYPE html PUBLIC "-//W3C//DTD XHTML 1.0 Transitional//EN"
 2. "http://www.w3.org/TR/xhtml1/DTD/xhtml1-transitional.dtd">
 3. <html xmlns="http://www.w3.org/1999/xhtml"
 4.       xmlns:ui="http://java.sun.com/jsf/facelets">
 5.    <head><title>IGNORED</title></head>
 6.    <body>
 7.       <ui:composition template="/templates/masterLayout.xhtml">
 8.          <ui:define name="windowTitle">
 9.             #{msgs.saturn}
10.          </ui:define>
11.
12.          <ui:define name="content">
13.             Saturn has rings made of ice and dust.
14.          </ui:define>
15.       </ui:composition>
16.    </body>
17. </html>
```

Facelets removes all tags *outside* the ui:composition tag—that is, the doctype declaration, html, head, title, and body tags. This is necessary because the ui:composition is replaced with the template that contains its own set of html, head, title, and body tags.

In fact, you could instead simply make a saturn.xhtml file with the following XML code:

```
<ui:composition template="/templates/masterLayout.xhtml"
    xmlns:ui="http://java.sun.com/jsf/facelets">
  <ui:define name="windowTitle">
    #{msgs.saturn}
  </ui:define>

  <ui:define name="content">
    Saturn has rings made of ice and dust.
  </ui:define>
</ui:composition>
```

This form is shorter and perhaps less confusing. However, you may not get as much help from your IDE with such a file as you would when editing a regular Facelets file. For that reason, it makes sense to include the composition inside a properly formatted XHTML page, as we have done in Listing 5–2.

The ui:define tags inside the ui:composition tag correspond to the ui:insert tags of the template shown in Listing 5–1. For example,

```
<ui:define name="content">
  Saturn has rings made of ice and dust.
</ui:define>
```

in the composition corresponds to

```
<ui:insert name="content"/>
```

in the template.

When the template is loaded, each ui:insert is replaced with the contents of the corresponding ui:define.

All of the pages in the planets application use the same template. The following examples show how the template is used for some of those pages. (Differences are shown in bold.)

mars.xhtml

```
<ui:composition template="/templates/masterLayout.xhtml">
  <ui:define name="windowTitle">
    #{msgs.mars}
  </ui:define>

  <ui:define name="content">
    Scientists believe that life may have existed on Mars in the past.
  </ui:define>
</ui:composition>
```

planetarium.xhtml

```
<ui:composition template="/templates/masterLayout.xhtml">
  <ui:define name="windowTitle">

  <ui:define name="content">
      #{msgs.planetariumWelcome}
  </ui:define>
</ui:composition>
```

login.xhtml

```
<ui:composition template="/templates/masterLayout.xhtml">
  <ui:define name="windowTitle">
      #{msgs.loginTitle}
  </ui:define>

  <ui:define name="heading">
      <ui:include src="/sections/login/header.xhtml"/>
  </ui:define>

  <ui:define name="sidebarLeft">
      <ui:include src="/sections/login/sidebarLeft.xhtml"/>
  </ui:define>

  <ui:define name="content">
      <h:form>
          <h:panelGrid columns="2">
            #{msgs.namePrompt}
            <h:inputText id="name" value="#{user.name}"/>
            #{msgs.passwordPrompt}
            <h:inputSecret id="password" value="#{user.password}"/>
          </h:panelGrid>
          <p>
            <h:commandButton value="#{msgs.loginButtonText}"
                          action="planetarium"/>
          </p>
      </h:form>
  </ui:define>
</ui:composition>
```

Note that the login.xhtml page overrides the defaults for the heading and sidebar.

Organizing Your Views

Fundamentally, templating splits a view into two XHTML pages: one that defines common functionality (a template), and another that defines functionality that differs between views (a composition).

From this simple templating technique, you can construct user interfaces that are very malleable and extensible. Let's take a look at the bigger picture for the planets application to see how.

Figure 5–3 shows the files that comprise the template and views for the planet application.

```
📂 web
    📄 earth.xhtml
    📄 jupiter.xhtml
    📄 login.xhtml
    📄 mars.xhtml
    📄 mercury.xhtml
    📄 neptune.xhtml
    📄 planetarium.xhtml
    📄 saturn.xhtml
    📄 uranus.xhtml
    📄 venus.xhtml
▼ 📂 sections
    ▼ 📂 login
          📄 header.xhtml
          📄 sidebarLeft.xhtml
    ▼ 📂 planetarium
          📄 header.xhtml
          📄 sidebarLeft.xhtml
▼ 📂 templates
          📄 masterLayout.xhtml
```

Figure 5–3   The planets application's pages, sections, and template

Not only does the planets application split views into a common template and compositions, but each piece of content is also split out into its own file; for example, the login and planetarium views have one file each for the header, and sidebar. Those individual pieces of content are included by each view with the ui:include tag. For example, the login page includes its header like this:

```
<ui:define name="heading">
  <ui:include src="sections/login/header.xhtml"/>
</ui:define>
```

Defining individual pieces of content in their own files makes it easy to locate code when you make changes to a view. For example, if you want to change something in the login view's sidebar, you know to edit sections/login/sidebar-Left.xhtml, instead of having to search for that sidebar definition in one long file. Splitting out sections makes it easy to read, understand, and modify your pages, as each file contains a small amount of markup.

In our pages, we did not use separate files for the content sections. If you prefer, you can factor out the content section into a separate Facelets file, such as /sections/login/content.xhtml.

> NOTE: Smalltalk advocates a design pattern known as Composed Method. That pattern urges you to write small, atomic methods from which you compose your application. Small, atomic methods are much easier to write, read, and extend than long methods with a lot of functionality. It's also easier to replace or modify functionality when that functionality is composed of small snippets of code.
>
> With JSF 2.0, you can use the Composed Method pattern to implement your views. Carving your views into small XHTML files that perform a single clear function, such as displaying a login form, makes it easer to implement, maintain, and extend your application's views.

To complete our exploration of how the planets application uses Facelets templating, let's take a look at the files under the sections directory. The files in this directory contain page sections that are included in a template.

Listings 5–3 through 5–5 show the XHTML markup that creates the login view's header, menu, and content.

The header for the login view looks like this:

The Planetarium

The implementation of that header is shown in Listing 5–3.

Notice that the content (in this case, the text for the heading) is placed inside a ui:composition tag that does not specify a template.

Here, we use ui:composition for a tactical reason: to discard the surrounding XHTML tags.

Listing 5–3   planets/web/sections/login/header.xhtml

```
 1. <!DOCTYPE html PUBLIC "-//W3C//DTD XHTML 1.0 Transitional//EN"
 2. "http://www.w3.org/TR/xhtml1/DTD/xhtml1-transitional.dtd">
 3. <html xmlns="http://www.w3.org/1999/xhtml"
 4.       xmlns:ui="http://java.sun.com/jsf/facelets">
 5.     <head><title>IGNORED</title></head>
 6.     <body>
 7.         <ui:composition>
 8.             <div class="header">
 9.                 #{msgs.loginHeading}
10.             </div>
11.         </ui:composition>
12.     </body>
13. </html>
```

If it wasn't for the ui:composition tag, you would wind up with multiple <html> tags, because then <ui:include src="/sections/login/header.xhtml"> would include the entire file.

As a general rule, whenever you include content using the ui:include tag, wrap the included content in a ui:composition tag.

NOTE: As already mentioned, you need not put the surrounding XHTML tags into the file that is being included. You still want to place the contents— which usually consists of a sequence of tags— inside a ui:composition tag so that the included file is proper XML.

Here is the sidebar for the login view:

Welcome to The Planetarium. Please log in.

The login sidebar is implemented as shown in Listing 5–4.

Listing 5–4   planets/web/sections/login/sidebarLeft.xhtml

```
1. <!DOCTYPE html PUBLIC "-//W3C//DTD XHTML 1.0 Transitional//EN"
2. "http://www.w3.org/TR/xhtml1/DTD/xhtml1-transitional.dtd">
3. <html xmlns="http://www.w3.org/1999/xhtml"
4.     xmlns:ui="http://java.sun.com/jsf/facelets"
5.     xmlns:h="http://java.sun.com/jsf/html">
6.    <head><title>IGNORED</title></head>
7.    <body>
8.      <ui:composition>
9.         <div class="welcome">
10.            #{msgs.loginWelcome}
11.            <div class="welcomeImage">
12.               <h:graphicImage library="images" name="Saturn.gif"/>
13.            </div>
14.         </div>
15.      </ui:composition>
16.    </body>
17. </html>
```

Finally, the content area of the login page looks like this:

```
┌──────────────────────────────────────────────────┐
│                                                    │
│   Please log in                                    │
│                                                    │
│   Name     │ William                      │        │
│   Password │              │                        │
│                                                    │
│   ( Log In )                                       │
│                                                    │
└──────────────────────────────────────────────────┘
```

The content section is included in the login.xhtml page—see Listing 5–5.

Listing 5–5   planets/web/login.xhtml

```
1. <!DOCTYPE html PUBLIC "-//W3C//DTD XHTML 1.0 Transitional//EN"
2. "http://www.w3.org/TR/xhtml1/DTD/xhtml1-transitional.dtd">
3. <html xmlns="http://www.w3.org/1999/xhtml"
4.     xmlns:h="http://java.sun.com/jsf/html"
5.     xmlns:ui="http://java.sun.com/jsf/facelets">
6.    <head><title>IGNORED</title></head>
7.    <body>
8.      <ui:composition template="/templates/masterLayout.xhtml">
9.         <ui:define name="windowTitle">
10.            #{msgs.loginTitle}
11.         </ui:define>
```

```
12.
13.        <ui:define name="heading">
14.           <ui:include src="/sections/login/header.xhtml"/>
15.        </ui:define>
16.
17.        <ui:define name="sidebarLeft">
18.           <ui:include src="/sections/login/sidebarLeft.xhtml"/>
19.        </ui:define>
20.
21.        <ui:define name="content">
22.           <h:form>
23.              <h:panelGrid columns="2">
24.                 #{msgs.namePrompt}
25.                 <h:inputText id="name" value="#{user.name}"/>
26.                 #{msgs.passwordPrompt}
27.                 <h:inputSecret id="password" value="#{user.password}"/>
28.              </h:panelGrid>
29.              <p>
30.                 <h:commandButton value="#{msgs.loginButtonText}"
31.                                  action="planetarium"/>
32.              </p>
33.           </h:form>
34.        </ui:define>
35.     </ui:composition>
36.  </body>
37. </html>
```

Now let's take a look at the planetarium content.

Listings 5–6 through 5–8 show the XHTML markup that creates the planetarium view's header, menu, and content.

Listing 5–6   planets/web/sections/planetarium/header.xhtml

```
1. <!DOCTYPE html PUBLIC "-//W3C//DTD XHTML 1.0 Transitional//EN"
2. "http://www.w3.org/TR/xhtml1/DTD/xhtml1-transitional.dtd">
3. <html xmlns="http://www.w3.org/1999/xhtml"
4.       xmlns:ui="http://java.sun.com/jsf/facelets">
5.    <head><title>IGNORED</title></head>
6.    <body>
7.       <ui:composition>
8.          <div class="header">
9.             #{msgs.planetariumHeading}
10.         </div>
11.      </ui:composition>
12.   </body>
13. </html>
```

Listing 5–7 planets/web/sections/planetarium/sidebarLeft.xhtml

```
1. <!DOCTYPE html PUBLIC "-//W3C//DTD XHTML 1.0 Transitional//EN"
2. "http://www.w3.org/TR/xhtml1/DTD/xhtml1-transitional.dtd">
3. <html xmlns="http://www.w3.org/1999/xhtml"
4.     xmlns:ui="http://java.sun.com/jsf/facelets"
5.     xmlns:h="http://java.sun.com/jsf/html"
6.     xmlns:corejsf="http://corejsf.com/facelets">
7.     <head><title>IGNORED</title></head>
8.     <body>
9.        <ui:composition>
10.          <h:form>
11.             <corejsf:planet name="mercury"
12.                            image="#{resource['images:Mercury.gif']}"/>
13.             <corejsf:planet name="venus"
14.                            image="#{resource['images:Venus.gif']}"/>
15.             <corejsf:planet name="earth"
16.                            image="#{resource['images:Earth.gif']}"/>
17.             <corejsf:planet name="mars"
18.                            image="#{resource['images:Mars.gif']}"/>
19.             <corejsf:planet name="jupiter"
20.                            image="#{resource['images:Jupiter.gif']}"/>
21.             <corejsf:planet name="saturn"
22.                            image="#{resource['images:Saturn.gif']}"/>
23.             <corejsf:planet name="uranus"
24.                            image="#{resource['images:Uranus.gif']}"/>
25.             <corejsf:planet name="neptune"
26.                            image="#{resource['images:Neptune.gif']}"/>
27.          </h:form>
28.        </ui:composition>
29.     </body>
30. </html>
```

Listing 5–8 planets/web/planetarium.xhtml

```
1. <!DOCTYPE html PUBLIC "-//W3C//DTD XHTML 1.0 Transitional//EN"
2. "http://www.w3.org/TR/xhtml1/DTD/xhtml1-transitional.dtd">
3. <html xmlns="http://www.w3.org/1999/xhtml"
4.     xmlns:ui="http://java.sun.com/jsf/facelets">
5.     <head><title>IGNORED</title></head>
6.     <body>
7.        <ui:composition template="/templates/masterLayout.xhtml">
8.          <ui:define name="windowTitle">
9.             #{msgs.planetariumTitle}
10.          </ui:define>
11.
```

```
12.          <ui:define name="content">
13.             #{msgs.planetariumWelcome}
14.          </ui:define>
15.      </ui:composition>
16.    </body>
17. </html>
```

The planetarium sections are similar to the login sections—each section is a composition that defines a piece of the planetarium view.

Notice the use of the `corejsf:planet` tag in Listing 5–7. We will discuss that tag, and Facelets custom tags in general, in the section "Custom Tags" on page 195.

Decorators

The template that you have seen in the preceding section defined a page by laying out individual parts. When using the template, you specify the contents of each part. This is similar to the Tiles framework (`http://tiles.apache.org`) that can be used with Struts and JSF 1.x.

When you have a complex set of pages, the Tiles approach gives you a lot of flexibility. But for a simple application, it seems rather complex to think of each page as an assembly of sections. Decorators are a more content-centric approach. You write your pages as usual, but you surround the contents with a `ui:decorate` tag that has a `template` attribute. The decorator approach is the Facelets analog of the Sitemesh framework (`http://www.opensymphony.com/sitemesh/`). In Sitemesh, as with decorators, you first design your content and then you decorate it.

In its simplest form, a decorator can be used like this:

```
<!DOCTYPE html PUBLIC "-//W3C//DTD XHTML 1.0 Transitional//EN"
    "http://www.w3.org/TR/xhtml1/DTD/xhtml1-transitional.dtd">
<html xmlns="http://www.w3.org/1999/xhtml"
      xmlns:h="http://java.sun.com/jsf/html"
      xmlns:ui="http://java.sun.com/jsf/facelets">
  <head><title>#{msgs.loginTitle}</title></head>
  <body>
      <ui:decorate template="/templates/masterDecorator.xhtml">
        <!-- Contents to be decorated -->
        <h:form>
            <h:panelGrid columns="2">
                #{msgs.namePrompt}
                <h:inputText id="name" value="#{user.name}"/>
                #{msgs.passwordPrompt}
                <h:inputSecret id="password" value="#{user.password}"/>
```

```
                </h:panelGrid>
                <p>
                    <h:commandButton value="#{msgs.loginButtonText}"
                        action="planetarium"/>
                </p>
            </h:form>
        </ui:decorate>
    </body>
</html>
```

The template decorates its contents in some way, such as with a header and a left sidebar. Note that the tags outside the ui:decorate are *not* trimmed off (as they would be with ui:composition). Here, the page author specifies the page title directly in the page, without templating.

The template is defined like this:

```
Optional XHTML header
<ui:composition>
    <h:outputStylesheet library="css" name="styles.css" target="body"/>
    <div id="heading">
        <ui:insert name="heading">Default header</ui:insert>
    </div>

    <div id="sidebarLeft">
        <ui:insert name="sidebarLeft">Default sidebar</ui:insert>
    </div>
    <div id="content">
        <ui:insert/>
    </div>
</ui:composition>
Optional XHTML footer
```

Note the <ui:insert/> tag without a name attribute. It inserts all children of the ui:decorate tag.

Also note the ui:composition tag that surrounds the layout instructions in the template. We do not want the XHTML header and footer tags as part of the template—the page that is being decorated already has its own XHTML tags.

With decorators, as with compositions, you can override defaults with ui:define tags, like this:

```
<ui:decorate template="/templates/masterDecorator.xhtml">
    <ui:define name="heading">Special Header</ui:define>
    Body
</ui:decorate>
```

The difference between ui:composition and ui:decorator is mostly conceptual. You can achieve the same effects with either tag. Facelets simply considers them complementary constructs: ui:composition trims all surrounding contents, whereas ui:decorator doesn't (and therefore requires a ui:composition in the template).

Parameters

When you invoke a template, you can supply arguments in two ways: with ui:define and with the ui:param tag. As you have already seen, ui:define is used to provide markup that is inserted into the template. In contrast, ui:param sets an EL variable for use in a template, like this:

```
<ui:composition template="templates/masterTemplate.xhtml">
  <ui:param name="currentDate" value="#{someBean.currentDate}"/>
</ui:composition>
```

In the corresponding template, you can access the parameter with an EL expression, like this:

```
...
<body>
  Today's date: #{currentDate}"/>
</body>
...
```

The ui:param tag can also be used as a child of a ui:include tag.

Custom Tags

You have now seen how to lay out user interface elements with *templates*. In addition, Facelets allows you to define *custom tags*. A custom tag looks like a regular JSF tag, but it uses the Facelets composition mechanism to insert content into your page.

For example, the planet links in the sidebar of the planets application are created by a custom tag, shown in Listing 5–7 on page 192, like this:

```
<corejsf:planet name="#{mercury}"/>
```

The corejsf:planet tag creates a link with an image of the appropriate planet, as shown in the menu in Figure 5–2 on page 182. When the user clicks on the link, the application shows information about the selected planet.

Implementing a custom Facelets tag with JSF 2.0 is a two-step process:

1. Implement the custom tag (or component) in an XHTML file.

2. Declare the custom tag in a tag library descriptor.

Listing 5–9 shows the implementation of the corejsf:planet tag.

Listing 5–9   planets/web/WEB-INF/tags/corejsf/planet.xhtml

```
 1. <!DOCTYPE html PUBLIC "-//W3C//DTD XHTML 1.0 Transitional//EN"
 2. "http://www.w3.org/TR/xhtml1/DTD/xhtml1-transitional.dtd">
 3.
 4. <html xmlns="http://www.w3.org/1999/xhtml"
 5.      xmlns:h="http://java.sun.com/jsf/html"
 6.      xmlns:ui="http://java.sun.com/jsf/facelets">
 7.   <h:head><title>IGNORED</title></h:head>
 8.   <h:body>
 9.     <ui:composition>
10.       <div class='#{name == planetarium.selectedPlanet ?
11.             "planetImageSelected" : "planetImage"}'>
12.         <h:commandLink action="#{planetarium.changePlanet(name)}">
13.           <h:graphicImage value="#{image}"/>
14.         </h:commandLink>
15.         <ui:insert name="content1"/>
16.       </div>
17.     </ui:composition>
18.   </h:body>
19. </html>
```

When the user clicks on the link created by the custom tag, the changePlanet method of the Planetarium class is invoked. That method simply navigates to the selected planet. The Planetarium class is shown in Listing 5–10.

Listing 5–10   planets/src/com/corejsf/Planetarium.java

```
 1. package com.corejsf;
 2.
 3. import java.io.Serializable;
 4. import javax.inject.Named;
 5.   // or import javax.faces.bean.ManagedBean;
 6. import javax.enterprise.context.RequestScoped;
 7.   // or import javax.faces.bean.RequestScoped;
 8.
 9. @Named // or @ManagedBean
10. @RequestScoped
11. public class Planetarium implements Serializable {
12.   private String selectedPlanet;
13.
14.   public String getSelectedPlanet() { return selectedPlanet; }
15.
```

```
16.  public String changePlanet(String newValue) {
17.     selectedPlanet = newValue;
18.     return selectedPlanet;
19.  }
20. }
```

In order to use the corejsf:planet tag, it must be declared in a *tag library file*. This file defines:

- A namespace for the tags in this library (such as http://corejsf.com/facelets, which is mapped to a prefix, such as corejsf:, in the page using the tags)
- A name for each tag (such as planet)
- The location of the template (here, tags/corejsf/planet.xhtml)

Listing 5–11 shows the listing for the tag library file.

Listing 5–11 planets/web/WEB-INF/corejsf.taglib.xml

```
1. <?xml version="1.0"?>
2. <!DOCTYPE facelet-taglib PUBLIC
3.     "-//Sun Microsystems, Inc.//DTD Facelet Taglib 1.0//EN"
4.     "http://java.sun.com/dtd/facelet-taglib_1_0.dtd">
5. <facelet-taglib>
6.   <namespace>http://corejsf.com/facelets</namespace>
7.   <tag>
8.     <tag-name>planet</tag-name>
9.     <source>tags/corejsf/planet.xhtml</source>
10.   </tag>
11. </facelet-taglib>
```

Next, specify the location of the tag library file in web.xml:

```
<context-param>
    <param-name>facelets.LIBRARIES</param-name>
    <param-value>/WEB-INF/corejsf.taglib.xml</param-value>
</context-param>
```

If you use multiple tag library files, separate them with semicolons.

You can also package a set of Facelets tags as a JAR file. Place the template files and any required resources into the JAR file. Then place the tag library file into the META-INF directory. It doesn't matter what name you give to the tag library file, provided its name ends with taglib.xml.

Implementing custom Facelets tags with JSF 2.0 is a simple matter, and it is highly recommended for factoring out repetitive markup.

Note, however, that custom Facelets tags are not as powerful as full-fledged JSF components. In particular, you cannot attach functionality, such as validators or listeners, to a Facelets custom tag. (See Chapters 7 and 8 for more information about validators and event listeners.) For example, we cannot add an action listener to the corejsf:planet tag. JSF 2.0 addresses this concern with a more advanced component mechanism, called composite components. We discuss composite components in Chapter 9.

Components and Fragments

The template for the planet custom tag defines a ui:composition. When you use the tag, it is replaced with the child elements of the composition. If you change ui:composition in Listing 5–9 on page 196 to the ui:component tag, then the child elements are placed *inside a JSF component*. The component is then added to the view.

You can supply id, binding, and rendered attributes with the ui:component tag. There are two reasons why you might want to do this. You can programmatically manipulate the component if you use the binding attribute to bind it to a bean. Moreover, you can conditionally render the component by setting the rendered attribute to a value expression.

Similarly, the ui:fragment tag is an analog to ui:decorate that generates a component. You can use a fragment inside a ui:composition or ui:component to conditionally include children:

```
<ui:fragment rendered="#{name == planetarium.selectedPlanet}">
    Conditionally included children
</ui:fragment>
```

Loose Ends

In this section, we look at the remaining tags from Table 5–1 on page 180, with the exception of ui:repeat, which is covered in the next chapter. We finish the section with a note on whitespace handling in Facelets.

<ui:debug>

When you place the ui:debug tag in a Facelets page, a debug component is added to the component tree for that page. If the user types a hotkey, which by default is CTRL+SHIFT+d, JSF opens a window and displays the state of the component tree and the application's scoped variables. Figure 5–4 shows that debug window.

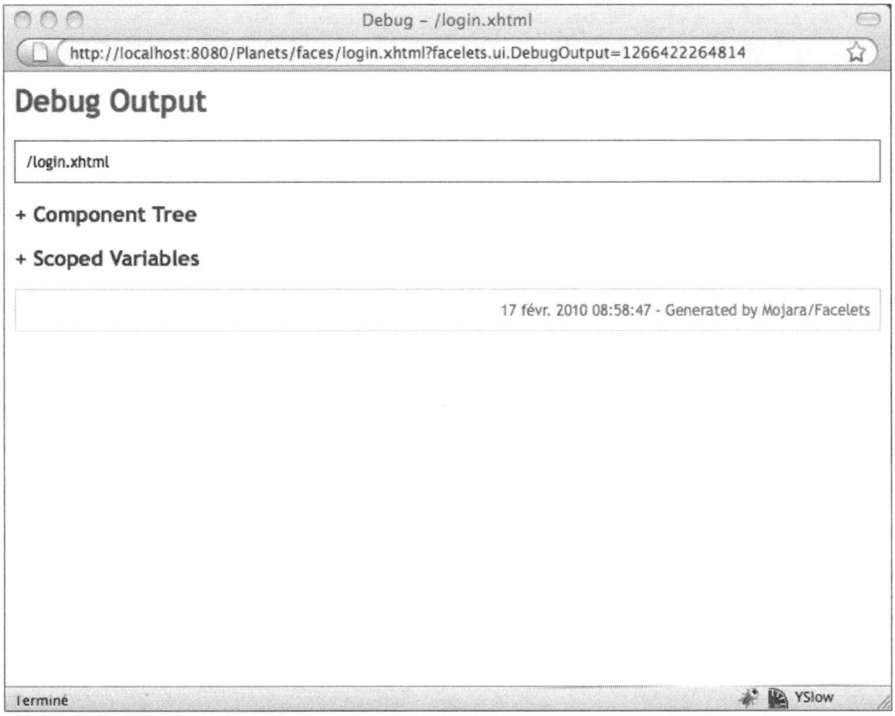

Figure 5–4   Facelets debug output

You can click on Component Tree or Scoped Variables, to show the component tree or the application's scoped variables, respectively, as shown in Figure 5–5.

The ui:debug tag also lets you redefine the hotkey that brings up the Debug Output window, with a hotkey attribute, like this:

```
<ui:debug hotkey="i"/>
```

The preceding use of ui:debug redefines the hotkey to CTRL+SHIFT+i.

The ui:debug tag is useful during development, so developers can instantly see the current page's component tree and the application's scoped variables; however, you will probably want to remove the tag in production. For that reason, we recommend that you put the ui:debug tag in a template, where it is specified in one place, and shared among many views, instead of replicating the tag in each view's XHTML page.

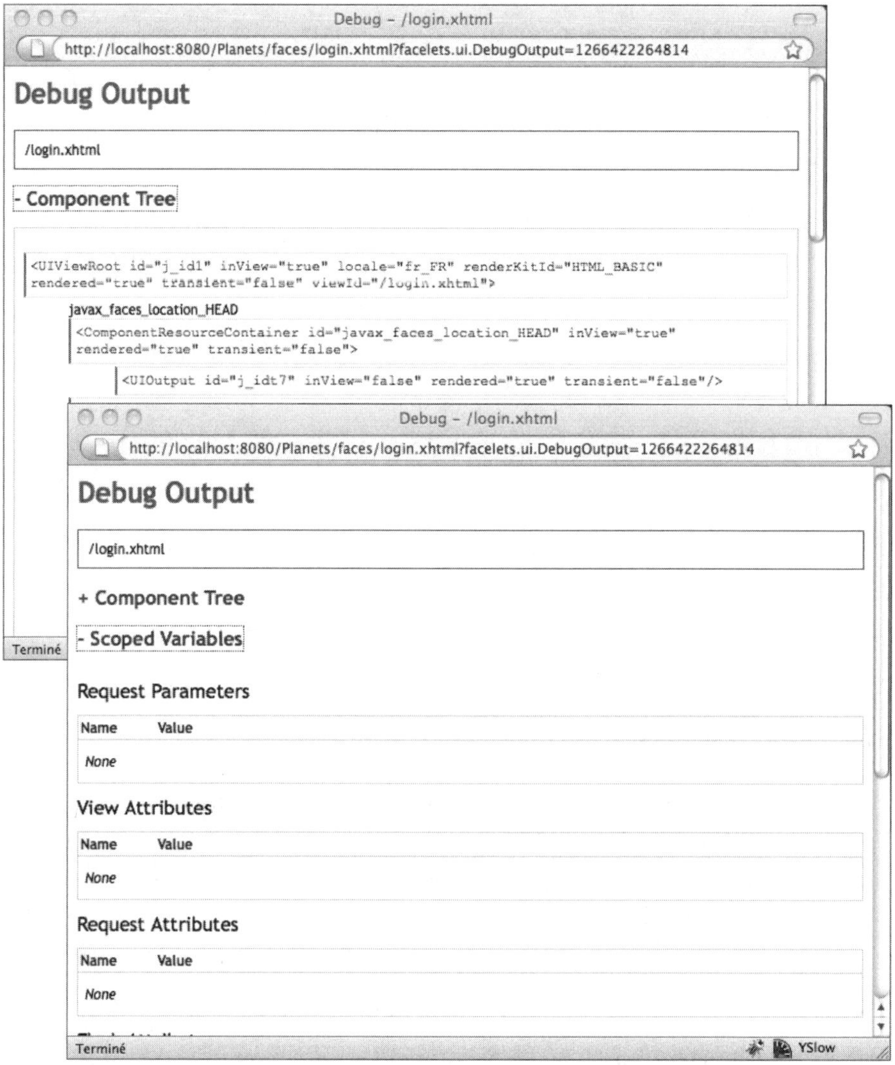

Figure 5–5 Examining the component tree and scoped variables

<ui:remove>

Sometimes, to find out which part of a JSF page causes a stack trace, you may want to use the time-honored divide-and-conquer strategy of commenting out parts of the page to isolate the offending component.

Somewhat surprisingly, the XML comments `<!-- ... -->` are not useful for this purpose. For example, if you comment out a button in an XHTML page, like this:

```
<!-- <h:commandButton id="loginButton"
  value="#{msgs.loginButtonText}"
  action="planetarium"/> -->
```

JSF will *process the value expression* `#{msgs.loginButtonText}`, and place the result, as a comment, in the generated HTML page. Assuming that `#{msgs.loginButtonText}` evaluates to Log In, you will see the following in the generated HTML page:

```
<!-- <h:commandButton id="loginButton"
  value="Log In"
  action="planetarium"/> -->
```

If the `getLoginButtonText` method throws an exception, then the XML comments don't help you at all.

Since Facelets is not JSP, you cannot use a JSP comment `<%-- ... --%>` either.

Instead, use `ui:remove`, like this:

```
<ui:remove>
  <h:commandButton id="loginButton"
    value="#{msgs.loginButtonText}"
    action="planetarium"/>
</ui:remove>
```

You may wonder why Facelets processes value expressions in XML comments. This feature was meant for use in JavaScript code inside comments. Actually, you should use the `script` tag, not XML comments, to include JavaScript code in your page, like this:

```
<script type="text/javascript">
  <![CDATA[
  Javascript code
  ]]>
</script>
```

This is a better solution since you can locate and process the scripts with XML tools.

 NOTE: If you set the context parameter `javax.faces.FACELETS_SKIP_COMMENTS` to `true` in `web.xml`, then XML comments are skipped. This is a sensible setting that you should consider for your projects.

Handling Whitespace

The handling of whitespace in Facelets pages can be a bit surprising. By default, whitespace is trimmed around components. For example, consider the tags:

```
<h:outputText value="#{msgs.name}"/>
<h:inputText value="#{user.name}"/>
```

They are separated by whitespace (the newline after the `h:outputText` and the spaces before `h:inputText`). Facelets won't turn that whitespace into a text component. This is a good thing—otherwise the tag sequence would not work correctly inside an `h:panelGrid`.

However, if you have two links in a row, the whitespace handling is unintuitive. The tags

```
<h:commandLink value="Previous" .../> <h:commandLink value="Next" .../>
```

yield links <u>PreviousNext</u> with no space in between. The remedy is to add a space with a value expression `#{' '}`.

Conclusion

Facelets is a much more powerful display technology than JSP. Facelets was expressly implemented for JSF, so it does not suffer from incompatibility with JSF, as with corner cases using JSP with JSF.

Like Tiles, Facelets gives you the ability to implement modular user interfaces that are easy to understand, modify, and extend, using the built-in templating capabilities. Facelets also gives you the ability to decorate sections of a page, further separating concerns between basic content and decorations. Finally, Facelets gives you a number of utility tags, including `ui:debug`, which make implementing JSF pages much easier than with JSP.

DATA TABLES

Topics in This Chapter

Chapter 6

Classic web applications deal extensively in tabular data. In the days of old, HTML tables were preferred for that task, in addition to acting as page layout managers. That latter task has, for the most part, been subsequently rendered to CSS, but displaying tabular data is still big business.

This chapter discusses the h:dataTable tag, a capable but limited component that lets you manipulate tabular data.

NOTE: The h:dataTable tag represents a capable component/renderer pair. For example, you can easily display JSF components in table cells, add headers and footers to tables, and manipulate the look and feel of your tables with CSS classes. However, h:dataTable is missing some high-end features that you might expect out of the box. For example, if you want to sort table columns, you will have to write some code to carry that out. See "Sorting and Filtering" on page 234 for more details on how to do that.

The Data Table Tag—h:dataTable

The h:dataTable tag iterates over *data* to create an HTML *table*. Here is how you use it:

```
<h:dataTable value="#{items}" var="item">
  <h:column>
    <!-- left column components -->
    #{item.aPropertyName}
  </h:column>

  <h:column>
    <!-- next column components -->
    <h:commandLink value="#{item.anotherPropertyName}" action="..."/>
  </h:column>

  <!-- add more columns, as desired -->
</h:dataTable>
```

The value attribute represents the data over which h:dataTable iterates; that data must be one of the following:

- A Java object
- An array
- An instance of java.util.List
- An instance of java.sql.ResultSet
- An instance of javax.servlet.jsp.jstl.sql.Result
- An instance of javax.faces.model.DataModel

As h:dataTable iterates, it makes each item in the array, list, result set, etc., available within the body of the tag. The name of the item is specified with h:dataTable's var attribute. In the preceding code fragment, each item (item) of a collection (items) is made available, in turn, as h:dataTable iterates through the collection. You use properties from the current item to populate columns for the current row.

You can also specify any Java object for h:dataTable's value attribute, although the usefulness of doing so is questionable. If that object is a scalar (meaning it is not a collection of some sort), h:dataTable iterates once, making the object available in the body of the tag.

The body of h:dataTable tags can contain only h:column tags; h:dataTable ignores all other component tags. Each column can contain an unlimited number of components (as well as optional header and footer facets, which we discuss in the next section).

h:dataTable pairs a UIData component with a Table renderer. That combination provides robust table generation that includes support for CSS styles, database access, custom table models, and more. We start our h:dataTable exploration with a simple table.

A Simple Table

Figure 6–1 shows a table of names.

Figure 6–1   A simple table

The directory structure for the application shown in Figure 6–1 is shown in Figure 6–2. The application's JSF page is given in Listing 6–1.

Figure 6–2   The directory structure for the simple table

In Listing 6–1, we use h:dataTable to iterate over an array of names. The last name followed by a comma is placed in the left column and the first name is placed in the right column.

Listing 6–2 shows the Name class. The array of names in this example is instantiated by a managed bean, which is shown in Listing 6–3.

Listing 6–1   simple/web/index.xhtml

```
1. <?xml version="1.0" encoding="UTF-8"?>
2. <!DOCTYPE html PUBLIC "-//W3C//DTD XHTML 1.0 Transitional//EN"
3. "http://www.w3.org/TR/xhtml1/DTD/xhtml1-transitional.dtd">
4. <html xmlns="http://www.w3.org/1999/xhtml"
5.       xmlns:h="http://java.sun.com/jsf/html">
6.   <h:head>
7.     <title>#{msgs.windowTitle}</title>
8.   </h:head>
9.   <h:body>
10.     #{msgs.pageTitle}
11.     <h:form>
12.       <h:dataTable value="#{tableData.names}" var="name">
13.         <h:column>
14.           #{name.last},
15.         </h:column>
16.
17.         <h:column>
18.           #{name.first}
19.         </h:column>
20.       </h:dataTable>
21.     </h:form>
22.   </h:body>
23. </html>
```

Listing 6–2   simple/src/java/com/corejsf/Name.java

```
1. package com.corejsf;
2.
3. import java.io.Serializable;
4.
5. public class Name implements Serializable {
6.    private String first;
7.    private String last;
8.
9.    public Name(String first, String last) {
10.       this.first = first;
11.       this.last = last;
12.    }
13.
```

```
14.    public void setFirst(String newValue) { first = newValue; }
15.    public String getFirst() { return first; }
16.
17.    public void setLast(String newValue) { last = newValue; }
18.    public String getLast() { return last; }
19. }
```

Listing 6–3 simple/src/java/com/corejsf/TableData.java

```
1. package com.corejsf;
2.
3. import java.io.Serializable;
4.
5. import javax.inject.Named;
6.    // or import javax.faces.bean.ManagedBean;
7. import javax.enterprise.context.SessionScoped;
8.    // or import javax.faces.bean.SessionScoped;
9. import javax.faces.model.ArrayDataModel;
10. import javax.faces.model.DataModel;
11.
12. @Named // or @ManagedBean
13. @SessionScoped
14. public class TableData implements Serializable {
15.    private static final Name[] names = new Name[] {
16.       new Name("William", "Dupont"),
17.       new Name("Anna", "Keeney"),
18.       new Name("Mariko", "Randor"),
19.       new Name("John", "Wilson")
20.    };
21.
22.    public Name[] getNames() { return names;}
23. }
```

The table in Figure 6–1 is intentionally vanilla. Throughout this chapter we will see how to add bells and whistles, such as CSS styles and column headers, to tables.

 CAUTION: h:dataTable data is row oriented—for example, the names in Listing 6–3 correspond to table rows, but the names say nothing about what is stored in each column—it is up to the page author to specify column content. Row-oriented data might be different from what you are used to; Swing table models, for example, keep track of what is in each row *and* column.

h:dataTable *Attributes*

h:dataTable attributes are listed in Table 6–1.

Table 6–1   Attributes for h:dataTable

Attribute	Description
bgcolor	Background color for the table
border	Width of the table's border
captionClass **JSF 1.2**	The CSS class for the table caption
captionStyle **JSF 1.2**	A CSS style for the table caption
cellpadding	Padding around table cells
cellspacing	Spacing between table cells
columnClasses	Comma-separated list of CSS classes for columns
dir	Text direction for text that does not inherit directionality; valid values: LTR (left to right) and RTL (right to left)
first	A zero-relative index of the first row shown in the table
footerClass	CSS class for the table footer
frame	Specification for sides of the frame surrounding the table; valid values: none, above, below, hsides, vsides, lhs, rhs, box, border
headerClass	CSS class for the table header
rowClasses	Comma-separated list of CSS classes for rows
rows	The number of rows displayed in the table, starting with the row specified with the first attribute; if you set this value to zero, all table rows will be displayed
rules	Specification for lines drawn between cells; valid values: groups, rows, columns, all
summary	Summary of the table's purpose and structure used for nonvisual feedback such as speech

Table 6–1   Attributes for `h:dataTable` **(cont.)**

Attribute	Description
`var`	The name of the variable created by the data table that represents the current item in the value
`binding, id, rendered, styleClass, value`	Basic
`lang, style, title, width`	HTML 4.0
`onclick, ondblclick, onkeydown, onkeypress, onkeyup, onmousedown, onmousemove, onmouseout, onmouseover, onmouseup`	DHTML events

The `binding` and `id` attributes are discussed in "IDs and Bindings" on page 108 of Chapter 4, and `rendered` attributes are discussed in "An Overview of the JSF HTML Tags" on page 105 of Chapter 4.

`h:dataTable` also comes with a full complement of DHTML event and HTML 4.0 pass-through attributes. You can read more about those attributes in Chapter 4.

The `first` attribute specifies a zero-relative index of the first visible row in the table. The `value` attribute points to the data over which `h:dataTable` iterates. At the start of each iteration, `h:dataTable` creates a request-scoped variable that you name with `h:dataTable`'s `var` attribute. Within the body of the `h:dataTable` tag, you can reference the current item with that name.

`h:column` *Attributes*

`h:column` attributes are listed in Table 6–2.

Table 6–2   Attributes for `h:column`

Attribute	Description
`footerClass` **JSF 1.2**	The CSS class for the column's footer
`headerClass` **JSF 1.2**	The CSS class for the column's header
`binding, id, rendered, styleClass, value`	Basic

Headers, Footers, and Captions

If you display a list of names as we did in "A Simple Table" on page 207, you need to distinguish last names from first names. You can do that with a column header, as shown in Figure 6–3.

Figure 6–3   Specifying column headers and footers

Besides headers, the table columns in Figure 6–3 also contain footers that indicate the data type of their respective columns; in this case, both columns are [alpha], for alphanumeric.

Column headers and footers are specified with facets, as shown here:

```
<h:dataTable>
   ...
   <h:column headerClass="columnHeader"
             footerClass="columnFooter">
      <f:facet name="header">
         <!-- header components go here -->
      </f:facet>

      <!-- column components go here -->

      <f:facet name="footer">
         <!-- footer components go here -->
      </f:facet>
   </h:column>
   ...
</h:dataTable>
```

h:dataTable places the components specified for the header and footer facets in the HTML table's header and footer, respectively. Notice that we use the h:column headerClass and footerClass attributes to specify CSS styles for column headers and footers, respectively.

To supply a table caption, add a caption facet, like this:

```
<h:dataTable ...>
  <f:facet name="caption">An Array of Names:</f:facet>
  ...
</h:dataTable>
```

If you add this facet to the table shown in Figure 6–3, you will see what is shown in Figure 6–4.

You can use captionStyle and captionClass to specify a style or CSS class, respectively, for the caption:

```
<h:dataTable ... captionClass="caption">
  <f:facet name="caption">An Array of Names:</f:facet>
  ...
</h:dataTable>
```

In the preceding code snippet, we used some plain text for the facet, but like any facet, you can specify a JSF component instead.

Figure 6–4   A table caption

The code for the JSF page shown in Figure 6–4 is given in Listing 6–4.

Listing 6–4   headersAndFooters/web/index.xhtml

```
 1. <?xml version="1.0" encoding="UTF-8"?>
 2. <!DOCTYPE html PUBLIC "-//W3C//DTD XHTML 1.0 Transitional//EN"
 3. "http://www.w3.org/TR/xhtml1/DTD/xhtml1-transitional.dtd">
 4. <html xmlns="http://www.w3.org/1999/xhtml"
 5.       xmlns:f="http://java.sun.com/jsf/core" xmlns:h="http://java.sun.com/jsf/html">
 6.   <h:head>
 7.     <h:outputStylesheet library="css" name="styles.css"/>
 8.     <title>#{msgs.windowTitle}</title>
 9.   </h:head>
10.   <h:body>
11.     <h:form>
12.       <h:dataTable value="#{tableData.names}" var="name"
13.                   captionStyle="font-size: 0.95em; font-style:italic"
14.                   style="width: 250px;">
15.
16.         <f:facet name="caption">An Array of Names</f:facet>
17.
18.         <h:column headerClass="columnHeader" footerClass="columnFooter">
19.           <f:facet name="header">#{msgs.lastnameColumn}</f:facet>
20.
21.           #{name.last},
22.
23.           <f:facet name="footer">#{msgs.alphanumeric}</f:facet>
24.         </h:column>
25.
26.         <h:column headerClass="columnHeader" footerClass="columnFooter">
27.           <f:facet name="header">#{msgs.firstnameColumn}</f:facet>
28.
29.           #{name.first}
30.
31.           <f:facet name="footer">#{msgs.alphanumeric}</f:facet>
32.         </h:column>
33.       </h:dataTable>
34.     </h:form>
35.   </h:body>
36. </html>
```

 TIP: To place multiple components in a table header or footer, you must
group them in an h:panelGroup tag or place them in a container component
with h:panelGrid or h:dataTable. If you place multiple components in a facet,
only the first component will be displayed.

Styles

h:dataTable has attributes that specify CSS classes for the following:

- The table as a whole (styleClass)
- Column headers and footers (headerClass and footerClass)
- Individual columns (columnClasses)
- Individual rows (rowClasses)

The table shown in Figure 6–5 uses styleClass, headerClass, and columnClasses.

Order Number	Order Date	Customer ID	Amount	Description
1	2002-05-20	1	129.99	Wristwatch
2	2002-05-21	1	19.95	Coffee grinder
3	2002-05-24	1	29.76	Bath towel
4	2002-05-23	1	39.34	Deluxe cheese grater
5	2002-05-22	2	56.75	Champagne glass set
6	2002-05-20	2	28.11	Instamatic camera
7	2002-05-22	2	38.77	Walkman
8	2002-05-21	2	56.76	Coffee maker
9	2002-05-23	2	21.47	Car wax
10	2002-05-21	2	16.8	Tape recorder
11	2002-05-24	2	25.44	Art brush set
12	2002-05-22	3	47.63	Game software

Figure 6–5 Applying styles to columns and headers

 NOTE: The h:dataTable rowClasses and columnClasses attributes are mutually exclusive. If you specify both, columnClasses has priority.

Styles by Column

Here is how the CSS classes in Figure 6–5 are specified:

```
<h:dataTable value="#{order.all}" var="order"
   styleClass="orders"
   headerClass="ordersHeader"
   columnClasses="oddColumn,evenColumn">
```

Those CSS classes are listed next.

```
.orders {
    border: thin solid black;
}
.ordersHeader {
    text-align: center;
    font-style: italic;
    color: Snow;
    background: Teal;
}
.oddColumn {
    height: 25px;
    text-align: center;
    background: MediumTurquoise;
}
.evenColumn {
    text-align: center;
    background: PowderBlue;
}
```

We specified only two column classes, but notice that we have five columns. In this case, h:dataTable reuses the column classes, starting with the first. By specifying only the first two column classes, we can set the CSS classes for odd and even columns. (When using the terms *odd* and *even* in this way, we assume that the first column is column 1.)

 CAUTION: We use color names, such as PowderBlue and Medium-Turquoise, in our style classes for the sake of illustration. You should prefer the equivalent hex constants because they are portable, whereas color names are not.

Styles by Row

You can use the rowClasses attribute to specify CSS classes by rows instead of columns, as illustrated in Figure 6–6. That data table is implemented like this:

```
<h:dataTable value="#{order.all}" var="order"
    styleClass="orders"
    headerClass="ordersHeader"
    rowClasses="oddRow,evenRow">
```

Like column classes, h:dataTable reuses row classes when the number of classes is less than the number of rows. In the preceding code fragment, we have taken advantage of this feature to specify CSS classes for odd and even rows.

Order Number	Order Date	Customer ID	Amount	Description
1	2002-05-20	1	129.99	Wristwatch
2	2002-05-21	1	19.95	Coffee grinder
3	2002-05-24	1	29.76	Bath towel
4	2002-05-23	1	39.34	Deluxe cheese grater
5	2002-05-22	2	56.75	Champagne glass set
6	2002-05-20	2	28.11	Instamatic camera
7	2002-05-22	2	38.77	Walkman
8	2002-05-21	2	56.76	Coffee maker
9	2002-05-23	2	21.47	Car wax
10	2002-05-21	2	16.8	Tape recorder
11	2002-05-24	2	25.44	Art brush set
12	2002-05-22	3	47.63	Game software

Figure 6–6   Applying styles to rows

The ui:repeat Tag JSF 2.0

Instead of the h:dataTable tag, you can use the ui:repeat tag. The ui:repeat tag repeatedly inserts its body into the page. You have to render the table markup yourself, like this:

```
<table>
  <ui:repeat value="#{tableData.names}" var="name">
  <tr>
    <td>#{name.last},</td>
    <td>#{name.first}</td>
  </tr>
  </ui:repeat>
</table>
```

We find that this gets a bit tedious, particularly when you have to worry about headers, footers, captions, and styles. But if you are familiar with HTML tables, there is nothing wrong with using ui:repeat instead of h:dataTable.

The ui:repeat tag has several attributes that can make it a better choice than h:dataTable in some situations.

The following attributes let you iterate over a subset of the collection:

- offset is the index at which the iteration starts (default: 0)
- step is the difference between successive index values (default: 1)
- size is the number of iterations (default: (size of the collection – offset) / step)

For example, if you want to show elements 10, 12, 14, 16, 18 of a collection, you use:

```
<ui:repeat ... offset="10" step="2" size="5">
```

The varStatus attribute sets a variable that reports on the iteration status. The iteration status has these properties:

- Boolean properties even, odd, first, and last, which are useful for selecting styles.

- Integer properties index, begin, step, and end, which give the index of the current iteration and the starting offset, step size, and ending offset. Note that begin = offset and end = offset + step × size, where offset and size are the attribute values from the ui:repeat tag.

The index property can be used for row numbers:

```
<table>
    <ui:repeat value="#{tableData.names}" var="name" varStatus="status">
    <tr>
        <td>#{status.index + 1}</td>
        <td>#{name.last},</td>
        <td>#{name.first}</td>
    </tr>
    </ui:repeat>
</table>
```

JSF Components in Tables

To this point, we have used only output components in table columns, but you can place any JSF component in a table cell. Figure 6–7 shows an application that uses a variety of components in a table.

h:dataTable iterates over data, so the table shown in Figure 6–7 provides a list of integers for that purpose. We use the current integer to configure components in the "Number", "Textfields", "Buttons", and "Menu" columns.

Components in a table are no different than components outside a table; you can manipulate them in any manner you desire, including conditional rendering with the rendered attribute, handling events, and the like.

The directory structure for the application shown in Figure 6–7 is shown in Figure 6–8. The JSF page is given in Listing 6–5. Listing 6–6 shows the managed bean that contains the model data: the numbers 1 through 5.

Using JSF Components in Tables - Mozilla Firefox

File Edit View History Bookmarks Tools Help

http://localhost:8080/components/

Number	Textfields	Buttons	Checkboxes	Links	Graphics	Menu	Radio Buttons	List Boxes
1	1	1	☐	1	·	1 ⬍	○ yes ○ no	yes maybe no ok
2	2	2	☐	2	··	2 ⬍	○ yes ○ no	yes maybe no ok
3	3	3	☐	3	···	3 ⬍	○ yes ○ no	yes maybe no ok
4	4	4	☐	4	::	4 ⬍	○ yes ○ no	yes maybe no ok
5	5	5	☐	5	::·	5 ⬍	○ yes ○ no	yes maybe no ok

Done

Figure 6–7   JSF components in table cells

📁 **components.war**
  📄 index.xhtml
  ▼ 📁 WEB-INF
    📄 beans.xml
    📄 faces-config.xml
    📄 web.xml
    ▼ 📁 classes
      ▼ 📁 com
        ▼ 📁 corejsf
          📄 messages.properties
  ▼ 📁 resources
    ▼ 📁 css
      📄 styles.css
    ▼ 📁 images
      📄 dice1.gif
      📄 dice2.gif
      📄 dice3.gif
      📄 dice4.gif
      📄 dice5.gif

Figure 6–8   Directory structure for the components example

Listing 6–5   components/web/index.xhtml

```
1. <?xml version="1.0" encoding="UTF-8"?>
2. <!DOCTYPE html PUBLIC "-//W3C//DTD XHTML 1.0 Transitional//EN"
3. "http://www.w3.org/TR/xhtml1/DTD/xhtml1-transitional.dtd">
4. <html xmlns="http://www.w3.org/1999/xhtml"
5.     xmlns:f="http://java.sun.com/jsf/core"
6.     xmlns:h="http://java.sun.com/jsf/html">
7.   <h:head>
8.     <h:outputStylesheet library="css" name="styles.css"/>
9.     <title>#{msgs.windowTitle}</title>
10.  </h:head>
11.  <h:body style="background: #eee">
12.    <h:form>
13.      <h:dataTable value="#{numberList}" var="number">
14.        <h:column>
15.          <f:facet name="header">#{msgs.numberHeader}</f:facet>
16.          #{number}
17.        </h:column>
18.        <h:column>
19.          <f:facet name="header">#{msgs.textfieldHeader}</f:facet>
20.          <h:inputText value="#{number}" size="3"/>
21.        </h:column>
22.        <h:column>
23.          <f:facet name="header">#{msgs.buttonHeader}</f:facet>
24.          <h:commandButton value="#{number}"/>
25.        </h:column>
26.        <h:column>
27.          <f:facet name="header">#{msgs.checkboxHeader}</f:facet>
28.          <h:selectBooleanCheckbox value="false"/>
29.        </h:column>
30.        <h:column>
31.          <f:facet name="header">#{msgs.linkHeader}</f:facet>
32.          <h:commandLink>#{number}</h:commandLink>
33.        </h:column>
34.        <h:column>
35.          <f:facet name="header">#{msgs.graphicHeader}</f:facet>
36.          <h:graphicImage library="images" name="dice#{number}.gif"
37.                          style="border: 0px"/>
38.        </h:column>
39.        <h:column>
40.          <f:facet name="header">#{msgs.menuHeader}</f:facet>
41.          <h:selectOneMenu>
42.            <f:selectItem itemLabel="#{number}" itemValue="#{number}"/>
43.          </h:selectOneMenu>
44.        </h:column>
```

```
45.              <h:column>
46.                 <f:facet name="header">#{msgs.radioHeader}</f:facet>
47.                 <h:selectOneRadio layout="lineDirection" value="nextMonth">
48.                    <f:selectItem itemValue="yes" itemLabel="yes"/>
49.                    <f:selectItem itemValue="no" itemLabel="no"/>
50.                 </h:selectOneRadio>
51.              </h:column>
52.              <h:column>
53.                 <f:facet name="header">#{msgs.listboxHeader}</f:facet>
54.                 <h:selectOneListbox size="4">
55.                    <f:selectItem itemValue="yes" itemLabel="yes"/>
56.                    <f:selectItem itemValue="maybe" itemLabel="maybe"/>
57.                    <f:selectItem itemValue="no" itemLabel="no"/>
58.                    <f:selectItem itemValue="ok" itemLabel="ok"/>
59.                 </h:selectOneListbox>
60.              </h:column>
61.           </h:dataTable>
62.        </h:form>
63.     </h:body>
64. </html>
```

Listing 6–6   components/web/WEB-INF/faces-config.xml

```
1. <?xml version="1.0"?>
2. <faces-config xmlns="http://java.sun.com/xml/ns/javaee"
3.     xmlns:xsi="http://www.w3.org/2001/XMLSchema-instance"
4.     xsi:schemaLocation="http://java.sun.com/xml/ns/javaee
5.        http://java.sun.com/xml/ns/javaee/web-facesconfig_2_0.xsd"
6.     version="2.0">
7.     <application>
8.        <resource-bundle>
9.           <base-name>com.corejsf.messages</base-name>
10.          <var>msgs</var>
11.       </resource-bundle>
12.    </application>
13.
14.    <managed-bean>
15.       <managed-bean-name>numberList</managed-bean-name>
16.       <managed-bean-class>java.util.ArrayList</managed-bean-class>
17.       <managed-bean-scope>session</managed-bean-scope>
18.       <list-entries>
19.          <value>1</value>
20.          <value>2</value>
21.          <value>3</value>
22.          <value>4</value>
23.          <value>5</value>
24.       </list-entries>
25.    </managed-bean>
26. </faces-config>
```

Editing Tables

The following two sample programs show you how to edit tables. We first show you how to edit individual table cells. Then we give an example of deleting table rows. The same technique would work for adding rows. When you implement commands that affect individual rows, your application needs to have a way of finding out which rows the user selected. Each example shows a different approach for identifying the user selections.

Editing Table Cells

To edit table cells, you provide an input component for the cell you want to edit. The application shown in Figure 6–9 allows editing of all its cells. You click a checkbox to edit a row and then click the "Save Changes" button to save your changes. From top to bottom, Figure 6–9 shows a cell being edited.

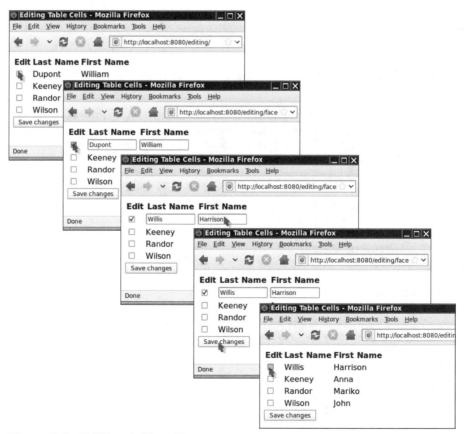

Figure 6–9   Editing table cells

The table cells in Figure 6–9 use an input component when the cell is being edited and an output component when it is not. The following code shows how that is implemented:

```
<h:dataTable value="#{tableData.names}" var="name">
  <!-- checkbox column -->
  <h:column>
    <f:facet name="header">
      <h:outputText value="#{msgs.editColumn}" style="font-weight: bold"/>
    </f:facet>

    <h:selectBooleanCheckbox value="#{name.editable}" onclick="submit()"/>
  </h:column>

  <!-- last name column -->
  <h:column>

    ...
    <h:inputText value="#{name.last}" rendered="#{name.editable}" size="10"/>

    <h:outputText value="#{name.last}" rendered="#{not name.editable}"/>
  </h:column>
  ...
</h:dataTable>
```

The preceding code fragment lists only the code for the checkbox and last name columns. The value of the checkbox corresponds to whether the current name is editable; if so, the checkbox is checked. Two components are specified for the last name column: an h:inputText and an h:outputText. If the name is editable, the input component is rendered. If the name is not editable, the output component is rendered.

Here we add an editable property to the Name class:

```
public class Name {
   private String first;
   private String last;
   private boolean editable;
   ...
   public boolean isEditable() { return editable; }
   public void setEditable(boolean newValue) { editable = newValue; }
}
```

The full listing for the JSF page shown in Figure 6–9 is given in Listing 6–7.

Listing 6-7   editing/web/index.xhtml

```
 1. <?xml version="1.0" encoding="UTF-8"?>
 2. <!DOCTYPE html PUBLIC "-//W3C//DTD XHTML 1.0 Transitional//EN"
 3. "http://www.w3.org/TR/xhtml1/DTD/xhtml1-transitional.dtd">
 4. <html xmlns="http://www.w3.org/1999/xhtml"
 5.       xmlns:f="http://java.sun.com/jsf/core"
 6.       xmlns:h="http://java.sun.com/jsf/html">
 7.   <h:head>
 8.     <title>#{msgs.windowTitle}</title>
 9.   </h:head>
10.   <h:body>
11.     <h:form>
12.       <h:dataTable value="#{tableData.names}" var="name">
13.         <h:column>
14.           <f:facet name="header">
15.             <h:outputText value="#{msgs.editColumn}"
16.                         style="font-weight: bold"/>
17.           </f:facet>
18.           <h:selectBooleanCheckbox value="#{name.editable}" onclick="submit()"/>
19.         </h:column>
20.         <h:column>
21.           <f:facet name="header">
22.             <h:outputText value="#{msgs.lastnameColumn}"
23.                         style="font-weight: bold"/>
24.           </f:facet>
25.           <h:inputText value="#{name.last}" rendered="#{name.editable}"
26.                       size="10"/>
27.           <h:outputText value="#{name.last}" rendered="#{not name.editable}"/>
28.         </h:column>
29.         <h:column>
30.           <f:facet name="header">
31.             <h:outputText value="#{msgs.firstnameColumn}"
32.                         style="font-weight: bold"/>
33.           </f:facet>
34.           <h:inputText value="#{name.first}" rendered="#{name.editable}"
35.                       size="10"/>
36.           <h:outputText value="#{name.first}" rendered="#{not name.editable}"/>
37.         </h:column>
38.       </h:dataTable>
39.       <h:commandButton value="#{msgs.saveChangesButtonText}"
40.                       action="#{tableData.save}"/>
41.     </h:form>
42.   </h:body>
43. </html>
```

NOTE: Table cell editing, as illustrated in the preceding section, works for all valid types of table data: Java objects, arrays, lists, result sets, and results. However, a database result set associated with a table must be *updatable* for the JSF implementation to update the database.

Deleting Rows JSF 2.0

When deleting or adding rows, it would be tedious to use an array to collect the row data. Use a list instead. We will simply use an ArrayList<Name> in our example.

Our sample application shows a link labeled "Delete" next to each row—see Figure 6–10. As in the editing example, there must be some way of finding out which row the user selected. In that example, we added an editable property to the Name class. That made the code quite simple, but it is not always a workable approach. If the Name class comes from the business logic of your application, you can't simply add properties to that class.

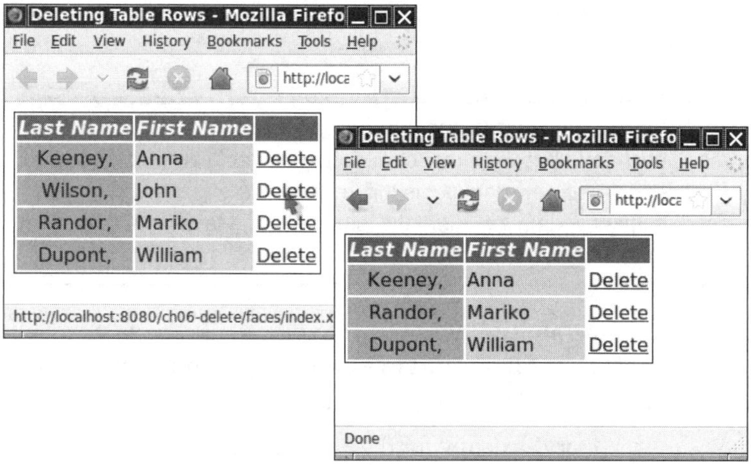

Figure 6–10   Deleting table rows

Instead, we want each link to identify the row to be deleted. In some web frameworks, you might craft links of the form /delete/*rowNumber* or delete?id=*someId*. You can do this in JSF, but since JSF 2.0, there is a much easier way. You simply pass the row item to the action method:

```
<h:dataTable value="#{tableData.names}" var="name" ...>
   ...
   <h:commandLink value="Delete" action="#{tableData.deleteRow(name)}">
   ...
</h:dataTable>
```

When the link is clicked, the deleteRow method is called with the current value of name, and the value is removed:

```
public String deleteRow(Name nameToDelete) {
   names.remove(nameToDelete);
   return null;
}
```

Note that we do not require that Name objects have IDs. We simply use the object itself. Of course, that object is not sent back and forth between the browser and the server. Instead, each component in a data table has an ID that contains its row number. These IDs are automatically generated when the data table is rendered. When a link is activated, its ID is sent to the server. When decoding the response, the data table loops again over the values, setting the name variable and regenerating the link IDs. When the matching link is encountered, its decode method is activated, and evaluates the expression #{tableData.deleteRow(name)} with the current value.

CAUTION: If the value of a data table has *request scope*, be sure that the data does not change between the rendering of the table and the decoding of the response. If the new data set is different, then the wrong row will be processed. If the new data set is empty, then no action takes place at all because no matching link is encountered.

Our example does not illustrate adding rows, but you can use the same idea to extend it. Provide "Add above" links next to each element, and then provide an additional link to add a row below the last one.

Figure 6–11 shows the directory structure for the application. Listings 6–8 and 6–9 provide the JSF page and the managed bean.

- 📁 **delete.war**
  - 📄 index.xhtml
  - ▼ 📁 WEB-INF
    - 📄 beans.xml
    - 📄 faces-config.xml
    - 📄 web.xml
    - ▼ 📁 classes
      - ▼ 📁 com
        - ▼ 📁 corejsf
          - 📄 Name.class
          - 📄 TableData.class
          - 📄 messages.properties
  - ▼ 📁 resources
    - ▼ 📁 css
      - 📄 styles.css

Figure 6–11   The directory structure for the delete example

Listing 6–8   delete/web/index.xhtml

```
1. <?xml version="1.0" encoding="UTF-8"?>
2. <!DOCTYPE html PUBLIC "-//W3C//DTD XHTML 1.0 Transitional//EN"
3. "http://www.w3.org/TR/xhtml1/DTD/xhtml1-transitional.dtd">
4. <html xmlns="http://www.w3.org/1999/xhtml"
5.       xmlns:ui="http://java.sun.com/jsf/facelets"
6.       xmlns:f="http://java.sun.com/jsf/core"
7.       xmlns:h="http://java.sun.com/jsf/html">
8.   <h:head>
9.     <h:outputStylesheet library="css" name="styles.css"/>
10.    <title>#{msgs.windowTitle}</title>
11.   </h:head>
12.   <h:body>
13.     <h:form>
14.       <h:dataTable value="#{tableData.names}" var="name" styleClass="names"
15.                   headerClass="namesHeader" columnClasses="last,first">
16.         <h:column>
17.           <f:facet name="header">#{msgs.lastColumnHeader}</f:facet>
18.           #{name.last},
19.         </h:column>
20.         <h:column>
21.           <f:facet name="header">#{msgs.firstColumnHeader}</f:facet>
22.           #{name.first}
23.         </h:column>
24.         <h:column>
25.           <h:commandLink value="Delete"
```

```
26.                              action="#{tableData.deleteRow(name)}"/>
27.          </h:column>
28.        </h:dataTable>
29.      </h:form>
30.    </h:body>
31. </html>
```

Listing 6–9	delete/src/java/com/corejsf/TableData.java

```
 1. package com.corejsf;
 2.
 3. import java.io.Serializable;
 4. import java.util.ArrayList;
 5. import java.util.Arrays;
 6.
 7. import javax.inject.Named;
 8.    // or import javax.faces.bean.ManagedBean;
 9. import javax.enterprise.context.SessionScoped;
10.    // or import javax.faces.bean.SessionScoped;
11.
12. @Named // or @ManagedBean
13. @SessionScoped
14. public class TableData implements Serializable {
15.    private ArrayList<Name> names = new ArrayList<Name>(Arrays.asList(
16.       new Name("Anna", "Keeney"),
17.       new Name("John", "Wilson"),
18.       new Name("Mariko", "Randor"),
19.       new Name("William", "Dupont")
20.    ));
21.
22.    public ArrayList<Name> getNames() {
23.       return names;
24.    }
25.
26.    public String deleteRow(Name nameToDelete) {
27.       names.remove(nameToDelete);
28.       return null;
29.    }
30. }
```

Database Tables

Databases store information in tables, so the JSF data table component is a good fit for showing data stored in a database. In this section, we show you how to display the results of a database query.

Figure 6–12 shows a JSF application that displays a database table.

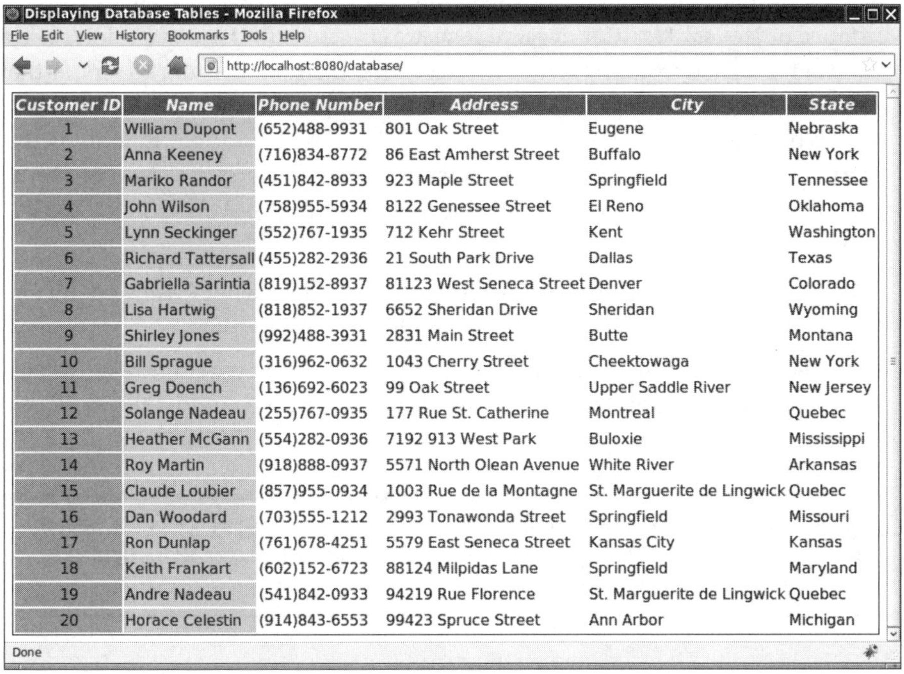

Customer ID	Name	Phone Number	Address	City	State
1	William Dupont	(652)488-9931	801 Oak Street	Eugene	Nebraska
2	Anna Keeney	(716)834-8772	86 East Amherst Street	Buffalo	New York
3	Mariko Randor	(451)842-8933	923 Maple Street	Springfield	Tennessee
4	John Wilson	(758)955-5934	8122 Genessee Street	El Reno	Oklahoma
5	Lynn Seckinger	(552)767-1935	712 Kehr Street	Kent	Washington
6	Richard Tattersall	(455)282-2936	21 South Park Drive	Dallas	Texas
7	Gabriella Sarintia	(819)152-8937	81123 West Seneca Street	Denver	Colorado
8	Lisa Hartwig	(818)852-1937	6652 Sheridan Drive	Sheridan	Wyoming
9	Shirley Jones	(992)488-3931	2831 Main Street	Butte	Montana
10	Bill Sprague	(316)962-0632	1043 Cherry Street	Cheektowaga	New York
11	Greg Doench	(136)692-6023	99 Oak Street	Upper Saddle River	New Jersey
12	Solange Nadeau	(255)767-0935	177 Rue St. Catherine	Montreal	Quebec
13	Heather McGann	(554)282-0936	7192 913 West Park	Buloxie	Mississippi
14	Roy Martin	(918)888-0937	5571 North Olean Avenue	White River	Arkansas
15	Claude Loubier	(857)955-0934	1003 Rue de la Montagne	St. Marguerite de Lingwick	Quebec
16	Dan Woodard	(703)555-1212	2993 Tonawonda Street	Springfield	Missouri
17	Ron Dunlap	(761)678-4251	5579 East Seneca Street	Kansas City	Kansas
18	Keith Frankart	(602)152-6723	88124 Milpidas Lane	Springfield	Maryland
19	Andre Nadeau	(541)842-0933	94219 Rue Florence	St. Marguerite de Lingwick	Quebec
20	Horace Celestin	(914)843-6553	99423 Spruce Street	Ann Arbor	Michigan

Figure 6–12 Displaying database tables

The JSF page shown in Figure 6–12 uses `h:dataTable`, like this:

```
<h:dataTable value="#{customerBean.all}" var="customer"
   styleClass="customers"
   headerClass="customersHeader"
   columnClasses="custid,name">
      <h:column>
      <f:facet name="header">#{msgs.customerIdHeader}</f:facet>
      #{customer.Cust_ID}
   </h:column>
   <h:column>
      <f:facet name="header">#{msgs.nameHeader}</f:facet>
      #{customer.Name}
   </h:column>
   ...
</h:dataTable>
```

The `customerBean` is a managed bean that knows how to connect to a database and perform a query of all customers in the database. The `CustomerBean.all` method performs that query.

When working with a database, the value you specify for h:dataTable is an instance of java.sql.ResultSet or javax.servlet.jsp.jstl.Result. However, don't use a result set returned from the Statement.executeQuery method. In order to render that result set, the underlying database connection has to stay open. But then you don't have a chance to close it. A better way is to use a wrapper that holds the query result, such as javax.sql.CachedRowSet or javax.servlet.jsp.jstl.Result (which was invented before CachedRowSet became a part of Java 5). We use a CachedRowSet in our example.

The preceding JSF page accesses column data by referencing column names—for example, #{customer.Cust_ID} references the Cust_ID column.

The directory structure for the database example is shown in Figure 6–13. The web page and managed bean for the application are given in Listings 6–10 and 6–11.

NOTE: Here we assume that you are familiar with setting up a data source with your application server. If not, please turn to Chapter 12 for detailed information.

Figure 6–13   Directory structure for the database example

Listing 6–10   database/web/index.xhtml

```
1. <?xml version="1.0" encoding="UTF-8"?>
2. <!DOCTYPE html PUBLIC "-//W3C//DTD XHTML 1.0 Transitional//EN"
3. "http://www.w3.org/TR/xhtml1/DTD/xhtml1-transitional.dtd">
4. <html xmlns="http://www.w3.org/1999/xhtml"
5.       xmlns:f="http://java.sun.com/jsf/core"
6.       xmlns:h="http://java.sun.com/jsf/html">
7.   <h:head>
8.     <h:outputStylesheet library="css" name="styles.css"/>
9.     <title>#{msgs.pageTitle}</title>
10.   </h:head>
11.   <h:body>
12.     <h:form>
13.       <h:dataTable value="#{customerBean.all}" var="customer"
14.                    styleClass="customers" headerClass="customersHeader"
15.                    columnClasses="custid,name">
16.         <h:column>
17.           <f:facet name="header">#{msgs.customerIdHeader}</f:facet>
18.           #{customer.Cust_ID}
19.         </h:column>
20.         <h:column>
21.           <f:facet name="header">#{msgs.nameHeader}</f:facet>
22.           #{customer.Name}
23.         </h:column>
24.         <h:column>
25.           <f:facet name="header">#{msgs.phoneHeader}</f:facet>
26.           #{customer.Phone_Number}
27.         </h:column>
28.         <h:column>
29.           <f:facet name="header">#{msgs.addressHeader}</f:facet>
30.           #{customer.Street_Address}
31.         </h:column>
32.         <h:column>
33.           <f:facet name="header">#{msgs.cityHeader}</f:facet>
34.           #{customer.City}
35.         </h:column>
36.         <h:column>
37.           <f:facet name="header">#{msgs.stateHeader}</f:facet>
38.           #{customer.State}
39.         </h:column>
40.       </h:dataTable>
41.     </h:form>
42.   </h:body>
43. </html>
```

| Listing 6–11 | database/src/java/com/corejsf/CustomerBean.java |

```java
1. package com.corejsf;
2.
3. import java.sql.Connection;
4. import java.sql.ResultSet;
5. import java.sql.SQLException;
6. import java.sql.Statement;
7.
8. import javax.annotation.Resource;
9. import javax.inject.Named;
10.    // or import javax.faces.bean.ManagedBean;
11. import javax.enterprise.context.RequestScoped;
12.    // or import javax.faces.bean.RequestScoped;
13. import javax.sql.DataSource;
14. import javax.sql.rowset.CachedRowSet;
15.
16. @Named // or @ManagedBean
17. @RequestScoped
18. public class CustomerBean {
19.    @Resource(name="jdbc/mydb")
20.    private DataSource ds;
21.
22.    public ResultSet getAll() throws SQLException {
23.       Connection conn = ds.getConnection();
24.       try {
25.          Statement stmt = conn.createStatement();
26.          ResultSet result = stmt.executeQuery("SELECT * FROM Customers");
27.          // return ResultSupport.toResult(result);
28.          CachedRowSet crs = new com.sun.rowset.CachedRowSetImpl();
29.             // or use an implementation from your database vendor
30.          crs.populate(result);
31.          return crs;
32.       } finally {
33.          conn.close();
34.       }
35.    }
36. }
```

Table Models

When you use a Java object, array, list, result set, or JSTL result object to represent table data, h:dataTable wraps those objects in a model that extends the javax.faces.model.DataModel class. All of those model classes, listed below, reside in the javax.faces.model package:

- ArrayDataModel
- ListDataModel
- ResultDataModel
- ResultSetDataModel
- ScalarDataModel

You don't usually need to know about the model when you use an h:dataTable, but in the following sections, we show you three problems that can be solved by accessing the model: rendering row numbers, finding the row that a user selected, and sorting table rows.

Rendering Row Numbers

Suppose you want to render row numbers, like this:

	Last Name	First Name
1	Keeney,	Anna
2	Wilson,	John
3	Randor,	Mariko
4	Dupont,	William

The JSF data table does not have an easy mechanism for producing these numbers. You display different content in each row by using the variable declared with the var attribute. That variable contains the row data, but not the line number (unless each row value happens to have the line number).

However, the DataModel class has a method getRowIndex that yields the current row number. You can access this method from a JSF page, as long as your application provides a table model instead of a collection. For example, you can change the TableData class as follows:

```
public class TableData implements Serializable {
   private static final Name[] names = new Name[] {
      new Name("William", "Dupont"),
      new Name("Anna", "Keeney"),
      new Name("Mariko", "Randor"),
      new Name("John", "Wilson")
   };
   private DataModel<Name> model = new ArrayDataModel<Name>(names);
   public DataModel<Name> getNames() { return model; }
}
```

Note that the getNames method returns a DataModel<Name> instead of a Name[] array.

Then add a column:

```
<h:dataTable value="#{tableData.names}" var="name">
   <h:column>#{tableData.names.rowIndex + 1}</h:column>
   <h:column>#{name.last},</h:column>
   <h:column>#{name.first}</h:column>
</h:dataTable>
```

This technique has one significant disadvantage: it ties your managed beans to the JSF API. See "The ui:repeat Tag" on page 217 for an alternative approach.

Finding the Selected Row

Another reason to expose the DataModel instead of the underlying collection is to find the selected row in an action or action listener. Consider again the example "Deleting Rows" on page 225, with a link in a data table:

```
<h:dataTable value="#{tableData.names}" var="name">
   ...
   <h:commandLink value="Delete" action="{tableData.deleteRow}"/>
   ...
</h:dataTable>
```

In the deleteRow method, you want to know which row contains the link that the user selected. We previously solved this problem by passing the row value as a parameter: action="{tableData.deleteRow(name)}".

However, prior to JSF 2.0, it was not posssible to pass parameters to an action method. Instead, you can retrieve the current item by calling the getRowData method of the DataModel class. For example:

```
public String deleteRow() {
   Name nameToDelete = model.getRowData();
   names.remove(nameToDelete);
   return null;
}
```

Sorting and Filtering

To sort or filter tables with h:dataTable, you need to implement a table model that decorates one of the table models listed on page 233. Figure 6–14 shows what it means to decorate a table model.

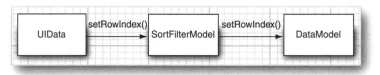

Figure 6–14   Data model filter

When the JSF implementation renders or decodes table data, it invokes methods on the table model. When you decorate that model, your model intercepts those method calls, giving the illusion that the data is sorted.

Figure 6–15 shows our basic table rewritten to support sortable table columns.

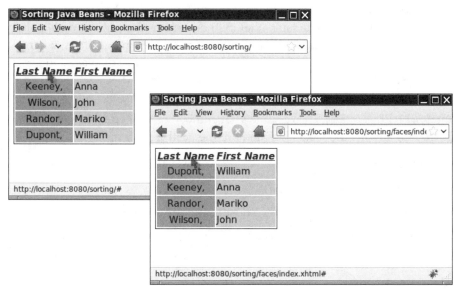

Figure 6–15   Sorting table columns

The application sorts table columns by decorating a table data model. First, we specify the h:dataTable's value attribute, like this:

```
<h:dataTable value="#{tableData.names}" var="name" ...>
```

The TableData.names method returns a data model:

```
public class TableData {
   private SortFilterModel<Name> filterModel;
   private static final Name[] names = {
      new Name("Anna", "Keeney"),
      new Name("John", "Wilson"),
      new Name("Mariko", "Randor"),
      new Name("William", "Dupont"),
   };

   public TableData() {
      filterModel = new SortFilterModel<Name>(new ArrayDataModel(names));
   }
   public DataModel<Name> getNames() {
```

```
            return filterModel;
        }
    }
```

When the `tableData` object is created, it creates an `ArrayDataModel` instance, passing it the array of names. That is the *original* model. Then the `TableData` constructor wraps that model in a *sorting* model. When the `getNames` method is subsequently called to populate the data table, that method returns the sorting model. The sorting model contains a regular model and an array of integers `rows`, where `rows[i]` indicates the index of the model data that should be displayed in the *i*th row. To sort the array in different ways, we sort the row indexes.

To understand the implementation details, you need to know a bit about the `DataModel` API. A `DataModel` has a somewhat cumbersome interface to get at a data item. First invoke the `setRowIndex` method, then call `getRowData`:

```
DataModel<Name> model = ...;
model.setRowIndex(currentIndex);
Name current = model.getRowData();
```

We intercept the call to `setRowIndex`, substituting the sorted index:

```
public class SortFilterModel<E> extends DataModel<E> {
    private DataModel<E> model;
    private Integer[] rows;
    ...
    public SortFilterModel(DataModel<E> model) {
        this.model = model;
        initializeRows();
    }
    private void initializeRows() {
        int rowCnt = model.getRowCount();
        if (rowCnt != -1) {
            rows = new Integer[rowCnt];
            for(int i = 0; i < rowCnt; i++) rows[i] = i;
        }
    }
    public void setRowIndex(int rowIndex) {
        if (0 <= rowIndex && rowIndex < model.getRowCount())
            model.setRowIndex(rows[i]);
        else
            model.setRowIndex(rowIndex);
    }
    ...
}
```

To sort, the caller needs to supply a data comparator. The sort filter model uses that comparator to rearrange the row index array. You can see the details in Listing 6–13 on page 238. (You may wonder why we used Integer instead of int for the rows. The reason is that we can use Arrays.sort with a custom comparator only for an Integer[] array, not for an int[] array.)

The directory structure for the sorting example is shown in Figure 6–16. Listings 6–12 through 6–14 provide the JSF page, sorting model, and the managed bean.

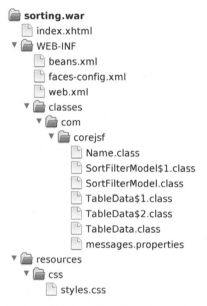

Figure 6–16   **The directory structure for the sorting example**

NOTE: The JSF specification recommends that concrete DataModel classes provide at least two constructors: a no-argument constructor that calls setWrappedData(null) and a constructor that passes wrapped data to setWrappedData(). See Listing 6–13 on page 238 for an example of those constructors.

Listing 6–12   sorting/web/index.xhtml

```
1. <?xml version="1.0" encoding="UTF-8"?>
2. <!DOCTYPE html PUBLIC "-//W3C//DTD XHTML 1.0 Transitional//EN"
3. "http://www.w3.org/TR/xhtml1/DTD/xhtml1-transitional.dtd">
4. <html xmlns="http://www.w3.org/1999/xhtml"
5.       xmlns:f="http://java.sun.com/jsf/core"
6.       xmlns:h="http://java.sun.com/jsf/html">
7.    <h:head>
8.       <h:outputStylesheet library="css" name="styles.css"/>
9.       <title>#{msgs.windowTitle}</title>
10.   </h:head>
11.   <h:body>
12.      <h:form>
13.         <h:dataTable value="#{tableData.names}" var="name" styleClass="names"
14.                     headerClass="namesHeader" columnClasses="last,first">
15.            <h:column>
16.               <f:facet name="header">
17.                  <h:commandLink action="#{tableData.sortByLast}">
18.                     #{msgs.lastColumnHeader}
19.                  </h:commandLink>
20.               </f:facet>
21.               #{name.last},
22.            </h:column>
23.            <h:column>
24.               <f:facet name="header">
25.                  <h:commandLink action="#{tableData.sortByFirst}">
26.                     #{msgs.firstColumnHeader}
27.                  </h:commandLink>
28.               </f:facet>
29.               #{name.first}
30.            </h:column>
31.         </h:dataTable>
32.      </h:form>
33.   </h:body>
34. </html>
```

Listing 6–13   sorting/src/java/com/corejsf/SortFilterModel.java

```
1. package com.corejsf;
2.
3. import java.util.Arrays;
4. import java.util.Comparator;
5.
6. import javax.faces.model.DataModel;
7.
```

```
8. public class SortFilterModel<E> extends DataModel<E> {
9.     private DataModel<E> model;
10.    private Integer[] rows;
11.
12.    public SortFilterModel() { // mandated by JSF spec
13.        setWrappedData(null);
14.    }
15.    public SortFilterModel(E[] names) { // recommended by JSF spec
16.        setWrappedData(names);
17.    }
18.    public SortFilterModel(DataModel<E> model) {
19.        this.model = model;
20.        initializeRows();
21.    }
22.
23.    private E getData(int row) {
24.        int originalIndex = model.getRowIndex();
25.        model.setRowIndex(row);
26.        E thisRowData = model.getRowData();
27.        model.setRowIndex(originalIndex);
28.        return thisRowData;
29.    }
30.
31.    public void sortBy(final Comparator<E> dataComp) {
32.        Comparator<Integer> rowComp = new
33.        Comparator<Integer>() {
34.            public int compare(Integer r1, Integer r2) {
35.                E e1 = getData(r1);
36.                E e2 = getData(r2);
37.                return dataComp.compare(e1, e2);
38.            }
39.        };
40.        Arrays.sort(rows, rowComp);
41.    }
42.
43.    public void setRowIndex(int rowIndex) {
44.        if (0 <= rowIndex && rowIndex < rows.length)
45.            model.setRowIndex(rows[rowIndex]);
46.        else
47.            model.setRowIndex(rowIndex);
48.    }
49.
50.    // The following methods delegate to the decorated model
51.
52.    public boolean isRowAvailable() {
53.        return model.isRowAvailable();
54.    }
```

```
55.    public int getRowCount() {
56.        return model.getRowCount();
57.    }
58.    public E getRowData() {
59.        return model.getRowData();
60.    }
61.    public int getRowIndex() {
62.        return model.getRowIndex();
63.    }
64.    public Object getWrappedData() {
65.        return model.getWrappedData();
66.    }
67.    public void setWrappedData(Object data) {
68.        model.setWrappedData(data);
69.        initializeRows();
70.    }
71.    private void initializeRows() {
72.        int rowCnt = model.getRowCount();
73.        if (rowCnt != -1) {
74.            rows = new Integer[rowCnt];
75.            for(int i = 0; i < rowCnt; ++i) rows[i] = i;
76.        }
77.    }
78. }
```

Listing 6–14 sorting/src/java/com/corejsf/TableData.java

```
1. package com.corejsf;
2.
3. import java.io.Serializable;
4. import java.util.Comparator;
5.
6. import javax.inject.Named;
7.    // or import javax.faces.bean.ManagedBean;
8. import javax.enterprise.context.SessionScoped;
9.    // or import javax.faces.bean.SessionScoped;
10. import javax.faces.model.DataModel;
11. import javax.faces.model.ArrayDataModel;
12.
13. @Named // or @ManagedBean
14. @SessionScoped
15. public class TableData implements Serializable {
16.    private SortFilterModel<Name> filterModel;
17.    private static final Name[] names = {
18.        new Name("Anna", "Keeney"),
19.        new Name("John", "Wilson"),
```

```
20.       new Name("Mariko", "Randor"),
21.       new Name("William", "Dupont"),
22.    };
23.
24.    public TableData() {
25.       filterModel = new SortFilterModel<Name>(new ArrayDataModel<Name>(names));
26.    }
27.    public DataModel<Name> getNames() {
28.       return filterModel;
29.    }
30.
31.    public String sortByFirst() {
32.       filterModel.sortBy(new Comparator<Name>() {
33.          public int compare(Name n1, Name n2) {
34.             return n1.getFirst().compareTo(n2.getFirst());
35.          }
36.       });
37.       return null;
38.    }
39.
40.    public String sortByLast() {
41.       filterModel.sortBy(new Comparator<Name>() {
42.          public int compare(Name n1, Name n2) {
43.             return n1.getLast().compareTo(n2.getLast());
44.          }
45.       });
46.       return null;
47.    }
48. }
```

API `javax.faces.model.DataModel<E>`

- `int getRowCount()`
  Returns the total number of rows, if known; otherwise, it returns –1. The `ResultSetDataModel` always returns –1 from this method.

- `int getRowIndex()`
  Returns the index of the current row.

- `void setRowIndex(int index)`
  Sets the current row index and updates the scoped variable representing the current item in the collection (that variable is specified with the `var` attribute of `h:dataTable`).

- `E getRowData()`
  Returns the data associated with the current row.

- `boolean isRowAvailable()`
  Returns true if there is valid data at the current row index.
- `Iterator<E> iterator()` **JSF 2.0**
  Returns an iterator that visits all rows.
- `void addDataModelListener(DataModelListener listener)`
  Adds a data model listener that is notified when the row index changes.
- `void removeDataModelListener(DataModelListener listener)`
  Removes a data model listener.
- `void setWrappedData(Object obj)`
  Sets the object that a data model wraps.
- `Object getWrappedData()`
  Returns a data model's wrapped data.

Scrolling Techniques

There are two ways to scroll through tables with lots of rows: with a scrollbar or with some other type of control that moves through the rows. We explore both techniques in this section.

Scrolling with a Scrollbar

Scrolling with a scrollbar is the simplest solution. Wrap your h:dataTable in an HTML div, like this:

```
<div style="overflow:auto; width:100%; height:200px;">
   <h:dataTable...>
      <h:column>
         ...
      </h:column>
      ...
   </h:dataTable>
</div>
```

The application shown in Figure 6–17 is identical to the application discussed in "Database Tables" on page 228, except that the data table is placed in a scrollable div, as shown above.

Scrollbars are nice from a usability standpoint, but they can be expensive for large tables because all the table data is loaded at once. A less resource-intensive alternative is to scroll through tables with pager widgets, an approach that requires only one page of data at a time.

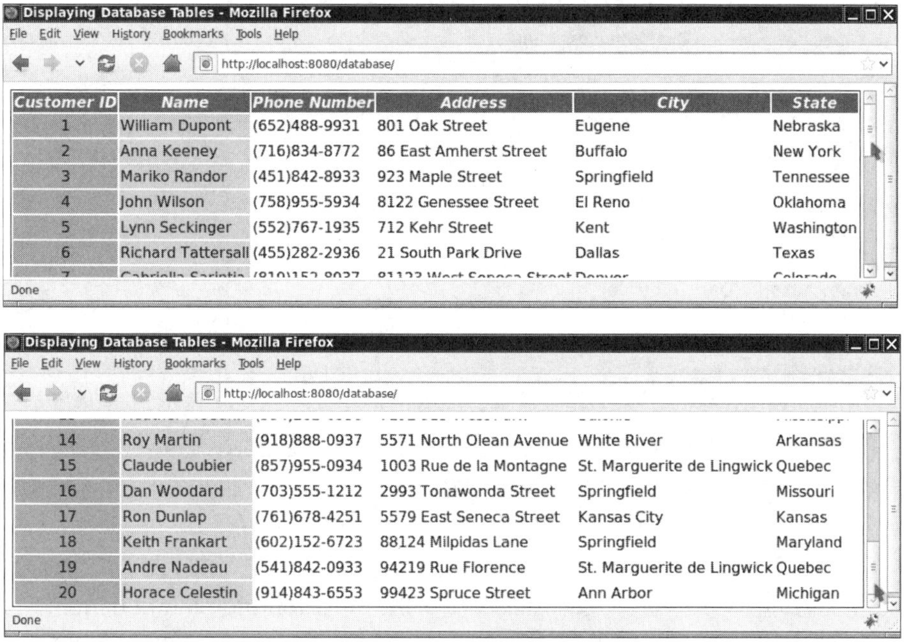

Figure 6–17   Scrolling a table with a scrollable div

Scrolling with Pager Widgets

Scrolling with pager widgets is more efficient than scrolling with a scrollable div, but it is also considerably more complex. In Chapter 13, we show you how to implement a pager widget that you can use with any table created with h:dataTable (see "How do I show a large data set, one page at a time?" on page 568 of Chapter 13). Figure 6–18 shows an example of that pager.

The application shown in Figure 6–18 uses a data table that displays the ISO country codes for locales. We obtain that list by calling java.util.Locale.getISO-Countries(), a static method that returns an array of strings.

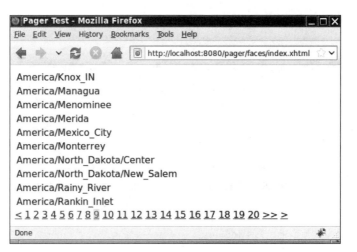

Figure 6–18   Scrolling with a JSF pager

Conclusion

You have now seen how to use h:dataTable, the most complex component in the standard JSF component set. In the next chapter, we show you how your application can react to user and system events.

CONVERSION AND VALIDATION

Chapter

In this chapter, we discuss how form data is converted to Java objects and how the conversion results are checked for correctness. The JSF container carries out these steps before updating the model, so you can rest assured that invalid inputs will never end up in the business logic.

We first look at the concepts behind the conversion and validation process. Then we discuss the standard tags that JSF provides for conversion and validation. These tags suffice for the most common needs. Next, you see how to supply your own conversion and validation code for more complex scenarios.

It is also possible to implement custom tags—reusable converters and validators that can be configured by page authors. However, implementing custom tags requires significantly more programming. We cover the necessary techniques in the last part of this chapter.

Overview of the Conversion and Validation Process

Let us look at user input in slow motion as it travels from the browser form to the beans that make up the business logic.

First, the user fills in a field of a web form. When the user clicks the submit button, the browser sends the value to the server, using an HTTP request. We call this value the *request value*.

In the Apply Request Values phase, the JSF implementation stores the request values in component objects. (Recall that each input tag of the JSF page has a corresponding component object.) A value stored in the component object is called a *submitted value*.

Of course, all request values are *strings*—after all, the client browser sends the strings that the user supplies. On the other hand, the web application deals with arbitrary types, such as int, Date, or even more sophisticated types. A *conversion* process transforms the incoming strings to those types. In the next section, we discuss conversion in detail.

The converted values are not immediately transmitted to the beans that make up the business logic. Instead, they are first stored inside the component objects as *local values*. After conversion, the local values are *validated*. Application designers can specify validation conditions—for example, that certain fields should have a minimum or maximum length. We begin our discussion of validation under "Using Standard Validators" on page 262. After all local values have been validated, the Update Model Values phase starts, and the local values are stored in beans, as specified by their value references.

You may wonder why JSF bothers with local values at all. Could not one simply store the request values directly in the model?

JSF uses a two-step approach to make it easier to preserve model integrity. As all programmers know only too well, users enter wrong information with distressing regularity. Suppose some of the model values had been updated before the first user error was detected. The model might then be in an inconsistent state, and it would be tedious to bring it back to its old state.

For that reason, JSF first converts and validates all user input. If errors are found, the page is redisplayed with the values that the user entered so that the user can try again. The Update Model Values phase starts only if all validations are successful.

Figure 7–1 shows the journey of a field value from the browser to the server-side component object and finally to the model bean.

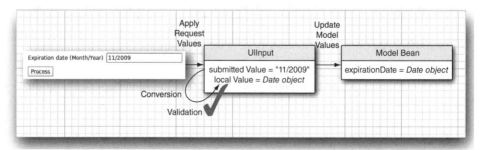

Figure 7–1 A value travels from the browser to the model

Using Standard Converters

In the first part of this chapter, we cover the converters and validators that are part of the JSF library.

Conversion of Numbers and Dates

A web application stores data of many types, but the web user interface deals exclusively with strings. For example, suppose the user needs to edit a Date object that is stored in the business logic. First, the Date object is converted to a string that is sent to the client browser to be displayed inside a text field. The user then edits the text field. The resulting string is returned to the server and must be converted back to a Date object.

The same situation holds, of course, for primitive types, such as int, double, or boolean. The user of the web application edits strings, and the JSF container needs to convert the string to the type required by the application.

To see a typical use of a built-in converter, imagine a web application that processes payments (see Figure 7–2). The payment data includes:

- The amount to be charged
- The credit card number
- The credit card expiration date

Figure 7–2   Processing payments

We attach a converter to the text field and tell it to format the current value with at least two digits after the decimal point:

```
<h:inputText value="#{payment.amount}">
  <f:convertNumber minFractionDigits="2"/>
</h:inputText>
```

The f:convertNumber converter is one of the standard converters supplied by the JSF implementation.

The second field in this screen does not use a converter. (Later in this chapter, we attach a custom converter.) The third field uses an f:convertDateTime converter whose pattern attribute is set to the string MM/yyyy. (The pattern string format is documented in the API documentation for the java.text.SimpleDateFormat class.)

```
<h:inputText value="#{payment.date}">
  <f:convertDateTime pattern="MM/yyyy"/>
</h:inputText>
```

In the result.xhtml page, we show the inputs that the user provided, using a different converter for the payment amount:

```
<h:outputText value="#{payment.amount}">
  <f:convertNumber type="currency"/>
</h:outputText>
```

This converter automatically supplies a currency symbol and decimal separators (see Figure 7–3).

Figure 7–3   Displaying the payment information

Converters and Attributes

Tables 7–1 and 7–2 show the standard converters and their attributes.

> NOTE: If you use a value expression whose type is either a primitive type, or, starting with JSF 1.2, an enumerated type or BigInteger/BigDecimal, then you do not need to specify any converter. The JSF implementation automatically picks a standard converter. However, you need to specify an explicit converter for Date values.

Table 7–1 Attributes of the f:convertNumber Tag

Attribute	Type	Value
type	String	number (default), currency, or percent
pattern	String	Formatting pattern, as defined in java.text.DecimalFormat
maxFractionDigits	int	Maximum number of digits in the fractional part
minFractionDigits	int	Minimum number of digits in the fractional part
maxIntegerDigits	int	Maximum number of digits in the integer part
minIntegerDigits	int	Minimum number of digits in the integer part
integerOnly	boolean	True if only the integer part is parsed (default: false)
groupingUsed	boolean	True if grouping separators are used (default: true)
locale	java.util.Locale or String	Locale whose preferences are to be used for parsing and formatting
currencyCode	String	ISO 4217 currency code, such as USD or EUR, for selecting a currency converter
currencySymbol	String	This string is passed to DecimalFormat.setDecimalFormatSymbols, overriding the locale-based symbol; not recommended—use currencyCode instead

Table 7–2   **Attributes of the** `f:convertDateTime` **Tag**

Attribute	Type	Value
type	String	date (default), time, or both
dateStyle	String	default, short, medium, long, or full
timeStyle	String	default, short, medium, long, or full
pattern	String	Formatting pattern, as defined in java.text.SimpleDateFormat
locale	java.util.Locale or String	Locale whose preferences are to be used for parsing and formatting
timeZone	java.util.TimeZone	Time zone to use for parsing and formatting; if you do not supply a time zone, the default is GMT Note: As of JSF 2.0, you can change the default to TimeZone.getDefault() by setting javax.faces.DATETIMECONVERTER _DEFAULT_TIMEZONE_IS_SYSTEM_TIMEZONE to true in web.xml.

The converter Attribute

An alternate syntax for attaching a converter to a component is to add the converter attribute to the component tag. You specify the ID of the converter like this:

```
<h:outputText value="#{payment.date}" converter="javax.faces.DateTime"/>
```

This is equivalent to using `f:convertDateTime` with no attributes:

```
<h:outputText value="#{payment.date}">
   <f:convertDateTime/>
</h:outputText>
```

A third way of specifying the converter would be as follows:

```
<h:outputText value="#{payment.date}">
   <f:converter converterId="javax.faces.DateTime"/>
</h:outputText>
```

All JSF implementations must define a set of converters with predefined IDs:

- javax.faces.DateTime (used by f:convertDateTime)
- javax.faces.Number (used by f:convertNumber)

- `javax.faces.Boolean, javax.faces.Byte, javax.faces.Character, javax.faces.Double, javax.faces.Float, javax.faces.Integer, javax.faces.Long, javax.faces.Short` (automatically used for primitive types and their wrapper classes)
- `javax.faces.BigDecimal, javax.faces.BigInteger` (automatically used for `BigDecimal`/`BigInteger`)

Additional converter IDs can be configured in an application configuration file (see "Specifying Converters" on page 279 for details).

 CAUTION: When the value of the `converter` attribute is a string, then the value indicates the ID of a converter. However, if it is a value expression, then its value must be a *converter object*—an object of a class that implements the `Converter` interface. That interface is introduced under "Implementing Custom Converter Classes" on page 275.

NOTE: As of JSF 1.2, the `f:convertNumber`, `f:convertDateTime`, and `f:converter` tags have an optional `binding` attribute. This allows you to tie a converter instance to a backing bean property of type `javax.faces.convert.Converter`.

Conversion Errors

When a conversion error occurs, the JSF implementation carries out the following actions:

- The component whose conversion failed posts a *message* and declares itself invalid. (You will see in the following sections how to display the message.)
- The JSF implementation redisplays the current page immediately after the Process Validations phase has completed. The redisplayed page contains all values that the user provided—no user input is lost.

This behavior is generally desirable. If a user provides an illegal input for, say, a field that requires an integer, then the web application should not try to use that illegal input. The JSF implementation automatically redisplays the current page, giving the user another chance to enter the value correctly.

However, you should avoid overly restrictive conversion options for *input* fields. For example, consider the "Amount" field in our example. Had we used a currency format, then the current value would have been nicely formatted. But suppose a user enters 100 (without a leading $ sign). The currency formatter will complain that the input is not a legal currency value. That is too strict for human use.

To overcome this problem, you can program a custom converter. A custom converter can format a value prettily, yet be lenient when interpreting human input. Custom converters are described in the section "Implementing Custom Converter Classes" on page 275.

TIP: When gathering input from the user, you should either use a lenient converter or redesign your form to be more user friendly. For example, rather than forcing users to format the expiration date as MM/yyyy, you can supply two input fields, one for the month and another for the year.

Displaying Error Messages

You want your users to see the messages that are caused by conversion and validation errors. Add h:message tags whenever you use converters and validators.

Normally, you want to show the error messages next to the components that reported them (see Figure 7–4). Give an ID to the component and reference that ID in the h:message tag. As of JSF 1.2, you also need to supply a component label that is displayed in the error message:

```
<h:inputText id="amount" label="#{msgs.amount}" value="#{payment.amount}"/>
<h:message for="amount"/>
```

For JSF 1.1, omit the label attribute.

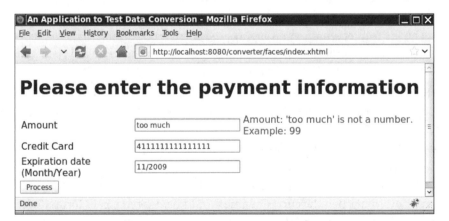

Figure 7–4   Displaying a conversion error message

The h:message tag takes a number of attributes to describe the appearance of the message (see "Messages" on page 171 of Chapter 4 for details). Here, we discuss only the attributes that are of particular interest for error reporting.

A message has two versions: *summary* and *detail*.

For the number converter, the detail error message shows the label of the component, the offending value, and a sample of a correct value, like this:

Amount: 'too much' is not a number. Example: 99

The summary message omits the example.

NOTE: In JSF 1.1, the converters displayed a generic message "Conversion error occurred."

By default, the h:message tag shows the detail and hides the summary. If you want to show the summary message instead, use these attributes:

```
<h:message for="amount" showSummary="true" showDetail="false"/>
```

CAUTION: If you use a standard converter, display either the summary message or the detail message, but not both—the messages are nearly identical. You do not want your users to ponder an error message that reads "...is not a number ... is not a number. Example: 99".

TIP: If you do not use an explicit f:convertNumber converter, but instead rely on the standard converters for numeric types, use the summary message and not the detail message. The detail messages give *far too much* detail. For example, the standard converter for double values has this detail message: "... must be a number between 4.9E-324 and 1.7976931348623157E308. Example: 1999999".

Usually, you will want to show error messages in a different color. You use the styleClass or style attribute to change the appearance of the error message:

```
<h:messages styleClass="errorMessage"/>
```

or

```
<h:message for="amount" style="color:red"/>
```

We recommend that you use styleClass and a stylesheet instead of a hardcoded style.

Of course, you can also place the message tags inside a div element and style that element with CSS.

Displaying All Error Messages

It is uncommon to have multiple messages for one component, but it can happen. The h:message tag produces only the *first* message. Unfortunately, you do not know whether the first message is the most useful one for the user. While no tag shows all messages for a particular component, you can show a listing of all messages from all components with the h:messages tag.

By default, the h:messages tag shows the message summary instead of the message detail. This behavior is opposite from that of the h:message tag.

The default value of the layout attribute for h:messages is "list", which yields an unnumbered list whose appearance you can control with a stylesheet. Alternatively, you can up the messages vertically by using:

```
<h:messages layout="table"/>
```

TIP: The h:messages tag is useful for debugging. Whenever your JSF application stalls at a particular page and is unwilling to move on, add an <h:messages/> tag to see if a failed conversion or validation is the culprit. In JSF 2.0, an <h:messages/> child is automatically added to the view if the project stage is set to Development.

CAUTION: In JSF 1.1, the default behavior was to concatenate all messages. Moreover, the error messages did not include the message label. That made the h:messages tag far less useful because users were left wondering which of their inputs caused an error.

Changing the Text of Standard Error Messages

Sometimes, you may want to change the standard conversion messages for your entire web application. Table 7–3 shows the most useful standard messages. Note that all detail message keys end in _detail. To save space, the table does not list separate summary and detail strings when the summary string is a substring of the detail string. Instead, the additional detail phrase is set in italics. In most messages, {0} is the invalid value, {1} is a sample valid value, and {2} is the component label; however, for the Boolean converter, {1} is the component label.

To replace a standard message, set up a message bundle, as explained in Chapter 2. Add the replacement message, using the appropriate key from Table 7–3.

Suppose you do not want to fuss with input labels or example values when the f:convertNumber converter reports an error. Add the following definition to a message bundle:

```
javax.faces.converter.NumberConverter.NUMBER_detail=''{0}'' is not a number.
```

Then set the base name of the bundle in a configuration file (such as faces-config.xml):

```
<faces-config>
  <application>
    <message-bundle>com.corejsf.messages</message-bundle>
  </application>
  ...
</faces-config>
```

You need only specify the messages that you want to override.

> NOTE: This message bundle is not the same as the resource bundles that are accessed with the resource-bundle tag in faces-config.xml. Those bundles are mapped to a variable that you can use in value expressions. The bundle referenced by the message-bundle tag is used for messages produced by the application.

Table 7–3   Standard Conversion Error Messages

Resource ID	Default Text
javax.faces.converter.IntegerConverter.INTEGER	{2}: "{0}" must be a number consisting of one or more digits.
javax.faces.converter.IntegerConverter.INTEGER_detail	{2}: "{0}" must be a number between -2147483648 and 2147483647. *Example: {1}*
javax.faces.converter.DoubleConverter.DOUBLE	{2}: "{0}" must be a number consisting of one or more digits.
javax.faces.converter.DoubleConverter.DOUBLE_detail	{2}: "{0}" must be a number between 4.9E-324 and 1.7976931348623157E308. *Example: {1}*

Table 7–3 Standard Conversion Error Messages (cont.)

Resource ID	Default Text
javax.faces.converter.BooleanConverter.BOOLEAN_detail	{1}: "{0}" must be 'true' or 'false'. *Any value other than 'true' will evaluate to 'false'.*
javax.faces.converter.BigDecimal-Converter.BIGINTEGER_detail	"{0}" must be a number consisting of one or more digits. *Example: {1}*
javax.faces.converter.BigDecimal-Converter.BIGDECIMAL_detail	"{0}" must be a signed decimal number *consisting of zero or more digits, that may be followed by a decimal point and fraction. Example: {1}*
javax.faces.converter.NumberConverter.NUMBER_detail	{2}: "{0}" is not a number. *Example: {1}*
javax.faces.converter.NumberConverter.CURRENCY_detail	{2}: "{0}" could not be understood as a currency value. *Example: {1}*
javax.faces.converter.NumberConverter.PERCENT_detail	{2}: "{0}" could not be understood as a percentage. *Example: {1}*
javax.faces.converter.DateTimeConverter.DATE_detail	{2}: "{0}" could not be understood as a date. *Example: {1}*
javax.faces.converter.DateTimeConverter.TIME_detail	{2}: "{0}" could not be understood as a time. *Example: {1}*
javax.faces.converter.DateTimeConverter.PATTERN_TYPE	{1}: A 'pattern' or 'type' attribute must be specified to convert the value "{0}".
javax.faces.converter.EnumConverter.ENUM	{2}: "{0}" must be convertible to an enum.
javax.faces.converter.EnumConverter.ENUM_detail	{2}: "{0}" must be convertible to an enum from the enum that contains the constant "{1}".
javax.faces.converter.EnumConverter.ENUM_NO_CLASS_detail	{1}: "{0}" must be convertible to an enum from the enum, but no enum class provided.

NOTE: In JSF 1.1, the generic message "Conversion error occurred" has key javax.faces.component.UIInput.Conversion.

Using a Custom Error Message

Starting with JSF 1.2, you can provide a custom converter error message for a component. Set the `converterMessage` attribute of the component whose value is being converted. For example:

```
<h:inputText ... converterMessage="Not a valid number."/>
```

 CAUTION: Unlike the message strings of the preceding section, these message attributes are taken literally. Placeholders, such as {0}, are not replaced.

A Complete Converter Example

We are now ready for our first complete example. Figure 7–5 shows the directory structure of the application. This web application asks the user to supply payment information (Listing 7–1) and then displays the formatted information on a confirmation screen (Listing 7–2). The messages are in Listing 7–3 and the bean class is in Listing 7–4.

```
converter.war
    index.xhtml
    result.xhtml
  ▼ WEB-INF
      beans.xml
      faces-config.xml
      web.xml
    ▼ classes
      ▼ com
        ▼ corejsf
            PaymentBean.class
            messages.properties
  ▼ resources
    ▼ css
        styles.css
```

Figure 7–5 Directory structure of the converter sample

Listing 7–1 `converter/web/index.xhtml`

```
1. <?xml version="1.0" encoding="UTF-8"?>
2. <!DOCTYPE html PUBLIC "-//W3C//DTD XHTML 1.0 Transitional//EN"
3. "http://www.w3.org/TR/xhtml1/DTD/xhtml1-transitional.dtd">
4. <html xmlns="http://www.w3.org/1999/xhtml"
5.       xmlns:f="http://java.sun.com/jsf/core"
6.       xmlns:h="http://java.sun.com/jsf/html">
7.   <h:head>
8.     <h:outputStylesheet library="css" name="styles.css"/>
9.     <title>#{msgs.title}</title>
10.  </h:head>
11.  <h:body>
12.    <h:form>
13.      <h1>#{msgs.enterPayment}</h1>
14.      <h:panelGrid columns="3">
15.        #{msgs.amount}
16.        <h:inputText id="amount" label="#{msgs.amount}"
17.                    value="#{payment.amount}">
18.          <f:convertNumber minFractionDigits="2"/>
19.        </h:inputText>
20.        <h:message for="amount" styleClass="errorMessage"/>
21.
22.        #{msgs.creditCard}
23.        <h:inputText id="card" label="#{msgs.creditCard}"
24.                    value="#{payment.card}"/>
25.        <h:message for="card" styleClass="errorMessage" />
26.
27.        #{msgs.expirationDate}
28.        <h:inputText id="date" label="#{msgs.expirationDate}"
29.                    value="#{payment.date}">
30.          <f:convertDateTime pattern="MM/yyyy"/>
31.        </h:inputText>
32.        <h:message for="date" styleClass="errorMessage"/>
33.      </h:panelGrid>
34.      <h:commandButton value="#{msgs.process}" action="result"/>
35.    </h:form>
36.  </h:body>
37. </html>
```

Listing 7–2 converter/web/result.xhtml

```
1. <?xml version="1.0" encoding="UTF-8"?>
2. <!DOCTYPE html PUBLIC "-//W3C//DTD XHTML 1.0 Transitional//EN"
3. "http://www.w3.org/TR/xhtml1/DTD/xhtml1-transitional.dtd">
4. <html xmlns="http://www.w3.org/1999/xhtml"
5.     xmlns:f="http://java.sun.com/jsf/core"
6.     xmlns:h="http://java.sun.com/jsf/html">
7.   <h:head>
8.     <h:outputStylesheet library="css" name="styles.css"/>
9.     <title>#{msgs.title}</title>
10.  </h:head>
11.  <h:body>
12.    <h:form>
13.      <h1>#{msgs.paymentInformation}</h1>
14.      <h:panelGrid columns="2">
15.        #{msgs.amount}
16.        <h:outputText value="#{payment.amount}">
17.          <f:convertNumber type="currency"/>
18.        </h:outputText>
19.
20.        #{msgs.creditCard}
21.        <h:outputText value="#{payment.card}"/>
22.
23.        #{msgs.expirationDate}
24.        <h:outputText value="#{payment.date}">
25.          <f:convertDateTime pattern="MM/yyyy"/>
26.        </h:outputText>
27.      </h:panelGrid>
28.      <h:commandButton value="#{msgs.back}" action="index"/>
29.    </h:form>
30.  </h:body>
31. </html>
```

Listing 7–3 converter/src/java/com/corejsf/messages.properties

```
1. title=An Application to Test Data Conversion
2. enterPayment=Please enter the payment information
3. amount=Amount
4. creditCard=Credit Card
5. expirationDate=Expiration date (Month/Year)
6. process=Process
7. back=Back
8. paymentInformation=Payment information
```

Listing 7–4 `converter/src/java/com/corejsf/PaymentBean.java`

```
1. package com.corejsf;
2.
3. import java.io.Serializable;
4. import java.util.Date;
5.
6. import javax.inject.Named;
7.    // or import javax.faces.bean.ManagedBean;
8. import javax.enterprise.context.SessionScoped;
9.    // or import javax.faces.bean.SessionScoped;
10.
11. @Named("payment") // or @ManagedBean(name="payment")
12. @SessionScoped
13. public class PaymentBean implements Serializable {
14.    private double amount;
15.    private String card = "";
16.    private Date date = new Date();
17.
18.    public void setAmount(double newValue) { amount = newValue; }
19.    public double getAmount() { return amount; }
20.
21.    public void setCard(String newValue) { card = newValue; }
22.    public String getCard() { return card; }
23.
24.    public void setDate(Date newValue) { date = newValue; }
25.    public Date getDate() { return date; }
26. }
```

Using Standard Validators

In the following sections, we discuss the standard JSF validators. You can also implement custom validators—see "Implementing Custom Validator Classes" on page 290.

Validating String Lengths and Numeric Ranges

It is easy to use JSF validators within JSF pages—add validator tags to the body of a component tag, like this:

```
<h:inputText id="card" value="#{payment.card}">
    <f:validateLength minimum="13"/>
</h:inputText>
```

The preceding code fragment adds a validator to a text field; when the text field's form is submitted, the validator makes sure that the string contains at least 13 characters. When validation fails (in this case, when the string has 12 or fewer characters), validators generate error messages associated with the guilty component. These messages can later be displayed in a JSF page by the h:message or h:messages tag.

JavaServer Faces has built-in mechanisms that let you carry out the following validations:

- Checking the length of a string
- Checking limits for a numerical value (for example, > 0 or ≤ 100)
- Checking against a regular expression (since JSF 2.0)
- Checking that a value has been supplied

Table 7–4 lists the standard validators that are provided with JSF. You saw the string length validator in the preceding section. To validate numerical input, you use a range validator. For example:

```
<h:inputText id="amount" value="#{payment.amount}">
  <f:validateLongRange minimum="10" maximum="10000"/>
</h:inputText>
```

The validator checks that the supplied value is ≥ 10 and ≤ 10000.

All the standard range validator tags have minimum and maximum attributes. You need to supply one or both of these attributes.

Table 7–4   Standard Validators

JSP Tag	Validator Class	Attribute[a]	Validates
f:validateDoubleRange	DoubleRangeValidator	minimum, maximum	A double value within an optional range
f:validateLongRange	LongRangeValidator	minimum, maximum	A long value within an optional range
f:validateLength	LengthValidator	minimum, maximum	A String with a minimum and maximum number of characters
f:validateRequired **JSF 2.0**	RequiredValidator		The presence of a value
f:validateRegex **JSF 2.0**	RegexValidator	pattern	A String against a regular expression

Table 7–4　Standard Validators (cont.)

JSP Tag	Validator Class	Attribute[a]	Validates
f:validateBean	BeanValidator	validation-Groups	Specifies validation groups for bean validators (see the JSR 303 specification for details)

a. You can disable any validator by setting the Boolean disabled attribute.

Checking for Required Values

To check that a value is supplied, you can nest a validator inside the input component tag:

```
<h:inputText id="date" value="#{payment.date}">
    <f:validateRequired/>
</h:inputText>
```

Alternatively, you can simply use the attribute required="true" in the input component:

```
<h:inputText id="date" value="#{payment.date}" required="true"/>
```

The f:validateRequired tag was introduced in JSF 2.0. It simply sets the required attribute of the enclosing component to true.

CAUTION: If the required attribute is not set and a user supplies a blank input, then no validation occurs at all! Instead, the blank input is interpreted as a request to leave the existing value unchanged.

As of JSF 2.0, you can change this behavior by setting the context parameter javax.faces.INTERPRET_EMPTY_STRING_SUBMITTED_VALUES_AS_NULL to true in web.xml.

An alternate syntax for attaching a validator to a component is to use the f:validator tag. You specify the ID of the validator and the validator parameters like this:

```
<h:inputText id="card" value="#{payment.card}">
    <f:validator validatorId="javax.faces.validator.LengthValidator">
        <f:attribute name="minimum" value="13"/>
    </f:validator>
</h:inputText>
```

Yet another way of specifying the validator is with a validator attribute to the component tag (see "Validating with Bean Methods" on page 294).

NOTE: As of JSF 1.2, the f:validateLength, f:validateLongRange, f:validate-DoubleRange, and f:validator tags have an optional binding attribute. This allows you to tie a validator instance to a backing bean property of type javax.faces.validator.Validator.

Displaying Validation Errors

Validation errors are handled in the same way as conversion errors. A message is added to the component that failed validation, the component is invalidated, and the current page is redisplayed immediately after the Process Validations phase has completed.

You use the h:message or h:messages tag to display the validation errors. For details, see "Displaying Error Messages" on page 254.

As of JSF 1.2, you can supply a custom message for a component by setting the requiredMessage or validatorMessage attribute, like this:

```
<h:inputText id="card" value="#{payment.card}" required="true"
    requiredMessage="#{msgs.cardRequired}"
    validatorMessage="#{msgs.cardInvalid}">
  <f:validateLength minimum="13"/>
</h:inputText>
```

You can also globally override the default validator messages shown in Table 7–5. Define a message bundle for your application and supply messages with the appropriate keys, as shown under "Changing the Text of Standard Error Messages" on page 256.

NOTE: In JSF 1.1, the input label was not included in the validation messages. The key for the "not in range" messages was javax.faces.validator.NOT_IN_RANGE.

CAUTION: The standard message for the LengthValidator is likely to be confusing to users. For example, if you set a minimum length of 5 for a zip code, and a user enters "9410", the error message is: "Value is less than allowable minimum of 5."

Table 7–5   Standard Validation Error Messages

Resource ID	Default Text	Reported By
javax.faces.component. UIInput.REQUIRED	{0}: Validation Error: Value is required.	UIInput with required attribute when value is missing.
javax.faces.validator. DoubleRangeValidator.NOT_IN_RANGE javax.faces.validator. LongRangeValidator.NOT_IN_RANGE	{2}: Validation Error: Specified attribute is not between the expected values of {0} and {1}.	DoubleRangeValidator and Long-RangeValidator when value is out of range and both minimum and maximum are specified.
javax.faces.validator. DoubleRangeValidator.MAXIMUM javax.faces.validator. LongRangeValidator.MAXIMUM	{1}: Validation Error: Value is greater than allowable maximum of "{0}".	DoubleRangeValidator or Long-RangeValidator when value is out of range and only maximum is specified.
javax.faces.validator. DoubleRangeValidator.MINIMUM javax.faces.validator. LongRangeValidator.MINIMUM	{1}: Validation Error: Value is less than allowable minimum of "{0}".	DoubleRangeValidator or Long-RangeValidator when value is out of range and only minimum is specified.
javax.faces.validator. DoubleRangeValidator.TYPE javax.faces.validator. LongRangeValidator.TYPE	{0}: Validation Error: Value is not of the correct type.	DoubleRangeValidator or Long-RangeValidator when value cannot be converted to double or long.
javax.faces.validator. LengthValidator.MAXIMUM	{1}: Validation Error: Value is greater than allowable maximum of "{0}".	LengthValidator when string length is greater than maximum.
javax.faces.validator. LengthValidator.MINIMUM	{1}: Validation Error: Value is less than allowable minimum of "{0}".	LengthValidator when string length is less than minimum.
javax.faces.validator. BeanValidator.MESSAGE	{0}	A validator from the Bean Validation Framework. See the JSR 303 specification for details about customizing messages.

Bypassing Validation

As you saw in the preceding examples, validation errors (as well as conversion errors) force a redisplay of the current page. This behavior can be problematic with certain navigation actions. Suppose, for example, you add a Cancel button to a page that contains required fields. If the user clicks

"Cancel", leaving a required field blank, then the validation mechanism kicks in and forces the current page to be redisplayed.

It would be unreasonable to expect your users to fill in required fields before they are allowed to cancel their input. Fortunately, a bypass mechanism is available. If a command has the `immediate` attribute set, then the command is executed during the Apply Request Values phase.

Thus, you would implement a Cancel button like this:

```
<h:commandButton value="Cancel" action="cancel" immediate="true"/>
```

A Complete Validation Example

The following sample application shows a form that employs all the standard JSF validation checks: required fields, string length, and numeric limits. The application makes sure that values are entered in all fields, the amount is between $10 and $10,000, the credit card number has at least 13 characters, and the expiration date is supplied. Figure 7–6 shows typical validation error messages. A Cancel button is also provided to demonstrate the validation bypass.

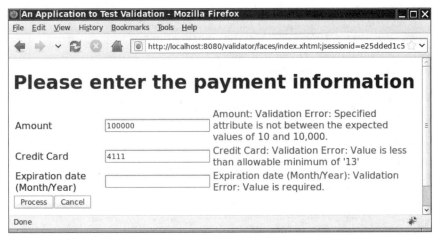

Figure 7–6   Typical validation error messages

Figure 7–7 shows the directory structure of the application. Listings 7–5 and 7–6 contain the JSF page with the validators and the page that is displayed when the request is canceled. (Note that no validation occurs when the user clicks the Cancel button.)

Figure 7–7   Directory structure of the validation example

Listing 7–5   `validator/web/index.xhtml`

```
1. <?xml version="1.0" encoding="UTF-8"?>
2. <!DOCTYPE html PUBLIC "-//W3C//DTD XHTML 1.0 Transitional//EN"
3. "http://www.w3.org/TR/xhtml1/DTD/xhtml1-transitional.dtd">
4. <html xmlns="http://www.w3.org/1999/xhtml"
5.      xmlns:f="http://java.sun.com/jsf/core"
6.      xmlns:h="http://java.sun.com/jsf/html">
7.    <h:head>
8.      <h:outputStylesheet library="css" name="styles.css"/>
9.      <title>#{msgs.title}</title>
10.   </h:head>
11.   <h:body>
12.     <h:form>
13.       <h1>#{msgs.enterPayment}</h1>
14.       <h:panelGrid columns="3">
15.         #{msgs.amount}
16.         <h:inputText id="amount" label="#{msgs.amount}"
17.                  value="#{payment.amount}" required="true">
18.           <f:convertNumber minFractionDigits="2"/>
19.           <f:validateDoubleRange minimum="10" maximum="10000"/>
20.         </h:inputText>
21.         <h:message for="amount" styleClass="errorMessage"/>
22.
23.         #{msgs.creditCard}
24.         <h:inputText id="card" label="#{msgs.creditCard}"
25.                  value="#{payment.card}" required="true"
```

```
26.                          requiredMessage="#{msgs.cardRequired}">
27.                <f:validateLength minimum="13"/>
28.              </h:inputText>
29.              <h:message for="card" styleClass="errorMessage"/>
30.
31.              #{msgs.expirationDate}
32.              <h:inputText id="date" label="#{msgs.expirationDate}"
33.                          value="#{payment.date}" required="true">
34.                <f:convertDateTime pattern="MM/yyyy"/>
35.              </h:inputText>
36.              <h:message for="date" styleClass="errorMessage"/>
37.            </h:panelGrid>
38.            <h:commandButton value="#{msgs.process}" action="result"/>
39.            <h:commandButton value="#{msgs.cancel}" action="canceled"
40.                            immediate="true"/>
41.          </h:form>
42.        </h:body>
43. </html>
```

Listing 7–6   validator/web/canceled.xhtml

```
1. <?xml version="1.0" encoding="UTF-8"?>
2. <!DOCTYPE html PUBLIC "-//W3C//DTD XHTML 1.0 Transitional//EN"
3. "http://www.w3.org/TR/xhtml1/DTD/xhtml1-transitional.dtd">
4. <html xmlns="http://www.w3.org/1999/xhtml"
5.      xmlns:f="http://java.sun.com/jsf/core"
6.      xmlns:h="http://java.sun.com/jsf/html">
7.    <h:head>
8.      <h:outputStylesheet library="css" name="styles.css"/>
9.      <title>#{msgs.title}</title>
10.   </h:head>
11.   <h:body>
12.     <h:form>
13.       #{msgs.canceled}
14.       <br/>
15.       <h:commandButton value="#{msgs.back}" action="index"/>
16.     </h:form>
17.   </h:body>
18. </html>
```

Bean Validation JSF 2.0

JSF 2.0 integrates with the *Bean Validation Framework* (JSR 303), a general framework for specifying validation constraints. Validations are attached to fields or property getters of a Java class, like this:

```
public class PaymentBean {
    @Size(min=13) private String card;
    @Future public Date getDate() { ... }
    ...
}
```

Table 7–6 shows the available annotations.

Table 7–6   Annotations in the Bean Validation Framework

Annotation	Attribute[a]	Purpose
@Null, @NotNull	None	Check that a value is null or not null.
@Min, @Max	The bound as a long	Check that a value is at least or at most the given bound. The type must be one of int, long, short, byte and their wrappers, BigInteger, BigDecimal. Note: double and float are not supported due to roundoff.
@DecimalMin, @DecimalMax	The bound as a String	As above. Can also be applied to a String.
@Digits	integer, fraction	Check that a value has, at most, the given number of integer or fractional digits. Applies to int, long, short, byte and their wrappers, BigInteger, BigDecimal, String.
@AssertTrue, @AssertFalse	None	Check that a Boolean value is true or false.
@Past, @Future	None	Check that a date is in the past or in the future.
@Size	min, max	Check that the size of a string, array, collection, or map is at least or at most the given bound.
@Pattern	regexp, flags	A regular expression and optional compilation flags.

a. All validation annotations have attributes message and groups. We do not discuss validation groups here.

The Bean Validation Framework has a significant advantage over page-level validation. Suppose your web application updates a bean in several pages. You don't need to add validation rules to each page, and you can be assured that validation is handled consistently.

To override the default messages, supply a file `ValidationMessages.properties` in the default (root) package of your application. You can override the standard messages, for example:

```
javax.validation.constraints.Min.message=Must be at least {value}
```

(instead of the unsightly default "Must be greater than or equal to ..."). To provide a custom message for a particular validation, reference the bundle key in the `message` attribute:

```
@Size(min=13, message="{com.corejsf.creditCardLength}")
private String card = "";
```

Then define the key in `ValidationMessages.properties`:

```
com.corejsf.creditCardLength=The credit card number must have at least 13 digits
```

> **NOTE:** If you use a Java EE 6 compatible application server, you automatically have access to a JSR 303 implementation. Otherwise, include the Hibernate Validator JAR files (`http://validator.hibernate.org/`) in the `WEB-INF/lib` directory.

We provide an example application that demonstrates bean validation (see Figure 7–8). The example is notable for its simplicity. The JSF pages are not concerned with validation. The model class, shown in Listing 7–7, contains the validation annotations.

Note the `@LuhnCheck` annotation that checks the digits of a credit card, using the Luhn formula.

> **NOTE:** The Luhn formula—developed by a group of mathematicians in the late 1960s—verifies and generates credit card numbers, as well as Social Insurance numbers for the Canadian government. The formula can detect whether a digit is entered wrongly or whether two digits were transposed. See the web site `http://www.merriampark.com/anatomycc.htm` for more information about the Luhn formula. For debugging, it is handy to know that the number 4111 1111 1111 1111 passes the Luhn check.

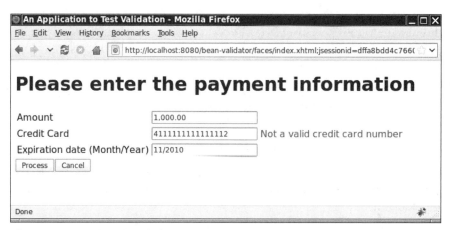

Figure 7–8   Luhn check failed

The @LuhnCheck annotation is a custom validator that we wrote for this book to demonstrate the extensibility of the Bean Validation Framework. To write a custom validator, you provide the following:

- An annotation (see Listing 7–8)
- A class that implements the ConstraintValidator interface (see Listing 7–9)
- Optionally, default messages in the ValidationMessages.properties file (see Listing 7–10)

Note the circular dependency between the annotation and the validator class. The annotation references the validator class:

```
@Constraint(validatedBy=LuhnCheckValidator.class)
public @interface LuhnCheck
```

The validator class references the annotation type:

```
public class LuhnCheckValidator implements ConstraintValidator<LuhnCheck, String>
```

The second type parameter of the ConstraintValidator interface is the type of the object that is being validated; in our case, a String. Therefore, the isValid method has a String parameter:

```
public boolean isValid(String value, ConstraintValidatorContext context) {
    return luhnCheck(value.replaceAll("\\D", "")); // remove non-digits
}
```

We won't go into the details of the Bean Validation Framework here. If you need to implement your own custom validation rules, you can simply follow this example.

Figure 7–9 shows the directory structure of this application.

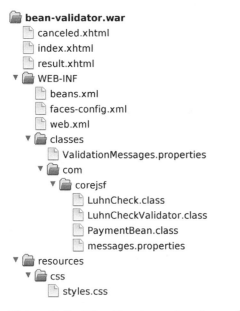

📁 **bean-validator.war**
  📄 canceled.xhtml
  📄 index.xhtml
  📄 result.xhtml
  ▼ 📁 WEB-INF
      📄 beans.xml
      📄 faces-config.xml
      📄 web.xml
      ▼ 📁 classes
          📄 ValidationMessages.properties
          ▼ 📁 com
              ▼ 📁 corejsf
                  📄 LuhnCheck.class
                  📄 LuhnCheckValidator.class
                  📄 PaymentBean.class
                  📄 messages.properties
  ▼ 📁 resources
      ▼ 📁 css
          📄 styles.css

Figure 7–9   The directory structure of the bean validation framework example

Listing 7–7   bean-validator/src/java/com/corejsf/PaymentBean.java

```
 1. package com.corejsf;
 2.
 3. import java.io.Serializable;
 4. import java.util.Date;
 5.
 6. import javax.inject.Named;
 7.    // or import javax.faces.bean.ManagedBean;
 8. import javax.enterprise.context.SessionScoped;
 9.    // or import javax.faces.bean.SessionScoped;
10. import javax.validation.constraints.Future;
11. import javax.validation.constraints.Max;
12. import javax.validation.constraints.Min;
13. import javax.validation.constraints.Size;
14.
15. @Named("payment") // or @ManagedBean(name="payment")
16. @SessionScoped
17. public class PaymentBean implements Serializable {
18.    @Min(10) @Max(10000)
19.    private double amount;
20.    @Size(min=13,message="{com.corejsf.creditCardLength}") @LuhnCheck
```

```
21.    private String card = "";
22.    @Future
23.    private Date date = new Date();
24.
25.    public void setAmount(double newValue) { amount = newValue; }
26.    public double getAmount() { return amount; }
27.
28.    public void setCard(String newValue) { card = newValue; }
29.    public String getCard() { return card; }
30.
31.    public void setDate(Date newValue) { date = newValue; }
32.    public Date getDate() { return date; }
33. }
```

Listing 7–8   bean-validator/src/java/com/corejsf/LuhnCheck.java

```
1. package com.corejsf;
2.
3. import java.lang.annotation.Documented;
4. import java.lang.annotation.Retention;
5. import java.lang.annotation.Target;
6. import javax.validation.Constraint;
7. import javax.validation.Payload;
8. import static java.lang.annotation.ElementType.*;
9. import static java.lang.annotation.RetentionPolicy.*;
10.
11. @Target({METHOD, FIELD})
12. @Retention(RUNTIME)
13. @Documented
14. @Constraint(validatedBy=LuhnCheckValidator.class)
15. public @interface LuhnCheck {
16.    String message() default "{com.corejsf.LuhnCheck.message}";
17.    Class[] groups() default {};
18.    Class<? extends Payload>[] payload() default {};
19. }
```

Listing 7–9   bean-validator/src/java/com/corejsf/LuhnCheckValidator.java

```
1. package com.corejsf;
2. import javax.validation.ConstraintValidator;
3. import javax.validation.ConstraintValidatorContext;
4.
5. public class LuhnCheckValidator implements ConstraintValidator<LuhnCheck, String> {
6.    public void initialize(LuhnCheck constraintAnnotation) {
7.    }
8.
```

```
 9.    public boolean isValid(String value, ConstraintValidatorContext context) {
10.        return luhnCheck(value.replaceAll("\\D", "")); // remove non-digits
11.    }
12.
13.    private static boolean luhnCheck(String cardNumber) {
14.        int sum = 0;
15.
16.        for(int i = cardNumber.length() - 1; i >= 0; i -= 2) {
17.            sum += Integer.parseInt(cardNumber.substring(i, i + 1));
18.            if(i > 0) {
19.                int d = 2 * Integer.parseInt(cardNumber.substring(i - 1, i));
20.                if(d > 9) d -= 9;
21.                sum += d;
22.            }
23.        }
24.
25.        return sum % 10 == 0;
26.    }
27. }
```

Listing 7–10 bean-validator/src/java/ValidationMessages.properties

```
1. javax.validation.constraints.Min.message=Must be at least {value}
2. com.corejsf.creditCardLength=The credit card number must have at least 13 digits
3. com.corejsf.LuhnCheck.message=Not a valid credit card number
```

Programming with Custom Converters and Validators

JSF standard converters and validators cover a lot of bases, but many web applications must go further. For example, you may need to convert to types other than numbers and dates or perform application-specific validation, such as checking a credit card.

In the following sections, we show you how to implement application-specific converters and validators. These implementations require a moderate amount of programming.

Implementing Custom Converter Classes

A *converter* is a class that converts between strings and objects. A converter must implement the Converter interface, which has the following two methods:

```
Object getAsObject(FacesContext context, UIComponent component, String newValue)
String getAsString(FacesContext context, UIComponent component, Object value)
```

The first method converts a string into an object of the desired type, throwing a ConverterException if the conversion cannot be carried out. This method is called when a string is submitted from the client, typically in a text field. The second method converts an object into a string representation to be displayed in the client interface.

To illustrate these methods, we develop a custom converter for credit card numbers. Our converter allows users to enter a credit card number with or without spaces. That is, we accept inputs of the following forms:

```
1234567890123456
1234 5678 9012 3456
```

Listing 7–11 shows the code for the custom converter. The getAsObject method of the converter strips out all characters that are not digits. It then creates an object of type CreditCard. If an error is found, then we generate a FacesMessage object and throw a ConverterException. We will discuss these steps in the next section, "Reporting Conversion Errors," on page 280.

The getAsString method of our converter makes an effort to format the credit card number in a way that is pleasing to the eye of the user. The digits are separated into the familiar patterns, depending on the credit card type. Table 7–7 shows the most common credit card formats.

Table 7–7   Credit Card Formats

Card Type	Digits	Format
MasterCard	16	5xxx xxxx xxxx xxxx
Visa	16	4xxx xxxx xxxx xxxx
Visa	13	4xxx xxx xxx xxx
Discover	16	6xxx xxxx xxxx xxxx
American Express	15	37xx xxxxxx xxxxx
American Express	22	3xxxxx xxxxxxxx xxxxxxxx
Diners Club, Carte Blanche	14	3xxxx xxxx xxxxx

In this example, the CreditCard class is minor; it contains just the credit card number (see Listing 7–12). We could have left the credit card number as a String object, reducing the converter to a formatter. However, most converters have a target type other than String. To make it easier for you to reuse this example, we use a distinct target type.

Listing 7–11 converter2/src/java/com/coresjf/CreditCardConverter.java

```java
1. package com.corejsf;
2.
3. import javax.faces.application.FacesMessage;
4. import javax.faces.component.UIComponent;
5. import javax.faces.context.FacesContext;
6. import javax.faces.convert.Converter;
7. import javax.faces.convert.ConverterException;
8. import javax.faces.convert.FacesConverter;
9.
10. @FacesConverter(forClass=CreditCard.class)
11. public class CreditCardConverter implements Converter {
12.     public Object getAsObject(FacesContext context, UIComponent component,
13.         String newValue) throws ConverterException {
14.         StringBuilder builder = new StringBuilder(newValue);
15.         boolean foundInvalidCharacter = false;
16.         char invalidCharacter = '\0';
17.         int i = 0;
18.         while (i < builder.length() && !foundInvalidCharacter) {
19.             char ch = builder.charAt(i);
20.             if (Character.isDigit(ch))
21.                 i++;
22.             else if (Character.isWhitespace(ch))
23.                 builder.deleteCharAt(i);
24.             else {
25.                 foundInvalidCharacter = true;
26.                 invalidCharacter = ch;
27.             }
28.         }
29.
30.         if (foundInvalidCharacter) {
31.             FacesMessage message = com.corejsf.util.Messages.getMessage(
32.                 "com.corejsf.messages", "badCreditCardCharacter",
33.                 new Object[]{ new Character(invalidCharacter) });
34.             message.setSeverity(FacesMessage.SEVERITY_ERROR);
35.             throw new ConverterException(message);
36.         }
37.
38.         return new CreditCard(builder.toString());
39.     }
40.
41.     public String getAsString(FacesContext context, UIComponent component,
42.         Object value) throws ConverterException {
43.         // length 13: xxxx xxx xxx xxx
44.         // length 14: xxxxx xxxx xxxxx
```

```
45.    // length 15: xxxx xxxxxx xxxxx
46.    // length 16: xxxx xxxx xxxx xxxx
47.    // length 22: xxxxxx xxxxxxxx xxxxxxxx
48.    String v = value.toString();
49.    int[] boundaries = null;
50.    int length = v.length();
51.    if (length == 13)
52.       boundaries = new int[]{ 4, 7, 10 };
53.    else if (length == 14)
54.       boundaries = new int[]{ 5, 9 };
55.    else if (length == 15)
56.       boundaries = new int[]{ 4, 10 };
57.    else if (length == 16)
58.       boundaries = new int[]{ 4, 8, 12 };
59.    else if (length == 22)
60.       boundaries = new int[]{ 6, 14 };
61.    else
62.       return v;
63.    StringBuilder result = new StringBuilder();
64.    int start = 0;
65.    for (int i = 0; i < boundaries.length; i++) {
66.       int end = boundaries[i];
67.       result.append(v.substring(start, end));
68.       result.append(" ");
69.       start = end;
70.    }
71.    result.append(v.substring(start));
72.    return result.toString();
73.    }
74. }
```

Listing 7–12   converter2/src/java/com/corejsf/CreditCard.java

```
1. package com.corejsf;
2.
3. import java.io.Serializable;
4.
5. public class CreditCard implements Serializable {
6.    private String number;
7.
8.    public CreditCard(String number) { this.number = number; }
9.    public String toString() { return number; }
10. }
```

Specifying Converters **JSF 2.0**

One mechanism for specifying converters involves a symbolic ID that you register with the JSF application. We will use the ID com.corejsf.Card for our credit card converter.

You associate the ID with the converter in one of two ways. Since JSF 2.0, you can use the @FacesConverter annotation:

```
@FacesConverter("com.corejsf.Card")
public class CreditCardConverter implements Converter
```

Before JSF 2.0, you had to place an entry into to faces-config.xml that associates the converter ID with the class that implements the converter:

```
<converter>
   <converter-id>com.corejsf.Card</converter-id>
   <converter-class>com.corejsf.CreditCardConverter</converter-class>
</converter>
```

In the following examples, we will assume that the card property of the Payment-Bean has type CreditCard, as shown in Listing 7–18 on page 289. Now we can use the f:converter tag and specify the converter ID:

```
<h:inputText value="#{payment.card}">
   <f:converter converterId="com.corejsf.Card"/>
</h:inputText>
```

Or, more succinctly, we can use the converter attribute:

```
<h:inputText value="#{payment.card}" converter="com.corejsf.Card"/>
```

Alternatively, if you are confident that your converter is appropriate for all conversions between String and CreditCard objects, then you can register it as the default converter for the CreditCard class.

Use the annotation:

```
@FacesConverter(forClass=CreditCard.class)
```

or the faces-config entry:

```
<converter>
   <converter-for-class>com.corejsf.CreditCard</converter-for-class>
   <converter-class>com.corejsf.CreditCardConverter</converter-class>
</converter>
```

Now you do not have to mention the converter any longer. It is automatically used whenever a value reference has the type CreditCard. For example, consider the tag:

```
<h:inputText value="#{payment.card}"/>
```

When the JSF implementation converts the request value, it notices that the target type is `CreditCard`, and it locates the converter for that class. This is the ultimate in converter convenience for the page author!

CAUTION: If you specify both the `value` and `forClass` attributes in the `FacesConverter` annotation, the latter is ignored.

 `javax.faces.convert.Converter`

- `Object getAsObject(FacesContext context, UIComponent component, String value)`
  Converts the given string value into an object that is appropriate for storage in the given component.

- `String getAsString(FacesContext context, UIComponent component, Object value)`
  Converts the given object, which is stored in the given component, into a string representation.

 `@javax.faces.convert.FacesConverter`

- `String value (Default: "")`
  The ID of the converter.

- `Class forClass (Default: Object.class)`
  The class for which this is a converter.

Reporting Conversion Errors

When a converter detects an error, it should throw a `ConverterException`. For example, the `getAsObject` method of our credit card converter checks whether the credit card contains characters other than digits or separators. If it finds an invalid character, it signals an error:

```
if (foundInvalidCharacter) {
  FacesMessage message = new FacesMessage(
    "Conversion error occurred. ", "Invalid card number. ");
  message.setSeverity(FacesMessage.SEVERITY_ERROR);
  throw new ConverterException(message);
}
```

The `FacesMessage` object contains the summary and detail messages that can be displayed with message tags.

javax.faces.application.FacesMessage

- FacesMessage(FacesMessage.Severity severity, String summary, String detail)

  Constructs a message with the given severity, summary, and detail. The severity is one of the constants SEVERITY_ERROR, SEVERITY_FATAL, SEVERITY_INFO, or SEVERITY_WARN in the FacesMessage class.

- FacesMessage(String summary, String detail)

  Constructs a message with severity SEVERITY_INFO and the given summary and detail.

- void setSeverity(FacesMessage.Severity severity)

  Sets the severity to the given level. The severity is one of the constants SEVERITY_ERROR, SEVERITY_FATAL, SEVERITY_INFO, or SEVERITY_WARN in the FacesMessage class.

javax.faces.convert.ConverterException

- ConverterException(FacesMessage message)
- ConverterException(FacesMessage message, Throwable cause)

  These constructors create exceptions whose getMessage method returns the summary of the given message and whose getFacesMessage method returns the given message.

- ConverterException()
- ConverterException(String detailMessage)
- ConverterException(Throwable cause)
- ConverterException(String detailMessage, Throwable cause)

  These constructors create exceptions whose getMessage method returns the given detail message and whose getFacesMessage method returns null.

- FacesMessage getFacesMessage()

  Returns the FacesMessage with which this exception object was constructed or returns null if none was supplied.

Getting Error Messages from Resource Bundles

Of course, for proper localization, you will want to retrieve the error messages from a message bundle.

Doing that involves some busywork with locales and class loaders:

1. Get the current locale.

    ```
    FacesContext context = FacesContext.getCurrentInstance();
    UIViewRoot viewRoot = context.getViewRoot();
    Locale locale = viewRoot.getLocale();
    ```

2. Get the current class loader. You need it to locate the resource bundle.

```
ClassLoader loader = Thread.currentThread().getContextClassLoader();
```

3. Get the resource bundle with the given name, locale, and class loader.

```
ResourceBundle bundle = ResourceBundle.getBundle(bundleName, locale, loader);
```

4. Get the resource string with the given ID from the bundle.

```
String resource = bundle.getString(resourceId);
```

However, there are several wrinkles in the process. We actually need two message strings: one for the summary and one for the detail messages. By convention, the resource ID of a detail message is obtained by addition of the string _detail to the summary key. For example:

```
badCreditCardCharacter=Invalid card number.
badCreditCardCharacter_detail=The card number contains invalid characters.
```

Moreover, converters are usually part of a reusable library. It is a good idea to allow a specific application to override messages. (You saw in "Changing the Text of Standard Error Messages" on page 256 how to override the standard converter messages.) Therefore, you should first attempt to locate the messages in the application-specific message bundle before retrieving the default messages.

Recall that an application can supply a bundle name in a configuration file, such as:

```
<faces-config>
  <application>
    <message-bundle>com.mycompany.myapp.messages</message-bundle>
  </application>
  ...
</faces-config>
```

The following code snippet retrieves that bundle name:

```
Application app = context.getApplication();
String appBundleName = app.getResourceBundle();
```

Look up your resources in this bundle before going to the library default.

Finally, you may want some messages to provide detailed information about the nature of the error. For example, you want to tell the user which character in the credit card number was objectionable. Message strings can contain placeholders {0}, {1}, and so on—for example:

```
The card number contains the invalid character {0}.
```

The java.text.MessageFormat class can substitute values for the placeholders:

```
Object[] params = ...;
MessageFormat formatter = new MessageFormat(resource, locale);
String message = formatter.format(params);
```

Here, the params array contains the values that should be substituted. (For more information about the MessageFormat class, see Cay Horstmann and Gary Cornell, *Core Java™*, 8th ed., Santa Clara, CA: Sun Microsystems Press/Prentice Hall, 2008, Vol. 2, Chapter 5.)

Ideally, much of this busywork should have been handled by the JSF framework. Of course, you can find the relevant code in the innards of the reference implementation, but the framework designers chose not to make it available to JSF programmers.

We provide the package com.corejsf.util with convenience classes that implement these missing pieces. Feel free to use these classes in your own code.

The com.corejsf.util.Messages class has a static method, getMessage, that returns a FacesMessage with a given bundle name, resource ID, and parameters:

```
FacesMessage message
  = com.corejsf.util.Messages.getMessage(
      "com.corejsf.messages", "badCreditCardCharacter",
      new Object[] { new Character(invalidCharacter) });
```

You can pass null for the parameter array if the message does not contain placeholders.

Our implementation follows the JSF convention of displaying missing resources as *???resourceId???*. See Listing 7–13 for the source code.

 NOTE: If you prefer to reuse the standard JSF message for conversion errors, call:

```
FacesMessage message = com.corejsf.util.Messages.getMessage(
    "javax.faces.Messages", "javax.faces.component.UIInput.CONVERSION", null);
```

---

javax.faces.context.FacesContext

- `static FacesContext getCurrentInstance()`
  Gets the context for the request that is being handled by the current thread, or null if the current thread does not handle a request.

- `UIViewRoot getViewRoot()`
  Gets the root component for the request described by this context.

javax.faces.component.UIViewRoot

- Locale getLocale()

Gets the locale for rendering this view.

Listing 7–13   converter2/src/java/com/corejsf/util/Messages.java

```
 1. package com.corejsf.util;
 2.
 3. import java.text.MessageFormat;
 4. import java.util.Locale;
 5. import java.util.MissingResourceException;
 6. import java.util.ResourceBundle;
 7. import javax.faces.application.Application;
 8. import javax.faces.application.FacesMessage;
 9. import javax.faces.component.UIViewRoot;
10. import javax.faces.context.FacesContext;
11.
12. public class Messages {
13.    public static FacesMessage getMessage(String bundleName, String resourceId,
14.       Object[] params) {
15.       FacesContext context = FacesContext.getCurrentInstance();
16.       Application app = context.getApplication();
17.       String appBundle = app.getMessageBundle();
18.       Locale locale = getLocale(context);
19.       ClassLoader loader = getClassLoader();
20.       String summary = getString(appBundle, bundleName, resourceId,
21.          locale, loader, params);
22.       if (summary == null) summary = "???" + resourceId + "???";
23.       String detail = getString(appBundle, bundleName, resourceId + "_detail",
24.          locale, loader, params);
25.       return new FacesMessage(summary, detail);
26.    }
27.
28.    public static String getString(String bundle, String resourceId,
29.          Object[] params) {
30.       FacesContext context = FacesContext.getCurrentInstance();
31.       Application app = context.getApplication();
32.       String appBundle = app.getMessageBundle();
33.       Locale locale = getLocale(context);
34.       ClassLoader loader = getClassLoader();
35.       return getString(appBundle, bundle, resourceId, locale, loader, params);
36.    }
37.
38.    public static String getString(String bundle1, String bundle2,
```

```
39.            String resourceId, Locale locale, ClassLoader loader,
40.            Object[] params) {
41.        String resource = null;
42.        ResourceBundle bundle;
43.
44.        if (bundle1 != null) {
45.            bundle = ResourceBundle.getBundle(bundle1, locale, loader);
46.            if (bundle != null)
47.                try {
48.                    resource = bundle.getString(resourceId);
49.                } catch (MissingResourceException ex) {
50.                }
51.        }
52.
53.        if (resource == null) {
54.            bundle = ResourceBundle.getBundle(bundle2, locale, loader);
55.            if (bundle != null)
56.                try {
57.                    resource = bundle.getString(resourceId);
58.                } catch (MissingResourceException ex) {
59.                }
60.        }
61.
62.        if (resource == null) return null; // no match
63.        if (params == null) return resource;
64.
65.        MessageFormat formatter = new MessageFormat(resource, locale);
66.        return formatter.format(params);
67.    }
68.
69.    public static Locale getLocale(FacesContext context) {
70.        Locale locale = null;
71.        UIViewRoot viewRoot = context.getViewRoot();
72.        if (viewRoot != null) locale = viewRoot.getLocale();
73.        if (locale == null) locale = Locale.getDefault();
74.        return locale;
75.    }
76.
77.    public static ClassLoader getClassLoader() {
78.        ClassLoader loader = Thread.currentThread().getContextClassLoader();
79.        if (loader == null) loader = ClassLoader.getSystemClassLoader();
80.        return loader;
81.    }
82. }
```

The Custom Converter Sample Application

Here are the remaining pieces of our next sample application. Figure 7–10 shows the directory structure. Listings 7–14 and 7–15 show the input and result pages. Look at the inputText and outputText tags for the credit card numbers to see the two styles of specifying a custom converter. (Both converter specifications could have been omitted if the converter had been registered to be the default for the CreditCard type.)

The custom converter is defined in the faces-config.xml file (Listing 7–16). The messages.properties file (shown in Listing 7–17) contains the error message for the credit card converter. Finally, Listing 7–18 shows the payment bean with three properties of type double, Date, and CreditCard.

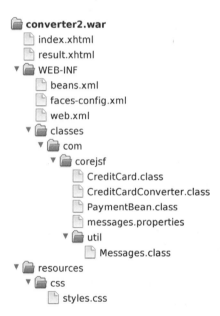

```
converter2.war
    index.xhtml
    result.xhtml
  WEB-INF
      beans.xml
      faces-config.xml
      web.xml
    classes
      com
        corejsf
            CreditCard.class
            CreditCardConverter.class
            PaymentBean.class
            messages.properties
          util
              Messages.class
  resources
    css
        styles.css
```

Figure 7–10 Directory structure of the custom converter example

Listing 7–14 converter2/web/index.xhtml

```
1. <?xml version="1.0" encoding="UTF-8"?>
2. <!DOCTYPE html PUBLIC "-//W3C//DTD XHTML 1.0 Transitional//EN"
3. "http://www.w3.org/TR/xhtml1/DTD/xhtml1-transitional.dtd">
4. <html xmlns="http://www.w3.org/1999/xhtml"
5.       xmlns:f="http://java.sun.com/jsf/core"
6.       xmlns:h="http://java.sun.com/jsf/html">
7.    <h:head>
```

```
8.       <h:outputStylesheet library="css" name="styles.css"/>
9.       <title>#{msgs.title}</title>
10.    </h:head>
11.    <h:body>
12.      <h:form>
13.        <h1>#{msgs.enterPayment}</h1>
14.        <h:panelGrid columns="3">
15.          #{msgs.amount}
16.          <h:inputText id="amount" label="#{msgs.amount}"
17.                       value="#{payment.amount}">
18.            <f:convertNumber minFractionDigits="2"/>
19.          </h:inputText>
20.          <h:message for="amount" styleClass="errorMessage"/>
21.
22.          #{msgs.creditCard}
23.          <h:inputText id="card" label="#{msgs.creditCard}"
24.                       value="#{payment.card}">
25.          </h:inputText>
26.          <h:message for="card" styleClass="errorMessage"/>
27.
28.          #{msgs.expirationDate}
29.          <h:inputText id="date" label="#{msgs.expirationDate}"
30.                       value="#{payment.date}">
31.            <f:convertDateTime pattern="MM/yyyy"/>
32.          </h:inputText>
33.          <h:message for="date" styleClass="errorMessage"/>
34.        </h:panelGrid>
35.        <h:commandButton value="#{msgs.process}" action="result"/>
36.      </h:form>
37.    </h:body>
38. </html>
```

Listing 7–15 converter2/web/result.xhtml

```
1. <?xml version="1.0" encoding="UTF-8"?>
2. <!DOCTYPE html PUBLIC "-//W3C//DTD XHTML 1.0 Transitional//EN"
3. "http://www.w3.org/TR/xhtml1/DTD/xhtml1-transitional.dtd">
4. <html xmlns="http://www.w3.org/1999/xhtml"
5.      xmlns:f="http://java.sun.com/jsf/core"
6.      xmlns:h="http://java.sun.com/jsf/html">
7.    <h:head>
8.      <h:outputStylesheet library="css" name="styles.css"/>
9.      <title>#{msgs.title}</title>
10.    </h:head>
11.    <h:body>
12.      <h:form>
13.        <h1>#{msgs.paymentInformation}</h1>
```

```
14.        <h:panelGrid columns="2">
15.           #{msgs.amount}
16.           <h:outputText value="#{payment.amount}">
17.              <f:convertNumber type="currency"/>
18.           </h:outputText>
19.
20.           #{msgs.creditCard}
21.           <h:outputText value="#{payment.card}"/>
22.           #{msgs.expirationDate}
23.           <h:outputText value="#{payment.date}">
24.              <f:convertDateTime pattern="MM/yyyy"/>
25.           </h:outputText>
26.        </h:panelGrid>
27.        <h:commandButton value="#{msgs.back}" action="index"/>
28.     </h:form>
29.   </h:body>
30. </html>
```

Listing 7–16 converter2/web/WEB-INF/faces-config.xml

```
 1. <?xml version="1.0"?>
 2. <faces-config xmlns="http://java.sun.com/xml/ns/javaee"
 3.     xmlns:xsi="http://www.w3.org/2001/XMLSchema-instance"
 4.     xsi:schemaLocation="http://java.sun.com/xml/ns/javaee
 5.        http://java.sun.com/xml/ns/javaee/web-facesconfig_2_0.xsd"
 6.     version="2.0">
 7.     <application>
 8.        <message-bundle>com.corejsf.messages</message-bundle>
 9.        <resource-bundle>
10.           <base-name>com.corejsf.messages</base-name>
11.           <var>msgs</var>
12.        </resource-bundle>
13.     </application>
14. </faces-config>
```

Listing 7–17 converter2/src/java/com/corejsf/messages.properties

```
 1. badCreditCardCharacter=Invalid card number.
 2. badCreditCardCharacter_detail=The card number contains the invalid character {0}.
 3. title=An Application to Test Data Conversion
 4. enterPayment=Please enter the payment information
 5. amount=Amount
 6. creditCard=Credit Card
 7. expirationDate=Expiration date (Month/Year)
 8. process=Process
 9. back=Back
10. paymentInformation=Payment information
```

Listing 7–18 converter2/src/java/com/corejsf/PaymentBean.java

```
1. package com.corejsf;
2.
3. import java.io.Serializable;
4. import java.util.Date;
5.
6. import javax.inject.Named;
7.    // or import javax.faces.bean.ManagedBean;
8. import javax.enterprise.context.SessionScoped;
9.    // or import javax.faces.bean.SessionScoped;
10.
11. @Named("payment") // or @ManagedBean(name="payment")
12. @SessionScoped
13. public class PaymentBean implements Serializable {
14.    private double amount;
15.    private CreditCard card = new CreditCard("");
16.    private Date date = new Date();
17.
18.    public void setAmount(double newValue) { amount = newValue; }
19.    public double getAmount() { return amount; }
20.
21.    public void setCard(CreditCard newValue) { card = newValue; }
22.    public CreditCard getCard() { return card; }
23.
24.    public void setDate(Date newValue) { date = newValue; }
25.    public Date getDate() { return date; }
26. }
```

Supplying Attributes to Converters

Every JSF component can store arbitrary attributes. You can set an attribute of the component to which you attach a converter; use the f:attribute tag. Your converter can then retrieve the attribute from its component. Here is how that technique would work to set the separator string for the credit card converter.

When attaching the converter, also nest an f:attribute tag inside the component:

```
<h:outputText value="#{payment.card}">
   <f:converter converterId="CreditCard"/>
   <f:attribute name="separator" value="-"/>
</h:outputText>
```

In the converter, retrieve the attribute as follows:

```
separator = (String) component.getAttributes().get("separator");
```

Later in this chapter, you will see a more elegant mechanism for passing attributes to a converter—writing your own converter tag.

API `javax.faces.component.UIComponent`

- `Map getAttributes()`
  Returns a mutable map of all attributes and properties of this component.

Implementing Custom Validator Classes

Implementing custom validator classes is similar to the process of implementing custom converters. Your validator class must implement the `javax.faces.validator.Validator` interface.

The `Validator` interface defines only one method:

```
void validate(FacesContext context, UIComponent component, Object value)
```

If validation fails, generate a `FacesMessage` that describes the error, construct a `ValidatorException` from the message, and throw it:

```
if (validation fails) {
   FacesMessage message = ...;
   message.setSeverity(FacesMessage.SEVERITY_ERROR);
   throw new ValidatorException(message);
}
```

The process is analogous to the reporting of conversion errors, except that you throw a `ValidatorException` instead of a `ConverterException`.

For example, Listing 7–19 on page 292 shows a validator that checks the digits of a credit card, using the Luhn formula. As described under "Getting Error Messages from Resource Bundles" on page 281, we use the convenience class `com.corejsf.util.Messages` to locate the message strings in a resource bundle.

API `javax.faces.validator.Validator`

- `void validate(FacesContext context, UIComponent component, Object value)`
  Validates the component to which this validator is attached. If there is a validation error, throw a `ValidatorException`.

Registering Custom Validators

Now that we have created a validator, we need to give it an ID. As with converter IDs, there are two choices. In JSF 2.0, you can use an annotation:

```
@FacesValidator("com.corejsf.Card")
public class CreditCardValidator implements Validator
```

Alternatively, you can register the validator in a configuration file (such as faces-config.xml), like this:

```
<validator>
    <validator-id>com.corejsf.Card</validator-id>
    <validator-class>com.corejsf.CreditCardValidator</validator-class>
</validator>
```

You specify the validator ID in the f:validator tag—for example, the following code fragment uses the credit card validator discussed above:

```
<h:inputText id="card" value="#{payment.card}" required="true">
    <f:converter converterId="com.corejsf.Card"/>
    <f:validator validatorId="com.corejsf.Card"/>
</h:inputText>
```

The f:validator tag uses the validator ID to look up the corresponding class, creates an instance of that class if necessary, and invokes its validate method.

 NOTE: JSF uses separate name spaces for converter and validator IDs. Thus, it is okay to have both a converter and a validator with the ID com.corejsf.Card.

 NOTE: JSF registers its standard validators with IDs javax.faces.LongRange, javax.faces.DoubleRange, javax.faces.Length, javax.faces.RegularExpression, javax.faces.Required, and javax.faces.Bean.

The remainder of the sample application is straightforward. Figure 7–11 shows the directory structure, and Listing 7–20 contains the JSF page.

The f:validator tag is useful for simple validators that do not have parameters, such as the credit validator discussed above. If you need a validator with properties that can be specified in a JSF page, you should implement a custom tag for your validator. You will see how to do that in the section "Implementing Custom Validator Classes" on page 290.

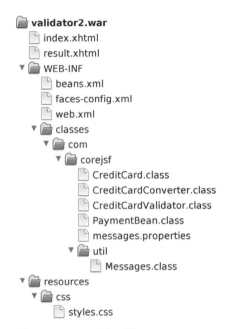

📁 **validator2.war**
  📄 index.xhtml
  📄 result.xhtml
  ▼ 📁 WEB-INF
      📄 beans.xml
      📄 faces-config.xml
      📄 web.xml
      ▼ 📁 classes
          ▼ 📁 com
              ▼ 📁 corejsf
                  📄 CreditCard.class
                  📄 CreditCardConverter.class
                  📄 CreditCardValidator.class
                  📄 PaymentBean.class
                  📄 messages.properties
                  ▼ 📁 util
                      📄 Messages.class
  ▼ 📁 resources
      ▼ 📁 css
          📄 styles.css

Figure 7–11   The directory structure of the custom validator example

Listing 7–19   validator2/src/java/com/corejsf/CreditCardValidator.java

```java
1. package com.corejsf;
2.
3. import javax.faces.application.FacesMessage;
4. import javax.faces.component.UIComponent;
5. import javax.faces.context.FacesContext;
6. import javax.faces.validator.FacesValidator;
7. import javax.faces.validator.Validator;
8. import javax.faces.validator.ValidatorException;
9.
10. @FacesValidator("com.corejsf.Card")
11. public class CreditCardValidator implements Validator {
12.    public void validate(FacesContext context, UIComponent component,
13.       Object value) {
14.      if(value == null) return;
15.      String cardNumber;
16.      if (value instanceof CreditCard)
17.        cardNumber = value.toString();
18.      else
19.        cardNumber = value.toString().replaceAll("\\D", ""); // remove non-digits
20.      if(!luhnCheck(cardNumber)) {
21.        FacesMessage message
```

```
22.              = com.corejsf.util.Messages.getMessage(
23.                 "com.corejsf.messages", "badLuhnCheck", null);
24.           message.setSeverity(FacesMessage.SEVERITY_ERROR);
25.           throw new ValidatorException(message);
26.       }
27.    }
28.
29.    private static boolean luhnCheck(String cardNumber) {
30.       int sum = 0;
31.
32.       for(int i = cardNumber.length() - 1; i >= 0; i -= 2) {
33.          sum += Integer.parseInt(cardNumber.substring(i, i + 1));
34.          if(i > 0) {
35.             int d = 2 * Integer.parseInt(cardNumber.substring(i - 1, i));
36.             if(d > 9) d -= 9;
37.             sum += d;
38.          }
39.       }
40.
41.       return sum % 10 == 0;
42.    }
43. }
```

Listing 7–20 validator2/web/index.xhtml

```
1. <?xml version="1.0" encoding="UTF-8"?>
2. <!DOCTYPE html PUBLIC "-//W3C//DTD XHTML 1.0 Transitional//EN"
3. "http://www.w3.org/TR/xhtml1/DTD/xhtml1-transitional.dtd">
4. <html xmlns="http://www.w3.org/1999/xhtml"
5.       xmlns:f="http://java.sun.com/jsf/core"
6.       xmlns:h="http://java.sun.com/jsf/html">
7.    <h:head>
8.       <h:outputStylesheet library="css" name="styles.css"/>
9.       <title>#{msgs.title}</title>
10.   </h:head>
11.   <h:body>
12.      <h:form>
13.         <h1>#{msgs.enterPayment}</h1>
14.         <h:panelGrid columns="3">
15.            #{msgs.amount}
16.            <h:inputText id="amount" label="#{msgs.amount}"
17.                         value="#{payment.amount}">
18.               <f:convertNumber minFractionDigits="2"/>
19.            </h:inputText>
20.            <h:message for="amount" styleClass="errorMessage"/>
21.
```

```
22.        #{msgs.creditCard}
23.        <h:inputText id="card" label="#{msgs.creditCard}"
24.                     value="#{payment.card}" required="true">
25.          <f:converter converterId="com.corejsf.Card"/>
26.          <f:validator validatorId="com.corejsf.Card"/>
27.        </h:inputText>
28.        <h:message for="card" styleClass="errorMessage"/>
29.
30.        #{msgs.expirationDate}
31.        <h:inputText id="date" label="#{msgs.expirationDate}"
32.                     value="#{payment.date}">
33.          <f:convertDateTime pattern="MM/yyyy"/>
34.        </h:inputText>
35.        <h:message for="date" styleClass="errorMessage"/>
36.      </h:panelGrid>
37.      <h:commandButton value="#{msgs.process}" action="result"/>
38.    </h:form>
39.  </h:body>
40. </html>
```

 @javax.faces.validator.FacesValidator

- String value

  The ID of the converter.

Validating with Bean Methods

In the preceding section, you saw how to implement a validation class. However, you can also add the validation method to an existing class and invoke it through a method expression, like this:

```
<h:inputText id="card" value="#{payment.card}"
   required="true" validator="#{payment.luhnCheck}"/>
```

The payment bean must then have a method with the exact same signature as the validate method of the Validator interface:

```
public class PaymentBean {
   ...
   public void luhnCheck(FacesContext context, UIComponent component, Object value) {
      ... // same code as in the preceding example
   }
}
```

Why would you want to do this? There is one major advantage. The validation method can access other instance variables of the class. You saw an example in the section, "Supplying Attributes to Converters" on page 289.

On the downside, this approach makes it more difficult to move a validator to a new web application, so you would probably only use it for application-specific scenarios.

CAUTION: The value of the validator attribute is a *method expression*, whereas the seemingly similar converter attribute specifies a *converter ID* (if it is a string) or a *converter object* (if it is a value expression). As Emerson said, "A foolish consistency is the hobgoblin of little minds."

Validating Relationships between Multiple Components

The validation mechanism in JSF was designed to validate a *single* component. However, in practice, you often need to ensure that related components have reasonable values before letting the values propagate into the model. For example, as we noted earlier, it is not a good idea to ask users to enter a date into a single text field. Instead, you would use three different text fields, for the day, month, and year, as in Figure 7–12.

If the user enters an illegal date, such as February 30, you would want to show a validation error and prevent the illegal data from entering the model.

Figure 7–12   Validating a relationship involving three components

You can solve this problem with the following approach. Attach the validator to the last of the components. By the time its validator is called, the preceding components have passed validation and had their local values set. The last component has passed conversion, and the converted value is passed as the Object parameter of the validation method.

To carry out this approach, the validator of the last component needs to have access to the other components. You can achieve that access by giving ID values to the other components. Then you can use the findComponent method of the UIComponent class to locate them:

```
public class BackingBean {
    ...
    public void validateDate(FacesContext context, UIComponent component,
            Object value) {
        UITnput dayInput = (UIInput) component.findComponent("day");
        UIInput monthInput = (UIInput) component.findComponent("month");
        int d = ((Integer) dayInput.getLocalValue()).intValue();
        int m = ((Integer) monthInput.getLocalValue()).intValue();
        int y = ((Integer) value).intValue();

        if (!isValidDate(d, m, y)) {
            FacesMessage message = ...;
            throw new ValidatorException(message);
        }
    }
    ...
}
```

Note that the value lookup is a bit asymmetric. The last component does not yet have the local value set because it has not passed validation.

An alternative approach is to attach the validator to a *hidden input field* that comes after all other fields on the form:

```
<h:inputHidden id="datecheck" validator="#{bb.validateDate}"
    value="needed"/>
```

The hidden field is rendered as a hidden HTML input field. When the field value is posted back, the validator kicks in. (It is essential that you supply some field value. Otherwise, the component value is never updated.) With this approach, the validation function is more symmetrical since all other form components already have their local values set.

 NOTE: In Chapter 8, you will see another approach: a listener to the PostValidateEvent that checks the three components.

> **NOTE:** It would actually be worthwhile to write a custom date component that renders three input fields and has a single value of type Date. That single component could then be validated easily. However, the technique of this section is useful for any form that needs validation across fields.

Implementing Custom Converter and Validator Tags

The custom converters and validator classes that you saw in the preceding sections have a shortcoming: They do not allow attributes. For example, we may want to specify a separator character for the credit card converter so that the page designer can choose whether to use dashes or spaces to separate the digit groups. Specifically, we would like page designers to use tags, such as the following:

```
<h:outputText value="#{payment.card}">
   <corejsf:convertCreditcard separator="-"/>
</h:outputText>
```

In other words, custom converters should have the same capabilities as the standard f:convertNumber and f:convertDateTime tags. To achieve this, you need to implement a custom converter tag. In this section, you will learn how to implement your own converter and validator tags.

You need to define custom converter and validator tags in a tag descriptor file. You have already encountered these descriptor files in Chapter 5. You can set the file location in web.xml, like this:

```
<context-param>
  <param-name>javax.faces.FACELETS_LIBRARIES</param-name>
  <param-value>/WEB-INF/corejsf.taglib.xml</param-value>
</context-param>
```

Alternatively, if you want to package your tags to that they are usable in other projects, you place them inside a JAR file and add the tag descriptor file into the META-INF directory.

Listing 7–21 shows the descriptor file that describes a custom converter and validator.

Listing 7–21 custom-tags/web/WEB-INF/corejsf.taglib.xml

```
 1. <?xml version="1.0" encoding="UTF-8"?>
 2. <facelet-taglib version="2.0"
 3.    xmlns="http://java.sun.com/xml/ns/javaee"
 4.    xmlns:xsi="http://www.w3.org/2001/XMLSchema-instance"
 5.    xsi:schemaLocation="http://java.sun.com/xml/ns/javaee
 6.    http://java.sun.com/xml/ns/javaee/web-facelettaglibary_2_0.xsd">
 7.    <namespace>http://corejsf.com</namespace>
 8.    <tag>
 9.       <tag-name>convertCreditCard</tag-name>
10.       <converter>
11.          <converter-id>com.corejsf.CreditCard</converter-id>
12.       </converter>
13.    </tag>
14.    <tag>
15.       <tag-name>validateCreditCard</tag-name>
16.       <validator>
17.          <validator-id>com.corejsf.CreditCard</validator-id>
18.       </validator>
19.    </tag>
20. </facelet-taglib>
```

You simply supply the converter or validator ID for the given tag name.

Listing 7–22 on page 299 shows the full converter class. Note the setSeparator method that is called when a separator is provided in the tag.

When implementing converters or validators that have state, you need to make sure that the state can be saved. The easiest way of accomplishing that is to implement the Serializable interface and follow the usual rules for Java serialization. (For more information on state saving, please see Chapter 11.)

In our sample application, we also provide a validator tag for carrying out the Luhn check. We use that validator in the following way:

```
<h:inputText id="card" value="#{payment.card}" required="true">
   <corejsf:validateCreditCard errorDetail="#{msgs.creditCardError}"/>
</h:inputText>
```

By default, the validator displays an error message that complains about failing the Luhn check. If your application's audience includes users who are unfamiliar with that terminology, you will want to change the message. We give you attributes errorSummmary and errorDetail for this purpose.

You will find the validator code in Listing 7–23. Note the setErrorSummary and setErrorDetail methods for setting the tag attributes.

Figure 7–13 shows the application's directory structure. Listing 7–24 shows the JSF page.

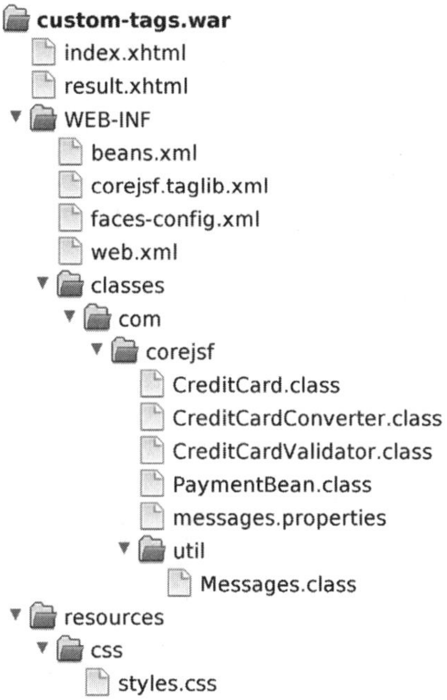

- 📁 **custom-tags.war**
  - 📄 index.xhtml
  - 📄 result.xhtml
  - ▼ 📁 WEB-INF
    - 📄 beans.xml
    - 📄 corejsf.taglib.xml
    - 📄 faces-config.xml
    - 📄 web.xml
    - ▼ 📁 classes
      - ▼ 📁 com
        - ▼ 📁 corejsf
          - 📄 CreditCard.class
          - 📄 CreditCardConverter.class
          - 📄 CreditCardValidator.class
          - 📄 PaymentBean.class
          - 📄 messages.properties
          - ▼ 📁 util
            - 📄 Messages.class
  - ▼ 📁 resources
    - ▼ 📁 css
      - 📄 styles.css

Figure 7–13 Directory structure of the thoroughly validating application

Listing 7–22 custom-tags/src/java/com/corejsf/CreditCardConverter.java

```
 1. package com.corejsf;
 2.
 3. import java.io.Serializable;
 4. import javax.faces.component.UIComponent;
 5. import javax.faces.context.FacesContext;
 6. import javax.faces.convert.Converter;
 7. import javax.faces.convert.ConverterException;
 8. import javax.faces.convert.FacesConverter;
 9.
10. @FacesConverter("com.corejsf.CreditCard")
11. public class CreditCardConverter implements Converter, Serializable
12. {
13.    private String separator;
14.
15.    public void setSeparator(String newValue) { separator = newValue; }
16.
```

```
17.    public Object getAsObject(
18.        FacesContext context,
19.        UIComponent component,
20.        String newValue)
21.        throws ConverterException {
22.        StringBuilder builder = new StringBuilder(newValue);
23.        int i = 0;
24.        while (i < builder.length()) {
25.            if (Character.isDigit(builder.charAt(i)))
26.                i++;
27.            else
28.                builder.deleteCharAt(i);
29.        }
30.        return new CreditCard(builder.toString());
31.    }
32.
33.    public String getAsString(
34.        FacesContext context,
35.        UIComponent component,
36.        Object value)
37.        throws ConverterException {
38.        // length 13: xxxx xxx xxx xxx
39.        // length 14: xxxxx xxxx xxxxx
40.        // length 15: xxxx xxxxxx xxxxx
41.        // length 16: xxxx xxxx xxxx xxxx
42.        // length 22: xxxxxx xxxxxxxx xxxxxxxx
43.        if (!(value instanceof CreditCard))
44.            throw new ConverterException();
45.        String v = ((CreditCard) value).toString();
46.        String sep = separator;
47.        if (sep == null) sep = " ";
48.        int[] boundaries = null;
49.        int length = v.length();
50.        if (length == 13)
51.            boundaries = new int[] { 4, 7, 10 };
52.        else if (length == 14)
53.            boundaries = new int[] { 5, 9 };
54.        else if (length == 15)
55.            boundaries = new int[] { 4, 10 };
56.        else if (length == 16)
57.            boundaries = new int[] { 4, 8, 12 };
58.        else if (length == 22)
59.            boundaries = new int[] { 6, 14 };
60.        else
61.            return v;
62.        StringBuilder result = new StringBuilder();
63.        int start = 0;
```

```
64.     for (int i = 0; i < boundaries.length; i++) {
65.        int end = boundaries[i];
66.        result.append(v.substring(start, end));
67.        result.append(sep);
68.        start = end;
69.     }
70.     result.append(v.substring(start));
71.     return result.toString();
72.  }
73.}
```

Listing 7–23 custom-tags/src/java/com/corejsf/CreditCardValidator.java

```
1. package com.corejsf;
2.
3. import java.io.Serializable;
4. import java.text.MessageFormat;
5. import java.util.Locale;
6.
7. import javax.faces.application.FacesMessage;
8. import javax.faces.component.UIComponent;
9. import javax.faces.context.FacesContext;
10. import javax.faces.validator.FacesValidator;
11. import javax.faces.validator.Validator;
12. import javax.faces.validator.ValidatorException;
13.
14. @FacesValidator("com.corejsf.CreditCard")
15. public class CreditCardValidator implements Validator, Serializable {
16.     private String errorSummary;
17.     private String errorDetail;
18.
19.     public void validate(FacesContext context, UIComponent component,
20.            Object value) {
21.        if(value == null) return;
22.        String cardNumber;
23.        if (value instanceof CreditCard)
24.           cardNumber = value.toString();
25.        else
26.           cardNumber = getDigitsOnly(value.toString());
27.        if(!luhnCheck(cardNumber)) {
28.           FacesMessage message
29.             = com.corejsf.util.Messages.getMessage(
30.                "com.corejsf.messages", "badLuhnCheck", null);
31.           message.setSeverity(FacesMessage.SEVERITY_ERROR);
32.           Locale locale = context.getViewRoot().getLocale();
33.           Object[] params = new Object[] { value };
34.           if (errorSummary != null)
```

```
35.              message.setSummary(
36.                  new MessageFormat(errorSummary, locale).format(params));
37.          if (errorDetail != null)
38.              message.setDetail(
39.                  new MessageFormat(errorDetail, locale).format(params));
40.          throw new ValidatorException(message);
41.      }
42.  }
43.
44.  public void setErrorSummary(String newValue) {
45.      errorSummary = newValue;
46.  }
47.
48.  public void setErrorDetail(String newValue) {
49.      errorDetail = newValue;
50.  }
51.
52.  private static boolean luhnCheck(String cardNumber) {
53.      int sum = 0;
54.
55.      for(int i = cardNumber.length() - 1; i >= 0; i -= 2) {
56.          sum += Integer.parseInt(cardNumber.substring(i, i + 1));
57.          if(i > 0) {
58.              int d = 2 * Integer.parseInt(cardNumber.substring(i - 1, i));
59.              if(d > 9) d -= 9;
60.              sum += d;
61.          }
62.      }
63.
64.      return sum % 10 == 0;
65.  }
66.
67.  private static String getDigitsOnly(String s) {
68.      StringBuilder digitsOnly = new StringBuilder ();
69.      char c;
70.      for(int i = 0; i < s.length (); i++) {
71.          c = s.charAt (i);
72.          if (Character.isDigit(c)) {
73.              digitsOnly.append(c);
74.          }
75.      }
76.      return digitsOnly.toString ();
77.  }
78. }
```

Listing 7-24   `custom-tags/web/index.xhtml`

```
1. <?xml version="1.0" encoding="UTF-8"?>
2. <!DOCTYPE html PUBLIC "-//W3C//DTD XHTML 1.0 Transitional//EN"
3. "http://www.w3.org/TR/xhtml1/DTD/xhtml1-transitional.dtd">
4. <html xmlns="http://www.w3.org/1999/xhtml"
5.       xmlns:h="http://java.sun.com/jsf/html"
6.       xmlns:f="http://java.sun.com/jsf/core"
7.       xmlns:corejsf="http://corejsf.com">
8.   <h:head>
9.       <h:outputStylesheet library="css" name="styles.css"/>
10.      <title>#{msgs.title}</title>
11.   </h:head>
12.   <h:body>
13.     <h:form>
14.       <h1>#{msgs.enterPayment}</h1>
15.       <h:panelGrid columns="2">
16.         #{msgs.amount}
17.         <h:inputText id="amount" value="#{payment.amount}">
18.             <f:convertNumber minFractionDigits="2"/>
19.         </h:inputText>
20.
21.         #{msgs.creditCard}
22.         <h:inputText id="card" value="#{payment.card}" required="true">
23.             <corejsf:validateCreditCard
24.                   errorDetail="#{msgs.creditCardError}"/>
25.         </h:inputText>
26.
27.         #{msgs.expirationDate}
28.         <h:inputText id="date" value="#{payment.date}">
29.             <f:convertDateTime pattern="MM/yyyy"/>
30.         </h:inputText>
31.       </h:panelGrid>
32.       <h:messages styleClass="errorMessage"
33.                   showSummary="false" showDetail="true"/>
34.       <br/>
35.       <h:commandButton value="Process" action="result"/>
36.     </h:form>
37.   </h:body>
38. </html>
```

Conclusion

As you have seen, JSF provides extensive and extensible support for conversion and validation. You can use the JSF standard converter and validators with one line of code in your JSF pages, or you can supply your own logic if more complex conversions or validations are needed. Finally, you can define your own conversion and validation tags.

EVENT HANDLING

Topics in This Chapter

Chapter 8

Web applications often need to respond to user events, such as selecting items from a menu or clicking a button. For example, you might want to respond to the selection of a country in an address form by changing the locale and reloading the current page to better accommodate your users.

Typically, you register event handlers with components—for example, you might register a value change listener with a menu in a JSF page, like this:

```
<h:selectOneMenu valueChangeListener="#{form.countryChanged}"...>
    ...
</h:selectOneMenu>
```

In the preceding code, the method binding #{form.countryChanged} references the countryChanged method of a bean named form. That method is invoked by the JSF implementation after the user makes a selection from the menu. Exactly when that method is invoked is one topic of discussion in this chapter.

JSF supports four kinds of events:

- Value change events
- Action events
- Phase events
- System events (since JSF 2.0)

Value change events are fired by *editable value holders*—such as h:inputText, h:selectOneRadio, and h:selectManyMenu—when the component's value changes.

Action events are fired by *action sources*—for example, h:commandButton and h:commandLink—when the button or link is activated. Phase events are routinely fired by the JSF life cycle. JSF 2.0 adds a large number of system events. Some of the system events are of interest to application programmers. For example, it is now possible to carry out an action before a view or component is rendered.

 NOTE: Keep in mind that all JSF events are executed *on the server*. When you provide an event handler in a JSF page, you tell the JSF implementation that you want the event to be handled, at the appropriate place in the life cycle, when the server processes the user input from your page.

Events and the JSF Life Cycle

Requests in JSF applications are processed by the JSF implementation with a controller servlet, which in turn executes the JSF life cycle. Event handling in the JSF life cycle is shown in Figure 8–1.

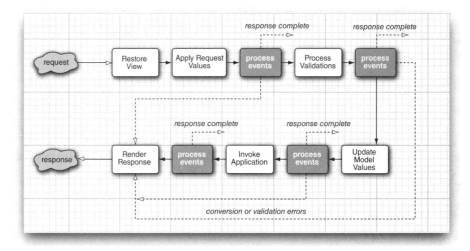

Figure 8–1   Event handling in the JSF life cycle

Starting with the Apply Request Values phase, the JSF implementation may create events and add them to an event queue during each life cycle phase. After those phases, the JSF implementation broadcasts queued events to registered listeners. Those events and their associated listeners are the focus of this chapter.

NOTE: Event listeners can affect the JSF life cycle in one of three ways:

1. Let the life cycle proceed normally.
2. Call the `renderResponse` method of the `FacesContext` class to skip the rest of the life cycle up to Render Response.
3. Call the `responseComplete` method of the `FacesContext` class to skip the rest of the life cycle entirely.

See "Immediate Components" on page 320 for an example of using the `renderResponse` method.

Value Change Events

Components in a web application often depend on each other. For example, in the application shown in Figure 8–2, the value of the "State" prompt depends on the "Country" menu's value. You can keep dependent components in synch with value change events, which are fired by input components after their new value has been validated.

Figure 8–2   Using value change events

The application in Figure 8–2 attaches a value change listener to the "Country" menu and uses the onchange attribute to force a form submit after the menu's value is changed:

```
<h:selectOneMenu value="#{form.country}" onchange="submit()"
    valueChangeListener="#{form.countryChanged}">
  <f:selectItems value="#{form.countries}" var="loc"
      itemLabel="#{loc.displayCountry}" itemValue="#{loc.country}"/>
</h:selectOneMenu>
```

Here, #{form.countries} is bound to an array of Locale objects.

When a user selects a country from the menu, the JavaScript submit function is invoked to submit the menu's form, which subsequently invokes the JSF life cycle. After the Process Validations phase, the JSF implementation invokes the form bean's countryChanged method. That method changes the view root's locale, according to the new country value:

```
public void countryChanged(ValueChangeEvent event) {
    for (Locale loc : countries)
        if (loc.getCountry().equals(event.getNewValue()))
            FacesContext.getCurrentInstance().getViewRoot().setLocale(loc);
}
```

Like all value change listeners, the preceding listener is passed a value change event. The listener uses that event to access the component's new value.

One more thing is noteworthy about this example. Notice that we add an onchange attribute whose value is submit() to our h:selectOneMenu tag. Setting that attribute means that the JavaScript submit function will be invoked whenever someone changes the selected value of the menu, which causes the surrounding form to be submitted.

That form submit is crucial because *the JSF implementation handles all events on the server*. If you take out the onchange attribute, the form will not be submitted when the selected menu item is changed, meaning that the JSF life cycle will never be invoked, our value change listener will never be called, and the locale will never be changed.

You may find it odd that JSF handles all events on the server, but remember that *you* can handle events on the client if you wish by attaching JavaScript to components with attributes, such as onblur, onfocus, onclick, and so on.

The directory structure for the application in Figure 8–2 is shown in Figure 8–3 and the application is shown in Listings 8–1 through 8–5.

API | **javax.faces.event.ValueChangeEvent**

- UIComponent getComponent()

  Returns the input component that triggered the event.

- Object getNewValue()

  Returns the component's new value, after the value has been converted and validated.

- Object getOldValue()

  Returns the component's previous value.

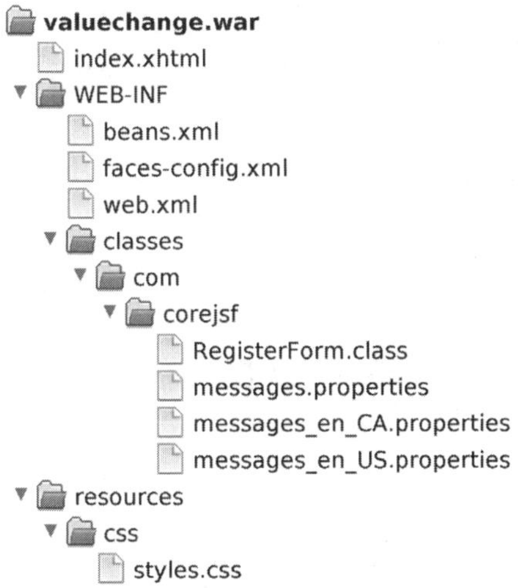

📁 **valuechange.war**
  📄 index.xhtml
▼ 📁 WEB-INF
    📄 beans.xml
    📄 faces-config.xml
    📄 web.xml
  ▼ 📁 classes
    ▼ 📁 com
      ▼ 📁 corejsf
        📄 RegisterForm.class
        📄 messages.properties
        📄 messages_en_CA.properties
        📄 messages_en_US.properties
▼ 📁 resources
  ▼ 📁 css
    📄 styles.css

Figure 8–3   **Directory structure for the value change example**

Listing 8–1 | valuechange/web/index.xhtml

```
1. <?xml version="1.0" encoding="UTF-8"?>
2. <!DOCTYPE html PUBLIC "-//W3C//DTD XHTML 1.0 Transitional//EN"
3. "http://www.w3.org/TR/xhtml1/DTD/xhtml1-transitional.dtd">
4. <html xmlns="http://www.w3.org/1999/xhtml"
5.       xmlns:f="http://java.sun.com/jsf/core"
6.       xmlns:h="http://java.sun.com/jsf/html">
7.    <h:head>
8.       <h:outputStylesheet library="css" name="styles.css"/>
9.       <title>#{msgs.windowTitle}</title>
10.   </h:head>
11.
12.   <h:body>
13.      <h:form>
14.         <span class="emphasis">#{msgs.pageTitle}</span>
```

```
15.        <h:panelGrid columns="2">
16.            #{msgs.streetAddressPrompt}
17.            <h:inputText value="#{form.streetAddress}"/>
18.
19.            #{msgs.cityPrompt}
20.            <h:inputText value="#{form.city}"/>
21.
22.            #{msgs.statePrompt}
23.            <h:inputText value="#{form.state}"/>
24.
25.            #{msgs.countryPrompt}
26.            <h:selectOneMenu value="#{form.country}" onchange="submit()"
27.                valueChangeListener="#{form.countryChanged}">
28.                <f:selectItems value="#{form.countries}" var="loc"
29.                itemLabel="#{loc.displayCountry}" itemValue="#{loc.country}"/>
30.            </h:selectOneMenu>
31.        </h:panelGrid>
32.        <h:commandButton value="#{msgs.submit}"/>
33.    </h:form>
34.    </h:body>
35. </html>
```

Listing 8–2   valuechange/src/java/com/corejsf/RegisterForm.java

```
 1. package com.corejsf;
 2.
 3. import java.io.Serializable;
 4. import java.util.LinkedHashMap;
 5. import java.util.Locale;
 6. import java.util.Map;
 7.
 8. import javax.inject.Named;
 9.    // or import javax.faces.bean.ManagedBean;
10. import javax.enterprise.context.SessionScoped;
11.    // or import javax.faces.bean.SessionScoped;
12. import javax.faces.context.FacesContext;
13. import javax.faces.event.ValueChangeEvent;
14.
15. @Named("form") // or @ManagedBean(name="form")
16. @SessionScoped
17. public class RegisterForm implements Serializable {
18.     private String streetAddress;
19.     private String city;
20.     private String state;
21.     private String country;
22.
23.     private static final Locale[] countries = { Locale.US, Locale.CANADA };
```

```
24.    public Locale[] getCountries() { return countries; }
25.
26.    public void setStreetAddress(String newValue) { streetAddress = newValue; }
27.    public String getStreetAddress() { return streetAddress; }
28.
29.    public void setCity(String newValue) { city = newValue; }
30.    public String getCity() { return city; }
31.
32.    public void setState(String newValue) { state = newValue; }
33.    public String getState() { return state; }
34.
35.    public void setCountry(String newValue) { country = newValue; }
36.    public String getCountry() { return country; }
37.
38.    public void countryChanged(ValueChangeEvent event) {
39.       for (Locale loc : countries)
40.          if (loc.getCountry().equals(event.getNewValue()))
41.             FacesContext.getCurrentInstance().getViewRoot().setLocale(loc);
42.    }
43. }
```

Listing 8–3 valuechange/web/WEB-INF/faces-config.xml

```
1. <?xml version="1.0"?>
2. <faces-config xmlns="http://java.sun.com/xml/ns/javaee"
3.    xmlns:xsi="http://www.w3.org/2001/XMLSchema-instance"
4.    xsi:schemaLocation="http://java.sun.com/xml/ns/javaee
5.       http://java.sun.com/xml/ns/javaee/web-facesconfig_2_0.xsd"
6.    version="2.0">
7.    <application>
8.       <resource-bundle>
9.          <base-name>com.corejsf.messages</base-name>
10.         <var>msgs</var>
11.      </resource-bundle>
12.   </application>
13. </faces-config>
```

Listing 8–4 valuechange/src/java/com/corejsf/messages_en_US.properties

```
1. windowTitle=Using Value Change Events
2. pageTitle=Please fill in your address
3.
4. streetAddressPrompt=Address
5. cityPrompt=City
6. statePrompt=State
7. countryPrompt=Country
8. submit=Submit address
```

Listing 8–5   `valuechange/src/java/com/corejsf/messages_en_CA.properties`

```
1. windowTitle=Using Value Change Events
2. pageTitle=Please fill in your address
3.
4. streetAddressPrompt=Address
5. cityPrompt=City
6. statePrompt=Province
7. countryPrompt=Country
8. submit=Submit address
```

Action Events

Action events are fired by buttons and links. As you saw in "Events and the JSF Life Cycle" on page 306, action events are fired during the Invoke Application phase, near the end of the life cycle.

You can add an action listener to an action source, like this:

```
<h:commandLink actionListener="#{bean.linkActivated}">
   ...
</h:commandLink>
```

Command components submit requests when they are activated, so there is no need to use onchange to force form submits as we did with value change events in "Value Change Events" on page 307. When you activate a button or link, the surrounding form is submitted and the JSF implementation subsequently fires action events.

It is important to distinguish between *action listeners* and *actions*. In a nutshell, actions are designed for business logic and participate in navigation handling, whereas action listeners typically perform user interface logic and do not participate in navigation handling.

Action listeners sometimes work in concert with actions when an action needs information about the user interface. For example, the application shown in Figure 8–4 uses an action and an action listener to react to mouse clicks by forwarding to a JSF page.

If you click on a president's face, the application forwards to a JSF page with information about that president. Note that an action alone cannot implement that behavior—an action can *navigate* to the appropriate page, but it cannot *determine* the appropriate page because it knows nothing about the image button in the user interface or the mouse click.

The application shown in Figure 8–4 uses a button with an image, like this:

```
<h:commandButton image="/resources/images/mountrushmore.jpg"
    actionListener="#{rushmore.handleMouseClick}"
    action="#{rushmore.act}"/>
```

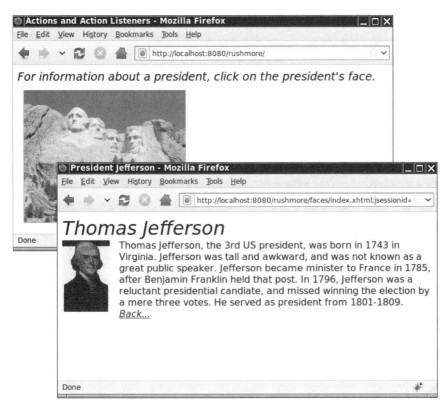

Figure 8–4   The Rushmore application

When you click a president, a listener—which has access to the mouse click coordinates—determines which president was selected. But the listener cannot affect navigation, so it stores an outcome corresponding to the selected president in an instance field:

```
public class Rushmore {
    private String outcome;
    private Rectangle washingtonRect = new Rectangle(70,30,40,40);
    private Rectangle jeffersonRect  = new Rectangle(115,45,40,40);
    private Rectangle rooseveltRect  = new Rectangle(135,65,40,40);
    private Rectangle lincolnRect    = new Rectangle(175,62,40,40);

    public void listen(ActionEvent e) {
```

```
FacesContext context = FacesContext.getCurrentInstance();
String clientId = e.getComponent().getClientId(context);
Map requestParams = context.getExternalContext().
   getRequestParameterMap();

int x = new Integer((String) requestParams.get(clientId + ".x")).intValue();
int y = new Integer((String) requestParams.get(clientId + ".y")).intValue();

outcome = null;

if (washingtonRect.contains(new Point(x,y)))
   outcome = "washington";

if (jeffersonRect.contains(new Point(x,y)))
   outcome = "jefferson";

if (rooseveltRect.contains(new Point(x,y)))
   outcome = "roosevelt";

if (lincolnRect.contains(new Point(x,y)))
   outcome = "lincoln";
   }
}
```

The action associated with the button uses the outcome to affect navigation:

```
public String act() {
   return outcome;
}
```

Note that the JSF implementation always invokes action listeners before actions.

NOTE: JSF insists that you separate user interface logic and business logic by refusing to give actions access to events or the components that fire them. In the preceding example, the action cannot access the client ID of the component that fired the event, information that is necessary for extraction of mouse coordinates from the request parameters. Because the action knows nothing about the user interface, we must add an action listener to the mix to implement the required behavior.

The directory structure for the application in Figure 8–4 is shown in Figure 8–5. The application is shown in Listings 8–6 through 8–9.

rushmore.war
- index.xhtml
- jefferson.xhtml
- lincoln.xhtml
- roosevelt.xhtml
- washington.xhtml
- ▼ WEB-INF
  - beans.xml
  - faces-config.xml
  - web.xml
  - ▼ classes
    - ▼ com
      - ▼ corejsf
        - Rushmore.class
        - messages.properties
- ▼ resources
  - ▼ css
    - styles.css
  - ▼ images
    - jefferson.jpg
    - lincoln.jpg
    - mountrushmore.jpg
    - roosevelt.jpg
    - washington.jpg

Figure 8–5   Directory structure for the Rushmore example

Listing 8–6   rushmore/web/index.xhtml

```
1. <?xml version="1.0" encoding="UTF-8"?>
2. <!DOCTYPE html PUBLIC "-//W3C//DTD XHTML 1.0 Transitional//EN"
3. "http://www.w3.org/TR/xhtml1/DTD/xhtml1-transitional.dtd">
4. <html xmlns="http://www.w3.org/1999/xhtml"
5.       xmlns:h="http://java.sun.com/jsf/html">
6.   <h:head>
7.     <h:outputStylesheet library="css" name="styles.css"/>
8.     <title>#{msgs.indexWindowTitle}</title>
9.   </h:head>
10.
11.   <h:body>
12.     <span class="instructions">#{msgs.instructions}</span>
13.     <h:form>
14.       <h:commandButton image="/resources/images/mountrushmore.jpg"
15.                   styleClass="imageButton"
16.                   actionListener="#{rushmore.handleMouseClick}"
17.                   action="#{rushmore.navigate}"/>
```

```
18.        </h:form>
19.      </h:body>
20.  </html>
```

Listing 8–7 rushmore/web/lincoln.xhtml

```
 1. <?xml version="1.0" encoding="UTF-8"?>
 2. <!DOCTYPE html PUBLIC "-//W3C//DTD XHTML 1.0 Transitional//EN"
 3. "http://www.w3.org/TR/xhtml1/DTD/xhtml1-transitional.dtd">
 4. <html xmlns="http://www.w3.org/1999/xhtml"
 5.       xmlns:f="http://java.sun.com/jsf/core" xmlns:h="http://java.sun.com/jsf/html">
 6.   <h:head>
 7.     <h:outputStylesheet library="css" name="styles.css"/>
 8.     <title>#{msgs.lincolnWindowTitle}</title>
 9.   </h:head>
10.
11.   <h:body>
12.     <h:form>
13.       <span class="presidentPageTitle">#{msgs.lincolnPageTitle}</span>
14.       <br/>
15.       <h:graphicImage library="images" name="lincoln.jpg" styleClass="leftImage"/>
16.       <span class="presidentDiscussion">#{msgs.lincolnDiscussion}</span>
17.       <br/>
18.       <h:commandLink action="index"
19.                  styleClass="backLink">${msgs.indexLinkText}</h:commandLink>
20.     </h:form>
21.   </h:body>
22. </html>
```

Listing 8–8 rushmore/src/java/com/corejsf/Rushmore.java

```
 1. package com.corejsf;
 2.
 3. import java.awt.Point;
 4. import java.awt.Rectangle;
 5. import java.util.Map;
 6.
 7. import javax.inject.Named;
 8.    // or import javax.faces.bean.ManagedBean;
 9. import javax.enterprise.context.RequestScoped;
10.    // or import javax.faces.bean.RequestScoped;
11. import javax.faces.context.FacesContext;
12. import javax.faces.event.ActionEvent;
13.
14. @Named // or @ManagedBean
15. @RequestScoped
```

```
16. public class Rushmore {
17.     private String outcome = null;
18.     private Rectangle washingtonRect = new Rectangle(70, 30, 40, 40);
19.     private Rectangle jeffersonRect = new Rectangle(115, 45, 40, 40);
20.     private Rectangle rooseveltRect = new Rectangle(135, 65, 40, 40);
21.     private Rectangle lincolnRect = new Rectangle(175, 62, 40, 40);
22.
23.     public void handleMouseClick(ActionEvent e) {
24.         FacesContext context = FacesContext.getCurrentInstance();
25.         String clientId = e.getComponent().getClientId(context);
26.         Map<String, String> requestParams
27.             = context.getExternalContext().getRequestParameterMap();
28.
29.         int x = new Integer((String) requestParams.get(clientId + ".x")).intValue();
30.         int y = new Integer((String) requestParams.get(clientId + ".y")).intValue();
31.
32.         outcome = null;
33.
34.         if (washingtonRect.contains(new Point(x, y)))
35.             outcome = "washington";
36.
37.         if (jeffersonRect.contains(new Point(x, y)))
38.             outcome = "jefferson";
39.
40.         if (rooseveltRect.contains(new Point(x, y)))
41.             outcome = "roosevelt";
42.
43.         if (lincolnRect.contains(new Point(x, y)))
44.             outcome = "lincoln";
45.     }
46.
47.     public String navigate() {
48.         return outcome;
49.     }
50. }
```

Listing 8–9   rushmore/src/java/com/corejsf/messages.properties

```
1. instructions=For information about a president, click on the president's face.
2.
3. indexWindowTitle=Actions and Action Listeners
4. indexLinkText=Back...
5. jeffersonWindowTitle=President Jefferson
6. rooseveltWindowTitle=President Roosevelt
7. lincolnWindowTitle=President Lincoln
8. washingtonWindowTitle=President Washington
```

```
 9.
10. jeffersonPageTitle=Thomas Jefferson
11. rooseveltPageTitle=Theodore Roosevelt
12. lincolnPageTitle=Abraham Lincoln
13. washingtonPageTitle=George Washington
14.
15. lincolnDiscussion=President Lincoln was known as the Great Emancipator because \
16. he was instrumental in abolishing slavery in the United States. He was born \
17. into a poor family in Kentucky in 1809, elected president in 1860 and \
18. assassinated by John Wilkes Booth in 1865.
19.
20. washingtonDiscussion=George Washington was the first president of the United \
21. States. He was born in 1732 in Virginia and was elected Commander in Chief of \
22. the Continental Army in 1775 and forced the surrender of Cornwallis at Yorktown \
23. in 1781. He was inaugurated on April 30, 1789.
24.
25. rooseveltDiscussion=Theodore Roosevelt was the 26th president of the United \
26. States. In 1901 he became president after the assassination of President \
27. McKinley. At only 42 years of age, he was the youngest president in US history.
28.
29. jeffersonDiscussion=Thomas Jefferson, the 3rd US president, was born in \
30. 1743 in Virginia. Jefferson was tall and awkward, and was not known as a \
31. great public speaker. Jefferson became minister to France in 1785, after \
32. Benjamin Franklin held that post. In 1796, Jefferson was a reluctant \
33. presidential candiate, and missed winning the election by a mere three votes. \
34. He served as president from 1801-1809.
```

Event Listener Tags

Up to now, we have added action and value change listeners to components
with the actionListener and valueChangeListener *attributes*, respectively. However,
you can also add action and value change listeners to a component with the
following tags:

- f:actionListener
- f:valueChangeListener

The f:actionListener *and* f:valueChangeListener *Tags*

The f:actionListener and f:valueChangeListener tags are analogous to the actionListener
and valueChangeListener attributes. For example, in Listing 8–1 on page 309, we
defined a menu like this:

```
<h:selectOneMenu value="#{form.country}" onchange="submit()"
    valueChangeListener="#{form.countryChanged}">
    <f:selectItems value="#{form.countryNames}"/>
</h:selectOneMenu>
```

Alternatively, we could use f:valueChangeListener, like this:

```
<h:selectOneMenu value="#{form.country}" onchange="submit()">
    <f:valueChangeListener type="com.corejsf.CountryListener"/>
    <f:selectItems value="#{form.countryNames}"/>
</h:selectOneMenu>
```

The tags have one advantage over the attributes: Tags let you attach multiple listeners to a single component.

Notice the difference between the values specified for the valueChangeListener attribute and the f:valueChangeListener tag in the preceding code. The former specifies a method binding, whereas the latter specifies a Java class. For example, the class referred to in the previous code fragment looks like this:

```
public class CountryListener implements ValueChangeListener {
    public void processValueChange(ValueChangeEvent event) {
        FacesContext context = FacesContext.getCurrentInstance();
        if ("US".equals(event.getNewValue()))
            context.getViewRoot().setLocale(Locale.US);
        else
            context.getViewRoot().setLocale(Locale.CANADA);
    }
}
```

Like all listeners specified with f:valueChangeListener, the preceding class implements the ValueChangeListener interface. That class defines a single method: void processValueChange(ValueChangeEvent).

The f:actionListener tag is analogous to f:valueChangeListener—the former also has a type attribute that specifies a class name; the class must implement the ActionListener interface. For example, in Listing 8–6 on page 315, we defined a button like this:

```
<h:commandButton image="mountrushmore.jpg"
    styleClass="imageButton"
    actionListener="#{rushmore.handleMouseClick}"
    action="#{rushmore.navigate}"/>
```

Instead of using the actionListener attribute to define our listener, we could have used the f:actionListener tag instead:

```
<h:commandButton image="mountrushmore.jpg" action="#{rushmore.navigate}">
    <f:actionListener type="com.corejsf.RushmoreListener"/>
</h:commandButton>
```

Action listener classes must implement the ActionListener interface, which defines a processAction method, so in the preceding code fragment, JSF will call RushmoreListener.processAction after the image button is activated.

You can specify multiple listeners with multiple f:actionListener or f:value-ChangeListener tags per component. For example, we could add another action listener to our previous example, like this:

```
<h:commandButton image="mountrushmore.jpg" action="#{rushmore.navigate}">
    <f:actionListener type="com.corejsf.RushmoreListener"/>
    <f:actionListener type="com.corejsf.ActionLogger"/>
</h:commandButton>
```

In the preceding code fragment, the ActionLogger class is a simple action listener that logs action events.

If you specify multiple listeners for a component, as we did in the preceding code fragment, the listeners are invoked in the following order:

1. The listener specified by the listener attribute

2. Listeners specified by listener tags, in the order in which they are declared

---

 NOTE: You may wonder why you must specify a method binding for listeners when you use the actionListener and valueChangeListener attributes, and why you must use a class name for listeners specified with f:actionListener and f:valueChangeListener tags. The mismatch between listener attributes and tags was an oversight on the part of the JSF expert group.

Immediate Components

In "Events and the JSF Life Cycle" on page 306, we saw that value change events are normally fired after the Process Validations phase, and action events are normally fired after the Invoke Application phase. Typically, that is the preferred behavior. You usually want to be notified of value changes only when they are valid, and actions should be invoked after all submitted values have been transmitted to the model.

But sometimes you want value change events or action events to fire at the beginning of the life cycle to bypass validation for one or more components. In "Using Immediate Input Components" on page 321 and "Bypassing Validation" on page 266 of Chapter 7, we make compelling arguments for such behavior. For now, we will look at the mechanics of how immediate events are delivered, as illustrated by Figure 8–6.

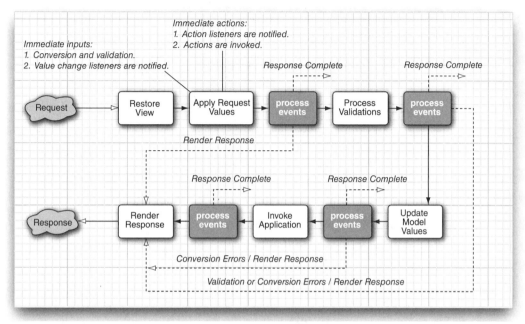

Figure 8–6   Event handling for immediate components

When a component has its immediate attribute set, it fires events after the Apply Request Values phase. An immediate input component performs conversion and validation earlier than usual, after completing the Apply Request Values phase. Then it fires a value change event. An immediate command component fires action listeners and actions earlier than usual, after the Apply Request Values phase. That process kicks in the navigation handler and circumvents the rest of the life cycle, moving directly to Render Response.

Using Immediate Input Components

Figure 8–7 shows the value change example discussed in "Value Change Events" on page 307. Recall that the application uses a value change listener to change the view's locale, which in turn changes the localized state prompt according to the selected locale.

Here we have made a seemingly innocuous change to that application: We added a required attribute to the Address field:

```
<h:inputText value="#{form.streetAddress}" required="true"/>
```

But that results in an error *when we select a country* without filling in the Address field (recall that the country menu submits its form when its value is changed).

The problem is this: We want validation to kick in when the submit button is activated, but not when the country is changed. How can we specify validation for one but not the other?

Figure 8–7   Unwanted validation

The solution is to make the country menu an *immediate* component. Immediate input components perform conversion and validation, and subsequently deliver value change events at the beginning of the JSF life cycle—after Apply Request Values—instead of after Process Validations.

We specify immediate components with the immediate attribute, which is available to all input and command components:

```
<h:selectOneMenu value="#{form.country}" onchange="submit()" immediate="true"
   valueChangeListener="#{form.countryChanged}">
   <f:selectItems value="#{form.countryNames}"/>
</h:selectOneMenu>
```

With the immediate attribute set to true, our menu fires value change events after Apply Request Values, well before any other input components are validated. You may wonder what good that does us if the other validations happen later instead of sooner—after all, the validations will still be performed and the validation error will still be displayed. To prevent validations for the other components in the form, we have one more thing to do, which is to call the renderResponse method of the FacesContext class at the end of our value change listener, like this:

```
private static final String US = "United States";
...
public void countryChanged(ValueChangeEvent event) {
   FacesContext context = FacesContext.getCurrentInstance();
```

```
   if (US.equals((String) event.getNewValue()))
      context.getViewRoot().setLocale(Locale.US);
   else
      context.getViewRoot().setLocale(Locale.CANADA);

   context.renderResponse();
}
```

The call to renderResponse skips the rest of the life cycle—including validation of the rest of the input components in the form—up to Render Response. Thus, the other validations are skipped and the response is rendered normally (in this case, the current page is redisplayed).

To summarize, you can skip validation when a value change event fires by doing the following:

1.   Adding an immediate attribute to your input tag
2.   Calling the renderResponse method of the FacesContext class at the end of your listener

Using Immediate Command Components

In Chapter 4 we discussed an application, shown in Figure 8–8, that uses command links to change locales.

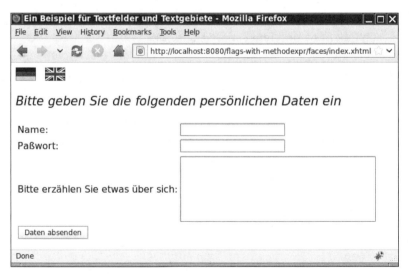

Figure 8–8   Changing locales with links

If we add a required validator to one of the input fields in the form, we will have the same problem we had with the application discussed in "Using Immediate Input Components" on page 321: The validation error will appear when we just want to change the locale by clicking a link. This time, however, we need an immediate *command* component instead of an immediate *input* component. All we need to do is add an immediate attribute to our h:commandLink tag, like this:

```
<h:commandLink action="#{localeChanger.germanAction}" immediate="true">
   <h:graphicImage library="images" name="de_flag.gif" style="border: 0px"/>
</h:commandLink>
```

Unlike value change events, we do not need to modify our listener to invoke FacesContext.renderResponse() because all actions, immediate or not, proceed directly to the Render Response phase, regardless of when they are fired.

Passing Data from the UI to the Server

The two flags in the application shown in Figure 8–8 are implemented with links. The link for the German flag is listed in the previous section. Here is the link for the British flag:

```
<h:commandLink action="#{localeChanger.englishAction}" immediate="true">
   <h:graphicImage library="images" name="en_flag.gif" style="border: 0px"/>
</h:commandLink>
```

Notice that each link has a different action: localeChanger.englishAction for the British flag and localeChanger.germanAction for the German flag. The implementations of those actions are minor:

```
public class LocaleChanger {
   public String germanAction() {
      FacesContext context = FacesContext.getCurrentInstance();
      context.getViewRoot().setLocale(Locale.GERMAN);
      return null;
   }

   public String englishAction() {
      FacesContext context = FacesContext.getCurrentInstance();
      context.getViewRoot().setLocale(Locale.ENGLISH);
      return null;
   }
}
```

Each action method sets the locale of the view root and returns null to indicate that the JSF implementation should reload the same page. Pretty simple.

But imagine if we supported many languages—for example, if we supported 100 languages, we would have to implement 100 actions, and each action would be identical to all the others except for the locale that it would set. Not so simple.

To reduce redundant code that we must write and maintain, it's better to pass the language code from the UI to the server. That way, we can write a single action or action listener to change the view root's locale. JSF gives us four mechanisms to pass information from the UI to the server:

- Method expression parameters (since JSF 2.0)
- The f:param tag
- The f:attribute tag
- The f:setPropertyActionListener tag (since JSF 1.2)

Now we take a look at each tag in turn to see how we can eliminate redundant code.

Method Expression Parameters JSF 2.0

Since JSF 2.0, method expressions can take parameters. Therefore, we can simply pass the desired locale as a value to the action method, like this:

```
<h:commandLink action="#{localeChanger.changeLocale('de')}">
    <h:graphicImage library="images" name="de_flag.gif" style="border: 0px"/>
</h:commandLink>
<h:commandLink action="#{localeChanger.changeLocale('en')}">
    <h:graphicImage library="images" name="en_flag.gif" style="border: 0px"/>
</h:commandLink>
```

On the server, the localeChanger method has a languageCode parameter to set the locale:

```
public class LocaleChanger {
    public String changeLocale(String languageChange) {
        FacesContext context = FacesContext.getCurrentInstance();
        context.getViewRoot().setLocale(new Locale(languageCode));
        return null;
    }
}
```

No matter how many flags links we add to our JSF page, our LocaleChanger is finished. No more redundant code.

The f:param Tag

The f:param tag lets you attach a parameter to a component. How the parameter is interpreted depends upon the type of component to which it is attached. For example, if you attach an f:param tag to an h:outputFormat tag, the parameter specifies placeholders, such as {0}, {1}, etc. If you attach an f:param tag to a command component, such as a button or a link, the parameter is turned into a request parameter. Here is how we can use the f:param tag for our flag example:

```
<h:commandLink immediate="true"
   action="#{localeChanger.changeLocale}">
   <f:param name="languageCode" value="de"/>
   <h:graphicImage library="images" name="de_flag.gif" style="border: 0px"/>
</h:commandLink>
<h:commandLink immediate="true"
   action="#{localeChanger.changeLocale}">
   <f:param name="languageCode" value="en"/>
   <h:graphicImage library="images" name="en_flag.gif" style="border: 0px"/>
</h:commandLink>
```

On the server, we access the languageCode request parameter to set the locale:

```
public class LocaleChanger {
   public String changeLocale() {
      FacesContext context = FacesContext.getCurrentInstance();
      String languageCode = getLanguageCode(context);
      context.getViewRoot().setLocale(new Locale(languageCode));
      return null;
   }
   private String getLanguageCode(FacesContext context) {
      Map<String, String> params = context.getExternalContext().
         getRequestParameterMap();
      return params.get("languageCode");
   }
}
```

The f:attribute Tag

Another way to pass information from the UI to the server is to set a component's attribute with the f:attribute tag. Here is how we do that with our flag example:

```
<h:commandLink immediate="true"
   actionListener="#{localeChanger.changeLocale}">
   <f:attribute name="languageCode" value="de"/>
   <h:graphicImage library="images" name="de_flag.gif" style="border: 0px"/>
</h:commandLink>
<h:commandLink immediate="true"
   actionListener="#{localeChanger.changeLocale}">
   <f:attribute name="languageCode" value="en"/>
   <h:graphicImage library="images" name="en_flag.gif" style="border: 0px"/>
</h:commandLink>
```

There are two things to notice here. First, we are using f:attribute to set an attribute on the link. That attribute's name is languageCode and its value is either en or de.

Second, we have switched from an action to an action listener. That is because action listeners are passed an event object that gives us access to the component that triggered the event; of course, that is one of our links. We need that component to access its languageCode attribute. Here is how it all hangs together on the server:

```
public class LocaleChanger {
   public void changeLocale(ActionEvent event) {
      UIComponent component = event.getComponent();
      String languageCode = getLanguageCode(component);
      FacesContext.getCurrentInstance()
          .getViewRoot().setLocale(new Locale(languageCode));
   }
   private String getLanguageCode(UIComponent component) {
      Map<String, Object> attrs = component.getAttributes();
      return (String) attrs.get("languageCode");
   }
}
```

This time, instead of pulling the language code out of a request parameter, we pull it out of a component attribute.

The f:setPropertyActionListener Tag

As we have seen, f:param and f:attribute are handy for passing information from the UI to the server, but those tags require us to manually dig the information out from a request parameter or component attribute, respectively.

The f:setPropertyActionListener tag, added in JSF 1.2, was designed to put an end to that digging. With f:setPropertyActionListener, the JSF implementation sets a property in your backing bean for you. Here is how it works for our flags example:

```
<h:commandLink immediate="true" action="#{localeChanger.changeLocale}">
   <f:setPropertyActionListener target="#{localeChanger.languageCode}" value="de"/>
   <h:graphicImage library="images" name="de_flag.gif" style="border: 0px"/>
</h:commandLink>
<h:commandLink immediate="true" action="#{localeChanger.changeLocale}">
   <f:setPropertyActionListener target="#{localeChanger.languageCode}" value="en"/>
   <h:graphicImage library="images" name="en_flag.gif" style="border: 0px"/>
</h:commandLink>
```

In the preceding JSP code, we tell the JSF implementation to set the languageCode property of the localeChanger bean with either de or en. Here is the corresponding implementation of the localeChanger bean:

```
public class LocaleChanger {
   private String languageCode;

   public String changeLocale() {
      FacesContext context = FacesContext.getCurrentInstance();
      context.getViewRoot().setLocale(new Locale(languageCode));
      return null;
   }
   public void setLanguageCode(String newValue) {
      languageCode = newValue;
   }
}
```

For this implementation of the LocaleChanger, we provide a languageCode write-only property that is set by the JSF implementation.

In the context of this example, method parameters are ostensibly the best choice for setting the localeChanger bean's languageCode property. They are easy to implement and understand. The f:setPropertyActionListener tag will probably find little use in JSF 2.0 applications. However, f:param and f:attribute have their place in other contexts, to set request parameters or component attributes.

Phase Events

The JSF implementation fires events, called *phase events*, before and after each life cycle phase. Those events are handled by phase listeners. Unlike value change and action listeners that you attach to individual components, a phase listener is attached to the view root. You can specify a phase listener for an individual page with a tag, such as the following, placed anywhere in that page:

```
<f:phaseListener type="com.corejsf.PhaseTracker"/>
```

Alternatively, you can specify global phase listeners in a faces configuration file, like this:

```
<faces-config>
   <lifecycle>
      <phase-listener>com.corejsf.PhaseTracker</phase-listener>
   </lifecycle>
</faces-config>
```

The preceding code fragment specifies only one listener, but you can specify as many as you want. Listeners are invoked in the order in which they are specified in the configuration file.

You implement phase listeners by means of the PhaseListener interface from the javax.faces.event package. That interface defines three methods:

- PhaseId getPhaseId()
- void afterPhase(PhaseEvent)
- void beforePhase(PhaseEvent)

The getPhaseId method tells the JSF implementation when to deliver phase events to the listener—for example, getPhaseId() could return PhaseId.APPLY_REQUEST_VALUES. In that case, beforePhase() and afterPhase() would be called once per life cycle: before and after the Apply Request Values phase. You could also specify PhaseId.ANY_PHASE, which really means *all phases*. Your phase listener's beforePhase and afterPhase methods will be called six times per life cycle: once each for each life cycle phase.

Alternatively, you can enclose a JSF page in an f:view tag with beforePhase or afterPhase attributes. These attributes must point to methods of with the signature void listener(javax.faces.event.PhaseEvent). They are invoked before every phase except for "Restore view". For example:

```
<f:view beforePhase="#{backingBean.beforeListener}">
    ...
</f:view>
```

Phase listeners are useful for debugging tools, and before JSF 2.0, they offered the only mechanism for writing custom components that were aware of the JSF life cycle. We expect that JSF 2.0 developers will prefer using the system events that are discussed in the next section.

System Events JSF 2.0

JSF 2.0 introduces a fine-grained notification system in which individual components as well as the JSF implementation notify listeners of many potentially interesting events. Table 8–1 lists the JSF system events.

Table 8–1   System Events

Event Class	Description	Source Type
PostConstructApplicationEvent PreDestroyApplicationEvent	Immediately after the application has started; immediately before it is about to be shut down	Application
PostAddToViewEvent PreRemoveFromViewEvent	After a component has been added to the view tree; before it is about to be removed	UIComponent
PostRestoreStateEvent	After the state of a component has been restored	UIComponent
PreValidateEvent PostValidateEvent	Before and after a component is validated	UIComponent
PreRenderViewEvent	Before the view root is about to be rendered	UIViewRoot
PreRenderComponentEvent	Before a component is about to be rendered	UIComponent
PostConstructViewMapEvent PreDestroyViewMapEvent	After the root component has constructed the view scope map; when the view map is cleared[a]	UIViewRoot
PostConstructCustomScopeEvent PreDestroyCustomScopeEvent	After a custom scope has been constructed; before it is about to be destroyed	ScopeContext
ExceptionQueuedEvent	After an exception has been queued	ExceptionQueuedEvent-Context

a. To monitor the life cycle of the application, session, and request maps, use a ServletContextListener, ServletHttpSessionListener, or ServletRequestListener.

There are four ways in which a class can receive system events:

- With the f:event tag:

```
<inputText value="#{...}">
    <f:event name="postValidate" listener="#{bean.method}"/>
</inputText>
```

The method must have the signature

```
public void listener(ComponentSystemEvent) throws AbortProcessingException
```

This is the most convenient way for listening to component or view events.

- With an annotation for a UIComponent or Renderer class:

```
@ListenerFor(systemEventClass=PreRenderViewEvent.class)
```

We discuss these classes in Chapter 11. This mechanism can be useful for component developers.

- By being listed as a system event listener in faces-config.xml:

```
<application>
   <system-event-listener>
      <system-event-listener-class>listenerClass</system-event-listener-class>
      <system-event-class>eventClass</system-event-class>
   </system-event-listener>
</application>
```

This mechanism is useful for installing a listener to application events.

- By calling the subscribeToEvent method of the UIComponent or Application class. This method is intended for framework developers, and we refer you to the JSF API for details.

In the following sections, we will discuss two typical examples of using system events.

Multi-Component Validation

As you have seen in Chapter 7, JSF does not have a mechanism for validating a group of components. For example, if you use day, month, and year input fields for entering a date, there is no natural way of validating the date as a whole. You can use the PostValidateEvent to overcome this limitation.

Here, we attach an event listener to the panel that contains the input components:

```
<h:panelGrid id="date" columns="2">
   <f:event type="postValidate" listener="#{bb.validateDate}"/>
   #{msgs.day}
   <h:inputText id="day" value="#{bb.day}" size="2" required="true"/>

   #{msgs.month}
   <h:inputText id="month" value="#{bb.month}" size="2" required="true"/>

   #{msgs.year}
```

```
    <h:inputText id="year" value="#{bb.year}" size="4" required="true"/>
</h:panelGrid>
<h:message for="date" styleClass="errorMessage"/>
```

In the event listener, we obtain the values that the user entered and check whether they form a valid date. If not, we add an error message to the component and call the renderResponse method:

```
public void validateDate(ComponentSystemEvent event) {
    UIComponent source = event.getComponent();
    UIInput dayInput = (UIInput) source.findComponent("day");
    UIInput monthInput = (UIInput) source.findComponent("month");
    UIInput yearInput = (UIInput) source.findComponent("year");
    int d = ((Integer) dayInput.getLocalValue()).intValue();
    int m = ((Integer) monthInput.getLocalValue()).intValue();
    int y = ((Integer) yearInput.getLocalValue()).intValue();
    if (!isValidDate(d, m, y)) {
        FacesMessage message = com.corejsf.util.Messages.getMessage(
            "com.corejsf.messages", "invalidDate", null);
        message.setSeverity(FacesMessage.SEVERITY_ERROR);
        FacesContext context = FacesContext.getCurrentInstance();
        context.addMessage(source.getClientId(), message);
        context.renderResponse();
    }
}
```

Note that the renderResponse method does not immediately render the response. The Process Validations phase is first completed; this includes processing of any post-validation event listeners. Then the response is rendered, and the current view is redisplayed with the error message (see Figure 8–9).

Figure 8–9   Using the PostValidateEvent **to validate a group of components**

Making Decisions before Rendering the View

Sometimes, you want to be notified before a view is rendered, for example, to load data, make changes to the components on a page, or to conditionally navigate to another page.

For example, you may want to make sure that a user has been logged in before showing a particular page. Enclose the page in an f:view tag and attach a listener:

```
<f:view>
    <f:event type="preRenderView" listener="#{user.checkLogin}"/>
    <h:head>
       <title>...</title>
    </h:head>
    <h:body>
       ...
    </h:body>
</f:view>
```

In the listener, check whether the user is logged in. If not, navigate to the login page:

```
public void checkLogin(ComponentSystemEvent event) {
    if (!loggedIn) {
        FacesContext context = FacesContext.getCurrentInstance();
        ConfigurableNavigationHandler handler = (ConfigurableNavigationHandler)
            context.getApplication().getNavigationHandler();
        handler.performNavigation("login");
    }
}
```

The following sample application combines the login check and the date validation. When you first load index.xhtml, the event handler instead navigates to login.xhtml. However, when you return to that page after login, it is displayed normally. After login, you can continue to the date entry view.

Figure 8–10 shows the directory structure of the application. Listings 8–10 and 8–11 show the pages with the f:event tags. Listings 8–12 and 8–13 contain the managed beans with the event handlers.

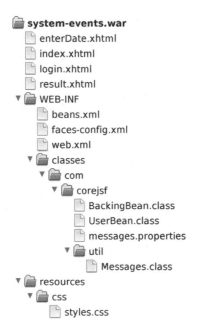

Figure 8–10   Directory structure of the system event demo application

Listing 8–10 system-events/web/index.xhtml

```
1. <?xml version="1.0" encoding="UTF-8"?>
2. <!DOCTYPE html PUBLIC "-//W3C//DTD XHTML 1.0 Strict//EN"
3. "http://www.w3.org/TR/xhtml1/DTD/xhtml1-strict.dtd">
4. <html xmlns="http://www.w3.org/1999/xhtml"
5.       xmlns:h="http://java.sun.com/jsf/html"
6.       xmlns:f="http://java.sun.com/jsf/core">
7.    <f:view>
8.      <f:event type="preRenderView" listener="#{user.checkLogin}"/>
9.      <h:head>
10.       <title>Welcome</title>
11.     </h:head>
12.     <h:body>
13.       <h3><h:outputText value="Welcome to JavaServer Faces, #{user.name}!" /></h3>
14.       <h:form>
15.         <h:commandButton value="Logout" action="#{user.logout}" />
16.         <h:commandButton value="Continue" action="enterDate" />
17.       </h:form>
18.     </h:body>
19.   </f:view>
20. </html>
```

Listing 8–11 system-events/web/enterDate.xhtml

```
1. <?xml version="1.0" encoding="UTF-8"?>
2. <!DOCTYPE html PUBLIC "-//W3C//DTD XHTML 1.0 Transitional//EN"
3. "http://www.w3.org/TR/xhtml1/DTD/xhtml1-transitional.dtd">
4. <html xmlns="http://www.w3.org/1999/xhtml"
5.       xmlns:f="http://java.sun.com/jsf/core"
6.       xmlns:h="http://java.sun.com/jsf/html">
7.    <h:head>
8.       <h:outputStylesheet library="css" name="styles.css"/>
9.       <title>#{msgs.title}</title>
10.   </h:head>
11.   <h:body>
12.      <h:form>
13.         <h1>#{msgs.enterDate}</h1>
14.         <h:panelGrid id="date" columns="2">
15.            <f:event type="postValidate" listener="#{bb.validateDate}"/>
16.            #{msgs.day}
17.            <h:inputText id="day" value="#{bb.day}" size="2"
18.                         required="true"/>
19.
20.            #{msgs.month}
21.            <h:inputText id="month" value="#{bb.month}"
22.                         size="2" required="true"/>
23.
24.            #{msgs.year}
25.            <h:inputText id="year" value="#{bb.year}"
26.                         size="4" required="true"/>
27.         </h:panelGrid>
28.         <h:message for="date" styleClass="errorMessage"/>
29.         <br/>
30.         <h:commandButton value="#{msgs.submit}" action="result"/>
31.         <h:commandButton value="#{msgs.back}" action="index" immediate="true"/>
32.      </h:form>
33.   </h:body>
34. </html>
```

Listing 8–12 system-events/src/java/com/corejsf/UserBean.java

```
1. package com.corejsf;
2.
3. import javax.faces.application.ConfigurableNavigationHandler;
4. import javax.inject.Named;
5.    // or import javax.faces.bean.ManagedBean;
6. import javax.enterprise.context.SessionScoped;
7.    // or import javax.faces.bean.SessionScoped;
```

```
 8. import javax.faces.context.FacesContext;
 9. import javax.faces.event.AbortProcessingException;
10. import javax.faces.event.ComponentSystemEvent;
11.
12. @Named("user") // or @ManagedBean(name="user")
13. @SessionScoped
14. public class UserBean {
15.    private String name = "";
16.    private String password;
17.    private boolean loggedIn;
18.
19.    public String getName() { return name; }
20.    public void setName(String newValue) { name = newValue; }
21.
22.    public String getPassword() { return password; }
23.    public void setPassword(String newValue) { password = newValue; }
24.
25.    public boolean isLoggedIn() { return loggedIn; }
26.
27.    public String login()  {
28.       loggedIn = true;
29.       return "index";
30.    }
31.
32.    public String logout() {
33.       loggedIn = false;
34.       return "login";
35.    }
36.
37.    public void checkLogin(ComponentSystemEvent event) {
38.       if (!loggedIn) {
39.          FacesContext context = FacesContext.getCurrentInstance();
40.          ConfigurableNavigationHandler handler = (ConfigurableNavigationHandler)
41.             context.getApplication().getNavigationHandler();
42.          handler.performNavigation("login");
43.       }
44.    }
45. }
```

Listing 8–13 system-events/src/java/com/corejsf/BackingBean.java

```
1. package com.corejsf;
2.
3. import java.io.Serializable;
4.
5. import javax.faces.application.FacesMessage;
6. import javax.inject.Named;
7.    // or import javax.faces.bean.ManagedBean;
8. import javax.enterprise.context.SessionScoped;
9.    // or import javax.faces.bean.SessionScoped;
10. import javax.faces.component.UIComponent;
11. import javax.faces.component.UIForm;
12. import javax.faces.component.UIInput;
13. import javax.faces.context.FacesContext;
14. import javax.faces.event.ComponentSystemEvent;
15. import javax.faces.validator.ValidatorException;
16.
17. @Named("bb") // or @ManagedBean(name="bb")
18. @SessionScoped
19. public class BackingBean implements Serializable {
20.    private int day;
21.    private int month;
22.    private int year;
23.
24.    public int getDay() { return day; }
25.    public void setDay(int newValue) { day = newValue; }
26.
27.    public int getMonth() { return month; }
28.    public void setMonth(int newValue) { month = newValue; }
29.
30.    public int getYear() { return year; }
31.    public void setYear(int newValue) { year = newValue; }
32.
33.    public void validateDate(ComponentSystemEvent event) {
34.       UIComponent source = event.getComponent();
35.       UIInput dayInput = (UIInput) source.findComponent("day");
36.       UIInput monthInput = (UIInput) source.findComponent("month");
37.       UIInput yearInput = (UIInput) source.findComponent("year");
38.       int d = ((Integer) dayInput.getLocalValue()).intValue();
39.       int m = ((Integer) monthInput.getLocalValue()).intValue();
40.       int y = ((Integer) yearInput.getLocalValue()).intValue();
41.       if (!isValidDate(d, m, y)) {
42.          FacesMessage message = com.corejsf.util.Messages.getMessage(
43.             "com.corejsf.messages", "invalidDate", null);
44.          message.setSeverity(FacesMessage.SEVERITY_ERROR);
```

```
45.        FacesContext context = FacesContext.getCurrentInstance();
46.        context.addMessage(source.getClientId(), message);
47.        context.renderResponse();
48.     }
49.  }
50.
51.  private static boolean isValidDate(int d, int m, int y) {
52.     if (d < 1 || m < 1 || m > 12) return false;
53.     if (m == 2) {
54.        if (isLeapYear(y)) return d <= 29;
55.        else return d <= 28;
56.     }
57.     else if (m == 4 || m == 6 || m == 9 || m == 11)
58.        return d <= 30;
59.     else
60.        return d <= 31;
61.  }
62.
63.  private static boolean isLeapYear(int y) {
64.     return y % 4 == 0 && (y % 400 == 0 || y % 100 != 0);
65.  }
66. }
```

Putting It All Together

We close out this chapter with an example of a poor man's implementation of a
tabbed pane. That example demonstrates event handling and advanced aspects
of using JSF HTML tags. Those advanced uses include the following:

- Nesting h:panelGrid tags
- Using facets
- Specifying tab indexing
- Adding tooltips to components with the title attribute
- Dynamically determining style classes
- Using action listeners
- Optional rendering
- Including JSF pages

JSF does not have a tabbed pane component, so if you want a tabbed pane in
your application, you have two choices: implement a custom component or
use existing tags—with a backing bean—to create an ad hoc tabbed pane.
Figure 8–11 shows the latter. The former is discussed in "Using Child Components and Facets" on page 457 of Chapter 11.

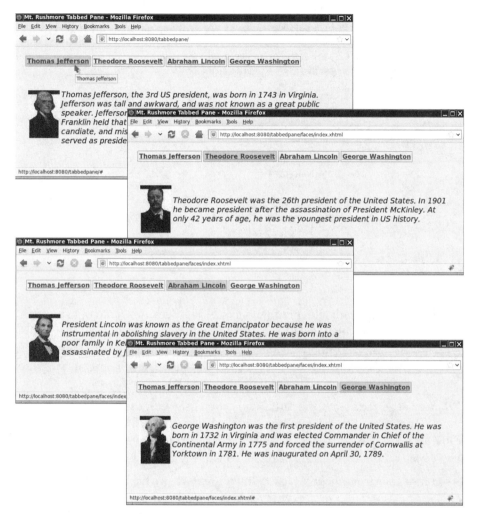

Figure 8–11 A poor man's tabbed pane

The tabbed pane shown in Figure 8–11 is implemented entirely with existing JSF HTML tags and a backing bean; no custom renderers or components are used. The JSF page for the tabbed pane looks like this:

```
...
<h:form>
   <h:panelGrid styleClass="tabbedPane" columnClasses="displayPanel">
      <!-- Tabs -->

      <f:facet name="header">
```

```
<h:panelGrid columns="4" styleClass="tabbedPaneHeader">
   <h:commandLink tabindex="1"
      title="#{msgs.jeffersonTooltip}"
      styleClass="#{tp.jeffersonStyle}"
      actionListener="#{tp.jeffersonAction}">
      #{msgs.jeffersonTab}
   </h:commandLink>
   ...
</h:panelGrid>
</f:facet>

<!-- Tabbed pane content -->

<ui:include src="washington.xhtml" />
<ui:include src="roosevelt.xhtml" />
<ui:include src="lincoln.xhtml" />
<ui:include src="jefferson.xhtml" />
</h:panelGrid>
</h:form>
...
```

The tabbed pane is implemented with h:panelGrid. Because we do not specify the columns attribute, the panel has one column. The panel's header—defined with an f:facet tag—contains the tabs, which are implemented with another h:panelGrid that contains h:commandLink tags for each tab. The only row in the panel contains the content associated with the selected tab.

When a user selects a tab, the associated action listener for the command link is invoked and modifies the data stored in the backing bean. Because we use a different CSS style for the selected tab, the styleClass attribute of each h:commandLink tag is pulled from the backing bean with a value reference expression.

As you can see from the top picture in Figure 8–11, we have used the title attribute to associate a tooltip with each tab. Another accessibility feature is the ability to move from one tab to another with the keyboard instead of the mouse. We implemented that feature by specifying the tabindex attribute for each h:commandLink.

The content associated with each tab is statically included with the JSP include directive. For our application, that content is a picture and some text, but you could modify the included JSF pages to contain any set of appropriate components. Notice that even though all the JSF pages representing content are included, only the content associated with the current tab is rendered. That is achieved with the rendered attribute—for example, jefferson.xhtml looks like this:

```
<h:panelGrid columns="2" columnClasses="presidentDiscussionColumn"
    rendered="#{tp.jeffersonCurrent}">
    <h:graphicImage value="/images/jefferson.jpg"/>
    <span class="tabbedPaneContent">"#{msgs.jeffersonDiscussion}"</span>
</h:panelGrid>
```

Figure 8–12 shows the directory structure for the tabbed pane application and Listings 8–14 through 8–17 show the most important files.

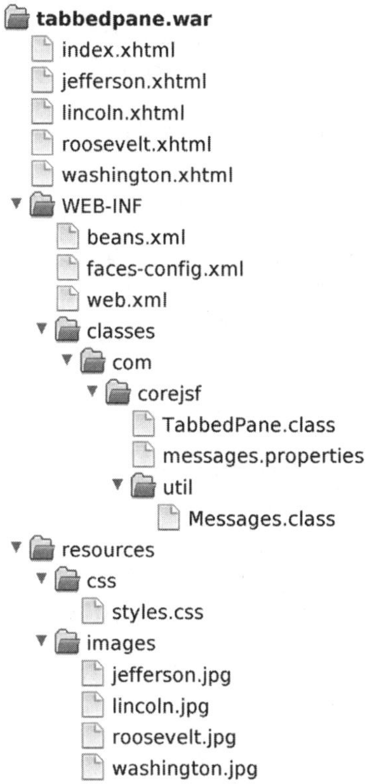

📁 **tabbedpane.war**
  📄 index.xhtml
  📄 jefferson.xhtml
  📄 lincoln.xhtml
  📄 roosevelt.xhtml
  📄 washington.xhtml
▼ 📁 WEB-INF
    📄 beans.xml
    📄 faces-config.xml
    📄 web.xml
  ▼ 📁 classes
    ▼ 📁 com
      ▼ 📁 corejsf
          📄 TabbedPane.class
          📄 messages.properties
        ▼ 📁 util
            📄 Messages.class
▼ 📁 resources
  ▼ 📁 css
      📄 styles.css
  ▼ 📁 images
      📄 jefferson.jpg
      📄 lincoln.jpg
      📄 roosevelt.jpg
      📄 washington.jpg

Figure 8–12   Directory structure for the tabbed pane example

Listing 8–14   tabbedpane/web/index.xhtml

```
1. <?xml version="1.0" encoding="UTF-8"?>
2. <!DOCTYPE html PUBLIC "-//W3C//DTD XHTML 1.0 Transitional//EN"
3. "http://www.w3.org/TR/xhtml1/DTD/xhtml1-transitional.dtd">
4. <html xmlns="http://www.w3.org/1999/xhtml"
5.      xmlns:ui="http://java.sun.com/jsf/facelets"
6.      xmlns:f="http://java.sun.com/jsf/core" xmlns:h="http://java.sun.com/jsf/html">
7.    <h:head>
```

```
8.      <h:outputStylesheet library="css" name="styles.css"/>
9.      <title>#{msgs.windowTitle}</title>
10.  </h:head>
11.
12.  <h:body>
13.     <h:form>
14.        <h:panelGrid styleClass="tabbedPane" columnClasses="displayPanel">
15.           <!-- Tabs -->
16.
17.           <f:facet name="header">
18.              <h:panelGrid columns="4" styleClass="tabbedPaneHeader">
19.                 <h:commandLink tabindex="1" title="#{msgs.jeffersonTooltip}"
20.                                styleClass="#{tp.jeffersonStyle}"
21.                                actionListener="#{tp.jeffersonAction}">
22.                    #{msgs.jeffersonTabText}
23.                 </h:commandLink>
24.
25.                 <h:commandLink tabindex="2" title="#{msgs.rooseveltTooltip}"
26.                                styleClass="#{tp.rooseveltStyle}"
27.                                actionListener="#{tp.rooseveltAction}">
28.                    #{msgs.rooseveltTabText}
29.                 </h:commandLink>
30.
31.                 <h:commandLink tabindex="3" title="#{msgs.lincolnTooltip}"
32.                                styleClass="#{tp.lincolnStyle}"
33.                                actionListener="#{tp.lincolnAction}">
34.                    #{msgs.lincolnTabText}
35.                 </h:commandLink>
36.
37.                 <h:commandLink tabindex="4" title="#{msgs.washingtonTooltip}"
38.                                styleClass="#{tp.washingtonStyle}"
39.                                actionListener="#{tp.washingtonAction}">
40.                    #{msgs.washingtonTabText}
41.                 </h:commandLink>
42.              </h:panelGrid>
43.           </f:facet>
44.
45.           <!-- Tabbed pane content -->
46.
47.           <ui:include src="washington.xhtml"/>
48.           <ui:include src="roosevelt.xhtml"/>
49.           <ui:include src="lincoln.xhtml"/>
50.           <ui:include src="jefferson.xhtml"/>
51.        </h:panelGrid>
52.     </h:form>
53.  </h:body>
54. </html>
```

Listing 8–15 tabbedpane/web/jefferson.xhtml

```
1. <?xml version="1.0" encoding="UTF-8"?>
2. <!DOCTYPE html PUBLIC "-//W3C//DTD XHTML 1.0 Transitional//EN"
3. "http://www.w3.org/TR/xhtml1/DTD/xhtml1-transitional.dtd">
4. <html xmlns="http://www.w3.org/1999/xhtml"
5.     xmlns:ui="http://java.sun.com/jsf/facelets"
6.     xmlns:h="http://java.sun.com/jsf/html">
7.   <ui:composition>
8.     <h:panelGrid columns="2" columnClasses="presidentDiscussionColumn"
9.                 rendered="#{tp.jeffersonCurrent}">
10.
11.       <h:graphicImage library="images" name="jefferson.jpg"/>
12.       <span class="tabbedPaneContent">#{msgs.jeffersonDiscussion}</span>
13.
14.     </h:panelGrid>
15.   </ui:composition>
16. </html>
```

Listing 8–16 tabbedpane/src/java/com/corejsf/messages.properties

```
1. windowTitle=Mt. Rushmore Tabbed Pane
2. lincolnTooltip=Abraham Lincoln
3. lincolnTabText=Abraham Lincoln
4. lincolnDiscussion=President Lincoln was known as the Great Emancipator because \
5.   he was instrumental in abolishing slavery in the United States. He was born \
6.   into a poor family in Kentucky in 1809, elected president in 1860 and \
7.   assassinated by John Wilkes Booth in 1865.
8.
9. washingtonTooltip=George Washington
10. washingtonTabText=George Washington
11. washingtonDiscussion=George Washington was the first president of the United \
12.   States. He was born in 1732 in Virginia and was elected Commander in Chief of \
13.   the Continental Army in 1775 and forced the surrender of Cornwallis at Yorktown \
14.   in 1781. He was inaugurated on April 30, 1789.
15.
16. rooseveltTooltip=Theodore Roosevelt
17. rooseveltTabText=Theodore Roosevelt
18. rooseveltDiscussion=Theodore Roosevelt was the 26th president of the United \
19.   States. In 1901 he became president after the assassination of President \
20.   McKinley. At only 42 years of age, he was the youngest president in US history.
21.
22. jeffersonTooltip=Thomas Jefferson
23. jeffersonTabText=Thomas Jefferson
24. jeffersonDiscussion=Thomas Jefferson, the 3rd US president, was born in \
25.   1743 in Virginia. Jefferson was tall and awkward, and was not known as a \
```

26. great public speaker. Jefferson became minister to France in 1785, after \
27. Benjamin Franklin held that post. In 1796, Jefferson was a reluctant \
28. presidential candiate, and missed winning the election by a mere three votes. \
29. He served as president from 1801-1809.

Listing 8-17 `tabbedpane/src/java/com/corejsf/TabbedPane.java`

```
1. package com.corejsf;
2.
3. import java.io.Serializable;
4.
5. import javax.inject.Named;
6.    // or import javax.faces.bean.ManagedBean;
7. import javax.enterprise.context.SessionScoped;
8.    // or import javax.faces.bean.SessionScoped;
9. import javax.faces.event.ActionEvent;
10.
11. @Named("tp") // or @ManagedBean(name="tp")
12. @SessionScoped
13. public class TabbedPane implements Serializable {
14.    private int index;
15.    private static final int JEFFERSON_INDEX = 0;
16.    private static final int ROOSEVELT_INDEX = 1;
17.    private static final int LINCOLN_INDEX = 2;
18.    private static final int WASHINGTON_INDEX = 3;
19.
20.    private String[] tabTooltips = { "jeffersonTooltip", "rooseveltTooltip",
21.        "lincolnTooltip", "washingtonTooltip" };
22.
23.    public TabbedPane() {
24.       index = JEFFERSON_INDEX;
25.    }
26.
27.    // action listeners that set the current tab
28.
29.    public void jeffersonAction(ActionEvent e) { index = JEFFERSON_INDEX;  }
30.    public void rooseveltAction(ActionEvent e) { index = ROOSEVELT_INDEX;  }
31.    public void lincolnAction(ActionEvent e) { index = LINCOLN_INDEX;     }
32.    public void washingtonAction(ActionEvent e) { index = WASHINGTON_INDEX; }
33.
34.    // CSS styles
35.
36.    public String getJeffersonStyle() { return getCSS(JEFFERSON_INDEX);  }
37.    public String getRooseveltStyle() { return getCSS(ROOSEVELT_INDEX);  }
38.    public String getLincolnStyle() { return getCSS(LINCOLN_INDEX);     }
39.    public String getWashingtonStyle() { return getCSS(WASHINGTON_INDEX); }
```

```
40.
41.    private String getCSS(int forIndex) {
42.        return forIndex == index ? "tabbedPaneTextSelected" : "tabbedPaneText";
43.    }
44.
45.    // methods for determining the current tab
46.
47.    public boolean isJeffersonCurrent() { return index == JEFFERSON_INDEX;  }
48.    public boolean isRooseveltCurrent() { return index == ROOSEVELT_INDEX;  }
49.    public boolean isLincolnCurrent() { return index == LINCOLN_INDEX;      }
50.    public boolean isWashingtonCurrent() { return index == WASHINGTON_INDEX; }
51. }
```

Conclusion

This example completes this chapter's introduction to event handling. In the
next chapter, you will see how to combine the standard JSF components into
your own composite components.

COMPOSITE COMPONENTS

JSF 2.0

Topics in This Chapter

Chapter 9

Unlike action-based frameworks, such as Struts or Ruby on Rails, JSF is component-based, which means you can implement components that you or others can reuse. Components are a powerful reuse mechanism.

JSF 1.0, however, nearly rendered components inconsequential, for two reasons. First, components were difficult to implement. You had to write Java code and specify XML configuration. You also had to have a good grasp of JSF's life cycle.

Second, JSF 1.0 made no provision for easily composing new components from existing ones. If you implemented a simple field component, with a prompt (h:outputText) and an input (h:inputText), you had to create and manipulate those components in Java code.

JSF 2.0 addresses both of those drawbacks by making it easier to implement custom components in Java code, and by providing a new facility for composing new components from existing ones. In this chapter, we take a look at the latter facility, known as *composite components*, in detail.

> 🗎 NOTE: JSF 2.0 refers to components that you implement with the composite library as *composite components*. JSF uses the term *composite* because you *compose* new components from existing components.
>
> Implementing composite components is easy. You don't have to write any Java code or specify any XML configuration. A simple XHTML file that defines a component will suffice for many composite component scenarios.

The Composite Tag Library

JSF 2.0 comes with a tag library for implementing composite components. By convention, developers use the composite: prefix for that library. To use the composite tag library, add a namespace declaration to an XHTML file, like this:

```
<html xmlns="http://www.w3.org/1999/xhtml"...
  xmlns:composite="http://java.sun.com/jsf/composite">
  ...
</html>
```

Once you have specified a namespace for the composite library, you can use any of the tags in Table 9–1.

> 🗎 NOTE: We distinguish between the *component author*, the developer who designs and implements a composite component, and *page authors*, the developers who use that component in their pages.

Table 9–1   Composite Component Tags

Tag	Description	Used In
interface	Contains other composite tags that expose a composite component's *attributes, action sources, value holders, editable value holders,* and *facets.*	N/A
implementation	Contains the XHTML markup that defines the component. Inside the implementation tag, the component author can access attributes with the expression #{cc.attrs.*attributeName*}.	N/A
attribute	Exposes an attribute of a component to page authors.	Interface

Table 9–1   Composite Component Tags (cont.)

Tag	Description	Used In
valueHolder	Exposes a component that holds a value to page authors.	Interface
editableValueHolder	Exposes a component that holds an editable value to page authors.	Interface
actionSource	Exposes a component that fires action events, such as a button or a link, to page authors.	Interface
facet	Declares that this component supports a facet with a given name.	Interface
extension	The component author can place this tag inside of any element in an interface. The extension tag can contain arbitrary XML.	Interface subelement
insertChildren	Inserts any child components specified by the page author.	Implementation
renderFacet	Renders a facet that was specified by the page author as a child component.	Implementation
insertFacet	Inserts a facet, specified by the page author, as a facet of the enclosing component.	Implementation

Composite components have interfaces and implementations, as evidenced by the first two tags in Table 9–1. Implementations are Facelet markup, using standard JSF tags. Interfaces let you expose configurable characteristics of your composite component.

For example, imagine a login composite component that's implemented as a form with name and password prompts, and a submit button. You would implement the login component with h:form, h:inputText, h:commandButton, etc., as you would any form in a Facelets view.

To be reusable, composite components need something more than just an implementation, however, because they must also be configurable. For example, for your login component, you would, more than likely, want to: customize the labels associated with the name and password fields; attach a validator onto one or both fields; and attach an action listener to the login component's submit button. You can do all of those things in your login component's interface.

Finally, in the end, you are creating components, so somehow you must register them with JSF. Fortunately, in JSF 2.0 that configuration is taken care of for you, as you'll see next.

Using Composite Components

To eliminate configuration, JSF 2.0 uses a naming convention for composite components. To illustrate that naming convention, we use a composite component shown in Figure 9–1, that displays information about the current HTTP request.

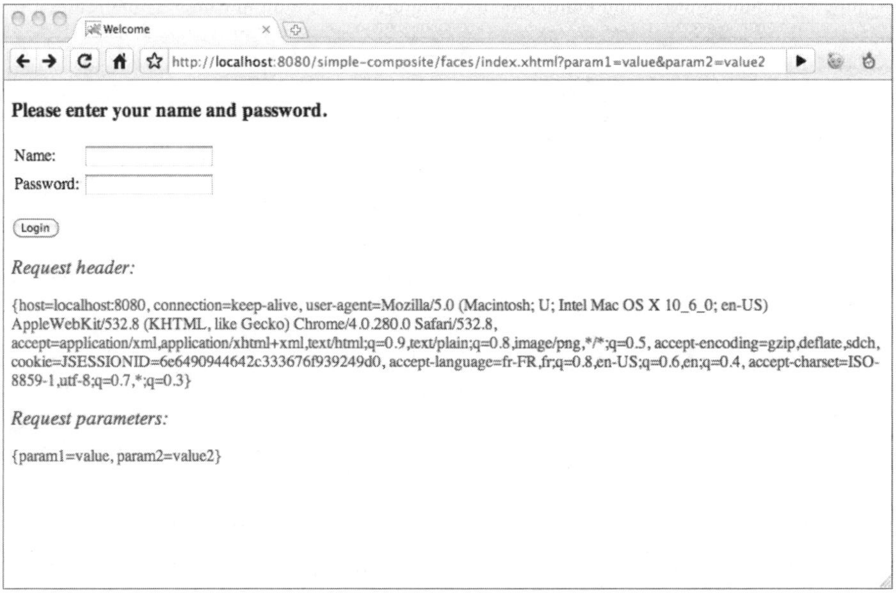

Figure 9–1 Using a debug component

The `<util:debug/>` custom component tag is near the bottom of Listing 9–1.

Listing 9–1   simple-composite/web/index.xhtml

```
1. <?xml version="1.0" encoding="UTF-8"?>
2. <!DOCTYPE html PUBLIC "-//W3C//DTD XHTML 1.0 Transitional//EN"
3. "http://www.w3.org/TR/xhtml1/DTD/xhtml1-transitional.dtd">
4. <html xmlns="http://www.w3.org/1999/xhtml"
5.     xmlns:h="http://java.sun.com/jsf/html"
6.     xmlns:util="http://java.sun.com/jsf/composite/util">
7.   <h:head>
8.     <title>Welcome</title>
9.   </h:head>
```

```
10.    <h:body>
11.       <h:form>
12.          <h3>Please enter your name and password.</h3>
13.          <table>
14.             <tr>
15.                <td>Name:</td>
16.                <td><h:inputText value="#{user.name}"/></td>
17.             </tr>
18.             <tr>
19.                <td>Password:</td>
20.                <td><h:inputSecret value="#{user.password}"/></td>
21.             </tr>
22.          </table>
23.          <p><h:commandButton value="Login" action="welcome"/></p>
24.       </h:form>
25.       <div style="color: red;">
26.          <util:debug />
27.       </div>
28.    </h:body>
29. </html>
```

To use a composite component, you must first declare a namespace. For example, in Listing 9–1, we declared a namespace named util:

```
<html xmlns="http://www.w3.org/1999/xhtml"
   xmlns:h="http://java.sun.com/jsf/html"
   xmlns:util="http://java.sun.com/jsf/composite/util">
```

You can use any name you want for the namespace, but the namespace's value must always start with http://java.sun.com/jsf/composite/.

The rest of the namespace's value points to the directory, under resources, where the composite component resides. Because our debug component is in the resources/util directory, as shown in Figure 9–2, the full value of the namespace must be http://java.sun.com/jsf/composite/util.

You use the prefix when you specify the component:

```
<util:debug/>
```

With a simple naming convention and the composite tag library, it's easy to use composite components. Now let's see how to implement them.

**Figure 9–2   The directory structure of the application with the debug
component**

Implementing Composite Components

Implementing composite components is almost as easy as using them; as
evidence, look at Listing 9–2, which shows the implementation of the debug
component used in Listing 9–1.

Listing 9–2   simple-composite/web/resources/util/debug.xhtml

```
1. <?xml version="1.0" encoding="UTF-8"?>
2. <!DOCTYPE html PUBLIC "-//W3C//DTD XHTML 1.0 Transitional//EN"
3.       "http://www.w3.org/TR/xhtml1/DTD/xhtml1-transitional.dtd">
4.
5. <html xmlns="http://www.w3.org/1999/xhtml"
6.    xmlns:composite="http://java.sun.com/jsf/composite">
7.
8.    <composite:interface/>
9.
10.    <composite:implementation>
11.       <div style="font-size: 1.2em; font-style: italic">
12.       Request header:
13.       </div>
14.
15.       <p>#{header}</p>
16.
17.       <div style="font-size: 1.2em; font-style: italic">
18.       Request parameters:
19.       </div>
20.
```

```
21.      <p>#{param}</p>
22.   </composite:implementation>
23. </html>
```

Like all composite components, the debug component has an *interface* and an *implementation*. A composite component's implementation is simply its markup, whereas the component's interface specifies component attributes so developers can configure composite components.

The debug component specifies nothing in its interface, which is a rare occurrence among composite components. Nearly all composite components expose attributes through their interfaces, so they can be configured, and therefore, reused, in different contexts.

Configuring Composite Components

Components are useful because they are reusable, and they are reusable because they can be configured for different circumstances. Consider icons like those shown in Figure 9–3.

Figure 9–3   Icons

Icons have two attributes: an image, and an action that gets invoked when you click the image. You can let page authors specify those two attributes like this:

```
<util:icon image="#{resource['images:back.jpg']}"
    actionMethod="#{user.logout}" />
```

The following icon.xhtml file defines a simple icon component:

```
<html xmlns="http://www.w3.org/1999/xhtml"
    xmlns:h="http://java.sun.com/jsf/html"
    xmlns:composite="http://java.sun.com/jsf/composite">

    <composite:interface>
        <composite:attribute name="image"/>
        <composite:attribute name="actionMethod"
            method-signature="java.lang.String action()" />
    </composite:interface>

    <composite:implementation>
        <h:form>
            <h:commandLink action="#{cc.attrs.actionMethod}">
                <h:graphicImage url="#{cc.attrs.image}" styleClass="icon" />
            </h:commandLink>
```

```
    </h:form>
  </composite:implementation>
</html>
```

In the icon's implementation, you access the image and actionMethod attributes with #{cc.attrs.image} and #{cc.attrs.actionMethod}, respectively. The cc represents the *composite component*, and cc.attrs receives special handling in the expression language to look up the component attributes. Thus, #{cc.attrs.*attributeName*} accesses the *attributeName* attribute of the composite component.

Note that the two attributes for the icon component are very different things: the image attribute "#{resource['images:back.jpg']}" is a *value expression*, whereas the actionMethod attribute "#{user.logout}" is a *method expression*. When the expression #{cc.attrs.*attributeName*} is evaluated, the JSF implementation checks whether the value with key *attributeName* is a value expression. If so, that expression is evaluated. Otherwise, the value associated with the key is simply returned.

NOTE: If a composite component attribute refers to a method expression, you must supply a method signature, so JSF knows that you're referring to a method name, and not the name of a property. That's the case for the icon's actionMethod in our example.

Attribute Types

As we did with icons, you can specify attributes with value expressions, like this:

```
<util:icon image="#{resource['images:back.jpg']}"
  actionMethod="#{user.logout}" />
```

By default, JSF assumes that attribute values are of type java.lang.Object. For example, in the preceding code, the value expression #{resource['images:back.jpg']} resolves to a URL, represented as a string: /*context-root*/faces/javax.faces.resource/back.jpg?ln=images. In fact, you could specify that string directly:

```
<util:icon image="/composite-login/faces/javax.faces.resource/back.jpg?ln=images"
  actionMethod="#{user.logout}" />
```

If you want a composite attribute to represent a subclass of java.lang.Object, you must tell JSF what the attribute's type is. One way to do that is to use the methodsignature attribute, of the composite:attribute tag, like we did in Listing 9–1. When you specify a method signature for an attribute, JSF resolves the attribute's value expression to a *method expression*, instead of an *object*.

Another way to specify an attribute's type is with the composite:attribute's type attribute. The type attribute must be specified with a fully qualified Java class name. So, for example, if you wanted a date attribute whose value was a Date object, you would do this: <composite:attribute name ="date" type="java.util.Date" />.

> NOTE: The composite:attribute tag's type and method-signature attributes both tell JSF that an attribute's value is something other than a string. With the type attribute, you can specify any type, whereas method-signature always indicates that the type is a JSF method expression object.
>
> The type and method-expression attributes for the composite:attribute tag are mutually exclusive, with type having priority over method-signature, should you inadvertently specify both attributes.

Required Attributes and Default Attribute Values

The icon component implemented in Listing 9–1 is pretty handy. You can make icons look and behave exactly as you wish. But, we can make icons more useful by:

• Requiring an image attribute

• Letting the page author specify a CSS class for the image

• Letting the page author trigger validation when an icon's action is invoked

Listing 9–3 shows an updated icon listing that implements the preceding features.

Listing 9–3 /composite-login/web/resources/util/icon.xhtml

```
1. <?xml version="1.0" encoding="UTF-8"?>
2. <!DOCTYPE html PUBLIC "-//W3C//DTD XHTML 1.0 Transitional//EN"
3.       "http://www.w3.org/TR/xhtml1/DTD/xhtml1-transitional.dtd">
4. <html xmlns="http://www.w3.org/1999/xhtml"
5.    xmlns:h="http://java.sun.com/jsf/html"
6.    xmlns:composite="http://java.sun.com/jsf/composite">
7.
8.    <composite:interface>
9.       <composite:attribute name="image" required="true" />
10.      <composite:attribute name="doValidation" default="false" />
11.      <composite:attribute name="styleClass" default="icon" />
12.      <composite:attribute name="actionMethod"
13.         method-signature="java.lang.String action()" />
```

```
14.  </composite:interface>
15.
16.  <composite:implementation>
17.  <h:form>
18.    <h:commandLink action="#{cc.attrs.actionMethod}"
19.      immediate="#{not cc.attrs.doValidation}">
20.
21.      <h:graphicImage url="#{cc.attrs.image}"
22.        styleClass="#{cc.attrs.styleClass}" />
23.
24.    </h:commandLink>
25.  </h:form>
26.  </composite:implementation>
27.
28. </html>
```

Although there are undoubtedly edge cases advocating invisible icons, we side with the vast majority of icon-related use cases by requiring page authors to provide an image, by virtue of the required attribute on the image's composite:attribute tag.

We also allow page authors to specify a CSS style for the icon's image with a styleClass attribute. We specify a default value of icon for that attribute.

Finally, we let the page author control whether clicking on an icon triggers input validation on the server. By default, an icon's link has it's immediate attribute set to true, where immediate indicates that validation should be skipped. If you want validation to occur when you click an icon, you must specify that explicitly, like this: <util:icon doValidation="true".../>.

Manipulating Server-Side Data

The icon component we showed you in Listing 9–1 is more interesting than the debug component we opened the chapter with because the icon component is configurable, and therefore more reusable, than the debug component. However, the icon component lacks something that many non-trivial composite components have: interaction with server-side data.

Figure 9–4 shows a login component that interacts with a managed bean.

The login component shown in Figure 9–4 can be used like this:

```
<util:login namePrompt="#{msgs.namePrompt}"
      passwordPrompt="#{msgs.passwordPrompt}"
        loginAction="#{user.login}"
      loginButtonText="#{msgs.loginButtonText}"
            user="#{user}"/>
```

The page author passes in a reference to the user managed bean, in addition to other attributes that configure the login component's prompts and button.

Figure 9–4 A login component

You can implement a simple login component as follows:

```
<html xmlns="http://www.w3.org/1999/xhtml"
    xmlns:h="http://java.sun.com/jsf/html"
    xmlns:ui="http://java.sun.com/jsf/facelets"
    xmlns:composite="http://java.sun.com/jsf/composite">

    <composite:interface>
        <composite:attribute user="user"/>

        <composite:attribute name="namePrompt"/>
        <composite:attribute name="passwordPrompt"/>

        <composite:attribute name="loginButtonText"/>
        <composite:attribute name="loginAction"
            method-signature="java.lang.String action()"/>
    </composite:interface>

    <composite:implementation>
        <h:form id="form">
            <h:panelGrid columns="2">
                #{cc.attrs.namePrompt}
                <h:inputText id="name" value="#{cc.attrs.user.name}"/>

                #{cc.attrs.passwordPrompt}
                <h:inputSecret id="password" value="#{cc.attrs.user.password}"/>
            </h:panelGrid>
            <p>
                <h:commandButton id="loginButton" value="#{cc.attrs.loginButtonText}"
                    action="#{cc.attrs.loginAction}"/>
            </p>
        </h:form>
    </composite:implementation>
</html>
```

The login component declares a user attribute, and uses that attribute for the name, #{cc.attrs.user.name}, and password, #{cc.attrs.user.password}, input values.

Passing a managed bean to a composite component is one strategy for interacting with server-side data. For the login component in Listing 9–3, however, that strategy results in tight coupling: The login component will only work with managed beans with properties named name and password.

To make the login component more accessible to a wider range of managed beans, perhaps ones with properties named username and passwd, for example, we can take a more fine-grained approach, like this:

```
<util:login namePrompt="#{msgs.namePrompt}"
    passwordPrompt="#{msgs.passwordPrompt}"
    name="#{user.username}"
    password="#{user.passwd}"
    loginAction="#{user.login}"
    loginButtonText="#{msgs.loginButtonText}"/>
```

Now, instead of giving the login component a user managed bean, and letting the component reference the bean's properties, we specify the bean's name and password properties directly. That means that this new version of the login component will work with managed beans with properties of any name.

You will need to make the following changes to the component definition:

```
<composite:interface>
    <composite:attribute name="name"/>
    <composite:attribute name="password"/>
    ...
</composite:interface>

<composite:implementation>
    ...
    #{cc.attrs.namePrompt}
    <h:inputText id="name" value="#{cc.attrs.name}"/>

    #{cc.attrs.passwordPrompt}
    <h:inputSecret id="password" value="#{cc.attrs.password}"/>
    ...
</composite:implementation>
```

Now page authors can associate individual properties of a managed bean, in our case #{user.username} and #{user.passwd}, with inputs created by the login component.

So now we have a backing bean (user) with properties (name and password) wired to inputs in a login component. The login component is beginning to look like a useful component. However, at this point it has one serious drawback that makes it less appealing than you might expect: You can't attach validators to the name and password inputs. You will see in the section "Exposing a Composite's Components" on page 360 how you can do exactly that.

Localizing Composite Components

Most of the time, you want to let page authors configure text displayed by your composite components, but sometimes you don't. For example, if we decide to sell some advertising space in our login component, and we are currently looking for eager advertisers, we can display some text at the bottom of the component, as shown in Figure 9–5.

Please log in

Name   Hiro

Password

(Log In)

This advertising space is available. Call 555-1212.

Figure 9–5   Localizing text in composite components

JSF 2.0 lets you associate a resource bundle with a composite component, so you can localize text that your composite component displays. In your composite component's directory, you create a properties file with the name *component_name*.properties, where *component_name* is the name of your composite component. For the login component, we created login.properties, as shown in Figure 9–6.

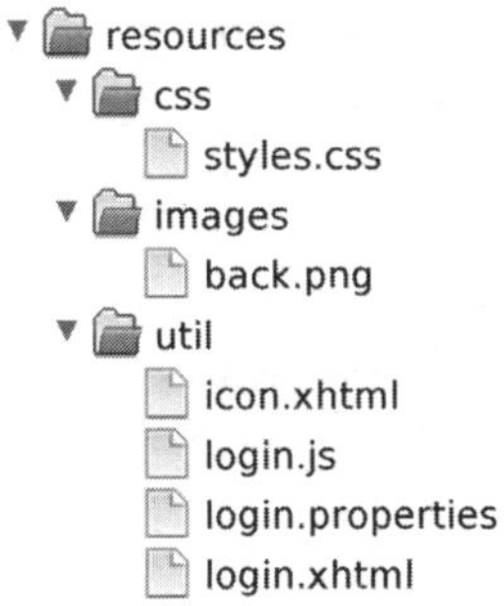

▼ 📁 resources
 ▼ 📁 css
    📄 styles.css
 ▼ 📁 images
    📄 back.png
 ▼ 📁 util
    📄 icon.xhtml
    📄 login.js
    📄 login.properties
    📄 login.xhtml

Figure 9–6   The login component's properties file

Our `login.properties` file only contains one key/value pair, as shown in Listing 9–4.

Listing 9–4 composite-login/web/resources/util/login.properties

```
1. footer=This advertising space is available. Call 555-1212.
```

Once you have a properties file, you can access its contents with the expression `#{cc.resourceBundleMap.`*key*`}` where *key* is the key from the properties file. In our login component, we did this:

```
<composite:implementation>
   ...
   <p>#{cc.resourceBundleMap.footer}</p>
   ...
</composite:implementation>
```

Exposing a Composite's Components

Now let's modify our login component so we can attach validators to the `name` and `password` inputs in the login component's form. The result of erring on the wrong side of one of those validators is shown in Figure 9–7.

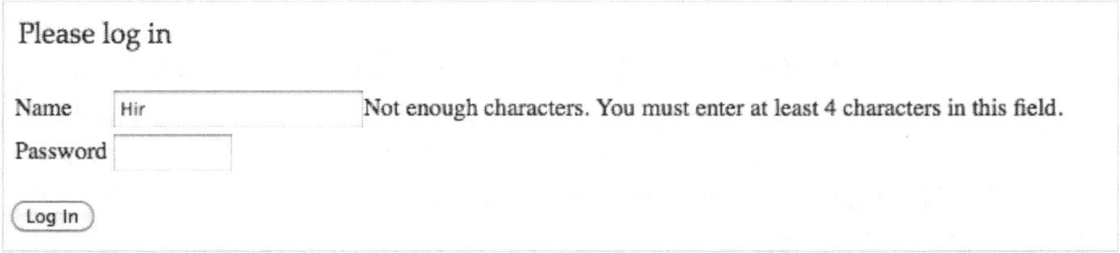

Figure 9–7 Adding a validator to one of the login component's inputs

We add three `composite:editableValueHolder` tags to our login component's interface. The first two refer to the `name` and `password` inputs, and the third refers to both inputs:

```
<composite:interface>
   <composite:editableValueHolder name="nameInput" targets="form:name"/>
   <composite:editableValueHolder name="passwordInput" targets="form:password"/>
   <composite:editableValueHolder name="inputs" targets="form:name form:password"/>
   ...
</composite:interface>
```

The `composite:editableValueHolder` exposes the components referenced by the targets attribute to the page author, under the name specified with the `name` attribute. The components are specified with component identifiers. Those identifiers are relative to the composite component, and since both inputs reside in a form, with the id `form`, we must prefix both component ids with `form:`.

Now that we've exposed the `name` and `password` input components to page authors, we can use those components like this:

```
<util:login namePrompt="#{msgs.namePrompt}"
      passwordPrompt="#{msgs.passwordPrompt}"
      name="#{user.name}"
      password="#{user.password}"
      loginAction="#{user.login}"
      loginButtonText="#{msgs.loginButtonText}">

  <f:validateLength maximum="10" for="inputs"/>
  <f:validateLength minimum="4" for="nameInput"/>
  <f:validator id="com.corejsf.Password" for="passwordInput"/>

</util:login>
```

In the preceding code snippet, we've added three validators to the inputs in the form component. The first two validators specify a maximum of 10 characters for both the `name` and `password` inputs, and a minimum of 4 characters for the `name` input. The third validator is a custom validator that we attach to the `password` input, that checks passwords for illegal characters. Figure 9–8 shows the result when that validation fails.

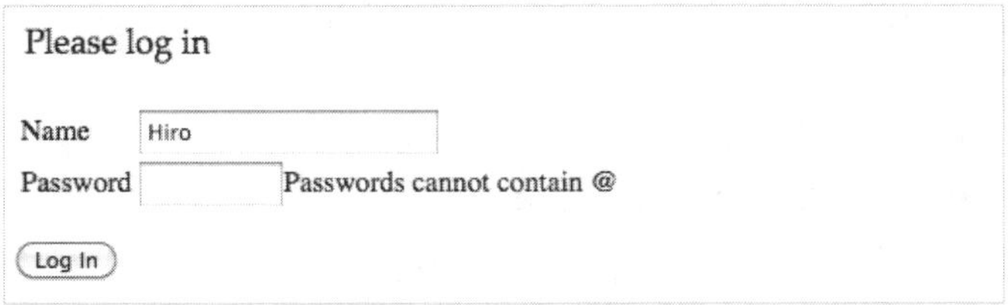

Please log in	
Name	Hiro
Password	Passwords cannot contain @
Log In	

Figure 9–8   Checking passwords for illegal characters (note: JSF clears the password input before showing the error message)

That validator attached to the `password` input is shown in Listing 9–5.

| **Listing 9–5** | composite-login/src/java/com/corejsf/PasswordValidator.java |

```
1. package com.corejsf;
2.
3. import javax.faces.application.FacesMessage;
4. import javax.faces.component.UIComponent;
5. import javax.faces.context.FacesContext;
6. import javax.faces.validator.FacesValidator;
7. import javax.faces.validator.Validator;
8. import javax.faces.validator.ValidatorException;
9.
10. @FacesValidator("com.corejsf.Password")
11. public class PasswordValidator implements Validator {
12.    public void validate(FacesContext context, UIComponent component, Object value)
13.          throws ValidatorException {
14.       String pwd = (String) value;
15.       if (pwd.contains("@")) {
16.          throw new ValidatorException(new FacesMessage("Passwords cannot contain @"));
17.       }
18.    }
19. }
```

The validator in the preceding listing is pretty simple-minded: it only checks for occurrences of @ in the password. You could easily expand the logic to add other checks.

NOTE: In the preceding example, we essentially aliased component identifiers, like this:

```
<composite:interface>
   ...
   <composite:editableValueHolder name="passwordInput"
      targets="form:password"/>
   <composite:editableValueHolder name="inputs"
      targets="form:name form:password"/>
   ...
</composite:interface>
```

The name attribute aliases the targets attribute, so page authors can refer to the name instead of the more unwieldly component id specified for the targets attribute:

```
<util:login ...>
   <f:validator binding="#{passwordValidator}" for="passwordInput"/>
   <f:validateLength maximum="10" for="inputs"/>
</util:login>
```

If no targets are supplied, the page author has to specify the full name of the component. For example, if the interface is

```
<composite:interface>
    <composite:editableValueHolder name="form:password"/> <!-- no target -->
    <composite:editableValueHolder name="inputs"
        targets="form:name form:password"/>
    ...
```

the password field is referenced like this:

```
<util:login...>
    <f:validator binding="#{passwordValidator}" for="form:password"/>
</util:login>
```

Exposing Action Sources

Besides composite:editableValueHolder, the composite tag library comes with two other tags that you can use to expose components contained in composite components to page authors: composite:valueHolder and composite:actionSource.

The composite:valueHolder tag exposes components, such as output components, that have a non-editable value. The composite:actionSource tag exposes components, such as buttons and links, that fire action events. For example, we can expose the login component's submit button:

```
<composite:interface>
    <composite:actionSource name="loginButton" targets="form:loginButton"/>
    ...
</composite:interface>"

<composite:implementation>
    ...
    <h:form id="form"... >
        ...
        <h:commandButton id="loginButton"
            value="#{cc.attrs.loginButtonText}"
            action="#{cc.attrs.loginAction}"/>
        ...
    </h:form>
</composite:implementation>
```

With the form's submit button exposed, page authors can use that button, like this:

```
<util:login ...>
    <f:actionListener for="loginButton" type="com.corejsf.LoginActionListener"/>
</util:login>
```

JSF 2.0 adds a for attribute to the f:actionListener. That attribute's value refers to an action source that is exposed in the surrounding login component.

As a result of attaching an action listener to the login component's submit button, when the user clicks the login component's submit button, JSF instantiates an instance of com.corejsf.LoginActionListener, and invokes it's processAction method.

In our sample application, we provide a LoginActionListener (shown in Listing 9–6) that checks whether the provided user name and password are valid. (In practice, it would be easier to handle login failure in the action method—we just want to show you the mechanics.)

Table 9–2 lists the tags that you can use in your composite component's interface section to expose the components contained in a composite component.

Table 9–2   Composite Component Tags

Interface Tag	Use the Component with These Tags in the Using Page
actionSource	f:actionListener
valueHolder	f:converter, f:convertDateTime, f:setPropertyActionListener, f:validate...
editableValueHolder	f:converter, f:convertDateTime, f:setPropertyActionListener, f:validate..., f:valueChangeListener

The right column in Table 9–2 lists tags that, like f:actionListener, have a for attribute that you can use to reference a component in a composite component that's been exposed through the component's interface with the tags in the left column in Table 9–2.

Listing 9–6   composite-login/src/java/com/corejsf/LoginActionListener.java

```
1. package com.corejsf;
2.
3. import javax.faces.application.FacesMessage;
4. import javax.faces.component.UIComponent;
5. import javax.faces.component.UIInput;
6. import javax.faces.context.FacesContext;
7. import javax.faces.event.AbortProcessingException;
8. import javax.faces.event.ActionEvent;
9. import javax.faces.event.ActionListener;
10.
11. public class LoginActionListener implements ActionListener {
```

```
12.    public void processAction(ActionEvent event) throws AbortProcessingException {
13.       UIComponent container = event.getComponent().getNamingContainer();
14.       String name = (String) ((UIInput)
15.          container.findComponent("form:name")).getValue();
16.       String pwd = (String) ((UIInput)
17.          container.findComponent("form:password")).getValue();
18.       if (Registrar.isRegistered(name, pwd)) return;
19.
20.       FacesContext context = FacesContext.getCurrentInstance();
21.       context.addMessage(container.getClientId(),
22.          new FacesMessage("Name and password are invalid. Please try again."));
23.       throw new AbortProcessingException("Invalid credentials");
24.    }
25. }
```

Facets

Adding objects such as listeners, converters, and validators to components inside a composite component is one way you can add functionality to a component. Another way to add functionality is to let page authors specify *facets* of a composite component.

A component uses facets if the component user needs to supply content in addition to the child components. For example, data tables have facets named header and footer, like this:

```
<h:dataTable ...>
   <f:facet name="header">#{msgs.tableHeader}</f:facet>
   ...
   <f:facet name="footer">#{msgs.tableFooter}</f:facet>
</h:dataTable>
```

You may want to provide facets in your own composite components. For example, with just a few lines of markup, you can add header and error facets to the login component, so a page author can do something like this:

```
<util:login ...>
   <f:facet name="header" styleClass="header">
      <div class="prompt">#{msgs.loginPrompt}</div>
   </f:facet>
   <f:facet name="error" styleClass="error">
      <h:messages layout="table" styleClass="error"/>
   </f:facet>
   ...
</util:login>
```

Here's how we implemented the header and error facets in the login component's defining page:

```
<composite:interface>
    ...
    <composite:facet name="header"/>
    <composite:facet name="error"/>
</composite:interface>

<composite:implementation>
    ...
    <composite:renderFacet name="header"/>
    <h:form ...>
    ...
    </h:form>
    <composite:renderFacet name="error"/>
</composite:implementation>
```

In the preceding code, we declared the facets in the component's interface with the composite:facet tag, and used the composite:renderFacet tag in the component's implementation, to render the facets.

The composite:renderFacet tag renders the supplied facet *as a child component*. If you want to insert it as a facet instead, use the composite:insertFacet tag, like this:

```
<composite:implementation>
    ...
    <h:dataTable>
        <composite:insertFacet name="header"/>
        ...
        <composite:insertFacet name="footer"/>
    </h:dataTable>
    ...
</composite:implementation>
```

Here, the header and footer become the data table's header and footer facets.

Children

Composite components are represented by tags. Sometimes it makes sense to allow content in the body of those tags. By default, if you put something in the body of a composite component's tag, JSF will just ignore that content, but you can use the <composite:insertChildren/> tag in your composite component's implementation to render the components in the body of your composite component's tag.

For example, with our login component, it might be convenient to let page authors add anything they want to the bottom of the component. A common use case would be to add a registration link to the login component, as depicted in Figure 9–9.

Please log in

Name   Hiro

Password

(Log In)

Register...

Figure 9–9   The login component, fitted with a registration link

In Figure 9–9, we've added a registration link, like this:

```
<util:login...>
    ...
    <f:facet name="header" styleClass="header">...</f:facet>
    <f:facet name="error" styleClass="error">...</f:facet>

    <!-- Child component -->
    <h:link>#{msgs.registerLinkText}</h:link>
</util:login>
```

In the login component's implementation, we use the composite:insertChildren tag to render the composite's children—i.e., any components other than facets, in the body of the composite's tag. For example, here's how we render child components after the error facet in our login component:

```
<composite:implementation>
    <composite:renderFacet name="header"/>
    <h:form ...>
    ...
    </h:form>
    <composite:renderFacet name="error"/>

    <composite:insertChildren/>
</composite:implementation>
```

JavaScript

It's often convenient to attach JavaScript to a component—for example, for client-side validation. JSF makes it easy to use JavaScript with the built-in JSF tags.

You can also use JavaScript with composite components that you develop. However, to do so effectively, you need to know how to access the client identifiers of HTML elements generated by your component.

Figure 9–10 shows client-side validation at work for the places login component. That validation uses some JavaScript.

Figure 9–10   Client-side validation for the login component

You can put JavaScript directly in the implementation section of a composite component, but to make things more modular, we placed the JavaScript for the login component in a file of its own. We load that JavaScript with the h:output-Script tag, and invoke a function from that JavaScript when the user submits the login form:

```
<composite:implementation>
  <h:outputScript library="util" name="login.js" target="head"/>
  <h:form id="form" onsubmit="return checkForm(this, '#{cc.clientId}')">
    ...
  </h:form>
  ...
</composite:implementation>
```

The checkForm() function takes two arguments: a reference to a form, and the client identifier of the composite component in which the form resides. That function uses the client identifier to access the composite component's form elements, as shown in Listing 9–7.

Listing 9–7   composite-login/web/resources/util/login.js

```
 1. function checkForm(form, ccId) {
 2.     var name = form[ccId + ':form:name'].value;
 3.     var pwd = form[ccId + ':form:password'].value;
 4.
 5.     if (name == "" || pwd == "") {
 6.         alert("Please enter name and password.");
 7.         return false;
 8.     }
 9.     return true;
10. }
```

Notice that we have to drill down to the inputs, through the composite component and the input's form. We can eliminate the form designation by telling JSF not to prepend the form's id, like this:

```
<h:form id="form" prependId="false"
    onsubmit="return checkForm(this, '#{cc.clientId}')">
```

Now we can access the name and password fields a little more easily:

```
var name = form[ccId + 'name'].value;
var pwd = form[ccId + 'password'].value;
```

Our sample application combines the techniques that we introduced in the preceding sections.

The final version of the component definition is shown in Listing 9–8. Listing 9–9 is the web page that uses the login component. The User class in Listing 9–10 represents the user that is being logged in. We provide a rudimentary registration service for demonstration purposes—see the book's companion code at http://corejsf.com for the implementation.

Listing 9–8 composite-login/web/resources/util/login.xhtml

```
1. <?xml version="1.0" encoding="UTF-8"?>
2. <!DOCTYPE html PUBLIC "-//W3C//DTD XHTML 1.0 Transitional//EN"
3.    "http://www.w3.org/TR/xhtml1/DTD/xhtml1-transitional.dtd">
4. <html xmlns="http://www.w3.org/1999/xhtml"
5.       xmlns:h="http://java.sun.com/jsf/html"
6.       xmlns:composite="http://java.sun.com/jsf/composite">
7.
8.    <composite:interface>
9.       <composite:editableValueHolder name="nameInput" targets="form:name"/>
10.      <composite:editableValueHolder name="passwordInput" targets="form:password"/>
11.      <composite:editableValueHolder name="inputs"
12.           targets="form:name form:password"/>
13.      <composite:actionSource name="loginButton" targets="form:loginButton"/>
14.
15.      <composite:attribute name="name"/>
16.      <composite:attribute name="password"/>
17.
18.      <composite:attribute name="namePrompt"/>
19.      <composite:attribute name="passwordPrompt"/>
20.
21.      <composite:attribute name="loginValidate"
22.         method-signature="void validateLogin(ComponentSystemEvent e)
23.             throws javax.faces.event.AbortProcessingException"/>
24.
25.      <composite:attribute name="loginAction"
26.         method-signature="java.lang.String action()"/>
27.
28.      <composite:facet name="heading"/>
29.      <composite:facet name="error"/>
30.   </composite:interface>
31.
32.   <composite:implementation>
33.      <h:outputScript library="components/util" name="login.js" target="head"/>
34.      <h:form id="form" onsubmit="return checkForm(this, '#{cc.clientId}')">
35.         <composite:renderFacet name="heading"/>
36.         <h:panelGrid columns="2">
37.            #{cc.attrs.namePrompt}
38.            <h:panelGroup>
39.               <h:inputText id="name" value="#{cc.attrs.name}"/>
40.               <h:message for="name"/>
41.            </h:panelGroup>
42.
43.            #{cc.attrs.passwordPrompt}
44.
45.            <h:panelGroup>
```

```
46.                  <h:inputSecret id="password" value="#{cc.attrs.password}" size="8"/>
47.                  <h:message for="password"/>
48.               </h:panelGroup>
49.             </h:panelGrid>
50.
51.             <p>
52.                <h:commandButton id="loginButton"
53.                   value="#{cc.attrs.loginButtonText}"
54.                   action="#{cc.attrs.loginAction}"/>
55.             </p>
56.
57.          </h:form>
58.
59.          <composite:renderFacet name="error"/>
60.
61.          <p><composite:insertChildren/></p>
62.
63.          <p>#{cc.resourceBundleMap.footer}</p>
64.       </composite:implementation>
65. </html>
```

Listing 9-9 composite-login/web/index.xhtml

```
1. <?xml version="1.0" encoding="UTF-8"?>
2. <!DOCTYPE html PUBLIC "-//W3C//DTD XHTML 1.0 Transitional//EN"
3.    "http://www.w3.org/TR/xhtml1/DTD/xhtml1-transitional.dtd">
4. <html xmlns="http://www.w3.org/1999/xhtml"
5.       xmlns:f="http://java.sun.com/jsf/core"
6.       xmlns:h="http://java.sun.com/jsf/html"
7.       xmlns:util="http://java.sun.com/jsf/composite/util"
8.       xmlns:ui="http://java.sun.com/jsf/facelets">
9.    <h:head>
10.       <title>#{msgs.loginHeading}</title>
11.       <h:outputStylesheet library="css" name="styles.css" />
12.    </h:head>
13.    <h:body>
14.       <util:login namePrompt="#{msgs.namePrompt}"
15.             passwordPrompt="#{msgs.passwordPrompt}"
16.             name="#{user.name}"
17.             password="#{user.password}"
18.             loginAction="#{user.login}"
19.             loginButtonText="#{msgs.loginButtonText}">
20.
21.          <f:validateLength minimum="4" for="nameInput"/>
22.          <f:validator validatorId="com.corejsf.Password" for="passwordInput"/>
23.          <f:actionListener type="com.corejsf.LoginActionListener" for="loginButton"/>
24.
```

```
25.        <f:facet name="heading" styleClass="header">
26.          <div class="prompt">#{msgs.loginPrompt}</div>
27.        </f:facet>
28.
29.        <f:facet name="error" styleClass="error">
30.          <h:messages layout="table" styleClass="error"/>
31.        </f:facet>
32.
33.        <!-- Child component -->
34.        <h:link outcome="register">#{msgs.registerLinkText}</h:link>
35.
36.      </util:login>
37.      <ui:debug/>
38.    </h:body>
39. </html>
```

Listing 9–10 composite-login/src/java/com/corejsf/User.java

```
 1. package com.corejsf;
 2.
 3. import java.io.Serializable;
 4. import javax.inject.Named;
 5.    // or import javax.faces.bean.ManagedBean;
 6. import javax.enterprise.context.SessionScoped;
 7.    // or import javax.faces.bean.SessionScoped;
 8.
 9. @Named // or @ManagedBean
10. @SessionScoped
11. public class User implements Serializable {
12.    private String name;
13.    private String password;
14.
15.    public User() { this("", ""); }
16.    public User(String name, String password) {
17.       this.name = name;
18.       this.password = password;
19.    }
20.
21.    public String getPassword() { return password; }
22.    public void setPassword(String newValue) { password = newValue; }
23.
24.    public String getName() { return name; }
25.    public void setName(String newValue) { name = newValue; }
26.
27.    public String register() {
28.       Registrar.register(name, password);
29.       return "welcome";
```

```
30.   }
31.
32.   public String login() {
33.       return "welcome";
34.   }
35.
36.   public String logout() {
37.       name = password = "";
38.       return "index";
39.   }
40. }
```

Backing Components

Sometimes, you want to have more control over the behavior of a composite component than you can achieve through XML declarations. To add Java code to a composite component, you supply a *backing component*. A backing component has these requirements:

*   It is a subclass of UIComponent.
*   It implements the NamingContainer marker interface.
*   Its family property has the value "javax.faces.NamingContainer".

We will discuss the UIComponent class and the notion of component families in detail in Chapter 11. This section gives you a simple, but typical example.

Consider a date component that uses three h:selectOneMenu components for the day, month, and year (see Figure 9–11).

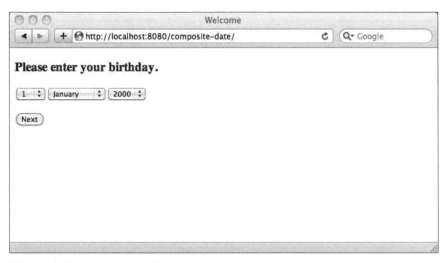

Figure 9–11   A composite date component

Using the techniques that you have already seen, it would be very easy to make such a component and expose the three child components, so that you can attach a value reference to each of them:

```
<util:date day="#{user.birthDate}" month="#{user.birthMonth}"
   year="#{user.birthYear}"/>
```

However, suppose your User class stores the date as a java.util.Date and not as three separate integers. After all, in object-oriented programming, you want to use classes whenever possible and not just store everything as numbers and strings.

It would be much better if the component had a single value of type Date:

```
<util:date value="#{user.birthDay}"/>
```

However, the Java Date class doesn't have property getters and setters for the day, month, and year. Therefore, we cannot simply use value expressions, such as #{cc.attrs.value.day}, inside our composite component. Instead, some Java code is needed to assemble a Date from its components. Therefore, we will provide a backing component.

There are two ways of designating a backing component for a composite component. The easiest is to follow a naming convention: use the class name *libraryName.componentName*. In our example, the class name is util.date—that is, a class date in a package util. (It's a bit odd to have a lowercase class name, but that's the price to pay for "convention over configuration".)

Alternatively, you can use the @FacesComponent annotation to specify a "component type", and then you specify that component type in the composite:interface declaration:

```
<composite:interface componentType="com.corejsf.Date">
```

We will discuss component types in Chapter 11. In this example, we follow the naming convention and provide a class util.date.

As you will see in Chapter 11, component classes that take user input should extend the UIInput class. Thus, our backing component has the following form:

```
package util;
...
public class date extends UIInput implements NamingContainer {
   public String getFamily() {
      return "javax.faces.NamingContainer";
   }
   ...
}
```

Before going further with the implementation of the backing component, have a look at the composite component definition in Listing 9–11.

Listing 9–11 composite-date/web/resources/util/date.xhtml

```
 1. <?xml version="1.0" encoding="UTF-8"?>
 2. <!DOCTYPE html PUBLIC "-//W3C//DTD XHTML 1.0 Transitional//EN"
 3.       "http://www.w3.org/TR/xhtml1/DTD/xhtml1-transitional.dtd">
 4.
 5. <html xmlns="http://www.w3.org/1999/xhtml"
 6.    xmlns:h="http://java.sun.com/jsf/html"
 7.    xmlns:composite="http://java.sun.com/jsf/composite"
 8.    xmlns:f="http://java.sun.com/jsf/core">
 9.
10.    <composite:interface>
11.       <composite:attribute name="value" type="java.util.Date"/>
12.    </composite:interface>
13.
14.    <composite:implementation>
15.       <h:selectOneMenu id="day" converter="javax.faces.Integer">
16.          <f:selectItems value="#{dates.days}"/>
17.       </h:selectOneMenu>
18.       <h:selectOneMenu id="month" converter="javax.faces.Integer">
19.          <f:selectItems value="#{dates.months]"/>
20.       </h:selectOneMenu>
21.       <h:selectOneMenu id="year" converter="javax.faces.Integer">
22.          <f:selectItems value="#{dates.years}"/>
23.       </h:selectOneMenu>
24.    </composite:implementation>
25. </html>
```

Here, the dates bean simply produces arrays of values 1 . . . 31, January . . . December, and 1900 . . . 2100—see Listing 9–12.

Listing 9–12 composite-date/src/java/com/corejsf/Dates.java

```
1. package com.corejsf;
2. import java.io.Serializable;
3. import java.text.DateFormatSymbols;
4. import java.util.LinkedHashMap;
5. import java.util.Map;
6. import javax.inject.Named;
7.    // or import javax.faces.bean.ManagedBean;
8. import javax.enterprise.context.ApplicationScoped;
9.    // or import javax.faces.bean.ApplicationScoped;
```

```
10.
11. @Named // or @ManagedBean
12. @ApplicationScoped
13. public class Dates implements Serializable {
14.     private int[] days;
15.     private int[] years;
16.     private Map<String, Integer> months;
17.
18.     private static int[] intArray(int from, int to) {
19.         int[] result = new int[to - from + 1];
20.         for (int i = from; i <= to; i++) result[i - from] = i;
21.         return result;
22.     }
23.
24.     public Dates() {
25.         days = intArray(1, 31);
26.         years = intArray(1900, 2100);
27.         months = new LinkedHashMap<String, Integer>();
28.         String[] names = new DateFormatSymbols().getMonths();
29.         for (int i = 0; i < 12; i++) months.put(names[i], i + 1);
30.     }
31.
32.     public int[] getDays() { return days; }
33.     public int[] getYears() { return years; }
34.     public Map<String, Integer> getMonths() { return months; }
35. }
```

When rendering the composite component, we need to set the day, month, and year values of the child components. This happens in the encodeBegin method:

```
public class date extends UIInput implements NamingContainer {
    ...
    public void encodeBegin(FacesContext context) throws IOException {
        Date date = (Date) getValue();
        Calendar cal = new GregorianCalendar();
        cal.setTime(date);
        UIInput dayComponent = (UIInput) findComponent("day");
        UIInput monthComponent = (UIInput) findComponent("month");
        UIInput yearComponent = (UIInput) findComponent("year");
        dayComponent.setValue(cal.get(Calendar.DATE));
        monthComponent.setValue(cal.get(Calendar.MONTH) + 1);
        yearComponent.setValue(cal.get(Calendar.YEAR));
        super.encodeBegin(context);
    }
    ...
}
```

When the form is submitted, we need to reconstitute the Date value from the day, month, and year. To find the correct place for this conversion, consider how the JSF life cycle starts:

1. The HTTP request delivers name/value pairs.
2. In the Apply Request Values phase, each of the h:selectOneMenu components sets its submitted value.
3. During validation, the component's submitted value is converted to the desired type, becoming the converted value. In our case, each h:selectOne-Menu component has an integer converter that converts the incoming string to an Integer.
4. If the converted value passes validation, it becomes the value of the component.

Now consider the composite component. It does not have a submitted value because there is nothing in the HTTP request that directly corresponds to the composite component. But we want it to have a converted value, so that we can attach validators to the composite component. Therefore, we compute the date in the getConvertedValue method:

```
public class date extends UIInput implements NamingContainer {
    ...
    protected Object getConvertedValue(FacesContext context, Object newSubmittedValue)
            throws ConverterException {
        UIInput dayComponent = (UIInput) findComponent("day");
        UIInput monthComponent = (UIInput) findComponent("month");
        UIInput yearComponent = (UIInput) findComponent("year");
        int day = (Integer) dayComponent.getValue();
        int month = (Integer) monthComponent.getValue();
        int year = (Integer) yearComponent.getValue();
        if (isValidDate(day, month, year))
            return new GregorianCalendar(year, month - 1, day).getTime();
        else
            throw new ConverterException(new FacesMessage(FacesMessage.SEVERITY_ERROR,
                "Invalid date", "Invalid date"));
    }
    ...
}
```

If the user provides an invalid date, such as February 30, a converter exception occurs. Note that this is *not* a validation error. For a Date, a validation error would be a date that is not in an expected date range. But if the user provides an input of February 30, we don't have a Date yet—the user input cannot be converted into one.

As it turns out, we do need to override the getSubmittedValue since a null submitted value is treated as a special case. We simply return the component itself— see Listing 9–15.

Using the component is very easy, as shown in Listing 9–13. We simply attach a Date-valued property; here, the birthday of the UserBean class in Listing 9–14. Note the @Past validation annotation of the birthday property. This annotation works seamlessly with our date component, validating the submitted Date value. If the user supplies a date that lies in the future, the application reverts to the old date and displays an error (Figure 9–12).

Figure 9–12 Trying to enter a date in the future is rejected with a validation error

Figure 9–13 shows the directory structure of the application.

As you can see, implementing a backing component requires some knowledge of the JSF component API, which we discuss in Chapter 11. However, it is much less work to add a small amount of code in a backing component than it would be to write a custom component from scratch.

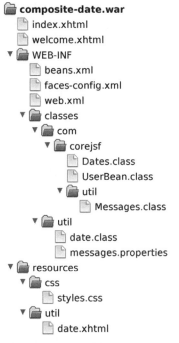

```
composite-date.war
    index.xhtml
    welcome.xhtml
    WEB-INF
        beans.xml
        faces-config.xml
        web.xml
        classes
            com
                corejsf
                    Dates.class
                    UserBean.class
                    util
                        Messages.class
            util
                date.class
                messages.properties
    resources
        css
            styles.css
        util
            date.xhtml
```

Figure 9–13   The directory structure of the composite date application

Listing 9–13   composite-date/web/index.xhtml

```
1. <?xml version="1.0" encoding="UTF-8"?>
2. <!DOCTYPE html PUBLIC "-//W3C//DTD XHTML 1.0 Transitional//EN"
3. "http://www.w3.org/TR/xhtml1/DTD/xhtml1-transitional.dtd">
4. <html xmlns="http://www.w3.org/1999/xhtml"
5.       xmlns:h="http://java.sun.com/jsf/html"
6.       xmlns:ui="http://java.sun.com/jsf/facelets"
7.       xmlns:util="http://java.sun.com/jsf/composite/util">
8.    <h:head>
9.       <title>Welcome</title>
10.       <h:outputStylesheet library="css" name="styles.css"/>
11.    </h:head>
12.    <h:body>
13.       <h:form>
14.          <h3>Please enter your birthday.</h3>
15.          <util:date id="date" value="#{user.birthday}"/>
16.          <br/><h:message for="date" styleClass="error"/>
17.          <p><h:commandButton value="Next" action="welcome"/></p>
18.       </h:form>
```

```
19.
20.    </h:body>
21. </html>
```

Listing 9-14 composite-date/src/java/com/corejsf/UserBean.java

```
 1. package com.corejsf;
 2.
 3. import java.io.Serializable;
 4. import java.util.Date;
 5. import java.util.GregorianCalendar;
 6. import javax.inject.Named;
 7.    // or import javax.faces.bean.ManagedBean;
 8. import javax.enterprise.context.SessionScoped;
 9.    // or import javax.faces.bean.SessionScoped;
10. import javax.validation.constraints.Past;
11.
12. @Named("user") // or @ManagedBean(name="user")
13. @SessionScoped
14. public class UserBean implements Serializable {
15.    private String name;
16.    private String password;
17.    @Past private Date birthday = new GregorianCalendar(2000, 0, 1).getTime();
18.
19.    public String getName() { return name; }
20.    public void setName(String newValue) { name = newValue; }
21.
22.    public String getPassword() { return password; }
23.    public void setPassword(String newValue) { password = newValue; }
24.
25.    public Date getBirthday() { return birthday; }
26.    public void setBirthday(Date newValue) { birthday = newValue; }
27. }
```

Listing 9-15 composite-date/src/java/util/date.java

```
 1. package util;
 2.
 3. import com.corejsf.util.Messages;
 4.
 5. import java.io.IOException;
 6. import java.util.Calendar;
 7. import java.util.Date;
 8. import java.util.GregorianCalendar;
 9. import java.util.Locale;
10. import java.util.ResourceBundle;
```

```
11. import javax.faces.application.FacesMessage;
12. import javax.faces.component.NamingContainer;
13. import javax.faces.component.UIInput;
14. import javax.faces.context.FacesContext;
15. import javax.faces.convert.ConverterException;
16.
17. public class date extends UIInput implements NamingContainer {
18.     public String getFamily() {
19.         return "javax.faces.NamingContainer";
20.     }
21.
22.     public void encodeBegin(FacesContext context) throws IOException {
23.         Date date = (Date) getValue();
24.         Calendar cal = new GregorianCalendar();
25.         cal.setTime(date);
26.         UIInput dayComponent = (UIInput) findComponent("day");
27.         UIInput monthComponent = (UIInput) findComponent("month");
28.         UIInput yearComponent = (UIInput) findComponent("year");
29.         dayComponent.setValue(cal.get(Calendar.DATE));
30.         monthComponent.setValue(cal.get(Calendar.MONTH) + 1);
31.         yearComponent.setValue(cal.get(Calendar.YEAR));
32.         super.encodeBegin(context);
33.     }
34.
35.     public Object getSubmittedValue() {
36.         return this;
37.     }
38.
39.     protected Object getConvertedValue(FacesContext context, Object newSubmittedValue)
40.             throws ConverterException {
41.         UIInput dayComponent = (UIInput) findComponent("day");
42.         UIInput monthComponent = (UIInput) findComponent("month");
43.         UIInput yearComponent = (UIInput) findComponent("year");
44.         int day = (Integer) dayComponent.getValue();
45.         int month = (Integer) monthComponent.getValue();
46.         int year = (Integer) yearComponent.getValue();
47.         if (isValidDate(day, month, year))
48.             return new GregorianCalendar(year, month - 1, day).getTime();
49.         else {
50.             FacesMessage message
51.                     = Messages.getMessage("util.messages", "invalidDate", null);
52.             message.setSeverity(FacesMessage.SEVERITY_ERROR);
53.             throw new ConverterException(message);
54.         }
55.     }
56.
57.     private static boolean isValidDate(int d, int m, int y) {
```

```
58.     if (d < 1 || m < 1 || m > 12) {
59.         return false;
60.     }
61.     if (m == 2) {
62.         if (isLeapYear(y)) {
63.             return d <= 29;
64.         } else {
65.             return d <= 28;
66.         }
67.     } else if (m == 4 || m == 6 || m == 9 || m == 11) {
68.         return d <= 30;
69.     } else {
70.         return d <= 31;
71.     }
72. }
73.
74. private static boolean isLeapYear(int y) {
75.     return y % 4 == 0 && (y % 400 == 0 || y % 100 != 0);
76. }
77. }
```

Packaging Composite Components in JARs

You can package your composite components in JAR files, so that other developers can use those components. All you have to do is put your composite component, and its artifacts, such as JavaScript, stylesheets, or properties files, under a META-INF directory in the JAR, as shown in Figure 9–14.

Figure 9–14   Packaging the icon and login components in a JAR file

Once you have a JAR file containing one or more composite components, simply put the JAR file on your classpath to use the components.

Conclusion

JSF's biggest selling point is that it's a component-based framework, and JSF 2.0 finally makes it simple to implement custom components: If you can implement a Facelets view, you can implement a composite component.

JSF 2.0 comes with extensive support for composite components, including support for processing facets and children.

Combined with the new Ajax capabilities of JSF 2.0, composite components enable JSF developers the ability to easily implement custom components that encapsulate Ajax.

AJAX

JSF 2.0

Topics in This Chapter

Chapter 10

Asynchronous JavaScript and XML (Ajax) used to be considered a luxury, both for users and developers, but today Ajax is essential for building compelling and competitive web applications.

JSF 2.0 has built-in Ajax support, with a standard JavaScript library. You can accesss that library in both your views and in your Java code.

You can handle most of the common Ajax use cases—such as field validation and progress indicators—with a tag from JSF's core library: f:ajax. Like other tags from JSF's core library, such as f:validator and f:converter, f:ajax attaches a *behavior* to a component. For example, here's how you would attach an Ajax behavior to a text input:

```
<h:inputText value="#{someBean.someProperty}">
    <f:ajax event="keyup" render="someOtherComponentId"/>
</h:inputText>
```

For each keyup event in the text input, JSF makes an Ajax call to the server, and processes the input's value. When the Ajax call returns, JSF renders a component with the identifier someOtherComponentId.

Ajax and JSF

Conceptually, Ajax is simple. In fact, Ajax requests differ from regular HTTP requests in only two ways:

1. Ajax *partially* processes forms on the server during the Ajax call.
2. Ajax *partially* renders Document Object Model (DOM) elements on the client after the Ajax call returns from the server.

This sequence of events is illustrated in Figure 10–1, which illustrates an Ajax call that validates a single input, presumably when the field loses focus.

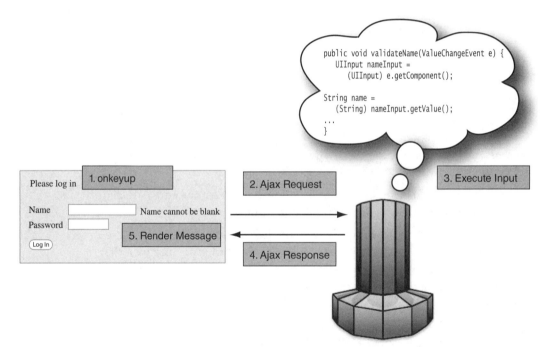

Figure 10–1   An Ajax request for validating an input field

In JSF, we deal in components, so we will define JSF Ajax like this:

> *JSF Ajax requests partially process components on the server, and partially render components on the client when the request returns.*

As you'll see in the next section, JSF integrates Ajax into its life cycle, which is the fundamental lifeblood of all JSF applications. That deep level of integration lets you handle Ajax requests in the same manner in which you handle other component behaviors, such as validation or conversion.

The JSF Life Cycle and Ajax

JSF 2.0 splits the JSF life cycle into two parts: *execute* (where components are executed) and *render*, as shown in Figure 10–2 and Figure 10–3, respectively. *On any given Ajax request, you specify a set of components that JSF executes, and another set of components that it renders.*

The execute part of the life cycle executes inputs on the server, and is represented by step 3 in Figure 10–1.

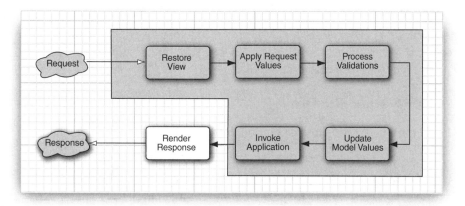

Figure 10–2   The execute portion of the JSF life cycle

The render part of the life cycle, illustrated by step 5 in Figure 10–1, renders components on the client. The render part of the life cycle is shown in Figure 10–3.

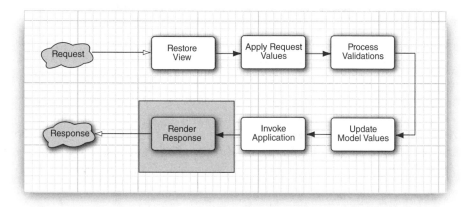

Figure 10–3   The render portion of the life cycle

As Figure 10–2 illustrates, when JSF executes a component on the server, it:

- Converts and validates the component's value (if the component is an input)
- Pushes valid input values to the model (if the component is wired to a bean property)
- Executes actions and action listeners (if the component is an action)

So JSF 2.0 effectively has two life cycles: one that executes components, and one that renders components. JSF always executes components first, and subsequently renders them.

For regular HTTP requests, all components in a form are both executed and rendered, whereas for Ajax requests, JSF executes one or more components, and renders zero or more components.

The JSF Ajax Recipe

Here's the recipe for using Ajax with JSF 2.0:

1. Associate a component and an event with an Ajax request.
2. Indentify components to execute on the server during the Ajax request.
3. Identify components to render after the Ajax request.

It typically takes a couple of lines of XML in an XHTML file, and perhaps a few lines of Java in a managed bean to implement most Ajax use cases, including, as you will see later in this chapter, validating inputs and showing progress bars.

You associate an Ajax call with an event, such as keyup or blur, fired by a specific component. Then you specify the components that you want to execute, and the components you want to render. For example, you can associate an Ajax call with an input, like this:

```
<h:inputText id="name" value="#{user.name}">
   <f:ajax event="blur" execute="@this" render="nameError"/>
</h:inputText>
```

The preceding code triggers an Ajax event when the input loses focus. That Ajax request *executes* the name component on the server—the @this value for the execute attribute refers to the f:ajax tag's surrounding input—and *renders* a component whose id is nameError on the client, when the Ajax call returns.

We could also execute and render multiple components, like this:

```
<h:inputText id="nameInput" value="#{user.name}">
  <f:ajax event="blur" execute="@this passwordInput"
                       render="nameError passwordError"/>
</h:inputText>

<h:outputText id="nameError"/>
...
<h:inputText id="passwordInput"/>
<h:outputText id="passwordError" value="#{user.passwordError}"/>
...
```

The preceding code executes the nameInput, and the passwordInput. It renders the nameError and passwordError components.

JSF's Ajax support is a low-level—but capable and comprehensive—Ajax implementation. The key to using Ajax with JSF is to keep in mind what it means to execute a component on the server during an Ajax call.

When JSF executes an input component, for example, it copies the input's value to a backing bean property. That changed property typically has a role in how the Ajax response is rendered: Perhaps it's a value that's simply redisplayed, or it could effectuate a more marked change to the user interface.

The f:ajax Tag

Page authors attach behaviors—such as validation—to JSF components with tags from JSF's core library. For example, here's how you validate that a text input has at least five characters:

```
<h:inputText value="#{user.name}">
  <f:validateLength minimum="5"/>
</h:inputText>
```

JSF's Ajax support follows suit. To attach Ajax behavior to a component, you add an f:ajax tag in the body of the component; for example:

```
<h:inputText id="name" value="#{user.name}">
  <f:ajax event="keyup" execute="@this" render="echo"/>
</h:inputText>
...
<h:outputText id="echo" value="#{user.name}"/>
```

The preceding markup attaches an Ajax behavior to the input. That behavior echoes whatever the user types in the name field, as shown in Figure 10–4.

For each keyup event fired by the input, JSF makes an Ajax call to the server. On the server, the Ajax call executes the name component (signified by the built-in @this keyword), and when the Ajax call returns, JSF renders only the echo component on the client.

The echo output text echoes the name input because, when JSF executes the name input on the server, it copies the name into the name input's associated backing bean property, the name field of a managed bean named user. Subsequently, JSF renders the echo field, which displays the newly updated user.name.

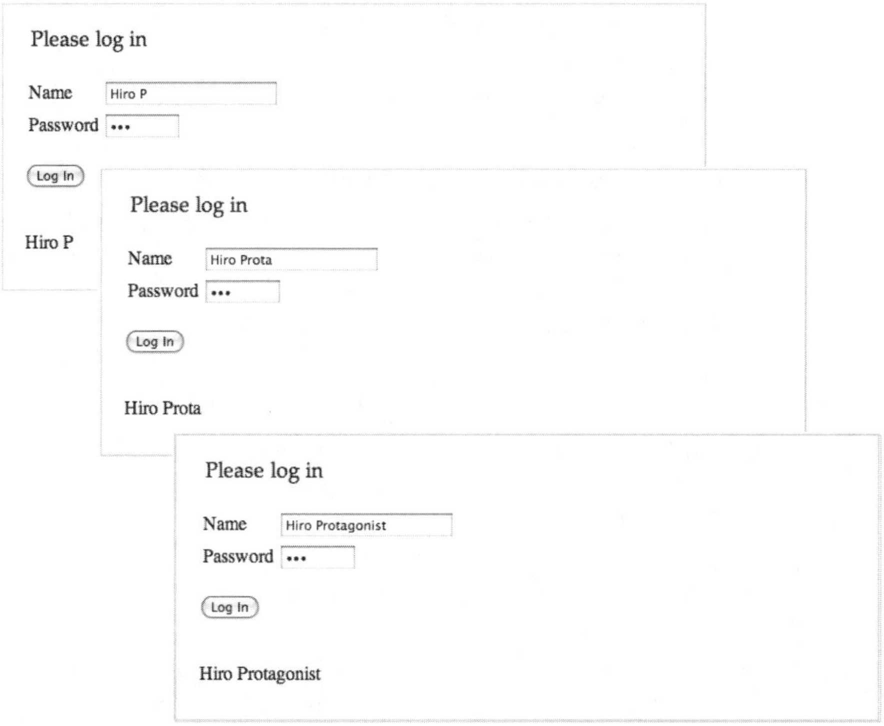

Figure 10–4   Using Ajax to echo an input as the user types

Most of the time, as is the case for our simple echo example, you want to execute an f:ajax tag's surrounding input component, so JSF executes @this by default. That default means we can omit execute="@this" from the preceding markup, like this:

```
<h:inputText id="name" value="#{user.name}">
    <f:ajax event="keyup" render="echo"/>        <!-- execute="@this" is implicit -->
</h:inputText>
```

Besides @this, you can also use @form, @all, or @none as values for the f:ajax tag's execute attribute, as you can see from Table 10–1, which lists the attributes for the f:ajax tag.

Table 10–1   f:ajax Tag Attributes

Attribute	Description
disabled	Disable the tag by specifying true for the disabled attribute.
event	The event that triggers the Ajax request. Event names can be JavaScript event names without the on prefix. For example, you would use event="blur" for the onblur event. Event names can also be the following component events: action and valueChange. Those names can be specified for command components (buttons and links) and inputs, respectively.
execute	A space-separated list of components that JSF executes on the server during the Ajax call. Valid keywords for the execute attribute are: @this @form @all @none If you don't specify an execute attribute, JSF uses @this as the default value.
immediate	If you set this attribute to true, JSF processes inputs early in the life cycle.
onerror	A JavaScript function that JSF calls if the Ajax call results in an error.
onevent	A JavaScript function that JSF calls for Ajax events. This function will be called three times during the lifetime of a successful Ajax call: begin complete success For a successful Ajax call, JSF invokes the onevent function when the Ajax call begins (begin), when it has been processed on the server (complete), and just before JSF renders the Ajax response (success). If there is an error during an Ajax request, JSF calls the onevent function after the Ajax request completes, and subsequently invokes the error handler referenced by the onevent attribute.

Table 10–1   f:ajax Tag Attributes (cont.)

Attribute	Description
listener	JSF invokes this listener's processAjaxBehavior method once during each Ajax call, in the Invoke Application phase of the life cycle (at the end of the execute portion of the life cycle).
	That method must have this signature: public void processAjax-Behavior(javax.faces.event.AjaxBehaviorEvent event) throws javax.faces.event.AbortProcessingException
render	A space-separated list of components that JSF renders on the client after the Ajax call returns from the server.
	You can use the same keywords (@all, @this, @form, and @none) that are valid for the execute attribute.
	If you do not specify the render attribute, it defaults to @none, meaning JSF will not render any components after the Ajax request completes.

Notice the naming convention JSF uses for events: Take the JavaScript event name, and strip the leading on. So onblur becomes blur, onkeyup becomes keyup, etc. Also notice that events can be the component events action and valueChange, instead of JavaScript events.

The onerror and onevent attributes are JavaScript functions that JSF calls when certain predetermined events happen in the Ajax life cycle. For a successful Ajax request, JSF invokes the onevent function three times: when the Ajax request begins, when it completes, and again after completion, for a successful request. JSF invokes the onerror JavaScript function after an unsuccessful Ajax request.

The value for the listener attribute is a method expression. JSF calls that Java method once per Ajax call (in the Invoke Application phase of the JSF life cycle).

Ajax Groups

As you saw in "The f:ajax Tag" on page 389, you put f:ajax tags inside a component tag, to associate an Ajax request with the component. JSF also lets you associate an Ajax request with a group of Ajax components by inverting that structure, like this:

```
<f:ajax>
    <h:form>
        <h:panelGrid columns="2">
            ...
            <h:inputText id="name" value="#{user.name}"/>
```

```
      ...
      <h:inputText id="password" value="#{user.password}"/>
      ...
      </h:commandButton value="Submit" action="#{user.login}"/>
    </h:panelGrid>
  </h:form>
</f:ajax>
```

The preceding markup Ajaxifies all of the components in the form. When the input values change, or when the user activates the button, JSF makes an Ajax request to the server. (Note that in the preceeding code listing, JSF will not render any components when the Ajax call returns because we did not specify a render attribute for the f:ajax tag.)

Some of the built-in JSF components have a default Ajax event. Table 10–2 shows default events for components that have a default event type.

Table 10–2　JSF Component's Default Ajax Event

Components	Default Ajax Event
Command buttons and links	action
Text inputs, text areas, secret inputs, and all of the select components	valueChange

JSF applies the default Ajax events listed in Table 10–2 if you don't explicitly specify an event. You can specify an event like this:

```
<f:ajax event="click">
  <h:form>
    ...
    <h:inputText id="name" value="#{user.name}">
    ...
    <h:inputText id="password" value="#{user.password}"/>
    ...
    <h:commandButton value="Submit" action="#{user.login}"/>
  </h:form>
</f:ajax>
```

So now the Ajax is only applicable for the click event—when you click on one of the inputs or the button, JSF fires an Ajax request. You can even nest f:ajax tags in one another, and the results are additive; for example:

```
<f:ajax event="click">
  <h:form>
    ...
    <h:inputText id="name" value="#{user.name}">
```

```
        ...
        <h:inputText id="password" value="#{user.password}"/>
        ...
        <h:commandButton value="Submit" action="#{user.login}">
            <f:ajax event="mouseover"/>
        </h:commandButton>
    </h:form>
</f:ajax>
```

In the preceding markup, JSF fires Ajax requests when the mouse hovers over the button, or the user activates the button.

Ajax Field Validation

All other things being equal, it's best to give users immediate validation feedback as they type in an input field. Field validation is a common Ajax use case.

Figure 10–5 shows an example of Ajax field validation. The name component has a validator that checks to see whether the name contains an underscore; if so, the validator thows a validator exception containing an error message.

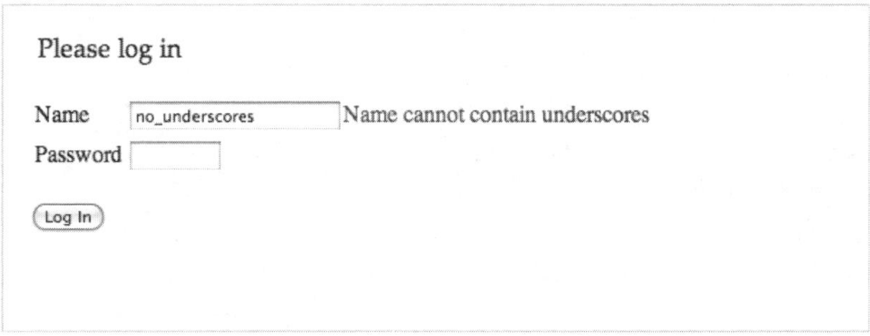

Please log in

Name   no_underscores   Name cannot contain underscores
Password

Log In

Figure 10–5   Ajax validation

Here's the markup for the name input, and an associated h:message tag:

```
<h:inputText id="name" value="#{user.name}" validator="#{user.validateName}">
    <f:ajax event="keyup" render="nameError"/>
</h:inputText>
<h:message for="name" id="nameError" style="color: red"s/>
```

For every keyup event in the name component, JSF makes an Ajax request and executes the name input.

When it executes the name input on the server, JSF invokes the input's validator, the validateName() method of a managed bean named user. The User class is provided in Listing 10–1.

Listing 10–1 `echo/src/java/com/corejsf/UserBean.java`

```
 1. package com.corejsf;
 2.
 3. import java.io.Serializable;
 4.
 5. import javax.enterprise.context.SessionScoped;
 6. import javax.faces.application.FacesMessage;
 7. import javax.faces.component.UIComponent;
 8. import javax.faces.context.FacesContext;
 9. import javax.faces.validator.ValidatorException;
10. import javax.inject.Named;
11.     // or import javax.faces.bean.SessionScoped;
12.
13. @Named("user") // or @ManagedBean(name="user")
14. @SessionScoped
15. public class UserBean implements Serializable {
16.     private String name = "";
17.     private String password;
18.
19.     public String getName() { return name; }
20.     public void setName(String newValue) { name = newValue; }
21.
22.     public String getPassword() { return password; }
23.     public void setPassword(String newValue) { password = newValue; }
24.
25.     public void validateName(FacesContext fc, UIComponent c, Object value) {
26.       if ( ((String)value).contains("_") )
27.         throw new ValidatorException(
28.           new FacesMessage("Name cannot contain underscores"));
29.     }
30. }
```

The `validateName()` method checks to see if the name contains an underscore; if so, the method throws a validator exception with an appropriate error message. Subsequently, when the Ajax request returns, JSF renders the `nameError` component, which shows the validator exception's message.

The preceeding markup makes an Ajax request for every keystroke in the `name` component, by virtue of the `event` attribute specified in the preceding markup.

You can reduce the number of Ajax requests, by making an Ajax request only when the `name` field loses focus, like this:

```
<h:inputText id="name" value="#{user.name}" validator="#{user.validateName}">
  <f:ajax event="blur" render="nameError"/>
</h:inputText>
```

Validating inputs with Ajax is a simple proposition. Now let's look at something a little more complicated.

Ajax Request Monitoring

You can monitor Ajax requests with the f:ajax tag's onevent attribute. That attribute's value must be a JavaScript function. JSF calls that function at each stage of an Ajax request: begin, complete, and success.

Figure 10-6 shows an application that monitors the Ajax validation of the name input discussed in "Ajax Field Validation" on page 394.

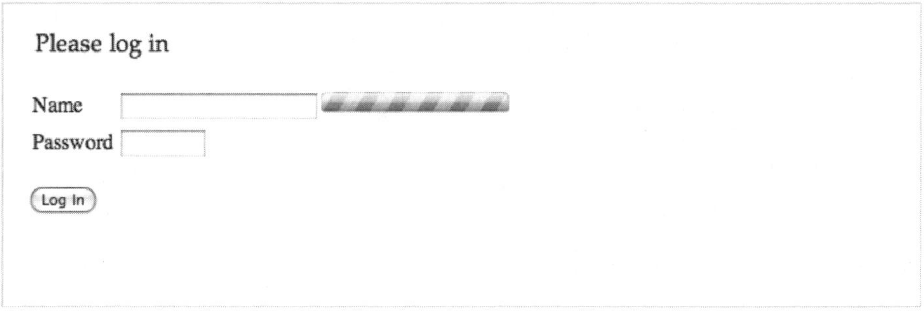

Figure 10–6   Ajax validation monitoring application

While the validation takes place on the server, the application shows an animated progress bar on the client. We should note that this example is somewhat artificial—in practice, validation typically does not take long enough to justify a progress bar.

When the Ajax call returns, the application hides the progress bar. Here's the pertinent markup:

```
<h:outputScript library="javascript" name="prototype-1.6.0.2.js"/>

<script type="text/javascript">
  function showProgress(data) {
    var inputId = data.source.id
    var progressbarId = inputId.substring(0, inputId.length - "name".length)
      + "pole";

    if (data.status == "begin")
      Element.show(progressbarId);
    else if (data.status == "success")
      Element.hide(progressbarId);
  }
```

```
</script>

<h:form id="form" prependId="false">
    ...
    <h:panelGrid columns="2">
        #{msgs.namePrompt}
        <h:panelGroup>
            <h:inputText id="name" value="#{user.name}"
                validator="#{user.validateName}">

            <f:ajax event="blur" render="nameError" onevent="showProgress"/>

            </h:inputText>

            <h:graphicImage id="pole"
                library="images" name="orange-barber-pole.gif"
                style="display: none"/>
            <h:message for="name" id="nameError"
                value="#{user.nameError}" style="color: red"/>
        </h:panelGroup>

    ...

    <p>
        <h:commandButton id="loginButton"
        value="#{msgs.loginButtonText}"
        action="#{user.loginAction}"/>
    </p>

    ...

</h:form>
```

In the preceding markup, we use the popular Prototype JavaScript library (see http://www.prototypejs.org/ for more information about Prototype) to show and hide the progress bar, with Prototype's Element object. We could implement the JavaScript to do that, but it requires browser-specific code that we'd rather not write. To use Prototype, we copied the Prototype JavaScript file to resources/javascript, and then we accessed that JavaScript with the h:outputScript tag.

We also added an f:ajax tag to the name component, and registered the Java-Script showProgress function as a callback. That function checks to see if the status of the Ajax request is begin; if so, the function shows the progress bar. On the other hand, if the Ajax request status is success—meaning the Ajax call returned and rendered successfully—the function hides the progress bar. More rigorous definitions of begin, success, and complete, are shown in Table 10–3.

Table 10–3   Data Object Attributes

Attribute	Description
begin	Just before JSF sends the Ajax call to the server.
success	Just after the Ajax response is rendered.
complete	For a successful call, JSF calls this method just after the execute portion of the life cycle, which by definition means just before the render portion. For errors, JSF calls this method just before it invokes the error handler. You typically set the error handler either with the onevent attribute of f:ajax or with the JSF JavaScript APIs.

JSF passes a data object to any JavaScript function that's registered with an Ajax call via f:ajax's onevent attribute. That data object's attributes are listed in Table 10–4.

Table 10–4   More Data Object Attributes

Attribute	Description
status	The status of the current Ajax call. Must be one of: begin, complete, or error.
type	Either event or status.
source	The DOM element that is the source of the event.
responseXML	The response to the Ajax request. This object is undefined in the begin phase of the Ajax request.
responseText	The XML response, as text. This object is also undefined in the begin phase of the Ajax request.
responseCode	The numeric response code of the Ajax request. Like responseXML and responseText, this object is undefined in the begin phase of the Ajax request.

JavaScript Namespaces

In "The f:ajax Tag" on page 389, we implemented a JavaScript function—show-Progress()—that uses Prototype to show and hide a DOM element. That method is fragile, however, because it can be overwritten by another JavaScript method of the same name.

It sounds plausible that someone might implement another JavaScript function named showProgress(), thereby replacing your version of the method with theirs. To prevent that replacement from happening, you could name your function something more unique, such as com.corejsf.showProgress().

With that strategy in mind for protecting our JavaScript method from being overwritten, we implement a simple map that serves as a namespace, and we define functions in that map[1]:

```
if (!com) var com = {}
if (!com.corejsf) {
    com.corejsf = {
        showProgress: function(data) {
            var inputId = data.source.id
            var progressbarId = inputId.substring(0, inputId.length - "name".length)
                + "pole";

            if (data.status == "begin")
                Element.show(progressbarId);
            else if (data.status == "success")
                Element.hide(progressbarId);
        }
    }
}
```

So now the caller accesses the function through the namespace, like this:

```
<f:ajax event="blur" render="nameError" onevent="com.corejsf.showProgress"/>
```

JavaScript namespacing not only prevents others from overwriting your functions, but it also indicates to readers of your code that you are a JavaScript coder of some substance.

NOTE: Besides creating an ad-hoc namespace by putting JavaScript *functions* in a map, you can also put *data* in a map.

Namespacing data is a consideration when you implement custom components that maintain data on the client. If you have multiple instances of the component, they will overwrite each other's data. Putting the data in a map, keyed by the client identifier of the component to which the data is associated, is a way to ensure that multiple Ajax-based custom components of the same type that store data on the client, can co-exist in a single page.

---

1. The map is actually an object literal—JavaScript does not have a map data structure—but semantically a JavaScript object literal is similar to a map.

Handling Ajax Errors

You can use f:ajax's onerror attribute to handle errors, like this:

```
<f:ajax onerror="handleAjaxError"/>
```

The value of the onerror attribute is a JavaScript function. JSF calls that function when there's an error during the processing of the Ajax request. Like f:ajax's onevent attribute, JSF passes the onerror function a data object. The values for that object are the same as the values for the data object that JSF passes to the event function, as listed in Table 10–4, except for the status property. Valid values for the status property are listed in Table 10–5.

Table 10–5   data.status Values for Error Functions

Attribute	Description
httpError	Response status null or undefined or status < 200 or status ≥ 300.
emptyResponse	There was no response from the server.
malformedXML	The response was not well-formed XML.
serverError	The Ajax response contains an error element from the server.

For errors, the data object also contains three properties not present for events:

*   description
*   errorName
*   errorMessage

So far in this chapter, we've shown you how to use f:ajax to implement some common Ajax use cases, such as validation and request monitoring. f:ajax is a simple, but versatile tool, especially with it's support for grouping; however, it's beneficial to know how it works beneath the covers. For that, we'll look at the JavaScript library that JSF uses to implement f:ajax, and we'll also look at what JSF Ajax responses look like.

Ajax Responses

The response from a JSF Ajax request is an XML document that tells JSF how to update the XHTML page from which the request was launched. That response is handled by the jsf.ajax.response() function. You can view JSF Ajax responses using Firebug in Firefox, as shown in Figure 10–7.

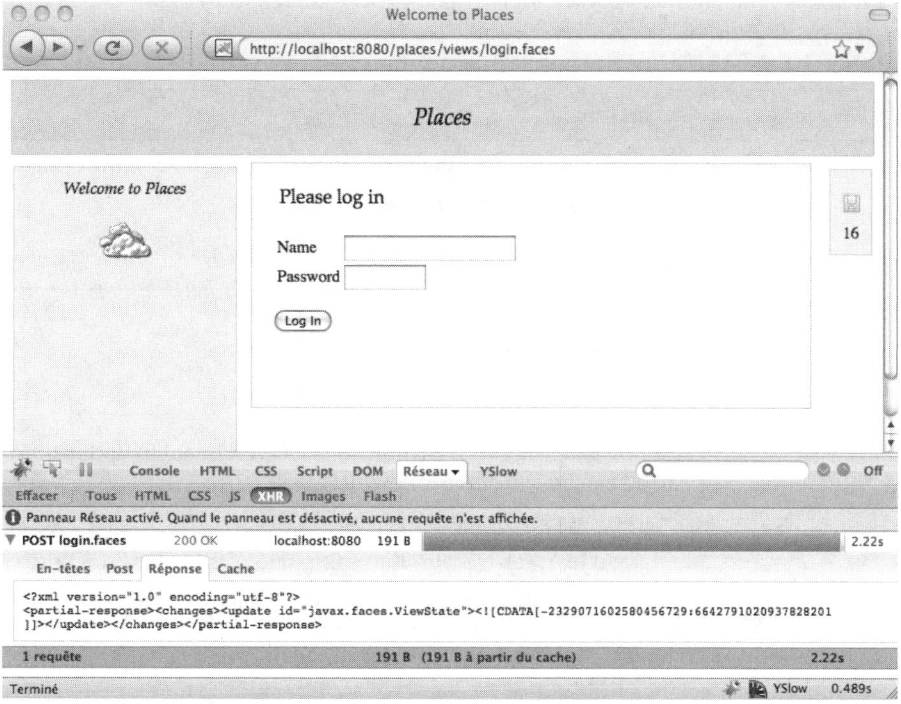

Figure 10–7   Viewing an Ajax response using Firebug

JSF's Ajax response is XML. For example, here is the response returned from the validation Ajax request discussed in "Ajax Field Validation" on page 394, when validation fails because the Name field contained an underscore:

```
<?xml version="1.0" encoding="utf-8"?>
<partial-response>
   <changes>
      <update id="j_idt18:nameError">
         <![CDATA[<span id="j_idt18:nameError" style="color: red">
            Name cannot contain underscores
         </span>]]>
      </update>

      <update id="javax.faces.ViewState">
         <![CDATA[-4047143760309857992:5238789135448605596]]>
      </update>
   </changes>
</partial-response>
```

Table 10–6 lists the valid XML elements for JSF Ajax responses.

Table 10–6   JSF Ajax Response Elements

Element	Description

insert	Inserts a DOM element with the specified ID before an existing element:
	
	`<insert id="insert id" before="before id">`
	`    <![CDATA[...]]>`
	`</insert>`

update	Updates a DOM element:
	
	`<update id="update id">`
	`    <![CDATA[...]]>`
	`</insert>`
	
	In addition to specifying a client ID of a DOM element to update, the update id can be one of the following:
	
	`javax.faces.ViewRoot`: updates the entire DOM
	
	`javax.faces.ViewState`: updates the entire state of the submitting form
	
	`javax.faces.ViewBody`: updates the body of the page

delete	Deletes the DOM element with the specified ID:
	
	`<delete id="delete id">`
	`    <![CDATA[...]]>`
	`</attribute>`

attributes	Updates one or more attributes of a DOM element:
	
	`<attributes id="element id">`
	`    <attribute name="attribute name" value="attribute value"/>`
	`    ...`
	`</attribute>`

error	Generates a server error with the enclosed name and message:
	
	`<error>`
	`    <error-name>fully qualified exception class</error-name>`
	`    <error-message>error message</error-message>`
	`    ...`
	`</error>`

redirect	Redirects the request to a new URL: `<redirect url="redirect url"/>`

In practice, the particulars of the Ajax response are somewhat academic unless you want to generate or process the response directly.

By default, JSF generates the response from changes that you make to the component tree during the Ajax response. For example, if you specify a component to render with h:ajax's `render` attribute, and you change that component's `style` attribute during an Ajax call, JSF generates a partial response that updates the DOM element associated with that component.

JSF processes the response with the `jsf.ajax.response()` function that's defined in the JavaScript that comes with JSF.

> NOTE: You can find the XML schema for JSF Ajax responses in Appendix A, section 1.3 of the JSF specification.

The JSF 2.0 JavaScript Library

The `f:ajax` tag is a convenient way to implement simple Ajax functionality. Because it's a tag, however, `f:ajax` offers limited functionality. But because that tag is built on JSF's built-in JavaScript library, you can use that JavaScript directly to implement more complicated Ajax scenarios.

You can access JSF's built-in JavaScript library in your XHTML files like this:

```
<h:outputScript library="javax.faces" name="jsf.js"/>
```

The library comes with a set of Ajax functions, listed in Table 10–7.

Table 10–7 `jsf.ajax` **Functions**

Function	Description
addOnError(callback)	A JavaScript function that JSF invokes when an Ajax call results in an error.
addOnEvent(callback)	A JavaScript function that JSF calls for Ajax events. This function will be called three times throughout the lifetime of a successful Ajax call: • begin • complete • success

Table 10–7   jsf.ajax **Functions (cont.)**

Function	Description
isAutoExec()	Returns true if the browser executes eval'd JavaScript.
request(source, event, options)	Sends an Ajax request. The arguments of this function correspond to f:ajax attributes.
response(request, context)	Processes the Ajax response. The response is XML.

The request() method sends an Ajax request to the server. That request is always:

- A POST to the surrounding form's action
- Asynchronous
- Queued with other Ajax requests

Because f:ajax uses the Ajax JavaScript API in Table 10–7, you can bypass that tag and use the API directly in your XHTML pages. For example, instead of:

```
<h:inputText...>
  <f:ajax event="blur" render="nameError" onevent="com.corejsf.showProgress"/>
</h:inputText>
```

You can do this:

```
<h:outputScript library="javax.faces" name="jsf.js"/>
```

```
<h:inputText
  onblur="jsf.ajax.request(this, event,
          { render: 'nameError',
            onevent: com.corejsf.showProgress
          })"/>
```

Notice one subtle difference between the preceding identical uses of f:ajax and the JavaScript API: f:ajax's attributes are always strings, whereas the onevent attribute of the options sent to jsf.ajax.request() is a method, not a string.

Table 10–8 lists the valid keys and values for jsf.ajax.request()'s options map.

Table 10–8 Keys and Values for the Options in
`jsf.ajax.request(source, event, options)`

Key	Value
execute	A space-separated list of components that JSF runs through the execute phase of the life cycle. Keywords: • `@this` • `@form` • `@all` • `@none`
render	A space-separated list of components that JSF will run through the render phase of the life cycle.
onevent	A JavaScript function that JSF calls for Ajax events. This function will be called three times throughout the lifetime of an Ajax call: • `begin` • `complete` • `success`
onerror	A JavaScript function that JSF will call if the Ajax call results in an error.

You can find extensive documentation for the JSF JavaScript library both in the JSF specification, and in the JavaScript documentation that comes with JSF. You can also download the JSF reference implementation source code, which includes the JavaScript library.

Besides specifying the things in Table 10–8 for an Ajax request, you can also add additional parameters for any Ajax request.

Passing Additional Ajax Request Parameters

Sometimes you need to perform additional operations in conjunction with an Ajax call. For example, in the autocomplete textbox component that we discuss in "Using Ajax in Composite Components" on page 409, we calculate the location of a listbox containing completion items, that we show under a text input. Then we pass that information along with the Ajax request, like this:

```
if (!com) var com = {};

if (!com.corejsf) {
   var focusLostTimeout;

      com.corejsf = {
         updateCompletionItems: function(input, event) {
            var keystrokeTimeout;

            var ajaxRequest = function() {
               jsf.ajax.request(input, event,
               { render: com.corejsf.getListboxId(input),
                     x: Element.cumulativeOffset(input)[0],
                     y: Element.cumulativeOffset(input)[1] + Element.getHeight(input)
               });
            }

            window.clearTimeout(keystrokeTimeout);
            keystrokeTimeout = window.setTimeout(ajaxRequest, 350);
         }, ...
      ...
   }
```

JSF passes any key/value pairs in the Ajax options that are not listed in
Table 10–8 to the Ajax request as parameters. The names of the parameters are
the keys, and the parameter values are the values associated with the key. In
the preceeding code, those values are the x and y values of the listbox. We use
Prototype's Element.cumulativeOffset() function to compute those coordinates.

For the preceding Ajax call, we use those x and y coordinates on the server, like
this:

```
package com.corejsf;

...

@ManagedBean()
@SessionScoped()
public class AutocompleteListener {
   ...
   private void setListboxStyle(int rows, Map<String, Object> attrs) {
      if (rows > 0) {
         Map<String, String> reqParams = FacesContext.getCurrentInstance()
            .getExternalContext().getRequestParameterMap();

         attrs.put("style", "display: inline; position: absolute; left: "
```

```
              + reqParams.get("x") + "px;" + " top: " + reqParams.get("y") + "px");
        }
        else
            attrs.put("style", "display: none;");
    }
    ...
}
```

Queueing Events

JSF automatically queues Ajax requests and executes those requests serially, so the last Ajax request always finishes before the next one starts.

However, JSF only queues Ajax calls—it does not queue regular HTTP requests. Because JSF does not queue regular HTTP requests, that means that mixing Ajax and HTTP requests can result in indeterminate behavior. For example, consider this:

```
<h:form>
    <h:inputText ...>
        <f:ajax onblur="..."/>
    </h:inputText>

    <h:commandButton value="submit" action="nextPage"/>
</h:form>
```

In the preceding markup, we have an Ajax input inside a form with a non-Ajax button. Consider what happens when the input has focus and the user clicks on the button: The input loses focus and starts an Ajax call, and immediately afterward, JSF makes a regular form submission as a result of the button activation. Does the Ajax call complete before the form submission? Perhaps, depending on how long the Ajax call takes, but odds are that the form submission will interrupt the Ajax call, and since the point of Ajax is to manipulate server-side data, it's easy to wind up in an indeterminate state.

The solution to mixing Ajax and regular HTTP requests is simple: Don't do it. Instead, make the regular HTTP request an Ajax request, too, and JSF will queue those Ajax calls, making sure that the first Ajax request finishes before the second begins. In the preceding markup, then, you would just Ajaxify the button:

```
<h:form>
    <h:inputText ...>
        <f:ajax onblur="..."/>
    </h:inputText>
```

```
    <h:commandButton value="submit" action="nextPage">
        <f:ajax/>
    </h:commandButton>
</h:form>
```

Coalescing Events

In general, Ajax can sometimes be tricky. For example, for an Ajax-enabled text input, a user could theoretically type fast enough to encounter a perceptible delay between fingers and display.

In such cases, you might want to coalesce Ajax calls so that you periodically make calls to the server, instead of making calls for every event. JSF 2.0 has no explicit support for coalescing Ajax calls, but it's simple to do yourself with a JavaScript timer. For example, the autocomplete component, discussed in "Using Ajax in Composite Components" on page 409, coalesces Ajax calls with a JavaScript function:

```
<h:inputText id="input" value="#{cc.attrs.value}"
    onkeyup="com.corejsf.updateCompletionItems(this, event)" ... />
```

The updateCompletionItems function coalesces events:

```
updateCompletionItems: function(input, event) {
    var keystrokeTimeout;
        var ajaxRequest = function() {
            jsf.ajax.request(input, event,
                { render: corejsf.getListboxId(input),
                        x: Element.cumulativeOffset(input)[0],
                        y: Element.cumulativeOffset(input)[1] + Element.getHeight(input)
                });
        }

        window.clearTimeout(keystrokeTimeout);
        keystrokeTimeout = window.setTimeout(ajaxRequest, 350);
    }
    ...
}
```

When a keyup event occurs in an input, we schedule an Ajax call in 350ms. If there is an ensuing keyup event within that 350ms, we cancel the previous Ajax call, and schedule a new one in 350ms. Therefore, we only submit an Ajax call to the server when the user pauses for 350ms or more between keystrokes.

Intercepting `jsf.ajax.request()`

JSF lets you associate a Java function with an Ajax request with `f:ajax`'s listener attribute, like this:

```
<h:inputText value="...">
   <f:ajax event="keyup" listener="#{someBean.someMethod}"/>
</h:inputText>
```

However, `f:ajax` only lets you add a listener for a particular event tied to a particular component. Sometimes, you may want to add some functionality to every Ajax request. The reasons for wanting to do so are myriad. Perhaps you want to add security to every Ajax call, or you want to log every Ajax call to the server. For that kind of functionality, JSF has no explicit solution.

In "JavaScript Namespaces" on page 398, we showed you how to use a map to implement an ad-hoc JavaScript namespace that helps protect your JavaScript functions from being intercepted by other functions with the same name.

JSF Ajax requests are implemented with a JavaScript function—`jsf.ajax.request()`, to be specific—and like any JavaScript function, it can be easily intercepted, like this:

```
var builtinAjaxRequestFunction = jsf.ajax.request;
jsf.ajax.request = function(c,e,o) {
    alert("hello")
    builtinAjaxRequestFunction(c,e,o)
    alert("bye")
}
```

After intercepting `jsf.ajax.request()` with the JavaScript above, every Ajax call, whether it initiates from an `f:ajax` tag or is invoked with `jsf.ajax.request()`, results in a call to the intercepted function, which in this case just shows alerts before and after the Ajax call to the server. You will probably want to modify the markup to do something more useful than just showing alerts.

Using Ajax in Composite Components

Arguably, the two most important features in JSF 2.0 are built-in Ajax, and support for composite components. Those features are easy to combine, making it simple to implement Ajax-based composite components. For example, Figure 10–8 shows an autocomplete textbox that's implemented as a JSF composite component with built-in Ajax.

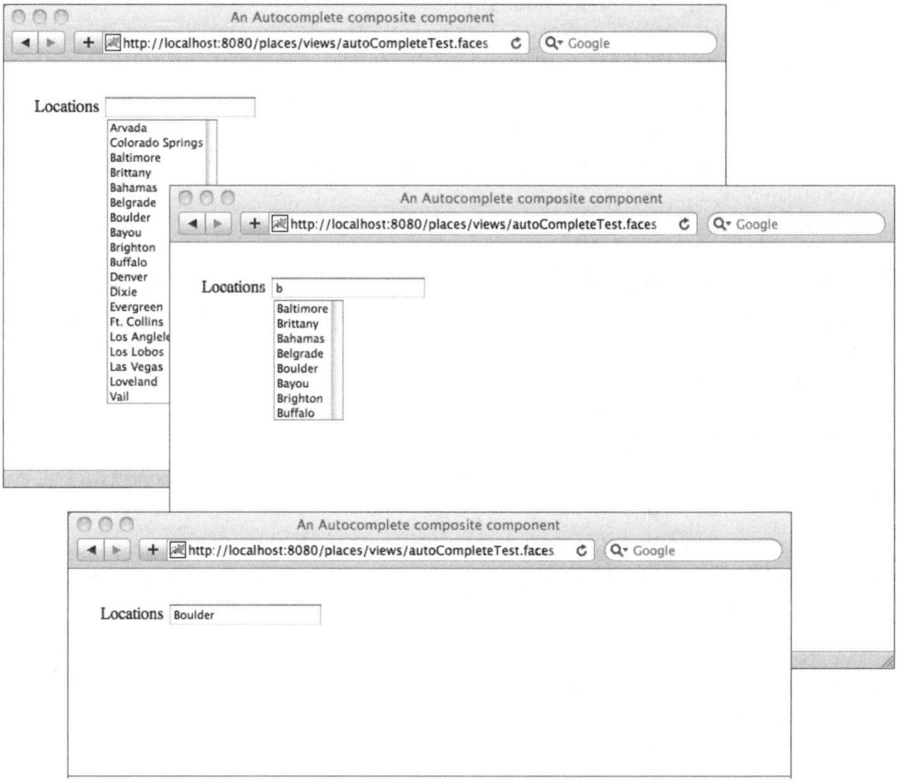

Figure 10–8 An autocomplete composite component

The autocomplete component consists of four files:

1. An XHTML file that defines the component's interface and implementation
2. A JavaScript file with code specific to the component
3. The JavaScript file for the Prototype JavaScript library
4. A Java class that implements listener methods for the autcomplete component's text input and listbox

The autocomplete component is also comprised of a text input and a listbox. Initially, the listbox is hidden.

Subsequently, in response to keyup events in the text input, JSF makes Ajax calls to the server. On the server, a value change listener associated with the text input checks the input's value against the list of completion items associated with the input, and populates the listbox with matching items. If there are any matching items, the value change listener sets the style of the listbox, so that it is displayed underneath the associated input.

Here's how we use the autocomplete component shown in Figure 10–8:

```
<html xmlns="http://www.w3.org/1999/xhtml"
    xmlns:f="http://java.sun.com/jsf/core"
    xmlns:h="http://java.sun.com/jsf/html"
    xmlns:util="http://java.sun.com/jsf/composite/util">

    <h:head><title>An Autocomplete composite component</title></h:head>

    <h:body>
        <div style="padding: 20px;">
            <h:form>
                <h:panelGrid columns="2">

                    Locations

                    <util:autoComplete value="#{user.city}"
                    completionItems="#{autoComplete.locations}" />

                </h:panelGrid>
            </h:form>
        </div>
    </h:body>
</html>
```

In the preceding markup, we simply declare a namespace for the component (util), and use the component's tag (util:autoComplete). The completionItems attribute points to a String[] property of an autoComplete managed bean. That bean has a simple implementation:

```
@ApplicationScoped
public class AutoComplete {
    public String[] getLocations() {
        return new String[] {
            "Arvada", "Colorado Springs", "Baltimore", "Brittany", "Bahamas",
            "Belgrade", "Boulder", "Bayou", "Brighton", "Buffalo", "Denver", "Dixie",
            "Evergreen", "Ft. Collins", "Los Angeles", "Los Lobos", "Las Vegas",
            "Loveland", "Vail"
        };
    }
}
```

Listings 10–2 through 10–4 show the code for the autocomplete component, including the definition of the component, and its associated JavaScript and backing bean.

There are a few things to note about the autocomplete component:

- Listing 10–2. The autocomplete component uses both f:ajax and the JSF JavaScript API.

- Listing 10–3. The autocomplete component adds two request parameters to an Ajax request: the x and y location for the upper left-hand corner of the listbox.

- Listing 10–3. The application coalesces keyup events, only firing an Ajax call when the user stops typing for 350ms. This avoids making many requests to the server when a fast typist has control of the text input.

- Listing 10–3. When the autocomplete's text input loses focus, the composite component hides the listbox.

- Listing 10–4. Each autocomplete component stores its list of completion items (the items shown in the listbox) in an attribute of the autocomplete component's listbox. That ensures that you can put multiple autocomplete components in a single page.

However, if the text input loses focus, the listbox never sees the item selection because the listbox was hidden when the input lost focus. So, using the same trick as coalsceing events, the composite component waits for 200ms when the input loses focus before actually hiding the listbox. That leaves the listbox visible when the user selects an item.

Listing 10–2 autoComplete/web/resources/util/autoComplete.xhtml

```
1. <!DOCTYPE html PUBLIC "-//W3C//DTD XHTML 1.0 Transitional//EN"
2. "http://www.w3.org/TR/xhtml1/DTD/xhtml1-transitional.dtd">
3. <html xmlns="http://www.w3.org/1999/xhtml"
4.     xmlns:ui="http://java.sun.com/jsf/facelets"
5.     xmlns:f="http://java.sun.com/jsf/core"
6.     xmlns:h="http://java.sun.com/jsf/html"
7.     xmlns:composite="http://java.sun.com/jsf/composite">
8.   <head><title>IGNORED</title></head>
9.   <body>
10.     <ui:composition>
11.       <composite:interface>
12.         <composite:attribute name="value" required="true"/>
13.         <composite:attribute name="completionItems" required="true"/>
14.       </composite:interface>
15.       <composite:implementation>
16.         <h:outputScript library="javascript"
17.             name="prototype-1.6.0.2.js" target="head"/>
18.         <h:outputScript library="javascript"
19.             name="autoComplete.js" target="head"/>
```

```
20.
21.        <h:inputText id="input" value="#{cc.attrs.value}"
22.          valueChangeListener="#{autocompleteListener.valueChanged}"
23.          onkeyup="com.corejsf.updateCompletionItems(this, event)"
24.          onblur="com.corejsf.inputLostFocus(this)"/>
25.
26.        <h:selectOneListbox id="listbox" style="display: none"
27.          valueChangeListener="#{autocompleteListener.completionItemSelected}"
28.          onfocus="com.corejsf.listboxGainedFocus()">
29.
30.          <f:selectItems value="#{cc.attrs.completionItems}"/>
31.          <f:ajax render="input"/>
32.
33.        </h:selectOneListbox>
34.      </composite:implementation>
35.    </ui:composition>
36.  </body>
37. </html>
```

Listing 10–3 autoComplete/web/resources/javascript/autoComplete.js

```
1. if (!com) var com = {}
2. if (!com.corejsf) {
3.    var focusLostTimeout
4.    com.corejsf = {
5.      errorHandler: function(data) {
6.          alert("Error occurred during Ajax call: " + data.description)
7.      },
8.
9.      updateCompletionItems: function(input, event) {
10.        var keystrokeTimeout
11.
12.        jsf.ajax.addOnError(com.corejsf.errorHandler)
13.
14.        var ajaxRequest = function() {
15.          jsf.ajax.request(input, event, {
16.            render: com.corejsf.getListboxId(input),
17.            x: Element.cumulativeOffset(input)[0],
18.            y: Element.cumulativeOffset(input)[1] + Element.getHeight(input)
19.          })
20.        }
21.
22.        window.clearTimeout(keystrokeTimeout)
23.        keystrokeTimeout = window.setTimeout(ajaxRequest, 350)
24.      },
25.
```

```
26.        inputLostFocus: function(input) {
27.          var hideListbox = function() {
28.            Element.hide(com.corejsf.getListboxId(input))
29.          }
30.
31.          focusLostTimeout = window.setTimeout(hideListbox, 200)
32.        },
33.
34.        getListboxId: function(input) {
35.          var clientId = new String(input.name)
36.          var lastIndex = clientId.lastIndexOf(":")
37.          return clientId.substring(0, lastIndex) + ":listbox"
38.        }
39.    }
40.}
```

Listing 10–4 autoComplete/src/java/com/corejsf/AutoCompleteListener.java

```
1. package com.corejsf;
2.
3. import java.util.ArrayList;
4. import java.util.List;
5. import java.util.Map;
6.
7. import javax.inject.Named;
8.    // or import javax.faces.bean.ManagedBean;
9. import javax.enterprise.context.SessionScoped;
10.    // or import javax.faces.bean.SessionScoped;
11. import javax.faces.component.UIInput;
12. import javax.faces.component.UISelectItems;
13. import javax.faces.component.UISelectOne;
14. import javax.faces.context.FacesContext;
15. import javax.faces.event.ValueChangeEvent;
16.
17.
18. @Named // @ManagedBean
19. @SessionScoped
20. public class AutocompleteListener {
21.    private static String COMPLETION_ITEMS_ATTR = "corejsf.completionItems";
22.
23.    public void valueChanged(ValueChangeEvent e) {
24.      UIInput input = (UIInput)e.getSource();
25.      UISelectOne listbox = (UISelectOne)input.findComponent("listbox");
26.
27.      if (listbox != null) {
28.        UISelectItems items = (UISelectItems)listbox.getChildren().get(0);
```

```
29.        Map<String, Object> attrs = listbox.getAttributes();
30.        List<String> newItems = getNewItems((String)input.getValue(),
31.           getCompletionItems(listbox, items, attrs));
32.
33.        items.setValue(newItems.toArray());
34.        setListboxStyle(newItems.size(), attrs);
35.      }
36.    }
37.
38.    private List<String> getNewItems(String inputValue, String[] completionItems) {
39.      List<String> newItems = new ArrayList<String>();
40.
41.      for (String item : completionItems) {
42.        String s = item.substring(0, inputValue.length());
43.        if (s.equalsIgnoreCase(inputValue))
44.          newItems.add(item);
45.      }
46.
47.      return newItems;
48.    }
49.
50.    private void setListboxStyle(int rows, Map<String, Object> attrs) {
51.      if (rows > 0) {
52.        Map<String, String> reqParams = FacesContext.getCurrentInstance()
53.           .getExternalContext().getRequestParameterMap();
54.
55.        attrs.put("style", "display: inline; position: absolute; left: "
56.           + reqParams.get("x") + "px;" + " top: " + reqParams.get("y") + "px");
57.      }
58.      else
59.        attrs.put("style", "display: none;");
60.    }
61.
62.    private String[] getCompletionItems(UISelectOne listbox,
63.      UISelectItems items, Map<String, Object> attrs) {
64.        String[] completionItems = (String[])attrs.get(COMPLETION_ITEMS_ATTR);
65.
66.        if (completionItems == null) {
67.          completionItems = (String[])items.getValue();
68.          attrs.put(COMPLETION_ITEMS_ATTR, completionItems);
69.        }
70.      return completionItems;
71.    }
72.
73.    public void completionItemSelected(ValueChangeEvent e) {
74.      UISelectOne listbox = (UISelectOne)e.getSource();
75.      UIInput input = (UIInput)listbox.findComponent("input");
```

```
76.
77.      if(input != null) {
78.        input.setValue(listbox.getValue());
79.      }
80.      Map<String, Object> attrs = listbox.getAttributes();
81.      attrs.put("style", "display: none");
82.    }
83. }
```

Conclusion

JSF 2.0 provides a solid Ajax infrastructure that you can use to implement rich user interfaces. At the highest level of abstraction, JSF provides the f:ajax tag, which lets you attach Ajax behaviors to components. The f:ajax tag results in uniformity with other JSF behaviors, such as validators and converters, which are also attached to components through an embedded tag from the core JSF library (f:validator and f:converter, respectively). That uniformity makes Ajax via the f:ajax tag very natural to JSF developers.

At the lowest level of abstraction, you can use JSF's JavaScript API (which JSF uses to implement the f:ajax tag) directly. Using the JavaScript API directly is a little more verbose than using the f:ajax tag, but it gives you much more flexibility because you can attach additional functionality to Ajax calls.

The built-in Ajax functionality in JSF 2.0 will suffice for many Ajax use cases. Future versions of JSF will undoubtedly build on that base of functionality by expanding the Ajax capabilities the framework provides.

CUSTOM COMPONENTS, CONVERTERS, AND VALIDATORS

Topics in This Chapter

Chapter

JSF provides a basic set of components for building HTML-based web applications, such as text fields, checkboxes, buttons, and so on. You saw in Chapter 9 how to compose these components into more advanced components. However, composite components are limited to relatively simple layouts. For example, you could not display a tree or a tabular calendar as a composite component. Fortunately, JSF makes it possible to build *custom components* with rich behavior.

The JSF API lets you implement custom components and associated tags with the same features as the JSF standard tags. For example, h:inputText uses a value expression to associate a text field's value with a bean property, so you could use a value expression of type java.util.Date in a calendar component. JSF standard input components fire value change events when their value changes, so you could fire value change events when a different date is selected in a calendar, for example.

We start the chapter with a spinner component (see Figure 11–1) that illustrates basic issues that you encounter in all custom components. We then enhance the spinner to show more advanced issues:

- "Using an External Renderer" on page 438
- "Processing Tag Attributes" on page 441
- "Encoding JavaScript" on page 453

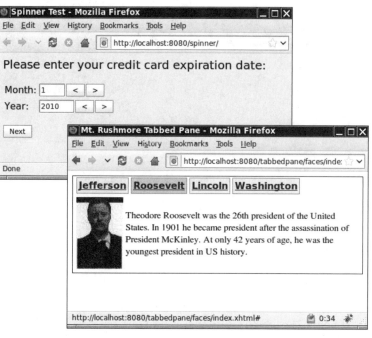

Figure 11–1   **The spinner and the tabbed pane**

We then turn to a tabbed pane component (also shown in Figure 11–1) that illustrates the following aspects of custom component development:

- "Processing SelectItem Children" page 460
- "Processing Facets" on page 461
- "Using Hidden Fields" on page 462
- "Saving and Restoring State" on page 468

Finally, we return to the spinner to show you how you can Ajax-enable your custom components—see "Building Ajax Components" on page 473.

Implementing a Component Class

When you provide a custom component, you need to implement a *component class* with the following responsibilities:

- To maintain the component state (for example, the minimum, maximum, and current value of a spinner)
- To *encode* the user interface by writing markup (in the case of the spinner, the HTML code for the input field and buttons)
- To *decode* HTTP requests (such as clicks on the spinner buttons)

By convention, the component class name has a UI prefix—for example, UISpinner.

Component classes can delegate encoding and decoding to a separate renderer. By using different renderers, you can support multiple clients, such as web browsers and cell phones. Initially, our spinner component will render itself, but in "Using an External Renderer" on page 438, we show you how to implement a separate renderer for the spinner.

A component class must be a subclass of the UIComponent class. That class defines over 40 abstract methods, so you will want to extend an existing class that implements them. You can choose from the classes shown in Figure 11–2.

You usually subclass one of the following three standard component classes:

- UIOutput, if your component displays a value, but does not allow the user to edit it
- UIInput, if your component reads a value from the user (such as the spinner)
- UICommand, if your component produces actions similar to a command button or link

If you look at Figure 11–2, you will find that these three classes implement interfaces that specify these distinct responsibilities:

- ValueHolder defines methods for managing a component value, a local value, and a converter.
- EditableValueHolder extends ValueHolder and adds methods for managing validators and value change listeners.
- ActionSource defines methods for managing action listeners.
- ActionSource2 defines methods for managing actions.

NOTE: The ActionSource2 interface was added in JSF 1.2. In JSF 1.1, the ActionSource interface handled both actions and action listeners.

The UIComponent class manages several important categories of data. These include:

- A list of *child components*. For example, the children of the h:panelGrid component are the components that are placed in the grid location. However, a component need not have any children.
- A map of *facet components*. Facets are similar to child components, but each facet has a key, not a position in a list. It is up to the component how to lay out its facets. For example, the h:dataTable component has header and footer facets.

- A map of *attributes*. This is a general-purpose map that you can use to store arbitrary key/value pairs.

- A map of *value expressions*. This is another general-purpose map that you can use to store arbitrary value expressions. For example, if a spinner tag has an attribute value="#{cardExpirationDate.month}", then the component stores a ValueExpression object for the given value expression under the key "value".

- A collection of *event listeners*. The listeners are notified when broadcasting an event whose source is this component.

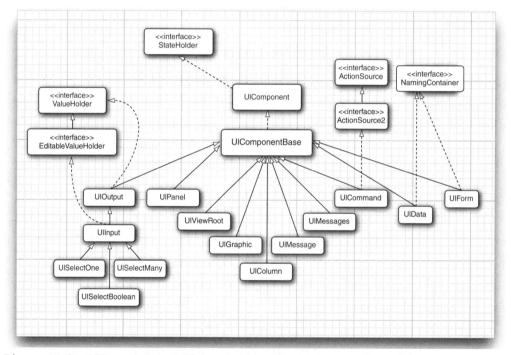

Figure 11–2   JSF component hierarchy (not all classes are shown)

Let us now look closely at the spinner component. A spinner lets you enter a number in a text field, either by typing it directly into the field or by activating an increment or decrement button. Figure 11–3 shows an application that uses two spinners for a credit card's expiration date, one for the month and another for the year.

In Figure 11–3, from top to bottom, all proceeds as expected. The user enters valid values, so navigation takes us to a designated JSF page that echoes those values.

Figure 11–3   Using the spinner component

Here is how you use corejsf:spinner:

```
<html xmlns="http://www.w3.org/1999/xhtml"
    xmlns:h="http://java.sun.com/jsf/html"
    xmlns:corejsf="http://corejsf.com">
...
<corejsf:spinner value="#{cardExpirationDate.month}"
    minimum="1" maximum="12" size="3"/>
...
<corejsf:spinner value="#{cardExpirationDate.year}"
    minimum="1900" maximum="2100" size="5"/>
```

The minimum and maximum attributes let you assign a range of valid values—for example, the month spinner has a minimum of 1 and a maximum of 12. You can also limit the size of the spinner's text field with the size attribute.

In the following sections, we will implement the UISpinner component that handles the responsibilities of encoding and decoding.

Encoding: Generating Markup

JSF components generate markup for their user interfaces. By default, the standard JSF components generate HTML. Components can do their own encoding, or they can delegate encoding to a separate renderer. The latter is the more elegant approach because it lets you plug in different renderers—for example to encode markup in something other than HTML. However, for simplicity, we will start out with a spinner that renders itself.

Components encode markup with three methods:

- encodeBegin()
- encodeChildren()
- encodeEnd()

The methods are called by JSF at the end of the life cycle, in the order in which they are listed above. JSF invokes encodeChildren only if a component returns true from its getRendersChildren method. (Most standard components return false, leaving it to the JSF implementation to render the children.)

For simple components, like our spinner, that do not have children, you do not need to implement encodeChildren. Because we do not need to worry what gets encoded before or after the children, we do all our encoding in encodeBegin.

The spinner generates HTML for a text field and two buttons; that HTML looks like this:

```
<input type="text" name="..." size="..." value="current value"/>
<input type="submit" name="..." value="<"/>
<input type="submit" name="..." value=">"/>
```

Here is how that HTML is encoded in UISpinner:

```
public void encodeBegin(FacesContext context) throws IOException {
    ResponseWriter writer = context.getResponseWriter();
    String clientId = getClientId(context);

    // Encode input field
    writer.startElement("input", this);
    writer.writeAttribute("name", clientId, null);
    Object v = getValue();
    if (v != null) writer.writeAttribute("value", v, "value");
    Object size = getAttributes().get("size");
    if (size != null) writer.writeAttribute("size", size, "size");
    writer.endElement("input");

    // Encode decrement button
    writer.startElement("input", this);
    writer.writeAttribute("type", "submit", null);
```

```
    writer.writeAttribute("name", clientId + ".less", null);
    writer.writeAttribute("value", "<", "value");
    writer.endElement("input");

    // Encode increment button
    ...
}
```

The `ResponseWriter` class is used for writing the markup. It has convenience methods for starting and ending HTML elements and for writing element attributes. The `startElement` and `endElement` methods produce the element delimiters. They keep track of child elements, so you do not have to worry about the distinction between `<input .../>` and `<input ...>...</input>`. The `writeAttribute` method writes an attribute name/value pair with the appropriate escape characters.

The last parameter of the `startElement` and `writeAttribute` methods is intended for tool support. You are supposed to pass the component object or attribute name, or `null` if the output does not directly correspond to a component or attribute. This parameter is not used by the reference implementation, but other implementations may replace the `ResponseWriter` and make use of it.

The `UISpinner.encodeBegin` method faces two challenges. First, it must get the current state of the spinner. The numerical value is easily obtained with the `getValue` method that the spinner inherits from `UIInput`. The size is retrieved from the component's attribute map, using the `getAttributes` method.

Second, the encoding method needs to come up with names for the HTML elements the spinner encodes. It calls the `getClientId` method to obtain the client ID of the component, which is composed of the ID of the enclosing form and the ID of this component, such as `_id1:monthSpinner`.

That identifier is created by the JSF implementation. The increment and decrement button names start with the client ID and end in `.more` and `.less`, respectively. Here is a complete example of the HTML generated by the spinner:

```
<input type="text" name="_id1:monthSpinner" value="1" size="3"/>
<input type="submit" name="_id1:monthSpinner.less" value="<"/>
<input type="submit" name="_id1:monthSpinner.more" value=">"/>
```

In the next section, we discuss how those names are used by the spinner's decode method.

javax.faces.component.UIComponent

- void encodeBegin(FacesContext context) throws IOException

  The method is called in the Render Response phase of the JSF life cycle, when the component's renderer type is null.

- String getClientId(FacesContext context)

  Returns the client ID for this component. The JSF framework creates the client ID from the ID of the enclosing form (or, more generally, the enclosing *naming container*) and the ID of this component.

- Map<String, Object> getAttributes()

  Returns a mutable map of component attributes and properties. You use this method to view, add, update, or remove attributes from a component. You can also use this map to view or update properties. The map's get and put methods check whether the key matches a component property. If so, the property getter or setter is called.

  As of JSF 1.2, the map also gets attributes that are defined by value expressions. If get is called with a name that is not a property or attribute but a key in the component's value expression map, then the value of the associated expression is returned.

> NOTE: The spinner is a simple component with no children, so its encoding is rather basic. For a more complicated example, see how the tabbed pane renderer encodes markup. That renderer is shown in Listing 11–11 on page 462.

> NOTE: JSF invokes a component's encodeChildren method if the component returns true from getRendersChildren. Interestingly, it does not matter whether the component actually has children—as long as the component's getRendersChildren method returns true, JSF calls encodeChildren even if the component has no children.

javax.faces.context.FacesContext

- ResponseWriter getResponseWriter()

  Returns a reference to the response writer. You can plug your own response writer into JSF if you want. By default, JSF uses a response writer that can write HTML tags.

javax.faces.context.ResponseWriter

- void startElement(String elementName, UIComponent component)

  Writes the start tag for the specified element. The component parameter lets tools associate a component and its markup. Currently, the JSF reference implementation ignores this attribute.

- void endElement(String elementName)

  Writes the end tag for the specified element.

- void writeAttribute(String attributeName, String attributeValue, String componentProperty)

  Writes an attribute and its value. This method can only be called between calls to startElement() and endElement(). The componentProperty is the name of the component property that corresponds to the attribute. This parameter is intended for tools and is not used by the JSF reference implementation.

Decoding: Processing Request Values

To understand the decoding process, keep in mind how a web application works. The server sends an HTML form to the browser. When the user submits the form, the browser sends back a POST request that consists of name/value pairs. That POST request is the only data that the server can use to interpret the user's actions inside the browser.

If the user clicks the increment or decrement button, the ensuing POST request includes the names and values of *all* text fields, but only the name and value of the *clicked* button. For example, if the user clicks the month spinner's increment button in the application shown in Figure 11–1 on page 420, the following request parameters are transferred to the server from the browser:

Name	Value
_id1:monthSpinner	1
_id1:yearSpinner	2010
_id1:monthSpinner.more	>

When our spinner decodes an HTTP request, it looks for the request parameter names that match its client ID and processes the associated values. The spinner's decode method is listed next.

```
public void decode(FacesContext context) {
    Map requestMap = context.getExternalContext().getRequestParameterMap();
    String clientId = getClientId(context);

    int increment;
    if (requestMap.containsKey(clientId + MORE)) increment = 1;
    else if (requestMap.containsKey(clientId + LESS)) increment = -1;
    else increment = 0;

    try {
        int submittedValue
            = Integer.parseInt((String) requestMap.get(clientId));
        int newValue = getIncrementedValue(submittedValue, increment);
        setSubmittedValue("" + newValue);
    }
    catch (NumberFormatException ex) {
        // let the converter take care of bad input, but we still have
        // to set the submitted value or the converter won't have
        // any input to deal with
        setSubmittedValue((String) requestMap.get(clientId));
    }
}
```

The decode method looks at the request parameters to determine which of the spinner's buttons, if any, triggered the request. If a request parameter named *clientId*.less exists, where *clientId* is the client ID of the spinner we are decoding, then we know that the decrement button was activated. If the decode method finds a request parameter named *clientId*.more, then we know that the increment button was activated.

If neither parameter exists, we know that the request was not initiated by the spinner, so we set the increment to zero. We still need to update the value—the user might have typed a value into the text field and clicked the "Next" button.

Our naming convention works for multiple spinners in a page because each spinner is encoded with the spinner component's client ID, which is guaranteed to be unique. If you have multiple spinners in a single page, each spinner component decodes its own request.

Once the decode method determines that one of the spinner's buttons was clicked, it increments the spinner's value by 1 or –1, depending on which button the user activated. That incremented value is calculated by a private getIncrementedValue method:

```
private int getIncrementedValue(int submittedValue, int increment) {
    Integer minimum = toInteger(getAttributes().get("minimum"));
    Integer maximum = toInteger(getAttributes().get("maximum"));
```

```
    int newValue = submittedValue + increment;

    if ((minimum == null || newValue >= minimum.intValue()) &&
        (maximum == null || newValue <= maximum.intValue()))
        return newValue;
    else
        return submittedValue;
}
```

The getIncrementedValue method checks the value the user entered in the spinner against the spinner's minimum and maximum attributes.

Here, we use a helper method toInteger that converts an attribute value to an integer. Keep in mind that an attribute value can be an arbitrary Object. The attribute could have been set as a string:

```
minimum="1"
```

In that case, it is an object of type String. Alternatively, it could have been the result of a value expression:

```
minimum="#{someBean.someProperty}"
```

If the property value has type int or Integer, the attribute has type Integer. The toInteger method deals with these cases:

```
private static Integer toInteger(Object value) {
    if (value == null) return null;
    if (value instanceof Number) return ((Number) value).intValue();
    if (value instanceof String) return Integer.parseInt((String) value);
    throw new IllegalArgumentException("Cannot convert " + value);
}
```

After it gets the incremented value, the decode method calls the spinner component's setSubmittedValue method. That method stores the submitted value in the component.

Note that you set the submitted value as a *string*. The spinner component uses the standard JSF integer converter to convert strings to Integer objects, and vice versa. The UISpinner constructor simply calls setConverter, like this:

```
public class UISpinner extends UIInput {
    public UISpinner() {
        setConverter(new IntegerConverter()); // to convert the submitted value
        setRendererType(null);                // this component renders itself
    }
    ...
}
```

The spinner's decode method traps invalid inputs in a NumberFormatException catch clause. Instead of reporting the error, it sets the component's submitted value to the user input. Later on in the JSF life cycle, the standard integer converter will try to convert that value and will generate an appropriate error message for bad input.

Listing 11–1 contains the complete code for the UISpinner class.

Listing 11–1 spinner/src/java/com/corejsf/UISpinner.java

```
1. package com.corejsf;
2.
3. import java.io.IOException;
4. import java.util.Map;
5.
6. import javax.faces.component.FacesComponent;
7. import javax.faces.component.UIInput;
8. import javax.faces.context.FacesContext;
9. import javax.faces.context.ResponseWriter;
10. import javax.faces.convert.IntegerConverter;
11.
12. @FacesComponent("com.corejsf.Spinner")
13. public class UISpinner extends UIInput {
14.     private static final String MORE = ".more";
15.     private static final String LESS = ".less";
16.
17.     public UISpinner() {
18.         setConverter(new IntegerConverter()); // to convert the submitted value
19.         setRendererType(null); // this component renders itself
20.     }
21.
22.     public void encodeBegin(FacesContext context) throws IOException {
23.         ResponseWriter writer = context.getResponseWriter();
24.         String clientId = getClientId(context);
25.
26.         encodeInputField(writer, clientId);
27.         encodeDecrementButton(writer, clientId);
28.         encodeIncrementButton(writer, clientId);
29.     }
30.
31.     public void decode(FacesContext context) {
32.         Map<String, String> requestMap
33.             = context.getExternalContext().getRequestParameterMap();
34.         String clientId = getClientId(context);
35.
36.         int increment;
37.         if (requestMap.containsKey(clientId + MORE)) increment = 1;
```

```
38.       else if(requestMap.containsKey(clientId + LESS)) increment = -1;
39.       else increment = 0;
40.
41.       try {
42.          int submittedValue
43.             = Integer.parseInt((String) requestMap.get(clientId));
44.
45.          int newValue = getIncrementedValue(submittedValue, increment);
46.          setSubmittedValue("" + newValue);
47.       }
48.       catch(NumberFormatException ex) {
49.          // let the converter take care of bad input, but we still have
50.          // to set the submitted value, or the converter won't have
51.          // any input to deal with
52.          setSubmittedValue((String) requestMap.get(clientId));
53.       }
54.   }
55.
56.   private void encodeInputField(ResponseWriter writer, String clientId)
57.         throws IOException {
58.      writer.startElement("input", this);
59.      writer.writeAttribute("name", clientId, null);
60.
61.      Object v = getValue();
62.      if (v != null) writer.writeAttribute("value", v, "value");
63.
64.      Object size = getAttributes().get("size");
65.      if (size != null) writer.writeAttribute("size", size, "size");
66.
67.      writer.endElement("input");
68.   }
69.
70.   private void encodeDecrementButton(ResponseWriter writer, String clientId)
71.         throws IOException {
72.      writer.startElement("input", this);
73.      writer.writeAttribute("type", "submit", null);
74.      writer.writeAttribute("name", clientId + LESS, null);
75.      writer.writeAttribute("value", "<", "value");
76.      writer.endElement("input");
77.   }
78.
79.   private void encodeIncrementButton(ResponseWriter writer, String clientId)
80.         throws IOException {
81.      writer.startElement("input", this);
82.      writer.writeAttribute("type", "submit", null);
83.      writer.writeAttribute("name", clientId + MORE, null);
84.      writer.writeAttribute("value", ">", "value");
85.      writer.endElement("input");
```

```
86.    }
87.
88.    private int getIncrementedValue(int submittedValue, int increment) {
89.       Integer minimum = toInteger(getAttributes().get("minimum"));
90.       Integer maximum = toInteger(getAttributes().get("maximum"));
91.       int newValue = submittedValue + increment;
92.
93.       if ((minimum == null || newValue >= minimum.intValue()) &&
94.          (maximum == null || newValue <= maximum.intValue()))
95.          return newValue;
96.       else
97.          return submittedValue;
98.    }
99.
100.   private static Integer toInteger(Object value) {
101.      if (value == null) return null;
102.      if (value instanceof Number) return ((Number) value).intValue();
103.      if (value instanceof String) return Integer.parseInt((String) value);
104.      throw new IllegalArgumentException("Cannot convert " + value);
105.   }
106.}
```

 javax.faces.component.UIComponent

- void decode(FacesContext context)

  The method called by JSF at the beginning of the JSF life cycle—only if the component's renderer type is null, signifying that the component renders itself.

  The decode method decodes request parameters. Typically, components transfer request parameter values to component properties or attributes. Components that fire action events queue them in this method.

javax.faces.context.FacesContext

- ExternalContext getExternalContext()

  Returns a reference to a context proxy. Typically, the real context is a servlet or portlet context. If you use the external context instead of using the real context directly, your applications can work with servlets and portlets.

`javax.faces.context.ExternalContext`

* `Map getRequestParameterMap()`

   Returns a map of request parameters. Custom components typically call this method in `decode()` to see if they were the component that triggered the request.

 javax.faces.component.EditableValueHolder

* `void setSubmittedValue(Object submittedValue)`

   Sets a component's submitted value—input components have editable values, so `UIInput` implements the `EditableValueHolder` interface. The submitted value is the value the user entered, presumably in a web page. For HTML-based applications, that value is always a string, but the method accepts an `Object` reference in deference to other display technologies.

 javax.faces.component.ValueHolder

* `void setConverter(Converter converter)`

   Input and output components both have values and, therefore, both implement the `ValueHolder` interface. Values must be converted, so the `ValueHolder` interface defines a method for setting the converter. Custom components use this method to associate themselves with standard or custom converters.

The Tag Library Descriptor JSF 2.0

In addition to implementing a custom component class, you also need to provide a descriptor file that specifies how your custom component tags can be used in a JSF page.

JSF 2.0 NOTE: Because JSF 1.0 was built on top of JSP, custom component developers had to carry out a tremendous amount of tedious busywork for processing tags. This aspect of custom component development has been greatly simplified in JSF 2.0.

When you provide a custom component, you need to produce a tag library descriptor file that specifies:

* A namespace (such as `http://coresf.com`)
* For each tag, a name (such as `spinner`) and a *component type*

For example:

```
<facelet-taglib ...>
    <namespace>http://corejsf.com</namespace>
    <tag>
        <tag-name>spinner</tag-name>
        <component>
            <component-type>com.corejsf.Spinner</component-type>
        </component>
    </tag>
</facelet-taglib>
```

You have already encountered tag library descriptor files in Chapter 5. Recall that the file name must end in `taglib.xml`, for example `corejsf.taglib.xml`.

The component type is an identifier for the component class that must get mapped to the actual class. You can set the ID with an annotation of the component class:

```
@FacesComponent("com.corejsf.Spinner")
public class UISpinner extends UIInput
```

You can think of the component type as the analog of a converter or validator ID, which was described in Chapter 7.

Listing 11–2 on page 435 shows the descriptor file for the spinner component.

> NOTE: You can specify the names and types of the tag attributes in the taglib descriptor file, but that information is only for documentation purposes. It is *not* used by the JSF implementation.

You can set the file location in `web.xml`, like this:

```
<context-param>
    <param-name>javax.faces.FACELETS_LIBRARIES</param-name>
    <param-value>/WEB-INF/corejsf.taglib.xml</param-value>
</context-param>
```

In our simple example, we will use this approach.

However, if you want to package the spinner component so that it is reusable across multiple projects, you should provide a JAR file that can be added to the `WEB-INF/lib` directory of any web application.

You will want to make the JAR file self-contained so that users do not have to worry about editing tag library descriptor or configuration files. Follow these steps:

1. Place the tag library descriptor file into the META-INF directory.
2. If you need a faces-config.xml file, also place it into the META-INF directory.
3. Place any resources (such as images, scripts, or CSS files) into the META-INF/resources directory.
4. Avoid name clashes by using an appropriate prefix for the global names, such as component names, message keys, or loggers, used by your implementation.

You have now seen all the parts that are required for the spinner test application shown in Figure 11–1 on page 420. The directory structure is shown in Figure 11–4. Listings 11–3 and 11–4 show the JSF pages, and Listing 11–5 shows the managed bean class.

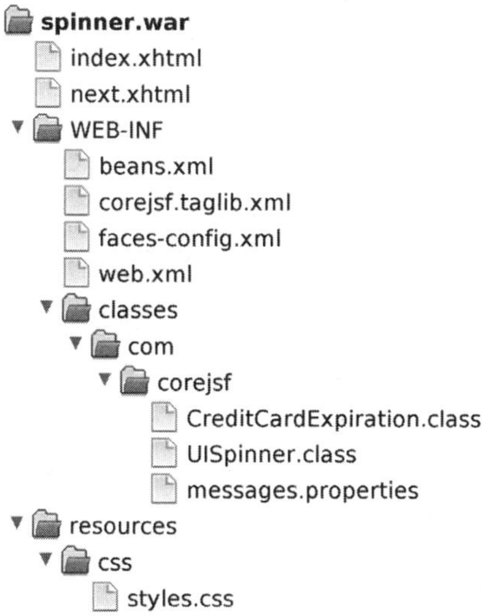

```
📁 spinner.war
   📄 index.xhtml
   📄 next.xhtml
▼ 📁 WEB-INF
      📄 beans.xml
      📄 corejsf.taglib.xml
      📄 faces-config.xml
      📄 web.xml
   ▼ 📁 classes
      ▼ 📁 com
         ▼ 📁 corejsf
               📄 CreditCardExpiration.class
               📄 UISpinner.class
               📄 messages.properties
▼ 📁 resources
   ▼ 📁 css
         📄 styles.css
```

Figure 11–4 Directory structure for the spinner example

Listing 11–2 spinner/web/WEB-INF/corejsf.taglib.xml

```
1. <?xml version="1.0" encoding="UTF-8"?>
2. <facelet-taglib version="2.0"
3.    xmlns="http://java.sun.com/xml/ns/javaee"
4.    xmlns:xsi="http://www.w3.org/2001/XMLSchema-instance"
5.    xsi:schemaLocation="http://java.sun.com/xml/ns/javaee
6.    http://java.sun.com/xml/ns/javaee/web-facelettaglibary_2_0.xsd">
7.    <namespace>http://corejsf.com</namespace>
8.    <tag>
9.       <tag-name>spinner</tag-name>
```

```
10.      <component>
11.          <component-type>com.corejsf.Spinner</component-type>
12.      </component>
13.    </tag>
14. </facelet-taglib>
```

Listing 11–3 spinner/web/index.xhtml

```
1. <?xml version="1.0" encoding="UTF-8"?>
2. <!DOCTYPE html PUBLIC "-//W3C//DTD XHTML 1.0 Transitional//EN"
3. "http://www.w3.org/TR/xhtml1/DTD/xhtml1-transitional.dtd">
4. <html xmlns="http://www.w3.org/1999/xhtml"
5.      xmlns:h="http://java.sun.com/jsf/html"
6.      xmlns:corejsf="http://corejsf.com">
7.    <h:head>
8.      <h:outputStylesheet library="css" name="styles.css"/>
9.      <title>#{msgs.windowTitle}</title>
10.   </h:head>
11.
12.   <h:body>
13.     <h:form id="spinnerForm">
14.       <h:outputText value="#{msgs.creditCardExpirationPrompt}"
15.                     styleClass="pageTitle"/>
16.       <p/>
17.       <h:panelGrid columns="3">
18.         #{msgs.monthPrompt}
19.         <corejsf:spinner value="#{cardExpirationDate.month}"
20.           id="monthSpinner" minimum="1" maximum="12" size="3"/>
21.         <h:message for="monthSpinner"/>
22.         #{msgs.yearPrompt}
23.         <corejsf:spinner value="#{cardExpirationDate.year}"
24.           id="yearSpinner" minimum="1900" maximum="2100" size="5"/>
25.         <h:message for="yearSpinner"/>
26.       </h:panelGrid>
27.       <p/>
28.       <h:commandButton value="#{msgs.nextButtonPrompt}" action="next"/>
29.     </h:form>
30.   </h:body>
31. </html>
```

Listing 11-4 spinner/web/next.xhtml

```
1. <?xml version="1.0" encoding="UTF-8"?>
2. <!DOCTYPE html PUBLIC "-//W3C//DTD XHTML 1.0 Transitional//EN"
3. "http://www.w3.org/TR/xhtml1/DTD/xhtml1-transitional.dtd">
4. <html xmlns="http://www.w3.org/1999/xhtml"
5.     xmlns:h="http://java.sun.com/jsf/html">
6.   <h:head>
7.     <h:outputStylesheet library="css" name="styles.css"/>
8.     <title>#{msgs.windowTitle}</title>
9.   </h:head>
10.  <h:body>
11.    <h:form>
12.      <h:outputText value="#{msgs.youEnteredPrompt}" styleClass="pageTitle"/>
13.      <p>#{msgs.expirationDatePrompt} #{cardExpirationDate.month} /
14.      #{cardExpirationDate.year}</p>
15.      <p><h:commandButton value="Try again" action="index"/></p>
16.    </h:form>
17.  </h:body>
18. </html>
```

Listing 11-5 spinner/src/java/com/corejsf/CreditCardExpiration.java

```
1. package com.corejsf;
2.
3. import java.io.Serializable;
4.
5. import javax.inject.Named;
6.     // or import javax.faces.bean.ManagedBean;
7. import javax.enterprise.context.SessionScoped;
8.     // or import javax.faces.bean.SessionScoped;
9.
10. @SessionScoped
11. @Named("cardExpirationDate") // or @ManagedBean(name="cardExpirationDate")
12. public class CreditCardExpiration implements Serializable {
13.    private int month = 1;
14.    private int year = 2010;
15.
16.    public int getMonth() { return month; }
17.    public void setMonth(int newValue) { month = newValue; }
18.
19.    public int getYear() { return year; }
20.    public void setYear(int newValue) { year = newValue; }
21. }
```

Using an External Renderer

In the preceding example, the `UISpinner` class was in charge of its own rendering. However, UI classes can delegate rendering to a separate class. When JSF was first created, it was envisioned to have renderers that encode markup other than HTML or decode input other than HTTP. This generality has never been seriously exploited, and we will not dwell on it. However, it still can be handy to separate component and renderer classes because you can reuse each of them separately.

Just like every component has an ID called the component type, every renderer has an ID called the *renderer type*.

The names of the standard HTML tags are meant to indicate the component type and the renderer type. For example, an `h:selectOneMenu` has component type `javax.faces.SelectOne` and renderer type `javax.faces.Menu`. Similarly, `h:selectManyMenu` has component type `javax.faces.SelectMany`, and it has the same renderer type, `javax.faces.Menu`.

Unfortunately, that naming scheme did not work so well. The renderer type for `h:input`**Text** and `h:output`**Text** is `javax.faces.`**Text**. But you can't render the input and output components in the same way. To render an `h:inputText` component, one writes an HTML `input` text field. To render an `h:outputText` tag, one just writes the text and possibly a `span`. The renderers have nothing in common!

So, instead of identifying renderers by individual components, renderers are determined by the *component family* and renderer type. For all standard JSF components, the component family is identical to the component type. (The distinction seems a bit pointless—it is just another example of "just in case" generality that is so pervasive in the JSF specification.)

The renderer type is specified in the tag library descriptor, like this:

```
<tag>
    <tag-name>spinner</tag-name>
    <component>
        <component-type>com.corejsf.Spinner</component-type>
        <renderer-type>com.corejsf.Spinner</renderer-type>
    </component>
</tag>
```

Use the `@FacesRenderer` annotation to specify the component family and renderer type for a renderer class:

```
@FacesRenderer(componentFamily="javax.faces.Input",
    rendererType="com.corejsf.Spinner")
public class SpinnerRenderer extends Renderer {
```

> NOTE: Component IDs and renderer IDs have separate namespaces. It is okay to use the same string as a component ID and a renderer ID.

It is also a good idea to set the renderer type in the component constructor:

```
public UISpinner() {
    ...
    setRendererType("com.corejsf.Spinner"); // this component has a renderer
}
```

Then the renderer type is properly set if a component is used programmatically, without the use of tags.

The final step is implementing the renderer itself. Renderers extend the javax.faces.render.Renderer class. That class has seven methods, four of which are familiar:

- void encodeBegin(FacesContext context, UIComponent component)
- void encodeChildren(FacesContext context, UIComponent component)
- void encodeEnd(FacesContext context, UIComponent component)
- void decode(FacesContext context, UIComponent component)

The renderer methods listed above are almost identical to their component counterparts except that the renderer methods take an additional argument: a reference to the component being rendered.

Since the renderer methods receive a reference to the component as a generic UIComponent parameter, you must apply a cast in order to use methods that are specific to your component. Rather than casting to a specific class, such as UISpinner, cast to one of the interface types ValueHolder, EditableValueHolder, ActionSource, or ActionSource2. That makes it easier to reuse your code in other renderers. For example, in the UISpinner renderer we use the EditableValueHolder interface.

Here are the remaining renderer methods:

- boolean getRendersChildren()
- String convertClientId(FacesContext context, String clientId)
- Object getConvertedValue(FacesContext context, UIComponent component, Object submittedValue)

The getRendersChildren method specifies whether a renderer is responsible for rendering its component's children. If that method returns true, the renderer's encodeChildren method will be called; if it returns false (the default behavior), the JSF implementation will not call that method and the children will be encoded separately.

The convertClientId method converts an ID string (such as _id1:monthSpinner) so that it can be used on the client—some clients may place restrictions on IDs, such as disallowing special characters. The default implementation returns the original ID string, and that is fine for HTML renderers.

The getConvertedValue method converts a component's submitted value from a string to an object. The default implementation in the Renderer class simply returns the submitted value. Unfortunately, that is a problem for components that use converters. When the spinner delegates to a renderer, it can no longer rely on the UIInput mechanism for conversion. Since the JSF API does not expose the conversion code, you must replicate it in any renderer that uses a converter. We placed that code in the static getConvertedValue method of the class com.corejsf.util.Renderers (see Listing 11–8 on page 450) and call it in the renderer's getConvertedValue method.

NOTE: The conversion code in UIInput resides in the protected UIInput.get-ConvertedValue method, which looks like this in the JSF 2.0 Reference Implementation:

```
// This code is from the javax.faces.component.UIInput class:
protected void getConvertedValue(FacesContext context, Object
    newSubmittedValue) throws ConverterException {
  Object newValue = newSubmittedValue;
  if (renderer != null) {
    newValue = renderer.getConvertedValue(context, this, newSubmittedValue);
  } else if (newSubmittedValue instanceof String) {
    Converter converter = getConverterWithType(context); // a private method
    if (converter != null) {
      newValue = converter.getAsObject(context, this,
        (String) newSubmittedValue);
    }
  }
  return newValue;
}
```

The private getConverterWithType method looks up the appropriate converter for the component value.

Because UIInput's conversion code is buried in protected and private methods, it is not available for a renderer to reuse. Custom components that use converters must duplicate the code—see, for example, the implementation of com.sun.faces.renderkit.html_basic.HtmlBasicInputRenderer in the reference implementation. Our com.corejsf.util.Renderers class provides the code for use in your own classes.

If you compare Listing 11–6 on page 446 and Listing 11–7 on page 447 with Listing 11–1 on page 430, you will see that we moved most of the code from the original component class to a new renderer class.

Processing Tag Attributes JSF 2.0

When you use a component tag in a JSF page, you supply tag attributes to specify the tag's properties. For example, the spinner tag has attributes for setting the minimum, maximum, and current value of the spinner. In our first example, we simply obtained the tag values from the component's attribute map.

In this section, we examine the handling of tag attributes in greater detail. A *tag handler* processes the tag attributes and their values. The default tag handler has rules for the most common attributes and takes a reasonable action for the attributes that it does not know. If that default is not appropriate for your component, you can add a custom handler.

To see why attribute handling is not trivial, consider the spinner tag from our first example:

```
<corejsf:spinner value="#{cardExpirationDate.month}" minimum="1" maximum="12" />
```

Note that the component must store the value expression #{cardExpiration-Date.month} without evaluating it. After all, whenever the JSF implementation decodes and converts a value, it must execute the setMonth property setter of the cardExpirationDate bean. The tag handler converts the string "#{cardExpiration-Date.month}" to a ValueExpression object and stores it in the component's value expression map, using the key "value". The UIInput class uses that value expression when it updates the model value after successful validation.

This is a special case that is hardwired into the default tag handler. If your component implements the ValueHolder interface, its value attribute is correctly handled. There are special cases for the following attributes:

- The value attribute of ValueHolder instances
- The validator and valueChangeListener attributes of EditableValueHolder instances
- The actionListener attribute of ActionSource instances
- The action attribute of ActionSource2 instances

However, the default handler knows nothing about our minimum and maximum attributes. First, the handler will look whether the component has property setters setMinimum or setMaximum. If so, it will invoke them, evaluating value expression strings and, if the target type is a numeric or Boolean type, converting string literals to the target type.

If there is no property setter, then the tag handler places the attribute name and value into the component's attribute map. It evaluates value expressions but does not convert strings.

This is what happens with the minimum and maximum attributes. They are stored in the component's attribute map, with values "1" and "12". Note that the values are strings, not numbers—the tag handler has no knowledge of the intended type.

To summarize, here is what the default tag handler does:

*   If the attribute is value, validator, valueChangeListener, action, or actionListener, use a special rule.
*   Else, if there is a property setter for the attribute, call it, evaluating value expressions and converting string values as necessary.
*   Else add an entry to the component's attribute map. Value expressions are evaluated, but strings are not converted.

Now consider the renderer that uses the tag attribute settings. In our spinner class, we use a call such as

```
component.getAttributes().get("minimum")
```

to retrieve the attribute values. However, there is more in this call than meets the eye. The map returned by the UIComponent.getAttributes method is smart: It accesses component properties, the attribute map, and the value reference map. For example, if you call the map's get method with an attribute whose name is "value", the getValue method is called. If the attribute name is "minimum", and there is no getMinimum method, the component's attribute map is queried for the entry with key "minimum".

To complete a long discussion, as a component author, you have to make a choice for your tag attributes. Either provide a property setter or use the attribute map. The property setter approach has a small advantage: you get automatic conversion from strings to numbers or Boolean values. The disadvantage is that you then need to worry about state saving. (See "Saving and Restoring State" on page 468.)

Supporting Value Change Listeners

If your custom component is an input component, you can fire value change events to interested listeners. For example, in a calendar application, you may want to update another component whenever a month spinner value changes.

Fortunately, it is easy to support value change listeners. The UIInput class automatically generates value change events whenever the input value has changed. Recall that there are two ways of attaching a value change listener. You can add one or more listeners with f:valueChangeListener, like this:

```
<corejsf:spinner ...>
   <f:valueChangeListener type="com.corejsf.SpinnerListener"/>
   ...
</corejsf:spinner>
```

Or you can use a valueChangeListener attribute:

```
<corejsf:spinner value="#{cardExpirationDate.month}"
   id="monthSpinner" minimum="1" maximum="12" size="3"
   valueChangeListener="#{cardExpirationDate.changeListener}"/>
```

In the sample program, we demonstrate the value change listener by keeping a count of all value changes that we display on the form (see Figure 11–5):

```
public class CreditCardExpiration {
   private int changes = 0;
   // to demonstrate the value change listener
   public void changeListener(ValueChangeEvent e) {
      changes++;
   }
}
```

Figure 11–5 Counting the value changes

Supporting Method Expressions

The special attributes valueChangeListener, validator, action, and actionListener automatically support method expressions. If you want to support method expressions for your own attributes, you have to do a bit of work.

We give you a slightly contrived example. The second version of our spinner supports attributes atMax and atMin that can be set to method expressions. The methods are called when a user tries to increment a spinner past its maximum or minimum. In our example program, we set the atMax attribute to a method that increments the year and sets the month to 1. Thus, if a user increments the current month past 12, the date is automatically set to January of the next year.

The JSF page contains the method reference:

```
<corejsf:spinner value="#{cardExpirationDate.month}"
    minimum="1" maximum="12" size="3"
    atMax="#{cardExpirationDate.incrementYear}" .../>
```

where the incrementYear method is defined like this:

```
@Named("cardExpirationDate")
public class CreditCardExpiration {
    ...
    public void incrementYear(ActionEvent event) { year++; month = 1; }
}
```

Unfortunately, the default tag handler cannot tell that "#{cardExpiration-Date.incrementYear}" is a method reference. This is a weakness of the EL API. Therefore, you must modify the tag handler. Here is how.

Supply a handler class SpinnerHandler and declare it in your tag library descriptor:

```
<facelet-taglib ...>
    <namespace>http://corejsf.com</namespace>
    <tag>
        <tag-name>spinner</tag-name>
        <component>
            <component-type>com.corejsf.Spinner</component-type>
            <renderer-type>com.corejsf.Spinner</renderer-type>
            <handler-class>com.corejsf.SpinnerHandler</handler-class>
        </component>
    </tag>
</facelet-taglib>
```

In the SpinnerHandler class, declare rules for handling the atMax and atMin attributes:

```
public class SpinnerHandler extends ComponentHandler {
    public SpinnerHandler(ComponentConfig config) { super(config); }

    protected MetaRuleset createMetaRuleset(Class<?> type) {
        return super.createMetaRuleset(type)
            .addRule(new MethodRule("atMax", Void.class, ActionEvent.class))
            .addRule(new MethodRule("atMin", Void.class, ActionEvent.class));
    }
}
```

The details of the createMetaRuleset method are a bit arcane, and we will not dwell upon it. If you need to support method expressions in your tag, you can simply follow this model.

The handler class sets the atMin and atMax attributes to MethodExpression objects. In the next section, we explain how to make use of them.

Queuing Events

Suppose the user reaches the maximum value of a spinner. We want to execute the atMax method expression, but we only want to do so after the request values have been submitted and validated. Executing the method expression immediately in the decode method is pointless since the model values will be overwritten with the submitted values.

To delay the execution of the method expression, we need to queue an event that the JSF implementation executes in the Invoke Application phase:

```
FacesEvent event = new ActionEvent(spinner);
event.setPhaseId(PhaseId.INVOKE_APPLICATION);
spinner.queueEvent(event);
```

If the minimum or maximum has been exceeded, the spinner renderer adds a MethodExpressionActionListener that was constructed with the atMin or atMax method expression. When the event is broadcast to the listener, the method is executed. The listener is removed when the component is rendered.

The details are a bit messy because the methods for adding and removing listeners are protected methods in UIComponent; see Listings 11–6 and 11–7.

NOTE: It is a bit unusual to install listeners dynamically in the renderer. With the standard actionListener attribute, the tag handler installs the listener.

The Sample Application

Figure 11–6 shows the directory structure of the second spinner application in which we use a separate renderer.

Listings 11–6 and 11–7 show the code for the spinner component and the renderer, respectively.

We rely on the Renderers convenience class in Listing 11–8 that contains the code for invoking the converter. (The Renderers class also contains a getSelectedItems method that we need later in this chapter—ignore it for now.)

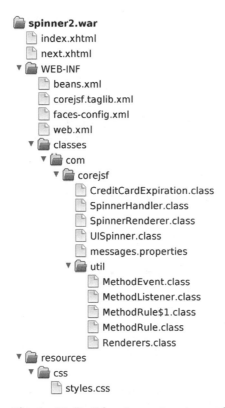

Figure 11–6   Directory structure of the revisited spinner example

Listing 11–6   spinner2/src/java/com/corejsf/UISpinner.java

```
1. package com.corejsf;
2.
3. import javax.faces.component.FacesComponent;
4. import javax.faces.component.UIInput;
5. import javax.faces.convert.IntegerConverter;
6. import javax.faces.event.FacesListener;
7.
8. @FacesComponent("com.corejsf.Spinner")
9. public class UISpinner extends UIInput {
10.    private FacesListener maxMinListener;
11.    public UISpinner() {
12.       setConverter(new IntegerConverter()); // to convert the submitted value
13.       setRendererType("com.corejsf.Spinner");
14.    }
15.
```

```
16.    public void addMaxMinListener(FacesListener listener) {
17.       if (listener != null) addFacesListener(listener);
18.       maxMinListener = listener;
19.    }
20.
21.    public void removeMaxMinListener() {
22.       if (maxMinListener != null) {
23.          removeFacesListener(maxMinListener);
24.          maxMinListener = null;
25.       }
26.    }
27. }
```

Listing 11–7   spinner2/src/java/com/corejsf/SpinnerRenderer.java

```
1. package com.corejsf;
2.
3. import java.io.IOException;
4. import java.util.Map;
5.
6. import javax.el.MethodExpression;
7. import javax.faces.component.EditableValueHolder;
8. import javax.faces.component.UIComponent;
9. import javax.faces.component.UIInput;
10. import javax.faces.context.FacesContext;
11. import javax.faces.context.ResponseWriter;
12. import javax.faces.convert.ConverterException;
13. import javax.faces.event.ActionEvent;
14. import javax.faces.event.ActionListener;
15. import javax.faces.event.FacesEvent;
16. import javax.faces.event.MethodExpressionActionListener;
17. import javax.faces.event.PhaseId;
18. import javax.faces.render.FacesRenderer;
19. import javax.faces.render.Renderer;
20.
21. @FacesRenderer(componentFamily="javax.faces.Input",
22.    rendererType="com.corejsf.Spinner")
23. public class SpinnerRenderer extends Renderer {
24.    private static final String MORE = ".more";
25.    private static final String LESS = ".less";
26.
27.    public Object getConvertedValue(FacesContext context, UIComponent component,
28.          Object submittedValue) throws ConverterException {
29.       return com.corejsf.util.Renderers.getConvertedValue(context, component,
30.          submittedValue);
31.    }
```

```
32.
33.    public void encodeBegin(FacesContext context, UIComponent spinner)
34.        throws IOException {
35.      ResponseWriter writer = context.getResponseWriter();
36.      String clientId = spinner.getClientId(context);
37.
38.      encodeInputField(spinner, writer, clientId);
39.      encodeDecrementButton(spinner, writer, clientId);
40.      encodeIncrementButton(spinner, writer, clientId);
41.
42.      ((UISpinner) spinner).removeMaxMinListener();
43.    }
44.
45.    public void decode(FacesContext context, UIComponent component) {
46.      EditableValueHolder spinner = (EditableValueHolder) component;
47.      Map<String, String> requestMap
48.        = context.getExternalContext().getRequestParameterMap();
49.      String clientId = component.getClientId(context);
50.
51.      int increment;
52.      if (requestMap.containsKey(clientId + MORE)) increment = 1;
53.      else if (requestMap.containsKey(clientId + LESS)) increment = -1;
54.      else increment = 0;
55.
56.      try {
57.        int submittedValue
58.          = Integer.parseInt((String) requestMap.get(clientId));
59.
60.        int newValue = getIncrementedValue(component, submittedValue,
61.          increment);
62.        spinner.setSubmittedValue("" + newValue);
63.      }
64.      catch(NumberFormatException ex) {
65.        // let the converter take care of bad input, but we still have
66.        // to set the submitted value, or the converter won't have
67.        // any input to deal with
68.        spinner.setSubmittedValue((String) requestMap.get(clientId));
69.      }
70.    }
71.
72.    private void encodeInputField(UIComponent spinner, ResponseWriter writer,
73.        String clientId) throws IOException {
74.      writer.startElement("input", spinner);
75.      writer.writeAttribute("name", clientId, null);
76.
77.      Object v = ((UIInput) spinner).getValue();
78.      if (v != null)
```

```
79.          writer.writeAttribute("value", v, "value");
80.
81.      Object size = spinner.getAttributes().get("size");
82.      if (size != null)
83.          writer.writeAttribute("size", size, "size");
84.
85.      writer.endElement("input");
86.   }
87.
88.   private void encodeDecrementButton(UIComponent spinner,
89.          ResponseWriter writer, String clientId) throws IOException {
90.      writer.startElement("input", spinner);
91.      writer.writeAttribute("type", "submit", null);
92.      writer.writeAttribute("name", clientId + LESS, null);
93.      writer.writeAttribute("value", "<", "value");
94.      writer.endElement("input");
95.   }
96.
97.   private void encodeIncrementButton(UIComponent spinner,
98.          ResponseWriter writer, String clientId) throws IOException {
99.      writer.startElement("input", spinner);
100.     writer.writeAttribute("type", "submit", null);
101.     writer.writeAttribute("name", clientId + MORE, null);
102.     writer.writeAttribute("value", ">", "value");
103.     writer.endElement("input");
104.  }
105.
106.  private int getIncrementedValue(UIComponent spinner, int submittedValue,
107.         int increment) {
108.     Integer minimum = toInteger(spinner.getAttributes().get("minimum"));
109.     Integer maximum = toInteger(spinner.getAttributes().get("maximum"));
110.     int newValue = submittedValue + increment;
111.
112.     ActionListener listener = null;
113.
114.     MethodExpression minMethod
115.        = (MethodExpression) spinner.getAttributes().get("atMin");
116.     if (minimum != null && newValue < minimum && minMethod != null) {
117.        listener = new MethodExpressionActionListener(minMethod);
118.        FacesEvent event = new ActionEvent(spinner);
119.        event.setPhaseId(PhaseId.INVOKE_APPLICATION);
120.        spinner.queueEvent(event);
121.     }
122.
123.     MethodExpression maxMethod
124.        = (MethodExpression) spinner.getAttributes().get("atMax");
125.     if (maximum != null && newValue > maximum && maxMethod != null) {
126.        listener = new MethodExpressionActionListener(maxMethod);
```

```
127.        FacesEvent event = new ActionEvent(spinner);
128.        event.setPhaseId(PhaseId.INVOKE_APPLICATION);
129.        spinner.queueEvent(event);
130.     }
131.
132.     ((UISpinner) spinner).addMaxMinListener(listener);
133.
134.     if ((minimum == null || newValue >= minimum.intValue()) &&
135.        (maximum == null || newValue <= maximum.intValue()))
136.        return newValue;
137.     else
138.        return submittedValue;
139.  }
140.
141.  private static Integer toInteger(Object value) {
142.     if (value == null) return null;
143.     if (value instanceof Number) return ((Number) value).intValue();
144.     if (value instanceof String) return Integer.parseInt((String) value);
145.     throw new IllegalArgumentException("Cannot convert " + value);
146.  }
147.}
```

Listing 11–8   spinner2/src/java/com/corejsf/util/Renderers.java

```
1. package com.corejsf.util;
2.
3. import java.util.ArrayList;
4. import java.util.Arrays;
5. import java.util.Collection;
6. import java.util.List;
7. import java.util.Map;
8.
9. import javax.el.ValueExpression;
10. import javax.faces.application.Application;
11. import javax.faces.component.UIComponent;
12. import javax.faces.component.UIForm;
13. import javax.faces.component.UISelectItem;
14. import javax.faces.component.UISelectItems;
15. import javax.faces.component.ValueHolder;
16. import javax.faces.context.FacesContext;
17. import javax.faces.convert.Converter;
18. import javax.faces.convert.ConverterException;
19. import javax.faces.model.SelectItem;
20.
21. public class Renderers {
22.    public static Object getConvertedValue(FacesContext context,
```

```
23.          UIComponent component, Object submittedValue)
24.          throws ConverterException {
25.       if (submittedValue instanceof String) {
26.          Converter converter = getConverter(context, component);
27.          if (converter != null) {
28.             return converter.getAsObject(context, component,
29.                   (String) submittedValue);
30.          }
31.       }
32.       return submittedValue;
33.    }
34.
35.    public static Converter getConverter(FacesContext context,
36.          UIComponent component) {
37.       if (!(component instanceof ValueHolder)) return null;
38.       ValueHolder holder = (ValueHolder) component;
39.
40.       Converter converter = holder.getConverter();
41.       if (converter != null)
42.          return converter;
43.
44.       ValueExpression expr = component.getValueExpression("value");
45.       if (expr == null) return null;
46.
47.       Class<?> targetType = expr.getType(context.getELContext());
48.       if (targetType == null) return null;
49.       // Version 1.0 of the reference implementation will not apply a converter
50.       // if the target type is String or Object, but that is a bug.
51.
52.       Application app = context.getApplication();
53.       return app.createConverter(targetType);
54.    }
55.
56.    public static String getFormId(FacesContext context, UIComponent component) {
57.       UIComponent parent = component;
58.       while (!(parent instanceof UIForm))
59.          parent = parent.getParent();
60.       return parent.getClientId(context);
61.    }
62.
63.    public static List<SelectItem> getSelectItems(UIComponent component) {
64.       ArrayList<SelectItem> list = new ArrayList<SelectItem>();
65.       for (UIComponent child : component.getChildren()) {
66.          if (child instanceof UISelectItem) {
67.             Object value = ((UISelectItem) child).getValue();
68.             if (value == null) {
69.                UISelectItem item = (UISelectItem) child;
```

```
70.            list.add(new SelectItem(item.getItemValue(),
71.                item.getItemLabel(),
72.                item.getItemDescription(),
73.                item.isItemDisabled()));
74.          } else if (value instanceof SelectItem) {
75.            list.add((SelectItem) value);
76.          }
77.        } else if (child instanceof UISelectItems) {
78.          Object value = ((UISelectItems) child).getValue();
79.          if (value instanceof SelectItem)
80.            list.add((SelectItem) value);
81.          else if (value instanceof SelectItem[])
82.            list.addAll(Arrays.asList((SelectItem[]) value));
83.          else if (value instanceof Collection<?>) {
84.            @SuppressWarnings("unchecked")
85.            Collection<SelectItem> values = (Collection<SelectItem>) value;
86.            list.addAll(values);
87.          }
88.          // warning
89.          else if (value instanceof Map<?, ?>) {
90.            for (Map.Entry<?, ?> entry : ((Map<?, ?>) value).entrySet())
91.              list.add(new SelectItem(entry.getKey(),
92.                "" + entry.getValue()));
93.          }
94.        }
95.      }
96.    return list;
97.  }
98. }
```

`javax.faces.component.UIComponent`

- ValueExpression getValueExpression(String name) **JSF 1.2**
  Returns the value expression associated with the given name.

`javax.faces.component.ValueHolder`

- Converter getConverter()
  Returns the converter associated with a component.

`javax.faces.context.FacesContext`

- ELContext getELContext() **JSF 1.2**
  Returns the "expression language context" object that is necessary for evaluating expressions.

A P I   `javax.el.ValueExpression`   **JSF 1.2**

- Class getType(ELContext context)

  Returns the type of this value expression.

A P I   `javax.faces.application.Application`

- Converter createConverter(Class targetClass)

  Creates a converter, given its target class. JSF implementations maintain a map of valid converter types, which you typically specify in a faces configuration file. If targetClass is a key in that map, this method creates an instance of the associated converter (specified as the value for the target-Class key) and returns it.

  If targetClass is not in the map, this method searches the map for a key that corresponds to targetClass's interfaces and superclasses, in that order, until it finds a matching class. Once a matching class is found, this method creates an associated converter and returns it. If no converter is found for the targetClass, its interfaces, or its superclasses, this method returns null.

Encoding JavaScript

The spinner component performs a roundtrip to the server every time you click one of its buttons. That roundtrip updates the spinner's value on the server. Those roundtrips can take a severe bite out of the spinner's performance, so in almost all circumstances, it is better to store the spinner's value on the client and update the component's value only when the form in which the spinner resides is submitted. We can do that with JavaScript that looks like this:

```
<input type="text" name="_id1:monthSpinner" value="1"/>

<script language="JavaScript">
   document.forms['_id1']['_id1:monthSpinner'].min = 1;
   document.forms['_id1']['_id1:monthSpinner'].max = 12;
</script>

<input type="button" value="<" onclick=
   "com.corejsf.spinner.spin(document.forms['_id1']['_id1:monthSpinner'], -1);"/>
<input type="button" value=">" onclick=
   "com.corejsf.spinner.spin(document.forms['_id1']['_id1:monthSpinner'], 1);"/>
```

The spin function is defined in a JavaScript file spinner-js/web/resources/javascript/spinner.js, shown in Listing 11–9 on page 454.

In order to ensure that the JavaScript resource is included in every JSF page using the spinner, you simply annotate the renderer with the @ResourceDependency annotation:

```
@FacesRenderer(...)
@ResourceDependency(library="javascript", name="spinner.js")
public class JSSpinnerRenderer extends Renderer
```

When you write JavaScript code that accesses fields in a form, you need to specify the field with an expression, such as:

```
document.forms['_id1']['_id1:monthSpinner']
```

The first array index is the client ID of the form, and the second index is the client ID of the component.

Obtaining the form ID is a common task, and we added a convenience method to the com.corejsf.util.Renderers class for this purpose:

```
public static String getFormId(FacesContext context, UIComponent component) {
    UIComponent parent = component;
    while (!(parent instanceof UIForm)) parent = parent.getParent();
    return parent.getClientId(context);
}
```

We will not go into the details of JavaScript programming here, but note that we are a bit paranoid about injecting global JavaScript functions and variables into an unknown page.

Rather than writing a global spin function, we define spin to be a method of the com.corejsf.spinner object. We use a similar approach with the minimum and maximum values of each spinner, adding min and max variables to each input field.

The spinner renderer that encodes the preceding JavaScript is shown in Listing 11–10.

Note that the UISpinner component is completely unaffected by this change. Only the renderer has been updated, thus demonstrating the power of pluggable renderers.

Listing 11–9 spinner-js/web/resources/javascript/spinner.js

```
1. if (!com) var com = {};
2. if (!com.corejsf) com.corejsf = {};
3. com.corejsf.spinner = {
4.    spin: function(field, increment) {
5.       var v = parseInt(field.value) + increment;
6.       if (isNaN(v)) return;
7.       if ('min' in field && v < field.min) return;
```

```
 8.        if ('max' in field && v > field.max) return;
 9.        field.value = v;
10.   }
11. };
```

Listing 11–10   spinner-js/src/java/com/corejsf/JSSpinnerRenderer.java

```
 1. package com.corejsf;
 2.
 3. import java.io.IOException;
 4. import java.text.MessageFormat;
 5. import java.util.Map;
 6.
 7. import javax.faces.application.ResourceDependency;
 8. import javax.faces.component.EditableValueHolder;
 9. import javax.faces.component.UIComponent;
10. import javax.faces.component.UIInput;
11. import javax.faces.context.FacesContext;
12. import javax.faces.context.ResponseWriter;
13. import javax.faces.convert.ConverterException;
14. import javax.faces.render.FacesRenderer;
15. import javax.faces.render.Renderer;
16.
17. @FacesRenderer(componentFamily="javax.faces.Input",
18.    rendererType="com.corejsf.Spinner")
19. @ResourceDependency(library="javascript", name="spinner.js")
20. public class JSSpinnerRenderer extends Renderer {
21.    public Object getConvertedValue(FacesContext context, UIComponent component,
22.         Object submittedValue) throws ConverterException {
23.      return com.corejsf.util.Renderers.getConvertedValue(context, component,
24.         submittedValue);
25.    }
26.
27.    public void encodeBegin(FacesContext context, UIComponent component)
28.         throws IOException {
29.      ResponseWriter writer = context.getResponseWriter();
30.      String clientId = component.getClientId(context);
31.      String formId = com.corejsf.util.Renderers.getFormId(context, component);
32.
33.      UIInput spinner = (UIInput) component;
34.      String min = component.getAttributes().get("minimum").toString();
35.      String max = component.getAttributes().get("maximum").toString();
36.      String size = component.getAttributes().get("size").toString();
37.
38.      writer.startElement("input", spinner);
39.      writer.writeAttribute("type", "text", null);
40.      writer.writeAttribute("name", clientId , null);
41.      writer.writeAttribute("value", spinner.getValue().toString(), "value");
```

```
42.      if (size != null) writer.writeAttribute("size", size , null);
43.      writer.endElement("input");
44.
45.      writer.startElement("script", spinner);
46.      writer.writeAttribute("language", "JavaScript", null);
47.      if (min != null) {
48.         writer.write(MessageFormat.format(
49.            "document.forms[''{0}''][''{1}''].min = {2};",
50.            formId, clientId, min));
51.      }
52.      if (max != null) {
53.         writer.write(MessageFormat.format(
54.            "document.forms[''{0}''][''{1}''].max = {2};",
55.            formId, clientId, max));
56.      }
57.      writer.endElement("script");
58.
59.      writer.startElement("input", spinner);
60.      writer.writeAttribute("type", "button", null);
61.      writer.writeAttribute("value", "<", null);
62.      writer.writeAttribute("onclick",
63.         MessageFormat.format(
64.            "com.corejsf.spinner.spin(document.forms[''{0}''][''{1}''], -1);",
65.            formId, clientId),
66.         null);
67.      writer.endElement("input");
68.
69.      writer.startElement("input", spinner);
70.      writer.writeAttribute("type", "button", null);
71.      writer.writeAttribute("value", ">", null);
72.      writer.writeAttribute("onclick",
73.         MessageFormat.format(
74.            "com.corejsf.spinner.spin(document.forms[''{0}''][''{1}''], 1);",
75.            formId, clientId),
76.         null);
77.      writer.endElement("input");
78.   }
79.
80.   public void decode(FacesContext context, UIComponent component) {
81.      EditableValueHolder spinner = (EditableValueHolder) component;
82.      Map<String, String> requestMap
83.         = context.getExternalContext().getRequestParameterMap();
84.      String clientId = component.getClientId(context);
85.      spinner.setSubmittedValue((String) requestMap.get(clientId));
86.      spinner.setValid(true);
87.   }
88. }
```

Using Child Components and Facets

The spinner discussed in the first half of this chapter is a simple component that has no children. To illustrate how a component can manage other components, we implement a tabbed pane, as shown in Figure 11–7.

The tabbed pane component differs from the tabbed pane implementation in Chapter 8 in an essential way. The implementation in Chapter 8 was ad hoc, composed of standard JSF tags, such as h:graphicImage and h:commandLink. We will now develop a reusable component that page authors can simply drop into their pages.

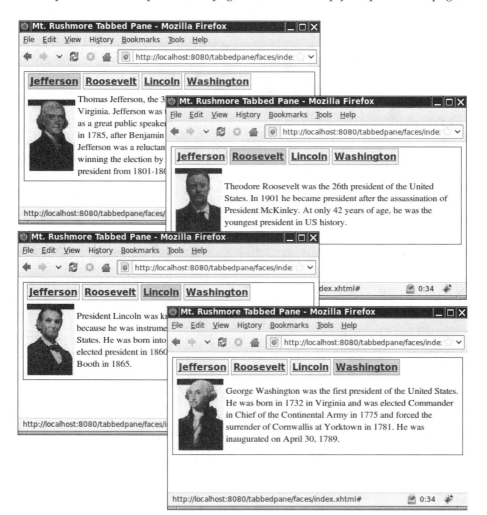

Figure 11–7 The tabbed pane component

You specify tabs with f:selectItem tags (or f:selectItems), the way the standard JSF menu and listbox tags specify menu or listbox items. These are children of the tabbed pane.

You specify tabbed pane content with a facet (which the renderer renders). For example, you could specify the content for the "Washington" tab in Figure 11–7 as washington. Then the renderer looks for a facet of the tabbed pane named washington. This use of facets is similar to the use of header and footer facets in the h:dataTable tag.

Here is a simple example of using the tabbed pane component:

```
<corejsf:tabbedPane >
    <f:selectItem itemLabel="Jefferson"  itemValue="jefferson"/>
    <f:selectItem itemLabel="Roosevelt"  itemValue="roosevelt"/>
    <f:selectItem itemLabel="Lincoln"    itemValue="lincoln"/>
    <f:selectItem itemLabel="Washington" itemValue="washington"/>
    <f:facet name="jefferson">
       <h:panelGrid columns="2">
          <h:graphicImage value="/images/jefferson.jpg"/>
          <h:outputText value="#{msgs.jeffersonDiscussion}"/>
       </h:panelGrid>
    </f:facet>
    <!-- three more facets -->
    ...
</corejsf:tabbedPane>
```

The preceding code results in a rather plain-looking tabbed pane, as shown in Figure 11–8.

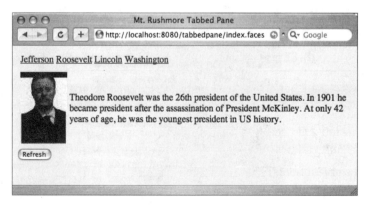

Figure 11–8 A plain tabbed pane

To get the effect shown in Figure 11–7, you can use CSS styles, like this:

```
<corejsf:tabbedPane styleClass="tabbedPane"
      tabClass="tab" selectedTabClass="selectedTab">
```

You can also use a single f:selectItems tag in lieu of multiple f:selectitem tags, like this:

```
<corejsf:tabbedPane styleClass="tabbedPane"
      tabClass="tab" selectedTabClass="selectedTab">
   <f:selectItems value="#{myBean.tabs}"/>
   ...
</corejsf:tabbedPane>
```

Here, the tabs are defined inside a bean.

In the previous example we directly specified the text displayed in each tab as select item labels: "Jefferson", "Roosevelt", etc. Before the tabbed pane renderer encodes a tab, it looks to see if those labels are keys in a resource bundle—if so, the renderer encodes the key's value. If the labels are not keys in a resource bundle, the renderer just encodes the labels as they are. You specify the resource bundle with the resourceBundle attribute, like this:

```
<corejsf:tabbedPane resourceBundle="com.corejsf.messages">
   <f:selectItem itemLabel="jeffersonTabText"  itemValue="jefferson"/>
   <f:selectItem itemLabel="rooseveltTabText"  itemValue="roosevelt"/>
   <f:selectItem itemLabel="lincolnTabText"    itemValue="lincoln"/>
   <f:selectItem itemLabel="washingtonTabText" itemValue="washington"/>
   ...
</corejsf:tabbedPane>
```

Notice the item labels—they are all keys in the messages resource bundle:

```
...
jeffersonTabText=Jefferson
rooseveltTabText=Roosevelt
lincolnTabText=Lincoln
washingtonTabText=Washington
...
```

Finally, the tabbed pane component fires an action event when a user selects a tab. You can use the f:actionListener tag to add one or more action listeners, or you can specify a method that handles action events with the tabbed pane's actionListener attribute, like this:

```
<corejsf:tabbedPane ... actionListener="#{tabbedPaneBean.presidentSelected}">
   <f:selectItems value="#{tabbedPaneBean.tabs}"/>
</corejsf:tabbedPane>
```

In the following sections, you will see how the tabbed pane features are implemented.

Processing SelectItem *Children*

The tabbed pane lets you specify tabs with f:selectItem or f:selectItems. Those tags create UISelectItem components and add them to the tabbed pane as children. Because the tabbed pane renderer has children and because it renders those children, it overrides getRendersChildren() and encodeChildren():

```
public boolean getRendersChildren() {
   return true;
}
public void encodeChildren(FacesContext context, UIComponent component)
      throws java.io.IOException {
   // if the tabbedpane component has no children, this method is still called
   if (component.getChildCount() == 0) {
      return;
   }
   ...
   for (SelectItem item : com.corejsf.util.Renderers.getSelectItems(component))
      encodeTab(context, writer, item, component);
      ...
   }
   ...
}
```

Generally, a component that processes its children contains code, such as the following:

```
for (UIComponent child : component.getChildren())
   processChild(context, writer, child, component);
```

However, our situation is more complex. Recall from Chapter 4 that you can specify a single select item, a collection of select items, an array of select items, or a map of Java objects as the value for the f:selectItems tag. Whenever your class processes children that are of type SelectItem or SelectItems, you need to deal with this mix of possibilities.

The com.corejsf.util.Renderers.getSelectItems method accounts for all those data types and synthesizes them into a list of SelectItem objects. You can find the code for the helper method in Listing 11–8 on page 450.

The encodeChildren method of the TabbedPaneRenderer calls the getSelectItems method and encodes each child into a tab. You will see the details in "Using Hidden Fields" on page 462.

Processing Facets

The tabbed pane uses facet names for the content associated with a particular tag. The `encodeEnd` method is responsible for rendering the selected facet:

```java
public void encodeEnd(FacesContext context, UIComponent component)
      throws java.io.IOException {
   ResponseWriter writer = context.getResponseWriter();
   UITabbedPane tabbedPane = (UITabbedPane) component;
   String content = tabbedPane.getContent();
   ...
   if (content != null) {
      UIComponent facet = component.getFacet(content);
      if (facet != null) {
         if (facet.isRendered()) {
            facet.encodeBegin(context);
            if (facet.getRendersChildren())
               facet.encodeChildren(context);
            facet.encodeEnd(context);
         }
      }
   }
}
```

The `UITabbedPane` class has an instance variable `content` that stores the facet name or URL of the currently displayed tab.

The `encodeEnd` method checks to see whether the content of the currently selected tab is the name of a facet of this component. If so, it encodes the facet by invoking its `encodeBegin`, `encodeChildren`, and `encodeEnd` methods. Whenever a renderer renders its own children, it needs to take over this responsibility.

 javax.faces.component.UIComponent

- `UIComponent getFacet(String facetName)`

  Returns a reference to the facet if it exists. If the facet does not exist, the method returns `null`.

- `boolean getRendersChildren()`

  Returns `true` if the component renders its children; otherwise, `false`. A component's `encodeChildren` method won't be called if this method does not return `true`. By default, `getRendersChildren` returns `false`.

- `boolean isRendered()`

  Returns the `rendered` property. The component is only rendered if the `rendered` property is `true`.

Using Hidden Fields

Each tab in the tabbed pane is encoded as a hyperlink, like this:

```
<a href="#" onclick="document.forms[formId][clientId].value=content;
    document.forms[formId].submit();"/>
```

When a user clicks a particular hyperlink, the form is submitted (the href value corresponds to the current page). Of course, the server needs to know which tab was selected. This information is stored in a *hidden field* that is placed after all the tabs:

```
<input type="hidden" name="clientId"/>
```

When the form is submitted, the name and value of the hidden field are sent back to the server, allowing the decode method to activate the selected tab.

The renderer's encodeTab method produces the hyperlink tags. The encodeEnd method calls encodeHiddenFields(), which encodes the hidden field. You can see the details in Listing 11–11.

When the tabbed pane renderer decodes the incoming request, it uses the request parameter, associated with the hidden field, to set the tabbed pane component's content.

We also queue an action event in order to invoke any attached action listeners:

```java
public void decode(FacesContext context, UIComponent component) {
    Map<String, String> requestParams =
        context.getExternalContext().getRequestParameterMap();
    String clientId = component.getClientId(context);
    String content = (String) (requestParams.get(clientId));
    if (content != null && !content.equals("")) {
        UITabbedPane tabbedPane = (UITabbedPane) component;
        tabbedPane.setContent(content);
    }
    component.queueEvent(new ActionEvent(component));
}
```

This completes the discussion of the TabbedPaneRenderer class. You will find the complete code in Listing 11–11.

Listing 11–11   tabbedpane/src/java/com/corejsf/TabbedPaneRenderer.java

```java
1. package com.corejsf;
2.
3. import java.io.IOException;
4. import java.util.Map;
5. import java.util.logging.Level;
```

```
 6. import java.util.logging.Logger;
 7. import javax.faces.component.UIComponent;
 8. import javax.faces.context.ExternalContext;
 9. import javax.faces.context.FacesContext;
10. import javax.faces.context.ResponseWriter;
11. import javax.faces.event.ActionEvent;
12. import javax.faces.model.SelectItem;
13. import javax.faces.render.FacesRenderer;
14. import javax.faces.render.Renderer;
15. import javax.servlet.ServletContext;
16. import javax.servlet.ServletException;
17. import javax.servlet.ServletRequest;
18. import javax.servlet.ServletResponse;
19.
20. // Renderer for the UITabbedPane component
21.
22. @FacesRenderer(componentFamily="javax.faces.Command",
23.    rendererType="com.corejsf.TabbedPane")
24. public class TabbedPaneRenderer extends Renderer {
25.    private static Logger logger = Logger.getLogger("com.corejsf.util");
26.
27.    // By default, getRendersChildren() returns false, so encodeChildren()
28.    // won't be invoked unless we override getRendersChildren() to return true
29.
30.    public boolean getRendersChildren() {
31.       return true;
32.    }
33.
34.    // The decode method gets the value of the request parameter whose name
35.    // is the client Id of the tabbedpane component. The request parameter
36.    // is encoded as a hidden field by encodeHiddenField, which is called by
37.    // encodeEnd. The value for the parameter is set by JavaScript generated
38.    // by the encodeTab method. It is the name of a facet or a JSP page.
39.
40.    // The decode method uses the request parameter value to set the
41.    // tabbedpane component's content attribute.
42.    // Finally, decode() queues an action event that's fired to registered
43.    // listeners in the Invoke Application phase of the JSF lifecycle. Action
44.    // listeners can be specified with the <corejsf:tabbedpane>'s actionListener
45.    // attribute or with <f:actionListener> tags in the body of the
46.    // <corejsf:tabbedpane> tag.
47.
48.    public void decode(FacesContext context, UIComponent component) {
49.       Map<String, String> requestParams
50.          = context.getExternalContext().getRequestParameterMap();
51.       String clientId = component.getClientId(context);
52.
```

```
53.        String content = (String) (requestParams.get(clientId));
54.        if (content != null && !content.equals("")) {
55.           UITabbedPane tabbedPane = (UITabbedPane) component;
56.           tabbedPane.setContent(content);
57.        }
58.
59.        component.queueEvent(new ActionEvent(component));
60.     }
61.
62.     // The encodeBegin method writes the starting <table> HTML element
63.     // with the CSS class specified by the <corejsf:tabbedpane>'s styleClass
64.     // attribute (if supplied)
65.
66.     public void encodeBegin(FacesContext context, UIComponent component)
67.            throws java.io.IOException {
68.        ResponseWriter writer = context.getResponseWriter();
69.        writer.startElement("table", component);
70.
71.        String styleClass = (String) component.getAttributes().get("styleClass");
72.        if (styleClass != null)
73.           writer.writeAttribute("class", styleClass, null);
74.
75.        writer.write("\n"); // to make generated HTML easier to read
76.     }
77.
78.     // encodeChildren() is invoked by the JSF implementation after encodeBegin().
79.     // The children of the <corejsf:tabbedpane> component are UISelectItem
80.     // components, set with one or more <f:selectItem> tags or a single
81.     // <f:selectItems> tag in the body of <corejsf:tabbedpane>
82.
83.     public void encodeChildren(FacesContext context, UIComponent component)
84.            throws java.io.IOException {
85.        // if the tabbedpane component has no children, this method is still
86.        // called
87.        if (component.getChildCount() == 0) {
88.           return;
89.        }
90.
91.        ResponseWriter writer = context.getResponseWriter();
92.        writer.startElement("thead", component);
93.        writer.startElement("tr", component);
94.        writer.startElement("th", component);
95.
96.        writer.startElement("table", component);
97.        writer.startElement("tbody", component);
98.        writer.startElement("tr", component);
99.
```

```
100.        for (SelectItem item : com.corejsf.util.Renderers.getSelectItems(component))
101.           encodeTab(context, writer, item, component);
102.
103.        writer.endElement("tr");
104.        writer.endElement("tbody");
105.        writer.endElement("table");
106.
107.        writer.endElement("th");
108.        writer.endElement("tr");
109.        writer.endElement("thead");
110.        writer.write("\n"); // to make generated HTML easier to read
111.     }
112.
113.     // encodeEnd() is invoked by the JSF implementation after encodeChildren().
114.     // encodeEnd() writes the table body and encodes the tabbedpane's content
115.     // in a single table row.
116.
117.     // The content for the tabbed pane can be specified as either a URL for
118.     // a JSP page or a facet name, so encodeEnd() checks to see if it's a facet;
119.     // if so, it encodes it; if not, it includes the JSP page
120.
121.     public void encodeEnd(FacesContext context, UIComponent component)
122.            throws java.io.IOException {
123.        ResponseWriter writer = context.getResponseWriter();
124.        UITabbedPane tabbedPane = (UITabbedPane) component;
125.        String content = tabbedPane.getContent();
126.
127.        writer.startElement("tbody", component);
128.        writer.startElement("tr", component);
129.        writer.startElement("td", component);
130.
131.        if (content != null) {
132.           UIComponent facet = component.getFacet(content);
133.           if (facet != null) {
134.              if (facet.isRendered()) {
135.                 facet.encodeBegin(context);
136.                 if (facet.getRendersChildren())
137.                    facet.encodeChildren(context);
138.                 facet.encodeEnd(context);
139.              }
140.           } else
141.              includePage(context, component);
142.        }
143.
144.        writer.endElement("td");
145.        writer.endElement("tr");
146.        writer.endElement("tbody");
```

```
147.
148.     // Close off the column, row, and table elements
149.     writer.endElement("table");
150.
151.     encodeHiddenField(context, writer, component);
152.   }
153.
154.   // The encodeHiddenField method is called at the end of encodeEnd().
155.   // See the decode method for an explanation of the field and its value.
156.
157.   private void encodeHiddenField(FacesContext context, ResponseWriter writer,
158.       UIComponent component) throws java.io.IOException {
159.     // write hidden field whose name is the tabbedpane's client Id
160.     writer.startElement("input", component);
161.     writer.writeAttribute("type", "hidden", null);
162.     writer.writeAttribute("name", component.getClientId(context), null);
163.     writer.endElement("input");
164.   }
165.
166.   // encodeTab, which is called by encodeChildren, encodes an HTML anchor
167.   // element with an onclick attribute which sets the value of the hidden
168.   // field encoded by encodeHiddenField and submits the tabbedpane's enclosing
169.   // form. See the decode method for more information about the hidden field.
170.   // encodeTab also writes out a class attribute for each tab corresponding
171.   // to either the tabClass attribute (for unselected tabs) or the
172.   // selectedTabClass attribute (for the selected tab).
173.
174.   private void encodeTab(FacesContext context, ResponseWriter writer,
175.       SelectItem item, UIComponent component) throws java.io.IOException {
176.     String tabText = getLocalizedTabText(component, item.getLabel());
177.     String content = (String) item.getValue();
178.
179.     writer.startElement("td", component);
180.     writer.startElement("a", component);
181.     writer.writeAttribute("href", "#", "href");
182.
183.     String clientId = component.getClientId(context);
184.     String formId = com.corejsf.util.Renderers.getFormId(context, component);
185.
186.     writer.writeAttribute("onclick",
187.     // write value for hidden field whose name is the tabbedpane's client Id
188.
189.         "document.forms['" + formId + "']['" + clientId + "'].value='"
190.             + content + "'; " +
191.
192.             // submit form in which the tabbedpane resides
193.             "document.forms['" + formId + "'].submit(); ", null);
```

```
194.
195.      UITabbedPane tabbedPane = (UITabbedPane) component;
196.      String selectedContent = tabbedPane.getContent();
197.
198.      String tabClass = null;
199.      if (content.equals(selectedContent))
200.         tabClass = (String) component.getAttributes().get("selectedTabClass");
201.      else
202.         tabClass = (String) component.getAttributes().get("tabClass");
203.
204.      if (tabClass != null)
205.         writer.writeAttribute("class", tabClass, null);
206.
207.      writer.write(tabText);
208.
209.      writer.endElement("a");
210.      writer.endElement("td");
211.      writer.write("\n"); // to make generated HTML easier to read
212.   }
213.
214.   // Text for the tabs in the tabbedpane component can be specified as
215.   // a key in a resource bundle, or as the actual text that's displayed
216.   // in the tab. Given that text, the getLocalizedTabText method tries to
217.   // retrieve a value from the resource bundle specified with the
218.   // <corejsf:tabbedpane>'s resourceBundle attribute. If no value is found,
219.   // getLocalizedTabText just returns the string it was passed.
220.
221.   private String getLocalizedTabText(UIComponent tabbedPane, String key) {
222.      String bundle = (String) tabbedPane.getAttributes().get("resourceBundle");
223.      String localizedText = null;
224.
225.      if (bundle != null) {
226.         localizedText = com.corejsf.util.Messages.getString(bundle, key, null);
227.      }
228.      if (localizedText == null)
229.         localizedText = key;
230.      // The key parameter was not really a key in the resource bundle,
231.      // so just return the string as is
232.      return localizedText;
233.   }
234.
235.   // includePage uses the servlet request dispatcher to include the page
236.   // corresponding to the selected tab.
237.
238.   private void includePage(FacesContext fc, UIComponent component) {
239.      ExternalContext ec = fc.getExternalContext();
240.      ServletContext sc = (ServletContext) ec.getContext();
```

```
241.     UITabbedPane tabbedPane = (UITabbedPane) component;
242.     String content = tabbedPane.getContent();
243.
244.     ServletRequest request = (ServletRequest) ec.getRequest();
245.     ServletResponse response = (ServletResponse) ec.getResponse();
246.     try {
247.         sc.getRequestDispatcher(content).include(request, response);
248.     } catch (ServletException ex) {
249.         logger.log(Level.WARNING, "Couldn't load page: " + content, ex);
250.     } catch (IOException ex) {
251.         logger.log(Level.WARNING, "Couldn't load page: " + content, ex);
252.     }
253.   }
254.}
```

Saving and Restoring State

The JSF implementation saves and restores the view state between requests. This state includes components, converters, validators, and event listeners. You need to make sure that your custom components can participate in the state saving process.

When your application saves the state on the server, then the view objects are held in memory. However, when the state is saved on the client, then the view objects are encoded and stored in a hidden field, in a very long string that looks like this:

```
<input type="hidden" name="javax.faces.ViewState" id="javax.faces.ViewState"
    value="rO0ABXNyACBjb20uc3VuLmZhY2VzLnV0aWwuVHJ1ZVN0cnVjdHVyZRRmG0QclWAgAgAETAAI...
    ...4ANXBwcHBwcHBwcHBwcHBxAH4ANXEAfgA1cHBwcHQABnN1Ym1pdHVxAH4ALAAAAAA=" />
```

Saving state on the client is required to support users who turn off cookies, and it reduces the amount of data that the server needs to store for each user of a web application.

One approach is to implement the saveState and restoreState methods of the StateHolder interface.

These methods have the following form:

```
public Object saveState(FacesContext context) {
    Object[] values = new Object[n];
    values[0] = super.saveState(context);
    values[1] = instance variable #1;
    values[2] = instance variable #2;
    ...
    return values;
}
```

```
public void restoreState(FacesContext context, Object state) {
    Object values[] = (Object[]) state;
    super.restoreState(context, values[0]);
    instance variable #1 = (Type) values[1];
    instance variable #2 = (Type) values[2];
    ...
}
```

Here, we assume that the values in the instance variables are serializable. If they are not, then you need to come up with a serializable representation of the component state.

NOTE: You may wonder why the implementors did not simply use the standard Java serialization algorithm. However, Java serialization, while quite general, is not necessarily the most efficient format for encoding component state. The JSF architecture allows JSF implementations to provide more efficient mechanisms.

TIP: If you store all of your component state as *attributes*, you do not have to implement the saveState and restoreState methods because component attributes are automatically saved by the JSF implementation. For example, the tabbed pane can use a content attribute instead of the content instance variable.

Then you do not need the UITabbedPane class at all. Use the UICommand superclass and declare the component class, like this:

```
<component>
    <component-type>com.corejsf.TabbedPane</component-type>
    <component-class>javax.faces.component.UICommand</component-class>
</component>
```

Partial State Saving JSF 2.0

JSF 2.0 provides an improved algorithm for state saving that is based on a simple observation. There is no need for the components of a page to store the initial state that is established when the view is constructed. After all, that state can be obtained by building the view again. Only the difference between the initial and current state needs to be saved. A StateHelper class tracks whether values have been added or changed after the view has been constructed.

If you want to benefit from partial state saving, you need to store your component properties in the component's state helper. The UITabbedPane class has one property: the facet name of the currently displayed tab. Here is how you can store that property in the state helper:

```
private enum PropertyKeys { content };

public String getContent() {
    return (String) getStateHelper().get(PropertyKeys.content);
}

public void setContent(String newValue) {
    getStateHelper().put(PropertyKeys.content, newValue);
}
```

When you use a state helper, you need not implement the saveState and restoreState methods.

To test why state saving is necessary, run this experiment:

1. Replace the getContent and setContent methods with

    ```
    private String content;

    public String getContent() { return content; }
    public void setContent(String newValue) { content = newValue; }
    ```

2. Activate client-side state saving by adding these lines to web.xml:

    ```
    <context-param>
        <param-name>javax.faces.STATE_SAVING_METHOD</param-name>
        <param-value>client</param-value>
    </context-param>
    ```

3. Add a button <h:commandButton value="Test State Saving"/> to index.faces.

4. Run the application and click a tab.

5. Click the "Test State Saving" button. The current page is redisplayed, but no tab is selected!

Listing 11–12 shows how the UITabbedPane class saves and restores its state. Listing 11–13 shows the JSF page for the tabbed pane application.

Listing 11–12   tabbedpane/web/index.xhtml

```
1. <?xml version="1.0" encoding="UTF-8"?>
2. <!DOCTYPE html PUBLIC "-//W3C//DTD XHTML 1.0 Transitional//EN"
3. "http://www.w3.org/TR/xhtml1/DTD/xhtml1-transitional.dtd">
4. <html xmlns="http://www.w3.org/1999/xhtml"
5.     xmlns:h="http://java.sun.com/jsf/html"
6.     xmlns:f="http://java.sun.com/jsf/core"
7.     xmlns:corejsf="http://corejsf.com">
```

```
 8.    <h:head>
 9.       <h:outputStylesheet library="css" name="styles.css"/>
10.       <title>#{msgs.windowTitle}</title>
11.    </h:head>
12.    <h:body>
13.       <h:form>
14.          <corejsf:tabbedPane styleClass="tabbedPane" tabClass="tab"
15.                              selectedTabClass="selectedTab">
16.             <f:facet name="jefferson">
17.                <h:panelGrid columns="2">
18.                   <h:graphicImage library="images" name="jefferson.jpg"/>
19.                   <h:outputText value="#{msgs.jeffersonDiscussion}"
20.                                 styleClass="tabbedPaneContent"/>
21.                </h:panelGrid>
22.             </f:facet>
23.             <f:facet name="roosevelt">
24.                <h:panelGrid columns="2">
25.                   <h:graphicImage library="images" name="roosevelt.jpg"/>
26.                   <h:outputText value="#{msgs.rooseveltDiscussion}"
27.                                 styleClass="tabbedPaneContent"/>
28.                </h:panelGrid>
29.             </f:facet>
30.             <f:facet name="lincoln">
31.                <h:panelGrid columns="2">
32.                   <h:graphicImage library="images" name="lincoln.jpg"/>
33.                   <h:outputText value="#{msgs.lincolnDiscussion}"
34.                                 styleClass="tabbedPaneContent"/>
35.                </h:panelGrid>
36.             </f:facet>
37.             <f:facet name="washington">
38.                <h:panelGrid columns="2">
39.                   <h:graphicImage library="images" name="washington.jpg"/>
40.                   <h:outputText value="#{msgs.washingtonDiscussion}"
41.                                 styleClass="tabbedPaneContent"/>
42.                </h:panelGrid>
43.             </f:facet>
44.
45.             <f:selectItem itemLabel="#{msgs.jeffersonTabText}"
46.                           itemValue="jefferson"/>
47.             <f:selectItem itemLabel="#{msgs.rooseveltTabText}"
48.                           itemValue="roosevelt"/>
49.             <f:selectItem itemLabel="#{msgs.lincolnTabText}"
50.                           itemValue="lincoln"/>
51.             <f:selectItem itemLabel="#{msgs.washingtonTabText}"
52.                           itemValue="washington"/>
53.          </corejsf:tabbedPane>
54.          <!-- <h:commandButton value="Test State Saving"/> -->
```

```
55.      </h:form>
56.    </h:body>
57. </html>
```

Listing 11–13 tabbedpane/src/java/com/corejsf/UITabbedPane.java

```
1. package com.corejsf;
2.
3. import javax.faces.component.FacesComponent;
4. import javax.faces.component.UICommand;
5.
6. @FacesComponent("com.corejsf.TabbedPane")
7. public class UITabbedPane extends UICommand {
8.    private enum PropertyKeys { content };
9.
10.    public String getContent() {
11.       return (String) getStateHelper().get(PropertyKeys.content);
12.    }
13.
14.    public void setContent(String newValue) {
15.       getStateHelper().put(PropertyKeys.content, newValue);
16.    }
17.
18. /*
19.    Use this version to test what happens when the component state is not saved.
20.
21.    private String content;
22.
23.    public String getContent() { return content; }
24.    public void setContent(String newValue) { content = newValue; }
25. */
26. }
```

javax.faces.component.StateHolder

- Object saveState(FacesContext context)
  Returns a Serializable object that saves the state of this object.

- void restoreState(FacesContext context, Object state)
  Restores the state of this object from the given state object, which is a copy of an object previously obtained from calling saveState.

- void setTransient(boolean newValue)
- boolean isTransient()
  Sets and gets the transient property. When this property is set, the state is not saved.

javax.faces.component.StateHelper JSF 2.0

- Object put(Serializable key, Object value)

  Puts a key/value pair into this state helper map and returns the previous value or null if there was none.

- Object get(Serializable key)

  Gets the value associated with key in this state helper map, or null if none is present.

Building Ajax Components JSF 2.0

There are two ways to add Ajax functionality to your custom components.

1. Embed Ajax into your custom component. Typically, you do that by implementing a custom renderer that generates JavaScript, which in turn uses the JSF 2.0 Ajax library to make Ajax calls.
2. Ajax-enable your custom component by supporting the f:ajax tag. Page authors can then use f:ajax to with your component to implement their own Ajax functionality.

Both options are equally valid. For example, you might want to implement a date picker that has pull-downs for month and day. When the user selects the month, your date picker would use Ajax to update the list of select items for the day pull-down. In that case, you would want to embed that Ajax functionality into your date picker.

It's also convenient for page authors if your custom components work with f:ajax, so that page authors can attach their own ad-hoc Ajax functionality to your custom components.

In the next two sections, we show you how to embed Ajax functionality into your custom components, and how to support f:ajax. We illustrate those techniques with a font spinner, as shown in Figure 11–9.

The font spinner is simple. When the user changes the spinner's value, we make an Ajax call to the server, and subsequently update the font size of the characters below the spinner to reflect the new font size.

The example shown Figure 11–9 uses a custom font spinner component that implements self contained Ajax. The page author just adds a corejsf:fontSpinner tag to the page, and the font spinner component takes care of all the Ajax details.

We also implemented a second example, that looks and behaves identically to the application shown in Figure 11–9, but the second example adds f:ajax support to the spinner discussed in "Encoding JavaScript" on page 453, and the Ajax functionality is implemented by the page author in an XHTML file.

We discuss both implementations of the font spinner in the next two sections.

Figure 11–9   A font spinner

Implementing Self-Contained Ajax in Custom Components

In our self-contained version of the font spinner, the font spinner encapsulates all of its Ajax functionality, so all a page author has to do is add the font spinner tag to a view:

```
<h:form id="spinnerForm">
  #{msgs.fontSizePrompt}
  <corejsf:fontSpinner value="#{fontSpecifics.size}"
    id="fontSpinner" minimum="1" maximum="100" size="3"/>
</h:form>
```

The value of the font spinner points to a property of a simple managed bean:

```
public class FontSpecifics implements Serializable {
  private int size = 1;
  public int getSize() { return size; }
  public void setSize(int size) { this.size = size; }
}
```

The font spinner is similar to the spinner component we discussed earlier in this chapter, except that we added the two-character display below the spinner. The interesting code is in the font spinner's renderer, which is given in Listing 11–14.

The font spinner renderer generates JavaScript that makes an Ajax call to the server. That JavaScript uses the built-in JavaScript library that comes with JSF 2.0. The renderer makes sure that the built-in JavaScript library is injected into the page with a ResourceDependency annotation:

```
@ResourceDependencies( {
  @ResourceDependency(library="javascript", name="spinner.js"),
  @ResourceDependency(library="javax.faces", name="jsf.js")
})
```

Notice that our font spinner actually requires two JavaScript libraries, so we use the ResourceDependencies annotation for that requirement.

Once we have the required JavaScript libraries, we create some JavaScript:

```
String ajaxScript = MessageFormat.format(
  "if(document.forms[''{0}''][''{1}''].value != '''') {2};",
  formId, clientId, getAjaxScript(context, spinner));
```

The script is generated by a getAjaxScript() method, but that script is only executed if the value of the spinner is not an empty string. That avoids the edge case where the spinner tries to display a 0 point font.

The getAjaxScript() method returns a script that makes an Ajax call. That script looks like this:

```
"jsf.ajax.request('" + component.getClientId() +
    "', null, { 'render': '" + component.getParent().getClientId() + "' })"
```

The script calls the jsf.ajax.request() function, with the spinner as the component that fired the Ajax call, and an unspecified event (the null parameter). The script also specifies that the parent of the spinner component (in this case, a form) is rendered after the Ajax call.

The font spinner renderer uses that generated JavaScript to make an Ajax call when there's a keyup event in the spinner's text input, and when there's an onclick event in the buttons.

The Ajax call made by the font spinner executes the spinner on the server, which stores the spinner's value in the spinner component. When the Ajax call returns, JSF renders the spinner, including the text displayed below the spinner:

```
writer.startElement("span", spinner);
String s = ((Integer) spinner.getValue()).toString();
writer.writeAttribute("style", "font-size: " + s + "em;", null);
writer.write("Aa");
writer.endElement("span");
```

The renderer adjusts the font size of the characters below the spinner to reflect the spinner's value.

Listing 11–14   spinner-ajax/src/java/com/corejsf/FontSpinnerRenderer.java

```
1. package com.corejsf;
2.
3. import java.io.IOException;
4. import java.text.MessageFormat;
5. import java.util.Map;
6.
7. import javax.faces.application.ResourceDependencies;
8. import javax.faces.application.ResourceDependency;
9. import javax.faces.component.EditableValueHolder;
10. import javax.faces.component.UIComponent;
11. import javax.faces.component.UIInput;
12. import javax.faces.context.FacesContext;
13. import javax.faces.context.ResponseWriter;
14. import javax.faces.convert.ConverterException;
15. import javax.faces.render.FacesRenderer;
16. import javax.faces.render.Renderer;
```

```
17.
18. @FacesRenderer(componentFamily="javax.faces.Input",
19.     rendererType="com.corejsf.FontSpinner")
20.
21. @ResourceDependencies( {
22.     @ResourceDependency(library="javascript", name="spinner.js"),
23.     @ResourceDependency(library="javax.faces", name="jsf.js")
24. })
25. public class FontSpinnerRenderer extends Renderer {
26.     public Object getConvertedValue(FacesContext context, UIComponent component,
27.         Object submittedValue) throws ConverterException {
28.       return com.corejsf.util.Renderers.getConvertedValue(context, component,
29.         submittedValue);
30.     }
31.
32.     public void encodeBegin(FacesContext context, UIComponent component)
33.         throws IOException {
34.       ResponseWriter writer = context.getResponseWriter();
35.       String clientId = component.getClientId(context);
36.       String formId = com.corejsf.util.Renderers.getFormId(context, component);
37.       UIInput spinner = (UIInput) component;
38.       String ajaxScript = MessageFormat.format(
39.         "if(document.forms[''{0}''][''{1}''].value != '''') {2};",
40.         formId, clientId, getChangeScript(context, spinner));
41.
42.       String min = component.getAttributes().get("minimum").toString();
43.       String max = component.getAttributes().get("maximum").toString();
44.       String size = component.getAttributes().get("size").toString();
45.
46.       writer.startElement("input", spinner);
47.       writer.writeAttribute("type", "text", null);
48.       writer.writeAttribute("name", clientId , null);
49.       writer.writeAttribute("id", clientId, null);
50.       writer.writeAttribute("value", spinner.getValue().toString(), "value");
51.       if (size != null) writer.writeAttribute("size", size , null);
52.
53.       writer.writeAttribute("onkeyup", ajaxScript, null);
54.       writer.endElement("input");
55.
56.       writer.startElement("script", spinner);
57.       writer.writeAttribute("language", "JavaScript", null);
58.       if (min != null) {
59.         writer.write(MessageFormat.format(
60.           "document.forms[''{0}''][''{1}''].min = {2};",
61.           formId, clientId, min));
62.       }
63.       if (max != null) {
```

```
64.         writer.write(MessageFormat.format(
65.            "document.forms[''{0}''][''{1}''].max = {2};",
66.            formId, clientId, max));
67.         }
68.      writer.endElement("script");
69.      writer.write(" em ");
70.
71.      String spinScript = MessageFormat.format(
72.         "com.corejsf.spinner.spin(document.forms[''{0}''][''{1}'']), -1);",
73.         formId, clientId);
74.
75.      writer.startElement("input", spinner);
76.      writer.writeAttribute("type", "button", null);
77.      writer.writeAttribute("value", "<", null);
78.      writer.writeAttribute("onclick",  spinScript + ajaxScript, null);
79.      writer.endElement("input");
80.
81.      spinScript = MessageFormat.format(
82.         "com.corejsf.spinner.spin(document.forms[''{0}''][''{1}'']), 1);",
83.         formId, clientId);
84.
85.      writer.startElement("input", spinner);
86.      writer.writeAttribute("type", "button", null);
87.      writer.writeAttribute("value", ">", null);
88.      writer.writeAttribute("onclick",  spinScript + ajaxScript, null);
89.      writer.endElement("input");
90.
91.      writer.startElement("br", spinner);
92.      writer.endElement("br");
93.
94.      writer.startElement("span", spinner);
95.      String s = ((Integer)spinner.getValue()).toString();
96.      writer.writeAttribute("style", "font-size: " + s + "em;", null);
97.      writer.write("Aa");
98.      writer.endElement("span");
99.   }
100.
101.  public void decode(FacesContext context, UIComponent component) {
102.     EditableValueHolder spinner = (EditableValueHolder) component;
103.     Map<String, String> requestMap
104.        = context.getExternalContext().getRequestParameterMap();
105.     String clientId = component.getClientId(context);
106.     spinner.setSubmittedValue((String) requestMap.get(clientId));
107.     spinner.setValid(true);
108.  }
109.
110.  protected final String getChangeScript(FacesContext context, UIInput component)
```

```
111.        throws IOException {
112.    return
113.      "jsf.ajax.request('" + component.getClientId() +
114.      "', null, { 'render': '" +
115.      component.getParent().getClientId() + "' })";
116.    }
117.}
```

Supporting f:ajax *in Custom Components*

In many cases, it makes sense to implement self-contained Ajax functionality in a custom component, as we did in the preceding section. However, it's also a good idea to support f:ajax for your custom components so that page authors can attach Ajax functionality to your custom components.

In this section we look at an alternate implementation of the font spinner that we discussed in the last section. Instead of embedding the Ajax functionality to update the character display when a user changes the spinner value, we let the page author specify that behavior:

```
<h:form id="spinnerForm">
    #{msgs.fontSizePrompt}
    <corejsf:spinner value="#{fontSpecifics.size}"
          id="fontSpinner" minimum="1" maximum="100" size="3">
        <f:ajax render="fontPreview"/>
    </corejsf:spinner>
    <br/>
    <h:outputText id="fontPreview" value="Aa"
          style="font-size: #{fontSpecifics.size}em"/>
</h:form>
```

In the preceding markup it's the page author, and not the spinner component, who creates the two-character display below the spinner. It's also the page author, and not the component, who implements the Ajax functionality, simply by adding an f:ajax tag to the spinner.

When the default Ajax event occurs in the spinner (indicating that the user changed the spinner's value), the client makes an Ajax call to the server, which stores the font size in a managed bean property. When that Ajax call returns, the client re-renders the two-character display, and specifies the font size of that output text to correspond to the value the user entered in the spinner.

To support f:ajax, custom components must implement the ClientBehaviorHolder interface. The f:ajax tag attaches client behaviors to the tag's surrounding component, so our spinner tag must be able to hold onto that client behavior: thus, the name of the interface.

The `ClientBehaviorHolder` interface defines four methods:

- `void addClientBehavior(String event, ClientBehavior behavior)`
- `Map<String, List<ClientBehavior>> getClientBehaviors()`
- `String getDefaultEventName()`
- `Collection<String> getEventNames()`

For your convenience, the `UIComponentBase` class (from which the spinner component ultimately inherits) provides default implementations of the four methods, even though `UIComponentBase` does not itself implement the `ClientBehaviorHolder` interface.

We are happy with the `UIComponentBase` implementations of `addClientBehavior()` and `getClientBehaviors()`, but we must tell JSF what events we support for Ajax calls, and what event is the default event that will trigger an Ajax call. In this case, the default event is `click`, so when a page author adds an `f:ajax` with no event specified to the spinner, JSF associates that Ajax behavior with the `click` event. Here is the `UISpinner` class:

```
@FacesComponent("com.corejsf.Spinner")
public class UISpinner extends UIInput implements ClientBehaviorHolder {
    private static List<String> eventNames = Arrays.asList("click");
    public UISpinner() {
        setConverter(new IntegerConverter()); // to convert the submitted value
        setRendererType("com.corejsf.JSSpinner");  // this component has a renderer
    }
    @Override public String getDefaultEventName() { return "click"; }
    @Override public Collection<String> getEventNames() { return eventNames; }
}
```

Most of the spinner's support for `f:ajax`, however, is implemented in the spinner's renderer, which is provided in Listing 11–15.

This version of the spinner renderer is similar to the renderer provided in Listing 11–14 on page 476. Both renderers generate JavaScript that makes an Ajax call, and both renderers attach that JavaScript to the spinner's input and buttons. So when the user performs a keyup in the spinner's input, or a click on one of the buttons, JSF makes an Ajax call to the server.

The difference between the two renderers is where they get the JavaScript that makes the Ajax call. The renderer listed in Listing 11–14 on page 476 generated the script directly by using the JSF 2.0 built-in JavaScript. However, the renderer in the preceding listing gets the script from a client behavior that `f:ajax` attached to the spinner component, like this:

```
public final String getAjaxScript(FacesContext context, UIInput component)
    throws IOException {
```

```
    String script = null;
    ClientBehaviorContext behaviorContext
       = ClientBehaviorContext.createClientBehaviorContext(context,
           component, "click", component.getClientId(context), null);

    Map<String,List<ClientBehavior>> behaviors =
       ((UIInput) component).getClientBehaviors();

    if (behaviors.containsKey("click"))
       script = behaviors.get("click").get(0).getScript(behaviorContext);
    return script;
}
```

In the preceding code, we are looking for the "click" behavior attached to the
spinner component. Remember that the spinner component told JSF that the
default Ajax event was a click, and the page author didn't explicitly specify an
event for the f:ajax tag, so JSF associates the f:ajax tag's behavior with the click
event. Of course, we are not being entirely honest with JSF because we execute
the "click" behavior's script not only when the user clicks the spinner's buttons,
but also when the user performs a key up event in the spinner's inputs. But
that's our business, and is none of JSF's concern.

Finally, the renderer in Listing 11–15 decodes all of the client behaviors
attached to the spinner component. Client behaviors, like components and renderers, are able to decode request parameters. In our example, the client behavior attached to our spinner by f:ajax does nothing when told to decode, so you
can remove the call to decodeBehaviors() in that renderer, and the example will
still work. However, it's a good idea to always decode all behaviors attached to
your custom component in case one or more of those behaviors needs to get
some information from the request when a call is made to the server.

Listing 11–15 spinner-ajax2/src/java/com/corejsf/JSSpinnerRenderer.java

```
 1. package com.corejsf;
 2.
 3. import java.io.IOException;
 4. import java.text.MessageFormat;
 5. import java.util.List;
 6. import java.util.Map;
 7.
 8. import javax.faces.application.ResourceDependencies;
 9. import javax.faces.application.ResourceDependency;
10. import javax.faces.component.EditableValueHolder;
11. import javax.faces.component.UIComponent;
12. import javax.faces.component.UIInput;
```

```
13. import javax.faces.component.behavior.ClientBehavior;
14. import javax.faces.component.behavior.ClientBehaviorContext;
15. import javax.faces.component.behavior.ClientBehaviorHolder;
16. import javax.faces.context.ExternalContext;
17. import javax.faces.context.FacesContext;
18. import javax.faces.context.ResponseWriter;
19. import javax.faces.convert.ConverterException;
20. import javax.faces.render.FacesRenderer;
21. import javax.faces.render.Renderer;
22.
23. @FacesRenderer(componentFamily="javax.faces.Input",
24.     rendererType="com.corejsf.Spinner")
25. @ResourceDependencies( {
26.     @ResourceDependency(library="javascript", name="spinner.js"),
27.     @ResourceDependency(library="javax.faces", name="jsf.js")
28. })
29. public class JSSpinnerRenderer extends Renderer {
30.     public Object getConvertedValue(FacesContext context, UIComponent component,
31.         Object submittedValue) throws ConverterException {
32.       return com.corejsf.util.Renderers.getConvertedValue(context, component,
33.         submittedValue);
34.     }
35.
36.     public void encodeBegin(FacesContext context, UIComponent component)
37.         throws IOException {
38.       ResponseWriter writer = context.getResponseWriter();
39.       String clientId = component.getClientId(context);
40.       String formId = com.corejsf.util.Renderers.getFormId(context, component);
41.       UIInput spinner = (UIInput) component;
42.       String ajaxScript = MessageFormat.format(
43.         "if(document.forms[''{0}''][''{1}''].value != '''') {2};",
44.         formId, clientId, getChangeScript(context, spinner));
45.
46.       String min = component.getAttributes().get("minimum").toString();
47.       String max = component.getAttributes().get("maximum").toString();
48.       String size = component.getAttributes().get("size").toString();
49.
50.       writer.startElement("input", spinner);
51.       writer.writeAttribute("type", "text", null);
52.       writer.writeAttribute("name", clientId , null);
53.       writer.writeAttribute("id", clientId, null);
54.       writer.writeAttribute("value", spinner.getValue().toString(), "value");
55.       if (size != null) writer.writeAttribute("size", size , null);
56.
57.       writer.writeAttribute("onkeyup", ajaxScript, null);
58.       writer.endElement("input");
59.
```

```
60.      writer.startElement("script", spinner);
61.      writer.writeAttribute("language", "JavaScript", null);
62.      if (min != null) {
63.         writer.write(MessageFormat.format(
64.            "document.forms[''{0}''][''{1}''].min = {2};",
65.            formId, clientId, min));
66.      }
67.      if (max != null) {
68.         writer.write(MessageFormat.format(
69.            "document.forms[''{0}''][''{1}''].max = {2};",
70.            formId, clientId, max));
71.      }
72.      writer.endElement("script");
73.
74.      String spinScript = MessageFormat.format(
75.         "com.corejsf.spinner.spin(document.forms[''{0}''][''{1}''], -1);",
76.         formId, clientId);
77.
78.      writer.startElement("input", spinner);
79.      writer.writeAttribute("type", "button", null);
80.      writer.writeAttribute("value", "<", null);
81.      writer.writeAttribute("onclick",  spinScript + ajaxScript, null);
82.      writer.endElement("input");
83.
84.      spinScript = MessageFormat.format(
85.         "com.corejsf.spinner.spin(document.forms[''{0}''][''{1}''], 1);",
86.         formId, clientId);
87.
88.      writer.startElement("input", spinner);
89.      writer.writeAttribute("type", "button", null);
90.      writer.writeAttribute("value", ">", null);
91.      writer.writeAttribute("onclick",  spinScript + ajaxScript, null);
92.      writer.endElement("input");
93.   }
94.
95.   public void decode(FacesContext context, UIComponent component) {
96.      EditableValueHolder spinner = (EditableValueHolder) component;
97.      Map<String, String> requestMap
98.         = context.getExternalContext().getRequestParameterMap();
99.      String clientId = component.getClientId(context);
100.     spinner.setSubmittedValue((String) requestMap.get(clientId));
101.     spinner.setValid(true);
102.
103.     decodeBehaviors(context, component);
104.   }
105.
106.   public final String getChangeScript(FacesContext context, UIInput component)
```

```
107.        throws IOException {
108.    String script = null;
109.      ClientBehaviorContext behaviorContext =
110.        ClientBehaviorContext.createClientBehaviorContext(context,
111.          component, "click", component.getClientId(context), null);
112.
113.      Map<String,List<ClientBehavior>> behaviors
114.        = ((UIInput)component).getClientBehaviors();
115.      if (behaviors.containsKey("click") )
116.        script = behaviors.get("click").get(0).getScript(behaviorContext);
117.      return script;
118.    }
119.
120.    public final void decodeBehaviors(FacesContext context, UIComponent component) {
121.      if (!(component instanceof ClientBehaviorHolder)) return;
122.      ClientBehaviorHolder holder = (ClientBehaviorHolder)component;
123.      Map<String, List<ClientBehavior>> behaviors = holder.getClientBehaviors();
124.      if (behaviors.isEmpty()) return;
125.
126.      ExternalContext external = context.getExternalContext();
127.      Map<String, String> params = external.getRequestParameterMap();
128.      String behaviorEvent = params.get("javax.faces.behavior.event");
129.
130.      if (behaviorEvent != null) {
131.        List<ClientBehavior> behaviorsForEvent = behaviors.get(behaviorEvent);
132.
133.        if (behaviors.size() > 0) {
134.          String behaviorSource = params.get("javax.faces.source");
135.          String clientId = component.getClientId();
136.          if (null != behaviorSource && behaviorSource.equals(clientId))
137.            for (ClientBehavior behavior: behaviorsForEvent)
138.              behavior.decode(context, component);
139.        }
140.      }
141.    }
142.}
```

Conclusion

You have now seen how to write a JSF custom component. Implementing custom components is a complex task, and it is a good idea to consider a composite component first. However, for components with rich behavior, a custom component is sometimes your only choice. You will see more examples in Chapter 13.

The next chapter shows you how to access external services, such as databases and email, from a JSF application.

EXTERNAL SERVICES

Chapter 12

In this chapter, you learn how to access external services from your JSF application. We show you how to access databases, send email, and connect to web services.

Database Access with JDBC

In the following sections, we give you a brief refresher of the Java Database Connectivity (JDBC) API. We assume that you are familiar with basic Structured Query Language (SQL) commands. A more thorough introduction to these topics can be found in Cay Horstmann and Gary Cornell, *Core Java™*, 8th ed., Santa Clara, CA: Sun Microsystems Press/Prentice Hall, 2008, Vol. 2, Chapter 4.

Issuing SQL Statements

To issue SQL statements to a database, you need a *connection* object. There are various methods of obtaining a connection. The most elegant one is to use a *data source*.

```
DataSource source = . . .;
Connection conn = source.getConnection();
```

The section "Accessing a Container-Managed Resource" on page 495 describes how to obtain a data source in the GlassFish and Tomcat containers. For now, we assume that the data source is properly configured to connect to your favorite database.

Once you have the `Connection` object, you create a `Statement` object that you use to send SQL statements to the database. You use the `executeUpdate` method for SQL statements that update the database and the `executeQuery` method for queries that return a result set:

```
Statement stat = conn.createStatement();
stat.executeUpdate("INSERT INTO Credentials VALUES ('troosevelt', 'jabberwock')");
ResultSet result = stat.executeQuery("SELECT * FROM Credentials");
```

The `ResultSet` class has an unusual iteration protocol. First you call the `next` method to advance the cursor to the first row. (The `next` method returns `false` if no further rows are available.) To get a field value as a string, you call the `getString` method. For example:

```
while (result.next()) {
    username = result.getString("username");
    password = result.getString("passwd");
    . . .
}
```

 NOTE: We use `passwd` as the column name throughout this chapter because `password` is a SQL reserved word, and some databases (such as PostgreSQL) do not allow it as a column name.

When you are done using the database, be certain to close the connection. To ensure that the connection is closed under all circumstances, even when an exception occurs, wrap the query code inside a try/finally block, like this:

```
Connection conn = source.getConnection();
try {
    . . .
}
finally {
    conn.close();
}
```

Of course, there is much more to the JDBC API, but these simple concepts are sufficient to get you started.

 NOTE: Here we show you how to execute SQL statements from your web application. This approach is fine for lightweight applications that have modest storage requirements. For complex applications, you would want to use an object-relational mapping technology, such as JPA (the Java Persistence API), which we discuss later in this chapter.

Connection Management

One of the more vexing issues for the web developer is the management of database connections. There are two conflicting concerns. First, opening a connection to a database can be time consuming. Several seconds may elapse for the processes of connecting, authenticating, and acquiring resources to be completed. Thus, you cannot simply open a new connection for every page request.

On the flip side, you cannot keep open a huge number of connections to the database. Connections consume resources, both in the client program and in the database server. Commonly, a database puts a limit on the maximum number of concurrent connections that it allows. Thus, your application cannot simply open a connection whenever a user logs on and leave it open until the user logs off. After all, your user might walk away and never log off.

One common mechanism for solving these concerns is to *pool* the database connections. A connection pool holds database connections that are already opened. Application programs obtain connections from the pool. When the connections are no longer needed, they are returned to the pool, but they are not closed. Thus, the pool minimizes the time lag of establishing database connections.

Implementing a database connection pool is not easy, and it certainly should not be the responsibility of the application programmer. As of version 2.0, JDBC supports pooling in a pleasantly transparent way. When you receive a pooled Connection object, it is actually instrumented so that its close method merely returns it to the pool. It is up to the application server to set up the pool and to give you a data source whose getConnection method yields pooled connections.

Each application server has its own way of configuring the database connection pool. The details are not part of any Java standard—the JDBC specification is completely silent on this issue. In the next section, we describe how to configure GlassFish and Tomcat for connection pooling. The basic principle is the same with other application servers, but of course the details may differ considerably.

To maintain the pool, it is still essential that you close every connection object when you are done using it. Otherwise the pool will run dry, and new physical connections to the database will need to be opened. Properly closing connections is the topic of the next section.

Plugging Connection Leaks

Consider this simple sequence of statements:

```
DataSource source = . . .;
Connection conn = source.getConnection();
Statement stat = conn.createStatement();
String command = "INSERT INTO Credentials VALUES ('troosevelt', 'jabberwock')";
stat.executeUpdate(command);
conn.close();
```

The code looks clean—we open a connection, issue a command, and immediately close the connection. But there is a fatal flaw. If one of the method calls throws an exception, the call to the close method never happens!

In that case, an irate user may resubmit the request many times in frustration, leaking another connection object with every click.

To overcome this issue, *always* place the call to close inside a finally block:

```
DataSource source = . . .;
Connection conn = source.getConnection();
try {
   Statement stat = conn.createStatement();
   String command = "INSERT INTO Credentials VALUES ('troosevelt', 'jabberwock')";
   stat.executeUpdate(command);
}
finally {
   conn.close();
}
```

This simple rule completely solves the problem of leaking connections.

The rule is most effective if you *do not combine* this try/finally construct with any other exception handling code. In particular, do not attempt to catch a SQLException in the same try block:

```
// we recommend that you do NOT do this
Connection conn = null;
try {
   conn = source.getConnection();
   Statement stat = conn.createStatement();
   String command = "INSERT INTO Credentials VALUES ('troosevelt', 'jabberwock')";
   stat.executeUpdate(command);
}
catch (SQLException) {
   // log error
}
```

```
finally {
   conn.close(); // ERROR
}
```

That code has two subtle mistakes. First, if the call to getConnection throws an exception, then conn is still null, and you can't call close. Moreover, the call to close can also throw an SQLException. You could clutter up the finally clause with more code, but the result is a mess. Instead, use two separate try blocks:

```
// we recommend that you use separate try blocks
try {
   Connection conn = source.getConnection();
   try {
      Statement stat = conn.createStatement();
      String command = "INSERT INTO Credentials VALUES ('troosevelt', 'jabberwock')";
      stat.executeUpdate(command);
   }
   finally {
      conn.close();
   }
}
catch (SQLException) {
   // log error
}
```

The inner try block ensures that the connection is closed. The outer try block ensures that the exception is logged.

> NOTE: Of course, you can also tag your method with throws SQLException and leave the outer try block to the caller. That is often the best solution.

Using Prepared Statements

A common optimization technique for JDBC programs is the use of the Prepared-Statement class. You use a *prepared statement* to speed up database operations if your code issues the same type of query multiple times. Consider the lookup of user passwords. You will repeatedly need to issue a query of the form:

```
SELECT passwd FROM Credentials WHERE username=...
```

A prepared statement asks the database to precompile a query—that is, parse the SQL statement and compute a query strategy. That information is kept with the prepared statement and reused whenever the query is reissued.

You create a prepared statement with the prepareStatement method of the Connection class. Use a ? character for each parameter:

```
PreparedStatement stat = conn.prepareStatement(
  "SELECT passwd FROM Credentials WHERE username=?");
```

When you are ready to issue a prepared statement, first set the parameter values:

```
stat.setString(1, name);
```

(Note that the index value 1 denotes the first parameter.) Then issue the statement in the usual way:

```
ResultSet result = stat.executeQuery();
```

At first glance, it appears as if prepared statements would not be of much benefit in a web application. After all, you close the connection whenever you complete a user request. A prepared statement is tied to a database connection, and all the work of establishing it is lost when the physical connection to the database is terminated.

However, if the physical database connections are kept in a pool, then there is a good chance that the prepared statement is still usable when you retrieve a connection. Many connection pool implementations will cache prepared statements.

When you call prepareStatement, the pool will first look inside the statement cache, using the query string as a key. If the prepared statement is found, then it is reused. Otherwise, a new prepared statement is created and added to the cache.

All this activity is transparent to the application programmer. You request PreparedStatement objects and hope that, at least some of the time, the pool can retrieve an existing object for the given query.

 CAUTION: You cannot keep a PreparedStatement object and reuse it beyond a single request scope. Once you close a pooled connection, all associated PreparedStatement objects also revert to the pool. Thus, you should not hang on to PreparedStatement objects beyond the current request. Instead, keep calling the prepareStatement method with the same query string, and chances are good that you will get a cached statement object.

NOTE: Even if you are not interested in performance, there is another good reason to use prepared statements: to guard against SQL injection attacks. When a query is formed by concatening SQL code and user input, a malicious user can supply SQL code in the input that modifies the meaning of the query. With a prepared statement, the user input is never interpreted as SQL.

Transactions

You can group a set of statements to form a *transaction*. The transaction can be *committed* when all has gone well. Or, if an error has occurred in one of them, it can be *rolled back* as if none of the statements had been issued.

You group statements into transactions for two reasons: *database integrity* and *concurrent access*. For example, suppose you want to transfer money from one bank account to another. Then, it is important to simultaneously debit one account and credit another. If the system fails after debiting the first account but before crediting the other account, the debit needs to be undone. Similarly, if there are two concurrent accesses to an account, they need to be serialized.

By default, a database connection is in *autocommit mode,* and each SQL statement is committed to the database as soon as it is executed. Once a statement is committed, you cannot roll it back. Turn off this default when you use transactions:

```
conn.setAutoCommit(false);
```

Execute queries and updates in the normal way. If all statements have been executed without error, call the commit method:

```
conn.commit();
```

However, if an error occurred, call:

```
conn.rollback();
```

Then, all statements until the last commit are automatically reversed. It is a bit painful to make sure that the call to the rollback method occurs when an exception is thrown. The following code outline guarantees this:

```
conn.setAutoCommit(false);
boolean committed = false;
try {
   database operations
   conn.commit();
   committed = true;
} finally {
   if (!committed) conn.rollback();
}
```

Using the Derby Database

To get started with the programs in this chapter, we recommend that you use the Apache Derby database that is a part of GlassFish and some versions of the JDK. (If you don't already have Derby, download Apache Derby from http://db.apache.org/derby.)

> NOTE: Oracle refers to the version of Apache Derby that is included in the JDK as JavaDB. To avoid confusion, we will call it Derby in this chapter.

The database server needs to be started before you can connect to it. The details depend on your database.

With the Derby database, follow these steps:

1. If you use GlassFish, simply run the following:

    glassfish/bin/asadmin start-database

    Otherwise, locate the file derbyrun.jar. With some versions of the JDK, it is contained in the *jdk*/db/lib directory, with others in a separate JavaDB installation directory. We denote the directory containing lib/derbyrun.jar with *derby*. Run the command:

    java -jar *derby*/lib/derbyrun.jar server start

2. Double-check that the database is working correctly. Create a file ij.properties that contains these lines:

    ```
    ij.driver=org.apache.derby.jdbc.ClientDriver
    ij.protocol=jdbc:derby://localhost:1527/
    ij.database=COREJSF;create=true
    ```

    Run Derby's interactive scripting tool (called ij) by executing:

    java -jar *derby*/lib/derbyrun.jar ij -p ij.properties

    Now you can issue SQL commands, such as:

    ```
    CREATE TABLE Greetings (Message VARCHAR(20));
    INSERT INTO Greetings VALUES ('Hello, World!');
    SELECT * FROM Greetings;
    DROP TABLE Greetings;
    ```

    Note that each command must be terminated by a semicolon. To exit, type:

    EXIT;

3. When you are done using the database, stop the server with the command:

    glassfish/bin/asadmin stop-database

    Or, if you don't use GlassFish:

    java -jar *derby*/lib/derbyrun.jar server shutdown

NOTE: If you use the GlassFish `asadmin` tool, your databases are located in the *glassfish*/databases directory. However, if you happen to have a file `derby.log` in the directory from which you issue the `asadmin` command, then they are created in that directory. If you don't use GlassFish, your databases are located in the directory from which you start Derby.

If you no longer need a database, simply stop the database server and remove the database directory.

If you use another database, you need to consult the documentation to find out how to start and stop your database server, and how to connect to it and issue SQL commands.

Configuring a Data Source

In the following sections, we show you how to configure a data source in your application server, such as GlassFish and Tomcat, and how to access the data source from a web application.

Accessing a Container-Managed Resource

Your application accesses a resource, such as a data source by a symbolic name (for example, `jdbc/mydb`). There are two ways for obtaining the resource from the name. The most elegant one is *resource injection*. You declare a field in a managed bean and mark it with an annotation, like this:

```
@Resource(name="jdbc/mydb") private DataSource source;
```

When the application server loads the managed bean, then the field is automatically initialized.

Table 12–1 lists the annotations that you can use to inject resources into a JSF managed bean.

CAUTION: The resources in Table 12–1 are *not serializable*. This is not a problem with CDI. The container will null out the injected resources before serializing a bean and reinject them after deserialization. However, when you use JSF managed beans and enable clustering, do not inject these resources into session- or application-scoped beans.

Table 12–1   Annotations for Resource Injection

Annotation	Resource Type
@Resource, @Resources	Arbitrary JNDI Resource
@WebServiceRef, @WebServiceRefs	Web Service Port
@EJB, @EJBs	EJB Session Bean
@PersistenceContext, @PersistenceContexts	Persistent Entity Manager
@PersistenceUnit, @PersistenceUnits	Persistent Entity Manager Factory

Configuring a Database Resource in GlassFish

GlassFish has a convenient web-based administration interface that you can use to configure a data source. Point your browser to http://localhost:4848 and log on. (The default username is admin and the default password is adminadmin.)

1.   Configure a database pool. Select "Connection Pools" and set up a new pool. Give a name to the pool, select a resource type (javax.sql.DataSource), and pick your database vendor (see Figure 12–1).

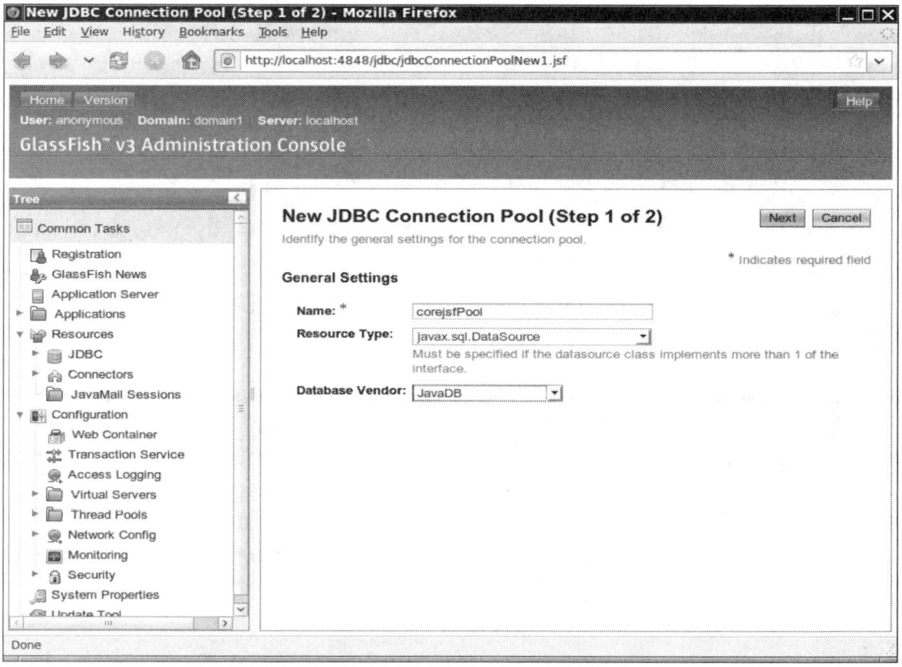

Figure 12–1   Configuring a connection pool in GlassFish

2.　On the next screen, you specify the data source class
(org.apache.derby.jdbc.ClientDataSource) and database connection
options such as username and password (see Figure 12–2).

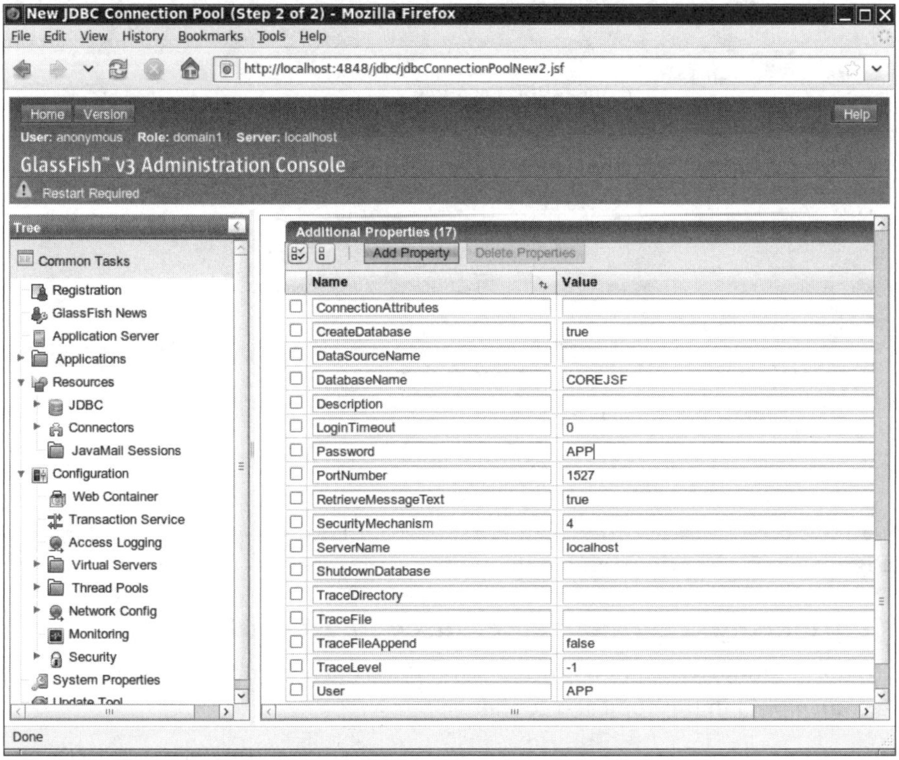

Figure 12–2　Specifying database connection options

3.　Next, you configure a new data source. Give it the name jdbc/mydb and
select the pool that you just set up (see Figure 12–3).

NOTE: If you aren't using the built-in Derby database, you need to place the
JAR file for the database driver file into the domains/domain1/lib/ext subdirectory of your GlassFish installation.

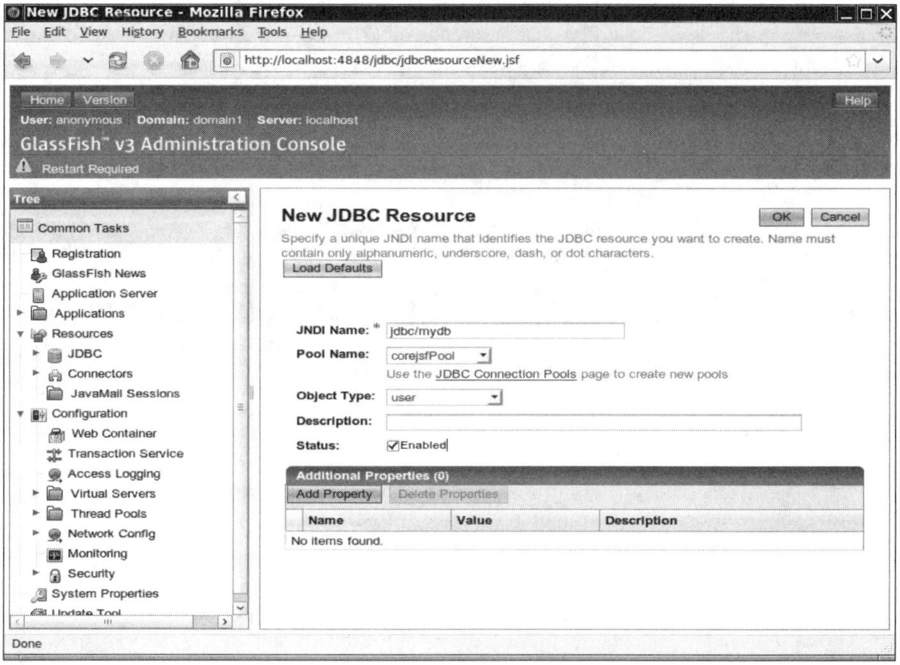

Figure 12–3   Configuring a data source

Configuring a Database Resource in Tomcat

In this section, we walk you through the steps of configuring a database resource pool in the Tomcat 6 container.

1. Copy the driver JAR file (`derbyclient.jar` for the Derby database) to the *tomcat*/`lib` directory.

2. Add a file `META-INF/context.xml` that defines the connection parameters. Here is an example for Derby:

```
<Context>
   <Resource
      name="jdbc/mydb"
      auth="Container"
      type="javax.sql.DataSource"
      username="APP"
      password="APP"
      driverClassName="org.apache.derby.jdbc.ClientDriver"
      url="jdbc:derby://localhost:1527/COREJSF;create=true"/>
</Context>
```

This configures the resource for a specific application.

3.   Add the following entry to your web.xml file:

```
<resource-ref>
    <res-ref-name>jdbc/mydb</res-ref-name>
    <res-type>javax.sql.DataSource</res-type>
    <res-auth>Container</res-auth>
</resource-ref>
```

 TIP: You can find detailed configuration instructions for a number of popular databases at http://jakarta.apache.org/tomcat/tomcat-6.0-doc/ jndi-datasource-examples-howto.html.

A Complete Database Example

In this example, we show you how to verify a username/password combination. As with the example program in Chapter 1, we start with a simple login screen (Figure 12–4). If the username/password combination is correct, we show a welcome screen (Figure 12–5). Otherwise, we prompt the user to try again (Figure 12–6). Finally, if a database error occurred, we show an error screen (Figure 12–7).

Thus, we have four JSF pages, shown in Listings 12–1 through 12–4. Listing 12–5 gives the code for the UserBean.

Figure 12–4   Login screen

Figure 12–5   Welcome screen

Figure 12–6   Authentication error screen

Figure 12–7   Internal error screen

In our simple example, we add the database code directly into the UserBean class. We place the code for database access into the separate method:

```
public void doLogin() throws SQLException
```

That method queries the database for the username/password combination and sets the loggedIn field to true if the username and password match. It then increments the login count that is displayed on the welcome page.

The button on the index.xhtml page references the login method of the user bean. That method calls the doLogin method and returns a result string for the navigation handler. The login method also deals with exceptions that the doLogin method reports.

We assume that the doLogin method is focused on the database, not the user interface. If an exception occurs, doLogin should report it and take no further action. The login method, on the other hand, logs exceptions and returns a result string "internalError" to the navigation handler.

```
public String login() {
   try {
      doLogin();
   }
   catch (SQLException ex) {
      logger.log(Level.SEVERE, "login failed", ex);
      return "internalError";
   }
   if (loggedIn)
      return "loginSuccess";
   else
      return "loginFailure";
}
```

Before running this example, you need to start your database and create a table named Credentials and add one or more username/password entries:

```
CREATE TABLE Credentials (username VARCHAR(20), passwd VARCHAR(20),
   logincount INTEGER)
INSERT INTO Credentials VALUES ('troosevelt', 'jabberwock', 0)
INSERT INTO Credentials VALUES ('tjefferson', 'mockturtle', 0)
```

You can then deploy and test your application.

Figure 12–8 shows the directory structure for this application, and Figure 12–9 shows the navigation map. The before mentioned application files follow in Listings 12–1 through 12–5.

 NOTE: Lots of things can go wrong with database configurations. If the application has an internal error, look at the log file. In GlassFish, the default log file is domains/domain1/logs/server.log. In Tomcat, it is logs/catalina.out.

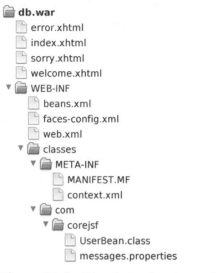

Figure 12–8 Directory structure of the database application

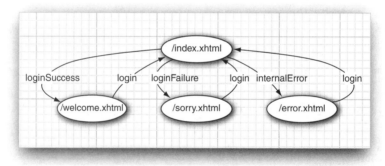

Figure 12–9 Navigation map of the database application

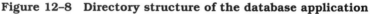

Listing 12–1 db/web/index.xhtml

```
1. <?xml version="1.0" encoding="UTF-8"?>
2. <!DOCTYPE html PUBLIC "-//W3C//DTD XHTML 1.0 Transitional//EN"
3. "http://www.w3.org/TR/xhtml1/DTD/xhtml1-transitional.dtd">
4. <html xmlns="http://www.w3.org/1999/xhtml"
5.     xmlns:f="http://java.sun.com/jsf/core" xmlns:h="http://java.sun.com/jsf/html">
6.    <h:head>
7.      <title>#{msgs.title}</title>
8.    </h:head>
9.    <h:body>
```

```
10.        <h:form>
11.          <h1>#{msgs.enterNameAndPassword}</h1>
12.          <h:panelGrid columns="2">
13.            #{msgs.name}
14.            <h:inputText value="#{user.name}"/>
15.
16.            #{msgs.password}
17.            <h:inputSecret value="#{user.password}"/>
18.          </h:panelGrid>
19.          <h:commandButton value="#{msgs.login}" action="#{user.login}"/>
20.        </h:form>
21.      </h:body>
22.  </html>
```

Listing 12–2   db/web/welcome.xhtml

```
1. <?xml version="1.0" encoding="UTF-8"?>
2. <!DOCTYPE html PUBLIC "-//W3C//DTD XHTML 1.0 Transitional//EN"
3. "http://www.w3.org/TR/xhtml1/DTD/xhtml1-transitional.dtd">
4. <html xmlns="http://www.w3.org/1999/xhtml"
5.       xmlns:f="http://java.sun.com/jsf/core" xmlns:h="http://java.sun.com/jsf/html">
6.    <h:head>
7.      <title>#{msgs.title}</title>
8.    </h:head>
9.    <h:body>
10.      <h:form>
11.        <p>#{msgs.welcome} <h:outputText value="#{user.name}"/>!</p>
12.        <p>
13.          <h:outputFormat value="#{msgs.visits}">
14.            <f:param value="#{user.count}"/>
15.          </h:outputFormat>
16.        </p>
17.
18.        <p><h:commandButton value="#{msgs.logout}" action="#{user.logout}"/>
19.        </p>
20.      </h:form>
21.    </h:body>
22. </html>
```

Listing 12–3   db/web/sorry.xhtml

```
1. <?xml version="1.0" encoding="UTF-8"?>
2. <!DOCTYPE html PUBLIC "-//W3C//DTD XHTML 1.0 Transitional//EN"
3. "http://www.w3.org/TR/xhtml1/DTD/xhtml1-transitional.dtd">
4. <html xmlns="http://www.w3.org/1999/xhtml"
5.       xmlns:f="http://java.sun.com/jsf/core" xmlns:h="http://java.sun.com/jsf/html">
```

```
 6.    <h:head>
 7.        <title>#{msgs.title}</title>
 8.    </h:head>
 9.    <h:body>
10.        <h:form>
11.            <h1>#{msgs.authError}</h1>
12.            <p>#{msgs.authError_detail}</p>
13.            <p><h:commandButton value="#{msgs.continue}" action="login"/></p>
14.        </h:form>
15.    </h:body>
16. </html>
```

Listing 12–4   db/web/error.xhtml

```
 1. <?xml version="1.0" encoding="UTF-8"?>
 2. <!DOCTYPE html PUBLIC "-//W3C//DTD XHTML 1.0 Transitional//EN"
 3. "http://www.w3.org/TR/xhtml1/DTD/xhtml1-transitional.dtd">
 4. <html xmlns="http://www.w3.org/1999/xhtml"
 5.        xmlns:f="http://java.sun.com/jsf/core" xmlns:h="http://java.sun.com/jsf/html">
 6.    <h:head>
 7.        <title>#{msgs.title}</title>
 8.    </h:head>
 9.    <h:body>
10.        <h:form>
11.            <h1>#{msgs.internalError}</h1>
12.            <p>#{msgs.internalError_detail}</p>
13.            <p><h:commandButton value="#{msgs.continue}" action="index"/></p>
14.        </h:form>
15.    </h:body>
16. </html>
```

Listing 12–5   db/src/java/com/corejsf/UserBean.java

```
 1. package com.corejsf;
 2.
 3. import java.io.Serializable;
 4. import java.sql.Connection;
 5. import java.sql.PreparedStatement;
 6. import java.sql.ResultSet;
 7. import java.sql.SQLException;
 8. import java.util.logging.Level;
 9. import java.util.logging.Logger;
10.
11. import javax.annotation.Resource;
12. import javax.inject.Named;
13.    // or import javax.faces.bean.ManagedBean;
```

```
14. import javax.enterprise.context.SessionScoped;
15.    // or import javax.faces.bean.SessionScoped;
16. import javax.sql.DataSource;
17.
18. @Named("user") // or @ManagedBean(name="user")
19. @SessionScoped
20. public class UserBean implements Serializable {
21.    private String name;
22.    private String password;
23.    private int count;
24.    private boolean loggedIn;
25.    private Logger logger = Logger.getLogger("com.corejsf");
26.
27.    @Resource(name="jdbc/mydb")
28.    private DataSource ds;
29.
30.    /*
31.    If your web container does not support resource injection, add this constructor:
32.    public UserBean()
33.    {
34.       try {
35.          Context ctx = new InitialContext();
36.          ds = (DataSource) ctx.lookup("java:comp/env/jdbc/mydb");
37.       } catch (NamingException ex) {
38.          logger.log(Level.SEVERE, "DataSource lookup failed", ex);
39.       }
40.    }
41.    */
42.
43.    public String getName() { return name; }
44.    public void setName(String newValue) { name = newValue; }
45.
46.    public String getPassword() { return password; }
47.    public void setPassword(String newValue) { password = newValue; }
48.
49.    public int getCount() { return count; }
50.
51.    public String login() {
52.       try {
53.          doLogin();
54.       }
55.       catch (SQLException ex) {
56.          logger.log(Level.SEVERE, "login failed", ex);
57.          return "internalError";
58.       }
59.       if (loggedIn)
60.          return "loginSuccess";
```

```
61.      else
62.        return "loginFailure";
63.    }
64.
65.    public String logout() {
66.      loggedIn = false;
67.      return "login";
68.    }
69.
70.    public void doLogin() throws SQLException {
71.      if (ds == null) throw new SQLException("No data source");
72.      Connection conn = ds.getConnection();
73.      if (conn == null) throw new SQLException("No connection");
74.
75.      try {
76.        conn.setAutoCommit(false);
77.        boolean committed = false;
78.        try
79.        {
80.          PreparedStatement passwordQuery = conn.prepareStatement(
81.            "SELECT passwd, logincount from Credentials WHERE username = ?");
82.          passwordQuery.setString(1, name);
83.
84.          ResultSet result = passwordQuery.executeQuery();
85.
86.          if (!result.next()) return;
87.          String storedPassword = result.getString("passwd");
88.          loggedIn = password.equals(storedPassword.trim());
89.          count = result.getInt("logincount");
90.
91.          PreparedStatement updateCounterStat = conn.prepareStatement(
92.            "UPDATE Credentials SET logincount = logincount + 1"
93.            + " WHERE USERNAME = ?");
94.          updateCounterStat.setString(1, name);
95.          updateCounterStat.executeUpdate();
96.
97.          conn.commit();
98.          committed = true;
99.        } finally {
100.          if (!committed) conn.rollback();
101.        }
102.      }
103.      finally {
104.        conn.close();
105.      }
106.    }
107.}
```

Using the Java Persistence Architecture

In the preceding section, you have seen how to access a database with JDBC. Nowadays, many programmers prefer to use an object/relational (O/R) mapper rather than raw SQL commands. The Java Persistence Architecture (JPA) provides a standard O/R mapper for the Java EE technology stack. In the following sections, we show you how your JSF applications can access a database through JPA.

A Crash Course in JPA

An O/R mapper translates between database tables and Java objects that you manipulate in your program. Your program never touches the database directly. In JPA, you use annotations to mark the classes that should be stored in the database. (These classes are called *entities*.) For example, here is a Credentials class with the requisite annotations:

```
@Entity public class Credentials {
    @Id private String username;
    private String passwd;
    private int loginCount;

    public Credentials() {}
    ...
}
```

For a class to be an entity, there are three requirements:

* The class must be annotated with @Entity.
* Each object must have a unique primary key, marked with the @Id annotation.
* The class must have a default constructor.

You use additional annotations to denote relationships between entities. For example, here is how you express the fact that each Person has one associated Credentials entity and zero or more associated roles:

```
@Entity public class Person {
    @OneToOne private Credentials creds;
    @OneToMany private Set<Role> roles;
    ...
}
```

The O/R mapper translates these annotations into foreign keys or join tables.

You use an *entity manager* to create, read, update, and delete entity objects. The following call adds a new entity to the database:

```
EntityManager em = ...; // See the following sections on how to initialize em
em.persist(entity);
```

To change an existing entity, modify the Java object and commit the current transaction. The changes are automatically saved. You remove an entity by calling `em.remove(entity)`.

To read data, you issue a query in JPQL, an object-oriented query language that is similar to SQL. For example, the following query finds the `Credentials` objects for a given username:

```
SELECT c FROM Credentials c WHERE c.username = :username
```

The colon indicates a parameter that should be set when issuing the query. Here is how to get the query results:

```
Query query = em.createQuery(
    "SELECT c FROM Credentials c WHERE c.username = :username")
    .setParameter("username", name);
@SuppressWarnings("unchecked")
List<Credentials> result = query.getResultList();
```

We use a `@SuppressWarnings` annotation because the `getResultList` method returns a raw `List`, and that list is assigned to a parameterized `List<Credentials>`. We want a list with the appropriate type parameter so that we can get the elements as `Credentials` objects.

Behind the scenes, the entity manager issues an SQL query, constructs `Credentials` objects from the result (or finds them in its cache), and returns them in a list.

We do not discuss the mapping annotations, the entity manager, or JPQL further; see Chapters 19 and 21 of the Java EE 6 tutorial at `http://java.sun.com/javaee/6/docs/tutorial/doc` for more information.

Using JPA in a Web Application

When using JPA in a web application, you need to deal with two issues:

1. Obtaining an entity manager
2. Handling transactions

As you will see in the next section, both of these issues are much simpler when you use an EJB session bean—but then you need to run a full EE application server, not just a web container.

To get an entity manager, you first obtain an entity manager factory, which the JSF implementation will inject into a managed bean. Place this annotated field into the managed bean class:

```
@PersistenceUnit(unitName="default") private EntityManagerFactory emf;
```

"Persistence units" are configured in an XML file jpa/src/java/META-INF/persistence.xml—see Listing 12–8. Each unit has a name (here, "default"), a data source, and various configuration parameters.

You obtain an entity manager by calling:

```
EntityManager em = emf.createEntityManager();
```

When you are done with the entity manager, call:

```
em.close();
```

> NOTE: In a request scoped managed bean, you can inject an entity manager directly (as shown in the next section). This is not feasible for other scopes because the entity manager is not threadsafe. However, the entity manager factory is threadsafe.

You should wrap any work with the entity manager into a transaction. Obtain a transaction manager with the injection:

```
@Resource private UserTransaction utx;
```

Then use this outline:

```
utx.begin();
em.joinTransaction();
boolean committed = false;
try {
    carry out work with em
    utx.commit();
    committed = true;
} finally {
    if (!committed) utx.rollback();
}
```

Our example program carries out the same work as the preceding program. However, it uses JPA to access the database instead of SQL. Listing 12–6 shows the Credentials entity. The UserBean is in Listing 12–7 (note the changed doLogin method). Listing 12–8 shows the persistence.xml file. In the WAR file, the persistence.xml file is inside the WEB-INF/classes/META-INF directory—see Figure 12–10.

> 📰 NOTE: While it is possible to add a JPA provider to Tomcat, the process is complex and we do not discuss it here. You should run this example on GlassFish or another Java EE application server.

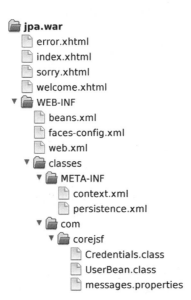

```
📁 jpa.war
   📄 error.xhtml
   📄 index.xhtml
   📄 sorry.xhtml
   📄 welcome.xhtml
 ▼ 📁 WEB-INF
      📄 beans.xml
      📄 faces-config.xml
      📄 web.xml
    ▼ 📁 classes
       ▼ 📁 META-INF
            📄 context.xml
            📄 persistence.xml
       ▼ 📁 com
          ▼ 📁 corejsf
               📄 Credentials.class
               📄 UserBean.class
               📄 messages.properties
```

Figure 12–10   Directory structure of the JPA demo application

Listing 12–6   jpa/src/java/com/corejsf/Credentials.java

```java
 1. package com.corejsf;
 2.
 3. import java.io.Serializable;
 4. import javax.persistence.Entity;
 5. import javax.persistence.Id;
 6.
 7. @Entity
 8. public class Credentials implements Serializable {
 9.    @Id
10.    private String username;
11.    private String passwd;
12.    private int loginCount;
13.
14.    public Credentials() {} // Required by JPA
15.
16.    public Credentials(String username, String password) {
```

```
17.        this.username = username;
18.        this.passwd = password;
19.    }
20.    public String getPasswd() { return passwd; }
21.    public String getUsername() { return username; }
22.    public int incrementLoginCount() { loginCount++; return loginCount; }
23. }
```

Listing 12–7   jpa/src/java/com/corejsf/UserBean.java

```
1. package com.corejsf;
2.
3. import java.io.Serializable;
4. import java.util.List;
5. import java.util.logging.Level;
6. import java.util.logging.Logger;
7.
8. import javax.annotation.Resource;
9. import javax.inject.Named;
10.    // or import javax.faces.bean.ManagedBean;
11. import javax.enterprise.context.SessionScoped;
12.    // or import javax.faces.bean.SessionScoped;
13. import javax.persistence.EntityManager;
14. import javax.persistence.EntityManagerFactory;
15. import javax.persistence.PersistenceUnit;
16. import javax.persistence.Query;
17. import javax.transaction.HeuristicMixedException;
18. import javax.transaction.HeuristicRollbackException;
19. import javax.transaction.NotSupportedException;
20. import javax.transaction.RollbackException;
21. import javax.transaction.SystemException;
22. import javax.transaction.UserTransaction;
23.
24. @Named("user") // or @ManagedBean(name="user")
25. @SessionScoped
26. public class UserBean implements Serializable {
27.    private String name;
28.    private String password;
29.    private int count;
30.    private boolean loggedIn;
31.
32.    @PersistenceUnit(unitName="default")
33.    private EntityManagerFactory emf;
34.
35.    @Resource
36.    private UserTransaction utx;
```

```
37.
38.    public String getName() { return name; }
39.    public void setName(String newValue) { name = newValue; }
40.
41.    public String getPassword() { return password; }
42.    public void setPassword(String newValue) { password = newValue; }
43.
44.    public int getCount() { return count; }
45.
46.    public String login() {
47.       try {
48.          doLogin();
49.       } catch (Exception ex) {
50.          Logger.getLogger("com.corejsf").log(Level.SEVERE, "login failed", ex);
51.          return "internalError";
52.       }
53.       if (loggedIn)
54.          return "loginSuccess";
55.       else
56.          return "loginFailure";
57.    }
58.
59.    public String logout() {
60.       loggedIn = false;
61.       return "login";
62.    }
63.
64.    public void doLogin() throws NotSupportedException, SystemException,
65.          RollbackException, HeuristicMixedException, HeuristicRollbackException {
66.       EntityManager em = emf.createEntityManager();
67.       try {
68.          utx.begin();
69.          em.joinTransaction();
70.          boolean committed = false;
71.          try {
72.             Query query = em.createQuery(
73.                "SELECT c FROM Credentials c WHERE c.username = :username")
74.                .setParameter("username", name);
75.             @SuppressWarnings("unchecked")
76.             List<Credentials> result = query.getResultList();
77.
78.             if (result.size() == 1) {
79.                Credentials c = result.get(0);
80.                if (c.getPasswd().trim().equals(password)) {
81.                   loggedIn = true;
82.                   count = c.incrementLoginCount();
83.                }
```

```
84.          }
85.          utx.commit();
86.          committed = true;
87.      } finally {
88.          if (!committed) utx.rollback();
89.      }
90.  } finally {
91.      em.close();
92.  }
93.  }
94. }
```

Listing 12–8   jpa/src/java/META-INF/persistence.xml

```
1. <?xml version="1.0" encoding="UTF-8"?>
2. <persistence version="1.0"
3.      xmlns="http://java.sun.com/xml/ns/persistence"
4.      xmlns:xsi="http://www.w3.org/2001/XMLSchema-instance"
5.      xsi:schemaLocation="http://java.sun.com/xml/ns/persistence
6.          http://java.sun.com/xml/ns/persistence/persistence_1_0.xsd">
7.  <persistence-unit name="default" transaction-type="JTA">
8.    <provider>org.eclipse.persistence.jpa.PersistenceProvider</provider>
9.    <jta-data-source>jdbc/mydb</jta-data-source>
10.   <exclude-unlisted-classes>false</exclude-unlisted-classes>
11.   <properties>
12.     <property name="eclipselink.ddl-generation" value="create-tables"/>
13.   </properties>
14.  </persistence-unit>
15. </persistence>
```

Using Managed Beans and Stateless Session Beans

We now move to a full EJB architecture where the JSF managed beans communicate with *stateless session beans*, objects that are managed by the application server. There is a significant benefit: By default, session bean methods are automatically transactional. The application server takes care of the transaction handling whenever a session bean method is invoked. Similarly, the application server takes care of threading, simply by providing a pool of beans and issuing one for each request. The beans are called stateless because they should keep no state between requests. That feature enables the application server to pick any available bean for a particular request, or to create new ones when needed.

 NOTE: In this section, we describe the simplified "no interface" version of session beans that is introduced in Java EE 6.

A stateless session bean is annoted with @Stateless. You inject an entity manager and simply use it, without declaring any transactions:

```
@Stateless public class CredentialsManager {
   @PersistenceContext(unitName="default") private EntityManager em;

   public int checkCredentials(String name, String password) {
      Query query = em.createQuery(...).setParameter("username", name);
      @SuppressWarnings("unchecked") List<Credentials> result
         = query.getResultList();
      ...
   }
}
```

Then inject the stateless session bean into one or more managed beans with the @EJB annotation:

```
@ManagedBean(name="user") @RequestScoped public class UserBean {
   @EJB private CredentialsManager cm;
   ...
   public String login() {
      count = cm.checkCredentials(name, password);
      ...
   }
}
```

This is a very straightforward programming model. You place the application logic into the managed beans and the business logic into the stateless session beans. The only drawback is that you need to transport a fair amount of data between the two types of beans. Traditionally, this problem was addressed with "data access objects", objects whose sole purpose is to transport data between architectural layers. Naturally, implementing and maintaining these objects is quite tedious. With EJB 3, you can use entity objects instead, but you have to be aware of a significant restriction.

When an entity object is returned from a stateless session bean to a JSF managed bean, it becomes *detached*. The entity manager no longer knows about the object. If the managed bean changes the entity, it must merge it back into the entity manager. That is usually achieved by a call to another session bean method, which calls em.merge(entity).

Detached entities have another issue. When an entity holds a collection of other entities, that collection is not a simple hash set or array list, but by default a *lazy collection* that only fetches elements on demand. If you want to send such an entity to a JSF managed bean, you need to ensure that the dependent entities are prefetched, usually by adding fetch instructions in the JPQL query.

If you use stateless session beans in your JSF application, you need to learn enough about EJB 3 entities to solve these issues, or you need to use data access objects. The next section shows how you can avoid this issue by using *stateful session beans*.

We continue our sample application, now implementing the same functionality with a managed bean (Listing 12–9) and a stateless session bean (Listing 12–10).

Listing 12–9   slsb/src/java/com/corejsf/UserBean.java

```
1. package com.corejsf;
2.
3. import java.io.Serializable;
4. import java.util.logging.Level;
5. import java.util.logging.Logger;
6.
7. import javax.ejb.EJB;
8. import javax.inject.Named;
9.    // or import javax.faces.bean.ManagedBean;
10. import javax.enterprise.context.SessionScoped;
11.    // or import javax.faces.bean.SessionScoped;
12.
13. @Named("user") // or @ManagedBean(name="user")
14. @SessionScoped
15. public class UserBean implements Serializable {
16.    private String name;
17.    private String password;
18.    private boolean loggedIn;
19.    private int count;
20.    private Logger logger = Logger.getLogger("com.corejsf");
21.
22.    @EJB private CredentialsManager cm;
23.
24.    public String getName() { return name; }
25.    public void setName(String newValue) { name = newValue; }
26.
27.    public String getPassword() { return password; }
28.    public void setPassword(String newValue) { password = newValue; }
29.
30.    public int getCount() { return count; }
31.
32.    public String login() {
33.       try {
34.          count = cm.checkCredentials(name, password);
35.          loggedIn = count > 0;
36.       } catch (Exception ex) {
```

```
37.          logger.log(Level.SEVERE, "login failed", ex);
38.          return "internalError";
39.        }
40.        if (loggedIn)
41.          return "loginSuccess";
42.        else
43.          return "loginFailure";
44.      }
45.
46.      public String logout() {
47.        loggedIn = false;
48.        return "login";
49.      }
50. }
```

Listing 12–10   slsb/src/java/com/corejsf/CredentialsManager.java

```
1. package com.corejsf;
2.
3. import java.util.List;
4.
5. import javax.ejb.Stateless;
6. import javax.persistence.EntityManager;
7. import javax.persistence.PersistenceContext;
8. import javax.persistence.Query;
9.
10. @Stateless
11. public class CredentialsManager {
12.    @PersistenceContext(unitName="default")
13.    private EntityManager em;
14.
15.    public int checkCredentials(String name, String password) {
16.      Query query = em.createQuery("SELECT c FROM Credentials c
17.        WHERE c.username = :username")
18.        .setParameter("username", name);
19.      @SuppressWarnings("unchecked")
20.      List<Credentials> result = query.getResultList();
21.      if (result.size() != 1) return 0;
22.      Credentials c = result.get(0);
23.      String storedPassword = c.getPasswd();
24.      if (password.equals(storedPassword.trim()))
25.        return c.incrementLoginCount();
26.      else
27.        return 0;
28.    }
29. }
```

Stateful Session Beans CDI

A stateless session bean is essentially a place to put one or more methods—it is a rather degenerate object. The EJB architecture also defines *stateful session beans*, which can hold state, just like regular Java objects. Of course, stateful session beans are much more heavyweight. The EJB container manages them, perhaps caching them or moving them to another server for load balancing. The container also provides for access control and transaction support when methods are invoked.

The Seam framework (http://seamframework.org) pioneered the ability to use stateful session beans instead of JSF managed beans. The Contexts and Dependency Injection (CDI) specification adds this capability to Java EE 6.

With CDI, your application can be composed of stateful session beans and entity beans, both managed by the EJB container. The JSF pages reference stateful session beans directly. Then the issue of detached entities goes away, and it becomes very simple to access the database from your web application. Of course, you are now relying on the EJB container to manage all your beans. For a simple single-server application, this is a significant overhead, even though EJB containers have become lighter weight and faster than they used to be. As your application grows, it is easier to cluster an EJB application, and the inventors of Seam argue that it is no less efficient.

Here is how you use a stateful session bean with JSF:

```java
@Named("user") @SessionScoped @Stateful
public class UserBean {
    private String name;
    @PersistenceContext(unitName="default") private EntityManager em;
    ...
    public String getName() { return name; } // Accessed in JSF page
    public void setName(String newValue) { name = newValue; }

    public String login() { // Called from JSF page
        doLogin();
        if (loggedIn) return "loginSuccess";
        else return "loginFailure";
    }

    public void doLogin() { // Accesses database
        Query query = em.createQuery(...).setParameter("username", name);
        @SuppressWarnings("unchecked") List<Credentials> result
            = query.getResultList();
        ...
    }
}
```

In the JSF page, you use #{user.name} and #{user.login} in the usual way.

Our sample application has now become extremely simple. The stateful session bean interacts with the JSF pages and the database—see Listing 12–11. The use of JPA has eliminated cumbersome SQL. Transaction handling is automatic.

Listing 12–11 sfsb/src/java/com/corejsf/UserBean.java

```
1. package com.corejsf;
2.
3. import java.util.List;
4. import java.util.logging.Level;
5. import java.util.logging.Logger;
6.
7. import javax.ejb.Stateful;
8. import javax.enterprise.context.SessionScoped;
9. import javax.inject.Named;
10. import javax.persistence.EntityManager;
11. import javax.persistence.PersistenceContext;
12. import javax.persistence.Query;
13.
14. @Named("user")
15. @SessionScoped
16. @Stateful
17. public class UserBean {
18.    private String name;
19.    private String password;
20.    private boolean loggedIn;
21.    private int count;
22.
23.    @PersistenceContext(unitName="default")
24.    private EntityManager em;
25.
26.    public String getName() { return name; }
27.    public void setName(String newValue) { name = newValue; }
28.
29.    public String getPassword() { return password; }
30.    public void setPassword(String newValue) { password = newValue; }
31.
32.    public int getCount() { return count; }
33.
34.    public String login() {
35.       try {
36.          doLogin();
37.       }
38.       catch (Exception ex) {
```

```
39.          Logger.getLogger("com.corejsf").log(Level.SEVERE, "login failed", ex);
40.          return "internalError";
41.       }
42.       if (loggedIn)
43.          return "loginSuccess";
44.       else
45.          return "loginFailure";
46.    }
47.
48.    public String logout() {
49.       loggedIn = false;
50.       return "login";
51.    }
52.
53.    public void doLogin() {
54.       Query query = em.createQuery(
55.          "SELECT c FROM Credentials c WHERE c.username = :username")
56.          .setParameter("username", name);
57.       @SuppressWarnings("unchecked")
58.       List<Credentials> result = query.getResultList();
59.       if (result.size() == 1) {
60.          Credentials c = result.get(0);
61.          String storedPassword = c.getPasswd();
62.          loggedIn = password.equals(storedPassword.trim());
63.          count = c.incrementLoginCount();
64.       }
65.    }
66. }
```

Container-Managed Authentication and Authorization

In the preceding sections, you saw how a web application can use a database to look up user information. It is up to the application to use that information appropriately, to allow or deny users access to certain resources. In this section, we discuss an alternative approach: *container-managed authentication*. This mechanism puts the burden of authenticating users on the application server.

It is much easier to ensure that security is handled consistently for an entire web application if the container manages authentication and authorization. The application programmer can then focus on the flow of the web application without worrying about user privileges.

NOTE: Most of the configuration details in this chapter are specific to Glass-Fish and Tomcat, but other application servers have similar mechanisms.

To protect a set of pages, you specify access control information in the web.xml file. For example, the following security constraint restricts all pages in the protected subdirectory to authenticated users who have the role of registereduser or invitedguest:

```
<security-constraint>
   <web-resource-collection>
      <url-pattern>/faces/protected/*</url-pattern>
      <url-pattern>/protected/*</url-pattern>
   </web-resource-collection>
   <auth-constraint>
      <role-name>registereduser</role-name>
      <role-name>invitedguest</role-name>
   </auth-constraint>
</security-constraint>
```

> NOTE: If you use extension mapping, then you do not add a /faces prefix to the URL pattern.

The role of a user is assigned during authentication. Roles, usernames, and passwords are stored in a user directory, which can be an LDAP directory, a database, or simply a text file.

Next, you need to specify how users authenticate themselves. The most flexible approach is form-based authentication. Add the following entry to web.xml:

```
<login-config>
   <auth-method>FORM</auth-method>
   <form-login-config>
      <form-login-page>/login.html</form-login-page>
      <form-error-page>/noauth.html</form-error-page>
   </form-login-config>
</login-config>
```

The form login configuration specifies a web page into which the user types the username and password. You are free to design any desired appearance for the login page, but you must include a mechanism to submit a request to j_security_check with request parameters named j_username and j_password. The following form will do the job:

```
<form method="POST" action="j_security_check">
   User name: <input type="text" name="j_username"/>
   Password:  <input type="password" name="j_password"/>
   <input type="submit" value="Login"/>
</form>
```

The error page can be any page at all.

When the user requests a protected resource, the login page is displayed (see Figure 12–11). If the user supplies a valid username and password, then the requested page appears. Otherwise, the error page is shown.

> NOTE: To securely transmit the login information from the client to the server, you should use SSL (Secure Sockets Layer). Configuring a server for SSL is beyond the scope of this book. For more information, turn to http://java.sun.com/developer/technicalArticles/WebServices/appserv8-1.html (GlassFish) or http://jakarta.apache.org/tomcat/tomcat-6.0-doc/ssl-howto.html (Tomcat).

Figure 12–11 Requesting a protected resource

You can also specify "basic" authentication by placing the following login configuration into web.xml:

```
<login-config>
    <auth-method>BASIC</auth-method>
    <realm-name>This string shows up in the dialog</realm-name>
</login-config>
```

In that case, the browser pops up a password dialog (see Figure 12–12). However, a professionally designed web site will probably use form-based authentication.

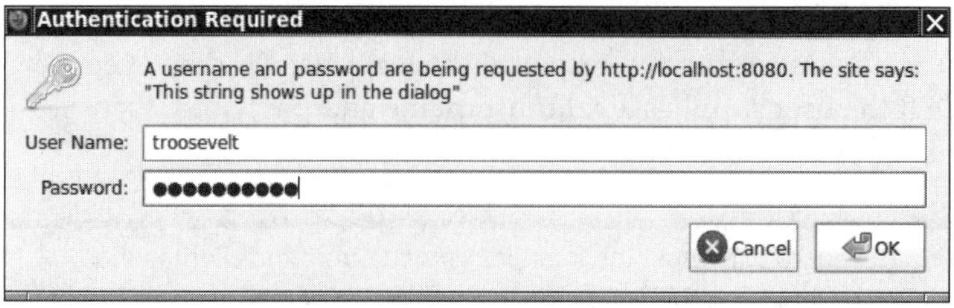

Figure 12–12   Basic authentication

The web.xml file describes only which resources have access restrictions and which roles are allowed access. It is silent on how users, passwords, and roles are stored. You configure that information by specifying a *realm* for the web application. A realm is any mechanism for looking up usernames, passwords, and roles. Application servers commonly support several standard realms that access user information from one of the following sources:

- An LDAP directory
- A relational database
- A file (such as Tomcat's conf/tomcat-users.xml)

In GlassFish, you use the administration interface to configure a realm. We will use a database realm and use our database of usernames and passwords. In the Configuration -> Security -> Realms menu, create a new realm called corejsfRealm (see Figure 12–13). Use the settings in Table 12–2 on page 524.

Make a Groups table in the COREJSF database with these instructions:

```
CREATE TABLE Groups (username VARCHAR(20), groupname VARCHAR(20));
INSERT INTO Groups VALUES ('troosevelt', 'registereduser');
INSERT INTO Groups VALUES ('troosevelt', 'invitedguest');
INSERT INTO Groups VALUES ('tjefferson', 'invitedguest');
```

By default, GlassFish wants to map the group names to role names. You can turn off the mapping in the GlassFish admin console. Select "Security" and check the option "Default Principal to Role Mapping". Or, you can provide a default mapping in a file WEB-INF/sun-web.xml with the following contents:

```
<?xml version="1.0" encoding="UTF-8"?>
<!DOCTYPE sun-web-app PUBLIC
    "-//Sun Microsystems, Inc.//DTD Application Server 9.0 Servlet 2.5//EN"
    "http://www.sun.com/software/appserver/dtds/sun-web-app_2_5-0.dtd">
<sun-web-app>
  <security-role-mapping>
    <role-name>registereduser</role-name>
```

```
        <group-name>registereduser</group-name>
    </security-role-mapping>
    <security-role-mapping>
        <role-name>invitedguest</role-name>
        <group-name>invitedguest</group-name>
    </security-role-mapping>
</sun-web-app>
```

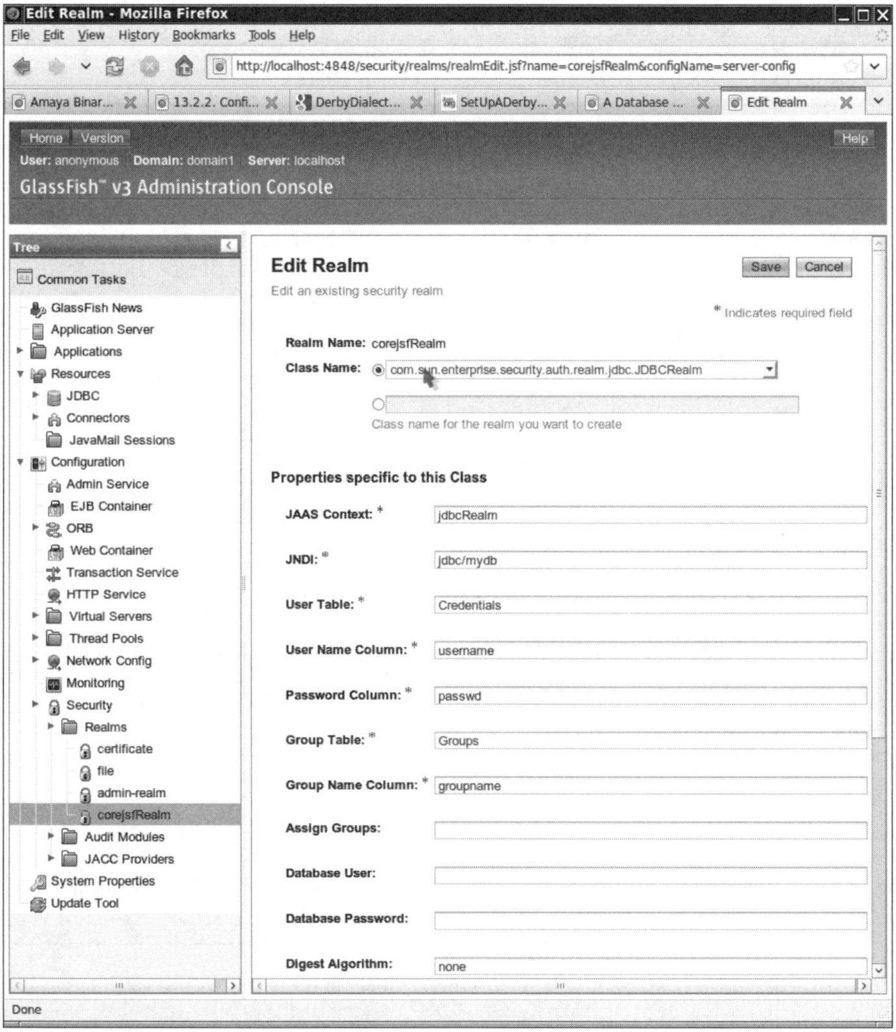

Figure 12–13   Specifying a realm in GlassFish

> **NOTE:** Setting up a realm can be frustrating because so many things must be set correctly, and by default, there are no error messages besides "login failure". Set `javax.enterprise.system.core.security.com.sun.enterprise.security.auth.realm.level` to `FINE` in *glassfish*/`domains/domain1/config/logging.properties` to get better error messages.

Table 12–2   Realm Settings for the Database

Property Name	Value	Notes
Class name	`com.sun.enterprise. security.auth.realm. jdbc.JDBCRealm`	
JAAS context	`jdbcRealm`	This context is defined in *glassfish*/`domains/domain1/config/login.conf`.
JNDI	`jdbc/mydb`	The JDBC resource for the user database—see "Configuring a Database Resource in GlassFish" on page 496.
User table	`Credentials`	Use the same table as for the database examples.
User name column	`username`	The colum name must be the same in the user and group tables.
Password column	`passwd`	Note that `password` is a reserved word in PostgreSQL.
Group table	`Groups`	
Group name column	`groupname`	
Digest algorithm	`none`	For a production system, hash the passwords. If you use `MD5`, you can get the hash by running `echo` *password* `|` `md5sum` .

To configure a realm in Tomcat, you supply a `Realm` element in the `conf/server.xml` file. Here is a typical example:

```
<Realm className="org.apache.catalina.realm.JDBCRealm" debug="99"
    driverName="org.apache.derby.jdbc.ClientDriver"
    connectionURL="jdbc:derby://localhost:1527/COREJSF"
```

```
connectionName="APP" connectionPassword="APP"
userTable="Credentials" userNameCol="username" userCredCol="passwd"
userRoleTable="Groups" roleNameCol="groupname"/>
```

See `http://tomcat.apache.org/tomcat-6.0-doc/realm-howto.html` for additional information about configuring a Tomcat realm.

Since the application server is in charge of authentication and authorization, there is nothing for you to program. Nevertheless, you may want to have programmatic access to the user information. The `HttpServletRequest` yields a small amount of information, in particular, the name of the user who logged in. You get the request object from the external context:

```
ExternalContext external
   = FacesContext.getCurrentInstance().getExternalContext();
HttpServletRequest request
   = (HttpServletRequest) external.getRequest();
String user = request.getRemoteUser();
```

You can also test whether the current user belongs to a given role. For example:

```
String role = "admin";
boolean isAdmin = request.isUserInRole(role);
```

> **NOTE:** Currently, there is no specification for logging off or for switching identities when using container-managed security. This is a problem, particularly for testing web applications. GlassFish and Tomcat use cookies to represent the current user. You need to quit and restart your browser (or at least clear personal data) whenever you want to switch your identity. We resorted to using the text-only Lynx browser for testing because it starts up much faster than a graphical web browser (see Figure 12–14).

We give you a skeleton application that shows container-managed security at work. When you access the protected resource `/faces/protected/welcome.xhtml` (Listing 12–12), then the authentication dialog of Listing 12–13 is displayed. You can proceed only if you enter a username and password of a user belonging to the `registereduser` or `invitedguest` role.

Upon successful authentication, the page shown in Figure 12–15 is displayed. The welcome page shows the name of the registered user and lets you test for role membership.

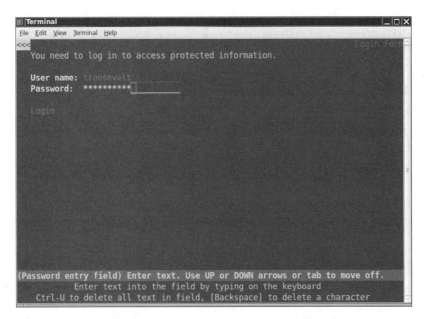

Figure 12–14   Using Lynx for testing a web application

Figure 12–15   Welcome page of the authentication test application

Listing 12–12   accesscontrol/web/protected/welcome.xhtml

```
1. <?xml version="1.0" encoding="UTF-8"?>
2. <!DOCTYPE html PUBLIC "-//W3C//DTD XHTML 1.0 Strict//EN"
3.    "http://www.w3.org/TR/xhtml1/DTD/xhtml1-strict.dtd">
4. <html xmlns="http://www.w3.org/1999/xhtml"
5.    xmlns:h="http://java.sun.com/jsf/html"
6.    xmlns:f="http://java.sun.com/jsf/core">
7. <h:head>
8.    <title>#{msgs.title}</title>
9. </h:head>
10. <h:body>
11.    <h:form>
12.       <p>#{msgs.youHaveAccess}</p>
13.       <h:panelGrid columns="2">
14.          #{msgs.yourUserName}
15.          <h:outputText value="#{user.name}" />
16.
17.          <h:panelGroup>
18.             #{msgs.memberOf}
19.             <h:selectOneMenu onchange="submit()" value="#{user.role}">
20.                <f:selectItem itemValue="" itemLabel="Select a role" />
21.                <f:selectItem itemValue="admin" itemLabel="admin" />
22.                <f:selectItem itemValue="manager" itemLabel="manager" />
23.                <f:selectItem itemValue="registereduser"
24.                   itemLabel="registereduser" />
25.                <f:selectItem itemValue="invitedguest" itemLabel="invitedguest" />
26.             </h:selectOneMenu>
27.          </h:panelGroup>
28.          <h:outputText value="#{user.inRole}" />
29.       </h:panelGrid>
30.    </h:form>
31. </h:body>
32. </html>
```

Listing 12–13   accesscontrol/web/login.html

```
1. <!DOCTYPE html PUBLIC "-//W3C//DTD XHTML 1.0 Strict//EN"
2.    "http://www.w3.org/TR/xhtml1/DTD/xhtml1-strict.dtd">
3. <html xmlns="http://www.w3.org/1999/xhtml">
4. <head>
5. <title>Login Form</title>
6. </head>
7.
8. <body>
9. <form method="post" action="j_security_check">
```

```
10. <p>You need to log in to access protected information.</p>
11. <table>
12.    <tr>
13.       <td>User name:</td>
14.       <td><input type="text" name="j_username" /></td>
15.    </tr>
16.    <tr>
17.       <td>Password:</td>
18.       <td><input type="password" name="j_password" /></td>
19.    </tr>
20. </table>
21. <p><input type="submit" value="Login" /></p>
22. </form>
23. </body>
24. </html>
```

Figure 12–16 shows the directory structure of the application. The web.xml file in Listing 12–14 restricts access to the protected directory. Listing 12–15 contains the page that is displayed when authorization fails. Listing 12–12 contains the protected page. You can find the code for the user bean in Listing 12–16 and the message strings in Listing 12–17.

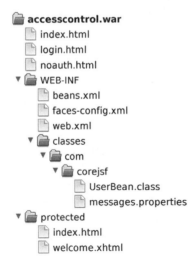

Figure 12–16   Directory structure of the access control application

Listing 12–14   accesscontrol/web/WEB-INF/web.xml

```
1. <?xml version="1.0" encoding="UTF-8"?>
2. <web-app xmlns:xsi="http://www.w3.org/2001/XMLSchema-instance"
3.       xmlns="http://java.sun.com/xml/ns/javaee"
4.       xmlns:web="http://java.sun.com/xml/ns/javaee/web-app_2_5.xsd"
5.       xsi:schemaLocation="http://java.sun.com/xml/ns/javaee
6.          http://java.sun.com/xml/ns/javaee/web-app_2_5.xsd"
7.       version="2.5">
8.    <servlet>
9.       <servlet-name>Faces Servlet</servlet-name>
10.       <servlet-class>javax.faces.webapp.FacesServlet</servlet-class>
11.    </servlet>
12.    <servlet-mapping>
13.       <servlet-name>Faces Servlet</servlet-name>
14.       <url-pattern>/faces/*</url-pattern>
15.    </servlet-mapping>
16.    <welcome-file-list>
17.       <welcome-file>index.xhtml</welcome-file>
18.    </welcome-file-list>
19.    <context-param>
20.       <param-name>javax.faces.PROJECT_STAGE</param-name>
21.       <param-value>Development</param-value>
22.    </context-param>
23.
24.    <security-constraint>
25.       <web-resource-collection>
26.          <web-resource-name>Protected Pages</web-resource-name>
27.          <url-pattern>/faces/protected/*</url-pattern>
28.          <url-pattern>/protected/*</url-pattern>
29.       </web-resource-collection>
30.       <auth-constraint>
31.          <role-name>registereduser</role-name>
32.          <role-name>invitedguest</role-name>
33.       </auth-constraint>
34.    </security-constraint>
35.
36.    <login-config>
37.       <auth-method>FORM</auth-method>
38.       <realm-name>corejsfRealm</realm-name>
39.       <form-login-config>
40.          <form-login-page>/login.html</form-login-page>
41.          <form-error-page>/noauth.html</form-error-page>
42.       </form-login-config>
43.    </login-config>
44.
```

```
45.    <security-role>
46.       <role-name>registereduser</role-name>
47.    </security-role>
48.    <security-role>
49.       <role-name>invitedguest</role-name>
50.    </security-role>
51. </web-app>
```

Listing 12–15   accesscontrol/web/noauth.html

```
1. <!DOCTYPE html PUBLIC "-//W3C//DTD XHTML 1.0 Strict//EN"
2.    "http://www.w3.org/TR/xhtml1/DTD/xhtml1-strict.dtd">
3. <html xmlns="http://www.w3.org/1999/xhtml">
4. <head>
5. <title>Authentication failed</title>
6. </head>
7.
8. <body>
9. <p>Sorry--authentication failed. Please try again.</p>
10. </body>
11. </html>
```

Listing 12–16   accesscontrol/src/java/com/corejsf/UserBean.java

```
1. package com.corejsf;
2.
3. import java.io.Serializable;
4. import java.util.logging.Logger;
5.
6. import javax.inject.Named;
7.    // or import javax.faces.bean.ManagedBean;
8. import javax.enterprise.context.SessionScoped;
9.    // or import javax.faces.bean.SessionScoped;
10. import javax.faces.context.ExternalContext;
11. import javax.faces.context.FacesContext;
12. import javax.servlet.http.HttpServletRequest;
13.
14. @Named("user") // or @ManagedBean(name="user")
15. @SessionScoped
16. public class UserBean implements Serializable {
17.    private String name;
18.    private String role;
19.    private static Logger logger = Logger.getLogger("com.corejsf");
20.
21.    public String getName() {
22.       if (name == null) getUserData();
```

```
23.        return name == null ? "" : name;
24.    }
25.
26.    public String getRole() { return role == null ? "" : role; }
27.    public void setRole(String newValue) { role = newValue; }
28.
29.    public boolean isInRole() {
30.        ExternalContext context
31.            = FacesContext.getCurrentInstance().getExternalContext();
32.        Object requestObject = context.getRequest();
33.        if (!(requestObject instanceof HttpServletRequest)) {
34.            logger.severe("request object has type " + requestObject.getClass());
35.            return false;
36.        }
37.        HttpServletRequest request = (HttpServletRequest) requestObject;
38.        return request.isUserInRole(role);
39.    }
40.
41.    private void getUserData() {
42.        ExternalContext context
43.            = FacesContext.getCurrentInstance().getExternalContext();
44.        Object requestObject = context.getRequest();
45.        if (!(requestObject instanceof HttpServletRequest)) {
46.            logger.severe("request object has type " + requestObject.getClass());
47.            return;
48.        }
49.        HttpServletRequest request = (HttpServletRequest) requestObject;
50.        name = request.getRemoteUser();
51.    }
52. }
```

Listing 12–17   accesscontrol/src/java/com/corejsf/messages.properties

```
1. title=Authentication successful
2. youHaveAccess=You now have access to protected information!
3. yourUserName=Your user name
4. memberOf=Member of
```

🅰🅿�🅸   *javax.servlet.HttpServletRequest*

- String getRemoteUser() **Servlet 2.2**

  Gets the name of the user who is currently logged in, or null if there is no such user.

- boolean isUserInRole(String role) **Servlet 2.2**

  Tests whether the current user belongs to the given role.

Sending Mail

It is fairly common to send mail in a web application. A typical example is a registration confirmation or password reminder. In this section, we give you a brief tutorial in the use of the JavaMail API in a JSF application.

The basic process is similar to using a database pool. You configure a mail resource in your application server or web container. Figure 12–17 shows how to use the GlassFish web interface.

Figure 12–17   Specifying mail session parameters in GlassFish

Table 12–3 shows settings for a GMail account. (You should double-check that GMail still accepts SMTP connections before trying out the sample program with your GMail account.)

 NOTE: For Tomcat instructions, see the section "JavaMail Sessions" in `http://tomcat.apache.org/tomcat-6.0-doc/jndi-resources-howto.html`.

 CAUTION: When specifying mail configuration parameters in GlassFish, you must replace periods with dashes. For example, `mail.auth` becomes `mail-auth`. Moreover, only parameters that start with `mail-` are placed into to the mail session properties.

Table 12–3 Mail Session Parameters

Parameter	Value	Notes
JNDI Name	`mail/gmailAccount`	Use this name in the `@Resource` annotation.
Mail Host	`smtp.gmail.com`	Substitute your SMTP server.
Default User	`your.account`	Your account name.
Default Return Address	`your.account@gmail.com`	The return address for your messages.
Transport Protocol	`smtps`	Use `smtp` if your server doesn't use SSL/TLS.
Transport Protocol Class	`com.sun.mail.smtp.SMTPSSLTransport`	Use `com.sun.mail.smtp.SMTPTransport` if your server doesn't use SSL/TLS.
Additional Parameter `mail-password`	`secret`	Substitute your own password and note the dash in the parameter name.
Additional Parameter `mail-auth`	`true`	Note the dash in the parameter name.

Choose a JNDI name for your mail resource and use it to inject a `javax.mail.Session` object:

```
@Resource(name = "mail/gmailAccount")
private Session mailSession;
```

When you are ready to send the message, use the following code outline:

```
MimeMessage message = new MimeMessage(mailSession);

Address toAddress = new InternetAddress(email address);
message.setRecipient(RecipientType.TO, toAddress);
message.setSubject(subject);
message.setText(message text);
message.saveChanges();

Transport tr = mailSession.getTransport();
String serverPassword = mailSession.getProperty("mail.password");
tr.connect(null, serverPassword);
tr.sendMessage(message, message.getAllRecipients());
tr.close();
```

Note how we retrieve the account password that we placed as an additional parameter when setting up the mail parameters.

 NOTE: Sending mail is notoriously error-prone since most mail servers restrict who can access them in order to combat spam. You may not be able to send mail through your corporate or university server from home, and most free web mail services no longer support SMTP connections. Another challenge with using JavaMail is getting the mail parameters right. If you run into problems, get the JavaMail distribution from http://java.sun.com/products/javamail/downloads and run the smtpsend test program. After you get the right parameters for your mail server with the test program, go back to the application server configuration.

Our sample program provides a registration service that is typical for web applications. A user picks a desired username and supplies an email address. The system generates a random password and emails the login information (see Figure 12–18). For simplicity, we skip the steps of checking that the username is available and of storing the credentials in the database.

Listing 12–18 shows the class that sends out the mail message. The index.xhtml page simply sets the name and emailAddress properties; we do not show it here. Listing 12–19 shows the message bundle.

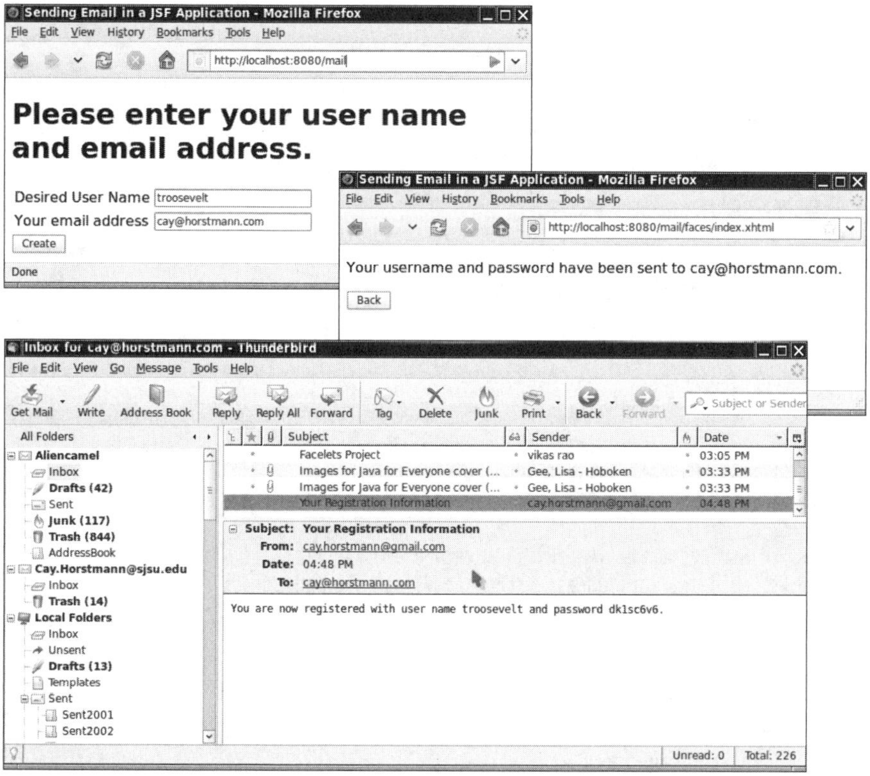

Figure 12–18 A JSF application that sends an email message

Listing 12–18   `mail/src/java/com/corejsf/NewAccount.java`

```
1. package com.corejsf;
2.
3. import java.io.Serializable;
4. import java.text.MessageFormat;
5. import java.util.ResourceBundle;
6. import java.util.logging.Level;
7. import java.util.logging.Logger;
8.
9. import javax.annotation.Resource;
10. import javax.inject.Named;
11.    // or import javax.faces.bean.ManagedBean;
12. import javax.enterprise.context.SessionScoped;
13.    // or import javax.faces.bean.SessionScoped;
14. import javax.mail.Address;
15. import javax.mail.MessagingException;
```

```
16. import javax.mail.Session;
17. import javax.mail.Transport;
18. import javax.mail.Message.RecipientType;
19. import javax.mail.internet.InternetAddress;
20. import javax.mail.internet.MimeMessage;
21.
22. @Named // or @ManagedBean
23. @SessionScoped
24. public class NewAccount implements Serializable {
25.    private String name;
26.    private String emailAddress;
27.    private String password;
28.
29.    @Resource(name="mail/gmailAccount")
30.    private Session mailSession;
31.
32.    public String getName() { return name; }
33.    public void setName(String newValue) { name = newValue; }
34.
35.    public String getEmailAddress() { return emailAddress; }
36.    public void setEmailAddress(String newValue) { emailAddress = newValue; }
37.
38.    public String create() {
39.       try {
40.          createAccount();
41.          sendNotification();
42.          return "done";
43.       }
44.       catch (Exception ex) {
45.          Logger.getLogger("com.corejsf").log(Level.SEVERE, "login failed", ex);
46.          return "error";
47.       }
48.    }
49.
50.    private void createAccount() {
51.       // Generate a random password; an 8-digit number in base 36.
52.       int BASE = 36;
53.       int LENGTH = 8;
54.       password = Long.toString((long)(Math.pow(BASE, LENGTH) * Math.random()), BASE);
55.       /*
56.        * In a real application, we would now make sure that the username is available
57.        * and save the username/password in a database.
58.        */
59.    }
60.
61.    private void sendNotification() throws MessagingException {
62.       ResourceBundle bundle = ResourceBundle.getBundle("com.corejsf.messages");
```

```
63.        String subject = bundle.getString("subject");
64.        String body = bundle.getString("body");
65.        String messageText = MessageFormat.format(body, name, password);
66.        mailSession.setDebug(true);
67.        MimeMessage message = new MimeMessage(mailSession);
68.
69.        Address toAddress = new InternetAddress(emailAddress);
70.        message.setRecipient(RecipientType.TO, toAddress);
71.        message.setSubject(subject);
72.        message.setText(messageText);
73.        message.saveChanges();
74.
75.        Transport tr = mailSession.getTransport();
76.        String serverPassword = mailSession.getProperty("mail.password");
77.        tr.connect(null, serverPassword);
78.        tr.sendMessage(message, message.getAllRecipients());
79.        tr.close();
80.    }
81. }
```

Listing 12–19   mail/src/java/com/corejsf/messages.properties

```
1. title=Sending Email in a JSF Application
2. enterNameAndEmail=Please enter your user name and email address.
3. name=Desired User Name
4. email=Your email address
5. emailSent=Your username and password have been sent to {0}.
6. internalError=Internal Error
7. internalError_detail=To our chagrin, an internal error has occurred. \
8.    Please report this problem to our technical staff.
9. create=Create
10. back=Back
11. subject=Your Registration Information
12. body=You are now registered with user name {0} and password {1}.
```

Using Web Services

When a web application needs to get information from an external source, it typically uses a remote procedure call mechanism. *Web services* have emerged as a popular technology for this purpose.

Currently, there are two different schools of thought on how to implement web services. The "WS-*" approach uses XML for requests and responses and has a well-developed (but complex) mechanism for encoding arbitrary data into XML. The "RESTful" approach encodes requests in URLs and responses in a choice of formats (XML, JSON, plain text, and so on, as specified in an HTTP header). It is up to the client how to read the response. There are merits to both approaches.

JSF has built-in support for consuming a WS-* web service, which we describe in this section.

We will look at a simple weather service described at `http://wiki.cdyne.com/wiki/index.php?title=CDYNE_Weather`. A primary attraction of web services is that they are language-neutral. We will access the service by using the Java programming language, but other developers can just as easily use C++ or PHP. A descriptor file, written in the Web Services Definition Language (WSDL), describes the services in a language-independent manner. For example, the WSDL for the CDYNE weather service (located at `http://ws.cdyne.com/WeatherWS/Weather.asmx?wsdl`) describes an `GetCityForecastByZIP` operation as follows:

```
<wsdl:operation name="GetCityForecastByZIP">
   <wsdl:input message="tns:GetCityForecastByZIPSoapIn"/>
   <wsdl:output message="tns:GetCityForecastByZIPSoapOut"/>
</wsdl:operation>
...
<wsdl:message name="GetCityForecastByZIPSoapIn">
   <wsdl:part name="parameters" element="tns:GetCityForecastByZIP"/>
</wsdl:message>
<wsdl:message name="GetCityForecastByZIPSoapOut">
   <wsdl:part name="parameters" element="tns:GetCityForecastByZIPResponse"/>
</wsdl:message>
```

Here is the definition of the `GetCityForecastByZIP` and `GetCityForecastByZIPResponse` type:

```
<s:element name="GetCityForecastByZIP">
   <s:complexType>
      <s:sequence>
         <s:element minOccurs="0" maxOccurs="1" name="ZIP" type="s:string"/>
      </s:sequence>
   </s:complexType>
</s:element>
```

This simply means that the service requires an optional string named `ZIP` as a parameter. The JAX-WS technology maps the WSDL type description to a Java type, in this case `String`.

The return type is more complex:

```
<s:element name="GetCityForecastByZIPResponse">
   <s:complexType>
      <s:sequence>
         <s:element minOccurs="0" maxOccurs="1" name="GetCityForecastByZIPResult"
```

```
          type="tns:ForecastReturn"/>
      </s:sequence>
    </s:complexType>
  </s:element>

  <s:complexType name="ForecastReturn">
    <s:sequence>
      <s:element minOccurs="1" maxOccurs="1" name="Success" type="s:boolean"/>
      <s:element minOccurs="0" maxOccurs="1" name="ResponseText" type="s:string"/>
      <s:element minOccurs="0" maxOccurs="1" name="State" type="s:string"/>
      <s:element minOccurs="0" maxOccurs="1" name="City" type="s:string"/>
      <s:element minOccurs="0" maxOccurs="1" name="WeatherStationCity"
          type="s:string"/>
      <s:element minOccurs="0" maxOccurs="1" name="ForecastResult"
          type="tns:ArrayOfForecast"/>
    </s:sequence>
  </s:complexType>
```

JAX-WS maps the return type to a Java class ForecastReturn with methods:

```
public boolean getSuccess()
public String getResponseText()
public String getState()
public String getCity()
public String getWeatherStationCity()
public ArrayOfForecast getForecastResult()
```

The ArrayOfForecast type is also defined in the WSDL file. The corresponding Java class has a method:

```
List<Forecast> getForecast()
```

Finally, the Forecast class has methods getDesciption [sic], getTemperatures, and so on. We aren't interested in the details of this particular service; what matters is that the WSDL file contains all the information needed to process the parameters and return values of the service.

To find out how to invoke the search service, locate the service element in the WSDL file:

```
<wsdl:service name="Weather">
  <wsdl:port name="WeatherSoap" binding="tns:WeatherSoap">
    <soap:address location="http://ws.cdyne.com/WeatherWS/Weather.asmx"/>
  </wsdl:port>
  ...
</wsdl:service>
```

This tells us that we need to make the call through a "port" object of type WeatherSoap that we obtain from a "service" object of type Weather.

You obtain the service object through dependency injection. Annotate a field with the @WebServiceRef annotation:

```
@WebServiceRef(wsdlLocation="http://ws.cdyne.com/WeatherWS/Weather.asmx?wsdl")
private Weather service;
```

Then call:

```
ForecastReturn ret = service.getWeatherSoap().getCityForecastByZIP(zip);
```

From the programmer's point of view, calling a WS-* web service is extremely simple. Just make a call to a Java method. Behind the scenes, the JAX-WS framework translates your parameter objects from Java to XML, sends the XML to the server (using a protocol called SOAP that you need not worry about), retrieves the result, and translates it from XML to Java.

The hardest part of using a web service is figuring out the parameter and return types, and that could be made easy by documenting them well.

Of course, you need to generate the classes that the service uses. The wsimport tool (included in recent versions of the JDK and in GlassFish) automatically generates the classes from the WSDL file. Unfortunately, it is a bit of a hassle to generate classes that implement the Serializable interface. Place this magic into a file jaxb-bindings.xml:

```
<?xml version="1.0" encoding="UTF-8"?>
<xs:schema xmlns:xs="http://www.w3.org/2001/XMLSchema"
    xmlns:jaxb="http://java.sun.com/xml/ns/jaxb"
    xmlns:xjc="http://java.sun.com/xml/ns/jaxb/xjc"
    elementFormDefault="qualified" attributeFormDefault="unqualified"
    jaxb:extensionBindingPrefixes="xjc" jaxb:version="2.1">
    <xs:annotation>
        <xs:appinfo>
            <jaxb:globalBindings>
                <xjc:serializable />
            </jaxb:globalBindings>
        </xs:appinfo>
    </xs:annotation>
</xs:schema>
```

Then run these commands:

```
wsimport -b jaxb-bindings.xml -p com.corejsf.ws
    http://ws.cdyne.com/WeatherWS/Weather.asmx?wsdl
jar cvf weather-ws.jar com/corejsf/ws/*.class
```

(The first command must be typed on a single line.) Place the resulting JAR file into the WEB-INF/lib directory of your JSF application.

Our sample application is straightforward. The user specifies a zip code and clicks the "Search" button (see Figure 12–19).

Figure 12–19 Searching for weather information

The service returns seven days worth of weather information (see Figure 12–20). This shows that the web service is successful. We leave it as the proverbial exercise for the reader to extend the functionality of the application.

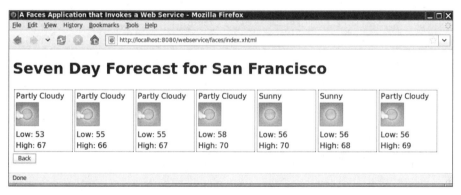

Figure 12–20 A weather forecast

The bean class in Listing 12–20 contains the call to the web service. We stash away the city and list of Forecast objects so that the success.xhtml page can display the result.

Listings 12–21 and 12–22 show the JSF pages. The success.xhtml page iterates over the Forecast objects that were obtained from the weather service.

> NOTE: The Forecast class really has a property named desciption. Please don't send us any error reports about that.

Listing 12–20   webservice/src/java/com/corejsf/WeatherBean.java

```
1. package com.corejsf;
2.
3. import java.util.List;
4.
5. import javax.inject.Named;
6.    // or import javax.faces.bean.ManagedBean;
7. import javax.enterprise.context.SessionScoped;
8.    // or import javax.faces.bean.SessionScoped;
9. import javax.xml.ws.WebServiceRef;
10.
11. import com.corejsf.ws.Forecast;
12. import com.corejsf.ws.ForecastReturn;
13. import com.corejsf.ws.Weather;
14. import java.io.Serializable;
15. import java.util.logging.Level;
16. import java.util.logging.Logger;
17.
18. @Named // or @ManagedBean
19. @SessionScoped
20. public class WeatherBean implements Serializable {
21.    @WebServiceRef(wsdlLocation="http://ws.cdyne.com/WeatherWS/Weather.asmx?wsdl")
22.    private Weather service;
23.
24.    private String zip;
25.    private String city;
26.    private List<Forecast> response;
27.
28.    public String getZip() { return zip; }
29.    public void setZip(String newValue) { zip = newValue; }
30.
31.    public List<Forecast> getResponse() { return response; }
32.    public String getCity() { return city; }
33.
34.    public String search() {
35.       try {
36.          ForecastReturn ret = service.getWeatherSoap().getCityForecastByZIP(zip);
37.          response = ret.getForecastResult().getForecast();
38.          for (Forecast f : response)
39.             if (f.getDesciption() == null || f.getDesciption().length() == 0)
40.                f.setDesciption("Not Available");
41.          city = ret.getCity();
42.          return "success";
43.       } catch(Exception e) {
44.          Logger.getLogger("com.corejsf").log(Level.SEVERE, "Remote call failed", e);
```

```
45.          return "error";
46.      }
47.  }
48. }
```

Listing 12–21   webservices/web/index.xhtml

```
1. <?xml version="1.0" encoding="UTF-8"?>
2. <!DOCTYPE html PUBLIC "-//W3C//DTD XHTML 1.0 Transitional//EN"
3. "http://www.w3.org/TR/xhtml1/DTD/xhtml1-transitional.dtd">
4. <html xmlns="http://www.w3.org/1999/xhtml"
5.      xmlns:h="http://java.sun.com/jsf/html">
6.    <h:head>
7.      <link href="styles.css" rel="stylesheet" type="text/css"/>
8.      <title>#{msgs.title}</title>
9.    </h:head>
10.   <h:body>
11.     <h:form>
12.       <h1>#{msgs.weatherSearch}</h1>
13.       #{msgs.zip}
14.       <h:inputText value="#{weatherBean.zip}"/>
15.       <h:commandButton value="#{msgs.search}" action="#{weatherBean.search}"/>
16.     </h:form>
17.   </h:body>
18. </html>
```

Listing 12–22   webservices/web/success.xhtml

```
1. <?xml version="1.0" encoding="UTF-8"?>
2. <!DOCTYPE html PUBLIC "-//W3C//DTD XHTML 1.0 Transitional//EN"
3. "http://www.w3.org/TR/xhtml1/DTD/xhtml1-transitional.dtd">
4. <html xmlns="http://www.w3.org/1999/xhtml"
5.      xmlns:h="http://java.sun.com/jsf/html"
6.      xmlns:f="http://java.sun.com/jsf/core"
7.      xmlns:ui="http://java.sun.com/jsf/facelets"
8.      xmlns:fn="http://java.sun.com/jsp/jstl/functions">
9.    <h:head>
10.     <title>#{msgs.title}</title>
11.   </h:head>
12.   <h:body>
13.     <h:form>
14.       <h1>
15.         <h:outputFormat value="#{msgs.searchResult}">
16.           <f:param value="#{weatherBean.city}"/>
17.         </h:outputFormat>
18.       </h1>
```

```
19.        <table>
20.          <tr>
21.            <ui:repeat value="#{weatherBean.response}" var="item">
22.              <td>
23.                <h:panelGrid columns="1"
24.                         style="width: 8em; border: thin dotted;">
25.                  <h:outputText value="#{item.desciption}"/>
26.                  <h:graphicImage library="images"
27.                      name="#{fn:replace(item.desciption, ' ', '')}.gif"/>
28.                  <h:outputText
29.                      value=
30.                      "#{msgs.low}: #{item.temperatures.morningLow}"/>
31.                  <h:outputText value=
32.                      "#{msgs.high}: #{item.temperatures.daytimeHigh}"/>
33.                </h:panelGrid>
34.              </td>
35.            </ui:repeat>
36.          </tr>
37.        </table>
38.        <h:commandButton value="#{msgs.back}" action="index"/>
39.      </h:form>
40.    </h:body>
41. </html>
```

Conclusion

You have now seen how your web applications can connect to external services, such as databases, email, and web services. Application servers provide common services for database connection pools, authentication realms, and so on. Dependency injection provides a convenient and portable mechanism for locating the classes that are needed to access these services.

How Do I . . . ?

Chapter 13

The preceding chapters covered the JSF technology in a systematic manner, organized by core concepts. However, every technology has certain aspects that defy systematic exposure, and JSF is no exception. At times, you will ask yourself "How do I . . . ?" and not find an answer, perhaps because JSF does not really offer support for the feature or because the solution is unintuitive. This chapter was designed to help out. We answer, in somewhat random order, common questions that we found in discussion groups or that we received from readers.

How do I find more components?

The JSF standard defines a minimal set of components. The only standard component that goes beyond basic HTML is the data table. This comes as a disappointment to anyone who is lured by the promise of JSF to be "Swing for the web".

You may well wonder why the JSF specification developers did not include a set of professionally designed components such as trees, date and time pickers, and the like. However, it takes tremendous skill to do this, and it is a skill that is entirely different from being able to produce a technology specification.

Here are several component libraries that are worth investigating.

- ICEfaces (http://icefaces.org) is an open source library of components with Ajax support. There is a Netbeans plugin for ICEfaces. Version 2 is compatible with JSF 2.0.

- RichFaces (http://www.jboss.org/jbossrichfaces/) is another open source component library. It is a part of the JBoss application server but can also be used separately. Version 4 is compatible with JSF 2.0.

- PrimeFaces (http://primefaces.org) and OpenFaces (http://openfaces.org) are two promising open source libraries with very rich selections of components.

- The ADF Faces component set by Oracle (http://oracle.com/technology/products/adf/adffaces) is free, but not open source. It too features a good set of well-designed components, includes Ajax functionality, and the ability to change the look and feel with skins.

- The Apache Trinidad library (http://myfaces.apache.org/trinidad) is an open source library that originated with an earlier version of ADF Faces that Oracle donated to the Apache foundation.

- The Apache Tomahawk library (http://myfaces.apache.org/tomahawk) has a number of non-visual components that are useful to solve specific JSF issues, but the visual components are not very attractive.

- The Java BluePrints project has developed a set of Ajax components (https://blueprints.dev.java.net/ajaxcomponents.html). These include autocompletion, Google map interfaces, pop-up balloons, a file upload with a progress indicator, and several other pretty and useful components.

You can find a listing of additional components at http://jsfcentral.com/products/components.

How do I support file uploads?

The users of your application may want to upload files, such as photos or documents (see Figure 13–1 and Figure 13–2).

Unfortunately, there is no standard file upload component in JSF. However, it turns out that it is fairly straightforward to implement one. The hard work has already been done by the folks at the Apache organization in the Commons file upload library (see http://jakarta.apache.org/commons/fileupload). We will show you how to incorporate the library into a JSF component.

> NOTE: The Tomahawk component set contains a file upload component with slightly different attributes from ours (see `http://myfaces.apache.org/tomahawk`). The article `http://today.java.net/pub/a/today/2006/02/09/file-uploads-with-ajax-and-jsf.html` shows how you can add an Ajax progress bar to a file upload component.

A file upload is different from all other form requests. When the form data (including the uploaded file) is sent from the client to the server, it is encoded with the "multipart/form-data" encoding instead of the usual "application/x-www-form-urlencoded" encoding.

Unfortunately, JSF does not handle this encoding at all. To overcome this issue, we install a *servlet filter* that intercepts a file upload and turns uploaded files into request attributes and all other form data into request parameters. (We use a utility method in the Commons file upload library for the dirty work of decoding a multipart/form-data request.)

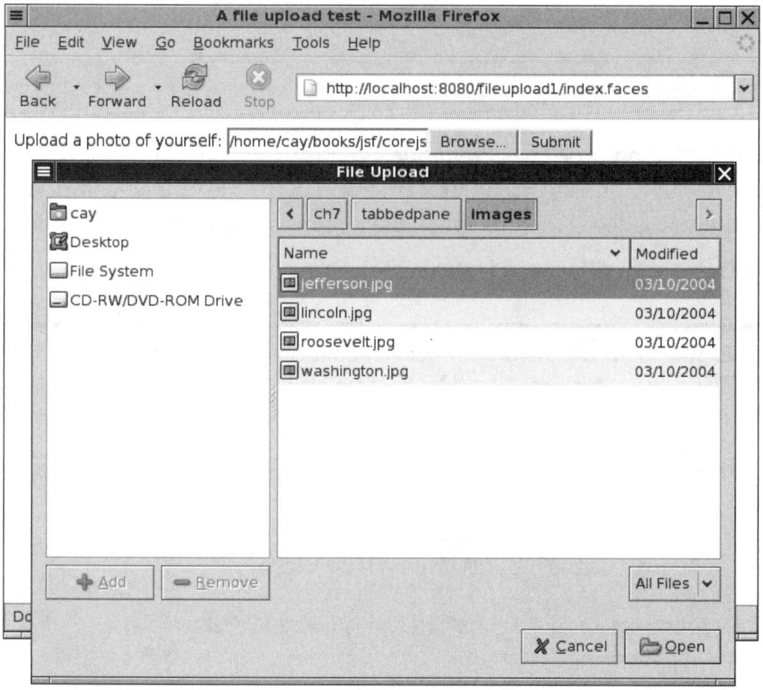

Figure 13–1 Uploading an image file

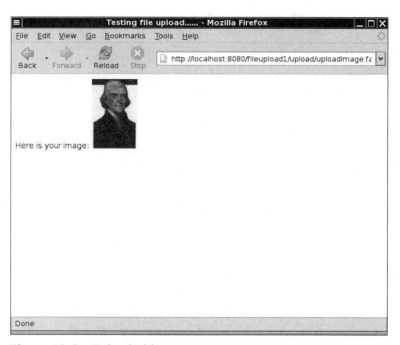

Figure 13–2   Uploaded image

The JSF application then processes the request parameters, blissfully unaware
that they were not URL encoded. The decode method of the file upload component
either places the uploaded data into a disk file or stores it in a value expression.

The code for the servlet filter is in Listing 13–1 on page 552.

 NOTE: You can find general information about servlet filters at
http://java.sun.com/products/servlet/Filters.html.

You need to install the filter in the web.xml file, using this syntax:

```
<filter>
   <filter-name>Upload Filter</filter-name>
   <filter-class>com.corejsf.UploadFilter</filter-class>
   <init-param>
      <param-name>com.corejsf.UploadFilter.sizeThreshold</param-name>
      <param-value>1024</param-value>
   </init-param>
</filter>
<filter-mapping>
   <filter-name>Upload Filter</filter-name>
```

```
    <url-pattern>/upload/*</url-pattern>
  </filter-mapping>
```

Alternatively, you can use an annotation:

```
@WebFilter(urlPatterns="/upload/*", initParams={
    @WebInitParam(name="com.corejsf.UploadFilter.sizeThreshold", value="1024")
})
public class UploadFilter
```

The filter uses the com.corejsf.UploadFilter.sizeThreshold initialization parameter to configure the file upload object. Files larger than 1024 bytes are saved to a temporary disk location rather than being held in memory. Our filter supports an additional initialization parameter, com.corejsf.UploadFilter.repositoryPath, the temporary location for uploaded files before they are moved to a permanent place. The filter sets the corresponding properties of the DiskFileUpload object of the Commons file upload library.

The filter mapping restricts the filter to URLs that start with /faces/upload/. Thus, we avoid unnecessary filtering of other requests.

Figure 13–3 shows the directory structure of the sample application.

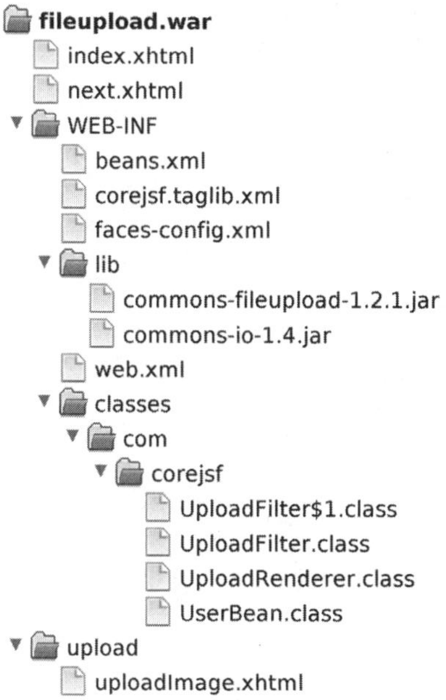

```
📁 fileupload.war
    📄 index.xhtml
    📄 next.xhtml
  ▼ 📁 WEB-INF
        📄 beans.xml
        📄 corejsf.taglib.xml
        📄 faces-config.xml
      ▼ 📁 lib
            📄 commons-fileupload-1.2.1.jar
            📄 commons-io-1.4.jar
        📄 web.xml
      ▼ 📁 classes
        ▼ 📁 com
          ▼ 📁 corejsf
                📄 UploadFilter$1.class
                📄 UploadFilter.class
                📄 UploadRenderer.class
                📄 UserBean.class
  ▼ 📁 upload
        📄 uploadImage.xhtml
```

Figure 13–3   The directory structure of the file upload application

Listing 13–1   fileupload/src/java/com/corejsf/UploadFilter.java

```
 1. package com.corejsf;
 2.
 3. import java.io.File;
 4. import java.io.IOException;
 5. import java.util.Collections;
 6. import java.util.Enumeration;
 7. import java.util.HashMap;
 8. import java.util.List;
 9. import java.util.Map;
10. import javax.servlet.Filter;
11. import javax.servlet.FilterChain;
12. import javax.servlet.FilterConfig;
13. import javax.servlet.ServletException;
14. import javax.servlet.ServletRequest;
15. import javax.servlet.ServletResponse;
16. import javax.servlet.annotation.WebFilter;
17. import javax.servlet.http.HttpServletRequest;
18. import javax.servlet.http.HttpServletRequestWrapper;
19. import org.apache.commons.fileupload.FileItem;
20. import org.apache.commons.fileupload.FileUploadException;
21. import org.apache.commons.fileupload.disk.DiskFileItemFactory;
22. import org.apache.commons.fileupload.servlet.ServletFileUpload;
23.
24. public class UploadFilter implements Filter {
25.    private int sizeThreshold = -1;
26.    private String repositoryPath;
27.
28.    public void init(FilterConfig config) throws ServletException {
29.       repositoryPath = config.getInitParameter(
30.          "com.corejsf.UploadFilter.repositoryPath");
31.       try {
32.          String paramValue = config.getInitParameter(
33.             "com.corejsf.UploadFilter.sizeThreshold");
34.          if (paramValue != null)
35.             sizeThreshold = Integer.parseInt(paramValue);
36.       }
37.       catch (NumberFormatException ex) {
38.          ServletException servletEx = new ServletException();
39.          servletEx.initCause(ex);
40.          throw servletEx;
41.       }
42.    }
43.
44.    public void destroy() {
45.    }
```

```
46.
47.    public void doFilter(ServletRequest request,
48.       ServletResponse response, FilterChain chain)
49.       throws IOException, ServletException {
50.
51.       if (!(request instanceof HttpServletRequest)) {
52.          chain.doFilter(request, response);
53.          return;
54.       }
55.
56.       HttpServletRequest httpRequest = (HttpServletRequest) request;
57.
58.       boolean isMultipartContent
59.          = ServletFileUpload.isMultipartContent(httpRequest);
60.       if (!isMultipartContent) {
61.          chain.doFilter(request, response);
62.          return;
63.       }
64.
65.       DiskFileItemFactory factory = new DiskFileItemFactory();
66.       if (sizeThreshold >= 0)
67.          factory.setSizeThreshold(sizeThreshold);
68.       if (repositoryPath != null)
69.          factory.setRepository(new File(repositoryPath));
70.       ServletFileUpload upload = new ServletFileUpload(factory);
71.
72.       try {
73.          @SuppressWarnings("unchecked") List<FileItem> items
74.             = (List<FileItem>) upload.parseRequest(httpRequest);
75.          final Map<String, String[]> map = new HashMap<String, String[]>();
76.          for (FileItem item : items) {
77.             String str = item.getString();
78.             if (item.isFormField())
79.                map.put(item.getFieldName(), new String[] { str });
80.             else
81.                httpRequest.setAttribute(item.getFieldName(), item);
82.          }
83.
84.          chain.doFilter(new
85.             HttpServletRequestWrapper(httpRequest) {
86.                public Map<String, String[]> getParameterMap() {
87.                   return map;
88.                }
89.                // busywork follows ... should have been part of the wrapper
90.                public String[] getParameterValues(String name) {
91.                   Map<String, String[]> map = getParameterMap();
92.                   return (String[]) map.get(name);
```

```
93.                    }
94.                    public String getParameter(String name) {
95.                        String[] params = getParameterValues(name);
96.                        if (params == null) return null;
97.                        return params[0];
98.                    }
99.                    public Enumeration<String> getParameterNames() {
100.                       Map<String, String[]> map = getParameterMap();
101.                       return Collections.enumeration(map.keySet());
102.                   }
103.                }, response);
104.        } catch (FileUploadException ex) {
105.            ServletException servletEx = new ServletException();
106.            servletEx.initCause(ex);
107.            throw servletEx;
108.        }
109.    }
110.}
```

Now we move on to the upload component. It supports two attributes: value and target. The value attribute denotes a value expression into which the file contents are stored. This makes sense for short files. More commonly, you will use the target attribute to specify the target location of the file.

The implementation of the FileUploadRenderer class in Listing 13–2 is straightforward. The encodeBegin method renders the HTML element. The decode method retrieves the file items that the servlet filter placed into the request attributes and disposes of them as directed by the tag attributes. The target attribute denotes a file relative to the server directory containing the root of the web application.

Finally, when using the file upload tag, you need to remember to set the form encoding to "multipart/form-data" (see Listing 13–3).

Listing 13–2 fileupload/src/java/com/corejsf/UploadRenderer.java

```
1. package com.corejsf;
2.
3. import java.io.File;
4. import java.io.IOException;
5. import java.io.InputStream;
6. import java.io.UnsupportedEncodingException;
7. import javax.el.ValueExpression;
8. import javax.faces.FacesException;
9. import javax.faces.component.EditableValueHolder;
10. import javax.faces.component.UIComponent;
```

```
11. import javax.faces.context.ExternalContext;
12. import javax.faces.context.FacesContext;
13. import javax.faces.context.ResponseWriter;
14. import javax.faces.render.FacesRenderer;
15. import javax.faces.render.Renderer;
16. import javax.servlet.ServletContext;
17. import javax.servlet.http.HttpServletRequest;
18. import org.apache.commons.fileupload.FileItem;
19.
20. @FacesRenderer(componentFamily="javax.faces.Input",
21.     rendererType="com.corejsf.Upload")
22. public class UploadRenderer extends Renderer {
23.     public void encodeBegin(FacesContext context, UIComponent component)
24.         throws IOException {
25.         if (!component.isRendered()) return;
26.         ResponseWriter writer = context.getResponseWriter();
27.
28.         String clientId = component.getClientId(context);
29.
30.         writer.startElement("input", component);
31.         writer.writeAttribute("type", "file", "type");
32.         writer.writeAttribute("name", clientId, "clientId");
33.         writer.endElement("input");
34.         writer.flush();
35.     }
36.
37.     public void decode(FacesContext context, UIComponent component) {
38.         ExternalContext external = context.getExternalContext();
39.         HttpServletRequest request = (HttpServletRequest) external.getRequest();
40.         String clientId = component.getClientId(context);
41.         FileItem item = (FileItem) request.getAttribute(clientId);
42.
43.         Object newValue;
44.         ValueExpression valueExpr = component.getValueExpression("value");
45.         if (valueExpr != null) {
46.             Class<?> valueType = valueExpr.getType(context.getELContext());
47.             if (valueType == byte[].class) {
48.                 newValue = item.get();
49.             }
50.             else if (valueType == InputStream.class) {
51.                 try {
52.                     newValue = item.getInputStream();
53.                 } catch (IOException ex) {
54.                     throw new FacesException(ex);
55.                 }
56.             }
57.             else {
```

```
58.            String encoding = request.getCharacterEncoding();
59.            if (encoding != null)
60.               try {
61.                  newValue = item.getString(encoding);
62.               } catch (UnsupportedEncodingException ex) {
63.                  newValue = item.getString();
64.               }
65.            else
66.               newValue = item.getString();
67.         }
68.         ((EditableValueHolder) component).setSubmittedValue(newValue);
69.         ((EditableValueHolder) component).setValid(true);
70.      }
71.
72.      Object target = component.getAttributes().get("target");
73.
74.      if (target != null) {
75.         File file;
76.         if (target instanceof File)
77.            file = (File) target;
78.         else {
79.            ServletContext servletContext
80.               = (ServletContext) external.getContext();
81.            String realPath = servletContext.getRealPath(target.toString());
82.            file = new File(realPath);
83.         }
84.
85.         try { // ugh--write is declared with "throws Exception"
86.            item.write(file);
87.         } catch (Exception ex) {
88.            throw new FacesException(ex);
89.         }
90.      }
91.   }
92. }
```

Listing 13–3   fileupload/web/upload/uploadImage.xhtml

```
1. <?xml version="1.0" encoding="UTF-8"?>
2. <!DOCTYPE html PUBLIC "-//W3C//DTD XHTML 1.0 Strict//EN"
3. "http://www.w3.org/TR/xhtml1/DTD/xhtml1-strict.dtd">
4. <html xmlns="http://www.w3.org/1999/xhtml"
5.    xmlns:h="http://java.sun.com/jsf/html"
6.    xmlns:corejsf="http://corejsf.com">
7. <h:head>
8.    <title>A file upload test</title>
9. </h:head>
```

```
10. <h:body>
11.    <h:form enctype="multipart/form-data">
12.       Upload a photo of yourself:
13.       <corejsf:upload target="upload/#{user.id}_image.jpg" />
14.       <h:commandButton value="Submit" action="/next" />
15.    </h:form>
16. </h:body>
17. </html>
```

How do I show an image map?

To implement a client-side image map, supply the usemap attribute with the h:outputImage element:

```
<h:outputImage value="image location" usemap="#aLabel"/>
```

You can then specify the map in HTML in the JSF page:

```
<map name="aLabel">
   <area shape="polygon" coords="..." href="...">
   <area shape="rect" coords="..." href="...">
   ...
</map>
```

However, this approach does not integrate well with JSF navigation. It would be nicer if the map areas acted like command buttons or links.

Chapter 13 of the Java EE 5 tutorial (http://java.sun.com/javaee/5/docs/tutorial/doc) includes sample map and area tags that overcome this limitation.

To see the image map in action, load the bookstore6 web application that is included with the tutorial (see Figure 13–4). Here is how the tags are used in the tutorial application:

```
<h:graphicImage id="mapImage" url="/template/world.jpg" alt="#{bundle.ChooseLocale}"
      usemap="#worldMap" />
<b:map id="worldMap" current="NAmericas" immediate="true" action="bookstore"
      actionListener="#{localeBean.chooseLocaleFromMap}"  >
   <b:area id="NAmerica" value="#{NA}" onmouseover="/template/world_namer.jpg"
      onmouseout="/template/world.jpg" targetImage="mapImage" />
   <b:area id="SAmerica" value="#{SA}" onmouseover="/template/world_samer.jpg"
      onmouseout="/template/world.jpg" targetImage="mapImage" />
      ...
</b:map>
```

The area values are defined in faces-config.xml, such as:

```
<managed-bean>
   <managed-bean-name> NA </managed-bean-name>
   <managed-bean-class> com.sun.bookstore6.model.ImageArea </managed-bean-class>
```

```
<managed-bean-scope> application </managed-bean-scope>
<managed-property>
    <property-name>coords</property-name>
    <value>
53,109,1,110,2,167,19,168,52,149,67,164,67,165,68,167,70,168,72,170,74,172,75,174,77,
175,79,177,81,179,80,179,77,179,81,179,81,178,80,178,82,211,28,238,15,233,15,242,31,
252,36,247,36,246,32,239,89,209,92,216,93,216,100,216,103,218,113,217,116,224,124,221,
128,230,163,234,185,189,178,177,162,188,143,173,79,173,73,163,79,157,64,142,54,139,53,
109
    </value>
</managed-property>
</managed-bean>
```

Alternatively, you can use a technique that we showed in Chapter 7. Put the image inside a command button, and process the x and y coordinates on the server side:

```
<h:commandButton image="..." actionListener="..."/>
```

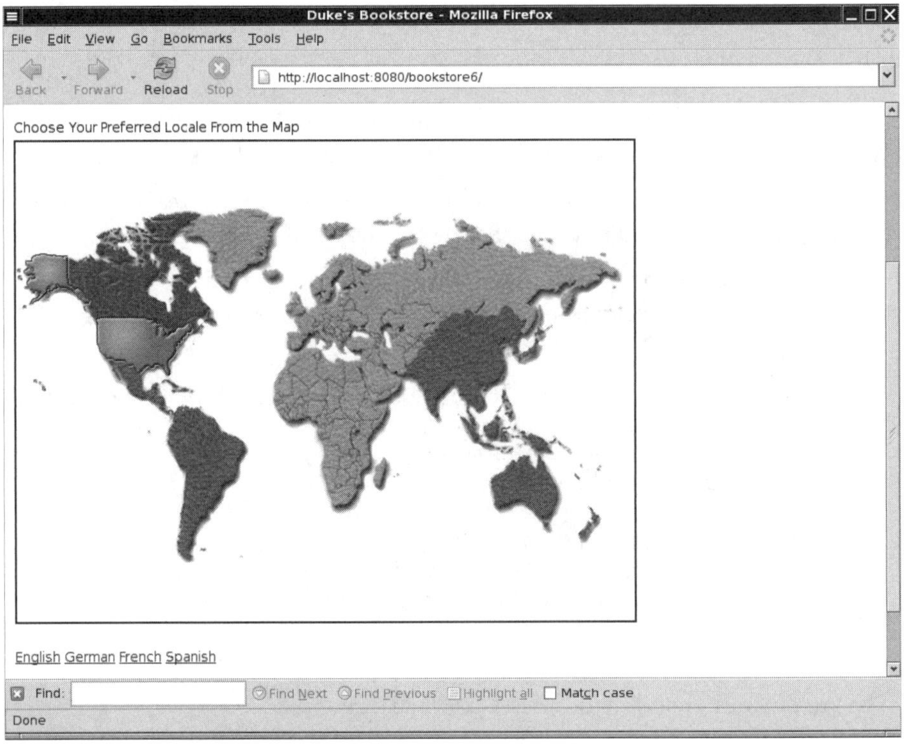

Figure 13–4   Image map sample component

Attach an action listener that gets the client ID of the button, attaches the suffixes .x and .y, and looks up the coordinate values in the request map. Process the values in any desired way. With this technique, the server application needs to know the geometry of the image.

How do I produce binary data in a JSF page?

Sometimes you will want to dynamically produce binary data, such as an image or a PDF file. It is difficult to do this in JSF because the default view handler sends text output to a writer, not a stream. It would theoretically be possible to replace the view handler, but it is far easier to use a helper servlet for producing the binary data. Of course, you still want to use the comforts of JSF—in particular, value expressions—to customize the output. Therefore, you want to provide a JSF tag that gathers the customization data and sends it to a servlet.

As an example, we implement a JSF tag that creates a chart image (see Figure 13–5). The image contains PNG-formatted data that was dynamically generated.

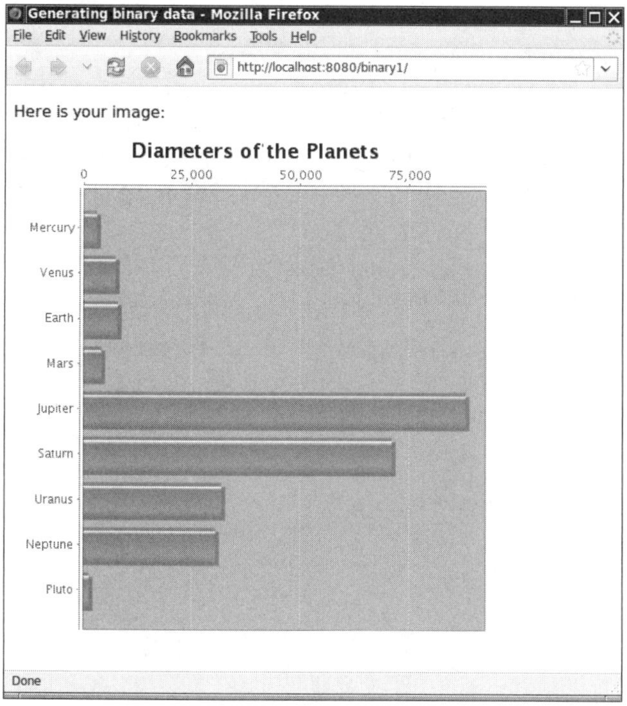

Figure 13–5   Producing binary data

Listing 13–4 includes the chart with the following tag:

```
<corejsf:chart width="500" height="500"
    title="Diameters of the Planets"
    names="#{planets.names}" values="#{planets.values}"/>
```

Here, names and values are value expression of type String[] and double[]. The renderer, whose code is shown in Listing 13–5, produces an image tag:

```
<img width="500" height="500" src="/binary/BinaryServlet?id=a unique ID" />
```

The image is produced by the BinaryServlet (see Listing 13–6).

To configure the servlet, add these lines to web.xml:

```
<servlet>
    <servlet-name>BinaryServlet</servlet-name>
    <servlet-class>com.corejsf.BinaryServlet</servlet-class>
</servlet>
<servlet-mapping>
    <servlet-name>BinaryServlet</servlet-name>
    <url-pattern>/BinaryServlet</url-pattern>
</servlet-mapping>
```

Alternatively, you can use an annotation:

```
@WebServlet("/BinaryServlet") public class BinaryServlet
```

Of course, the servlet needs to know the customization data. The renderer gathers the data from the component attributes in the usual way, bundles them into a transfer object (see Listing 13–8), and places the transfer object into the session map:

```
Map<String, Object> attributes = component.getAttributes();
Integer width = (Integer) attributes.get("width");
if (width == null) width = DEFAULT_WIDTH;
Integer height = (Integer) attributes.get("height");
if (height == null) height = DEFAULT_HEIGHT;
String title = (String) attributes.get("title");
if (title == null) title = "";
String[] names = (String[]) attributes.get("names");
double[] values = (double[]) attributes.get("values");

ChartData data = new ChartData();
data.setWidth(width);
data.setHeight(height);
data.setTitle(title);
data.setNames(names);
data.setValues(values);
```

```
String id = component.getClientId(context);
ExternalContext external = FacesContext.getCurrentInstance().getExternalContext();
Map<String, Object> session = external.getSessionMap();
session.put(id, data);
```

The servlet retrieves the transfer object from the session map and calls the transfer object's write method, which renders the image into the response stream:

```
HttpSession session = request.getSession();
String id = request.getParameter("id");
BinaryData data = (BinaryData) session.getAttribute(id);

response.setContentType(data.getContentType());
OutputStream out = response.getOutputStream();
data.write(out);
out.close();
```

To keep the servlet code general, we require that the transfer class implements an interface BinaryData (see Listing 13–7).

NOTE: To keep the code for generating the binary data short, we use the JFreeChart library (http://jfree.org/jfreechart) for generating the image. You need to add the jfreechart-*version*.jar and jcommon-*version*.jar files to the WEB-INF/lib directory. If you want to try out the code without the JFree-Chart library, use the ChartData class from the next example.

You use the same approach to generate any kind of binary data. The only difference is the code for writing data to the output stream.

Listing 13–4   binary1/web/index.xhtml

```
 1. <?xml version="1.0" encoding="UTF-8"?>
 2. <!DOCTYPE html PUBLIC "-//W3C//DTD XHTML 1.0 Transitional//EN"
 3. "http://www.w3.org/TR/xhtml1/DTD/xhtml1-transitional.dtd">
 4. <html xmlns="http://www.w3.org/1999/xhtml"
 5.      xmlns:h="http://java.sun.com/jsf/html" xmlns:corejsf="http://corejsf.com">
 6.    <h:head>
 7.      <title>Generating binary data</title>
 8.    </h:head>
 9.    <h:body>
10.      <h:form>
11.        <p>Here is your image:</p>
12.        <corejsf:chart width="500" height="500" title="Diameters of the Planets"
13.                       names="#{planets.names}" values="#{planets.values}"/>
14.      </h:form>
15.    </h:body>
16. </html>
```

Listing 13–5   binary1/src/java/com/corejsf/ChartRenderer.java

```
1. package com.corejsf;
2.
3. import java.io.IOException;
4. import java.util.Map;
5. import javax.faces.component.UIComponent;
6. import javax.faces.context.ExternalContext;
7. import javax.faces.context.FacesContext;
8. import javax.faces.context.ResponseWriter;
9. import javax.faces.render.FacesRenderer;
10. import javax.faces.render.Renderer;
11.
12. @FacesRenderer(componentFamily="javax.faces.Output",
13.       rendererType="com.corejsf.Chart")
14. public class ChartRenderer extends Renderer {
15.    private static final int DEFAULT_WIDTH = 200;
16.    private static final int DEFAULT_HEIGHT = 200;
17.
18.    public void encodeBegin(FacesContext context, UIComponent component)
19.       throws IOException {
20.       if (!component.isRendered()) return;
21.
22.       Map<String, Object> attributes = component.getAttributes();
23.       Integer width = toInteger(attributes.get("width"));
24.       if (width == null) width = DEFAULT_WIDTH;
25.       Integer height = toInteger(attributes.get("height"));
26.       if (height == null) height = DEFAULT_HEIGHT;
27.       String title = (String) attributes.get("title");
28.       if (title == null) title = "";
29.       String[] names = (String[]) attributes.get("names");
30.       double[] values = (double[]) attributes.get("values");
31.       if (names == null || values == null) return;
32.
33.       ChartData data = new ChartData();
34.       data.setWidth(width);
35.       data.setHeight(height);
36.       data.setTitle(title);
37.       data.setNames(names);
38.       data.setValues(values);
39.
40.       String id = component.getClientId(context);
41.       ExternalContext external
42.          = FacesContext.getCurrentInstance().getExternalContext();
43.       Map<String, Object> session = external.getSessionMap();
44.       session.put(id, data);
```

```
45.
46.        ResponseWriter writer = context.getResponseWriter();
47.        writer.startElement("img", component);
48.
49.        writer.writeAttribute("width", width, null);
50.        writer.writeAttribute("height", height, null);
51.        String path = external.getRequestContextPath();
52.        writer.writeAttribute("src", path + "/BinaryServlet?id=" + id, null);
53.        writer.endElement("img");
54.
55.        context.responseComplete();
56.    }
57.
58.    private static Integer toInteger(Object value) {
59.        if (value == null) return null;
60.        if (value instanceof Number) return ((Number) value).intValue();
61.        if (value instanceof String) return Integer.parseInt((String) value);
62.        throw new IllegalArgumentException("Cannot convert " + value);
63.    }
64. }
```

Listing 13–6   binary1/src/java/com/corejsf/BinaryServlet.java

```
1. package com.corejsf;
2.
3. import java.io.IOException;
4. import java.io.OutputStream;
5.
6. import javax.servlet.ServletException;
7. import javax.servlet.http.HttpServlet;
8. import javax.servlet.http.HttpServletRequest;
9. import javax.servlet.http.HttpServletResponse;
10. import javax.servlet.http.HttpSession;
11.
12. public class BinaryServlet extends HttpServlet {
13.    protected void processRequest(HttpServletRequest request,
14.        HttpServletResponse response)
15.        throws ServletException, IOException {
16.      HttpSession session = request.getSession();
17.      String id = request.getParameter("id");
18.      BinaryData data = (BinaryData) session.getAttribute(id);
19.
20.      response.setContentType(data.getContentType());
21.      OutputStream out = response.getOutputStream();
22.      data.write(out);
23.      out.close();
24.    }
```

```
25.
26.    protected void doGet(HttpServletRequest request, HttpServletResponse response)
27.        throws ServletException, IOException {
28.      processRequest(request, response);
29.    }
30.
31.    protected void doPost(HttpServletRequest request, HttpServletResponse response)
32.        throws ServletException, IOException {
33.      processRequest(request, response);
34.    }
35. }
```

Listing 13–7   binary1/src/java/com/corejsf/BinaryData.java

```
1. package com.corejsf;
2.
3. import java.io.IOException;
4. import java.io.OutputStream;
5.
6. public interface BinaryData {
7.    String getContentType();
8.    void write(OutputStream out) throws IOException;
9. }
```

Listing 13–8   binary1/src/java/com/corejsf/ChartData.java

```
1. package com.corejsf;
2.
3. import java.io.IOException;
4. import java.io.OutputStream;
5.
6. import org.jfree.chart.ChartFactory;
7. import org.jfree.chart.ChartUtilities;
8. import org.jfree.chart.JFreeChart;
9. import org.jfree.chart.plot.PlotOrientation;
10. import org.jfree.data.category.DefaultCategoryDataset;
11.
12. public class ChartData implements BinaryData {
13.    private int width, height;
14.    private String title;
15.    private String[] names;
16.    private double[] values;
17.
18.    private static final int DEFAULT_WIDTH = 200;
19.    private static final int DEFAULT_HEIGHT = 200;
20.
```

```
21.    public ChartData() {
22.        width = DEFAULT_WIDTH;
23.        height = DEFAULT_HEIGHT;
24.    }
25.
26.    public void setWidth(int width) {
27.        this.width = width;
28.    }
29.
30.    public void setHeight(int height) {
31.        this.height = height;
32.    }
33.
34.    public void setTitle(String title) {
35.        this.title = title;
36.    }
37.
38.    public void setNames(String[] names) {
39.        this.names = names;
40.    }
41.
42.    public void setValues(double[] values) {
43.        this.values = values;
44.    }
45.
46.    public String getContentType() {
47.        return "image/png";
48.    }
49.
50.    public void write(OutputStream out) throws IOException {
51.        DefaultCategoryDataset dataset = new DefaultCategoryDataset();
52.        for (int i = 0; i < names.length; i++)
53.            dataset.addValue(values[i], "", names[i]);
54.        JFreeChart chart = ChartFactory.createBarChart(
55.            title, // title
56.            "", // domain axis label
57.            "", // range axis label
58.            dataset,
59.            PlotOrientation.HORIZONTAL,
60.            false, // legend
61.            false, // tooltips
62.            false // urls
63.        );
64.
65.        ChartUtilities.writeChartAsPNG(out, chart, width, height);
66.    }
67. }
```

It is also possible to generate binary data directly from JSF, without a servlet. However, you must be very careful with the timing and grab the servlet output stream before the JSF implementation starts writing the response. Grabbing the servlet output stream cannot happen in a component renderer. A JSF component contributes to the page output, but it does not replace it.

Instead, we install a phase listener that is activated after the Restore View phase. It writes the binary data and then calls the responseComplete method to skip the other phases:

```
public class BinaryPhaseListener implements PhaseListener {
   public PhaseId getPhaseId() {
      return PhaseId.RESTORE_VIEW;
   }
   ...
   public void afterPhase(PhaseEvent event) {
      if (!event.getFacesContext().getViewRoot().getViewId()
            .startsWith("/binary")) return;
      HttpServletResponse servletResponse
         = (HttpServletResponse) external.getResponse();
      servletResponse.setContentType(data.getContentType());
      OutputStream out = servletResponse.getOutputStream();
      write data to out
      context.responseComplete();
   }
}
```

The filter action happens only with view IDs that start with /binary. As with the servlet solution, the key for the data transfer object is included as a GET parameter.

To trigger the filter, the image URL needs to be a valid JSF URL such as *appname*/binary.faces?id=*key* or *appname*/faces/binary?id=*key*. The exact type depends on the mapping of the Faces servlet. The renderer obtains the correct format from the view handler's getActionURL method:

```
ViewHandler handler = context.getApplication().getViewHandler();
String url = handler.getActionURL(context, "/binary");
```

Listing 13–9 shows the phase listener. The following element is required in faces-config.xml to install the listener:

```
<lifecycle>
   <phase-listener>com.corejsf.BinaryPhaseListener</phase-listener>
</lifecycle>
```

NOTE: In the example code, we generate the chart from scratch without using JFreeChart, illustrating that it doesn't matter how the binary data are generated.

Listing 13-9   binary2/src/java/com/corejsf/BinaryPhaseListener.java

```java
1. package com.corejsf;
2.
3. import java.io.IOException;
4. import java.io.OutputStream;
5. import java.util.Map;
6. import javax.faces.FacesException;
7. import javax.faces.context.ExternalContext;
8. import javax.faces.context.FacesContext;
9. import javax.faces.event.PhaseEvent;
10. import javax.faces.event.PhaseId;
11. import javax.faces.event.PhaseListener;
12. import javax.servlet.http.HttpServletResponse;
13.
14. public class BinaryPhaseListener implements PhaseListener {
15.    public static final String BINARY_PREFIX = "/binary";
16.
17.    public static final String DATA_ID_PARAM = "id";
18.
19.    public PhaseId getPhaseId() {
20.       return PhaseId.RESTORE_VIEW;
21.    }
22.
23.    public void beforePhase(PhaseEvent event) {
24.    }
25.
26.    public void afterPhase(PhaseEvent event) {
27.       if (!event.getFacesContext().getViewRoot().getViewId().startsWith(
28.          BINARY_PREFIX))
29.         return;
30.
31.       FacesContext context = event.getFacesContext();
32.       ExternalContext external = context.getExternalContext();
33.
34.       String id = (String) external.getRequestParameterMap().get(DATA_ID_PARAM);
35.       HttpServletResponse servletResponse =
36.          (HttpServletResponse) external.getResponse();
37.       try {
38.         Map<String, Object> session = external.getSessionMap();
```

```
39.          BinaryData data = (BinaryData) session.get(id);
40.          if (data != null) {
41.             servletResponse.setContentType(data.getContentType());
42.             OutputStream out = servletResponse.getOutputStream();
43.             data.write(out);
44.          }
45.       } catch (IOException ex) {
46.          throw new FacesException(ex);
47.       }
48.       context.responseComplete();
49.    }
50. }
```

How do I show a large data set, one page at a time?

As you saw in Chapter 6, you can add scrollbars to a table. However, if the table is truly large, you don't want it sent to the client in its entirety. Downloading the table takes a long time, and chances are that the application user wants to see only the first few rows anyway.

The standard user interface for navigating a large table is a *pager*, a set of links to each page of the table, to the next and previous pages, and if there are a great number of pages, to the next and previous batch of pages. Figure 13–6 shows a pager that scrolls through a large data set—the predefined time zones, obtained by a call to java.util.TimeZone.getAvailableIDs().

Unfortunately, JSF does not include a pager component. However, it is fairly easy to write one, and we give you the code to use or modify in your own applications.

The pager is a companion to a data table. You specify the ID of the data table, the number of pages that the pager displays, and the styles for the selected and unselected links. For example:

```
<h:dataTable id="timezones" value="#{bb.data}" var="row" rows="10">
   ...
</h:dataTable>
<corejsf:pager dataTableId="timezones" showpages="20"
selectedStyleClass="currentPage"/>
```

Suppose the user clicks the ">" link to move to the next page. The pager locates the data table and updates its first property, adding the value of the rows property. You will find that code in the decode method of the PagerRenderer in Listing 13–10.

The encode method is a bit more involved. It generates a set of links. Similar to a commandLink, clicking the link activates JavaScript code that sets a value in a hidden field and submits the form.

Listing 13–11 shows the index.xhtml page that generates the table and the pager. Listing 13–12 shows the trivial backing bean.

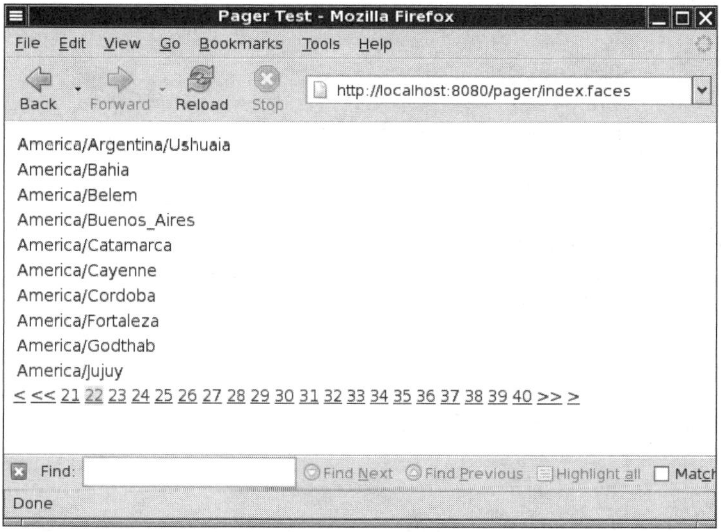

Figure 13–6   Table with a pager

> NOTE: The Apache Tomahawk dataScroller component offers similar functionality.

Listing 13–10   pager/src/java/com/corejsf/PagerRenderer.java

```
1. package com.corejsf;
2.
3. import java.io.IOException;
4. import java.util.Map;
5. import javax.faces.component.UIComponent;
6. import javax.faces.component.UIData;
7. import javax.faces.component.UIForm;
8. import javax.faces.context.FacesContext;
9. import javax.faces.context.ResponseWriter;
10. import javax.faces.render.FacesRenderer;
11. import javax.faces.render.Renderer;
```

```
12.
13. @FacesRenderer(componentFamily="javax.faces.Command",
14.     rendererType="com.corejsf.Pager")
15. public class PagerRenderer extends Renderer {
16.    public void encodeBegin(FacesContext context, UIComponent component)
17.        throws IOException {
18.        String id = component.getClientId(context);
19.        UIComponent parent = component;
20.        while (!(parent instanceof UIForm)) parent = parent.getParent();
21.        String formId = parent.getClientId(context);
22.
23.        ResponseWriter writer = context.getResponseWriter();
24.
25.        String styleClass = (String) component.getAttributes().get("styleClass");
26.        String selectedStyleClass
27.           = (String) component.getAttributes().get("selectedStyleClass");
28.        String dataTableId = (String) component.getAttributes().get("dataTableId");
29.        int showpages = toInt(component.getAttributes().get("showpages"));
30.
31.        // find the component with the given ID
32.
33.        UIData data = (UIData) component.findComponent(dataTableId);
34.
35.        int first = data.getFirst();
36.        int itemcount = data.getRowCount();
37.        int pagesize = data.getRows();
38.        if (pagesize <= 0) pagesize = itemcount;
39.
40.        int pages = itemcount / pagesize;
41.        if (itemcount % pagesize != 0) pages++;
42.
43.        int currentPage = first / pagesize;
44.        if (first >= itemcount - pagesize) currentPage = pages - 1;
45.        int startPage = 0;
46.        int endPage = pages;
47.        if (showpages > 0) {
48.           startPage = (currentPage / showpages) * showpages;
49.           endPage = Math.min(startPage + showpages, pages);
50.        }
51.        if (currentPage > 0)
52.           writeLink(writer, component, formId, id, "<", styleClass);
53.
54.        if (startPage > 0)
55.           writeLink(writer, component, formId, id, "<<", styleClass);
56.
57.        for (int i = startPage; i < endPage; i++) {
58.           writeLink(writer, component, formId, id, "" + (i + 1),
59.              i == currentPage ? selectedStyleClass : styleClass);
```

```
60.     }
61.
62.     if (endPage < pages)
63.       writeLink(writer, component, formId, id, ">>", styleClass);
64.
65.     if (first < itemcount - pagesize)
66.       writeLink(writer, component, formId, id, ">", styleClass);
67.
68.     // hidden field to hold result
69.     writeHiddenField(writer, component, id);
70.   }
71.
72.   private void writeLink(ResponseWriter writer, UIComponent component,
73.     String formId, String id, String value, String styleClass)
74.     throws IOException {
75.     writer.writeText(" ", null);
76.     writer.startElement("a", component);
77.     writer.writeAttribute("href", "#", null);
78.     writer.writeAttribute("onclick", onclickCode(formId, id, value), null);
79.     if (styleClass != null)
80.       writer.writeAttribute("class", styleClass, "styleClass");
81.     writer.writeText(value, null);
82.     writer.endElement("a");
83.   }
84.
85.   private String onclickCode(String formId, String id, String value) {
86.     return new StringBuilder().append("document.forms['")
87.       .append(formId).append("']['")
88.       .append(id).append("'].value='").append(value).append("'; document.forms['")
89.       .append(formId).append("'].submit(); return false;").toString();
90.   }
91.
92.   private void writeHiddenField(ResponseWriter writer, UIComponent component,
93.     String id) throws IOException {
94.     writer.startElement("input", component);
95.     writer.writeAttribute("type", "hidden", null);
96.     writer.writeAttribute("name", id, null);
97.     writer.endElement("input");
98.   }
99.
100.  public void decode(FacesContext context, UIComponent component) {
101.    String id = component.getClientId(context);
102.    Map<String, String> parameters
103.      = context.getExternalContext().getRequestParameterMap();
104.
105.    String response = (String) parameters.get(id);
106.    if (response == null || response.equals("")) return;
```

```
107.
108.     String dataTableId = (String) component.getAttributes().get("dataTableId");
109.     int showpages = toInt(component.getAttributes().get("showpages"));
110.
111.     UIData data = (UIData) component.findComponent(dataTableId);
112.
113.     int first = data.getFirst();
114.     int itemcount = data.getRowCount();
115.     int pagesize = data.getRows();
116.     if (pagesize <= 0) pagesize = itemcount;
117.
118.     if (response.equals("<")) first -= pagesize;
119.     else if (response.equals(">")) first += pagesize;
120.     else if (response.equals("<<")) first -= pagesize * showpages;
121.     else if (response.equals(">>")) first += pagesize * showpages;
122.     else {
123.        int page = Integer.parseInt(response);
124.        first = (page - 1) * pagesize;
125.     }
126.     if (first + pagesize > itemcount) first = itemcount - pagesize;
127.     if (first < 0) first = 0;
128.     data.setFirst(first);
129.   }
130.
131.   private static int toInt(Object value) {
132.     if (value == null) return 0;
133.     if (value instanceof Number) return ((Number) value).intValue();
134.     if (value instanceof String) return Integer.parseInt((String) value);
135.     throw new IllegalArgumentException("Cannot convert " + value);
136.   }
137.}
```

Listing 13–11   pager/web/index.xhtml

```
1. <?xml version="1.0" encoding="UTF-8"?>
2. <!DOCTYPE html PUBLIC "-//W3C//DTD XHTML 1.0 Transitional//EN"
3. "http://www.w3.org/TR/xhtml1/DTD/xhtml1-transitional.dtd">
4. <html xmlns="http://www.w3.org/1999/xhtml"
5.      xmlns:h="http://java.sun.com/jsf/html"
6.      xmlns:ui="http://java.sun.com/jsf/facelets"
7.      xmlns:corejsf="http://corejsf.com">
8.    <h:head>
9.      <h:outputStylesheet library="css" name="styles.css"/>
10.     <title>Pager Test</title>
11.   </h:head>
12.   <h:body>
```

```
13.      <ui:debug/>
14.      <h:form>
15.        <h:dataTable id="timezones" value="#{tz.data}" var="row" rows="10">
16.           <h:column>#{row}</h:column>
17.        </h:dataTable>
18.        <corejsf:pager dataTableId="timezones" showpages="20"
19.                       selectedStyleClass="currentPage"/>
20.      </h:form>
21.    </h:body>
22. </html>
```

Listing 13–12   `pager/src/java/com/corejsf/TimeZoneBean.java`

```
1. package com.corejsf;
2.
3. import javax.inject.Named;
4.    // or import javax.faces.bean.ManagedBean;
5. import javax.enterprise.context.RequestScoped;
6.    // or import javax.faces.bean.RequestScoped;
7.
8. @Named("tz") // or @ManagedBean(name="tz")
9. @RequestScoped
10. public class TimeZoneBean {
11.    private String[] data = java.util.TimeZone.getAvailableIDs();
12.    public String[] getData() { return data; }
13. }
```

How do I generate a pop-up window?

The basic method for a pop-up window is simple. Use the JavaScript calls:

```
popup = window.open(url, name, features);
popup.focus();
```

The features parameter is a string, such as:

```
"height=300,width=200,toolbar=no,menubar=no"
```

The pop-up window should be displayed when the user clicks a button or link. Attach a function to the onclick handler of the button or link, and have the function return false so that the browser does not submit the form or follow the link. For example:

```
<h:commandButton value="..." onclick="doPopup(this); return false;"/>
```

The doPopup function contains the JavaScript instructions for popping up the window. It is contained in a script tag inside the page header.

However, challenges arise when you need to transfer data between the main window and the pop-up.

Now we look at a specific example. Figure 13–7 shows a page with a pop-up window that lists the states of the USA or the provinces of Canada, depending on the setting of the radio buttons. The list is generated by a backing bean on the server.

How does the backing bean know which state was selected? After all, the form has not yet been posted back to the server when the user requests the pop-up. We show you two solutions—each of them is interesting in its own right and may give you ideas for solving similar problems.

In the first solution, we pass the selection parameter to the pop-up URL, like this:

```
window.open("popup.faces?country=" + country[i].value, "popup", features);
```

The popup.faces page retrieves the value of the country request parameter as param.country:

```
<h:dataTable value="#{bb.states[param.country]}" var="state">
```

Here, the states property of the backing bean bb yields a map whose index is the country name.

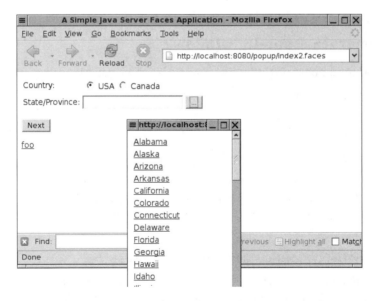

Figure 13–7   Popping up a window to select a state or province

The second solution (suggested by Marion Bass and Sergey Smirnov) is more involved, but also more powerful. In this technique, the pop-up window is first created as a blank window and then filled with the response to a JSF command.

The JSF command is issued by a form that contains a hidden field and an invisible link, like this:

```
<h:form id="hidden" target="popup">
  <h:inputHidden id="country" value="#{bb.country}"/>
  <h:commandLink id="go" action="showStates"/>
</h:form>
```

Note the following details:

*   The target of the form has the same name as the pop-up window. Therefore, the browser will show the result of the action inside the pop-up.
*   The hidden country field will be populated before the form is submitted. It sets the bb.country value expression. This enables the backing bean to return the appropriate set of states or provinces.
*   The action attribute of the command link is used by the navigation handler to select the JSF page that generates the pop-up contents.

The doPopup function initializes the hidden field and fires the link action:

```
document.getElementById("hidden:country").value = country[i].value;
document.getElementById("hidden:go").onclick(null);
```

The value of the selected state or province is transferred into the hidden field. When the hidden form is submitted, that value will be stored in the backing bean.

In this solution, the JSF page for the pop-up is more straightforward. The table of states or provinces is populated by the bean property call:

```
<h:dataTable value="#{bb.statesForCountry}" var="state">
```

The statesForCountry property takes the country property into account—it was set when the hidden form was decoded. This approach is more flexible than the first approach because it allows arbitrary bean properties to be set before the pop-up contents are computed.

With both approaches, it is necessary to send the pop-up data back to the original page. However, this can be achieved with straightforward JavaScript. The pop-up's opener property is the window that opened the pop-up. When the user clicks a link in the pop-up, the event handler sets the value of the corresponding text field in the original page:

```
opener.document.forms[formId][formId + ":state"].value = value;
```

How does the pop-up know the form ID of the original form? Here we take advantage of the flexibility of JavaScript. You can add instance fields to any object on-the-fly. We set an `openerFormId` field in the pop-up window when it is constructed:

```
popup = window.open(...);
popup.openerFormId = source.form.id;
```

When we are ready to modify the form variables, we retrieve it from the pop-up window, like this:

```
var formId = window.openerFormId;
```

These are the tricks that you need to know to deal with pop-up windows. The following example shows the two approaches that we discussed. The `technique1.xhtml`, `popup1.xhtml`, and `popup1.js` files in Listings 13–13 through 13–15 show the first approach, using a request parameter to configure the pop-up page.

The `technique2.xhtml`, `popup2.xhtml`, and `popup2.js` files in Listings 13–16 through 13–18 show the second approach, filling the pop-up page with the result of a JSF action. Listing 13–19 shows the backing bean.

Listing 13–13   popup/web/technique1.xhtml

```
1. <?xml version="1.0" encoding="UTF-8"?>
2. <!DOCTYPE html PUBLIC "-//W3C//DTD XHTML 1.0 Transitional//EN"
3. "http://www.w3.org/TR/xhtml1/DTD/xhtml1-transitional.dtd">
4. <html xmlns="http://www.w3.org/1999/xhtml"
5.     xmlns:h="http://java.sun.com/jsf/html"
6.     xmlns:f="http://java.sun.com/jsf/core">
7.    <h:head>
8.      <h:outputScript library="javascript" name="popup1.js"/>
9.      <title>Popup window technique 1</title>
10.   </h:head>
11.   <h:body>
12.     <h:form>
13.       <table>
14.         <tr>
15.           <td>Country:</td>
16.           <td><h:selectOneRadio id="country" value="#{bb.country}">
17.             <f:selectItem itemLabel="USA" itemValue="USA"/>
18.             <f:selectItem itemLabel="Canada" itemValue="Canada"/>
19.           </h:selectOneRadio></td>
20.         </tr>
21.         <tr>
22.           <td>State/Province:</td>
```

```
23.                <td><h:inputText id="state" value="#{bb.state}"/></td>
24.                <td><h:commandButton value="..."
25.                    onclick="doPopup(this); return false;"/></td>
26.              </tr>
27.            </table>
28.            <p><h:commandButton value="Next" action="index"/></p>
29.          </h:form>
30.        </h:body>
31. </html>
```

Listing 13–14   popup/web/popup1.xhtml

```
1. <?xml version="1.0" encoding="UTF-8"?>
2. <!DOCTYPE html PUBLIC "-//W3C//DTD XHTML 1.0 Transitional//EN"
3. "http://www.w3.org/TR/xhtml1/DTD/xhtml1-transitional.dtd">
4. <html xmlns="http://www.w3.org/1999/xhtml"
5.       xmlns:h="http://java.sun.com/jsf/html">
6.    <h:head>
7.      <h:outputScript library="javascript" name="popup1.js"/>
8.      <title>Select a state/province</title>
9.    </h:head>
10.   <h:body>
11.     <h:form>
12.       <h:dataTable value="#{bb.states[param.country]}" var="state">
13.         <h:column>
14.           <h:outputLink value="#" onclick="doSave('#{state}');">
15.             #{state}
16.           </h:outputLink>
17.         </h:column>
18.       </h:dataTable>
19.     </h:form>
20.   </h:body>
21. </html>
```

Listing 13–15   popup/web/resources/javascript/popup1.js

```
1. function doPopup(source) {
2.    country = source.form[source.form.id + ":country"];
3.    for ( var i = 0; i < country.length; i++) {
4.      if (country[i].checked) {
5.        popup = window.open("popup1.xhtml?country="
6.            + country[i].value, "popup",
7.            "height=300,width=200,toolbar=no,menubar=no,"
8.            + "scrollbars=yes");
9.        popup.openerFormId = source.form.id;
10.       popup.focus();
11.     }
```

```
12.     }
13. }
14.
15. function doSave(value) {
16.     var formId = window.openerFormId;
17.     opener.document.forms[formId][formId + ":state"].value = value;
18.     window.close();
19. }
```

Listing 13-16   popup/web/technique2.xhtml

```
 1. <?xml version="1.0" encoding="UTF-8"?>
 2. <!DOCTYPE html PUBLIC "-//W3C//DTD XHTML 1.0 Transitional//EN"
 3. "http://www.w3.org/TR/xhtml1/DTD/xhtml1-transitional.dtd">
 4. <html xmlns="http://www.w3.org/1999/xhtml"
 5.       xmlns:h="http://java.sun.com/jsf/html" xmlns:f="http://java.sun.com/jsf/core">
 6.   <h:head>
 7.     <h:outputScript library="javascript" name="popup1.js"/>
 8.     <title>Popup window technique 2</title>
 9.   </h:head>
10.   <h:body>
11.     <h:form>
12.       <table>
13.         <tr>
14.           <td>Country:</td>
15.           <td><h:selectOneRadio id="country" value="#{bb.country}">
16.             <f:selectItem itemLabel="USA" itemValue="USA"/>
17.             <f:selectItem itemLabel="Canada" itemValue="Canada"/>
18.           </h:selectOneRadio></td>
19.         </tr>
20.         <tr>
21.           <td>State/Province:</td>
22.           <td><h:inputText id="state" value="#{bb.state}"/></td>
23.           <td><h:commandButton value="..."
24.             onclick="doPopup(this); return false;"/></td>
25.         </tr>
26.       </table>
27.       <p><h:commandButton value="Next" action="index"/></p>
28.     </h:form>
29.
30.     <!-- This hidden form sends a request to a popup window. -->
31.     <h:form id="hidden" target="popup">
32.       <h:inputHidden id="country" value="#{bb.country}"/>
33.       <h:commandLink id="go" action="popup2"/>
34.     </h:form>
35.   </h:body>
36. </html>
```

Listing 13–17   popup/web/popup2.xhtml

```
1. <?xml version="1.0" encoding="UTF-8"?>
2. <!DOCTYPE html PUBLIC "-//W3C//DTD XHTML 1.0 Transitional//EN"
3. "http://www.w3.org/TR/xhtml1/DTD/xhtml1-transitional.dtd">
4. <html xmlns="http://www.w3.org/1999/xhtml"
5.       xmlns:h="http://java.sun.com/jsf/html">
6.   <h:head>
7.     <h:outputScript library="javascript" name="popup1.js"/>
8.     <title>Select a state/province</title>
9.   </h:head>
10.   <h:body>
11.     <h:form>
12.       <h:dataTable value="#{bb.statesForCountry}" var="state">
13.         <h:column>
14.           <h:outputLink value="#" onclick="doSave('#{state}');">
15.             #{state}
16.           </h:outputLink>
17.         </h:column>
18.       </h:dataTable>
19.     </h:form>
20.   </h:body>
21. </html>
```

Listing 13–18   popup/web/resources/javascript/popup2.js

```
1. function doPopup(source) {
2.    country = source.form[source.form.id + ":country"];
3.    for (var i = 0; i < country.length; i++) {
4.      if (country[i].checked) {
5.      popup = window.open("", "/faces/popup2.xhtml",
6.         "height=300,width=200,toolbar=no,menubar=no,scrollbars=yes");
7.      popup.openerFormId = source.form.id;
8.      popup.focus();
9.      document.getElementById("hidden:country").value = country[i].value;
10.      document.getElementById("hidden:go").onclick(null);
11.    }
12.  }
13. }
14.
15. function doSave(value) {
16.    var formId = window.openerFormId;
17.    opener.document.forms[formId][formId + ":state"].value = value;
18.    window.close();
19. }
```

Listing 13–19   popup/src/java/com/corejsf/BackingBean.java

```
1. package com.corejsf;
2.
3. import java.io.Serializable;
4. import java.util.HashMap;
5. import java.util.Map;
6.
7. import javax.inject.Named;
8.   // or import javax.faces.bean.ManagedBean;
9. import javax.enterprise.context.SessionScoped;
10.   // or import javax.faces.bean.SessionScoped;
11.
12. @Named("bb") // or @ManagedBean(name="bb")
13. @SessionScoped
14. public class BackingBean implements Serializable {
15.    private String country = "USA";
16.    private String state = "California";
17.    private static Map<String, String[]> states;
18.
19.    public String getCountry() { return country; }
20.    public void setCountry(String newValue) { country = newValue; }
21.
22.    public String getState() { return state; }
23.    public void setState(String newValue) { state = newValue; }
24.
25.    public Map<String, String[]> getStates() { return states; }
26.
27.    public String[] getStatesForCountry() { return (String[]) states.get(country); }
28.
29.    static {
30.       states = new HashMap<String, String[]>();
31.       states.put("USA",
32.          new String[] {
33.             "Alabama", "Alaska", "Arizona", "Arkansas", "California",
34.             "Colorado", "Connecticut", "Delaware", "Florida", "Georgia",
35.             "Hawaii", "Idaho", "Illinois", "Indiana", "Iowa", "Kansas",
36.             "Kentucky", "Louisiana", "Maine", "Maryland", "Massachusetts",
37.             "Michigan", "Minnesota", "Mississippi", "Missouri", "Montana",
38.             "Nebraska", "Nevada", "New Hampshire", "New Jersey", "New Mexico",
39.             "New York", "North Carolina", "North Dakota", "Ohio", "Oklahoma",
40.             "Oregon", "Pennsylvania", "Rhode Island", "South Carolina",
41.             "South Dakota", "Tennessee", "Texas", "Utah", "Vermont",
42.             "Virginia", "Washington", "West Virginia", "Wisconsin", "Wyoming"
43.          });
44.
```

```
45.      states.put("Canada",
46.        new String[] {
47.          "Alberta", "British Columbia", "Manitoba", "New Brunswick",
48.          "Newfoundland and Labrador", "Northwest Territories",
49.          "Nova Scotia", "Nunavut", "Ontario", "Prince Edward Island",
50.          "Quebec", "Saskatchewan", "Yukon"
51.        });
52.    }
53. }
```

How do I selectively show and hide parts of a page?

It is very common to show or hide parts of a page, depending on some condition. For example, when a user is not logged on, you may want to show input fields for the username and password. But if a user is logged on, you would want to show the username and a logout button.

It would be wasteful to design two separate pages that differ in this small detail. Instead, we want to include all components in our page and selectively display them.

You can solve this issue with the JSTL c:if or c:choose construct. If you prefer not to mix JSF and JSTL tags, it is easy to achieve the same effect with JSF alone.

If you want to enable or disable one component (or a container like a panel group), use the rendered property, such as:

```
<h:panelGroup rendered="#{userBean.loggedIn}">...</h:panelGroup>
```

If you want to switch between two component sets, you can use complementary rendered attributes:

```
<h:panelGroup rendered="#{!userBean.loggedIn}">...</h:panelGroup>
<h:panelGroup rendered="#{userBean.loggedIn}">...</h:panelGroup>
```

For more than two choices, it is best to use a component, such as panelStack in the Apache MyFaces components library (http://myfaces.apache.org/tomahawk). A panel stack is similar to the tabbed pane that you saw in Chapter 11, except that there are no tabs. Instead, one of the child components is selected programmatically.

With the panelStack, each child component must have an ID. The selectedPanel attribute specifies the ID of the child that is rendered:

```
<t:panelStack selectedPanel="#{userBean.status}">
  <h:panelGroup id="new">...</h:panelGroup>
  <h:panelGroup id="loggedIn">...</h:panelGroup>
  <h:panelGroup id="loggedOut">...</h:panelGroup>
</t:panelStack>
```

The getStatus method of the user bean should return a string "new", "loggedIn", or "loggedOut".

If you want to choose between two entirely different pages, you can use ui:include tags inside c:choose:

```
<c:choose>
    <c:when test="#{user.loggedIn}">
        <ui:include src="main.xhtml" />
    </c:when>
    <c:otherwise>
        <ui:include src="login.xhtml" />
    </c:otherwise>
</c:choose>
```

How do I customize error pages?

When you run an application in the "development" project stage and you encounter an error, you get an error message such as the one in Figure 13–8.

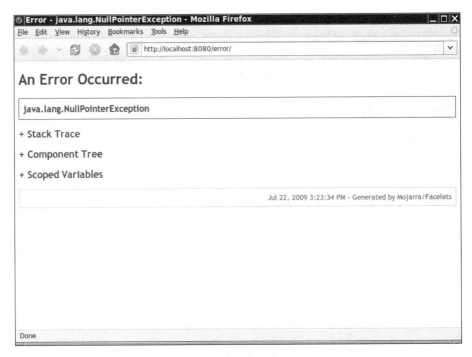

Figure 13–8   An error message in the development stage

You probably do not want your users to see that message in a production application. However, setting the project stage to "production" in web.xml makes matters worse—see Figure 13–9.

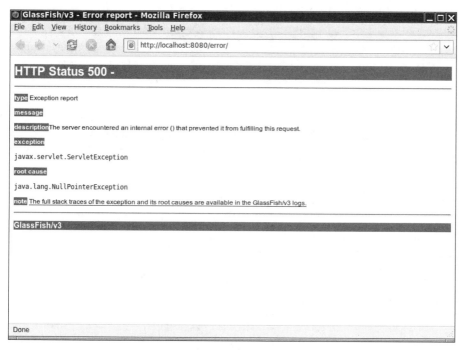

Figure 13–9   An error message in the production stage

You *really* don't want your users to see that page.

To substitue a better error page, use the error-page tag in the web.xml file. Specify either a Java exception class or an HTTP error code. For example:

```
<error-page>
    <exception-type>java.lang.Exception</exception-type>
    <location>/faces/exception.xhtml</location>
</error-page>
<error-page>
    <error-code>500</error-code>
    <location>/faces/error.xhtml</location>
</error-page>
<error-page>
    <error-code>404</error-code>
    <location>/faces/notfound.xhtml</location>
</error-page>
```

If an exception occurs and an error page matches its type, then the matching error page is displayed. Otherwise, an HTTP error 500 is generated.

If an HTTP error occurs and there is a matching error page, it is displayed. Otherwise, the default error page is displayed.

> CAUTION: If an error occurs while your application is trying to display a custom error page, the default error page is displayed instead. If your custom error page stubbornly refuses to appear, check the log files for messages relating to your error page.

When you use the error-page mechanism, several objects related to the error are placed in the request map (see Table 13–1). You can use these values to display information that describes the error.

Table 13–1 Servlet Exception Attributes

Key	Value	Type
javax.servlet.error.status_code	The HTTP error code	Integer
javax.servlet.error.message	A description of the error	String
javax.servlet.error.exception_type	The class of the exception	Class
javax.servlet.error.exception	The exception object	Throwable
javax.servlet.error.request_uri	The path to the application resource that encountered the error	String
javax.servlet.error.servlet_name	The name of the servlet that encountered the error	String

The following sample application uses this technique. We purposely produce a null pointer exception in the password property of the UserBean, resulting in the error report shown in Figure 13–10. Listing 13–20 shows the web.xml file that sets the error page to errorDisplay.xhtml (Listing 13–21).

Listing 13–22 shows the ErrorBean class. Its getStackTrace method assembles a complete stack trace that contains all nested exceptions.

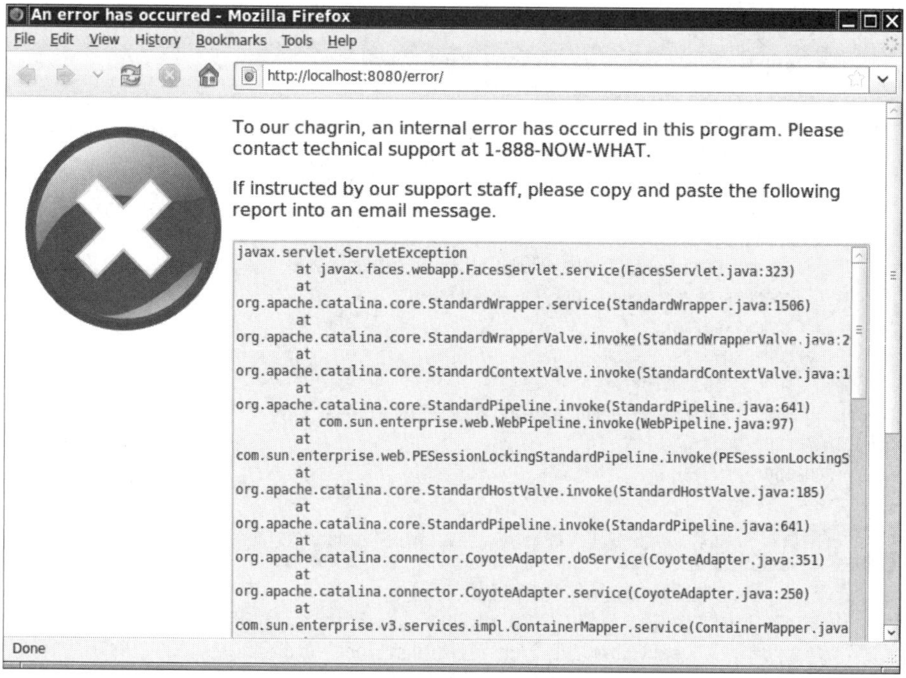

Figure 13–10   A customized error display

NOTE: If you use a custom error page, you can still include the standard Facelets error display in the development stage. Simply add the line:

```
<ui:include src="javax.faces.error.xhtml"/>
```

During production stage, the error display is suppressed.

Listing 13–20   error/web/WEB-INF/web.xml

```xml
1. <?xml version="1.0" encoding="UTF-8"?>
2. <web-app xmlns:xsi="http://www.w3.org/2001/XMLSchema-instance"
3.     xmlns="http://java.sun.com/xml/ns/javaee"
4.     xmlns:web="http://java.sun.com/xml/ns/javaee/web-app_2_5.xsd"
5.     xsi:schemaLocation="http://java.sun.com/xml/ns/javaee
6.       http://java.sun.com/xml/ns/javaee/web-app_2_5.xsd"
7.     version="2.5">
8.     <servlet>
9.       <servlet-name>Faces Servlet</servlet-name>
10.      <servlet-class>javax.faces.webapp.FacesServlet</servlet-class>
```

```
11.  </servlet>
12.  <servlet-mapping>
13.    <servlet-name>Faces Servlet</servlet-name>
14.    <url-pattern>/faces/*</url-pattern>
15.  </servlet-mapping>
16.  <welcome-file-list>
17.    <welcome-file>faces/index.xhtml</welcome-file>
18.  </welcome-file-list>
19.  <context-param>
20.    <param-name>javax.faces.PROJECT_STAGE</param-name>
21.    <param-value>Production</param-value>
22.  </context-param>
23.  <error-page>
24.    <error-code>500</error-code>
25.    <location>/faces/errorDisplay.xhtml</location>
26.  </error-page>
27. </web-app>
```

Listing 13–21 error/web/errorDisplay.xhtml

```
1. <?xml version="1.0" encoding="UTF-8"?>
2. <!DOCTYPE html PUBLIC "-//W3C//DTD XHTML 1.0 Transitional//EN"
3. "http://www.w3.org/TR/xhtml1/DTD/xhtml1-transitional.dtd">
4. <html xmlns="http://www.w3.org/1999/xhtml"
5.       xmlns:h="http://java.sun.com/jsf/html">
6.    <h:head>
7.       <title>#{msgs.errorTitle}</title>
8.    </h:head>
9.    <h:body>
10.      <h:form>
11.         <h:graphicImage library="images" name="error.png" style="float: left;"/>
12.         <p>#{msgs.errorOccurred}</p>
13.         <p>#{msgs.copyReport}</p>
14.         <h:inputTextarea value="#{error.stackTrace}" rows="40" cols="80"
15.                     readonly="true"/>
16.      </h:form>
17.   </h:body>
18. </html>
```

Listing 13–22 error/src/java/com/corejsf/ErrorBean.java

```
1. package com.corejsf;
2.
3. import java.io.PrintWriter;
4. import java.io.StringWriter;
5. import java.sql.SQLException;
```

```
 6. import java.util.Map;
 7.
 8. import javax.inject.Named;
 9.    // or import javax.faces.bean.ManagedBean;
10. import javax.enterprise.context.RequestScoped;
11.    // or import javax.faces.bean.RequestScoped;
12. import javax.faces.context.FacesContext;
13. import javax.servlet.ServletException;
14.
15. @Named("error") // or @ManagedBean(name="error")
16. @RequestScoped
17. public class ErrorBean {
18.    public String getStackTrace() {
19.       FacesContext context = FacesContext.getCurrentInstance();
20.       Map<String, Object> request
21.          = context.getExternalContext().getRequestMap();
22.       Throwable ex = (Throwable) request.get("javax.servlet.error.exception");
23.       StringWriter sw = new StringWriter();
24.       PrintWriter pw = new PrintWriter(sw);
25.       fillStackTrace(ex, pw);
26.       return sw.toString();
27.    }
28.
29.    private static void fillStackTrace(Throwable t, PrintWriter w) {
30.       if (t == null) return;
31.       t.printStackTrace(w);
32.       if (t instanceof ServletException) {
33.          Throwable cause = ((ServletException) t).getRootCause();
34.          if (cause != null) {
35.             w.println("Root cause:");
36.             fillStackTrace(cause, w);
37.          }
38.       } else if (t instanceof SQLException) {
39.          Throwable cause = ((SQLException) t).getNextException();
40.          if (cause != null) {
41.             w.println("Next exception:");
42.             fillStackTrace(cause, w);
43.          }
44.       } else {
45.          Throwable cause = t.getCause();
46.          if (cause != null) {
47.             w.println("Cause:");
48.             fillStackTrace(cause, w);
49.          }
50.       }
51.    }
52. }
```

How do I write my own client-side validation tag?

Suppose you have developed a JavaScript function for validation and tested it on multiple browsers. Now you would like to use it in your JSF applications. You need two tags:

1. A validator tag that is attached to each component that requires validation.
2. A component tag that generates the JavaScript code for validating all components on the form. The component tag must be added to the end of the form. Note that you cannot use a validator tag for this purpose. Only components can render output.

As an example, we show you how to make use of the credit card validation code in the Apache Commons Validator project. You can download the code from `http://jakarta.apache.org/commons/validator`.

We produce two tags: a `creditCardValidator` tag that can be added to any JSF input component and a component tag `validatorScript` that generates the required JavaScript code.

The `creditCardValidator` tag has two attributes. The `message` attribute specifies the error message template, such as:

```
{0} is not a valid credit card number
```

The `arg` attribute is the value that should be filled in for {0}, usually the field name. For example:

```
<corejsf:creditCardValidator
    message="#{msgs.invalidCard}" arg="#{msgs.primaryCard}"/>
```

The code for the validator is in Listing 13–23 on page 590. The validator class has two unrelated purposes: validation and error message formatting.

The class carries out a traditional server-side validation, independent of the client-side JavaScript code. After all, it is not a good idea to rely solely on client-side validation. Users may have deactivated JavaScript in their browsers. Also, automated scripts or web-savvy hackers may send unvalidated HTTP requests to your web application.

The `getErrorMessage` method formats an error message that will be included in the client-side JavaScript code. The error message is constructed from the `message` and `arg` attributes.

The `validatorScript` component is far more interesting (see Listing 13–24 on page 592). Its `encodeBegin` method calls the recursive `findCreditCardValidators` method, which walks the component tree, locates all components, enumerates their validators, checks which ones are credit card validators, and gathers them in a map object. The `writeValidationFunctions` method writes the JavaScript code that invokes the validation function on all fields with credit card validators.

You must place the `validatorScript` tag inside the form, like this:

```
<h:form id="paymentForm" onsubmit="return validatePaymentForm(this);">
    ...
    <corejsf:validatorScript functionName="validatePaymentForm"/>
</h:form>
```

Listing 13–25 on page 594 shows a sample JSF page. Figure 13–11 shows the error that is generated when a user tries to submit an invalid number.

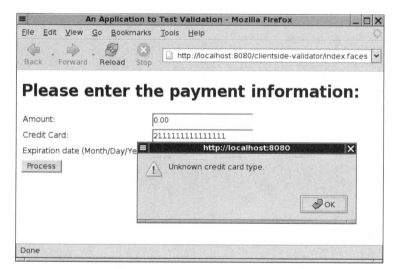

Figure 13–11   Client-side credit card validation

The details of the `writeValidationFunctions` method depend on the intricacies of the JavaScript code in the Commons Validator project.

First, the `writeValidationFunctions` method produces the validation function that is called in the `onsubmit` handler of the form:

```
var bCancel = false;
function functionName(form) { return bCancel || validateCreditCard(form); }
```

If a form contains "Cancel" or "Back" buttons, their `onclick` handlers should set the `bCancel` variable to true, to bypass validation.

The `validateCreditCard` function is the entry point into the Commons Validator code. It expects to find a function named *formName*_`creditCard` that constructs a configuration object. The writeValidationFunctions method generates the code for the creditCard function.

Unfortunately, the details are rather convoluted. The *formName_*creditCard function returns an object with one instance variable for each validated form element. Each instance field contains an array with three values: the ID of the form element, the error message to display when validation fails, and a validator-specific customization value. The credit card validator does not use this value; we supply the empty string.

The instance field names do not matter. In the writeValidationFunctions method, we take advantage of the flexibility of JavaScript and call the fields 0, 1, 2, and so on. For example:

```
function paymentForm_creditCard() {
   this[0] = new Array("paymentForm:primary",
      "Primary Credit Card is not a valid card number", "");
   this[1] = new Array("paymentForm:backup",
      "Backup Credit Card is not a valid card number", "");
}
```

If you design your own JavaScript functions, you can provide a saner mechanism for bundling up the parameters.

Listing 13–23 clientside-validator/src/java/com/corejsf/ CreditCardValidator.java

```
 1. package com.corejsf;
 2.
 3. import java.io.Serializable;
 4. import java.text.MessageFormat;
 5. import java.util.Locale;
 6. import javax.faces.application.FacesMessage;
 7. import javax.faces.component.UIComponent;
 8. import javax.faces.context.FacesContext;
 9. import javax.faces.validator.FacesValidator;
10. import javax.faces.validator.Validator;
11. import javax.faces.validator.ValidatorException;
12.
13. @FacesValidator("com.corejsf.CreditCard")
14. public class CreditCardValidator implements Validator, Serializable {
15.    private String message;
16.    private String arg;
17.
18.    public void setMessage(String newValue) { message = newValue; }
19.
20.    public void setArg(String newValue) { arg = newValue; }
```

```
21.    public String getArg() { return arg; }
22.
23.    public void validate(FacesContext context, UIComponent component,
24.          Object value) {
25.      if (value == null) return;
26.      String cardNumber;
27.      if (value instanceof CreditCard)
28.        cardNumber = value.toString();
29.      else
30.        cardNumber = getDigitsOnly(value.toString());
31.      if (!luhnCheck(cardNumber)) {
32.        FacesMessage message = new FacesMessage(FacesMessage.SEVERITY_ERROR,
33.          getErrorMessage(value, context), null);
34.        throw new ValidatorException(message);
35.      }
36.    }
37.
38.    public String getErrorMessage(Object value, FacesContext context) {
39.      Object[] params = new Object[] { value };
40.      if (message == null)
41.        return com.corejsf.util.Messages.getString(
42.            "com.corejsf.messages", "badLuhnCheck", params);
43.      else {
44.        Locale locale = context.getViewRoot().getLocale();
45.        MessageFormat formatter = new MessageFormat(message, locale);
46.        return formatter.format(params);
47.      }
48.    }
49.
50.    private static boolean luhnCheck(String cardNumber) {
51.      int sum = 0;
52.
53.      for (int i = cardNumber.length() - 1; i >= 0; i -= 2) {
54.        sum += Integer.parseInt(cardNumber.substring(i, i + 1));
55.        if(i > 0) {
56.          int d = 2 * Integer.parseInt(cardNumber.substring(i - 1, i));
57.          if(d > 9) d -= 9;
58.          sum += d;
59.        }
60.      }
61.
62.      return sum % 10 == 0;
63.    }
64.
65.    private static String getDigitsOnly(String s) {
66.      StringBuilder digitsOnly = new StringBuilder ();
67.      char c;
```

```
68.     for (int i = 0; i < s.length (); i++) {
69.        c = s.charAt (i);
70.        if (Character.isDigit(c)) {
71.           digitsOnly.append(c);
72.        }
73.     }
74.     return digitsOnly.toString ();
75.  }
76. }
```

Listing 13–24 clientside-validator/src/java/com/corejsf/
UIValidatorScript.java

```
1. package com.corejsf;
2.
3. import java.io.IOException;
4. import java.util.Map;
5. import java.util.LinkedHashMap;
6.
7. import javax.faces.application.ResourceDependency;
8. import javax.faces.component.EditableValueHolder;
9. import javax.faces.component.FacesComponent;
10. import javax.faces.component.UIComponent;
11. import javax.faces.component.UIComponentBase;
12. import javax.faces.context.FacesContext;
13. import javax.faces.context.ResponseWriter;
14. import javax.faces.validator.Validator;
15.
16. @FacesComponent("com.corejsf.ValidatorScript")
17. @ResourceDependency(library="javascript", name="validateCreditCard.js",
18.    target="head")
19. public class UIValidatorScript extends UIComponentBase {
20.    private Map<String, Validator> validators
21.       = new LinkedHashMap<String, Validator>();
22.
23.    public String getRendererType() { return null; }
24.    public String getFamily() { return null; }
25.
26.    private void findCreditCardValidators(UIComponent c, FacesContext context) {
27.       if (c instanceof EditableValueHolder) {
28.          EditableValueHolder h = (EditableValueHolder) c;
29.          for (Validator v : h.getValidators()) {
30.             if (v instanceof CreditCardValidator) {
31.                String id = c.getClientId(context);
32.                validators.put(id, v);
33.             }
34.          }
```

```
35.        }
36.
37.        for (UIComponent child : c.getChildren())
38.            findCreditCardValidators(child, context);
39.    }
40.
41.    private void writeScriptStart(ResponseWriter writer) throws IOException {
42.        writer.startElement("script", this);
43.        writer.writeAttribute("type", "text/javascript", null);
44.        writer.writeAttribute("language", "Javascript1.1", null);
45.        writer.write("\n<!--\n");
46.    }
47.
48.    private void writeScriptEnd(ResponseWriter writer) throws IOException {
49.        writer.write("\n-->\n");
50.        writer.endElement("script");
51.    }
52.
53.    private void writeValidationFunctions(ResponseWriter writer,
54.        FacesContext context) throws IOException {
55.        writer.write("var bCancel = false;\n");
56.        writer.write("function " );
57.        writer.write(getAttributes().get("functionName").toString());
58.        writer.write("(form) { return bCancel || validateCreditCard(form); }\n");
59.
60.        writer.write("function ");
61.        String formId = getParent().getClientId(context);
62.        writer.write(formId);
63.        writer.write("_creditCard() { \n");
64.        // for each field validated by this type, add configuration object
65.        int k = 0;
66.        for (String id : validators.keySet()) {
67.            CreditCardValidator v = (CreditCardValidator) validators.get(id);
68.            writer.write("this[" + k + "] = ");
69.            k++;
70.
71.            writer.write("new Array('");
72.            writer.write(id);
73.            writer.write("', '");
74.            writer.write(v.getErrorMessage(v.getArg(), context));
75.            writer.write("', '');\n"); // Third element unused for credit card validator
76.        }
77.        writer.write("}\n");
78.    }
79.
80.    public void encodeBegin(FacesContext context) throws IOException {
81.        ResponseWriter writer = context.getResponseWriter();
82.
83.        validators.clear();
```

```
84.     findCreditCardValidators(context.getViewRoot(), context);
85.
86.     writeScriptStart(writer);
87.     writeValidationFunctions(writer, context);
88.     writeScriptEnd(writer);
89.   }
90. }
```

Listing 13–25   clientside-validator/web/index.xhtml

```
1. <?xml version="1.0" encoding="UTF-8"?>
2. <!DOCTYPE html PUBLIC "-//W3C//DTD XHTML 1.0 Transitional//EN"
3. "http://www.w3.org/TR/xhtml1/DTD/xhtml1-transitional.dtd">
4. <html xmlns="http://www.w3.org/1999/xhtml"
5.      xmlns:h="http://java.sun.com/jsf/html" xmlns:f="http://java.sun.com/jsf/core"
6.      xmlns:corejsf="http://corejsf.com">
7.   <h:head>
8.     <h:outputStylesheet library="css" name="styles.css"/>
9.     <title>#{msgs.title}</title>
10.  </h:head>
11.  <h:body>
12.    <h:form id="paymentForm" onsubmit="return validatePaymentForm(this);">
13.      <corejsf:validatorScript functionName="validatePaymentForm"/>
14.      <h1>#{msgs.enterPayment}</h1>
15.      <h:panelGrid columns="3">
16.        #{msgs.amount}
17.        <h:inputText id="amount" value="#{payment.amount}">
18.          <f:convertNumber minFractionDigits="2"/>
19.        </h:inputText>
20.        <h:message for="amount" styleClass="errorMessage"/>
21.
22.        #{msgs.creditCard}
23.        <h:inputText id="card" value="#{payment.card}" required="true">
24.          <corejsf:creditCardValidator message="#{msgs.unknownType}"
25.                                       arg="#{msgs.creditCard}"/>
26.        </h:inputText>
27.        <h:message for="card" styleClass="errorMessage"/>
28.
29.        #{msgs.expirationDate}
30.        <h:inputText id="date" value="#{payment.date}">
31.          <f:convertDateTime pattern="MM/dd/yyyy"/>
32.        </h:inputText>
33.        <h:message for="date" styleClass="errorMessage"/>
34.      </h:panelGrid>
35.      <h:commandButton value="Process" action="result"/>
36.    </h:form>
37.  </h:body>
38. </html>
```

> NOTE: Unfortunately, the Commons Validator displays a pop-up when it finds a validation error. It would be nicer to place an error message next to the offending field. This feature is supported in Cagatay Civici's client-side validation package at `http://jsf-comp.sourceforge.net/components/clientvalidators/index.html`.

How do I configure my application?

Many applications require some configuration parameters, such as paths to external directories, default account names, and so on. Since these parameters need to be updated by application deployers, it is not a good idea to place them inside your application code.

A good place for supply configuration parameters is the `web.xml` file. Provide a set of `context-param` elements inside the `web-app` element, such as:

```
<web-app>
    <context-param>
        <param-name>URL</param-name>
        <param-value>ldap://localhost:389</param-value>
    </context-param>
    ...
</web-app>
```

To read a parameter, get the *external context* object. That object describes the execution environment that launched your JSF application. If you use a servlet container, then the external context is a wrapper around the `ServletContext` object. The `ExternalContext` class has a number of convenience methods to access properties of the underlying servlet context. The `getInitParameter` method retrieves a context parameter value with a given name:

```
ExternalContext external = FacesContext.getCurrentInstance().getExternalContext();
String url = external.getInitParameter("URL");
```

> CAUTION: Do not confuse `context-param` with `init-param`. The latter tag is used for parameters that a servlet can process at startup. It is unfortunate that the method for reading a context parameter is called `getInitParameter`.

Some applications prefer to process their own configuration files rather than using `web.xml`. The challenge is to locate the file because you do not know where the web container stores the files of your web application. In fact, the web container need not physically store your files at all—it can choose to read them out of the WAR file.

Instead, use the `getResourceAsStream` method of the `ExternalContext` class. For example, suppose you want to read `app.properties` in the `WEB-INF` directory of your application. Here is the required code:

```
FacesContext context = FacesContext.getCurrentInstance();
ExternalContext external = context.getExternalContext();
InputStream in = external.getResourceAsStream("/WEB-INF/app.properties");
```

How do I extend the JSF expression language?

Sometimes it is useful to extend the expression language. Consider, for example, an extension that allows us to look up forms and components by ID, such as:

```
view.loginForm
```

This is achieved by adding a *resolver* that processes an expression `base.property` (or the equivalent `base[property]`), where `base` is the string `"view"` and `property` is the form ID.

You extend the `ELResolver` class to implement a resolver. The key method is:

```
public Object getValue(ELContext context, Object base, Object property)
```

If your resolver knows how to resolve the expression `base.property`, then you call

```
context.setPropertyResolved(true);
```

and return the value of the expression.

There are several other methods for type inquiry and builder tool support; see the API documentation for details.

Now let us implement the resolver for form and component IDs. Consider, for example, the expression:

```
view.loginForm.password.value
```

We want to find the component with the ID `loginForm` inside the view root, then the component with the ID `password` inside the form, and then call its `getValue` method. Our resolver will handle expressions of the form *component.name*:

```
public class ComponentIdResolver extends ELResolver {
    public Object getValue(ELContext context, Object base, Object property) {
        if (base instanceof UIComponent && property instanceof String) {
            UIComponent r = ((UIComponent) base).findComponent((String) property);
            if (r != null) {
                context.setPropertyResolved(true);
                return r;
```

```
        }
      }
      return null;
    }
    ...
}
```

Note that our resolver is called to resolve the first two subexpressions (view.loginForm and view.loginForm.password). The last expression is resolved by the managed bean resolver that is part of the JSF implementation.

The initial expression view is a special case. Resolvers are called with base set to null and property set to the initial expression string. The JSF implicit object resolver resolves that expression, returning the UIViewRoot object of the page.

As another example, we build a resolver for system properties. For example, the expression

```
sysprop['java.version']
```

should return the result of calling

```
System.getProperty("java.version");
```

To make matters more interesting, the expression

```
sysprop.java.version
```

should also work. This custom resolver must handle the special case in which the base is null and the property is "sysprop". It must also deal with partially complete subexpressions, such as sysprop.java.

We collect the list of expressions in a nested class SystemPropertyResolver.Partial-Resolution. Our resolver distinguishes two cases:

1. If base is null and property is "sysprop", return an empty PartialResolution object.

2. If base is a PartialResolution object and property is a string, add the property to the end of the list. Then try to look up the system property whose key is the dot-separated concatenation of the list entries. If the system property exists, return it. Otherwise, return the augmented list.

The following code excerpt illustrates these cases:

```
public class SystemPropertyResolver extends ELResolver {
   public Object getValue(ELContext context, Object base, Object property) {
      if (base == null && "sysprop".equals(property)) {
         context.setPropertyResolved(true);
         return new PartialResolution();
```

```
      }
      if (base instanceof PartialResolution && property instanceof String) {
         ((PartialResolution) base).add((String) property);
         Object r = System.getProperty(base.toString());
         context.setPropertyResolved(true);
         if (r == null) return base;
         else return r;
      }
      return null;
   }
   ...
   public static class PartialResolution extends ArrayList<String> {
      public String toString() {
         StringBuilder r = new StringBuilder();
         for (String s : this) {
            if (r.length() > 0) r.append('.');
            r.append(s);
         }
         return r.toString();
      }
   }
}
```

To add the custom resolver to your JSF application, add elements, such as the following to faces-config.xml (or another application configuration file):

```
<application>
   <el-resolver>com.corejsf.ComponentIdResolver</el-resolver>
   ...
</application>
```

You will find the complete implementation for the two sample resolvers in the ch13/extending-el example of the companion code.

NOTE: In JSF 1.1, modifying the expression language is a bit more cumbersome. The JSF 1.1 implementation provides concrete subclasses of the abstract classes VariableResolver and PropertyResolver. A VariableResolver resolves the initial subexpression, and the PropertyResolver is in charge of evaluating the dot or bracket operator.

If you want to introduce your own variables, you supply your own variable resolver and specify it in the application configuration file, like this:

```
<application>
   <variable-resolver>
      com.corejsf.CustomVariableResolver
```

```
</variable-resolver>
   ...
</application>
```

In your resolver class, supply a constructor with a single parameter of type `VariableResolver`. Then the JSF implementation passes you its default variable resolver. This makes it straightforward to use the decorator pattern. Here is an example of a variable resolver that recognizes the variable name `sysprop`:

```
public class CustomVariableResolver extends VariableResolver {
   private VariableResolver original;

   public CustomVariableResolver(VariableResolver original) {
      this.original = original;
   }

   public Object resolveVariable(FacesContext context, String name) {
      if (name.equals("sysprop")) return System.getProperties();
      return original.resolveVariable(context, name);
   }
}
```

The implementation of a `PropertyResolver` is similar.

How do I add a function to the JSF expression language? JSF 2.0

You can add your own function to the JSF expression language by following this process:

1. Implement the function as a static method.
2. In a Facelets tag library file, map the function name to the implementation.

For example, suppose we want to define a function that reads a file and gets its contents. A typical use might be:

```
<p>Page source:</p><pre>#{corejsf:getFile("/index.xhtml")}</pre>
```

In Listing 13–26, the class implements the function as the static `ELFunctions.getFile` method.

Listing 13–26 extending-el/src/java/com/corejsf/ELFunctions.java

```
 1. package com.corejsf;
 2.
 3. import java.io.InputStream;
 4. import java.util.Scanner;
 5. import javax.faces.context.FacesContext;
 6.
 7. public class ELFunctions {
 8.    public static String getFile(String filename) {
 9.       FacesContext context = FacesContext.getCurrentInstance();
10.       java.util.logging.Logger.getLogger("com.corejsf").info("context=" + context);
11.       InputStream stream = context.getExternalContext().getResourceAsStream(filename);
12.       Scanner in = new Scanner(stream);
13.       java.util.logging.Logger.getLogger("com.corejsf").info("context=" + context);
14.       StringBuilder builder = new StringBuilder();
15.       while (in.hasNextLine()) { builder.append(in.nextLine()); builder.append('\n'); }
16.       return builder.toString();
17.    }
18. }
```

Listing 13–27 shows the tag library file.

Listing 13–27 extending-el/web/WEB-INF/corejsf.taglib.xml

```
 1. <?xml version="1.0" encoding="UTF-8"?>
 2. <facelet-taglib version="2.0"
 3.    xmlns="http://java.sun.com/xml/ns/javaee"
 4.    xmlns:xsi="http://www.w3.org/2001/XMLSchema-instance"
 5.    xsi:schemaLocation="http://java.sun.com/xml/ns/javaee
 6.    http://java.sun.com/xml/ns/javaee/web-facelettaglibary_2_0.xsd">
 7.    <namespace>http://corejsf.com</namespace>
 8.    <function>
 9.       <function-name>getFile</function-name>
10.       <function-class>com.corejsf.ELFunctions</function-class>
11.       <function-signature>
12.          java.lang.String getFile(java.lang.String)
13.       </function-signature>
14.    </function>
15. </facelet-taglib>
```

You can add your own methods to the JSF expression language by following the same recipe.

How do I monitor the traffic between the browser and the server?

It is often helpful to know what parameters the client sent back to the server when a form was submitted. Of course, you can simply embed the expression

    #{param}

in a page, and you will get a listing of the parameter names and values.

But particularly for debugging Ajax applications, it is better to monitor the entire traffic between client and server. Both Eclipse and Netbeans support this monitoring.

In Eclipse 3.5, the details depend on the server adapter. Here are the instructions for Glassfish:

1. Right-click on the server in the Servers tab and select Monitoring > Properties.
2. Click on Add and select port 8080 (see Figure 13–12).
3. Select Start.

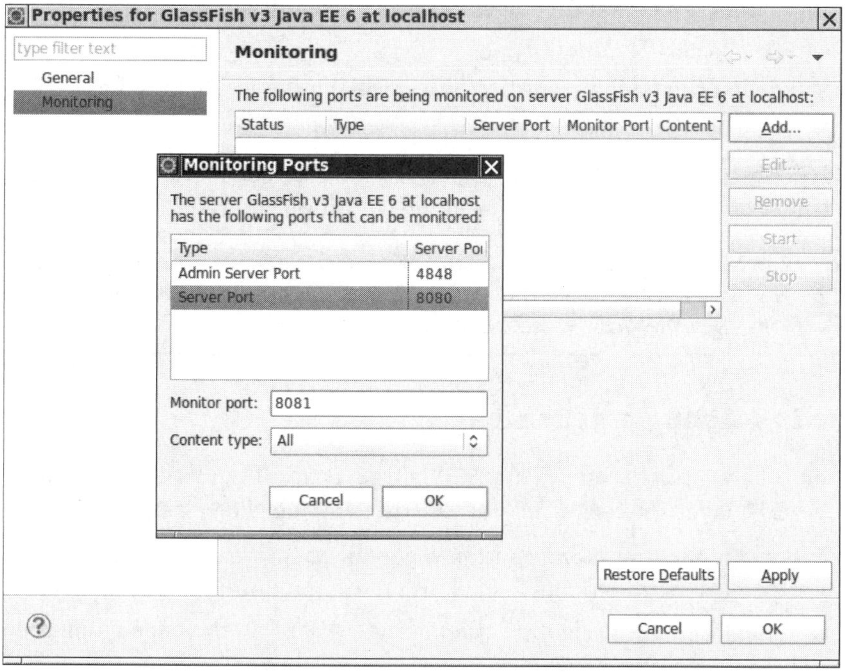

Figure 13–12   Activating HTTP monitoring in Eclipse

4.   Point your browser to `http://localhost:8081/`*contextRoot*. Eclipse intercepts the traffic on port 8081 and sends it to port 8080. More importantly, it displays the decoded requests and responses (see Figure 13–13).

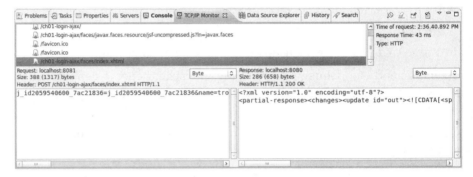

Figure 13–13   The HTTP monitor in action

With NetBeans 6.8 and Glassfish, follow these steps:

1.   Click the Services tab and expand the Servers node.

2.   Right-click the GlassFish entry and select Properties.

3.   Check "Use HTTP monitor".

4.   When you run your application, select the Window > Debugging > HTTP Server Monitor menu option.

Unlike Eclipse, Netbeans does not require you to change the port number in your URLs. Instead, it installs a filter in the web application.

   NOTE: You can also use a general-purpose TCP/IP sniffer such as Wireshark (http://www.wireshark.org/).

How do I debug a stuck page?

Sometimes, a JSF page seems "stuck". When you click the submit button, the page is redisplayed. Here is what you can do to debug such a page:

•   Make sure that the submit button is contained inside a `h:form`. If not, the page will be rendered, but clicking on the submit button has no effect.

•   Double-check the navigation rules to make sure that the page navigation is indeed set up properly.

- A common reason for a stuck page is a validation or conversion error. This is easy to check by placing a `<h:messages/>` tag on the page.

- If you still do not spot the error, install a phase tracker. You saw a simple implementation in Chapter 7, but for industrial-strength spying, check out FacesTrace from `http://code.google.com/p/primefaces-ext/`. It gives you a visual display of the phases (see Figure 13–14).

FacesTrace is easy to use. Add its JAR file and the Commons Logging JAR file to your web application's `WEB-INF/lib` directory. Add a namespace declaration to the `html` tag:

```
xmlns:ft="http://primefaces.prime.com.tr/facestrace"
```

Then add a tag at the end of your JSF page:

```
<ft:trace/>
```

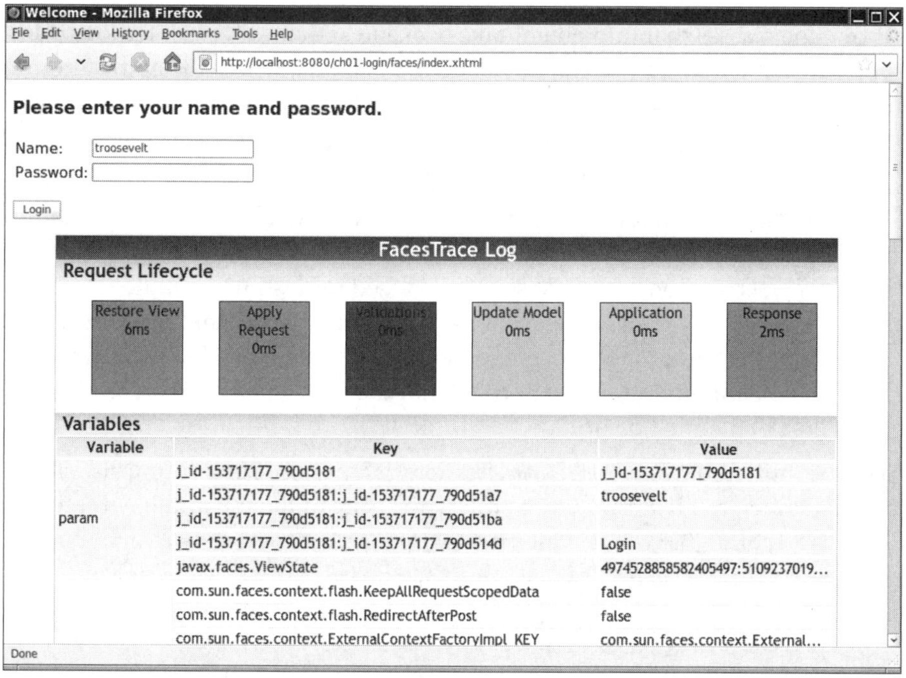

Figure 13–14   FacesTrace in action

How do I use testing tools when developing a JSF application?

You can test managed beans in isolation, by calling the methods that the JSF implementation would have called. For example, in a unit test, you might invoke the setName and setPassword method to simulate the decoding of the field values. Then invoke the login action method and check its return value. This is very much in the spirit of unit testing.

Problems arise when your managed bean is connected to backend systems; for example, a database. It is a good idea to separate out the database logic from the managed beans. This division arises naturally if you use EJB session beans for the database access. Then you can replace the EJB session beans with fake classes that simulate the database activity. Of course, your test harness needs to wire up the managed beans with the fake classes.

Providing classes that implement fake backend activities can get tedious. Most application servers can be run in "embedded" mode, where the application server runs in the same virtual machine as the test runner. This is quite a bit faster than starting up the application server and connecting to it remotely, and you can write tests that run against the actual backend.

Black-box test automation frameworks, such as HTMLUnit (http://htmlunit. sourceforge.net) or Selenium (http://seleniumhq.org), let you write scripts that simulate browser sessions. In a test script, you feed inputs into form fields, and submit forms, and analyze the response, in order to verify that the returned pages have certain properties. These frameworks have their use, but they also have significant limitations. In particular, if the user interface changes, tests often break and must be updated.

The JSFUnit framework (http://www.jboss.org/jsfunit) also runs your tests inside a full container, but it allows you to query the state of the JSF implementation. Here is a typical JSFUnit test method that verifies properties of a login page:

```
public void testInitialPage() throws IOException {
    JSFSession jsfSession = new JSFSession("/faces/index.xhtml");
    JSFServerSession server = jsfSession.getJSFServerSession();
    assertEquals("/index.xhtml", server.getCurrentViewID());
    UIComponent nameField = server.findComponent("name");
    assertTrue(nameField.isRendered());
    assertEquals("troosevelt", server.getManagedBeanValue("#{user.name}"));
}
```

You deploy JSFUnit tests with your web application, together with the JAR files for JSFUnit, Apache Cactus, and their dependencies.

A JSFUnit test can be run through a servlet that displays the test outcomes (see Figure 13–15). Alternatively, you can run the test from the command line. In that case, you must first start the application server. The JAR files on which JSFUnit depends must be on the class path, and you need to set the system property `cactus.contextURL` to the context URL of your application. You can either invoke the test runner with

```
-Dcactus.contextURL=http://localhost:8080/contextRoot
```

or add a static initializer

```
static {
    System.setProperty("cactus.contextURL", "http://localhost:8080/contextRoot");
}
```

to your JUnit test class.

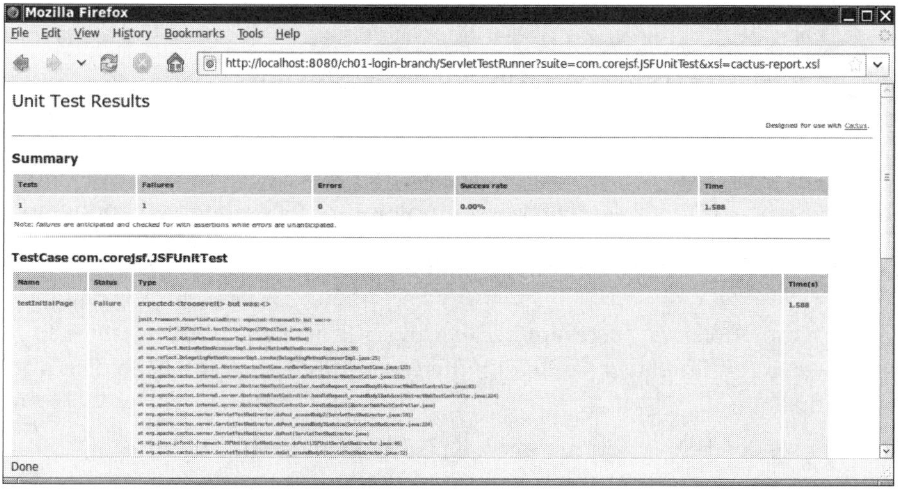

Figure 13–15   JSFUnit output

None of these approaches are a "silver bullet" for testing JSF applications. You should expect to use multiple approaches in your test suite.

How do I use Scala with JSF?

Scala (http://scala-lang.org) is a popular programming language for the Java Virtual Machine. Like Java, it is strongly typed and object-oriented, but it also supports functional programming. Many Java programmers are attracted to Scala because it requires less boilerplate for common constructs, such as properties. Of course, you can call any code in the Java library from Scala.

The following instructions refer to Java EE 6.

To implement a managed bean in Scala, simply annotate it, as you would in Java, but with the Scala annotation syntax. For example:

```
@Named{val value="user"} // or @ManagedBean{val name="user"}
@SessionScoped
class UserBean {
   @BeanProperty var name : String = ""
   @BeanProperty var password : String = ""
}
```

The @BeanProperty annotation generates Java getters and setters. You can now refer to EL expressions, such as #{user.name} in your JSF pages in the usual way.

You need the file scala-library.jar in the WEB-INF/lib directory.

To inject a stateless session bean into a managed bean, use:

```
@EJB private[this] var mySessionBean: MySessionBean = _
```

It is important that you annotate the session bean with @LocalBean:

```
@Stateless @LocalBean class MySessionBean { ... }
```

Alternatively, if you use a trait (for example, because you want to the flexibility of supplying a fake implementation for unit testing), use the @Local annotation:

```
@Local trait MySessionBean { ... }
@Stateless MySessionBeanImpl extends MySessionBean { ... }
```

These annotations are necessary because every Scala class implements an interface that is unrelated to EJB but interferes with the session bean discovery algorithm.

In your session beans, you can inject an entity manager like this:

```
@PersistenceContext private[this] var em: EntityManager = _
```

Your entity beans are annotated in the usual way. Add the @BeanProperty annotation for automatic getter and setter annotations. For example:

```
@Entity public class Credentials {
   @Id @BeanProperty var username : String = "";
   @BeanProperty var password : String = "";
}
```

Eclipse offers a good way of becoming familiar with Scala and JSF. Simply install the Scala plugin and add Scala classes to your web project in the usual way.

As you can see, using Scala with JSF and EJB is very straightforward. An immediate reward is not having to write getters and setters for the ubiquitous bean properties. As you become more familiar with Scala, you will appreciate other features that contribute to its conciseness and elegance, while keeping the benefits of strong typing and compatibility with Java.

How do I use Groovy with JSF?

Groovy (http://groovy.codehaus.org), inspired by Ruby, Smalltalk, and Python, is a another popular programming language for the Java Virtual Machine. Groovy is dynamically typed, and Groovy code can be more concise than the equivalent Java code because you can omit types of variables and parameters.

Almost any Java code is legal Groovy. That makes it simple to get started with Groovy in your JSF applications: Change the suffix of your code from .java to .groovy, and use the Groovy compiler to compile your Groovy code to a .class file. JSF deals in .class files, so it doesn't know, or care, that you are using Groovy to generate them.

The JSF reference implementation supports hot deployment of your Groovy code. See http://blogs.sun.com/rlubke/entry/groovy_mojarra for the configuration details. When you change a Groovy source file, the JSF implementation automatically recompiles it and deploys the class file to the web application. With Groovy and JSF, you get the same instant turnaround that developers using Ruby on Rails and PHP enjoy.

Of course, you will want to have IDE support. NetBeans supports Groovy out of the box. If you use Eclipse, you should install the Groovy Eclipse Plugin (http://groovy.codehaus.org/Eclipse+Plugin).

By default, the Groovy Eclipse Plugin sets the compiler output to /bin/groovy. You will probably want to set the output directory to WEB-INF/classes, which you can do with Eclipse preferences, as shown in Figure 13–16.

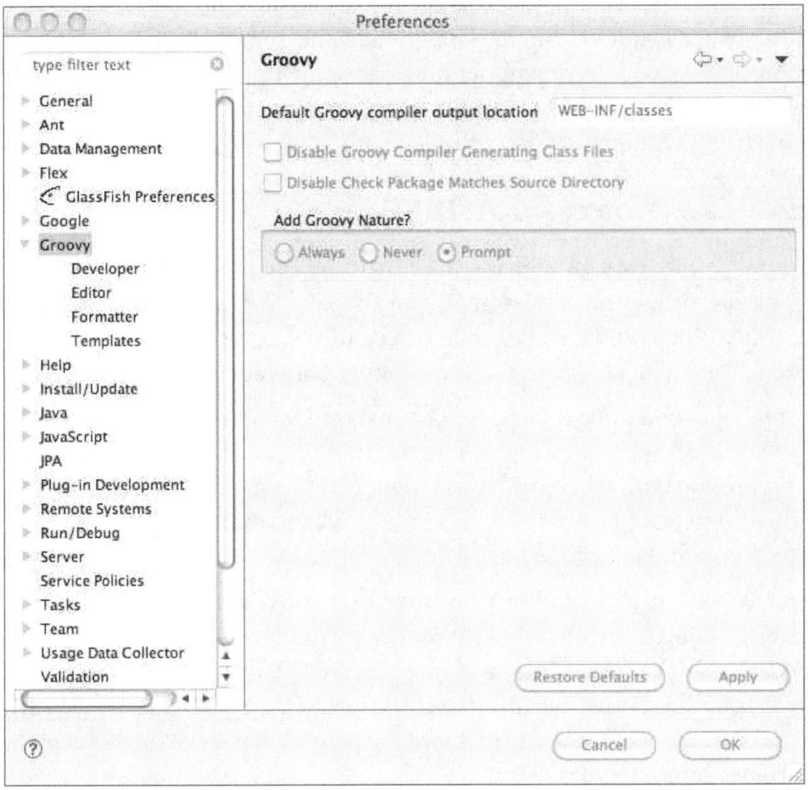

Figure 13–16   Changing the Groovy compiler output directory

Conclusion

You have now reached the end of this book. Along the way, you have learned how JSF enables the separation of page design and application logic, and how you can implement web applications simply by combining predefined components with your Java code. You have seen how JSF fits into the bigger picture of a Java EE application, and how to extend JSF when its built-in capabilities are insufficient for your tasks.

Index

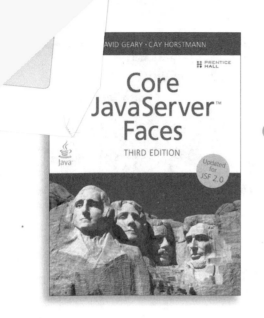

FREE Online Edition

Your purchase of **Core JavaServer™ Faces, Third Edition,** includes access to a free online edition for 45 days through the Safari Books Online subscription service. Nearly every Prentice Hall book is available online through Safari Books Online, along with more than 5,000 other technical books and videos from publishers such as Addison-Wesley Professional, Cisco Press, Exam Cram, IBM Press, O'Reilly, Que, and Sams.

SAFARI BOOKS ONLINE allows you to search for a specific answer, cut and paste code, download chapters, and stay current with emerging technologies.

Activate your FREE Online Edition at www.informit.com/safarifree

> **STEP 1:** Enter the coupon code: ZKETREH.

> **STEP 2:** New Safari users, complete the brief registration form.
> Safari subscribers, just log in.

If you have difficulty registering on Safari or accessing the online edition, please e-mail customer-service@safaribooksonline.com

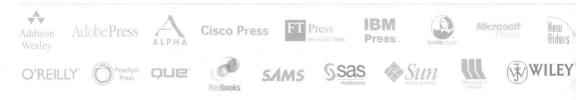